ACCOUNTING
Concepts and Applications

The Robert N. Anthony/Willard J. Graham Series in Accounting

ACCOUNTING
Concepts and Applications

BERNEY

of Accounting

Y J. GARSTKA

in the Practice of Accounting

e Yale School of Organization
agement

1984

RICHARD D. IRWIN, INC.
Homewood, Illinois   60430

ISBN 0–256–02964–4

Library of Congress Catalog Card No. 83–81169

Printed in the United States of America

1 2 3 4 5 6 7 8 9 0 K 1 0 9 8 7 6 5 4

Dedicated with Thanks to

Joyce Bailey Berney
Janet, Jennifer, and Stan Garstka

Preface

This introductory accounting text emphasizes accounting techniques and concepts and their use in analyzing financial statements and making managerial decisions.

The approach used in this textbook has been particularly successful in the following types of programs:

1. MBA, management and other professional schools such as law, engineering, hospital administration, and forestry.
2. Executive MBA and management programs.
3. Professional associations such as the Chartered Financial Analysts.
4. Selected upper level (juniors and seniors) liberal arts undergraduate school.
5. Executive training and development programs.

Each chapter contains problems which are procedural in nature and relate directly to the material covered in the text and short cases which emphasize concepts and are based on actual financial statements and events.

The flexible design of the text enables the instructor to teach a one or two semester (one to three quarters) introductory accounting course as well as a shorter executive development program in financial or managerial accounting.

Acknowledgments

All the problems and cases were written by the authors except for those which were generously contributed by our colleagues Ralph C. Jones, Professor Emeritus of Economics, Yale University; William P. Lyons, Associate Professor (Adjunct) and Arthur N. Haut, Lecturer in Accounting both of the Yale School of Organization and Management.

The authors are also indebted to Arthur N. Haut and William P. Lyons for their review of the manuscript and for the suggestions made by their students who used earlier versions of the manuscript.

Extremely valuable comments were made by the following reviewers: Anthony T. Krzystofik, University of Massachusetts; Gary A. Luoma, Georgia State University, Michael Sandretto, Harvard University, Jerry E. Trapnell, Louisiana State University, and particularly by our consulting editor, Robert N. Anthony, Harvard University. This is a better book because of the implementation of many of their recommendations.

We are also grateful to Jeanne Stone and Melinda DeMaio who were responsible for the production of this manuscript and to Roberta Sutkowski and Karen Eisenman who helped them.

Paul R. Berney
Stanley J. Garstka

Contents

General journal. Other books of original entry. Closing journal entry. The accounting cycle.

Problems and cases

3. Measuring and adjusting 46

1. Expenditures that affect more than one accounting period. 2. Receipts that affect more than one accounting period. 3. Revenues affecting the accounting period that have not been recorded. 4. Expenses affecting the accounting period that have not been recorded. Dividends. Correcting journal entries. Frequency of adjusting journal entries.

Problems and cases

4. Accounting principles 67

Accounting conventions and principles: *1. Entity. 2. Money measurement. 3. Going-concern. 4. Cost. 5. Objectivity. 6. Conservatism. 7. Consistency. 8. Materiality. 9. Disclosure. 10. Time period. 11. Revenue recognition. 12. Matching.* Opinion of the independent certified public accountant.

Problems and cases

5. Working capital 86

Current assets. Cash: *Compensating balances. Certificates of deposit.* Marketable securities: *Marketable equity securities. Marketable debt securities. The market value argument.* Accounts receivable: *Sales discounts (gross method). Sales discounts (net method). Sales returns and allowances. Uncollectible accounts receivable and the bad debt adjustment.* Short-term notes receivable. Prepaid expenses. Current liabilities. Accounts payable. Short-term notes payable. Current portion of long-term debt payable. Withholding and social security (FICA) taxes payable. Dividends payable. Federal income taxes payable. Unearned or deferred revenues. Accrued expenses.

Problems and cases

Inventory. Inventory valuation. Periodic inventory method. Gross profit method. Perpetual inventory method. Inventory cost flow methods: *1. Specific identification. 2. FIFO. 3. LIFO. 4. Weighted average.* Lower-of-cost-or-market rule (LCM). Comparison of the cost flow methods. Argument for use of the FIFO cost flow method. The argument for use of the LIFO cost flow method. Evaluation of LIFO. Financial statement disclosure. Inventories of manufacturing companies. Manufacturing flow of costs. Factory overhead. Cost of goods sold. Statement of cost of goods sold. Significance of the process.

Problems and cases

Property, plant, and equipment. The cost of plant and equipment. Maintenance, repairs, and improvements. Depreciation of plant and equipment—the allocation process. Methods of depreciation: *Straight-line depreciation. Units-of-production method. The declin-*

ing-balance method. Combination of declining-balance and straight-line depreciation. The sum-of-the-years'-digits method. Disposal of plant and equipment. Depreciation, federal income tax, and net income: *ACRS depreciation method. Comparison of ACRS and straight-line depreciation. Deferred income taxes.* Depreciation policy decisions. The investment tax credit: *The investment tax credit and financial reports.* Natural resources. Intangible assets.

Problems and cases

8. Long-term debt 170

Long-term notes payable (interest-bearing). Long-term notes payable (noninterest-bearing). Bonds: *Bond discount. Bond premium.* Bond issue costs. Straight-line amortization of bond discount and bond premium. Compound (effective) interest rate method of amortization of bond discount and premium. Bond retirements: *Callable bonds. Market purchases before maturity. Gains and losses on redemption of debt.* Bond conversion. Leases. Capital leases.

Problems and cases

9. Owners' equity. 204

Common stock: *Par value. No-par value stock. Underwriting.* Preferred stock: *Sale of preferred stock. Balance sheet format.* Treasury stock. Retained earnings. Cash dividends. Stock dividends. Stock splits. Appropriation of retained earnings. Financial disclosure. Book value of a share of common stock. Market price of a share of common stock. Earnings per (common) share: *Weighted average of common shares outstanding. Primary earnings per share. Fully diluted earnings per share.*

Problems and cases

10. Intercorporate investments and business combinations . . . 225

Cost method. Equity method. Consolidation method. Preparation of consolidated financial statements. Consolidated balance sheet. Consolidated income statement. Consolidated statement of changes in financial position: *Disclosure of principles of consolidation. Summary.* Business combinations: *Purchase method. Pooling of interests method. Example of purchase method. Example of pooling of interests method. Comparison of purchase and pooling of interests consolidated financial statements.* Disclosure on the financial statements of purchase and pooling of interests methods.

Problems and cases

11. Statement of changes in financial position 265

Major sources of working capital: *1. Operations. 2. Sale of noncurrent assets. 3. Long-term borrowing. 4. Issue of capital stock.* Major uses of working capital: *1. Capital expenditures. 2. Retirement of long-term debt. 3. Purchase of capital stock. 4. Payment of cash dividends.* All resources concept of statement of changes in financial position. Schedule of working capital accounts. Method of preparing a statement of changes in financial position: *Worksheet.* Funds defined as cash. Cash flow analysis. Uses of the statement of changes in financial position.

Problems and cases

12. Financial reporting and changing prices. 300

Constant-dollar (general price level) accounting: *Restatement of financial statements in constant dollars. Balance sheet. Income statement.* Current cost accounting (specific price changes): *Balance sheet. Income statement. Holding gains. Current costs and financial analysis.* SFAS 33, "Financial reporting and changing prices": *Example of* SFAS 33 *disclosure.*

Problems and cases

13. The income statement: A closer look. 326

The all-inclusive view of the income statement. Prior period adjustments: *Correction of errors. Compliance with accounting standards.* Extraordinary items: *Other income. Premature retirement of debt.* Accounting changes. Changes in accounting estimates. Discontinued operations. Accounting for income taxes: *Permanent differences. Timing differences. Deferred income taxes. Classification of deferred income taxes.* Income tax disclosure.

Problems and cases

14. Special topics (pensions, segment reporting, interim financial statements, and forecasts) 361

Pensions: *Types of pension plans. Terminology. Federal pension law.* Accounting for pensions: *Normal costs. Past service costs. Funding. Financial statement disclosure.* Segment reporting. *SFAS 14. Example of SFAS 14 disclosure.* Interim financial reports: *Operating costs. Income tax expense. LIFO inventories. Accounting changes, unusual items, extraordinary items. Interim financial reports. Sales. LIFO inventory. Operating costs. Review by independent certified public accountants.* Forecasts. SEC. FASB.

Problems and cases

15. Introduction to financial statement analysis 386

Financial ratio and comparative financial statement analysis. Liquidity (short-term solvency) measures: *LIFO and the current ratio. Summary. Acid-test (quick) ratio. Accounts receivable turnover ratio. Average accounts receivable collection period. Inventory turnover ratio. Defensive-interval and liquidity ratios.* Long-term solvency measures. Times-interest-earned. Profitability and operating efficiency measures: *Net profit margin on sales. Percentage income statement. Net profit margin excluding financing costs. Asset turnover ratio. Rate of return on assets. Current cost ROI.* Leverage: *Rate of return on common stockholders' equity.* Earnings per share. Price earnings ratio. Capitalization ratio. Dividend yield ratio. Uses of financial ratio and comparative financial statement analysis.

Problems and cases

16. Introduction to managerial accounting and absorption (full) costing 420

Cost accounting. Decision making. Budgeting and control. Performance evaluation. Absorption costing: *Fixed factory overhead costs. Variable factory overhead costs. Selling, general, and administrative costs.* Job order and process costing systems: *Job lot (job order) costing. Direct product costs. Factory overhead cost. Factory overhead variances. Variable factory overhead variance. Fixed factory over-*

head variance. *Variances and the income statement.* The influence of the level of production on income. Process costing: *Raw materials. Direct labor. Factory overhead. Inventories.* Further remarks.

Problems and cases

Standards. Manufacturing cost standards: *Factory overhead allocation—expected capacity. Factory overhead allocation—normal capacity.* Production variances: *Example of a standard cost system.* Raw material and direct labor production cost variances: *Raw material price variance. Raw material usage variance. Direct labor rate variance. Direct labor usage variance. Interpretation of direct labor variances.* Factory overhead variances: *Variable factory overhead variance. Variable factory overhead efficiency variance. Variable factory overhead spending variance. Fixed factory overhead variance. Fixed factory overhead budget variance. Fixed factory overhead volume variance.* Standard cost systems and financial statements.

Problems and cases

Cost pools, allocation rules, and cost objects: *Allocation of variable costs. Allocation of fixed costs. Combined overhead allocation rate. Example of cost allocation.* Joint product costs: Allocation: *Physical measures of output. Relative sales value of output. Approximate relative sales value of output.* Joint product costs: Decision making. Service department costs: Allocation: *Example of service department cost allocations. Fixed costs. Variable costs. Direct allocation method. Step-down allocation method. Reciprocal allocation method.* Service department costs: Decision making.

Problems and cases

19. The contribution approach to net income: Variable costing and break-even analysis 500

Variable costing: *Variable costing: Example. Comparison of variable costing and absorption costing. Contribution margin and the contribution format income statement. Variable costing and decision making. Sales equal production.* Break-even analysis: *Cost volume profit model and decision making. Break-even points and future cash flows. Noncash expenses. Assumptions made in break-even analysis.*

Problems and cases

20. Short-term decision making 520

Nonquantitative factors in decision making. Accrual accounting and cash flows. Income taxes and cash flows. Example: Incremental business: *Incremental cash inflows. Incremental cash outflows.* Incremental fixed costs. Example: Rent additional capacity: *Do nothing. Accept order and rent capacity. Accept order and do not rent.* Comprehensive example: Dropping a product: *Sales revenue. Cost of goods sold and inventories. Raw material cost. Direct labor cost. Variable overhead. Fixed factory overhead. Telephone costs. Personnel cost. Rent. Sales commissions. Administrative cost. Conclusion.* Constrained short-term decisions: *Linear programming.*

Problems and cases

21. Capital budgeting 541

Criteria for capital investment opportunities. Net present value. Discount rates and cash flows. Income taxes and cash flows: *Depreciation tax shield. Example. Investment tax credit. Research and development tax credit.* Summary of the capital budgeting process. Example: Equipment replacement: *Net acquisition cost of new machine. Direct labor costs. Depreciation tax shield. Salvage value of new machine. Training costs. Conclusion.* Changing inventory levels and overhead allocation rates and estimating cash flows. Alternatives to present value: *Payback period. Accounting rate of return. Internal rate of return.* Investment and financing decisions. Budget constraints. Appendix: Accelerated cost recovery system overview.

Problems and cases

22. Budgeting 572

The budget process: *Preparing the sales budget. Preparing production and inventory budgets. Physical budget. Cost budgets. Inventory. Pro forma income and cash flow. Master operating budget. Budgeted cash flows and planned financing.* The budget process: General comments: *Flexible budgets.* ZBB and PB: *Zero-base budgeting. Program budgeting.*

Problems and cases

ing profitability measures: Interpretation. Current cost and ROI.
Gross versus net book value. Graphical presentation of ROIs.

Problems and cases

1

Preparing and understanding financial statements

Accounting is the process of measuring, recording, and communicating economic information which aids users in making decisions.

Managerial accounting is concerned with providing information to all levels of management for planning, control, and decision making. It includes topics such as cost allocation, cost-volume-profit relationships, budgeting, alternative choice decisions, capital investment decisions, and performance evaluation. Chapters 16 to 25 of this book are devoted to managerial accounting.

Financial accounting provides information for external users such as short-term and long-term creditors who make decisions about loaning funds to an enterprise, investors who decide whether to buy or sell an enterprise's common stock, and a number of other users. Some other users of financial accounting information are management who use it as an aid in enterprise performance evaluation, government agencies who use it for regulatory purposes, and labor unions who use it for negotiation purposes.

2

Uniformity in general purpose external financial reports is obtained by requiring that they be prepared in accordance with standards called generally accepted accounting principles.

By law the Securities and Exchange Commission (SEC) has responsibility for setting accounting standards for business organizations in the United States. The SEC has delegated much of this responsibility to the Financial Accounting Standards Board (FASB), an independent private sector organization.

The three principal financial statements (balance sheet, income statement, and statement of changes in financial position), the generally accepted accounting principles that underlie their construction, and the interpretation of the financial information in the statements by users, is the subject of the financial accounting portion of this text (Chapters 1–15).

An analysis of the financial transactions of an enterprise (firm, company, organization) is necessary in order to prepare financial statements that will indicate the financial condition of the enterprise at a moment in time (balance sheet) and the results of the operations of the enterprise over a period of time (statement of income).

BALANCE SHEET

The balance sheet, also called the statement of financial condition and statement of financial position, consists of two main categories, *assets* and *equities*. Assets are resources of the enterprise that can be expressed in monetary terms. Enterprises acquire assets because they expect them to yield economic benefits in the future. Equities are monetary claims against those resources. There are two major types of equities or claims: those of outsiders (nonowners), which are called *liabilities*, and those of owners, which are called *owners' equity*. Liabilities are probable future sacrifices of economic benefits. They will require the enterprise to transfer assets or provide services in the future to meet present obligations. Owners' equity is the residual amount that belongs to the owners after deducting the liabilities from the assets. Owners' equity in a corporation is labeled stockholders' or shareholders' equity. In a partnership it is called partners' capital, and in an individual business the title usually used is proprietorship or net worth. The term *net worth* has also been used to identify owners' equity of all three types of organizations.

Assets expected to be converted into cash or consumed within one year or within the company's operating cycle, whichever is longer, are generally classified as *current*. An operating cycle is the average amount of time it takes a company to purchase or produce a product, sell it, and collect the cash from the sale.

Tangible assets with a life exceeding a year are generally classified as *fixed* assets (property, plant, or equipment).

Assets such as long-term investments and any other assets that do not fit into the current or fixed asset categories are classified under the heading *other assets*. Liabilities are also classified as *current* (to be paid within one year) and *long-term* (to be paid after one year). The relationship of current assets to current liabilities is a very important one because it indicates the firm's ability to pay its obligations on a current basis.

Recording the effect of transactions on the balance sheet

Every financial transaction of an enterprise can be recorded in terms of its effect on the balance sheet.

For example, assume that on August 15, 1984, a corporation (one form of a business enterprise) called Bailey's Drug Store, Inc., was organized to fill prescriptions and sell related merchandise. The owners of this corporation made an initial investment (the purchase of common stock from the corporation) of $40,000 on this date. Bailey's Drug Store, Inc., would record this *transaction* by increasing the asset, cash, $40,000, and increasing the owner's equity category, common stock, $40,000.

The balance sheet after this transaction will appear as in Illustration 1–1.

ILLUSTRATION 1–1

BAILEY'S DRUG STORE, INC.
Balance Sheet
August 15, 1984

Assets		Equities	
Cash	$40,000	Common stock	$40,000

Common stock is the title for the owners' investment in a corporation. It is documented by a written agreement (stock certificate) between the corporation and the stockholders.

On August 16, 1984, the company purchased display equipment in the amount of $10,000: $6,000 was paid in cash, and a $4,000, 12 percent per annum *note payable*, due in 90-days, was issued for the balance. The asset, *equipment*, was increased by $10,000; the asset *cash*, was decreased by $6,000; and the liability, *notes payable*, was increased by $4,000. The total assets of $44,000 are

4

equal to the claims against these assets of $44,000 (see Illustration 1–2).

ILLUSTRATION 1–2

BAILEY'S DRUG STORE, INC.
Balance Sheet
August 16, 1984

Assets		Equities	
Cash	$34,000	Notes payable	$ 4,000
Fixed assets:		Stockholders' equity:	
Equipment	10,000	Common stock	40,000
Total assets	$44,000	Total equities	$44,000

All resources (assets) are equal to the claims against these resources (equities).

$$\text{Assets} = \text{Equities}$$

Another way to state this equation is to say that owners' equity is equal to the total assets of the enterprise minus the claims of outsiders.

$$\text{Assets} - \text{Liabilities} = \text{Owners' Equity}$$

On August 16 the Bailey's Drug Store, Inc., paid the owner of the store they were renting $900; $300 was rent for the remainder of August, and $600 was a security deposit to be returned at the end of the two-year lease. On August 16 the rent paid in advance for the remainder of August is a current asset, *prepaid rent,* that will be used up on a daily basis as the month progresses. The $600 security deposit will exist until the end of the two-year lease; it is classified as an *other asset.*

The increase in these assets (prepaid rent of $300 and security deposit of $600) is offset by a decrease in the asset, cash, of $900. Total assets and the claims against them (equities) remain at $44,000 (see Illustration 1–3).

On August 17 the corporation purchased $25,000 of drugs and other merchandise for cash.

The drugs and other merchandise Bailey's is going to sell in the normal operation of its business are called *inventory.* Inventory

ILLUSTRATION 1–3

BAILEY'S DRUG STORE, INC.
Balance Sheet
August 16, 1984

Assets		Equities	
Current assets:		Current liabilities:	
Cash	$33,100	Notes payable	$ 4,000
Prepaid rent	300		
	33,400		
Fixed assets:			
Equipment	10,000		
Other assets:			
Security deposit	600	Stockholders' equity:	
		Common stock	40,000
Total assets	$44,000	Total equities	$44,000

is classified as a current asset because the intention is to sell it and convert it into cash in a current (usually no longer than one year) operating cycle. The increase in inventory is offset by a decrease in cash. The balance sheet after this transaction is shown in Illustration 1–4.

During the month of August the company sold $10,000 of the merchandise inventory for $13,500. The company's customers paid $8,000 and charged $5,500. This transaction results in an $8,000

ILLUSTRATION 1–4

BAILEY'S DRUG STORE, INC.
Balance Sheet
August 17,1984

Assets		Equities	
Current assets:		Current liabilities:	
Cash	$ 8,100	Notes payable	$ 4,000
Inventory	25,000		
Prepaid rent	300		
	33,400		
Fixed assets:			
Equipment	10,000		
Other assets:			
Security deposit	600	Stockholders' equity:	
		Common stock	40,000
Total assets	$44,000	Total equities	$44,000

increase in cash, a $5,500 increase in accounts receivable (amounts due from customers), and a $10,000 decrease in inventory. The net increase in assets of $3,500 ($8,000 + $5,500 − $10,000) represents the income (profit) on the sale of the merchandise.

The $13,500 sale is recognized in the period in which the sale is made rather than when *all* the cash is collected from the customers. This recognition method matches the total cost of the merchandise sold ($10,000) against the sales price ($13,500) and reflects the profit of $3,500 *in the period in which the sale was made.* Because the success of a business depends on its ability to generate sales, this system of matching is more accurate in measuring an enterprise's performance for a period of time than is a system based on cash receipts (collections) and cash disbursements (payments). A cash system could result in recording the cost of sales and the sale in different periods (if the cash disbursement and cash receipts are in different periods) or in recording both the cost of the sale and the sale in the same period, but in a period preceding or following the period in which the sale was made (cash disbursement and receipt precede the sale period, or cash disbursement and receipt follow the sale period).

Since profit (sales minus cost of merchandise sold) belongs to the owners (stockholders) their claim on the assets is increased by $3,500. Profits of corporations are recorded as increases in the stockholders' equity account, *retained earnings.* Losses and cash distributions to stockholders (cash dividends) are recorded as decreases in retained earnings. Partnerships often combine partners' investment, withdrawals, and profits and losses in one account called partners' capital. Individual owners also do not make a distinction between investments, withdrawals, and profits and losses and reflect all these transactions in a net worth or proprietorship account.

There is nothing tangible in the retained earnings account. Retained earnings is not a resource (asset) that may be used. It is only a claim of the owners.

The balance sheet after this transaction is shown in Illustration 1–5.

During the month of August, customers paid the $5,500 they owed Bailey's Drug Store. The current asset, cash, was increased $5,500, and the current asset, accounts receivable, was decreased by $5,500 (see Illustration 1–6).

The company purchased $9,000 of merchandise from a supplier (vendor) in August with the understanding that they would pay for it in 30 days.

The current asset, inventory, was increased by $9,000, and the

ILLUSTRATION 1–5

BAILEY'S DRUG STORE, INC.
Balance Sheet
August 31, 1984*

Assets		Equities	
Current assets:		Current liabilities:	
Cash	$16,100	Notes payable	$ 4,000
Accounts receivable	5,500		
Inventory	15,000		
Prepaid rent	300		
Total current assets	36,900		
		Stockholders' equity:	
Fixed assets:		Common stock	40,000
Equipment	10,000	Retained earnings	3,500
Other assets:		Total stockholders'	
Security deposit	600	equity	43,500
Total assets	$47,500	Total equities	$47,500

* For purposes of this balance sheet only, we are assuming that the sales occurred on August 31, the date this statement was prepared. Normally these sales would be made throughout the month.

current liability, accounts payable, was increased by $9,000 (see Illustration 1–7).

Accounts payable is the account title used for purchases of merchandise that will be paid for at a later date. The seller of merchan-

ILLUSTRATION 1–6

BAILEY'S DRUG STORE, INC.
Balance Sheet
August 31, 1984

Assets		Equities	
Current assets:		Current liabilities:	
Cash	$21,600	Notes payable	$ 4,000
Inventory	15,000		
Prepaid rent	300		
Total current assets	36,900	Stockholders' equity:	
Fixed assets:		Common stock	40,000
Equipment	10,000	Retained earnings	3,500
Other assets:		Total stockholders'	
Security deposit	600	equity	43,500
Total assets	$47,500	Total equities	$47,500

ILLUSTRATION 1-7

BAILEY'S DRUG STORE, INC.
Balance Sheet
August 31, 1984*

Assets		Equities	
Current assets:		Current liabilities:	
Cash	$21,600	Accounts payable	$ 9,000
Inventory	24,000	Notes payable	4,000
Prepaid rent	300	Total current	
Total current		liabilities	13,000
assets	45,900	Stockholders' equity:	
Fixed assets:		Common stock	40,000
Equipment	10,000	Retained earnings	3,500
Other assets:		Total stockholders'	
Security deposit	600	equity	43,500
Total assets	$56,500	Total equities	$56,500

* For purposes of this balance sheet only, we are assuming that the purchases occurred on August 31, the date this statement was prepared, rather than during the month.

dise will usually indicate the terms of payment. For example, a term of payment indicated by 2/10, n/30 means a 2 percent cash discount is allowed if the invoice (bill) is paid in 10 days and the full amount is due in 30 days.

During the period from August 15, 1984, to August 31, 1984, Bailey's paid its employees wages of $1,500 for work performed during this period.

The asset, cash, decreased by $1,500, and retained earnings decreased by $1,500. Wages for services performed reduces the owners' income and is recorded as a *decrease* in retained earnings (see Illustration 1-8).

Other financial events

In order to prepare an accurate balance sheet on August 31, 1984, the company will have to recognize and record other financial events which occurred during the month of August.

The rent Bailey's prepaid for the period August 15 to August 31 has expired, and it is necessary to recognize that Bailey's Drug Store, Inc., no longer has an asset in the amount of $300. They would reflect this by decreasing the prepaid rent to zero and by decreasing retained earnings by $300. The $300 rent for August 15 to August 31, 1984, is a reduction in the amount of the owners' income and reduces retained earnings.

ILLUSTRATION 1–8

BAILEY'S DRUG STORE, INC.
Balance Sheet
August 31, 1984

Assets			Equities		
Current assets			Current liabilities		
Cash		$20,100	Accounts payable		$ 9,000
Inventory		24,000	Notes payable		4,000
Prepaid rent		300	Total current		
Total current			liabilities		13,000
assets		44,400	Stockholders' equity:		
Fixed assets:			Common stock		40,000
Equipment		10,000	Retained earnings		2,000
Other assets:			Total stockholders'		
Security deposit		600	equity		42,000
Total assets		$55,000	Total equities		$55,000

A portion of the cost of the equipment also has to be assigned to the period August 15 to August 31, 1984. The cost of the equipment is allocated in the same manner as the prepaid rent. It has been determined that the useful life of the equipment is 40 months.

The equipment was used for half of the month of August, so Bailey's Drug Store, Inc., would reduce retained earnings by $125 ($10,000 ÷ 40 months = $250 per month or $125 for a half month). This allocation of the cost of a fixed asset to an accounting period which it benefits is called *depreciation*. The other part of this transaction is a reduction in the asset, equipment. The equipment would now be recorded at $10,000 less $125, or $9,875. It has been a convention in accounting to show this allocation of cost in a separate category called *accumulated depreciation* (allowance for depreciation) rather than to show it as a direct reduction from the equipment category. The balance in accumulated depreciation is the total amount of depreciation accumulated from the date the equipment was purchased to the date of the particular balance sheet being prepared.

As of August 31, a half month's interest, or .5% on the 12 percent note payable, has accrued with time. This amounts to $20 ($4,000 × 0.5% = $20) for the half month period from August 16 to August 31. Bailey's Drug Store, Inc., would reduce retained earnings (owners' income) by this amount. The other part of this transaction would be to recognize that the company has an additional liability called *interest payable* in the amount of $20 on August 31, 1984. The August 31, 1984, balance sheet (see Illustration 1–9)

ILLUSTRATION 1–9

BAILEY'S DRUG STORE, INC.
Balance Sheet
August 31, 1984

Assets

Current assets:
Cash ... $20,100
Inventory ... 24,000
Total current assets ... 44,100

Fixed assets:
Equipment ... 10,000
Less: Accumulated depreciation ... 125
Total fixed assets ... 9,875

Other assets:
Security deposit ... 600
Total assets ... $54,575

Equities

Current liabilities:
Accounts payable ... $ 9,000
Notes payable ... 4,000
Interest payable ... 20
Total current liabilities ... 13,020

Stockholders' equity:
Common stock ... 40,000
Retained earnings ... 1,555
Total stockholders' equity ... 41,555
Total equities ... $54,575

reflects the entries for the expiration of the prepaid rent, the depreciation of equipment, and the accrual of interest.

The balance sheet indicates that Bailey's Drug Store assets total $54,575 and their liabilities total $13,020. The residual amount of $41,555 ($54,575 − $13,020) belongs to the owners and is labeled stockholders' equity. The stockholders' original investment was $40,000, and the increase in their claim attributable to net income (net earnings, net profits), which is recorded in the retained earnings account, is $1,555.

The balance sheet shows only the financial condition of Bailey's Drug Store at a particular moment in time—August 31, 1984. It indicates that retained earnings and stockholders' equity have increased by the amount of the net income, but it does not give us the details of how the net income was earned.

In order to better evaluate the financial accomplishment of the enterprise, we would like to know not only the amount of the net income but the composition of all the items that increased net income and all the items that decreased net income.

INCOME STATEMENT

The statement that presents all the items that increase and decrease net income is called the *income statement* (profit and loss statement, net earnings statement). It is a dynamic statement and measures the results of operations of an enterprise for a period of time. It differs from the balance sheet, which is a static statement that measures the financial condition of the enterprise at a moment in time. The statement of income measures the results of operations between two balance sheet dates. In the Bailey's Drug Store problem, it would measure the results of operations from the inception of the corporation on August 15, 1984, to August 31, 1984, the date when we prepared our latest balance sheet.

In order to prepare a statement of income as well as a balance sheet on a current basis, it is necessary to expand the entries made directly to retained earnings into separate categories called *revenues* and *expenses*. Revenues are increases in net income that arise from the major ongoing operations of the enterprise. Expenses are decreases in net income that pertain to carrying out the major ongoing activities of the enterprise. Increases in income from peripheral activities of the firm are classified as gains rather than revenues, and decreases in income from peripheral activities are classified as losses rather than expenses.

Recording the effect of transactions on the balance sheet and income statement

Each financial transaction will have to be analyzed in terms of assets, liabilities, owners' equity, and the new categories of revenues and expenses. The revenues and expenses are temporary categories, and they exist only to aid us in preparing a statement of income. At the end of each accounting period the balances in the revenue and expense accounts will be transferred to retained earnings.

In the Bailey's Drug Store example, sales is a *revenue* (it increases net income), and cost of merchandise sold, wages, rent, depreciation, and interest are expenses (they all decrease net income).

To prepare an income statement for Bailey's Drug Store for the period August 15, 1984, to August 31, 1984, we have to analyze the transactions that affect net income differently than when we prepared only a balance sheet and put all revenue and expense items directly into retained earnings.

1. Sales to customers of $10,000 of merchandise for $13,500:

In terms of balance sheet only:

Increase cash	$ 8,000
Increase accounts receivable	5,500
Decrease inventory	10,000
Increase retained earnings	3,500

In a complete accounting system resulting in a balance sheet and a statement of income:

Increase cash	8,000
Increase accounts receivable	5,500
Increase sales (increases income)	13,500
Increase cost of merchandise sold (decreases income)	10,000
Decrease inventory	10,000

Sales of $13,500 minus cost of merchandise sold of $10,000 is nothing more than an expansion for purposes of income statement preparation of the increase of $3,500 in retained earnings.

2. The company paid wages of $1,500 for work performed:

In terms of balance sheet only:

Decrease retained earnings	$ 1,500
Decrease cash	1,500

In a complete accounting system resulting in a balance sheet and income statement:

Increase wages expense	1,500
Decrease cash	1,500

The increase in the expense account, wages expense, has the same effect as a decrease in retained earnings.

3. Expiration of the prepaid rent of $300:

In terms of balance sheet only:

Decrease retained earnings	$300
Decrease prepaid rent	300

In a complete accounting system resulting in a balance sheet and income statement:

Increase rent expense	300
Decrease prepaid rent	300

An increase in the rent expense account (reduction of net income) has the same effect as a decrease in retained earnings.

4. Depreciation of equipment of $125:

In terms of balance sheet only:

Decrease retained earnings	$125
Increase accumulated depreciation (deduction from the fixed asset account, equipment)	125

In a complete accounting system resulting in a balance sheet and income statement:

Increase depreciation expense	125
Increase accumulated depreciation	125

The increase in depreciation expense has the same effect as a decrease in retained earnings.

5. Interest expense of $20:

In terms of balance sheet only:

Decrease retained earnings .... $ 20
Increase interest payable   20

In a complete accounting system resulting in a balance sheet and income statement:

Increase interest expense   20
Increase interest payable   20

The increase in interest expense has the same effect as a decrease in retained earnings.

With this additional information, we are now able to prepare a statement of income (Illustration 1–10) for Bailey's Drug Store for the period August 15, 1984, to August 31, 1984, as well as the balance sheet (Illustration 1–9) on August 31, 1984.

ILLUSTRATION 1–10

BAILEY'S DRUG STORE, INC.
Statement of Income
For the Period August 15 to August 31, 1984

Sales		$13,500
Cost of merchandise sold		10,000
Gross profit*		3,500
Other expenses:		
Wages	$1,500	
Rent	300	
Depreciation	125	
Interest	20	1,945
Net income (profit)		$ 1,555

* Gross profit or gross margin is the difference between the sales revenue and the cost of the merchandise sold.

PROBLEMS AND CASES

1–1 The Jennifer Corporation

All the balance sheet categories of the Jennifer Corporation on December 31, 1984, are listed below:

Notes payable	$ 9,350
Cash	12,670
Accounts receivable	9,270
Equipment and furniture	30,650
Accounts payable	5,600
Inventory	22,735

Accumulated depreciation—equipment and furniture	$15,325
Common stock	40,000
Prepaid rent	1,200
Retained earnings	?
Security deposit—rent	700
Interest payable	450

Required:

1. Calculate the amount of retained earnings on December 31, 1984.

2. Prepare a balance sheet on December 31, 1984.

1–2 The Jones Company

Mr. Jones organized the Jones Company as a proprietorship and began business in September 1984. Shown below are a series of balance sheets showing the position of the company at four different points in time during the first few days of operation.

	(A)	(B)	(C)	(D)
Assets				
Cash	$10,000	$ 7,000	$ 9,000	$ 7,000
Accounts receivable	–0–	–0–	5,000	3,000
Merchandise	–0–	8,000	4,000	4,000
Total assets	$10,000	$15,000	$18,000	$14,000
Equities				
Note payable—bank	$ 3,000	$ 3,000	$ 3,000	$ 2,000
Accounts payable	–0–	5,000	5,000	2,000
Total liabilities	3,000	8,000	8,000	4,000
Proprietorship	7,000	7,000	10,000	10,000
Total equities	$10,000	$15,000	$18,000	$14,000

Required:

1. Balance sheet *(A)* was prepared immediately after the company was organized. Describe the transactions that occurred prior to its preparation.

2. Describe the transactions which account for the changes between:
a. Balance sheets *(A)* and *(B)*.
b. Balance sheets *(B)* and *(C)*.
c. Balance sheets *(C)* and *(D)*.

1–3 La Cabine Style Shop

On January 1, 1984, Jean Moe started La Cabine Style Shop with an investment of $55,000. During the month of January 1984 she prepared the following balance sheets:

LA CABINE STYLE SHOP
Balance Sheet
January 1, 1984

Assets		Equities	
Cash	$55,000	Jean Moe, net worth	$55,000

LA CABINE STYLE SHOP
Balance Sheet
January 1, 1984

Assets		Equities	
Current assets:		Current liabilities:	
Cash	$90,000	12% Note payable—	
		bank	$35,000
		Owner's equity:	
		Jean Moe, net worth	55,000
Total assets	$90,000	Total equities	$90,000

[handwritten: got a 35,000 loan 12%]

LA CABINE STYLE SHOP
Balance Sheet
January 1, 1984

Assets		Equities	
Current assets:		Current liabilities:	
Cash	$53,000	12% Note payable—	
Inventories	25,000	bank	$35,000
Total current assets ...	78,000		
Fixed assets:		Owner's equity:	
Equipment	12,000	Jean Moe, net worth	55,000
Total assets	$90,000	Total equities	$90,000

[handwritten: bought inv & equip.]

LA CABINE STYLE SHOP
Balance Sheet
January 31, 1984

Assets		Equities	
Current assets:		Current liabilities:	
Cash	$66,000	12% Note payable—	
Accounts		bank	$35,000
receivable	7,000		
Inventories	13,000		
Total current assets ...	86,000		
Fixed assets:		Owner's equity:	
Equipment	12,000	Jean Moe, net worth	63,000
Total assets	$98,000	Total equities	$98,000

[handwritten: cash 13,000 acc. 7000 sales 20,000 cgs - 12,000 8000 to ref. earning; Δ in inven; fixed]

LA CABINE STYLE SHOP
Balance Sheet
January 31, 1984

Assets		Equities	
Current assets:		Current liabilities:	
Cash	$66,000	12% Note payable—	
Accounts		bank	$35,000
receivable	7,000	Interest payable	350
Inventories	13,000	Rent payable	500
Total current assets	86,000	Wages payable	1,000
		Total current	
Fixed assets:		liabilities	36,850
Equipment	12,000		
Less: Accumulated			
depreciation	200	Owner's equity:	
Total fixed		Jean Moe, net worth	60,950
assets	11,800		
Total assets	$97,800	Total equities	$97,800

Required:

1. Analyze each balance sheet and describe any changes from the previous balance sheet. For example, the appropriate description for the first balance sheet would be: On January 1, 1984, Jean Moe started La Cabine Style Shop as a sole proprietorship with a cash investment of $55,000.

2. Prepare an income statement for La Cabine Style Shop for the month of January 1984.

3. Was La Cabine Style Shop successful in January 1984?

1-4 Richardson's Hardware Store, Inc.

Listed below are *all* the categories of the Richardson Corporation on December 31, 1984. The amounts in the categories reflect the recording of all the events for the period except for the transfer of net income (revenues − expenses) for 1984 to retained earnings.

Rent payable	$ 300
Cash	8,350
Sales	225,000
Accounts receivable	12,500
Depreciation expense	8,000
Retained earnings (12/31/83)	22,135
Inventory	13,125
Prepaid insurance	900
Interest payable	1,000
Insurance expense	1,260
Equipment and furniture	80,000
Cost of merchandise sold	155,000

⌐Interest expense	$	4,000
Accounts payable		7,600
Accumulated depreciation—equipment		
and furniture		20,000
⌐Rent expense		3,600
⌐Wages and salary expense		35,000
Salaries and wages payable		700
Common stock		45,000

Required:

1. Prepare an income statement for the year ended December 31, 1984.

2. Prepare a balance sheet on December 31, 1984.

3. Richardson Corporation has asked a local bank to loan them $25,000 for 90 days at market interest rates. Assume you are the bank loan officer. Would you make the loan? Explain why or why not and indicate what other information, if any, you would like to have before making the loan decision.

1–5 Art's Discount Store

The balance sheet of Art's Discount Store on November 30, 1984, was as follows:

ART'S DISCOUNT STORE
Balance Sheet
November 30, 1984

Assets

Cash	$26,300
Accounts receivable	8,500
Inventory	32,200
Total assets	$67,000

Equities

Accounts payable	$ 7,500
Notes payable—bank	15,000
Net worth—Art Swerz	44,500
Total equities	$67,000

Required:

1. You are to record the effect of the following December occurrences, and prepare both a balance sheet on December 31, 1984, and an income statement for the month of December 1984. You may use any format you feel is appropriate to accumulate the information to prepare the balance sheet and income statement.

a. Paid creditors $5,000 of amount owned them.

b. Collected $6,000 of the amount owed by customers.

c. Sold merchandise inventory with a cost of $7,500 for $15,000. The customers paid $12,500 in cash and charged $2,500.

d. Art withdrew $2,500 from the store's bank account. He also took merchandise for his personal use. The merchandise cost $400 and had a sales price of $800. Note: Art's Discount Store is a proprietorship, and the owner's investment and withdrawals and the store's profit and losses are all reflected in the net worth category.

e. Ordered merchandise costing $3,600 from Johnson Electric Company.

f. Paid wages of $2,000 covering the entire month of December to the sales clerk. Art didn't pay himself any stipulated salary for the month of November. He felt his services were worth approximately $3,000 a month.

g. Paid the $15,000 principal amount of the note plus $200 interest for the month of December.

h. Paid $1,500 for three months rent in advance on December 1.

i. Received the $3,600 of merchandise ordered from Johnson Electric Company. Art expects to pay the bill in January 1985.

j. Art Swerz was offered $64,000 for his equity in the store by a large discount chain. He rejected the offer but was pleased that the store had acquired goodwill.

k. Incorporated Art's Discount Store. Art Swerz received $46,400 in common stock for his equity in the store.

l. Art Swerz sold half of his stock to his friend Stan Gotkus for $32,000 (half of the $64,000 he was offered for the store).

2. Would you have invested $32,000 for a 50 percent ownership in Art's Discount Store?

1–6 Henderson Brothers Service Station

For 23 years Pete King had owned a service station located off U.S. Highway 1 in Dedham, Massachusetts. On February 1, 1984, King celebrated his 60th birthday and announced his intention to retire and move to Florida as soon as he could find a buyer for his service station.

Two brothers, Ed and Richard Henderson, saw King's newspaper ad for the sale of the station and drove to Dedham on a Saturday to investigate. They liked what they saw. The station was easily visible and accessible from U.S. Highway 1 and also occupied a prime location on the town's main thoroughfare. It was obvious to them that King had taken great pride in the station; the grounds were immaculate, and the building and equipment appeared to be well-maintained and clean. The Henderson brothers also noted the steady flow of morning customers into the station.

The Hendersons arranged a meeting with King for the following Monday to discuss a possible purchase. At the meeting, King indicated that he expected $98,000 for his business. He showed the Hendersons his figures for the preceding five years. Net income from the station during that period ranged from a low of $16,500 in 1980 to a high of $28,400 in 1983. King said that this net income was derived mainly from gasoline sales and minor auto repairs. He expressed the belief that if major repairs were also performed, sales and income could probably be doubled. King had not done major repairs because he had been satisfied with his results and had wished to keep the operation small.

The Henderson brothers declared their desire to buy the station, but they indicated that they had only $40,000 in cash. By this time, King was eager to sell his station and retire. He proposed to settle for $40,000 in cash and a 20-year mortgage loan on the remaining $58,000, which would be secured by the station and bear a 15 percent per annum interest rate. It was to be paid in 40 semiannual payments of principal plus interest on the unpaid balance.

Ed and Richard Henderson agreed to these terms, and on April 1, 1984, the sale papers were signed and the ownership was transferred. King and his wife moved to Florida. The Henderson brothers took over the service station as equal partners, each having contributed half of the purchase price. The sale price included $18,500 for the land, $50,000 for the building and improvements, $12,000 for tools and equipment, and $17,500 for inventory (gasoline, oil, tires, parts).

The brothers planned to expand the business by providing major repairs but soon discovered that in order to do so they would need a heavy duty hydraulic lift costing $5,600. Since the bank refused to lend this sum, Richard Henderson contributed $4,000 and Ed $1,600, and they purchased the hydraulic lift on July 1, 1984.

After six months of ownership, the Hendersons called Mr. Benson, a local accountant, to help them determine how they had done. Benson determined the following as of September 30, 1984:

a. There was $289 in the cash register and $3,286 in the checking account.
b. Customers owed the service station $1,200.
c. Unpaid bills due suppliers amounted to $700.
d. The physical inventory of gasoline, oil, tires, and parts amounted to $15,800.
e. The six-month payment of $5,800 for principal and interest on the loan was made on September 30, 1984.
f. The buildings and improvements had an estimated useful life of 35 years.
g. The tools and equipment had an estimated useful life of 10 years.

Required:

1. Prepare a balance sheet for the Henderson Brothers Service Station as of April 1, 1984.

2. Prepare a balance sheet as of September 30, 1984.

3. What were the equities (capital accounts) of Ed and Richard Henderson on September 30, 1984? (In partnership law, the partners share equally

in profits and losses unless there is an agreement by the partners to share them in a different manner).

4. If the partnership was dissolved on September 30, 1984, do you suppose the partners would receive an amount equal to their capital account? Explain.

2

Mechanics of accounting

The simple system we used for Bailey's Drug Store, Inc., to prepare a balance sheet and income statement was adequate because we had to analyze and classify only a few transactions. When there are many transactions, it is necessary to have a written analysis of each transaction and how it is recorded in the financial statements. We need a system that will analyze and record the transactions as they occur and transfer the increases and decreases to the correct category. In accounting, these categories are called *accounts*. Individual accounts are kept on separate sheets in a book, or on a computer tape in automated systems, called a *general ledger*.

In practice, each general ledger account would have a number. The listing of all the accounts of the enterprise is called the *chart of accounts*. The number of accounts in the chart of accounts will depend on how much information management wishes to and is required to generate for the preparation of financial statements. The numerical range for a small company might be as follows:

Assets	100–199
Liabilities	200–299
Stockholders' equity	300–399
Revenues	400–499
Expenses	500–699

GENERAL LEDGER

Listed below are the general ledger accounts of Bailey's Drug Store, Inc.

Cash	Interest Payable
Accounts Receivable	Common Stock
Inventory	Retained Earnings
Prepaid Rent	Sales
Equipment	Cost of Merchandise Sold
Accumulated Depreciation	Wages Expense
Security Deposit	Rent Expense
Accounts Payable	Depreciation Expense
Notes Payable	Interest Expense

The terms assets, current assets, fixed assets, other assets, equities, current liabilities, stockholders' equity, and revenues and expenses are not account titles. They are headings for groups of accounts used in the balance sheet or income statement. The five major groupings of accounts are assets, liabilities, owners' equity, revenues, and expenses.

a. Cash is a current asset account.
b. Equipment is a fixed-asset account.
c. Accumulated depreciation is a contra fixed asset account or deduction from a fixed asset account.
d. Accounts payable is a current liability account.
e. Retained earnings is an owners' equity account.
f. Sales is a revenue account.
g. Rent expense is an expense account.

The number of accounts in the general ledger will be determined by the amount of detail the enterprise's management wishes to accumulate. For example, management could have one general ledger account called *miscellaneous expense,* which includes bank charges, office supplies, and telephone expense, or they could have three separate accounts called *bank charges, office supplies,* and *telephone expense.*

Generally, it is good practice to accumulate the information in as many accounts as is economically feasible in the general ledger. It is always possible to reclassify and combine accounts for purposes of preparing financial statements.

The general ledger account for cash for Bailey's Drug Store, Inc., would appear as in Illustration 2–1.

The Ref. (reference) column indicates the book of original entry (CR = cash receipts book, CD = cash disbursements book) from which the transaction was posted. Books of original entry and the process of posting are explained later in this chapter.

For purposes of solving classroom problems, we use only the cen-

ILLUSTRATION 2–1

		Cash		
Date	Ref.	Increases	Decreases	Balance
1984				
Aug. 15	CR	40,000		40,000
16	CD		6,000	34,000
17	CD		900	33,100
17	CD		25,000	8,100
31	CR	8,000		16,100
31	CR	5,500		21,600
31	CD		1,500	20,100

ILLUSTRATION 2–2

Cash	
Increases	Decreases

Cash	
40,000	6,000
8,000	900
5,500	25,000
	1,500

ter, or *increases* and *decreases* portions of the formal general ledger account. This center portion of the general ledger account is called a *T-account* (see Illustration 2–2).

The $20,100 balance in the cash T(general ledger)-account is obtained by subtracting the $33,400 total of the decreases side of the account from the $53,500 total of the increases side of the account.

The accounting profession in the United States has decided that assets should have left-side balances and be on the *left side of the balance sheet,* and equities (liabilities and owners' equity) should have right-side balances and be on the *right side of the balance sheet.* (In some formal balance sheet presentations, assets are listed at the top of the page and equities on the bottom.) The basic accounting equation is assets (accounts with left-side balances) are equal to equities (accounts with right-side balances):

Assets = Equities

It was also decided by the accounting profession *that increases in assets accounts would be recorded on the left side, decreases on the right side.* To maintain the balance sheet equation of left-side account balances = right-side account balances, we would have to treat equity accounts in exactly the opposite fashion from asset accounts. Increases would be recorded on the right side and decreases on the left side.

Asset Accounts		=	Equity Accounts	
Increases	Decreases		Decreases	Increases

RECORDING TRANSACTIONS IN THE GENERAL LEDGER ACCOUNTS

Bailey's Drug Store, Inc., transactions in general ledger (T-account) form would appear as follows:

1. Initial investment by stockholders of $40,000.

Asset Accounts		=	Equity Accounts	
Cash			**Common Stock**	
(1) 40,000				(1) 40,000

The increase in the asset account, Cash, is recorded as a left-side entry. It is equal to an increase in the stockholders' equity account, Common Stock, which is recorded as a right-side entry.

2. The company purchases display equipment in the amount of $10,000; $6,000 was paid in cash and a $4,000, 12 percent, 90-day note was given for the balance.

Asset Accounts			=	Equity Accounts	
Cash				**Notes Payable**	
(1) 40,000	(2)	6,000			(2) 4,000
Equipment				**Common Stock**	
(2) 10,000					(1) 40,000

The $10,000 increase in the asset account, Equipment, is a left-side entry. It is equal to the right-side entries of $6,000 which reduces the asset account, Cash, and $4,000 which increases the liability account, Notes payable.

The balance in an account is the difference between the total of the increases minus the decreases. The Cash balance is $34,000. It is a left-side balance because the left-side entry of $40,000 exceeds the right-side entry of $6,000.

Total assets, (Cash, $34,000; Equipment, $10,000) of $44,000 are equal to total equities, (Notes Payable, $4,000; Common Stock, $40,000) of $44,000.

3. The company paid $300 rent for August and gave the landlord a $600 security deposit.

Asset Accounts			=	Equity Accounts		
Cash				**Notes Payable**		
(1)	40,000	(2) 6,000			(2)	4,000
		(3) 900				
Prepaid Rent				**Common Stock**		
(3)	300				(1)	40,000
Equipment						
(2)	10,000					
Security Deposit						
(3)	600					

The increases in the asset accounts, Prepaid Rent and Security Deposit, are reflected by left-side entries which are offset by a decrease (right-side entry) in the asset account, Cash.

4. On August 17, Bailey's purchased $25,000 worth of drugs and other merchandise for cash.

Asset Accounts			=	Equity Accounts		
Cash				**Notes Payable**		
(1)	40,000	(2) 6,000			(2)	4,000
		(3) 900				
		(4) 25,000				
Inventory						
(4)	25,000					
Prepaid Rent				**Common Stock**		
(3)	300				(1)	40,000
Equipment						
(2)	10,000					
Security Deposit						
(3)	600					

The increase (left-side entry) in the asset account, Inventory, is equal to the decrease (right-side entry) in the asset account, Cash.

Accounts with left-side balances are Cash, $8,100 [$40,000 − ($6,000 + $900 + $25,000)]; Inventory $25,000; Prepaid Rent, $300; Equipment, $10,000; and Security Deposit $600. Accounts with right-side balances are Notes Payable, $4,000, and Common Stock, $40,000. Total assets of $44,000 are equal to total equities of $44,000.

5. During the month of August the company sold $10,000 of the merchandise inventory to customers for $13,500. The customers paid $8,000 and charged $5,500.

Asset Accounts				=	Equity Accounts		
Cash					**Notes Payable**		
(1)	40,000	(2)	6,000			(2)	4,000
(5)	8,000	(3)	900				
		(4)	25,000				
Accounts Receivable					**Common Stock**		
(5)	5,500					(1)	40,000
Inventory					**Sales**		
(4)	25,000	(5)	10,000			(5)	13,500
Prepaid Rent					**Cost of Merchandise Sold**		
(3)	300				(5)	10,000	
Equipment							
(2)	10,000						
Security Deposit							
(3)	600						

Left-side entries are made to reflect the increase of $8,000 in the asset account, Cash, and $5,500 in the asset account, Accounts Receivable. These left-side entries are balanced by a right-side entry of $13,500 to the revenue account, Sales. *Increases in revenue accounts are recorded on the right-hand side because revenues increase net income and net income increases the owners' equity. Increases in owners' equity are right-side entries.* The increase of $10,000 in the expense account, Cost of Merchandise Sold, is balanced by a $10,000 decrease in the asset account, Inventory. *Increases in expense accounts are recorded on the left-hand side because expenses decrease net income and owners' equity.*

6. During the month of August the customers paid the $5,500 they owed Bailey's Drug Store, Inc.

Asset Accounts			=	Equity Accounts		
	Cash				**Notes Payable**	
(1)	40,000	(2)	6,000		(2)	4,000
(5)	8,000	(3)	900			
(6)	5,500	(4)	25,000			
	Accounts Receivable				**Common Stock**	
(5)	5,500	(6)	5,500		(1)	40,000
	Inventory				**Sales**	
(4)	25,000	(5)	10,000		(5)	13,500
	Prepaid Rent				**Cost of Merchandise Sold**	
(3)	300			(5)	10,000	
	Equipment					
(2)	10,000					
	Security Deposit					
(3)	600					

The increase in the asset, Cash, is balanced by the decrease in another asset, Accounts Receivable.

7. During the month of August the company purchased $9,000 of merchandise on account.

	Asset Accounts			=	Equity Accounts		

	Cash				Accounts Payable	
(1)	40,000	(2)	6,000		(7)	9,000
(5)	8,000	(3)	900			
(6)	5,500	(4)	25,000			

	Accounts Receivable				Notes Payable	
(5)	5,500	(6)	5,500		(2)	4,000

	Inventory				Common Stock	
(4)	25,000	(5)	10,000		(1)	40,000
(7)	9,000					

	Prepaid Rent			Sales	
(3)	300			(5)	13,500

	Equipment			Cost of Merchandise Sold	
(2)	10,000		(5)	10,000	

	Security Deposit	
(5)	600	

The increase in the asset account, Inventory, is balanced by an increase in the liability account, Accounts Payable.

Total assets of $56,500, that is, Cash, $21,600; Inventory, $24,000; Prepaid Rent, $300; Equipment, $10,000; and Security Deposit, $600 are equal to total equites of $56,500 representing Accounts Payable, $9,000; Notes Payable, $4,000; Common Stock, $40,000; and net income which increases Retained Earnings by $3,500 [Sales ($13,500) − Cost of Merchandise Sold ($10,000)].

8. Bailey's Drug Store paid its employees wages of $1,500 for work performed from August 15, 1984, to August 31, 1984.

	Asset Accounts			=		Equity Accounts	

	Cash					Accounts Payable	
(1)	40,000	(2)	6,000			(7)	9,000
(5)	8,000	(3)	900				
(6)	5,500	(4)	25,000				
		(8)	1,500				

	Accounts Receivable					Notes Payable	
(5)	5,500	(6)	5,500			(2)	4,000

	Inventory					Common Stock	
(4)	25,000	(5)	10,000			(1)	40,000
(7)	9,000						

	Prepaid Rent					Sales	
(3)	300					(5)	13,500

	Equipment					Cost of Merchandise Sold	
(2)	10,000				(5)	10,000	

	Security Deposit					Wages Expense	
(3)	600				(8)	1,500	

The increase in wages expense, which is a reduction in net income, is recorded by a left-side entry. It is balanced by a decrease in cash, a right-side entry.

Debits and credits

Accountants call left-side entries *debits* and right-side entries *credits.*

In the recording of accounting transactions there is no meaning for debit (abbreviated Dr.) other than left or for credit (abbreviated Cr.) other than right.

Debits which are always left-side entries increase assets and decrease liabilities and owners' equity.

Credits which are always right-side entries increase liabilities and owners' equity and decrease assets.

Increases in revenue accounts, which increase net income and therefore increase owners' equity, are recorded as credits. Increases in expense accounts, which decrease net income and therefore decrease owners' equity, are recorded as debits.

When used as a verb debit means to make an entry to the left-hand side of an account; credit means to make an entry to the right-hand side of an account.

9. The prepaid rent from August 15 to August 31 has expired. Debit (left-side entry) Rent Expense to record the increase in this expense account, and credit (right-side entry) Prepaid Rent to record the decrease in this asset account.

Asset Accounts				=	Equity Accounts		
Cash					**Accounts Payable**		
(1)	40,000	(2)	6,000			(7)	9,000
(5)	8,000	(3)	900				
(6)	5,500	(4)	25,000				
		(8)	1,500				
Accounts Receivable					**Notes Payable**		
(5)	5,500	(6)	5,500			(2)	4,000
Inventory					**Common Stock**		
(4)	25,000	(5)	10,000			(1)	40,000
(7)	9,000						
Prepaid Rent					**Sales**		
(3)	300	(9)	300			(5)	13,500
Equipment					**Cost of Merchandise Sold**		
(2)	10,000				(5)	10,000	
Security Deposit					**Wages Expense**		
(3)	600				(8)	1,500	
					Rent Expense		
					(9)	300	

10. Depreciation of the equipment for the last half of August, $125.

Debit Depreciation Expense to record the increase in this expense account, and credit Accumulated Depreciation—Equipment, which results in a decrease in the asset, equipment.

It is customary to accumulate the reductions in fixed asset accounts due to depreciation in this special contra fixed asset account called Accumulated Depreciation rather than directly deducting it from the fixed asset account, Equipment. This makes it possible to see both the original cost of the fixed asset and the total amount of depreciation accumulated from the purchase date of the fixed asset.

Asset Accounts			=	Equity Accounts		
Cash				**Accounts Payable**		
(1)	40,000	(2)	6,000		(7)	9,000
(5)	8,000	(3)	900			
(6)	5,500	(4)	25,000			
		(8)	1,500			

Accounts Receivable				**Notes Payable**		
(5)	5,500	(6)	5,500		(2)	4,000

Inventory				**Common Stock**		
(4)	25,000	(5)	10,000		(1)	40,000
(7)	9,000					

Prepaid Rent				**Sales**		
(3)	300	(9)	300		(5)	13,500

Equipment				**Cost of Merchandise Sold**		
(2)	10,000			(5)	10,000	

Accumulated Depreciation— Equipment				**Wages Expense**		
		(10)	125	(8)	1,500	

Security Deposit				**Rent Expense**		
(3)	600			(9)	300	

				Depreciation Expense		
				(10)	125	

11. Interest expense from August 16 to August 31 is recorded on the books.

Debit interest expense (see p. 33) and credit interest payable. This entry matches the interest expense for the last 15 days of August with the revenues earned during the same period of time.

Asset Accounts = *Equity Accounts*

Cash

(1)	40,000	(2)	6,000
(5)	8,000	(3)	900
(6)	5,500	(4)	25,000
		(8)	1,500

Accounts Payable

(7)	9,000

Accounts Receivable

(5)	5,500	(6)	5,500

Interest Payable

(11)	20

Inventory

(4)	25,000	(5)	10,000
(7)	9,000		

Notes Payable

(2)	4,000

Prepaid Rent

(3)	300	(9)	300

Common Stock

(1)	40,000

Equipment

(2)	10,000

Sales

(5)	13,500

Accumulated Depreciation—Equipment

(10)	125

Cost of Merchandise Sold

(5)	10,000

Security Deposit

(3)	600

Wages Expense

(8)	1,500

Rent Expense

(9)	300

Depreciation Expense

(10)	125

	Interest Expense	
(11)	20	

TRIAL BALANCE

It is good practice, prior to the preparation of the financial statements, to prove that all the accounts with debit balances are equal to all the accounts with credit balances. This unclassified listing of accounts is called a *trial balance.* The trial balance proves that the books are arithmetically correct. It does not prove that the balance in each account is correct as we could have made a debit and credit of the same amount to the wrong general ledger accounts and still be arithmetically in balance.

The August 31, 1984, trial balance for Bailey's Drug Store, Inc., is shown in Illustration 2–3.

ILLUSTRATION 2–3

BAILEY'S DRUG STORE, INC.
Trial Balance
August 31, 1984

	Dr. (Debit)	Cr. (Credit)
Cash	$20,100	
Inventory	24,000	
Equipment	10,000	
Accumulated depreciation		$ 125
Security deposit	600	
Accounts payable		9,000
Interest payable		20
Notes payable		4,000
Common stock		40,000
Sales		13,500
Cost of merchandise sold	10,000	
Wages expense	1,500	
Rent expense	300	
Depreciation expense	125	
Interest expense	20	
Totals	$66,645	$66,645

BOOKS OF ORIGINAL ENTRY

In order to maintain a chronological financial history of the enterprise, each transaction is first recorded in a *book of original entry* and then transferred or posted to the general ledger accounts.

General journal

It is possible to enter all the transactions in one book of original entry called a *general journal.* The format to be followed in making a *general journal entry* is to first list the general ledger account(s) to be debited at the left-hand margin. The general ledger account(s) to be credited is indented on the line below the account to be debited. The amount to be debited is listed in the money column on the left, and the amount to be credited is listed in the money column to the right. Usually a simple explanation of the journal entry is written under the accounts debited and credited.

All general journal entries for Bailey's Drug Store, Inc., made prior to their posting to the general ledger accounts are shown in Illustration 2–4.

ILLUSTRATION 2–4

GENERAL JOURNAL

Date		Accounts	Debit	Credit
1984 Aug.	15	Cash	40,000	
		Common Stock		40,000
		Issued $40,000 common stock to Joyce Bailey.		
	16	Equipment	10,000	
		Cash		6,000
		Notes Payable		4,000
		Purchased equipment from Heath Co., paid $4,000 cash and a 12%, 90-day note.		
	16	Prepaid Rent	300	
		Security Deposit	600	
		Cash		900
		Rent for 8/16 to 8/31 plus a $600 security deposit.		
	17	Inventory	25,000	
		Cash		25,000
		Purchased merchandise from McKesson and Robbins.		
	31	Cash	8,000	
		Accounts Receivable	5,500	
		Sales		13,500
		Sales for 8/15–8/31		
	31	Cost of Merchandise Sold	10,000	
		Inventory		10,000
		Cost of merchandise sold for 8/15–8/31.		

ILLUSTRATION 2–4 *(concluded)*

GENERAL JOURNAL

Date	Accounts	Debit	Credit
31	Cash	5,500	
	Accounts Receivable		5,500
	Collection of accounts receivable.		
31	Inventory	9,000	
	Accounts payable		9,000
	Purchases from Star Wholesalers, terms 30/n.		
31	Wages Expense	1,500	
	Cash		1,500
	Wages for 8/15–8/31.		
31	Rent Expense	300	
	Prepaid Rent		300
	To record the expiration of the prepaid rent.		
31	Depreciation Expense	125	
	Accumulated Depreciation		125
	To record depreciation for 15 days.		
31	Interest Expense	20	
	Interest Payable		20
	To record interest expense for 15 days.		

Other books of original entry

If a company had a large number of transactions each month,
posting from the general journal to the general ledger would become very time-consuming and cumbersome. This would be particularly true for transactions that are repetitive in nature, such as
sales, purchases, cash receipts, and cash disbursements. To solve
this problem and to segregate similar types of transactions for purposes of analysis, separate books or journals of original entry are
used for each of these major types of transactions. For example,
using a *cash receipts* journal makes it possible to post the monthly
total for cash receipts to the Cash account in the general ledger
instead of having to post each individual cash receipt, as would
be necessary if we used only a general journal to record all transactions. It also accumulates all the cash receipts for the month in
one journal. An example of a cash receipts journal is shown in
Illustration 2–5.

ILLUSTRATION 2–5

CASH RECEIPTS JOURNAL

Date	Received from	Cash Debit	Accounts Receivable Credit	Sales Credit	Miscellaneous Account	Amount Credit
8/15/84	Joyce Bailey	40,000			Common Stock	40,000
8/17/84	Cash sales	1,000		1,000		
8/19/84	Cash sales	2,000		2,000		
8/21/84	Customers	2,500	2,500			
8/22/84	Cash sales	3,000		3,000		
8/25/84	Customers	2,000	2,000			
8/27/84	Cash sales	1,500		1,500		
8/29/84	Customers	1,000	1,000			
8/31/84	Cash sales	500		500		
		53,500	5,500	8,000		40,000

With a cash receipts journal Bailey's would only post the $53,500 debit to the general ledger, Cash account for August. They would not have to post the individual amounts comprising this cash total. The $5,500 would be credited to the general ledger account, Accounts Receivable. In order to know how much each customer owes, the store will also have to keep a record for each customer in a separate accounts receivable ledger.

The $8,000 will be posted as a credit to the Sales account. In order to determine the profitability of each type of merchandise they were selling, Bailey's could also have a separate general ledger account and column in the cash receipts journal for Sales—Pharmacy, Sales—Wine and Liquor, Sales—Greeting Cards, and Sales—Sundries instead of one sales column.

The $40,000 is posted as a credit to the Common Stock account.

If a separate journal is used for cash receipts, cash disbursements, sales, and purchases, the general journal will only be used for adjustments and corrections to general ledger accounts. Bailey's entries for rent, depreciation, and interest are examples of *adjusting journal entries.*

CLOSING JOURNAL ENTRY

A special general journal entry which is made once a year is called the *closing journal entry.* The purpose of this entry is to transfer the balances of all the revenue and expense accounts (net income or net loss for the year) to retained earnings.

Let us assume that the revenue and expense accounts for Bailey's Drug Store, Inc., at the end of their first year of operations were as follows:

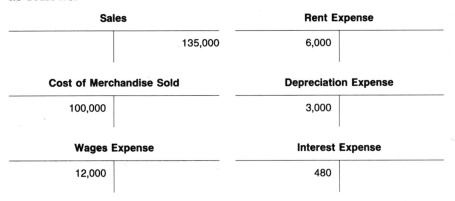

Sales		Rent Expense	
	135,000	6,000	

Cost of Merchandise Sold		Depreciation Expense	
100,000		3,000	

Wages Expense		Interest Expense	
12,000		480	

The closing journal entry to close out the revenue and expense accounts and transfer the net income to retained earnings is shown in Illustration 2–6.

ILLUSTRATION 2–6

GENERAL JOURNAL

Date		Accounts	Debit	Credit
1985 July	31	Sales	135,000	
		Cost of Merchandise Sold		100,000
		Wages Expense		12,000
		Rent Expense		6,000
		Depreciation Expense		3,000
		Interest Expense		480
		Retained Earnings		13,520
		To close the revenue and expense accounts for the fiscal year ended July 31, 1985.		

After the closing entry is posted, the revenue and expense accounts will all have a zero balance, and the net income of $13,520 will be transferred to the retained earnings account.

Retained Earnings

	(c)	13,520

Sales			**Rent Expense**		
(c)	135,000	135,000	6,000	(c)	6,000

Cost of Merchandise Sold			**Depreciation Expense**		
100,000	(c)	100,000	3,000	(c)	3,000

Wages Expense			**Interest Expense**		
12,000	(c)	12,000	480	(c)	480

The closing entry is made in order to prevent more than one year's totals from accumulating in the revenue and expense accounts.

Asset, liability, and owners' equity accounts are not closed at the end of the year because they represent either a resource of the company or a claim against company resources. The balance sheet account, retained earnings, will contain all of the net income earned from the inception of the enterprise less any distributions made to the owners. If this account has a debit balance, it is labeled deficit rather than retained earnings.

THE ACCOUNTING CYCLE

The accounting cycle may be represented schematically as follows:

Transactions
↓
Analyze transactions
↓
Record transactions in books of original entry
↓
Post books of original entry to the general ledger
↓
Analyze general ledger accounts and prepare
adjusting and correcting journal entries
↓
Post adjusting and correcting journal entries
to the general ledger
↓

↓

Prepare balance sheet and income statement
from the general ledger

↓

Prepare closing journal entry and post
it to the general ledger

The routine aspects of the accounting cycle (recording transactions and posting them to the general ledger accounts) are generally done by bookkeepers. Accountants focus on the more analytical aspects of the accounting cycle (analyses of the transactions and general ledger accounts and preparation of financial statements).

PROBLEMS AND CASES

2-1 Joyce Markets

Part A—Prepare a journal entry for each of the following *transactions* of Joyce Markets, a sole proprietorship which sells fruits and vegetables.

Dec.   1 Joyce Bailey started the company with a cash contribution of $25,000.

Purchased fixtures with a 10-year life from the Heath Company for $16,000. Paid them $10,000 in cash and gave them a $6,000, 12%, 120-day note.

Paid 3 months rent in advance. The rent is $450 a month.

Purchased $15,000 of fruits and vegetables from the Jones Company for cash.

1–31 Sold fruits and vegetables with a cost of $9,000 for $15,000. The customers paid us $10,000 in cash and charged $5,000.

Collected $4,000 of accounts receivable.

Paid wages of $1,000 to a store clerk for all the work he did in December.

Purchased $5,200 of fruits and vegetables from Jones Company on credit.

Joyce Bailey withdrew $1,000 in cash and took fruit and vegetables for her personal use which cost $200 and had a retail price of $300.

Part B. Joyce Bailey is interested in preparing a balance sheet on December 31 and an income statement for the month of December. She asks you to make all the necessary *adjusting* general journal entries in order to enable her to prepare these financial statements. She also wants you to explain to her why these journal entries have to be made prior to preparing the financial statements.

2-2 Rochette Corporation

Listed below are all of the general ledger accounts of the Rochette Corporation on December 31, 1985, after all transactions and adjusting journal entries have been recorded but before the closing journal entry was made.

Cash	$ 18,500
Sales	250,000
Wages Payable	300
Rent Expense	4,800
Interest Expense	1,600
Accounts Receivable	35,000
Income Taxes Payable	6,500
Prepaid Expenses	2,800
Furniture and Equipment	22,000
Accounts Payable	18,000
Inventory	58,400
Long-Term Notes Payable	10,000
Accumulated Depreciation	5,000
Income Tax Expense	26,000
Cost of Merchandise Sold	150,000
Common Stock	50,000
Depreciation Expense	2,500
Wages Expense	15,000
Retained Earnings (12/31/84)	18,500
Insurance Expense	2,800
Selling Expenses	19,300
Interest Payable	400

Required:

1. Prepare the December 31, 1985, closing journal entry.

2. Prepare Rochette's balance sheet as of December 31, 1985, and its income statement for the year ended December 31, 1985.

2-3 The Downtown Book Store, Inc.

The following transactions for the Downtown Book Store, Inc., occurred for the month of December 1984:

1984
Dec. 1 Issued $35,000 of common stock for cash and commenced operations.

Invested $10,000 in a money market fund. The corporation can draw cash out of this money market fund (which earns interest of 10%) at any time.

Paid $2,000 to the owner of the building in which the store will be located. Rent is $500 a month, and the owner required a month's security deposit.

Elected Joe Ryder president of the corporation at a salary of $500 a week.

Purchased books with an invoice price of $18,000. Paid cash of $17,640. The book distributor allowed a 2% cash discount for prompt payment.

Purchased store fixtures for $12,000. Gave the vendor an $8,000, 12%, 90-day note and $4,000 in cash. The fixtures have an estimated life of 10 years.

Hired a sales clerk for $200 a week.

1–31 Sold books with a cost of $12,000 for $18,000. Customers paid $13,000 in cash and owed $5,000 on December 31.

Paid Joe Ryder $2,000 and the sales clerk $800 for work performed for the period December 1 to December 24. Wages for the last week in December will be paid in January 1985.

Paid the utility bills for December, $350.

Purchased books for $8,000. The invoice requires payment in January 1985.

Received notice that $83.33 interest had been credited to the money market fund account.

Required:

1. Make general journal entries for all of the December transactions.

2. Make the adjusting general journal entries you think are necessary in order to prepare a balance sheet on December 31, 1984, and an income statement for the month of December. Note: Banks calculate interest on loans as if there were 360 days in a year.

3. Post the journal entries to T-(general ledger) accounts.

4. Prepare a balance sheet as of December 31, 1984, and an income statement for the month of December 1984.

5. Was the Downtown Book Store, Inc., successful in 1984?

2–4 Typo Company

During January 1984, Al Jones and Donna Cestario were reviewing the results of operations of the Typo Company, Inc., a duplicating, typing, and bindery service. They formed the corporation on January 1, 1984, and commenced business as Typo Company, Inc., on that date. The corporation selected the year ending December 31 for reporting purposes.

A summary of the transactions that took place from January 1, 1984, to December 31, 1984, is given below:

a. On January 1, 1984, Al Jones Paid $24,000 for 240 shares, and Donna Cestario paid $12,000 for 120 shares of Typo Company, Inc., common stock.

b. Sales made to customers amounted to $94,673; $9,030 of these sales were made at the end of December 1984 and were not collected until January of 1985.

c. Wages and salaries paid to employees (including $13,000 to Al Jones and $15,000 to Donna Cestario) for work performed through December 27, 1984, amounted to $40,500. Wages and salaries of $850 (including $250 for Al and $300 for Donna) for the last three days of December 1984 were paid on January 6, 1985.

d. Rent paid for the office was $4,550—$350 a month plus a security deposit of $350 which was paid on January 1, 1984.

e. Typo purchased $9,635 on paper during the year. It still owed for $850 of this paper on December 31, 1984. An inventory of paper on December 31, 1984, indicated there was still $2,800 of paper on hand.

f. Rental of the duplicating machines for 1984 was $32,678. Of this amount, $2,720 was unpaid on December 31, 1984.

g. Miscellaneous expenses incurred and paid for the year were $982.

h. Corporation income taxes for 1984, which will be paid in 1985, amounted to $1,250.

Required:

1. Prepare general journal entries for each of the transactions.

2. Post the journal entries to the general ledger (T-account form) accounts.

3. Prepare a statement of income for Typo Company, Inc., for the period January 1, 1984, to December 31, 1984.

4. Prepare a balance sheet as of December 31, 1984.

5. Was the Typo Company, Inc., successful in 1984?

6. Was it a good investment for the stockholders?

2–5 Total Toy Store

The Total Toy Store sold "Beautiful Baby," an incredible toy doll that could do virtually everything a real infant could. It walked, talked, and cried. The doll cost Total Toy $19.50, and the company sold it for $26. *For purposes of this problem we assume that $19.50 is Total Toy's only cost.*

The company realized the importance of prompt shipments of its dolls and had a policy of always maintaining an inventory equal to 50 dolls more than the number of dolls sold during the previous 30 days. Because Total Toy was a new company, their suppliers required them to pay their bills promptly. Total Toy's customers paid them on a 30-day basis.

On January 31, after one month's operations, their balance sheet was as follows:

TOTAL TOY COMPANY
Balance Sheet
January 31, 1984

Assets		*Equities*	
Cash	$2,925	Common stock	$7,800
Accounts		Retained	
receivable	2,600	earnings	650
Inventory	2,925		
Total assets	$8,450	Total equities	$8,450

Mr. Total, the president, was pleased that they had made a profit of $650 on January sales of 100 dolls. He predicted that sales would increase at a rate of 50 dolls a month for the next six months.

His predictions were correct for February. The company sold 150 dolls, collected their accounts receivable, and ordered and paid for an inventory of 200 dolls in anticipation of March sales.

The predictions for March sales of 200 dolls and April sales of 250 dolls were also correct. Collections, payments to suppliers, and inventory purchases were made as expected.

Total was discussing the profits of $4,550 for the four months with his sales manager when the bookkeeper told him that the company's bank balance was zero and they needed funds in order to continue operating in May.

Required:

1. Make journal entries to record each transaction and post them to the general ledger accounts.

2. Prepare a balance sheet on April 30, 1984, and an income statement for the period January 1 to April 30, 1984.

3. How is it possible for a company that starts with $7,800 in invested capital and has profitable sales for a period of four months to have a zero bank balance?

4. How much does the company need to borrow right away to sustain an increase in sales of 50 dolls a month for the remainder of the year?

2–6 Ye Old Spirit Shoppe

For 15 years, Jack Crawford had worked as the manager of one of the 16 Tick Tock Liquor Stores in Jacksonville, Florida. In late 1984, Crawford decided to go into business for himself and began searching for a good location for his own retail liquor store. In October he found what he thought to be an ideal location: a 2,500-square-foot store in a newly opened shopping center on a busy intersection. Crawford asked the leasing agent to reserve the space for him while he applied for a city retail liquor license. The application was approved, and Crawford opened Ye Old Spirit Shoppe on November 1, 1984.

Crawford realized that the first few months of business would be difficult, and therefore he planned to limit expenses to absolute essentials. He hoped to avoid the cost of an accountant by preparing his own financial statements and tax returns. On December 5, 1984, Crawford sat down at his desk to evaluate his first month of business. The following is a chronology of the store's November operations:

1984
Nov. 1 Jack Crawford opened a checking account at the Sunshine National Bank in the name of Ye Old Spirit Shoppe and deposited $25,000.

Signed a two-year lease calling for rent of $650 a month, to be paid in advance each month. Gave the leasing agent a check for the November rent.

Issued a $760 check to pay for a city retail liquor license for the remainder of the calendar year.

Arranged a $250,000 business liability insurance policy, and wrote a $504 check to pay for the first year's coverage.

Purchased and paid $1,800 for a new cash register. The salesman told Crawford that the other store owners were getting 10 years' use out of this type of register.

Accepted delivery of refrigerated display equipment costing $9,900. Made a $2,900 down payment, and signed a promissory note agreeing to pay the remainder on October 31, 1985, with interest at 12% per annum. Crawford expected the equipment to last 15 years.

Received $18,600 of wine, liquor, and beer from a local wholesaler who expected payment within 60 days. Crawford gave the delivery man a $150 check as a deposit on 10 beer kegs.

9 Hired a salesclerk, agreeing to pay him at a rate of $250 a week. Payment was to be made once a month.

26 Ordered, but did not receive, another shipment of liquor and beer of $4,600 from wholesaler. The terms of payment were the same as the previous order.

27 Took 22 bottles of table wine out of inventory and distributed them to his friends and relatives as a Thanksgiving gift. The wine's cost was $165, and its retail sales value was $220.

1–30 During November, Crawford had deposited a total of $10,890 in the Sunshine National Bank. This sum included $8,150 in cash sales and $2,740 in collections on credit sales. The amount owed by customers (accounts receivable) at the end of the month was $1,500.

30 Sent the liquor wholesaler a check for $9,500 and paid the December rent.

Received, but did not pay, $350 in utility and telephone bills for November.

Paid the salesclerk's salary for three weeks, deducting $45 from his check for the breakage of a case of wine the clerk had carelessly dropped.

Crawford wrote himself a $850 check on the business bank account for personal use and cashed it at the bank. Crawford was previously paid $300 a week when he was the manager of the Tick Tock Liquor Stores.

Crawford and his clerk took a physical inventory by counting the unsold merchandise. After multiplying the quantities of wine, liquor, and beer by their unit wholesale cost, Crawford found that he had $9,750 in inventory.

Required:

1. Prepare general journal entries for all the transactions and make all the necessary adjusting journal entries in order to prepare a balance sheet on November 30, 1984, and an income statement for the month of November.

2. Post the journal entries to general ledger accounts.

3. Prepare the November 30, 1984, balance sheet and the November 1984 income statement.

4. Was Ye Old Spirit Shoppe successful in November?

3

Measuring and adjusting

After the transactions for cash receipts, cash disbursements, sales, and purchases have been recorded and posted, it is necessary to analyze the general ledger accounts and make the appropriate adjusting journal entries. This is done to ensure that the balance sheet reflects all the assets and equities in existence on the balance sheet date and that the income statement includes all the revenue and expense accounts applicable to the time frame covered.

Typical adjusting journal entries preceding the preparation of the balance sheet and income statement are for:

1. Expenditures that affect more than one accounting period.
2. Receipts that affect more than one accounting period.
3. Revenues affecting the accounting period that have not been recorded.
4. Expenses affecting the accounting period that have not been recorded.

1. EXPENDITURES THAT AFFECT MORE THAN ONE ACCOUNTING PERIOD

Companies make expenditures in order to acquire assets and services. The expenditures are made in cash or by exchanging other assets or by incurring a liability.

The portion of the expenditure that is allocated to a particular accounting period is an expense of that period.

Assume that on April 1, 1984, the Rogers Hardware Store, Inc., purchases a $25,000 fire insurance policy to cover the contents of its store from the Security Insurance Company. Rogers pays Security a premium of $360 for this policy, which provides coverage for a 36-month period commencing April 1, 1984.

On April 1, 1984, the expenditure is recorded in the cash disbursement book as follows:

Unexpired (Prepaid) Insurance 360
    Cash 360

The general ledger accounts for this transaction are:

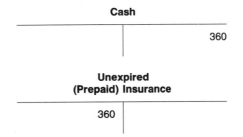

Rogers elects to report its income using a fiscal year which ends on June 30. A fiscal year is a period of 12 consecutive months. If the fiscal year ends on December 31, it is also called a calendar year.

On June 30, 1984, Rogers will have to make an adjusting entry to the unexpired insurance general ledger account to reflect the expiration of the insurance coverage and record the expense for the months of April, May, and June 1984.

The appropriate adjusting journal entry is:

Insurance Expense 30
    Unexpired Insurance 30
    To record expired insurance, April, May, and June 1984.

After posting this entry the affected general ledger accounts correctly reflect unexpired insurance of $330 (33 months at $10 per month) on June 30, 1984, and insurance expense of $30 (3 months at $10 per month) for the fiscal year ended June 30, 1984.

Unexpired Insurance		Insurance Expense	
360	30	30	

General ledger accounts on July 1, 1984, the first day of the next fiscal year are:

Unexpired Insurance		Insurance Expense	
360	30	30	30*

* Closed to retained earnings 6/30/84.

The balance in the Insurance Expense account after the June 30, 1984, closing entry is posted is zero ($30 − $30 = 0).

The appropriate adjusting journal entry for the next fiscal year, which ends on June 30, 1985, is:

Insurance Expense 120
    Unexpired Insurance 120
  To record expired insurance fiscal year ending (FYE) 6/30/85.

The general ledger accounts after this entry is made are:

Unexpired Insurance		Insurance Expense	
360	30	30	30
	120	120	

The balance in the unexpired insurance account is $210 ($360 − $150). This is correct because it is the unexpired amount on the balance sheet date, June 30, 1985. (July 1, 1985, to March 31, 1987, when the policy expires, is 21 months; 21 × $10 = $210.)

The expense account is correct because it represents expenses for the months of July 1, 1984, to June 30, 1985 (12 months × $10 = $120).

On May 1, 1984, Rogers Hardware Store purchases display equipment on account for $24,000. The equipment is estimated to have a 10-year life and is not expected to have any salvage value at the end of that time.[1]

---

[1] For purposes of this chapter we consider depreciation to be calculated on a straight-line basis. Other depreciation methods will be discussed in Chapter 7.

On May 1, the transaction is recorded:

Equipment 24,000
    Accounts Payable   24,000
Purchase of equipment from Jones Brothers.

The appropriate adjusting journal entry on June 30, 1984, to reflect the cost of the equipment allocated to May and June operations is:

Depreciation Expense 400
    Accumulated Depreciation—Equipment.............   400
To record depreciation (5/1/84–6/30/84).

Equipment		Accounts Payable	
24,000			24,000

Accumulated Depreciation—Equipment		Depreciation Expense	
	400	400	

The depreciation expense of $400 is the appropriate amount for the months of May and June 1984 ($24,000 ÷ 10 = $2,400 per year or $200 per month). The $24,000 in the asset account, Equipment, minus the $400 in the contra-asset account, Accumulated Depreciation—Equipment, equals $23,600 the amount to be allocated to future periods.

The depreciation expense for the subsequent fiscal year ended June 30, 1985, will be $2,400 because the equipment will be used for the entire year.

On January 1, 1984, Rogers Hardware purchases office supplies for $700. Although the bookkeeper knows that this is an asset on January 1, 1984, he expects that supplies will be all used up on June 30, 1984, and therefore debits the $700 to Office Supplies Expense rather than the asset account, Office Supplies Inventory.

On January 1, 1984, the following entry to record the transaction is made:

Office Supplies Expense 700
    Cash   700
To record purchase of office supplies.

The posted general ledger accounts are:

Cash		Office Supplies Expense	
	700	700	

On June 30, 1984 a count of all the office supplies on hand is made. This inventory of office supplies, which is valued at cost, amounted to $200.

The appropriate adjusting journal entry should reflect an asset of $200 and expense for the period of $500 ($700 − $200).

Office Supplies Inventory 200
    Office Supplies Expense 200
    To record the 6/30/84 office supplies inventory.

Office Supplies Inventory		Office Supplies Expense	
200		700	200

If the bookkeeper had followed the procedure of debiting the asset account on January 1, 1984, instead of the expense account, the general ledger account before adjustment would be:

Office Supplies Inventory	
700	

and the appropriate adjustment would be:

Office Supplies Expense 500
    Office Supplies Inventory 500
    To record use of $500 of office supplies.

Office Supplies Inventory		Office Supplies Expense	
700	500	500	

Regardless of which method the bookkeeper used to record the initial transaction the appropriate adjusting entry will result in an office supplies inventory of $200 on June 30, 1984, and office supplies expense of $500 for the year ended June 30, 1984.

2. RECEIPTS THAT AFFECT MORE THAN ONE ACCOUNTING PERIOD

Rogers Hardware rents a portion of its store to a concessionaire who makes keys. The rent is $150 a month. On June 1, 1984, the date the lease was signed, the concessionaire paid $450 rent for the months of June, July, and August 1984.

On June 1, 1984, the transaction is recorded:

Cash 450
    Rent Received in Advance   450
    To record the collection of three months' rent received
    in advance.

The $450 rent received in advance is a liability on June 1, 1984, because Rogers Hardware has the obligation to provide the floor space to the concessionaire for the months of June, July and August.

Cash		Rent Received in Advance	
450			450

On June 30, 1984, the store has a liability of $300 for the months of July and August and has earned rental income of $150 for the month of June.

The appropriate journal entry on June 30, 1984, is:

Rent Received in Advance 150
    Rent Revenue (Income)   150
    To record rent income for June.

Rent Received in Advance	
150	450

Rent Revenue (Income)	
	150

The general ledger accounts reflect the liability of $300 ($450 − $150) on June 30, 1984, and rental income of $150 for the year ended June 30, 1984.

Rent Received in Advance is called a *deferred income account.* It is a liability account which will become income in the future. Two other examples of deferred income accounts are unearned magazine subscriptions and advance payments made by customers. Subscriptions are paid for in advance and do not become earned income until the magazines are delivered. Advance payments become income when the merchandise is delivered or the services contracted for are performed.

3. REVENUES AFFECTING THE ACCOUNTING PERIOD THAT HAVE NOT BEEN RECORDED

Toro Manufacturing Company agrees to pay Rogers Hardware a special commission of $25 for every lawn mower they sell during a six-month promotion period commencing April 1, 1984. Payment is to be made at the end of the six-month period. From April 1, 1984, to June 30, 1984, Rogers Hardware sells 200 lawn mowers.

No entry is made on April 1, 1984, the date of the agreement, as no monetary transaction has taken place.

The appropriate adjusting entry on June 30, 1984, is the one that reflects the fact that Rogers Hardware has earned $5,000 (200 × $25) in commissions for the period April 1, 1984, to June 30, 1984, for the 200 lawn mowers they sold and has an asset, commissions receivable, of $5,000.

```
Commissions Receivable ........................... 5,000
     Commission Revenue (Income) ..................        5,000
     To record commissions earned (4/1/84–6/30/84).
```

Commissions Receivable		Commission Revenue	
5,000			5,000

Failure to make this entry would result in the $5,000 earned in the fiscal year ended June 30, 1984, becoming revenue in the fiscal year ended June 30, 1985, when the commissions are paid. Revenue and net income would be understated by $5,000 in the fiscal year ended June 30, 1984, and overstated by $5,000 in the fiscal year ended June 30, 1985.

On September 30, 1984, Toro Manufacturing paid Rogers Hardware $12,500 for 500 lawn mowers sold for the period April 1, 1984, to September 30, 1984.

The transaction is recorded:

```
Cash ............................................... 12,500
     Commissions Receivable .......................        5,000
     Commission Revenue ...........................        7,500
     To record cash received from Toro Manufacturing
     as commission for the sale of 500 lawn mowers.
```

Cash	
(2) 12,500	

Commissions Receivable			Commission Revenue		
(1)	5,000	(2) 5,000	5,000*	(1)	5,000
				(2)	7,500

*Closed to retained earnings on 6/30/84.

The adjustment to record on the books, or accrue, the unrecorded commission revenue of $5,000 in the fiscal year ended June 30, 1984, results in commission revenue being recorded in the year in which it is earned: $5,000 in the fiscal year ended June 30, 1984, and $7,500 in the fiscal year ended June 30, 1985.

Another example of this type of adjustment is the accrual of interest revenue on notes receivable that is earned but not paid during the particular time period.

4. EXPENSES AFFECTING THE ACCOUNTING PERIOD THAT HAVE NOT BEEN RECORDED

On May 16, 1984, Rogers Hardware borrowed $5,000 from the bank. The note was for four months at a 12 percent annual rate of interest.

The transaction is recorded on May 16, 1984:

Cash 5,000
  Notes Payable   5,000
To record a 12%, $5,000 note from the First Bank.

Cash	Notes Payable
5,000	5,000

On June 30, 1984, an adjusting journal entry has to be made to accrue on the books the interest expense for the period May 16, 1984, to June 30, 1984.

Interest rates are customarily stated on an annual basis. This note is 12 percent per year, or 1 percent per month. For the period May 15, 1984, to June 30, 1984, the interest expense is $75 (.015 × $5,000).

Interest Expense 75
  Accrued Interest Payable   75
To accrue interest 5/16/84–6/30/84 on the 12%, $5,000 four-month note.

54

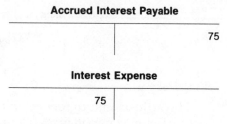

Accrued Interest Payable

| | 75 |

Interest Expense

| 75 | |

If we did not make this adjusting entry to accrue interest expense, net income for the fiscal year ended June 30, 1984, would be overstated by $75.

Accrued Interest Payable is a current liability on the June 30, 1984, balance sheet. It will be eliminated when the note and interest are paid on September 15, 1984.

Notes Payable	5,000	
Accrued Interest Payable	75	
Interest Expense	125	
Cash		5,200

To record payment on 9/15/84 of $5,000, 12%, four-month note.

General ledger accounts on September 15, 1984, after the above entry has been posted:

Cash

| (1) | 5,000 | (3) | 5,200 |

Notes Payable

| (3) | 5,000 | (1) | 5,000 |

Accrued Interest Payable

| (3) | 75 | (2) | 75 |

Interest Expense

| (2) | 75 | | 75* |
| (3) | 125 | | |

* Closed to retained earnings on 6/30/84.

Wages paid Rogers' employees for work done by them in the fiscal year ended June 30, 1984, amounted to $25,000.

Wages Expense	25,000	
Cash		25,000

To record payment for wages earned by employees in the fiscal year ended (FYE) 6/30/84.

The general ledger accounts are:

Cash		Wages Expense	
	25,000	25,000	

Rogers Hardware Store's weekly payroll is paid on Tuesday for the week ended the preceding Saturday. The payroll for the week ended Saturday, June 30, 1984 was $500.

The appropriate adjusting entry on June 30, 1984 is:

Wages Expense 500
    Wages Payable 500
    To accrue wages for the week ended June 30, 1984.

Wages Payable	
	500

Wages Expense	
25,000	
500	

Wages expense for the year ended June 30, 1984, is $25,500. It has to include wages earned but unpaid for the week ended June 30, 1984, if we are to match wage expense for the fiscal year ended June 30, 1984, against the revenues for the same time period.

On July 3, 1984, the wages of $500 are paid:

Wages Payable 500
    Cash 500

Cash		Wages Payable	
	500	500	500

This entry eliminates the liability for wages payable which was accrued on June 30, 1984.

Federal corporate income tax for the year ended June 30, 1984, was $1,800. This tax has to be paid by September 15, 1984.

The appropriate adjusting entry on June 30, 1984 is:

Income Tax Expense 1,800
    Accrued Income Tax Payable 1,800
    To accrue federal corporate income tax for the year
    ended 6/30/84.

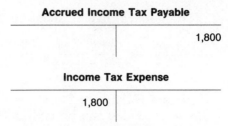

Accrued Income Tax Payable

	1,800

Income Tax Expense

1,800	

The income tax expense for the year ended June 30, 1984, has to be recorded and matched against the income for the year ended June 30, 1984.

When the income tax is paid on September 15, 1985, Roger's would make the following entry:

Accrued Income Tax Payable........................ 1,800
    Cash   1,800

Cash		**Accrued Income Tax Payable**	
	1,800	1,800	1,800

This entry eliminates the June 30, 1984, liability.

DIVIDENDS

When a company declares a cash dividend an entry is made to reflect this transaction. Cash dividends are a *distribution of earnings* to a company's stockholders and become a legal liability when they are declared by the board of directors. Dividends are not a cost of operations and are therefore not reflected on the income statement as an expense.

On June 30, 1984, the board of directors declared dividends to stockholders in the amount of $5,000. The dividends were to be paid on July 15, 1984.

The appropriate adjusting entry on June 30, 1984, is:

Retained Earnings 5,000
    Dividends Payable   5,000
  To record declaration of dividend to be paid
  7/15/84.

Dividends Payable

	5,000

Retained Earnings

5,000	

The debit is made to Retained Earnings to indicate a distribution to stockholders of previously earned net income. The credit is to Dividends Payable and indicates the company has a liability to pay the stockholders $5,000.

When the dividends are paid on July 15, 1984, we would make the following entry:

```
Dividends Payable ................................  5,000
    Cash .........................................          5,000
```

Cash		Dividends Payable	
	5,000	5,000	5,000

This entry eliminates the June 30, 1984, liability.

CORRECTING JOURNAL ENTRIES

An analysis of the general ledger accounts may reveal the need for a correcting journal entry due to an improper analysis or inaccurate posting of a transaction.

The bookkeeper charged the purchase of a new machine that cost $12,000 to Repairs Expense in error.

Cash		Repairs Expense	
	12,000	12,000	

The journal entry to correct this error is:

```
Machinery .......................................  12,000
    Repairs Expense .............................          12,000
    To reclassify charge of $12,000 incorrectly made
    to Repairs Expense.
```

Machinery		Repairs Expense	
12,000		12,000	12,000

After this correcting journal entry the Repairs Expense account has a zero balance ($12,000 − $12,000 = $0), and the asset account, Machinery, is $12,000.

At the end of the accounting period the bookkeeper will also make an adjusting journal entry to record depreciation expense on the $12,000 machine.

FREQUENCY OF ADJUSTING JOURNAL ENTRIES

Adjusting journal entries are required in order to measure accurately the amount of assets and equities on the balance sheet date and reflect all the revenues and expenses for the time frame covered by the income statement.

The company will have to prepare adjusting entries whenever they prepare financial statements.

PROBLEMS AND CASES

3-1 Understanding general ledger accounts

Indicate which of the following items is the *best* answer to the following situations. The check mark in the general ledger accounts indicates the balance in the account at the beginning of the period.

1.

Accrued Interest Payable		Interest Expense	
	1,500	400	
	1,500✓	1,800	
	1,800		

   a. Interest expense for this period is $400.
   b. Interest expense for this period is $1,800.
   c. Interest charges for previous periods were paid to the extent of $1,800 in cash during this period.
   d. Interest accrued during this period to be paid next period amounted to $1,800.
   e. None of the above applies.

2. Assets of the Yung Corporation at the beginning of the year were $400,000. Assets at the end of the year were $450,000.

   a. Our operations for the year were a failure.
   b. Our operations for the year must have been successful.
   c. Stockholders' equity has increased.
   d. Stockholders' equity has decreased.
   e. None of the above applies.

3.

Wages Payable	
21,000	7,000✓
	19,000

   a. Wages earned for the period were $26,000.

b. Wages earned in this period to be paid in a future period were $5,000.

c. Wages paid in cash for this period amounted to $7,000.

d. Wages paid in cash for this period amounted to $19,000.

e. None of the above applies.

4.

Deferred (Unearned) Subscription Income		Subscription Income	
160,300	90,000✓		160,300
	196,800		

a. Subscription income for the period was $196,800.

b. Subscription income for the period was $286,800.

c. Subscriptions sold this period to be delivered in future periods amounted to $196,800.

d. Subscriptions to be delivered in future periods amounted to $126,500.

e. None of the above applies.

5.

Retained Earnings	
7,000	12,000✓
	10,000

a. Net income from operations for this period was $3,000.

b. Dividends declared during this period were $10,000.

 c. Total stockholders' equity at the end of the year was $15,000.

d. Net income from operations for this period was $10,000.

e. None of the above applies.

6.

Increase in assets during the year.............	$2,120
Increase in liabilities during the year	1,520
Dividends declared and paid during the year....	760

The net income for the year was:

a. $160.

b. A loss of $160.

c. $2,880.

d. $600.

e. $1,360.

f. Some other amount.

7.

Accrued Interest Receivable		Interest Income (Revenue)	
✓120	120		160
240			240

a. Interest income (revenue) for this period was $240.
b. Interest accrued during this period was $160.
c. Interest collected in cash during this period was $280.
d. Interest income (revenue) for this period was $360.
✓e. None of the above applies.

3-2 Valencia Italian Ice Company

The Valencia Italian Ice Company commenced operations on October 1, 1984. Mr. Gelato, the sole stockholder and only full-time employee of Valencia, provided us with the following information about the company's *first month* of operations.

	October 1, 1984	October 31, 1984
Cash in bank	$ 350	$ 390
Amounts due from customers		
(accounts receivable)	–0–	875
Inventory	1,600	2,150
Prepaid (unexpired) insurance.	–0–	660
Prepaid rent	1,200	900
Accounts payable (for inventory).	–0–	1,200
Wages payable	–0–	300
Common stock	3,150	3,150
Retained earnings	–0–	?
Analysis of Valencia's checkbook		
for the month of October:		
Cash receipts:		
Received from customers		$3,500
Cash payments:		
Accounts payable (merchandise)	$2,350	
For one-year fire insurance		
policy (effective 10/1/84)	720	
Wages (Mr. Gelato)	390	
Total cash payments		3,460
Increase in cash during October		$ 40

Required:

1. Prepare a balance sheet on October 31, 1984.

2. Prepare an income statement for the month of October.

3. Was Valencia successful in October 1984?

3-3   Snake Eyes Retail Store

Comparative balance sheets for the Snake Eyes Retail Store for 1983 and 1984 are listed below:

	December 31	
	1983	1984
Assets		
Cash	$ 150	$ 180
Accounts receivable from customers	300	380
Merchandise inventory	450	500
Total current assets	900	1,060
Plant and equipment, net of accumulated depreciation	750	780
Total assets	$1,650	$1,840
Equities		
Accounts payable to suppliers of merchandise	$ 200	$ 260
Common stock	1,000	1,000
Retained earnings	450	580
Total equities	$1,650	$1,840

The following data relate to 1984:

a. Collections from credit customers, $2,000; cash sales $500.
b. Payments to suppliers of merchandise, $1,000.
c. Purchases of equipment (all paid in cash), $50.
d. Dividends paid to shareholders (all paid in cash), $40.
e. No plant and equipment was retired or sold during the year.

Required:

1. Compute depreciation expense for 1984.

2. Compute sales revenues for 1984.

3. Compute the cost of merchandise sold for 1984.

4. Compute net income for 1984.

3-4   Panhandlers, Inc.

Panhandlers, Inc., is a retail store that sells gourmet cookware.

The *balances* in the general ledger accounts on December 31, 1984, after all the transactions for the year have been posted but *before the year-end adjusting journal entries* have been made, are listed below:

62

Accounts with Debit Balances

Cash	$ 41,204
Accounts receivable	25,000
Inventory	188,400
Unexpired insurance	1,800
Furniture, fixtures, and equipment	42,000
Wages expense	22,950 ⁊450
Officer's salary	30,600 +600
Rent expense	8,100
Utilities expense	4,140
Interest expense	1,125
Miscellaneous expense	3,156
Totals	$368,475

Accounts with Credit Balances

Accumulated depreciation—furniture, fixtures, and equipment	$ 12,600
Accounts payable	14,050
15% note payable	10,000
Common stock	28,000
Retained earnings	18,225
Sales	285,600
Totals	$368,475

Additional information:

a. The furniture, fixtures, and equipment purchased on January 1, 1981, are estimated to have a useful life of 10 years.

b. The December 31, 1984, inventory was $23,000.

c. Unexpired insurance on December 31, 1984, amounted to $1,200.

d. Wages earned but not paid on December 31, 1984, were $450.

e. Officer's salary earned but not paid on December 31, 1984, was $600.

f. The 15% note payable was issued on March 31, 1984.

g. Corporate federal income tax rates for 1984 were 15 percent on the first $25,000 of taxable income and 18 percent on the next $25,000 of taxable income. For purposes of this problem taxable income is defined as net income before corporate federal income taxes.

Required:

1. Set up T-accounts for the December 31, 1984, general ledger balances.

2. Make the required adjusting journal entries for the year ended December 31, 1984, and post them to the T-accounts. You may add any additional general ledger accounts you feel are necessary.

3. Prepare the closing journal entry and post it to the T-accounts.

4. Prepare an income statement for 1984 and a balance sheet as of December 31, 1984.

5. Calculate the ratio of gross profit to sales, net income to sales, and net income to stockholders' equity.

6. Did Panhandler's, Inc., have a successful year?

3-5   Medi Shoppe, Inc.

Medi Shoppe, Inc., a discount health and beauty aid store, was incorporated in late 1983 and opened for business on January 2, 1984. The balance sheet as of that date is shown below:

MEDI SHOPPE, INC.
Balance Sheet
January 2, 1984

Assets

Current assets:

Cash	$ 2,240	
Inventory	39,200	
Total current assets	41,440	

Fixed assets:

Building	98,000	
Furniture and fixtures	24,360	
Total assets	$163,800	

Equities

Current liabilities:

Accounts payable	$ 16,800	
Notes payable to bank	21,000	
Total current liabilities	37,800	
Mortgage on building	70,000	
Common stock	56,000	
Total equities	$163,800	

The common stock was all owned by Theresa Weber. A checkbook was the only record that Weber kept to record Medi Shoppe, Inc.'s business transactions.

At the end of the first year of operations, Weber asked Roberta Anderson, a local CPA, to help prepare the annual financial statement required by the bank.

Anderson examined the Medi Shoppe checkbook and obtained the accompanying information:

MEDI SHOPPE, INC.
Record of Cash Receipts and Disbursements
1984*

Cash receipts:

Cash sales	$377,720
Collections from customers (these customers had received the merchandise but had not paid for it at the time of sale)	115,360
Total cash receipts	$493,080

Cash disbursements:

Advertising	$ 7,280
Insurance	2,800
Interest on bank loan	1,470
Maintenance and repairs	5,740
Merchandise purchases	302,400
Partial bank loan repayment on December 31, 1984	4,200
Payment of accounts payable	16,800
Property taxes	5,460
Selling expenses	19,880
Utilities	11,340
Wages and salaries	99,400
Total cash disbursements	$476,770

* Source: Medi Shoppe, Inc., checkbook.

She also examined the file of unpaid bills to suppliers and unpaid customer accounts. While looking through the files, she also discovered other information she felt needed to be considered in preparing financial statements. This information is listed below:

a. Unpaid bills to suppliers (representing merchandise purchases)—$13,720.

b. Unpaid customer accounts—$9,940.

c. Interest at the rate of 8 percent on the mortgage was payable annually on January 1. No interest had been paid.

d. Wages and salaries were paid monthly on the third working day of the next month. Wages and salaries earned in December, but not yet paid, totaled $8,680.

e. Of the total insurance premium of $2,800 paid in 1984, $1,120 was for a health insurance policy expiring December 31, 1984, and $1,680 was for a fire insurance policy which was effective for three years, expiring December 31, 1986.

f. The estimated life of the store building was 35 years. The furniture and fixtures had an estimated life of 10 years.

g. An inventory of merchandise on hand at the end of the year revealed goods in the store costing $58,800.

h. Interest at the annual rate of 7 percent on the bank loan was payable quarterly on the last day of each quarter. There were no delinquent interest charges in 1984.

i. Federal income tax rates for 1984 were:
15 percent for the first $25,000 of taxable income.
18 percent for the next $25,000 of taxable income.
30 percent for the next $25,000 of taxable income.
40 percent for the next $25,000 of taxable income.
46 percent for all taxable income over $100,000.

Required:

1. Prepare a statement of income for 1984 and a balance sheet as of December 31, 1984.

2. Was 1984 a successful year for Medi Shoppe, Inc.? For Theresa Weber?

--------------- **3–6 Acton Racing, Inc.** ---------------

"Bill, I have just reviewed the track's management contract with Management Group, Inc. (Exhibit 1), and the schedule of average daily handle (gross receipts) and racing days for the first six months of the year (Exhibit 2). I am having difficulty determining the correct balance sheet and income statement figures for the management fee. My confusion is caused by the recent decision of the Racing Commission to allow the track (Acton Racing, Inc.) to operate for the entire year. The track will be open for 150 racing days for the period July 1, 1984, to December 31, 1984, in addition to the 152 racing days just completed for the first half of the year. I would really appreciate it if you could go over the possibilities with me."

This request was made by Sal Berns, staff accountant for Rogers and Rogers, a Massachusetts certified public accounting firm, to his supervisor, Bill Myers. The accounting firm was conducting an audit of Acton Racing, Inc., for the period January 1, 1984, to June 30, 1984. The Massachusetts Racing Commission required semiannual reports from Acton Racing. These reports were to include an unqualified opinion rendered by Acton Racing's auditors.

The books of Acton Racing, Inc., reflected an expense for management fees of $120,000 ($20,000 paid per month) for the period ended June 30, 1984. There was no liability for management fees payable recorded on the June 30, 1984, balance sheet.

EXHIBIT 1. **Excerpts from a Contract between Acton Racing, Inc., and Management Group, Inc.**

Acton Racing, Inc., agrees to compensate Management Group, Inc. for managerial services provided as follows:

1. In the event that racing is conducted at the Acton Track for 100 days or less, $150,000 per year.

2. For all racing days in excess of 100 days, 0.5 percent of the handle on each day that the handle is in excess of $225,000, provided, however, that the total amount paid to Management Group, Inc., shall not exceed $250,000 per year.

3. Compensation shall be paid to the Management Group, Inc., during the continuation of the racing meet or meets run during the year at the rate of $20,000 per month, with the balance, if any, to be paid within 30 days after the completion of the annual audit of Acton Racing, Inc., by its certified public accountant.

EXHIBIT 2

1984	Average Daily Handle*	Racing Days
January	$380,000	25
February	420,000	24
March	475,000	26
April	460,000	26
May	410,000	26
June	325,000	25
		152

* For purposes of this problem, you may assume that the daily handle is equal to the average handle.

Required:

1. Assume you are Bill Myers. Explain to Sal Berns the amounts you think should be recorded on the June 30, 1984, financial statements. Your explanation should include a computation of the June 30, 1984, liability and the expense for the six-month period ended June 30, 1984.

2. What journal entry would you suggest Acton Racing, Inc., make on their books as of June 30, 1984.

4

Accounting principles

The purpose of accounting principles or standards is to ensure that financial statements prepared by accountants are relevant, reliable, comparable, and comprehensible.

Generally accepted accounting principles are established primarily by the Financial Accounting Standards Board (FASB) or the Securities and Exchange Commission (SEC).

The FASB promulgates new accounting principles and modifies existing principles in releases called Statements of Financial Accounting Standards (SFAS). These SFASs are based upon extensive research, preparation of exposure drafts, and responses to the exposure drafts by interested parties who are preparers and users of financial statements.

The SEC is the federal government agency charged with administering regulations relating to the disclosure of financial information by corporations whose stock is publicly traded. For the most part the SEC has delegated rule-making authority to the FASB. The SEC publishes its views on accounting matters in pronouncements that were called Accounting Series Releases (ASRs) until April 1, 1982, and Financial Reporting Releases after that date.

Prior to the establishment of the FASB in 1973 generally accepted accounting principles were formulated by the Committee on Accounting Procedures (CAP), 1939–59, and Accounting Principles Board (APB), 1959–73, of the American Institute of Certified Public Accountants (AICPA). In contrast to the APB, which was a large (18 to 21 members), part-time committee of the AICPA, the FASB is an independent board of 7 full-time members. Board members are well paid and are required to sever all relationships with their prior employers. Board membership is represented by a broad range of financial statement users as well as members of the public accounting profession.

The 51 accounting research bulletins issued by CAP and the 31 opinions previously issued by the APB were adopted by the FASB as being authoritative. The FASB has issued a large number of statements of financial accounting standards since its founding (approximately 70 at the end of 1982). These statements set standards for reporting particular financial transactions by firms.

ACCOUNTING CONVENTIONS AND PRINCIPLES

Some of the major assumptions, conventions, and principles that underlie the preparation of financial statements are:

1. Entity.
2. Money measurement.
3. Going-concern.
4. Cost.
5. Objectivity.
6. Conservatism.
7. Consistency.
8. Materiality.
9. Disclosure.
10. Time period.
11. Revenue recognition.
12. Matching.

1. Entity

An accounting entity is defined as a self-contained accounting unit that prepares its own financial statements.

The entity's financial statements present its operating performance and financial position and not that of its owners, creditors, or other related parties.

The financial statements of the local grocery store, which is organized as a proprietorship, would only report the results of operations and financial position of the grocery store and would exclude any of the owner's non-grocery store transactions.

A law partnership would prepare financial statements that reflect the results of operations and financial position of the law practice, not the net worth of the individual partners.

A corporation manufacturing and selling automobiles would prepare financial statements that relate to the financial activities of the corporation. It would not report the financial position or results of operations of each individual stockholder or of the workers or of the union that represents the workers.

A municipality would prepare financial reports about its financial activities and not that of its voters, taxpayers, creditors, or the organizations from whom it receives grants.

The entity principle enables the reader of financial statements to evaluate the performance of each specific accounting unit.

2. Money measurement

This principle stipulates that only events that can be measured in a common monetary unit will be expressed in the financial statements. In the United States the monetary measurement unit used is the dollar. Using the dollar as a common measurement unit, we can add such diverse items as 10,000 pounds of raw materials that cost $50,000, a machine that cost $75,000, and a cash account of $20,000. The total of $145,000 indicates in terms of one unit of value what the company owns.

One problem with the money measurement principle is that events which cannot be measured in dollars are not recorded even though they may have important implications for the enterprise's future success or failure. Examples include the retiring of a successful chief executive officer, the introduction of new personnel practices to increase productivity, or the threat of a strike against the company.

3. Going–concern

Financial accounting assumes that an accounting entity will operate for a period of time long enough to carry out its current plans and commitments. This assumption of continuity means that assets will be consumed in operations rather than liquidated. The presumption of a going-concern provides the rationale for recording assets at their cost rather than their liquidation value.

4. Cost

The cost principle requires assets to be recorded at their acquisition cost. All subsequent accounting for these assets is based on this acquisition or historical cost price regardless of how much the market value of these assets fluctuates.

For example, assume a company purchases a building with an

estimated life of 25 years for $500,000 in 1983. A 1988 appraisal of the building indicates that its fair market value is now $750,000.

The building is recorded on the books at its historical cost of $500,000, and depreciation expense of $20,000 ($500,000 ÷ 25 years) is recorded on the income statement each year for 25 years despite the fact that the current replacement cost of the building has increased to $750,000 in 1988 and annual depreciation expense based on that value would be $37,500 ($750,000 ÷ 20) for the next 20 years.

Some accountants argue that a balance sheet based on current replacement cost is a more useful presentation of the financial position of the company than one based on historical cost. They also claim expenses based on an allocation of the current replacement cost rather than the historical cost of assets more accurately reflects the value of the assets consumed to generate revenues.

Other members of the accounting profession, who support the cost principle, argue that users will have more confidence in financial statements based on objective measurements that can be verified.

In addition to preparing financial statements using the historical cost model, most large corporations are also required by *SFAS No. 33,* "Financial Reporting and Changing Prices," to disclose supplementary information using current replacement costs.

5. Objectivity

Accounting is based on measurements that are objective. An objective measurement can be independently verified and is not based on personal bias or judgment.

A rationale for recording assets at their cost rather than their current market value is that the acquisition or historical cost of an asset can usually be objectively verified by reference to the amount paid for it at the time of purchase, whereas the current market value of an asset may be based on the judgment of the person making the valuation and is not easily verified.

For example, assume a machine is purchased for $50,000 on December 31, 1984. Two years later the company hires an appraiser to determine the market or current value of the asset. Based on an estimate of the future earning power of the asset, one appraiser values the asset at $65,000. Another appraiser, using a different valuation method and personal judgment might value this asset at a figure that is lower or higher than $65,000. The current market value of $65,000 determined by the appraiser is more subjective and not so easily verified as the $50,000 historical cost value, which was determined in a more objective manner.

6. Conservatism

When there is more than one acceptable method of valuing an asset or reporting income this concept presumes that a company will choose the method which is the most *conservative:* results in the lowest asset value and the smallest income figure.

An illustration of this concept is its application to the valuing of inventory. Conservatism states that inventory should be valued at the *lower* of cost or market.

Assume that on the balance sheet date a company has inventory which cost $25,000 and has a replacement cost of $20,000. Following the conservatism convention the company would make the following adjusting journal entry.

Cost of Sales—Inventory Adjustment................. 5,000
    Inventory   5,000
    To write inventory down to current replacement cost.

This journal entry has the effect of stating inventory at its current replacement cost of $20,000 and reducing income for the period by $5,000 despite the fact that the inventory has not been sold.

Conservatism as applied to inventory valuation results in historical cost being used when current replacement cost is equal to or greater than historical cost and current replacement cost being used when it is lower than the acquisition price of the inventory.

Many accountants question the logic of a concept that uses neither historical nor current replacement cost on a consistent basis.

7. Consistency

The consistency principle presumes, that once a company selects an accounting method or policy from among available alternatives, it will continue to use it in the future.

The knowledge that accounting methods have been applied on a consistent basis makes it possible for the readers of financial statements to compare the financial position and results of operations of an accounting entity over time.

Changes in accounting methods should be made only when the change provides more relevant information to the users of the financial statements than the method currently used. Full disclosure of any significant change in accounting methods including the cumulative effect of the change on net income should be included in the financial statements.

A summary of a company's significant accounting policies are usually listed as the first footnote to its financial statements.

Readers of financial statements should understand that the consistency concept applies only to individual companies and not to industries. To compare financial statements of companies within an industry the reader should ascertain from the footnotes what accounting policies are used by each company.

8. Materiality

This principle refers to the accountants primary concern with the treatment of items and events that are significant in their impact on the financial statement.

The application of the materiality concept allows a company to depart from the use of generally accepted accounting principles in situations where the principle or method chosen does not result in a significant misstatement of the financial statements.

For example, a $9.98 pencil sharpener can be recorded as an expense rather than an asset at the time it is purchased because it involves less record keeping than recording it as an asset and depreciating it over its life, and it does not result in material misstatement of the financial statements.

What is material has never been specifically defined in the accounting literature and is largely a matter of judgment. The FASB defines materiality in the following manner:[1]

> The magnitude of an omission or misstatement of accounting information that, in the light of surrounding circumstances, makes it probable that the judgment of a reasonable person relying on the information would have been changed by the omission or misstatement.

9. Disclosure

This principle requires disclosure in the financial statements or the accompanying footnotes of all material financial information relevant to users in appraising the financial position and results of operations of a company.

Full and adequate disclosure encompasses all significant financial information including the disclosure of events that occur after the balance sheet date but prior to the issuing of the financial statements. For example, a company that had a major law suit filed against it on January 10, 1985, would be required to disclose this fact in its financial statements, which were issued on February 15, 1985, for the year ended December 31, 1984.

---

[1] FASB, *Statement of Financial Accounting Concepts No. 2,* "Qualitative Characteristics of Accounting Information" (Stamford, Conn., May 1980).

10. Time period

This principle states that the indefinite life of an accounting entity assumed by the going-concern principle will be subdivided into shorter time periods for financial reporting purposes.

One year is the accounting period used for the preparation of financial statements distributed to investors, creditors, and other users of the financial statements.

While most companies prepare financial statements for a 12-month period ending on December 31, a number of them choose years ending in the months that coincide with the end of their natural business cycle. Department stores, for example, generally select a fiscal year ended January 31 because it coincides with the end of their heaviest selling period in December and prior to the time they start buying inventory for the spring season.

In addition to annual reports many companies also prepare monthly, quarterly, and semiannual financial reports. Companies listed on major stock exchanges are required by the SEC to publish quarterly reports.

Readers of financial reports should be aware that financial statements prepared for a period of a year or less require estimates and assumptions which would not be required if the company were reporting on the entire life of an accounting entity. For example, companies have to estimate the life of an asset in order to determine the amount of depreciation that will be allocated to a particular accounting period.

11. Revenue recognition

Revenue can be defined as the increase in net assets (assets minus liabilities) which results from the sale of goods, rendering of services, or other activities that constitute the entity's major ongoing operations.[2]

For example, when a company sells merchandise to a customer it recognizes revenue in an amount equal to the increase in the asset account, Accounts Receivable.

Accounts Receivable xxx
    Sales xxx

When a company provides services to a customer who has paid in advance, the company recognizes revenue equal to the decrease in the liability account, Deferred Revenue—Advance Payments:

Deferred Revenue—Advance Payments xxx
    Revenue xxx

---

[2] FASB, *Statement of Financial Accounting Concepts No. 3,* "Elements of Financial Statements of Business Enterprises" (Stamford, Conn., December 1980).

The revenue recognition process requires the determination of the amount of revenue realized during the time frame covered by the financial statements. Revenue is realized in the financial statements at that point in the earnings process called the *critical event,* when revenue has been earned and is capable of objective measurement. The *accrual basis of accounting* requires that revenues be included in the income statement when the critical event occurs and requires expenses to be recognized when they are incurred so that they can be matched against the revenues.

For revenues that accrue with time, it is not difficult to compute how much of the earning process has taken place. For example, a company that issued a 12 percent, $100,000 note receivable on October 1, 1984, would recognize revenue of $3,000 ($100,000 $\times$ 12% $\times$ $\frac{3}{12}$) on its income statement for the year ended December 31, 1984.

The journal entry to *accrue* the interest revenue is:

Accrued Interest Receivable	3,000	
Interest Revenue		3,000
To accrue 3 months' interest on the $100,000, 12% note receivable.		

Determining the critical event for sales, which depend on economic activity rather than the passage of time, is more difficult. A manufacturing company purchases raw materials and then applies production costs to the raw materials in order to make them into a finished product that they sell to their customers who pay for them at a later date. Should revenue be recognized as the manufacturing company is proceeding through the production process? Or would it be more appropriate to recognize the revenue at the point that the sale is made? Or the point when the cash is collected from the customer?

The rule used in accounting is that revenue is recognized—the critical event occurs—when substantially all the costs and efforts necessary to generate the revenue have been incurred and the amount to be received is virtually certain.

For the manufacturing company in our example revenue is recognized when the sale is made to the customer. For a company rendering services revenue would be recognized when the services are performed.

Exceptions to this general rule of recognizing revenue at the point of sale are for long-term contracts and for certain installment sales.

For long-term construction projects, which cover periods in excess of one year, revenue can be recognized on a percentage-of-completion basis rather than waiting until the total contract is completed, as long as an irrevocable contract has been signed, total revenues to be received are known with reasonable certainty, and the amount of costs to be incurred in completion of the project are able to be accurately estimated. This method provides a more satisfactory measure of revenue on an annual basis than the point-of-sale or completed-contract method, which would lump a number of years' revenues in the year the contract is completed.

Installment sales are sales that allow the customer to pay in installments over a period of time. In some cases of installment sales, for example, in sales of undeveloped real estate, there is considerable uncertainty as to whether the total amount of the sale will be collected. In these cases, where there is uncertainty as to the amount to be collected, the installment sales revenue recognition method is considered to be appropriate. This method recognizes a percentage of the revenues and expenses relating to the sale based on cash collections. For example, if 30 percent of the real estate sale is collected in the accounting period, 30 percent of the profit related to the sale will be recognized in the accounting period.

12. Matching

Closely related to the revenue recognition principle is the matching principle. It states that all expenses incurred in order to earn the revenue will be recorded in the same period as the revenue.

The objectively determined residual of the matching process (revenues minus expenses) is defined as income by accountants. This definition of income is different from economic income or income taxable for federal income taxes. Economic income is generally defined as the amount that can be consumed or distributed by an entity, leaving itself as well off at the end of the period as it was at the beginning of the period. Taxable income is the amount determined in accordance with the federal income tax law.

Expenses can be defined as outflows or other using up of assets or incurrences of liabilities during a period from delivering or producing goods, rendering services, or carrying out other activities that constitute the entity's major ongoing operation.[3]

For example, when a company sells merchandise to a customer it recognizes the expense, cost of merchandise sold, in an amount equal to the decrease in the asset, inventory.

```
Cost of Merchandise Sold ............................ xxx
     Inventory .......................................          xxx
```

---

[3] Ibid.

When sales commissions are earned during the period but have not been paid the company recognizes an expense for sales commissions equal to an increase in the liability, accrued sales commissions payable.

Sales Commissions	xxx	
Accrued Sales Commissions Payable		xxx

Cost of merchandise sold and sales commissions are recorded as expenses in the same period in which the sale is recorded.

Some expenses, such as insurance expense, administrative salaries, and interest expense, cannot be directly matched against revenues and are recorded as expenses *in the period* in which they are incurred. For example, a company borrowed $100,000 from the bank on October 1, 1984, agreeing to pay 12 percent interest. The company would *accrue* $3,000 as interest expense on its income statement for the year ended December 31, 1984.

Interest Expense	3,000	
Accrued Interest Payable		3,000
To accrue 3 months' interest on $100,000, 12% note payable.		

OPINION OF THE INDEPENDENT CERTIFIED PUBLIC ACCOUNTANT

Companies hire independent certified public accountants to audit the financial statements they prepare.

The independent certified public accountant's opinion is an integral part of the company's financial statements. Considering the extensive investigation that precedes it, the audit opinion is very short. Generally it consists of two paragraphs: the first relates to the scope of the examination, and the second presents the CPA's opinion of the financial statements. A typical opinion might be:

> We have examined the balance sheets of the XYZ Company as of September 30, 19X2 and 19X1, and the related statements of income, retained earnings, and changes in financial position each of the three years in the period ended September 30, 19X2. Our examination was made in accordance with generally accepted auditing standards and accordingly included such tests of the accounting records and such other auditing procedures as we considered necessary in the circumstances.
>
> In our opinion, the above financial statements present fairly the financial position of the XYZ Company at September 30, 19X2 and 19X1, and the results of its operations and the changes in its financial position for the three years in the period ended September 30, 19X2, in conformity with generally accepted accounting principles applied on a basis consistent with that of the preceding year.

The independent CPA's opinion indicates that the financial statements fairly present the financial position and results of operations of a company. "Fairly presents" has generally been interpreted to mean that there are no *material* errors in the financial statements.

If the auditor is not satisfied that the financial statements are fairly presented in accordance with GAAP, the audit opinion is modified to denote the reasons for the dissatisfaction.

PROBLEMS AND CASES

4–1   Crackerjohn Corporation

CRACKERJOHN CORPORATION
Comparative Balance Sheets
December 31, 1984, and 1983

	1984	1983
Assets		
Cash	$ 4,000	$ 8,000
Other current assets	22,000	24,000
Property, plant, and equipment (net of depreciation)	24,000	24,000
Total assets	$50,000	$56,000
Equities		
Current liabilities	$12,000	$20,000
Common stock	24,000	24,000
Retained earnings	14,000	12,000
Total equities	$50,000	$56,000

CRACKERJOHN CORPORATION
Statement of Income and Increase in Retained Earnings
For the Year Ended December 31, 1984

Sales	$60,000
Cost of goods sold	35,000
Gross profit	25,000
Selling, general, and administrative expense	20,000
Net income (before income taxes)	5,000
Income taxes	2,000
Net income	3,000
Dividends	1,000
Increase in retained earnings	$ 2,000

Required:

In reviewing the above statements the sales manager of Crackerjohn Corporation made the following observations. You are to comment on each of these observations.

1.   The balance sheet of December 31, 1984, must be incorrect because it shows assets of only $50,000. The inventories alone could be sold for $24,000, and we had an offer of $40,000 for the plant last week.

2.   We really don't have to be too concerned about the company's cash position. If an emergency arises, we can always use the retained earnings.

3.   Sales for the year must be understated. A tabulation of all the sales orders obtained by the salespeople for 1984 amounted to $65,000, and there were no sales returns, allowances, or discounts.

4.   These statements are all fouled up. The income statement shows net income of $3,000 for the year, and yet the assets of the company are less now than they were at the beginning of the year.

5.   Included in selling, general, and administrative expenses on the income statement is an item of $1,400 for property taxes. I don't understand why this should be included, as these property taxes don't have to be paid until next month.

4–2 Propper Manufacturing Company

The Propper Manufacturing Company wants to obtain a bank loan for additional working capital (current assets minus current liabilities) to finance expansion. The bank has requested an income statement for the current year. Propper's treasurer has provided the president with the accompanying income statement to submit to the bank:

Sales		$832,100
Dividend income		12,300
Extraordinary gain on condemnation of land		28,400
		872,800
Less:		
Selling expenses	$101,100	
Cost of goods sold	532,200	
Advertising expenses	13,700	
Loss on obsolescence of inventories	34,000	
Loss on discontinued operations	48,600	
Administrative expenses	73,400	803,000
Income before income taxes		69,800
Income taxes (45% tax rate)		31,410
Net income		$ 38,390

Required:

1.   How would you rewrite (recast) this income statement in order to focus on Propper's ongoing operations?

2.   What figure on your recasted income statement should the banker focus on? Why?

3.   What other information would you require Propper to submit if you were the bank officer?

4-3 Stirling Homex Corporation

STIRLING HOMEX CORPORATION AND CONSOLIDATED SUBSIDIARIES
Consolidated Balance Sheets
July 31, 1971
With Comparative Figures for 1970

	1971	1970
Assets		
Current assets:		
Cash	$ 3,196,457	$ 2,778,077
Preferred stock proceeds receivable	19,000,000	—
Receivables (Note 3)	37,845,572	15,486,119
Inventories:		
Raw materials, work in process, and salable merchandise at lower of cost (first-in, first-out) or replacement market	2,614,200	2,167,603
Land held for development or sale, at cost	1,878,343	1,583,621
Prepaid expenses and other current assets	226,530	124,765
Total current assets	$64,761,102	$22,140,185
Investment in unconsolidated subsidiary	$ 1,134,579	—
Long-term receivables	4,225,349	$ 541,124
Property, plant, and equipment at cost, less accumulated depreciation and amortization: 1971—$733,705; 1970—$230,921	9,426,941	5,245,745
Deferred charges, less accumulated amortization: 1971—$586, 011; 1970—$153,894	2,558,792	944,109
	$82,106,763	$28,871,163
Liabilities and Stockholders' Equity		
Current liabilities:		
Current portion of long-term debt	$ 295,630	$ 333,036
Notes payable to banks—unsecured (1971, 6 to 6½ percent; 1970, 8 to 8½ percent)	37,700,000	11,700,000
Accounts payable	4,025,254	2,480,834
Due to unconsolidated subsidiary	76,894	—
Accrued expenses and other liabilities	577,377	232,819
Current and deferred income taxes	3,528,125	1,387,338
Total current liabilities	$46,203,280	$16,134,027
Long-term debt	$ 236,588	$ 496,489
Deferred income taxes	2,098,767	587,265
Option deposit on land contract	235,000	—
Stockholders' equity:		
$2.40 cumulative convertible preferred stock: Authorized 500,000 shares, $1 par value; shares subscribed; 1971—500,000 (aggregate involuntary liquidation value, $20 million); 1970—none	500,000	—
Common stock: Authorized 15 million shares, $.01 par value; shares issued: 1971—8,909,200; 1970—8,897,400	89,092	88,974
Additional paid-in capital	26,554,453	8,446,738
Retained earnings	6,370,333	3,117,670
	$33,513,878	$11,653,382
Less treasury stock at cost (60,000 shares)	180,750	—
Total stockholders' equity	$33,333,128	$11,653,382
Commitments and contingencies		
	$82,106,763	$28,871,163

STIRLING HOMEX CORPORATION AND CONSOLIDATED SUBSIDIARIES
Consolidated Statement of Income
Year Ended July 31, 1971
With Comparative Figures for 1970

	1971	1970
Revenues:		
Manufacturing division—trade (Note 3)	$29,482,271	$16,492,770
Installation division (Note 3):		
Trade	7,230,878	5,601,357
Affiliate	—	459,941
Equity in undistributed net income of subsidiary	134,579	—
Total revenues	$36,847,728	$22,554,068
Costs and expenses:		
Cost of sales:		
Manufacturing division	$17,729,078	$ 9,919,327
Installation division	6,601,413	5,240,388
Administrative and selling expenses	4,048,113	2,390,604
Interest expense	1,838,461	648,181
Total costs and expenses	$30,217,065	$18,198,500
Income before federal and state income taxes	$ 6,630,663	$ 4,355,568
Federal and state income taxes:		
Current	$ 368,000	$ 1,965,982
Deferred	3,010,000	354,397
	$ 3,378,000	$ 2,320,379
Net income	$ 3,252,663	$ 2,035,189
Average common shares outstanding	8,881,938	8,649,482
Earnings per common share	$ .37	$ .24

Notes to Consolidated Financial Statements, July 31, 1971:

Note 3: Receivables—The company enters into various modular housing sales contracts which contain an allocation of the sales price between modules (based upon published price lists) and installation work. Sales of modules (Manufacturing Division) are recognized when units are manufactured and assigned to specific contracts. Installation work (Installation Division) is recorded on the percentage of completion method. The contracts generally provide for payment upon completion and receipt of all approvals necessary for occupancy, or for payment upon completion of each respective phase. "Unbilled" receivables represent recorded sales on contracts in progress for which billings will be rendered in the future in accordance with the contracts.

	July 31, 1971	July 31, 1970
Contract receivables:		
Billed	$10,382,626	$10,559,145
Unbilled	24,633,799	4,626,370
Total	$35,016,425	$15,185,515
Income tax refund receivable	2,498,672	—
Current portion of long-term receivables	12,500	17,500
Other receivables	317,975	283,104
	$37,845,572	$15,486,119

Substantially all sales are to local housing authorities and sponsors who qualify for financial assistance from federal agencies of the U.S. government or who have made arrangements for long-term financing. In light of this, no provision for doubtful accounts is considered necessary.

Required:

1.   When does Stirling Homex recognize revenue? What do you think is the appropriate critical event for the Manufacturing Division? For the Installation Division?

2.   The staff of the Securities and Exchange Commission in reviewing Stirling Homex's 1971 registration statement for the issue of preferred stock to the public questioned the validity of recognizing revenue in advance of the date the customer was invoiced and asked Stirling Homex to revise its financial statements to defer recognition of revenue to the point at which the amount recorded was validly billable to customers.*

Recast Stirling Homex's income statement for the fiscal year ended July 31, 1971, and its balance sheet as of July 31, 1971, in accordance with the SEC request. Assume for purpose of this calculation that the increase in 1971 unbilled current receivables, $20,007,429, was included in 1971 sales and that unbilled current receivables are approximately 80 percent from the Manufacturing Division and 20 percent from the Installation Division.

3.   Do you agree with the SEC? Would present and potential shareholders be better served if the SEC required revenue to be recognized when it was validly billable? Explain.

4–4 Hyquest Corporation

On June 31, 1981, the Hyquest Corporation sold for $1,500,000 its Santa Fe, New Mexico, land, building, and improvements. This property had a book value at the date of sale of $1,105,000. The terms of the sale required the purchaser to pay $150,000 at the date of sale and give Hyquest a 14 percent first mortgage note payable in six annual installments plus interest on the unpaid balance commencing on June 30, 1982.

In accordance with generally accepted accounting principles† Hyquest was required to report this transaction as an installment sale.

Required:

1.   Assume that there were no selling costs and the total profit on the transaction was $395,000 ($1,500,000 − 1,105,000). How much of this profit will be recognized in 1981? 1982? 1986?

2.   Do you believe that this installment sales method is better than recognizing the entire $395,000 profit in 1981? Why?

3.   Make the journal entry on June 30, 1981, to record the installment sale.

4.   Make the journal entry on June 30, 1982, to record the annual principal and interest payment and accrued income.

---

* SEC, *Accounting Series Release No. 173* (Washington, D.C., July 2, 1975).

† *AICPA Accounting Guide,* "Accounting for Profit Recognition on Sales of Real Estate."

4-5 Optimal University

Roger Denudo, the controller of Optimal University, asks your advice in helping him decide when to accrue expenses for staff vacations and sick pay benefits and sabbatical leaves for professors.

a. The university policy is that all staff members receive two weeks vacation after one year's service with an additional day's vacation for each additional year's service. Employees who leave Optimal before the end of their first year of employment do not receive any vacation pay. All other employees are paid for all their unused vacation days when they leave the employment (voluntarily or involuntarily) of Optimal University.

b. Each staff member is entitled to four days' sick pay benefits after one year's employment with one additional day for each additional year's service. Unused sick days are not paid to the employee at the time of termination.

c. Professors receive a one-year, fully paid sabbatical every seven years.

Required:

1. When should Optimal University record an employee's vacation pay as an expense? In the year the vacation is earned (work performed) or the year the vacation is taken or paid? Why?

2. How should they treat the forfeiture of vacation days for employees who leave Optimal before the end of their first year of employment?

3. When should they record sick pay as an expense? In the year the sick pay is earned or paid? Why?

4. Should they record sabbaticals as expense in the year it is taken, or should they accrue it as an expense over seven years?

5. Would your treatment of the sabbatical expense be different if the professor was required to do research as a requirement of the sabbatical leave? If there were no conditions attached to the granting of the sabbatical?

4-6 AMAX, Inc.

AMAX, Inc., is a diversified minerals and energy development company with worldwide operations. The Company explores for, mines, refines, and sells a wide variety of minerals and metals and has substantial interests in coal, oil, and natural gas. AMAX's principal products are molybdenum, coal, iron ore, copper, lead, zinc, petroleum and natural gas, potash, phosphates, nickel, tungsten, silver, and magnesium. Through Alumax, Inc., a 50 percent-owned affiliate, AMAX is also involved in the production of aluminum and the fabrication and marketing of aluminum products.

Required:

1. A number of the possibilities that exist for recognizing revenue related to molybdenum are listed below. Explain why each of these methods

is appropriate or inappropriate in measuring AMAX's annual net income and suggest any other revenue recognition method you think is superior to those listed.

a. Record all the revenue at the time AMAX discovers the molybdenum deposits. Revenue equals the difference between current market price and estimated cost per ton.

b. Record revenue as the company mines and processes the molybdenum and adds value to the product. If a ton is 50 percent finished, 50 percent of the profit would be recognized.

c. Record all the revenue at the time the molybdenum is processed and placed in inventory ready for sale.

d. Record all the revenue when it sells the molybdenum to a customer.

e. Record all the revenue when it collects the receivable from the customer.

2. Refer to AMAX's December 31, 1981, consolidated statement of financial position (balance sheet) and a statement taken from the first page of their annual report titled "Here's What You Own." Assume that you could obtain the market price of each of the items listed in "Here's What You Own" from quotations on the commodities exchanges.

a. Would the resources per share stated at market price times the number of common shares outstanding be equal to the amount of assets less liabilities and preferred stock recorded on the statement of financial position?

b. Assume you are a potential investor in AMAX, Inc. Which valuation method for mining resources—historical cost or market value of reserves—would you find most useful in deciding whether to purchase the company's common stock? Can you suggest a different valuation method you think is superior to either of these methods?

AMAX, INC.
Consolidated Statements of Financial Position
At December 31, 1981

Assets

Cash and equivalent	$ 40,600
Accounts receivable	352,400
Inventories	820,100
Prepaid expenses and other current assets	64,000
Current assets	1,277,100
Investments—	
Alumax, Inc.	295,100
Other affiliates accounted for by the equity method	174,600
Investments accounted for by the cost method	56,100
Property, plant, and equipment, less accumulated depreciation and depletion; **$951,900** (1980—$802,100)	3,584,500
Other assets	61,200
	$5,448,600

Liabilities and deferred credits

Accounts payable, trade	$ 153,100
Other liabilities and accruals	182,700
Income and other taxes	166,400
Short-term borrowings	175,500
Advances under equipment leases	
Current maturities of long-term debt	113,500
Current liabilities	791,200
Long-term debt	1,234,700
Proceeds from sale of future production	355,900
Capital lease obligations	
Other long-term liabilities and reserves	122,600
Unearned revenue	85,700
Minority interests	27,000
Deferred income taxes	25,600
	2,642,700

Contingencies and commitments

Capital stock and retained earnings

Series C and D sinking fund preferred	250,000
Series B nonsinking fund convertible preferred	200
Common stock of $1 par value—	
Authorized 150,000 shares	
Issued—**63,094** (1980—62,084) shares	63,100
In treasury, at cost	(200)
Paid-in capital	1,004,900
Retained earnings	1,487,900
	$5,448,600

HERE'S WHAT YOU OWN*

Molybdenum	11.9 tons of ore		Phosphates	9.0 tons of ore
Tungsten	0.25 tons of ore		Copper	3.5 tons of ore
Coal	52.7 tons		Lead and zinc	0.5 tons of ore
Petroleum	0.2 barrels		Silver	0.19 tons of ore
Iron ore	7.1 long tons of ore		Natural gas	3,644 cubic feet
Potash	1.2 tons of ore			

* A composite investment for each share was created by dividing the number of common shares issued at December 31, 1981 (63,094,089), into the relevant reserve data for each mineral as prepared for the AMAX Form 10-K Report for 1981.

For example, they obtained 11.9 tons of molybdenum ore per share of common stock by dividing their estimated molybdenum reserves of approximately 750.8 million tons by 63,094,089 shares outstanding on December 31, 1981.

4–7 Morrison-Knudsen Company

Morrison-Knudsen Company provides engineering, design, construction, and construction-management services on a worldwide basis in addition to developing commercial real estate, building and repairing naval and commercial ships, and engaging in a number of specialized industrial operations.

Construction and engineering projects have been performed by "M-K" in all 50 states and nearly 75 foreign countries. Generally, these operations include large-scale and/or highly complex projects, which relatively few firms are capable of undertaking.

In the footnotes to its 1981 annual financial statements Morrison-Knudsen disclosed the following revenue recognition policy:

> *Recognition of Revenue:* The company recognizes revenue on construction and engineering contracts, including substantially all of its joint venture contracts, on the percentage-of-completion method based on the proportion of costs incurred on the contract to total estimated contract costs. Revenue on new ship construction contracts is recognized on the percentage-of-completion method based on the proportion of manhours incurred on the contract to total estimated manhours. Revisions in contract revenue and cost estimates are reflected in the accounting period when known. Provision is made currently for estimated losses on uncompleted contracts. Claims for additional revenue are recognized when settled.

Required:

Assume that on April 1, 1983, M-K entered into a contract with Saudi Arabia to build an office building for $5.25 million. The agreement stated that the building had to be completed in 21 months and that $5.25 million price was firm and Saudi Arabia would not pay for any cost overruns. It was also agreed that Saudi Arabia would make progress payments of $250,000 on the last day of each month commencing with April 30, 1983.

On April 1, 1983, M-K estimated that they would make a profit of $1.575 million on the Saudi contract.

As of December 31, 1983, M-K incurred costs of $3.15 million on the contract and they received $2.25 million from the Saudi government as payment on account which they credited to this account.

The contract was completed as expected on December 31, 1984, but costs for the contract exceeded those originally anticipated: 1984 costs incurred were $1.5 million, and the total profit on the contract was $.6 million ($5.25 − $3.15 + $1.5). The Saudi government paid the $3 million balance due on the contract in 1984.

1. Calculate the profit earned by M-K on the Saudi contract in 1983 and 1984 using the percentage-of-completion method that the company uses for contracts of this type.

2. Calculate the profit that would have been earned by M-K in 1983 and 1984 if they used the completed contract method to report revenue on this contract.

3. Which method most accurately measures net earnings (profit) for a company like M-K?

5

Working capital

Working capital is defined as current assets minus current liabilities. It is a measure of a company's short-term liquidity and is often used by present and potential creditors and investors in assessing the company's ability to pay its current obligations.

CURRENT ASSETS

Current assets are assets that are expected to be converted into cash or consumed during an operating cycle or one year whichever is longer. An operating cycle is the average amount of time it takes a company to purchase or produce a product, sell it, and collect the cash from the sale.

Cash, marketable securities, accounts receivable, short-term notes receivable, inventories (covered in Chapter 6), and prepaid expenses are the major current assets.

CASH

Cash is immediately available to pay obligations and is the most liquid current asset. The cash account on the balance sheet includes cash on hand, cash in checking accounts, cash in savings accounts, and all other readily available funds.

Compensating balances

Many banks require borrowers to maintain a minimum or *compensating* balance in connection with a loan agreement. For example, one of the conditions of a $2 million, 12 percent loan made by the Second Bank to Jelly Corporation legally requires it to maintain a compensating balance in its checking account equal to 10 percent of the face amount of the loan.[1] Since the $200,000 compensating balance is restricted and not fully available for payment of Jelly Corporation's obligations, it should be disclosed as a *separate item* in the current assets section of the balance sheet. Compensating balances for long-term loans should be listed in the noncurrent assets section of the balance sheet.

Certificates of deposit

Certificates of deposit (CDs) are loans made by a company or an individual to a bank. The bank promises to repay the CDs with interest on their maturity date. Because they can be converted into cash quickly and inexpensively they are often classified as cash on the balance sheet. CDs that cannot be rapidly converted into cash should be classified separately on the balance sheet if the amount is material.

MARKETABLE SECURITIES

In order to earn additional revenue companies often make temporary short-term investments in marketable securities with cash that is not needed for current operations.

The characteristics of marketable securities are that in addition to paying interest or dividends they are readily marketable and can easily be converted into cash.

Examples of marketable securities are *marketable equity securities,* which are ownership securities (common stock) of companies that trade in a national securities market, and *marketable debt securities,* which are government and corporate obligations (long-term notes and bonds) that trade on national securities exchanges.

---

[1] The effect of the compensating balance is to reduce the amount borrowed from $2,000,000 to $1,800,000 ($2,000,000 − $200,000) and increase the interest rate to 13.33 percent $\left(\frac{12\% \times \$2,000,000}{\$1,800,000}\right)$.

Marketable equity securities

At the time of their acquisition marketable equity securities are recorded at cost. On the balance sheet date they are valued at the lower of cost or market on a portfolio basis.[2]

Assume that Waddell Corporation purchased the following short-term investments in marketable equity securites in 1984:

January 20, 1984—purchased 3,000 shares of General Motors Corporation at a cost of $105,750

May 26, 1984—purchased 2,000 shares of General Electric Company at a cost of 121,400

August 31, 1984—purchased 5,000 shares of GATX, Inc., at a cost of 132,400

The journal entries on Waddell's books are:

Marketable Equity Securities....................	105,750	
Cash		105,750

To record purchase of 3,000 shares of General Motors Corporation.

Marketable Equity Securities....................	121,400	
Cash		121,400

To record purchase of 2,000 shares of General Electric Company.

Marketable Equity Securities....................	132,400	
Cash		132,400

To record purchase of 5,000 shares of GATX, Inc.

On December 31, 1984, the cost and market values of the securities in Waddell's portfolio are:

	Cost	Market	Unrealized Gain (Loss)
General Motors Corporation	$105,750	$100,000	$(5,750)
General Electric Company	121,400	122,000	600
GATX, Inc.	132,400	132,400	–0–
	$359,550	$354,400	$(5,150)

---

[2] FASB, *Statement of Financial Accounting Standards No. 12,* "Accounting for Certain Marketable Securities" (Stamford, Conn., December 1975).

Because the market value of the *total* portfolio ($354,400) is lower than the cost of the total portfolio ($359,550), an entry is made to reduce the portfolio to market:

Unrealized Loss—Marketable Equity
   Securities 5,150
     Allowance for Valuation Loss—
      Marketable Equity Securities   5,150
To recognize loss on write down to market of market-
able equity securities.

Marketable Equity Securities		Unrealized Loss or Gain Marketable Equity Securities	
105,750		(a)	5,150
121,400			
132,400			

Allowance for Valuation Loss— Marketable Equity Securities	
	(a) 5,150

These are all claims

The temporary investment in marketable equity securities of $354,400 ($359,550 − $5,150) is carried at aggregate market value, and the $5,150 unrealized loss on marketable equity securities is treated as an expense on the 1984 income statement.

If the market value of the portfolio increases in subsequent periods, the marketable equity securities portfolio can be increased but only to the extent of original cost. For example, assume that no purchases or sales of marketable equity securities are made in 1985 and the market value of Waddell's portfolio is now $363,000.

General Motors Corporation	$104,000
General Electric Company	123,000
GATX, Inc.	136,000
	$363,000

The $363,000 market value of the aggregate portfolio on December 31, 1984, exceeds the book value of $354,400 ($359,500 − $5,150) by $8,600. The journal entry on December 31, 1984, is for $5,150 rather than $8,600 because the aggregate portfolio cannot be stated above its original cost of $359,550.

Allowance for Valuation Loss—
    Marketable Equity Securities 5,150
      Unrealized Gain—Marketable
        Equity Securities 5,150
To recognize gain on write up of marketable equity
securities to *cost*.

Marketable Equity Securities			Unrealized Gain— Marketable Equity Securities			
105,750		(a)	5,150			5,150*
121,400					(b)	5,150
132,400						

Allowance for Valuation Loss— Marketable Equity Securities			
(b)	5,150	(a)	5,150

* 1984 expense closed to retained earnings.

The following footnote from the 1981 annual financial report of the Dayco Corporation is a good example of disclosure related to marketable securities.

> *Marketable Securities:* Marketable securities are carried at the lower of aggregate portfolio costs or market values. Marketable securities had a cost basis of $16,400,000 and $11,054,000 at October 31, 1981, and 1980, respectively.
> To reduce the carrying value of the marketable securities portfolio to market, which was lower than cost, a provision of $3,920,000 was charged to income for the year ended October 31, 1981. The provisions to income for the years ended October 31, 1980, and 1979 were not material. These provisions had no impact on cash flow.

Marketable debt securities

Many companies value marketable debt securities at cost or market, whichever is lower, on a portfolio basis even though *FASB Statement No. 12* only relates to marketable equity securities. The alternative generally accepted accounting method is to value marketable debt securities at cost with a write down to market only for substantial declines that are deemed not to be temporary.[3]

The market value argument

Many accountants argue that market value of securities is more relevant in determining the liquidity of the firm and gives better

---

[3] AICPA, *Accounting Research Bulletin No. 43,* "Restatement and Revision of Accounting Research Bulletins Nos. 1–42"* (New York, 1953), chapter 3A, paragraph 9.

disclosure than the conservative lower of cost or market method of *FASB No. 12,* which reflects market value when the portfolio value exceeds cost.

In the case of marketable equity and debt securities, market value is reliable as well as relevant because the price of the securities may be objectively determined by reference to quotations on national securities markets.

Marketable securities are listed after cash on the balance sheet because they are liquid and easily converted to cash.

ACCOUNTS RECEIVABLE

Accounts receivable are usually valued at the amount expected to be collected from the customer.

The customary accounting procedure is to record accounts receivable at their gross sales price at the time of sale and then adjust this amount for sales discounts, sales returns and allowances, and estimated uncollectible accounts receivable.

Sales discounts (gross method)

Sales (cash) discounts are usually offered as an inducement for prompt payment of an invoice.

Assume that on March 1, Fish Corporation sells merchandise to the James Company for $25,000 with payment terms of 2/10 net 30 (discount of 2 percent if paid in 10 days, no discount if paid after 10 days, full amount due within 30 days).

The entry on March 1 is:

```
Accounts Receivable ............................. 25,000
    Sales ........................................             25,000
    To record sale to James Company.
```

The entry on March 8 when the James Company pays its bill is:

```
Cash ............................................ 24,500
Sales Discounts ................................    500
    Accounts Receivable .........................            25,000
    To record cash receipt from James Company.
```

If the James Company paid the bill on March 25 the entry would be:

```
Cash ............................................ 25,000
    Accounts Receivable .........................            25,000
```

[handwritten margin note: is this a asset or a claim — claim, right?]

Sales discounts (net method)

An alternative method of treating sales discounts is to record the sale at the net amount of $24,500 and record the $500 as interest revenue (sales discounts forfeited) if the accounts receivable isn't paid within 10 days.

The entry on March 1 is:

```
Accounts Receivable .............................  24,500
        Sales ..........................................          24,500
```

If the James Company pays their bill on March 8 the journal entry is:

```
Cash .............................................  24,500
        Accounts Receivable ..........................          24,500
```

If the bill is paid on March 25 the journal entry is:

```
Cash .............................................  25,000
        Accounts Receivable ..........................          24,500
        Sales Discounts Forfeited .....................             500
```

Although the net method of recording sales discounts describes the transaction better, it is rarely used because it requires more record keeping and the amount of the discounts involved are not material enough to have an impact on net income.

Sales returns and allowances

Sales returns or allowances are given to customers for merchandise that they have returned because the merchandise was defective or unsuitable.

The entry is:

```
Sales Returns and Allowances .........................  xxx
        Accounts Receivable ..............................          xxx
        To record return of merchandise.
```

The sales return and allowances account is a contra (deduction from) sales account.

Uncollectible accounts receivable and the bad debt adjustment

The amount of credit sales the company estimates is going to be uncollectible is deducted from gross sales and from accounts receivable.

Allowance method for estimating bad debts. The following example describes the process of recording uncollectible accounts receivable using the allowance method for estimating bad debts.

Assume that for the fiscal year ended June 30, 1985, Bailey's Drug Store had sales of $500,000; $200,000 of the sales were for cash and $300,000 were charge sales. The merchandise sold cost Bailey's $375,000.

The journal entries to record these transactions are:

(a) Cash 200,000
     Accounts Receivable 300,000
       Sales   500,000
     To record sales for the year (in practice
     sales would be recorded on a daily basis
     and posted to the general ledger monthly).

(b) Cost of Merchandise Sold.................. 375,000
       Inventory   375,000
     To record cost of the merchandise sold.

During the fiscal year, collections of accounts receivable amount to $205,000.

(c) Cash 205,000
       Accounts Receivable   205,000
     To record collection of receivables.

The general ledger accounts would appear as follows:

Cash				Sales	
(a)	200,000			(a)	500,000
(c)	205,000				

Accounts Receivable				Cost of Merchandise Sold	
(a)	300,000	(c)	205,000	(b)	375,000

Inventory	
(b)	375,000

Bailey's *estimates* that it will probably not collect $4,500 of the charge sales made in the fiscal year ended June 30, 1985. They are unable to determine which of the charge customers will not pay, but based on past experience they estimate that 1½ percent of charge sales or $4,500 (.015 × $300,000) will not be collected.[4]

The appropriate adjusting entry is:

(d) Bad Debt Expense (Sales—Bad Debt
     Adjustment) 4,500
          Allowance for Uncollectible
          Accounts Receivable   4,500
     To record estimated uncollectible accounts for
     the FYE 6/30/84.

Accounts Receivable			Sales	
300,000	205,000			500,000

Allowance for Uncollectible Accounts Receivable			Cost of Merchandise Sold	
	(d)	4,500	375,000	

Bad Debt Expense	
(d) 4,500	

The debit to bad debt expense of $4,500 records the expense for estimated bad debts in the year the sales are made and results in the matching of revenue and expense.

Accounts receivable cannot be credited at this time for the $4,500 because we do not know which of the store's customers will default. To solve this problem, an account called *Allowance for Uncollectible (or Doubtful) Accounts Receivable* is created. This account is a contra asset account. It is deducted from the asset account, Accounts Receivable.

The formal balance sheet would show:

Accounts receivable $95,000
    Less: Allowance for uncollectible
        accounts receivable   4,500
            Net accounts receivable $90,500

---

[4] Another method of estimating bad debts for the year is based on the accounts receivable balance rather than on charge sales. Accounts receivable are classified by the length of time they are past due and estimates of their collectibility are made. This process is called "aging accounts receivable." The allowance for uncollectible accounts is then adjusted to make sure it is large enough to cover all estimated uncollectible accounts receivable.

The balance sheet discloses to the reader that the store is owed $95,000 by customers and that it expects to collect $90,500 of this amount.

Sometime in the future, when Bailey's Drug Store finds out from their attorney that Bob Roberts's $200 account cannot be collected, the following entry is made:

(e) Allowance for Uncollectible Accounts
         Receivable 200
             Accounts Receivable   200
     To write off Bob Roberts's account as uncollectible.

Accounts Receivable

300,000	205,000
(e)	200

Allowance for Uncollectible Accounts Receivable

(e) 200	4,500

The entry to Accounts Receivable can be made now because the specific customer has been identified. In an accounts receivable ledger that lists each individual's accounts receivable, we would indicate on Bob Roberts's account that his balance was written off as uncollectible.

The balance sheet after the write-off would show:

Accounts receivable	$94,800
Less: Allowance for uncollectible accounts receivable	4,300
Net accounts receivable ...	$90,500

The store is now saying it is owed $94,800 and expects to collect $90,500. There is no effect from the write-off of an uncollectible account on the net amount of accounts receivable expected to be collected.

Direct write-off method of reordering bad debts.   Another possibility in handling bad debts would be to record the expense in the year the accounts receivable became worthless. The problem with this *direct write-off method* is that it can result in the bad debt expense being recorded in a year other than the one in which the sale has occurred. In order to match revenue and expense properly, we should estimate the expense in the year the charge sale is made.

Bad debt recoveries. Sometimes, but not often, accounts that have been written off as uncollectible are collected at a later date. Assume that we collect $50 at a later date from Roberts. The appropriate entry is to correct the write-off and treat the receipt as a collection of receivables. This entry should also be reflected on Roberts's individual accounts receivable card in the subsidiary ledger.

Accounts Receivable	50	
Allowance for Uncollectible Accounts		
Receivable		50
To correct the write-off of $50 of Roberts's account receivable.		
Cash	50	
Accounts Receivable		50
To record the collection of $50 on Roberts's account receivable.		

Sales discounts, sales returns and allowances, and the bad debt adjustment are contra revenue accounts not expense accounts. The preferred income statement disclosure is:

They're not expenses.

Sales			xxxxxx
Less: Sales discount		xxxx	
Sales returns and allowances		xxxx	
Sales—bad debt adjustment		xxxx	xxxxx
Net sales			xxxxxx

Accounts receivable follow marketable securities in the balance sheet. The expectation is that the net realizable value (accounts receivable minus allowance for uncollectible accounts receivable) will be collected in cash within 30 to 60 days depending on the company's credit terms.

SHORT-TERM NOTES RECEIVABLE

Notes are written promises to pay a certain sum of money on demand or on a specified date.

The issuer of the note is called the *maker,* and the recipient to whom the payment will be made is called the *payee.*

Makers record the payments specified in the note as notes payable. Payees record them as notes receivable.

Notes receivable often require the payment of interest in addition to the face amount of the note. Short-term notes receivable are classified as current assets because they will be converted to cash within one year of the balance sheet date.

Assume that on December 1, Rogers Corporation received a $10,000, 15 percent, 60-day note from Joslow, Inc., in payment of an account receivable. Rogers prepares financial statements on a calendar-year basis.

The appropriate journal entries for the note are:

```
Dec.  1   Notes Receivable .........................  10,000
              Accounts Receivable .................            10,000
          To record receipt of the note.


      31   Accrued Interest Receivable .............     125
              Interest Revenue .....................              125
          To accrue interest revenue for year
          ended December 31 (15% × $10,000 ×
          30/360).*


Jan. 30   Cash.....................................  10,250
              Accrued Interest Receivable..........              125
              Interest Revenue .....................             125
              Note Receivable .....................           10,000
          To record payment of the note.
```

* For purposes of computing interest, lenders often assume a year consists of 360 days.

Short-term notes receivable and accrued interest receivable are listed after accounts receivable in the current asset section of the balance sheet.

PREPAID EXPENSES

Prepaid expenses are not expenses. They are unexpired costs that are expected to benefit future periods, and they will become expenses in those periods.

On June 30, 1984, the Rogers Company purchases a three-year fire insurance policy for $3,600. The policy protects Rogers for the period June 30, 1984, to June 30, 1987.

The appropriate journal entries are:

```
June 30, 1984   Unexpired (prepaid) Insurance .......  3,600
                    Cash ...........................            3,600
                To record purchase of fire insurance
                policy.
```

> Dec. 31, 1984   Insurance Expense 600
>   Unexpired Insurance   600
>   Insurance expense 6/30/84–12/31/84.

On December 31, 1984, the prepaid expense, unexpired insurance is $3,000 ($3,600 − $600). Of this, $1,200 is a current asset because it will expire within one year of the balance sheet date, and $1,800, which provides insurance coverage for 1986 and 1987, is noncurrent.

In practice the entire $3,000 is considered to be a current asset primarily because the prepaid amounts are generally immaterial.

Prepaid expenses are valued at their cost and follow inventories on the balance sheet.

Current assets on the balance sheet are listed in order of liquidity: cash, marketable securities, receivables, inventories, and prepayments.

CURRENT LIABILITIES

Current liabilities are liabilities that are expected to be paid within an operating cycle or one year, whichever is longer. They adopt the same time frame as the current assets used to pay them.

Included in current liabilities are accounts payable, short-term notes payable, current installment of long-term debt payable, withholding and social security taxes payable, dividends payable, federal income taxes payable, unearned or deferred revenues, and accrued expenses.

ACCOUNTS PAYABLE

Accounts payable are valued at the amount expected to be paid to vendors.

Customary accounting procedure is to use the gross method and record accounts payable at the invoice price at the time of the purchase and adjust this amount for purchase (cash) discounts and purchase returns and allowances.

Assume that on March 1, James Company purchases merchandise costing $25,000 with payment terms of 2/10 net 30 from Fish Corporation.

The entry on March 1, using the gross method of recording purchase (cash) discounts, is:

> Inventory* 25,000
>   Accounts Payable   25,000
> To record purchase of merchandise from Fish Corporation.

* Some companies use a separate purchases account; the amount in this account is subsequently transferred to the inventory account.

The entry on March 8 when James Company pays its bill is:

Accounts Payable 25,000
    Cash   24,500
    Purchase Discounts   500
  To record payment of the invoice.

If James Company paid the bill on March 25, the entry would be:

Accounts Payable 25,000
    Cash   25,000

Alternatively James could have recorded the purchases using the net method.
The entry on March 1 is:

Inventory 24,500
    Accounts Payable   24,500

If James pays the bill on March 8 the journal entry is:

Accounts Payable 24,500
    Cash   24,500

If they pay the bill on March 25 the journal entry is:

Accounts Payable 24,500
Purchase Discounts Lost   500
    Cash   25,000

Purchase discounts lost would be recorded as a financial (other) expense on the income statement.

Although the net method is more accurate in its valuation of the cost of inventory (it treats financing cost as a period expense rather than a production cost), it is not generally used in practice because it requires more record keeping and the amount of purchase discounts are not usually material.

Purchase returns and allowances for merchandise that is defective or returned are recorded as follows:

Accounts Payable xxx
    Purchase Returns and Allowances   xxx

Purchase discounts and purchase returns and allowances are contra (deduction from) gross purchases and are not revenue accounts.

[handwritten margin note: For things that you return.]

Purchases (addition to inventory during the year)		xxxx
Less:		
Purchase discounts	xx	
Purchase returns and allowances	xx	xx
Net purchases		xxx

SHORT-TERM NOTES PAYABLE

Companies issue notes to creditors for goods and services and to banks for cash loans. Unlike accounts payable, which are oral agreements, notes payable are formal, written promises to pay specified amounts on certain dates.

The journal entries to record notes payable to creditors are symmetrical to the entries we made for notes receivable earlier in the chapter. Joslow would record the $10,000, 15 percent, 60-day note payable issued to Rogers Corporation on December 1 as follows:

Dec.	1	Accounts Payable 10,000	
		Notes Payable	10,000
		To record issue of note.	
	31	Interest Expense 125	
		Accrued Interest Payable.............	125
		To accrue interest expense for the year ended Decmber 31.	
Jan.	31	Notes Payable 10,000	
		Accrued Interest Payable 125	
		Interest Expense 125	
		Cash	10,250
		To record payment of note and interest.	

The entries for interest-bearing bank loans are shown in Chapter 3.

Notes that are expected to be paid within one year are classified as current liabilities on the balance sheet.

CURRENT PORTION OF LONG-TERM DEBT PAYABLE

The amount of long-term debt to be paid within one year of the balance sheet date is classified as a current liability.[5]

---

[5] In cases where a company intends to refinance (replace it with new long-term debt) and can demonstrate it has the ability to complete the refinancing within the operating cycle, they should not list the debt as a current liability. See *FASB No. 6,* "Classification of Short-Term Obligations Expected to Be Refinanced" (Stamford, Conn., 1975).

The Zypo Company borrows $100,000 from the Third Bank on December 31, 1984. The loan requires Zypo to make 20 semiannual principal payments commencing June 30, 1984, plus pay interest on the unpaid balance at a rate of 12 percent.

The journal entry to record the transaction on December 31, 1984 is:

```
Cash ...........................................  100,000
    Long-Term Notes Payable ..................              100,000
    To record 12% long-term loan from Third Bank.
```

On the December 31, 1984, balance sheet $10,000, due within one year of the balance sheet date, is classified as a current liability and $90,000 as a long-term liability.

```
Current liabilities:
    Current installments on Third Bank 12% Notes Payable ...............  $10,000
Long-term liabilities:
    Third Bank 12% notes payable ....................................   90,000
```

No liability is recorded for interest on this note because interest accrues with time and there is no interest due on December 31, 1984.

WITHHOLDING AND SOCIAL SECURITY (FICA)[6] TAXES PAYABLE

The U.S. government requires organizations to withhold federal income taxes and social security taxes from the pay of employees. When the taxes are deducted from the employees' pay they are liabilities of the organization, which must pay the amount withheld to the U.S. government.

For example, assume that for the first week in January 1982, Art Stan, who works for the Paul Corporation, earned gross wages of $400. It was determined that, based on current federal income tax rates and the number of his dependents, $100 should be withheld for income taxes.

The journal entry on Paul's book is:

---

[6] Social security taxes are withheld in accordance with the Federal Insurance Contribution Act and are called FICA taxes. The tax was 6.7 percent on the first $32,400 of wages in 1982.

```
1.  Wages Expense ................................ 400.00
        Withholding Taxes Payable ...............        100.00
        FICA Tax Payable (6.7% of $400) ..........         26.80
        Wages Payable ...........................         273.20
    To record payroll.
```

The FICA also assesses employers an amount equal to what was deducted from the employees' pay. The entry to accrue this expense is:

```
2.  FICA Tax Expense ...........................  26.80
        FICA Tax Payable ........................         26.80
    To accrue FICA taxes.
```

The $26.80 is an expense because it is a cost of operations that has to be paid by the employer.

The entries to record the payment to the government and wages to Art Stan are:

```
3.  Withholding Taxes Payable ...................  100.00
    FICA Taxes Payable (2 × $26.80) ..............   53.60
        Cash ....................................         153.60
    Payment of payroll taxes to the federal govern-
    ment.

4.  Wages Payable .............................  273.20
        Cash ....................................         273.20
    Payment of Art Stan's wages.
```

The general ledger accounts for these transactions.

Cash				Withholding Taxes Payable			
		(3)	153.60	(3)	100	(1)	100
		(4)	273.20				

FICA Tax Payable			
(3)	53.60	(1)	26.80
		(2)	26.80

Wages Payable			
(4)	273.20	(1)	273.20

Wages Expense	
(1)	400

FICA Tax Expense	
(2)	26.80

DIVIDENDS PAYABLE

Dividends payable in cash are recorded as a liability at the time they are authorized to be paid by the board of directors. On that date stockholders become creditors of the corporation in an amount equal to the dividend declaration. Cash dividends payable are classified as current liabilities because they are paid within one year from the date they are declared.

FEDERAL INCOME TAXES PAYABLE

Federal income taxes are levied on the taxable income of businesses. Taxable income is calculated based on the Internal Revenue Code and sometimes differs from income calculated using generally accepted accounting principles. The income of a business owned by proprietors or partnerships is not taxed separately but is included in the individual's tax return.

Corporate federal income tax rates for 1984 were:

Taxable Income	Tax Rate
$ 1–$ 25,000	15%
$25,001–$ 50,000	18%
$50,001–$ 75,000	30%
$75,001–$100,000	40%
Over $100,000	46%

Corporations are required by law to make quarterly tax payments in advance based on their estimate of taxable income for the year. Any unpaid amounts are paid half in 75 days and half 135 days after the end of the year. Penalties are assessed by the Internal Revenue Service for underestimation of income.

Federal income taxes payable are current liabilities because they will be paid within one year from the balance sheet date.

UNEARNED OR DEFERRED REVENUES

Unearned or deferred revenues arise from advance payments for goods and services. In Chapter 3 we made the entries for the deferred revenue account, Rent Paid in Advance.

Another example of a deferred (unearned) revenue account would be Advance Payments for Magazine Subscriptions.

On December 1, 1984, the Scripto Company sells 1,000 annual subscriptions of its monthly magazine for $12.

On December 1, 1984, the entry is:

Cash 12,000
        Unearned Subscriptions 12,000
    To record sale of subscriptions.

104

Unearned Subscriptions is a liability account because Scripto must provide future services (delivery of magazines) to discharge this obligation.

On December 31, 1984, when the first issue is sent to subscribers, the entry is

```
Unearned Subscriptions ...........................  1,000
    Subscription Revenue ..........................          1,000
    To record delivery of the December issue to subscri-
    bers.
```

This entry recognizes the revenue earned and reduces the liability by the delivery of the December issue.

Unearned or deferred revenue accounts are classified as current liabilities when the required services will be provided within one year or an operating cycle, whichever is longer.

ACCRUED EXPENSES

In order to match expenses against revenues companies must accrue all expenses that apply to the accounting period but have not been paid on the balance sheet date.

Examples of accruals for interest and wage expense are shown in Chapter 3. An entry was made earlier in this chapter to accrue FICA tax expense.

Accrued expenses are current liabilities because they will be paid within one year of the balance sheet date.

PROBLEMS AND CASES

5-1 King Company

The balance in King Company's Accounts Receivable account at the end of its first year of operations on December 31, 1985, was $22,000.

An analysis by the company's accountant revealed that 90 percent of all credit sales in 1985 were collected and that no accounts receivable were written off as uncollectible. The accountant figured that ½ of 1 percent credit sales was a reasonable estimate of uncollectible accounts receivable.

On February 21, 1986, it was determined that Mr. Lucky's accounts receivable of $900, which was nine months old, was uncollectible and should be written off.

On July 30, 1986, Mr. Lucky, who had been fortunate in winning $50,000 in the Connecticut lottery, paid King the $900 previously written off.

Required:

1. Make the following journal entries.

a. The estimate of bad debt expense for the year ended December 31, 1985.

b. The write-off of Mr. Lucky's accounts receivable on February 21, 1986.

c. The recovery (collection) of the $900 from Mr. Lucky which was previously written off.

2. Do you agree with King Company's policy of estimating bad debts as a percentage of credit sales? Sure

5-2 White-Out Company

Make journal entries for the following transactions of the White-Out Company, which sells appliances. White-Out records purchases in a general ledger account, Purchases—White Goods, and uses the gross method to record discounts.

July 1 Purchased 10 washing machines from the General Electric Company at $324 per machine with payment terms of 2/10 net 30.

8 Purchased 20 stoves at $263 each from Roper, Inc. Terms 2/10 net 30.

9 Paid General Electric's invoice.

11 Returned 3 stoves with defective pilot lights to Roper.

23 Paid Roper's invoice and took the 2 percent cash discount.

30 Notified by Roper that it was improper to take the 2 percent cash discount and that they were disallowing it. White-Out put the amount of the disallowed discount in accounts payable.

5-3 Roper, Inc.

1. Make the journal entries to record Roper's sales to the White-Out Company in Problem 5-2 using both the gross and net method of recording sales discounts.

2. Which method do you think is more accurate in measuring net income?

5-4 Dayco Corporation

The following footnote was taken from the 1981 annual report of the Dayco Corporation.

Marketable Securities: Marketable securities are carried at the lower of aggregate portfolio costs or market values. Marketable securities had a cost basis of $16,400,000 and $11,054,000 at October 31, 1981 and 1980, respectively.

To reduce the carrying value of the marketable securities portfolio to market, which was lower than cost, a provision of $3,920,000 was charged to income for the year ended October 31, 1981. The provisions to income for the years ended October 31, 1980 and 1979 were not material. These provisions had no impact on cash flow.

For purposes of this problem you may assume there was no allowance for valuation account contra to marketable securities on October 31, 1981.

Required:

1. What journal entry did Dayco make on October 31, 1981, to reduce the carrying value of its marketable securities portfolio to market, which was lower than cost.

2. Assume that during the fiscal year ended October 31, 1982, Dayco purchased marketable securities at a cost of $3,400,000 and sold marketable securities with a cost of $1,000,000 for $1,250,000. Make the journal entries to record the purchase and sale of marketable securities for the year.

3. Assume further that the market value of Dayco's marketable securities portfolio was $19,800,000 on October 31, 1982. What journal entry, if any, should Dayco make on October 31, 1982?

4. Do you believe the accounting treatment of marketable equity securities required by *FASB 12* results in a better measurement of income and cash flows than valuing them at historical cost? Market value?

5–5   Venetian Publishing Company, Inc.

The Venetian Publishing Company published a monthly magazine that was only available by subscription. The subscription price for 12 monthly issues was $12.

The trial balance (general ledger account balance) on December 31, 1984, after all transactions have been recorded but before *year-end adjusting entries,* is listed below:

VENETIAN PUBLISHING COMPANY, INC.
Trial Balance
December 31, 1984

Account Titles	Debit	Credit
Cash	$ 192,600	
Accounts receivable—subscriptions	592,000	
Allowance for bad debts		$ 4,500
Paper inventory	530,000	
Supplies inventory	76,000	
Unexpired insurance	34,800	
Furniture, fixtures, and equipment	1,066,000	
Accumulated depreciation—furniture, fixtures, and equipment		140,000
Accounts payable		95,600
Unearned (deferred) subscriptions		2,868,000
Notes payable		200,000
Common stock		70,000
Retained earnings		75,600
Advertising income		636,000
Production salaries	422,700	
Factory rent	180,000	
Light, heat, and power	74,600	
Maintenance and repairs	86,500	
Sales salaries, and commissions	268,200	
Administrative salaries	337,600	
Interest expense	10,000	
Miscellaneous, general, and administrative expense	218,700	
Totals	$4,089,700	$4,089,700

An analysis of these general ledger accounts by Venetian's accountant prior to the preparation of financial statements revealed the following:

Cash. Reconciliation of the bank statement and other analysis indicates that the cash balance reflected in the general ledger account is correct and doesn't need adjustment.

Accounts receivable and allowance for bad debts. An adjusting entry is necessary to estimate bad debts for 1984 and to calculate the allowance for bad debts on December 31, 1984. The company's bad debt policy is based on past experience and relates to the age of the accounts receivable on the balance sheet date.

Age of Receivables	Percent Estimated to Be Uncollectible
0– 30 days	.5
21– 60 days	1.0
61– 90 days	2.5
91–120 days	5.0
Over 120 days	10.0

For example, Venetian would expect 10 percent of all accounts receivable over 120 days old not to be collected.

An analysis of the general ledger accounts and the aging of the accounts receivable on December 31, 1984, are shown below:

Accounts Receivable—Subscriptions

Balance 1/1/84	$ 152,000
Charge sales 1984	1,968,000
	2,120,000
Collections 1984	1,520,000
Uncollectible accounts written off 1984	8,000
Balance 12/31/84	$ 592,000

Allowance for Bad Debts

Balance 1/1/84	$ 12,500
Uncollectible accounts written off in 1984	8,000
Balance 12/31/84	$ 4,500

December 31, 1984, Aging of Accounts Receivable

0– 30 days	$ 300,000
61– 60 days	90,000
61– 90 days	80,000
91–120 days	70,000
Over 120 days	52,000
	$ 592,000

Paper inventory. An adjusting entry is necessary to reflect the December 31, 1984, physical inventory of $156,000. The appropriate expense account for the paper used is Printing Materials Consumed.

Supplies inventory. An adjusting entry is necessary to reflect the December 31, 1984, inventory of $44,600. The appropriate expense account for supplies used is Supplies Expense.

Unexpired (prepaid) insurance. An adjusting entry is necessary to reflect the insurance coverage that has expired in 1984.

A schedule of all the insurance policies in force on December 31, 1984 is as follows:

Policy Dates	Types of Coverage	Premium
1/1/84 to 12/31/84	Workers' compensation	$ 7,200
6/30/83 to 6/30/86	Liability $100,000/1,000,000	18,000
1/1/84 to 12/31/86	Fire and extended coverage	12,600

The appropriate expense account for expired insurance is Insurance Expense.

Furniture, fixtures, and equipment and accumulated depreciation. An adjusting entry is necessary to record depreciation expense for 1984. A listing of the furniture, fixtures, and equipment is shown below:

Date of Acquisition	Cost	Accumulated Depreciation 12/31/83	Depreciation Method	Estimated Life
1/1/80	$ 200,000	$ 80,000	Straight-line	10
6/30/82	400,000	60,000	Straight-line	10
6/30/84	350,000	–0–	Straight-line	10
12/31/84	116,000	–0–	Straight-line	10
Total	$1,066,000	$140,000		

Accounts payable. The list of unpaid vendors' invoices is in agreement with the balance in the general ledger account, and no adjusting entry is necessary.

Unearned subscriptions (deferred income). An adjusting entry is necessary to reflect magazines delivered in 1984.

The first issue of a subscription is delivered in the month following the receipt of the subscription. For example, if a subscription is received in February, the March issue will be the first one delivered to the subscriber.

An analysis of the unearned subscription account on December 31, 1984 is as follows:

Balance 1/1/84 (subscriptions sold in 1983; magazine to be delivered in 1984)	$ 900,000
Subscriptions sold in 1984	1,968,000
Balance 12/31/84	$2,868,000

1984 Subscriptions

Date Sold	Number Sold	Amount
January	8,000	$ 96,000
February	10,000	120,000
March	10,000	120,000
April	8,000	96,000
May	10,000	120,000
June	11,000	132,000
July	12,000	144,000
August	15,000	180,000
September	15,000	180,000
October	20,000	240,000
November	20,000	240,000
December	25,000	300,000
Total	164,000	$1,968,000

The appropriate income account for magazines delivered is Subscription Income.

Notes payable. An adjustment is necessary to accrue the appropriate amount of interest expense on December 31, 1984.

Date Note Issued	Amount	Interest Rate	Interest Paid	Note Due
4/1/84	$200,000	10%	Quarterly	4/1/85

Common stock. No adjusting entry is necessary.

Retained earnings. An analysis of this account prior to the year-end closing journal entry is:

Retained earnings 1/1/84	$175,600
Dividends declared and paid in 1984	100,000
	$ 75,600

Income and expense accounts. An analysis of these accounts indicates that $12,500 of sales salaries was charged to the Administrative Salaries account in error and an adjusting entry has to be made for the following payroll, which was earned for the week ended December 31 and will be paid on January 4, 1985.

Production salaries	$ 8,100
Sales salaries	4,000
Administrative salaries	6,500
	$18,600*

Income tax expense. An adjusting entry is necessary to record income tax expense for the year ended December 31, 1984.

Income tax rates for 1984 are:

15 percent for the first $25,000 of taxable income.*

18 percent for the next $25,000 of taxable income.

30 percent for the next $25,000 of taxable income.

40 percent for the next $25,000 of taxable income.

46 percent for all taxable income over $100,000.

Required:

1. Prepare a general ledger (T-account form) that includes all the accounts in the December 13, 1984, trial balance.

2. Prepare all the necessary adjusting journal entries and post these entries to the general ledger (T-accounts). Add any additional accounts you feel are necessary.

3. Prepare and post the closing journal entry.

4. Prepare an income statement for the year ended December 31, 1984 and a balance sheet as of December 31, 1984.

5. Was the Venetian Publishing Company successful in 1984?

5-6 Associated Hardware

For the past 10 years, two brothers, Frank and Roger Johnson, had operated a hardware store in a suburb of Boston. Although they kept only mini-

---

* For purposes of this problem disregard payroll taxes and assume taxable income is income minus expenses before income taxes.

mal accounting records, it seemed to them that they had been very successful. The store was always busy, and each partner had been able to draw
a salary of $31,500.

In January 1985, Roger was offered a managerial position with a large
chain store operation on the West Coast. To help Roger make a decision,
the two brothers decided to carefully evaluate the value of their business
as of December 31, 1984. They hired a professional accountant, Roberta
Franks, to prepare a balance sheet as of December 31, 1984, and an income
statement for the past year.

Franks first prepared the accompanying trial balance as of January 1,
1984.

ASSOCIATED HARDWARE
Trial Balance
January 1, 1984

Account Titles	Debit	Credit
Cash	$ 29,925	
Accounts receivable	10,185	
Inventory	219,450	
Prepaid insurance	1,890	
Store fixtures and equipment	21,000	
Accumulated depreciation—equipment		$ 8,400
Accounts payable		7,795
Wages payable		235
Salaries payable		1,000
Capital—Roger Johnson		132,510
Capital—Frank Johnson		132,510
Totals	$282,450	$282,450

Franks then examined the checkbook and bank statements for the year
and prepared the accompanying list of cash receipts and disbursements:

Cash receipts:
Cash sales $210,000
Collections of charge sales
(accounts receivable) 7,875
Mortgage proceeds from Sunshine
Bank 42,000
Total cash receipts $259,875

Cash disbursements:
Payments to suppliers
(accounts payable)................. $ 96,000
Property taxes 420
Miscellaneous store expenses 3,675
Salaries—partners 63,000
Wages—employees 15,750
Utilities 9,450
Shipping expense 3,135
Payment—warehouse 51,870
Rent 3,780
Total cash disbursements......... $247,080

Excess of receipts over
disbursements .... $ 12,795

Her examination also revealed the following additional information:

a. The prepaid insurance on the January 1, 1984, trial balance was for a fire contents policy that would provide coverage until June 30, 1985.

b. Associated Hardware pays rent for the hardware store at a rate of $315 per month.

c. The accounts receivable at the end of the year were $13,230. Included in this amount was $622 due from one customer and owed for over one year. Further investigation revealed that the customer had moved out of town, and collection of this amount was considered unlikely.

d. Accounts payable on December 31, 1984, were $7,035.

e. Wages of $300 and partners' salaries of $1,200 for the week ended December 31, 1984, were not paid until January 4, 1985.

f. Because of the water damage that occurred during the winter and the need for additional space, the brothers purchased a building to be used as a warehouse on June 30, 1984.

   The closing statement for the purchase revealed the following:

Land	$ 8,190
Building	44,100
	52,290
Less: Property taxes, January 1, 1984, to June 30, 1984	420
Total	$51,870

The 1984 property taxes are assessed based on a tax list date of January 1, 1984, with semiannual payments of the tax on July 1, 1984, and January 1, 1985. Associated Hardware made a payment of $420 representing one half of the year's tax on July 1, 1984.

g. They financed the building with partnership cash and a 10 percent mortgage note payable for $42,000 taken out with the Sunshine Bank on June 30, 1984. This note payable is called a *mortgage* note because the bank received the building as security for the payment of the note. The mortgage is payable in 40 equal semiannual principal payments with interest on the unpaid balance. Payments are to be made on January 1 and July 1 of each year.

h. Depreciation rates for the fixed assets were estimated as follows: store fixtures and equipment, 10 percent; warehouse, 2 percent.

i. The inventory on December 31, 1984, was counted and priced at $192,000. *Included* in the inventory figure were hardware tools that cost Associated $1,920, which had been ruined by water damage caused by flooding last January. Roger felt that this damaged inventory did not have any resale value. In the course of the discussion about the inventory, Frank remembered that they had donated a Toro lawnmower, which cost them $521, to the high school. This lawnmower had a regular retail price of $837.

Required:

1.   Prepare an income statement for the year ended December 31, 1984.

2.   Prepare a balance sheet as of December 31, 1984.

3.   What is the minimum salary Roger should request from the chain store in order for him to consider leaving Associated Hardware?

4.   If he leaves, how much should Frank pay him for half interest in the partnership?

6

Working capital—inventories

Inventory consists of all the goods owned by a merchandising company that it expects to sell in the normal operations of its business. A manufacturing company's inventories consist of goods that are finished and available for sale (finished goods), goods that are partially processed (goods or work in process), raw materials that will be used directly in the manufacture of the finished goods, and supplies that will be used indirectly in the manufacturing process.

Inventory is classified as a current asset because the expectation is that it will be sold and converted into cash within one year or the company's operating cycle, whichever is longer.

For most manufacturing and merchandising companies, inventory is often the single largest current asset. The Cost of Goods Sold account, which represents the inventory sold, frequently is the largest expense in the income statement. At the date of acquisition, inventory items are recorded in accordance with the cost principle. Subsequently, when they are sold, their cost is matched with revenue in accordance with the matching principle.

INVENTORY VALUATION

Inventory value is determined by multiplying the quantity of inventory items on hand by their unit prices. The unit prices are determined by using one of the inventory cost flow methods described later in this chapter.

PERIODIC INVENTORY METHOD

The *periodic inventory method* determines the ending inventory quantity by an actual physical count of goods on hand on the balance sheet date. The value of the inventory on the balance sheet date (ending inventory) is determined by multiplying the units counted times the appropriate unit prices.

Cost of goods sold is computed by subtracting the ending inventory from the goods that were available for sale (beginning inventory plus purchases).

Beginning Inventory + Purchases − Ending Inventory = Cost of Goods Sold

---

The assumption using this formula is that all goods not in the ending inventory have been sold. In actual practice this will result in losses due to pilferage and evaporation being treated as cost of goods sold.

An illustration of the cost of goods sold section of the income statement for a merchandising company that uses the periodic inventory method is as follows:

COMPANY X
Cost of Goods Sold
For the Year Ended December 31, 1984

Beginning inventory		$ 450,000
Add:		
Purchases (gross invoice price)	$2,125,000	
Freight-in	42,500	
	2,167,500	
Deduct: Purchase returns and discounts	54,000	
Net purchases		2,113,500
Goods available for sale		2,563,500
Less: Ending inventory		822,300
Cost of goods sold		$1,741,200

The cost of inventory purchases includes the invoice cost of the merchandise plus all freight or related costs to get it to the company. To obtain net purchases for the period, purchase discounts and purchase returns should be subtracted from gross purchases.

At the end of the accounting period prior to the taking of the ending inventory, the Merchandise Inventory general ledger account would appear as follows:

Merchandise Inventory

Beginning balance	450,000	Purchase returns and discounts	54,000
Gross purchases	2,125,000		
Freight-in	42,500		

The periodic inventory taken at the end of the year showed merchandise on hand with a cost of $822,300. A journal entry is necessary to adjust the inventory account to $822,300 and to reflect a cost of goods sold of $1,741,200 ($2,563,500 − $822,300).

Cost of Goods Sold	1,741,200	
Merchandise Inventory		1,741,200
To record cost of goods sold.		

The relevant general ledger accounts would appear as follows:

Merchandise Inventory				**Cost of Goods Sold**	
Beginning balance	450,000	54,000	.....Purchase returns and discounts		
Gross purchases.....	2,125,000				
Freight-in	42,500	1,741,200	.....Cost of..... goods sold	1,741,200	

One disadvantage of the periodic inventory method is that a physical inventory must be taken each time financial statements are prepared. A physical inventory is usually taken at the end of each year, but many companies use the gross profit or gross margin method of estimating their inventories and cost of goods sold for interim financial statements (prepared for a period of less than one year).

GROSS PROFIT METHOD

The gross profit method uses the estimated gross profit percentage to determine the cost of goods sold and ending inventory.

The Miniature Dress Company's sales, purchases, and inventory accounts for the first quarter of 1985 prior to the preparation of financial statements are as follows:

Inventory		Sales	
10,000			200,000
Purchases 142,500			

The company's management estimates that the gross profit (margin) percentage (gross profit/sales) for the first quarter is 40 percent.

Sales − Cost of Goods Sold = Gross Profit
100% −   60%   =   40%
Cost of Goods Sold   = $120,000 (60% of $200,000)

Cost of Goods Sold = Beginning Inventory + Purchases − Ending Inventory
     $120,000   = $10,000   + $142,500 − Ending Inventory
Ending Inventory   = $32,500 ($10,000 + $142,500 − $120,000)

The company would make the following journal entry:

Cost of Goods Sold 120,000
    Inventory   120,000
  To record cost of inventory sold.

The general ledger accounts after this entry is posted:

Inventory		Cost of Goods Sold		Sales	
10,000	120,000	120,000			200,000
142,500					

PERPETUAL INVENTORY METHOD

Under a perpetual inventory method the purchase and sale of each unit is identified and recorded. At the same time the journal entry is made to record a sale, the matching entry is made to record the cost of the sale.

Assume that a company has sales of $10,000 and that the perpetual inventory indicates that the cost of these sales is $7,000. The following journal entries summarize the entries made at the time of these sales.

Accounts Receivable 10,000
    Sales   10,000
  To record sales.

Cost of Goods Sold 7,000
    Inventory   7,000
  To record the cost of sales.

The advantage of the perpetual inventory method over the periodic inventory method is that it enables a company to determine the cost of the goods sold at the time of sale rather than waiting to the end of the accounting period for a physical inventory. It also maintains an updated value for inventory. The knowledge of what items were sold and the amount you have in inventory is extremely useful in planning the amount of inventory that has to be purchased or produced in the future.

For example, some supermarkets and major department stores maintain a perpetual inventory by the use of electronic point-of-sale cash registers. The registers indicate the number and cost of each item sold in the store. By reference to the information generated by the register, supermarkets can determine sales and the amount of inventory by item on a daily basis and use this information to plan future inventory levels.

The disadvantage of the perpetual inventory method is that it requires more record keeping and is more costly than the periodic inventory method.

Companies should weigh the costs of the perpetual inventory method against its benefits in order to determine whether to use it or the periodic inventory method.

INVENTORY COST FLOW METHODS

During any given period inventory may be purchased or manufactured at different unit costs. When the inventory is sold, the company must determine which items remain in the inventory.

For items such as automobiles that can be specifically identified, it is not difficult to determine the cost of the unit sold. In most cases, all the units of inventory are physically the same, and it is extremely difficult and costly to ascertain whether the unit that was taken off the shelf or out of the storeroom was one of the older units or one of the newer units.

Generally accepted accounting principles require the *consistent* use of the inventory cost flow method that most clearly reflects periodic income.[1]

This means that the basis for the selection of a particular method is not the actual physical flow of goods but the method that best matches cost with revenue.

The four major cost flow methods are:

1. Specific identification.
2. First-in, first-out (FIFO).

---

[1] AICPA, *Accounting Research Bulletin No. 43*, "Restatement and Revision of Accounting Research Bulletins Nos. 1–42" (New York, 1953), chapter 4.

3. Last-in, first-out (LIFO).
4. Weighted average.

To illustrate these cost flow methods assume the data in Illustration 6–1 applies to the purchase and sale of a single item.

ILLUSTRATION 6–1

		Units Received	Unit Cost	Units Sold	Units on Hand
Dec. 1	Inventory	100	$100		100
4	Purchase	80	120		180
10	Sale			110	70
16	Purchase	150	140		220
19	Sale			160	60
26	Purchase	90	150		150

1. Specific identification

The specific identification cost flow method identifies a specific cost with each item in the inventory.

For example, an automobile dealer would keep a perpetual inventory cost card for each automobile in the inventory. This card would record the cost of the particular automobile and identify it by reference to its engine number, model, color, and other distinguishable characteristics.

On the date the automobile is sold, the cost of the particular car is transferred from inventory to cost of goods sold.

In cases where the inventory units can be easily identified the specific identification cost flow method results in the appropriate match of the cost of goods sold with sales on a physical flow basis.

When the specific identification cost flow method is used for units that are physically alike but have different costs, it can result in the manipulation of net income. A high or low cost for the year could be "specifically assigned" to the units sold depending on whether management wanted to maximize, minimize, or average net income.

In our illustration management could "specifically identify" the 110 units sold on December 10 in a number of different ways: 80 at $120 and 30 at $100; 100 at $100 and 10 at $120; or any combination thereof depending on their profit-reporting objective.

2. FIFO

The FIFO inventory cost flow method assumes that the first goods purchased or manufactured are the first ones sold. Cost of goods sold is valued at the oldest unit prices, and inventory is valued at the most recent prices.

In our illustration the 150 units in the ending inventory (periodic method) are the last 150 units purchased.

Ending Inventory:

90 units at $150		$13,500
60 units at $140		8,400
150 units		$21,900

The cost of goods sold is determined by subtracting the ending inventory from the cost of goods available for sale (beginning inventory plus purchases).

Beginning inventory (100 units at $100)		$10,000
Plus purchases:		
December 4—80 units at $120		9,600
December 16—150 units at $140		21,000
December 26—90 units at $150		13,500
Total cost of goods available for sale		54,100
Deduct ending inventory (150 units):		
90 units at $150	$13,500	
60 units at $140	8,400	21,900
Cost of goods sold		$32,200

If the company had used the perpetual inventory method instead of the periodic inventory method the company would cost out the units when they were sold instead of waiting until the end of the year.

Cost of Goods Sold:

December 10—110 units sold	$100 \times \$100 = $	$10,000
	$10 \times \$120 = $	1,200
December 19—160 units sold	$70 \times \$120 = $	8,400
	$90 \times \$140 = $	12,600
		$32,200
Inventory:		
$60 \times \$140$		$ 8,400
$90 \times \$150$		13,500
		$21,900

The perpetual and periodic inventory methods result in the same cost of goods sold and inventory values under the FIFO cost flow method.

3. LIFO

The last-in, first-out inventory cost flow method assumes that the latest goods purchased are the goods sold. Cost of goods sold is valued at the most recent prices, and inventory is valued at the oldest prices.

The 150 units in the ending inventory are the first 150 units purchased.

100 units at $100	$10,000
50 units at $120	6,000
	$16,000

Cost of goods sold are the most recent purchases.

Total cost of goods available for sale (from the preceding example)		$54,100
Deduct ending inventory:		
100 units at $100	$10,000	
50 units at $120	6,000	16,000
Cost of goods sold		$38,100

When the periodic inventory method is used the LIFO cost flow *disregards* the dates when the units are purchased or sold and calculates the ending inventory on the basis of total units. In our illustration the 150 units in the ending inventory are assumed to come from the most recent purchases (100 in beginning inventory plus 50 purchased on December 4) regardless of the fact that those units may have actually been sold.

The perpetual inventory method requires the transfer to cost of goods sold of the most recent costs at the time of the sale and results in a different value than the periodic method, which is applied on a theoretical or total unit basis.

Cost of Goods Sold:		
December 10—110 units sold	$80 \times \$120 =$	$ 9,600
	$30 \times \$100 =$	3,000
December 19—160 units sold	$150 \times \$140 =$	21,000
	$10 \times \$100 =$	1,000
		$34,600
Inventory:		
90 units at $150		$13,500
60 units at $100		6,000
		$19,500

During periods of rising prices the perpetual inventory method should result in lower cost of goods sold, higher net income, and larger income taxes than the periodic inventory method. Because income tax savings are one of the main reasons for using LIFO the perpetual inventory method is rarely used with this cost flow method.

4. Weighted average

The weighted average cost flow method assumes that an average unit cost is a representative cost of all items available for sale during the period.

Total cost of goods available for sale (from the preceding example)		$54,100
Total units available for sale (beginning inventory plus total purchases)	420	
Average unit cost ($54,100 ÷ 420) = $128.81		
Ending inventory = Number of units × Average unit cost = 150 × $128.81		19,321
Cost of goods sold = Number of units × Average unit cost = 270 × $128.81		$34,779

The weighted average method generally produces cost of goods sold and inventory values in between those produced by the FIFO and LIFO methods.

LOWER-OF-COST-OR-MARKET RULE (LCM)

In all cost flow methods the principle of conservatism requires that year-end inventory be written down whenever the market price of the units in inventory is less than the historical cost of the units.

Market price for purposes of this rule is usually defined as current replacement cost, but it should not exceed net realizable value (estimated selling price in the ordinary course of business less reasonably predictable costs of completion and disposal) or be less than net realizable value reduced by an allowance for a normal profit margin.[2]

For income tax purposes companies that use the LIFO cost flow method may not use the lower-of-cost-or-market rule.

To illustrate how the LCM rule works, let us assume that the market price of the inventory dropped to $130 per unit at the end of the accounting period on December 31. Using our sample data

---

[2] Ibid, Paragraph 8.

and assuming that the company was using FIFO, we see that a year-end write-down must be made in accordance with the LCM rule.

Calculation:
Current ending inventory, FIFO

90 units at $150	$13,500	
60 units at $140	8,400	$21,900

Current ending inventory, at market prices

90 units at $130	11,700	
60 units at $130	7,800	19,500
Write-down		$ 2,400

The write-down would increase cost of goods sold for the period and would reduce the amount shown in inventory on the balance sheet by the same amount.

Many accountants question the logic of writing inventory down to current replacement cost but not writing it up when current replacement cost is greater than historical cost. They argue that current replacement cost is a more relevant figure for investors and creditors in estimating the liquidity of a company and measuring income.

COMPARISON OF THE COST FLOW METHODS

All of the four cost flow methods illustrated are in accordance with generally acceptable accounting principles as long as they are applied on a consistent basis. They are all also acceptable for the computation of federal income taxes. The Internal Revenue Service requires that a company using the LIFO inventory cost flow method for financial reporting also use it for income tax purposes and that the company obtain permission to switch from the LIFO inventory cost flow method to another cost flow method.

A summary of the cost of goods sold and inventory values (periodic inventory) using the different cost flow methods is listed in the following table. In periods of rising prices LIFO will usually result in cost of goods sold which is higher than the other methods. Reported earnings and income taxes will be lower using LIFO as will the inventory which will be valued at the oldest prices.

	Cost of Goods Sold	Inventory
FIFO	$32,200	$21,900
LIFO	$38,100	$16,000
Weighted average	$34,779	$19,321
Specific identification*		

* Depends on how items are specifically identified.

If inventory levels are not maintained and the company is forced to sell old (low-cost) inventory purchased in a prior period, the cost of goods sold using LIFO could be lower than the other methods.

ARGUMENT FOR USE OF THE FIFO COST FLOW METHOD

As long as prices remain constant, both the FIFO method and LIFO method give the same results. When unit prices change, however, the two methods provide significant differences in inventory valuation, cost of goods sold, and net income.

In the post-World War II economic era, rising prices have been prevalent throughout the world. With rising prices, FIFO matches the lowest (oldest) costs against sales revenue and values inventory on the balance sheet at the most recent purchase prices.

Proponents of FIFO generally point to the fact that the balance sheet account, Inventory, is more realistic under FIFO and the current ratio (current assets divided by current liabilities—a key measure of corporate short-term liquidity) and other measures related to current assets are not distorted. They also argue that FIFO more closely approximates the actual physical flow of most goods.

Managements of some companies have chosen to use the FIFO inventory cost flow method during periods of rising prices because it results in higher net income and earnings per share than the other cost flow methods. This is particularly true in companies where management compensation is based on net income.

THE ARGUMENT FOR USE OF THE LIFO COST FLOW METHOD

Under LIFO, during a period of rising prices, the most recent (highest) costs are matched with sales revenue (most recent sales prices), and inventory is valued at the oldest (lowest) costs. The argument in favor of LIFO (apart from tax considerations) is that it states cost of goods sold in relatively current dollars and more correctly reports net income on a current-dollar basis than the other inventory cost flow methods.

Proponents of LIFO suggest that in a period of rising prices, other methods of inventory valuation produce misleading and fictitious profits because a portion of such profits must be used to replace, at higher costs, the units sold from inventory.

EVALUATION OF LIFO

A number of factors have contributed to an increase in the use of the LIFO cost flow method. Historically, managements have not been inclined to use LIFO because of its depressing effect on reported earnings. The Internal Revenue Service has permitted the use of LIFO but requires companies that adopt LIFO inventory valuation for tax purposes to also use it on the company's books. This eliminates the possibility of using FIFO for annual report purposes (with higher earnings and better inventory values) and LIFO for tax purposes (better income measurement and lower tax payments). During the 1974–75 recession, however, corporate management looked at the tax and other benefits of LIFO with renewed interest because of a need for increased cash flow and the belief that their published earnings reports were having little impact on the market prices of their securities.[3] Companies using the LIFO method receive improved cash flows from tax savings. Under LIFO, during periods of rising prices and assuming inventory levels don't decrease, cost of goods sold is higher and reported net income is lower than it would be under an alternative method of inventory costing; consequently, federal and state income taxes will be lower resulting in a cash savings.

Many financial analysts and accounting theoreticians have challenged the quality of non-LIFO earnings. They have raised the question of the validity of these earnings when the inventory units sold have to be replaced at higher prices. They also question the payment of higher federal income taxes by companies that don't use LIFO since this results in the depletion of cash that would otherwise be available for capital expenditures and dividend distributions. The magnitude of the cash savings obtained through the use of LIFO was addressed by the Dayco Corporation in the Management's Discussion and Analysis section of their 1981 annual report.

LIFO

In 1974, when it became evident that we had entered a long-term high inflation period, Dayco switched to the LIFO (last-in, first-out) method of valuing substantially all inventories. We believe this change was necessary in order to match costs and revenues properly, even though our reported net earnings and rates of return have been lower than they would have been had we continued using a FIFO (first-in, first-out) inventory valuation method, as shown in the following supplementary table:

---

[3] Some of the empirical research on the relationship between accounting changes and stock prices indicates that stock prices do not decline when a company switches from FIFO to LIFO. This is probably due to the detailed disclosure of the change and the increased cash flow under LIFO due to tax savings.

	1981	1980	1979	1978	1977
LIFO net earnings (000's)*	$ 9,043	$ 8,642	$21,126	$17,328	$13,623
After-tax LIFO provision (000's)	5,875	5,664	6,592	1,688	2,189
Pro-forma FIFO net earnings (000's)	$14,918	$14,306	$27,718	$19,016	$15,812
Actual LIFO primary EPS on earnings from operations*	$1.53	$1.51	$3.87	$3.52	$3.00
FIFO/LIFO EPS difference	1.01	1.01	1.22	.35	.50
Pro-forma FIFO primary EPS on earnings from operations*	$2.54	$2.52	$5.09	$3.87	$3.50
Return on average shareholders' equity					
—LIFO*	6.1%	6.1%	16.4%	14.4%	15.7%
—FIFO*	10.0%	10.0%	20.8%	17.7%	17.7%
Return on average total capital					
—LIFO*	6.1%	5.0%	9.1%	8.4%	8.0%
—FIFO*	7.6%	6.7%	11.0%	9.0%	8.8%

* Before extraordinary item

In other words, our reported results look different than those of similar companies (which stayed on FIFO) simply due to the way we record our inventories.

However, there is a hidden benefit of LIFO, because our taxing authorities permit us to deduct the LIFO provision on our tax returns. We believe that a dollar saved in taxes is as good for our shareholders as a dollar earned (after taxes) from operations.

We have estimated the net present value of the tax benefits to Dayco from using LIFO. To do this, we used the very conservative assumptions of (a) an average annual projected LIFO tax benefit of $1,500,000 plus the existing tax savings of $18,750,000 and (b) an average after tax rate of return of 8 percent. The present tax benefit, combined with the estimated future tax benefit discounted at 8 percent, yields a value to the Corporation in today's dollars of approximately $46,-000,000 or $7.89 per share.

Some of the advantage of more accurate income measurement and better cash flow with the use of LIFO (through the reduction of income taxes) can be lost in subsequent years if inventory quantities are reduced so that the base inventory or other low-cost layers are liquidated. Low-cost inventory would flow into cost of goods sold to be matched with current sales revenue, resulting in a gross profit that includes a large gain on holding inventory.

Dayco made the following disclosure on the liquidating of LIFO inventories in the notes to its 1981 annual report.

During the last two years, in reaction to downturns in demand for certain products, the Corporation reduced inventory levels related to these products. These reductions resulted in a liquidation of LIFO inventories carried at costs prevailing in prior years. Without these reductions costs of sales (net of taxes) would have been higher by approximately $1,532,000 ($1,259,000 in 1980) or $.26 per share ($.22 per share in 1980).

Except for unusual situations where there is a strike or a product is being phased out, well-financed companies can ensure that they do not invade the base inventory by making year-end purchases.

FINANCIAL STATEMENT DISCLOSURE

Companies must disclose the inventory cost flow method they use in the footnotes to the financial statements. An example of this disclosure is from a recent General Electric annual report.

INVENTORIES

Substantially all manufacturing inventories located in the U.S. are valued on a last-in, first-out, or LIFO, basis. Manufacturing inventories outside the U.S. are generally valued on a first-in, first-out, or FIFO, basis. Valuations are based on the cost of material, direct labor and manufacturing overhead, and do not exceed net realizable values. Certain indirect manufacturing expenses are charged directly to operating costs during the period incurred, rather than being inventoried.

Full disclosure of any change in an inventory cost flow method including its effect on net income must also be disclosed. An example of this type of disclosure is taken from the annual report of Dana Corporation.

CHANGES IN ACCOUNTING

In 1981 Dana changed its method of accounting for inventories from the first-in, first-out (FIFO), or average cost method to the last-in, first-out (LIFO) method for all domestic inventories which were not already on LIFO. This change was made because management believes LIFO more clearly reflects income by providing a better matching of current costs against current revenues. The change had the effect of reducing inventories at December 31, 1981 $27,739,000 and reducing net income $14,424,000 and net income per share of common stock $.41 for the year then ended. There is no cumulative effect on prior years since the December 31, 1980 inventories accounted for on the FIFO basis are the beginning LIFO inventories.

FASB Statement 33, "Financial Reporting and Changing Prices," October 1979, requires the largest corporations to make a supplementary disclosure in their financial statements of the current cost of inventory and cost of goods sold calculated using current prices. This disclosure will make it possible to obtain current inventory values for companies who use the LIFO inventory cost flow methods and to calculate cost of goods sold on a current cost basis for companies who use the FIFO inventory cost flow method.

The difference between the current cost of the inventory and the LIFO cost of the inventory is often identified as the LIFO reserve. This disclosure enables companies to segregate profits from holding inventory (current cost of inventory minus acquisition cost of inventory), called holding gains or losses, from operating profits (sales minus current costs of inventory sold).

INVENTORIES OF MANUFACTURING COMPANIES

The measurement of cost of goods sold in a manufacturing company is more complex than in a merchandising (purchase inventory) concern because the manufacturer applies direct labor and factory costs to the raw materials in order to convert them into finished goods. Generally accepted accounting principles require the manufacturing company to include in cost of goods sold the cost of raw materials used, the cost of direct labor applied, and all other factory costs.

In the manufacturing firm, the product often is manufactured in one period for delivery to customers in a later period. All manufacturing costs during the production process are charged to the asset account, Inventory, and are expensed through the Cost of Goods Sold account only when the sale is made.

MANUFACTURING FLOW OF COSTS

The flow of costs in the manufacturing concern is described below:

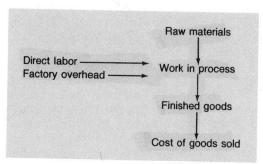

Raw materials cost includes all the costs necessary to put the material into production. Only the materials that become part of the product are included in raw materials.

Direct labor is the labor used to convert the raw material into the finished product. Direct labor cost includes only the wages of the people working directly on the product; for example, production workers on the assembly line.

Factory overhead, the third element of cost of manufacturing, encompasses all factory costs other than raw materials and direct labor. Included is the cost of indirect labor, which represents the wages and benefits earned by employees. Examples are factory supervisors, forklift operators, and the plant manager, who do not work directly on the product but whose services are closely related to the production process.

Factory overhead also includes depreciation on the production machinery and factory building, factory utilities and supplies, factory rent if applicable, and insurance and taxes on the assets used in the manufacturing operation.

The production and sales cycle of a manufacturing company may be illustrated by means of a line graph:

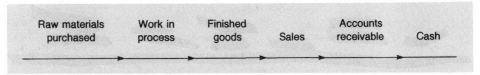

It begins when raw materials are purchased and ends when cash is collected from the sale of the goods that have been manufactured.

A diagram of the manufacturing flow in a hacksaw blade factory is shown in Illustration 6–2.

The raw material inventory is composed of large rolls of steel banding material in varying thicknesses. On command from the Production Control Office, a roll is sent to Station 1. The entire continuous roll of steel banding material is machine serrated, giv-

ILLUSTRATION 6–2. **Manufacturing Facility—Hood Hacksaw Company**

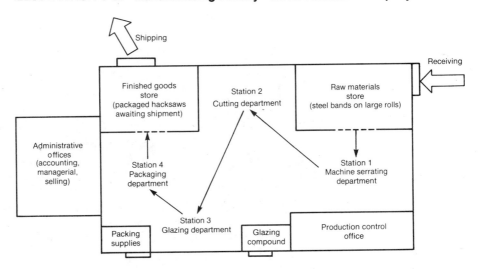

ing the band its sawtooth edge. The serrated roll is then sent to the cutting department where it is machine cut in varying lengths, generally 9 to 12 inches. After Station 2, the cut material is sanded, cleaned, and glazed with a chemical compound in the Glazing Department. On completion, the finished hacksaw blades are sent to Station 4 for special packing instructions. From packaging, the blades are sent to the Finished Goods area where, if there is an open order, they are immediately shipped; otherwise, inventory is placed on the shelf and is available for sale.

The accounting for the cost of the hacksaw blade follows the flow of the product through the factory. For example, let us assume a beginning raw materials inventory of $22,000. During the period, $49,000 of steel banding material was purchased. The entry recording the purchase would be:

Raw Materials Inventory	49,000	
Accounts Payable		49,000
To record raw materials purchased.		

During the period, $65,000 of the raw materials inventory was put into production (that is, sent to Station 1). The entry reflecting this is:

Work in Process Inventory	65,000	
Raw Materials Inventory		65,000
To record raw materials transferred to production.		

The raw materials inventory general ledger account, after the above transactions, would appear as follows:

	Raw Materials Inventory		
Beginning balance	22,000	65,000	.....To work in process inventory
Purchases	49,000		

The next item to consider is the wages of the production workers (direct labor). These wages are charged to the asset account, Work in Process Inventory. Factory labor is being used to create an asset (in this case hacksaw blades), and the cost of such labor does not become an expense until the hacksaw blades are sold. This differs from the wages of the office employees, which are not a part of the inventory cost and are expenses in the period incurred.

During the period, the production direct labor cost was $34,000. The appropriate entry would be:

```
Work in Process Inventory ........................ 34,000
    Wages Payable ................................           34,000
To record direct labor earned.
```

FACTORY OVERHEAD

The third item of manufacturing cost is factory overhead. Factory overhead represents all those costs associated with the manufacturing process other than raw materials and direct labor. During the period under review, indirect labor wages totaled $18,000, the factory rent was $4,000, and depreciation on the machinery was $3,500. Depreciation on factory machinery is a part of the cost of making the product and will be charged to the Work in Process Inventory account. Other miscellaneous manufacturing costs for light, heat, power, and manufacturing supplies totaled $13,000.

The entries reflecting these transactions would be:

```
Work in Process Inventory ........................ 18,000
    Wages Payable ................................           18,000
To record indirect factory labor earned.

Work in Process Inventory ........................  4,000
    Rent Payable .................................            4,000
To record factory rent.

Work in Process Inventory ........................  3,500
    Accumulated Depreciation—Factory ...........            3,500
To record depreciation on factory machinery.

Work in Process Inventory ........................ 13,000
    Accounts Payable ............................           13,000
To record miscellaneous manufacturing costs.
```

Goods manufactured during the period are moved to the finished goods area in the factory. The accounting entry is:

```
Finished Goods Inventory ......................... 93,500
    Work in Process Inventory ...................           93,500
To transfer cost of goods finished.
```

This transfer of costs indicates that some partially manufactured goods (work in process) have been converted into finished goods.

Partially manufactured goods will be located throughout the factory on the last day of the period. The balance in the Work in Process account ($44,000 in our illustration) represents the cost of unfinished hacksaw blades in various stages of production at that time.

The general ledger account for work in process inventory after posting the above entries is:

Work in Process Inventory

Beginning balance	0	93,500	. . . . Transferred to finished
Raw materials	65,000		goods inventory
Direct labor	34,000		
Factory overhead:			
Indirect labor	18,000		
Rent	4,000		
Depreciation	3,500		
Miscellaneous	13,000		

COST OF GOODS SOLD

The finished goods inventory account represents the total manufacturing cost of the goods available for sale. To complete our example, assume hacksaw blades sold during the period cost $87,000. The entry to record this is:

Cost of Goods Sold   87,000
        Finished Goods Inventory   87,000
    To transfer finished goods sold.

The balance of $6,500 in the finished goods inventory account represents the cost of the finished goods.

Finished Goods Inventory

Beginning balance	0	87,000	. . Transferred to cost of goods sold
From work in process . .	93,500		

STATEMENT OF COST OF GOODS SOLD

The operating cycle of this manufacturing company is now completed. The cycle consists of purchasing materials, processing them into finished goods, and selling them to customers. The flow of manufacturing costs through the accounts can be summarized in the statement of cost of goods sold. See Illustration 6–3.

SIGNIFICANCE OF THE PROCESS

Merchandising companies purchase their product (inventory) in the finished form. Manufacturing companies produce their product by adding direct labor and other factory costs to raw materials. All costs of manufacturing are *product costs* and become expenses in the accounting period in which the product is sold.

ILLUSTRATION 6-3

THE HOOD HACKSAW COMPANY
Statement of Cost of Goods Sold
For X Months Ended December 31, 19XX

Raw materials:

Beginning raw material inventory	$ 22,000
Raw material purchases	49,000
	71,000
Less: Ending raw materials	6,000
Cost of material used	65,000
Direct labor	34,000
Factory overhead:	
Indirect labor	18,000
Rent	4,000
Depreciation	3,500
Other	13,000
Total manufacturing cost	137,500
Plus: Beginning work in process inventory	–0–
Less: Ending work in process inventory	44,000
Cost of goods manufactured	93,500
Plus: Beginning finished goods inventory	–0–
Less: Ending finished goods inventory	6,500
Cost of goods sold	$ 87,000

PROBLEMS AND CASES

6-1 Gotkers Manufacturing

The following information was taken from the records of the Gotkers Manufacturing Company, for the year ended December 31, 1985.

Office salaries	$ 18,000
Purchases—raw materials	67,320
Freight-in (raw materials)	8,000
Sales salaries and commissions	22,000
Direct labor	102,540
Factory overhead (includes indirect labor, rent, equipment depreciation, and factory supplies)	151,270
Other selling expenses	36,000
Other general and administrative expenses	47,000
Purchase returns and discounts on raw materials	1,800
Inventories:	
Raw materials—1/1/85	15,000
Raw materials—12/31/85	10,500
Work in process—1/1/85	42,000
Work in process—12/31/85	48,500
Finished goods—1/1/85	32,000
Finished goods—12/31/85	34,000

Required:

From the above information prepare a statement of cost of goods sold for the year ended December 31, 1985.

6-2 Zorbo Manufacturing Company

The Zorbo Manufacturing Company manufactures one product. A summary of its activities for 1984 is as follows:

	Units	Amount
Sales	80,000	$800,000
Material inventory:		
1/1/84		40,000
12/31/84		32,000
Work in process inventory:		
1/1/84		55,000
12/31/84		72,000
Finished goods:		
1/1/84	16,000	64,000
12/31/84	24,000	?
Material purchases		152,000
Direct labor		145,000
Manufacturing (factory) costs		108,000
Selling expenses		50,000
General and administrative expenses		40,000

Required:

1. Calculate total manufacturing cost for 1984.

2. Calculate the cost of goods manufactured (finished), the number of units manufactured (finished), and the cost per unit.

3. Calculate the cost of goods *sold* for the year. The company uses the LIFO inventory costing method for its finished goods inventory.

6-3 Yeastall Pharmaceutical Company

The Yeastall Pharmaceutical Company manufactures vitamin pills containing brewer's yeast extract. On the first of March the company had on hand raw materials that cost $324,000, finished pills and containers costing $600,000, and partially processed pills embodying a total of $448,000 worth of raw materials, direct labor, and manufacturing overhead.

During March, receipts of additional materials totaled $680,000, and $948,000 worth of material was put into production. Direct labor applying to March production was $500,000, and manufacturing overhead totaled

$292,000. At the end of March partially processed pills on hand represented $36,000 in materials, $24,000 in direct labor, and $16,000 of manufacturing overhead. Pills costing $1,930,000 were shipped to customers during March.

Required: 1740,000

1. What was the total factory (manufacturing) cost for March?
2. What was the cost of goods finished? ~~1,930,000~~ 2,112,000
3. What was the cost of goods sold?   1930,000
4. What was the finished goods inventory on March 31?

782,000

6–4   The Rasholm Chemical Corporation

The Rasholm Chemical Corporation is a producer of molding-powder pellets, a basic raw material used in the manufacture of Plexiglas sheets. On January 1, 1984, the accounts of the Rasholm Corporation were as follows:

Account Titles	Debit	Credit
Cash	$ 55,500	
Accounts receivable	72,000	
Raw materials	25,500	
Work in process	9,750	
Finished goods	31,500	
Land	18,000	
Buildings	90,000	
Accumulated depreciation—buildings		$ 9,000
Equipment	120,000	
Accumulated depreciation—equipment....		48,000
Accounts payable		19,500
Notes payable		30,000
Accrued interest payable...............		1,800
Wages payable		1,500
Common stock		225,000
Retained earnings		87,450
	$422,250	$422,250

A summary of business operations for the ensuing quarter follows:

a. Raw materials purchased on account, $180,000.
b. Direct labor cost, $147,000.
c. Indirect labor cost, $91,500.
d. General manufacturing costs paid by check, $58,500.
e. Depreciation on equipment is 20 percent a year and is all chargeable to factory overhead.
f. Depreciation on the building is 5 percent a year (80 percent of the

building space is used for manufacturing operations, 10 percent for general administration, and 10 percent for the sales staff).

g. General and administrative expenses, paid in cash, $58,500. Selling expenses, paid in cash, $48,000.

h. Notes payable bear interest at the rate of 12 percent.

i. Raw materials put into production during the quarter, $163,500.

j. Fully manufactured goods transferred to finished goods, $414,000.

k. Sales on account, $540,000. Cost of goods shipped to customers totaled $363,000.

l. Collection of accounts receivable, $480,000.

m. Cash disbursements made:
   (1). Accounts payable—$136,500.
   (2). Wages payable—$231,000.

n. The federal income tax rate is 50 percent.

Required:

1. Prepare a statement of cost of goods sold and an income statement for the period January 1 to March 31, 1984.

2. Prepare a balance sheet as of March 31, 1984.

6–5 Devlin Corporation

The Devlin Corporation, a diversified distribution company, purchases cartons of canned tennis balls (three balls per can) from the Questor Company and markets the balls under the Devlin brand name.

Purchase and sales data for Devlin's first three years of business are shown in the accompanying table.

		1983
Sales		19,200 cartons at $54/carton
Purchases	February	6,500 cartons at $27
	July	10,000 cartons at $29
	September	8,000 cartons at $35
		1984
Sales		24,000 cartons at $64/carton
Purchases	January	9,000 cartons at $37
	June	10,000 cartons at $39
	September	6,500 cartons at $42
		1985
Sales		29,000 cartons at $70/carton
Purchases	June	11,000 cartons at $45
	August	7,500 cartons at $48
	September	8,000 cartons at $50

Required:

1. Calculate the year-end inventories and prepare income statements for each of the three years using:

a. FIFO.
b. LIFO.

2. Assuming an income tax rate of 50 percent, compute the tax savings associated with the LIFO method in each year.

Which method would you prefer, assuming you were:

a. The general manager (being paid a bonus based on earnings). FIFO
b. A bank creditor. LIFO
c. A present shareholder. FIFO
d. A prospective shareholder. FIFO
e. A labor union official. FIFO
f. An Internal Revenue Service agent. LIFO

6–6 Bulldog Corporation

The Bulldog Corporation, which uses the average cost method of inventory valuation, reported net income (profit) before income taxes as follows:

1984 .... $5,000
1985 8,000

The corporation's president was disappointed with the net income figures and was curious to know what the results would have been had they used the FIFO or LIFO method of inventory valuation instead of the average cost method. To help you make this calculation, she had the controller prepare the following table of inventory valuations:

	Average cost	LIFO	FIFO
		Inventory method	
January 1, 1984	$40,000	$38,000	$41,000
December 31, 1984	42,000	36,000	44,000
December 31, 1985	44,000	34,000	49,000

Required:

1. Calculate Bulldog's net income before taxes using FIFO and LIFO instead of average cost.

2. During the period January 1, 1984, to December 31, 1985, the purchasing power of the dollar declined approximately 25 percent. The president of the Bulldog Corporation was concerned because the company sells merchandise that is extremely sensitive to changes in the price level. She wants

you to answer the following questions, which will help her understand the impact of inflation on inventories.

a. Which inventory valuation method would reflect the best measurement of net income from operations for the two-year period? Why?
b. Which inventory valuation method would give the most accurate measurement of inventory on the December 31, 1985, balance sheet? Why?

6-7 Binney and Smith

The summary of significant accounting policies section of Binney and Smith's, manufacturer of Crayola products, 1981 annual report contains the following disclosure of how the company accounts for inventory.
Inventories at December 31 are summarized as follows:

	1981	1980	1979
Raw materials	$10,039,000	$ 9,898,000	$ 8,067,000
Work in process	2,608,000	2,087,000	2,000,000
Finished goods	14,827,000	11,935,000	9,482,000
Total	27,474,000	23,920,000	19,549,000
Less: LIFO reserve	3,487,000	1,491,000	—
Total inventories	$23,987,000	$22,429,000	$19,549,000

Effective January 1, 1980, the company changed its method of determining inventory costs for domestic inventories from the first-in, first-out (FIFO) method to the last-in, first out (LIFO) method. The LIFO method has the effect of minimizing the impact of price level changes upon inventory valuation and generally matches current annual costs against current revenues in the statement of earnings. The use of this method of accounting had the effect of reducing inventories at December 31, 1980, by $1,491,000 and net earnings for the year then ended by $765,000 ($.22 per share). There is no cumulative effect of the change on prior years, since the December 31, 1979, inventory as previously reported ia also the amount of the beginning inventory under the LIFO method.

Required:

1. If Binney and Smith had used FIFO instead of LIFO as an inventory cost flow method for 1980 and 1981, how much larger or smaller would net earnings for 1981 have been? Assume a state and federal income tax rate of 51 percent for 1980 and 1981.

2. If Binney and Smith had used FIFO instead of LIFO for 1980 and 1981, how much larger or smaller would *total assets* have been on December 31, 1981?

3. Does the LIFO cost flow method result in a better measure of income than the FIFO method? opinion - who knows

4. Why do you think Binney and Smith switched from FIFO to LIFO?
less taxes.

────────────── ## 6–8   LIFO versus FIFO ──────────────────────────────

Read the attached article from *The Wall Street Journal,* dated January 19, 1981. Do you agree with the author's premise that firms using the FIFO inventory cost flow method are paying millions of dollars in additional income taxes that they would not be required to pay if they used the LIFO inventory cost flow method?

Now read *The Wall Street Journal* article, dated February 9, 1981. Does this article refute the argument presented in the January 19, 1981, article?

PAYING FIFO TAXES: YOUR FAVORITE CHARITY

In one of the most puzzling rituals of American business behavior, thousands of U.S. companies are once again preparing their annual reports using FIFO rather than LIFO inventory accounting. By so doing, they will pay as extra taxes funds which could be used for expansion, capital replacement or dividends.

Under FIFO, or the first-in, first-out assumption, inventory costs flow through the firm as if on a conveyor belt. Costs are assigned to units sold in the same order the costs entered inventory. As a result, during periods of rising prices, older and thus *lower* costs are subtracted from revenues when determining reported (and taxable) earnings.

In contrast, under LIFO, or the last-in, first-out assumption, inventory costs are accumulated as if on a coal pile, with the newest costs being removed from the top and assigned to units sold. Unless a cost layer is liquidated by depleting inventories, it can remain in the base of the pile indefinitely. Thus, during periods of rising prices older and lower costs can remain in the balance sheet inventory accounts while the newer and *higher* costs are used to calculate earnings. Compared to FIFO, reported earnings in most cases drop. But so do taxable earnings. The company can keep more cash for itself and for shareholders.

According to their latest annual reports, three long-time LIFO users— Amoco, General Electric, and U.S. Steel—have together saved more than $3 billion in taxes compared to what they would have paid using FIFO.

LIFO was deemed acceptable for tax purposes in 1939, and it's been used widely in selected industries, notably steel and petroleum, since the late 1940s. A large number of firms switched to LIFO in 1974, a year of high inflation. And for 1980, American Hospital Supply, Eli Lilly, Clorox and Williams Cos., among others, have announced they're making the switch.

Yet the vast majority of companies continue to use FIFO. Some managers are perhaps reluctant to incur additional LIFO bookkeeping costs. Some have perhaps dismissed LIFO's tax advantages in light of variable year-end inventory levels or less than galloping prices. Others may believe that since LIFO would result in lower reported earnings, stockholders are content to pay the extra LIFO taxes.

How much extra are stockholders willing to pay? In a forthcoming study in the "Supplement to the Journal of Accounting Research, 1980," I compare the inventory levels and accounts of 105 New York Stock Exchange firms which used FIFO, with those of 105 competitors that adopted LIFO between 1973 and 1975. From 1974 to 1978, by my estimates, the 105 FIFO firms paid an average of nearly *$26 million* each in additional federal income taxes, thanks to their policy of sticking with FIFO. For 1974 alone, these additional taxes averaged nearly $12 million per firm—more than 1½ percent of sales.

Indeed there are good reasons to suspect that the additional taxes paid by FIFO firms put them at a competitive disadvantage. The accompanying table compares estimates of the additional taxes paid by six FIFO firms, with the amounts saved by direct competitors that adopted LIFO or extended its use in 1974.

FIFO firms, of course, do not typically disclose the additional taxes they have paid. I have estimated these amounts, however, using industry-specific price indexes and assumptions about procurement, to come up with the difference between FIFO- and LIFO-based earnings. The additional FIFO taxes shown in the table equal these differences multiplied by the corporate income tax rate (then 48 percent).

The estimates of additional FIFO taxes assume that LIFO is applicable to all of a FIFO firm's inventories. As a result, these amounts may be overstated for firms like Smith International which hold significant portions of their inventories in other countries where LIFO is not permitted. However, the amounts that have been saved by LIFO competitors may understate the potential savings in cases like American Stores where LIFO has been adopted for only a portion of domestic inventories.

The amounts presented suggest that a number of firms have paid millions of dollars each in additional taxes by using FIFO rather than LIFO for domestic inventories. It is unlikely that bookkeeping costs could account for such sums. And fears of negative stockholder reaction appear unfounded in light of the efficient markets research documenting investor preferences for cash flows. While there are some unusual circumstances (like falling prices or inventory levels) in which LIFO could yield smaller cash flows, it is puzzling why so many firms in so many industries have continued to use FIFO.

Perhaps companies sticking to FIFO are showing their support for some worthy federal program. But wouldn't it make more sense to contribute some LIFO tax savings to a favorite *tax-deductible* charity? Or perhaps I have ignored an important LIFO cost or FIFO benefit. If so, please let me know.

	1974–1978 ($ millions)	
FIFO Firms LIFO Competitors	Additional FIFO Taxes	LIFO Tax Savings
Federal Paper Board	$ 8	
Mead Corp.		$ 46
J. P. Stevens	29	
Burlington Inds.		44
Cone Mill		28
Jewel Companies	36	
American Stores		18
Masco Corp.	15	
Wallace-Murray		13
Minn. Mining & Mfg.	118	
Eastman Kodak		204
Smith International	32	
Dresser Inds.		125
Hughes Tool Co.		22

Source: Gary C. Biddle, *The Wall Street Journal,* January 19, 1981. Reprinted by permission of *The Wall Street Journal,* © Dow Jones & Company, Inc. (1981). All rights reserved.

LIFO'S BOON OF CASH CAN BACKFIRE WHEN COMPANIES REDUCE INVENTORIES

LIFO accounting increases cash available to companies. Right? After all, it trims corporate taxes by reducing reported profits. Right. But not always.

In the fourth quarter, for instance, LIFO accounting increased profits of some companies and raised their tax payments, thereby reducing the cash they had left to spend.

Last-in, first-out inventory accounting, commonly known as LIFO, is an accounting technique designed to minimize the impact of inflation on inventory values, and thus avoid income taxes on phantom inventory profits. It works pretty well for most companies in these inflationary times. However, it can backfire when companies reduce inventories, as many did after the recession clobbered sales in the second quarter.

Wallace Murray Corp., for instance, obtained $1.2 million of its fourth quarter profit from favorable LIFO adjustments because of inventory profit. That was a big part of its earnings increase to $11 million from the year-earlier $8.5 million. Interlake Inc. picked up $5.6 million from LIFO in the fourth quarter, which provided all its profit increase to $19.4 million from $13.7 million.

Accountants can explain the reason in mind-numbing detail, but LIFO's effect basically depends on whether a company is using LIFO or just adopting it and whether inventories are growing or shrinking.

For many years, most companies operated under a first-in, first-out system, or FIFO. They assumed that the first items purchased or manufactured were the first sold. Then came the 1973–74 inflation.

Replacing inventory. Suddenly, companies found themselves selling an item from inventory that cost $1 and replacing it with one that cost $1.25. As companies continued this replacement, inventory values soared. Companies had to pay income taxes on the increased value just as though it were cash in the bank.

To avoid that tax load, many companies switched to LIFO, which produces lower reported profits than FIFO in any inflationary period because the company is always selling the most recent—and thus most expensive—inventory.

In 1980, companies cut profits if they adopted LIFO, extended LIFO to additional divisions or merely increased inventories of units already on LIFO. But companies that used LIFO accounting in 1979 and reduced inventories during 1980 got a profit bonus.

Boosted the economy. Because of the cuts in 1980, companies dipped into the low-cost inventories that would have been sold in 1979 or earlier if they had remained on FIFO. That made 1980 profit margins abnormally large and forced the companies to pay some of the income taxes they had avoided by moving to LIFO in the first place.

An unexpected effect of LIFO came late last year, when the accounting method boosted the economy slightly. Businessmen don't like to pay taxes very much, so some decided late last fall to rebuild inventories a bit to minimize LIFO profits. High interest rates kept executives from being very aggressive about it, but they did buy a little extra raw material in the final weeks of the year that they knew they'd need in early 1981.

Steel warehouses in December, for example, boosted inventories 4 percent to bring them back to the level at the start of 1980, according to a survey by the Steel Service Center Institute, a trade group. Part of the motivation was to avoid a LIFO profit that would raise taxes, said Andrew G. Sharkey, president.

General Tire & Rubber Co. did the same thing, said M. G. O'Neil, president. Despite accelerating some raw materials purchases, General Tire picked up $2.4 million of pretax LIFO profit in the fourth quarter ended Nov. 30, bringing the total for the year to $6.4 million. Taxes took about $2.9 million of that.

Economists figure that the anticipatory buying wasn't a huge factor in the fourth quarter's surprisingly strong 5 percent annual rate of growth in the gross national product, the total output of goods and services. But they say the buying did have some inpact. Of course, resulting purchases and production were borrowed from the 1981 first quarter, so that the wheels of industry are turning a bit more slowly this period.

6-9 The Wolohan Lumber Company

The Wolohan Lumber Company merchandises building materials. It was founded in 1964 when three supply centers were opened and by 1974 had grown into a six-state chain of 26 one-stop retail centers.

Each of these centers distributes more than 3,000 different products, including nearly every item used in constructing, remodeling, or maintaining a home. Sales are divided evenly between professional contractors and retail customers.

Required:

Read the following exhibits and answer the following questions:

1. Comment on the president's letter. Do you think the president is more concerned with corporate liquidity and cash flow, or reported profits? Which is more important?

2. Comment on the company's explanation (Exhibit 3) of the impact of LIFO versus FIFO. Have any significant ramifications been ignored?

3. Compare Wolohan's performance in 1974 to its 1973 performance. In which year was the company more successful? Why?

4. Comment on the auditor's opinion (Exhibit 6). Do you agree that the financial statements of Wolohan Lumber are fairly presented?

EXHIBIT 1

THE WOLOHAN LUMBER COMPANY
Financial Highlights
Year Ended December 31,

	1974*	1973
Sales	$72,349,076	$66,924,517
Gross profit	15,785,869	13,516,983
Income before income taxes	2,008,859	2,432,329
Net income	1,007,859	1,200,329
Per share:†		
Net income	$ .49	$ .59
Shareholders' equity	6.39	6.00
Dividend	.10	.05
Financial position at year-end		
Working capital	9,191,316	7,012,855
Total assets	22,974,635	24,010,080
Long-term debt	5,400,517	3,426,699
Total liabilities	9,936,409	11,775,713
Shareowners' equity	13,038,226	12,234,367
Key ratios and percentages		
Current ratio	3.2:1	1.9:1
Gross profit margin	21.8%	20.2%
Operating margin	3.9%	4.3%
Pretax profit margin	2.8%	3.6%
Return on sales	1.4%	1.8%
Return on shareowners' equity	8.2%	10.8%

* In 1974, the company changed its method of accounting for substantially all of its inventories for the first-in, first-out (Fifo) method to the last-in, first-out (Lifo) method. This was done because the adoption of the Lifo method during a period of rising costs provides a better matching of current costs with current sales, and at the same time permits a substantial reduction in the cash outlay for income taxes. The effect on reported earnings for the year was a decrease of $514,000, or $.25 per share.

† Calculated on 2,040,000 shares outstanding both years.

EXHIBIT 2. **Excerpts from the President's Letter**

To Our Shareowners:

The year that ended December 31, 1974, presented an operating environment marked by more numerous and serious problems than our industry has faced for many years. A persisting inflation that increased operating costs . . . high interest rates that discouraged home buying . . . a continuing decline in home building . . . rising energy costs . . . continued shortages of some materials . . . an erosion of consumer confidence . . . many industry layoffs, and other difficulties . . . all of which resulted in seriously slowing our economy.

Despite this environment—as a result of the steps taken to increase sales, to more effectively control profit margins on those sales, and to better manage assets and expenses so as to improve our return—we feel that our performance was satisfactory.

Sales of Wolohan Lumber Co. were $72.3 million, the ninth consecutive

EXHIBIT 2 *(concluded)*
year they climbed to record highs, and an 8.1 percent increase from 1973's to $66.9 million.

Net income was $1 million, equivalent to 49 cents a share, 16 percent less than 1973's $1.2 million, equivalent to 59 cents a share. It should be noted, however, that in 1974, the company changed its method of accounting for substantially all of its inventories from the first-in, first-out (Fifo) method to the last-in, first-out (Lifo) method. This was done because the adoption of the Lifo method during a period of rising costs provides a better matching of current costs with current sales, and at the same time permits a substantial reduction in the cash outlay for income taxes. The effect on reported earnings for the year was a decrease of $514,000, or 25 cents a share. The two methods are described later in the report.

Shareowners' equity rose 6.6 percent to $13 million ($6.39 per share), from $12.2 million ($6 per share) the year before.

We opened two building materials retail centers—one in Terre Haute, Indiana; the other in Saginaw, Michigan—a central warehouse operation in Madison, Wisconsin, and a second roof-truss manufacturing facility in Clarks Hill, Indiana.

Many of our operating ratios were lower, 1974 versus 1973, as a result of the inventory accounting change. Our return on sales went from 1.8 percent to 1.4 percent; our return on assets from 5.4 percent to 4.0 percent; our return on shareowners' equity from 10.8 percent to 8.2 percent; our operating profit margin from 4.3 percent to 3.9 percent; and our net profit margin before taxes from 3.6 percent to 2.8 percent. But here, too, it should be noted that without that accounting change, these ratios would have shown improvement.

Therefore, in October, the Board of Directors felt it appropriate to declare a 10-cent dividend, payable November 29, 1974, up from 5 cents a share the year before.

Richard V. Wolohan
President

EXHIBIT 3. **LIFO versus FIFO**

Shareowners of hundreds of corporations have been made conscious lately of two strange-sounding words—new to many of them—Lifo and Fifo. What do they mean? Why are companies switching from one to the other? What is the impact of each on reported earnings and cash available to the company?

Both refer to methods of inventory accounting. Fifo stands for first-in, first-out; Lifo, for last-in, first-out.

To illustrate how the two methods work, assume a merchant buys five cases of nails over a period of time with progressive costs of $1, $2, $3, $4, and $5. Their total cost to him, then, and the value of the five cases if one assumes no sales have been made yet from the inventory, under each accounting method is $15 ($1 + $2 + $3 + $4 + $5).

EXHIBIT 3 *(concluded)*

If three cases were sold at $10 each, this would be the impact:

	Fifo		Lifo	
Sales	$30	($10 × 3)	$30	($10 × 3)
Cost of sales	6	($1 + $2 + $3)	12	($5 + $4 + $3)
Pre tax earnings	24		18	
Taxes	12	($24 × 50%)	9	(18 × 50%)
Net earnings	$12		$ 9	

Although gross sales stay the same under each method, taxes on earnings in this simplified example would be 25 percent less using Lifo.

Note the value of the inventory left on hand under each method:

	Fifo	Lifo
Cost value	$9 ($15 − $6, cost of sales, or cases costing $4 and $5)	$3 ($15 − $12, cost of sales, or cases costing $1 and $2).

The value of inventory on hand, which is also subject to taxes, is 66.7 percent less under Lifo.

Note, too, the cash available to the company under each method.

	Fifo	Lifo
Sales	$30	$30
Addition to inventories	15	15
	15	15
Taxes....................................	12	9
Cash available to the company	$ 3	$ 6

The cash available to the company, in this example, is 100 percent greater under Lifo.

To sum up, these are the major effects of switching from traditional Fifo inventory accounting to Lifo:

---

1. Most visibly: Reported earnings are lower. This means that comparisons with previous years when earnings were based on FIFO are less favorable. This may affect the price of the shares—though less than normally in today's depressed market.
2. The cost of sales now reflects more accurately the rising cost of replacement.
3. Taxes are reduced.
4. Cash available to the company for growth is now greater—at a time when money is not only costly but difficult to obtain.

(This is a much-simplified explanation, of course. In practice, there are other important factors involved, with advantages and disadvantages not always so obvious, and legal complexities involved in the change.)

EXHIBIT 4

THE WOLOHAN LUMBER COMPANY
Statement of Income and Retained Earnings
Years Ended December 31, 1974, and 1973

	1974	1973
Net sales	$72,349,076	$66,924,517
Other income	118,749	109,919
	$72,467,825	$67,034,436
Costs and expenses:		
Cost of sales	56,563,207	53,407,534
Selling and administrative expenses	13,084,690	10,747,210
Interest on long-term debt	447,457	171,950
Other interest	363,612	275,413
	$70,458,966	$64,602,107
Income before income taxes	$ 2,008,859	$ 2,432,329
Income Taxes:		
Current:		
Federal	747,000	904,000
State	154,000	178,000
Deferred federal and state	100,000	150,000
	$ 1,001,000	$ 1,232,000
Net income:		
(per share, based on 2,040,000 shares:		
1974—$.49; 1973—$.59)	$ 1,007,859	$ 1,200,329
Retained earnings at beginning of year	6,023,959	4,925,630
	$ 7,031,818	$ 6,125,959
Cash dividends paid:		
(per share: 1974—$.10; 1973—$.05)	204.00	102.000
Retained earnings at end of year	$ 6,827,818	$ 6,023,959

EXHIBIT 5

THE WOLOHAN LUMBER COMPANY
Balance Sheet
December 31, 1974 and 1973

	1974	1973
Assets		
Current assets:		
Cash	$ 1,205,227	$ 970,195
Trade receivables, less allowance for doubtful		
accounts (1974—$111,000; 1973—$93,100)	3,732,412	3,594,613
Inventories (less adjustment to last-in, first-out		
cost of $1,069,000 in 1974) (Note B)	8,335,392	10,404,921
Prepaid expenses and other current accounts	11,125	49,088
Total current assets	$13,284,156	$15,018,817
Other assets	77,387	56,405
Properties:		
Land	1,542,050	1,507,850
Land improvements	1,921,907	1,622,593
Buildings	6,209,750	5,559,119
Equipment	2,342,317	1,901,833
Construction in progress	–0–	123,644
Allowances for depreciation (deduction)	(2,402,932)	(1,780,181)
	$ 9,613,092	$ 8,934,858
	$22,974,635	$24,010,080
Liabilities and Stockholders' Equity		
Current liabilities:		
Notes payable to banks	$ –0–	$ 3,000,000
Trade accounts payable	2,228,880	3,248,788
Employee compensation	868,857	615,971
Accrued expenses	467,776	449,861
Federal and state income taxes................	1,146	139,348
Current portion of long-term debt	526,181	551,994
Total current liabilities	$ 4,092,840	$ 8,005,962
Long-term debt (Less portion classified as		
current liability)............................	5,400,517	3,426,699
Deferred income taxes	443,052	343,052
Stockholders' equity:		
Common stock, par value $1 a share:		
Authorized—3,000,000 shares	2,040,000	2,040,000
Outstanding—2,040 shares		
Additional paid-in capital	4,170,408	1,170,408
Retained Earnings...........................	6,827,818	6,023,959
	$13,038,226	$12,234,367
	$22,974,635	$24,010,080

Notes to Financial Statements:

Note B: Change in Accounting Method—Effective January 1, 1974, the company changed its method of determining the cost of substantially all inventories from the first-in, first-out (Fifo) method to the last-in, first-out (Lifo) method. The change reduced net income for 1974 by $514,400 ($.25 a share). Prior years' earnings are not affected since the ending inventories under the Fifo method at December 31, 1973, represent the beginning inventories for 1974 under the Lifo method.

The company believes that the adoption of Lifo during a period of rising costs provides a better matching of current costs with current scales, and at the same time permits a substantial reduction in the cash outlay for income taxes.

EXHIBIT 6. **The Auditor's Report**

Board of Directors
Wolohan Lumber Co.
Saginaw, Michigan

We have examined the balance sheet of Wolohan Lumber Co. as of December 31, 1974, and 1973, and the related statements of income and retained earnings and changes in financial position for the years then ended. Our examinations were made in accordance with generally accepted auditing standards and, accordingly, included such tests of the accounting records and such other auditing procedures as we considered necessary in the circumstances.

In our opinion, the financial statements referred to above present fairly the financial position of Wolohan Lumber Co. at December 31, 1974, and 1973, and the results of its operations and changes in financial position for the years then ended, in conformity with generally accepted accounting principles consistently applied during the period except for the change, with which we concur, in the method of determining inventory cost as described in Note B to the financial statements.

Ernst & Ernst

7

Property, plant, and equipment, natural resources and intangibles

PROPERTY, PLANT, AND EQUIPMENT

Land, buildings, building improvements, machinery, trucks, furniture, fixtures, tools, and office equipment are long-lived assets which are classified on the balance sheet as fixed assets or more descriptively as property, plant, and equipment.

Fixed assets are acquired because they are expected to produce benefits (earn revenue) for the enterprise in future accounting periods. Unlike inventory, they are not held for resale in the normal course of business.

The acquisition of fixed assets represents a major commitment of the economic resources of the firm. Accounting for fixed assets is concerned with problems related to:

1. The cost of acquiring the assets.
2. The allocation of the acquisition cost of the assets to operations over the estimated useful life of the asset in a systematic and rational manner.
3. The treatment of maintenance, repairs, and improvements.
4. The disposal of the asset by sale, exchange, or retirement.

150

THE COST OF PLANT AND EQUIPMENT

The cost of plant and equipment includes all reasonable expenditures necessary to put it into operating use. For example, assume that a company purchases a machine for $50,000 at terms of 1/10, n/60, freight to be paid by the buyer. The machine requires specialized electrical wiring and must be mounted on a concrete support.

The cost of the machine would be:

Purchase price	$50,000
Less: 1% cash discount	500
Net purchase price	49,500
Freight	300
Electrical wiring	1,250
Concrete support construction	825
Total asset cost	$51,875

The journal entries would be:

Machinery	49,500	
Cash		49,500
To record the net cash paid on purchase.		

Machinery	300	
Cash		300
To record freight payment.		

Machinery	2,075	
Cash		2,075
To record machinery installation costs.		

all to machinery

MAINTENANCE, REPAIRS, AND IMPROVEMENTS

Maintenance and repairs costs influence the length of life of assets and, together with the depreciation charges, constitute the full cost of using a depreciable asset. Normal repairs and maintenance do not increase the original expected productive capacity of the fixed asset and are charged to expense in the period incurred. Expenditures that do increase the productive capacity of the fixed asset are called improvements or betterments and are capitalized (recorded as a fixed asset). Improvements are allocated to future periods as part of the depreciation charge. In practice it is often hard to make an exact judgment as to whether an expenditure is a repair of improvement.

152

DEPRECIATION OF PLANT AND EQUIPMENT— THE ALLOCATION PROCESS

An important characteristic of fixed assets, other than land, is that although they can be kept in usable operating condition for some time, eventually they are no longer productive and are retired from service. The purpose of depreciation is to recognize that the fixed assets have a limited useful life and to allocate the cost of these assets to the accounting periods they benefit.

The journal entry to allocate the cost of a fixed asset not used in manufacturing (sales, administration) to the period benefited is:

```
Depreciation Expense ............................... xxx
     Accumulated Depreciation ......................... xxx
```

The journal entry to allocate the cost of fixed asset used in manufacturing is:

```
Work in Process (Depreciation) ....................... xxx
     Accumulated Depreciation ......................... xxx
```

Depreciation cost on nonmanufacturing assets appears in the income statement as an expense of the current period. The depreciation cost on manufacturing assets becomes part of the product (inventory) cost and becomes an expense when the product is sold.

The accumulated depreciation account is a contra asset account; it is deducted from the related asset account. The preferred balance sheet presentation is:

```
Equipment ......................... $1,200,000
Less: Accumulated depreciation ......     500,000
     Net equipment ................ $  700,000
```

METHODS OF DEPRECIATION

To calculate the periodic depreciation charge, three items must be considered:

1. The depreciation base, which is the acquisition cost of the asset plus all costs necessary to get the asset ready for operation, less any salvage value expected to be recovered when the asset is ultimately sold, traded in, or scrapped.
2. The estimated useful service life of the asset, which is generally determined by past experience with similar assets.
3. The manner in which the cost expires over the useful life of the assets.

There are several methods available for computing the manner in which asset cost is allocated to each period. The most common ones are:

1. The straight-line depreciation method.
2. The units-of-production method.
3. The declining-balance method.
4. Combination of declining-balance and straight-line method.
5. The sum-of-the-years'-digits method.

Straight-line depreciation

The straight-line depreciation method assumes that the cost of the asset expires as a steady (straight-line) function of time. The formula is:

$$\text{Depreciation/Year} = \frac{\text{Cost} - \text{Salvage Value}}{\text{Estimated Useful Life in Years}}$$

For example, if a machine costing $20,000 has an estimated life expectancy of six years and a salvage value of $2,000, the annual depreciation charge would be ($20,000 − $2,000)/6 = $3,000.

The straight-line method owes its popularity primarily to its simplicity. It assumes level operating efficiency and level maintenance procedures.

Units-of-production method

This method assumes the useful life is best estimated by the number of units produced by the asset. Under this method, a depreciation rate per unit is calculated:

$$\text{Rate of Depreciation/Unit} = \frac{\text{Cost} - \text{Salvage Value}}{\begin{array}{c}\text{Estimated Units of Production}\\\text{during Service Life}\end{array}}$$

For example, a machine costing $1,200 is purchased and is expected to produce 1,000 widgets during its service life. Its salvage value is $300. The amount of depreciation in 1984, if 300 widgets were produced, is:

$$\frac{\$1,200 - \$300}{1,000} = \$.90 \text{ per widget produced}$$

$$300 \times \$.90 = \$270, \text{ depreciation expense in 1984}$$

The declining-balance method

The declining-balance method assumes that as assets grow older they become less efficient and their earning power declines. This method is called an accelerated or fast write-off method because it results in larger depreciation charges during the early years of asset life with gradually decreasing charges in later years.

Under the double-declining-balance (DDB) method, a uniform rate, computed at twice the straight-line rate, is applied in each period to the net book value or carrying value (cost less accumulated depreciation) of the asset. Salvage value is not taken into account in making the computation for double-declining-balance depreciation. Declining-balance rates less than twice the straight-line rate (175 or 150 percent of the straight-line rate) are also used in practice.

To illustrate the double-declining-balance method, assume that a machine was purchased on January 1, 1984, for $5,000, and that it had an estimated life of five years with a salvage value of $200 at the end of five years. The depreciation rate under the double-declining balance method would be 40 percent (1/5 years × 2), and this rate would be applied each year to the net book value of the asset. The annual depreciation charges would be calculated as shown in Illustration 7–1.

ILLUSTRATION 7–1

Year	Original Cost	Accumulated Depreciation as of January 1	Net Book (Carrying) Value as of January 1	Depreciation Rate	Depreciation Charge for the Year
1984	$5,000	–0–	$5,000	.40	$2,000
1985	5,000	$2,000	3,000	.40	1,200
1986	5,000	3,200	1,800	.40	720
1987	5,000	3,920	1,080	.40	432
1988	5,000	4,352	648	.40	259

Combination of declining-balance and straight-line depreciation

Some companies that use declining-balance depreciation switch to straight-line depreciation for the year that straight-line depreciation of the remaining depreciable cost exceeds declining-balance depreciation. This switch also results in the asset being depreciated down to its estimated salvage value.

In our example a switch would occur starting with 1986 when double-declining-balance depreciation would be $432 (.40 × $1,080) and straight-line depreciation is $440. The net book value of the machine at the end of 1986 is $1,080 ($5,000 − $3,920). Straight-line depreciation for 1987 and 1988 would be $1,080 − $200 (salvage value)/2 = $440.

The sum-of-the-years'-digits method

The sum-of-the-years'-digits (SOYD) method allocates the cost of the fixed assets as follows:

1. Determine the sum of the digits. If the useful life of the asset is five years, the sum of the digits is: $1 + 2 + 3 + 4 + 5 = 15$. The formula for the sum of the digits is $(n/2)(n + 1)$, where n equals the useful life of the asset.

$$\frac{5}{2} \times (5 + 1) = 15$$

2. Determine the depreciation rate. It is expressed by a fraction whose numerator is the years in reverse order (5,4,3,2,1), and whose denominator is the sum of the digits as computed above. Thus, depreciation rates for a five-year asset are 5/15, 4/15, 3/15, 2/15, and 1/15, a total of 15/15.
3. Compute the depreciation charge for the period-depreciation rate times cost minus salvage value.

To illustrate, consider an asset costing $5,000 purchased January 1, 1984, which has an estimated life of five years and an estimated salvage value of $200. The sum-of-the-years'-digits calculation is shown in Illustration 7–2.

[handwritten margin note: you'd have to make out a schedule when you bought the machinery!]

ILLUSTRATION 7–2

Year	Cost Minus Salvage Value	Remaining Life in Years	Depreciation Rate Fraction	Annual Depreciation Charge
1984	$4,800	5	5/15	$1,600
1985	4,800	4	4/15	1,280
1986	4,800	3	3/15	960
1987	4,800	2	2/15	640
1988	4,800	1	1/15	320
Total				$4,800

DISPOSAL OF PLANT AND EQUIPMENT

An asset may be disposed of by sale, by being traded in as part of the purchase price of a replacement, or simply by being discarded or scrapped. The accounting treatment to reflect the retirement or disposal of an asset involves a three-step process:

1. The asset must be depreciated to the date of disposal.
2. The cost of the disposed asset must be removed from the asset account, and the accumulated depreciation associated with the asset must be removed from the accumulated depreciation account. An asset may still be kept in service after it is fully depreciated. In that event, the asset remains on the books, and no further depreciation is taken. Only at the time of disposition is it necessary to remove the asset and its associated accumulated depreciation from the accounts.
3. Any difference between the proceeds received on the disposal of an asset and its net book value is recorded as a gain or loss. Gains, but not losses, on *trade-ins of similar assets* are treated as an adjustment (decrease) in the cost of the new asset rather than a gain on the disposal of the asset traded in.[1]

To illustrate, assume the machinery account includes $4,000 as the original cost of a machine bought July 1, 1984, with a four-year useful life and no salvage value. Depreciation on a straight-line basis through December 31, 1986 (2.5 years), totals $2,500. If the machine is to be sold on July 1, 1987, for $800, then the following entries must be made on July 1:

Depreciation 500
    Accumulated Depreciation 500
  To record depreciation on machine (January 1 to June 30, 1987).

Cash 800
Accumulated Depreciation 3,000
Loss on Sale of Fixed Asset 200
    Machinery 4,000
  To record disposal of equipment at a loss.

Because the company received $800 for an asset with a net book value of $1,000 ($4,000 − $3,000), the company will recognize a loss on sale of $200. The loss may be attributable to unexpected obsolescence or simply to errors in estimating the salvage value or estimated life. If the asset had been sold for more than its book value, a gain on the sale would be recognized.

Gains or losses of this type are not from the major ongoing operations of the company and are classified as nonoperating income or expense on the income statement.

---

[1] AICPA, *Accounting Principles Board Opinion No. 29* "Accounting for Nonmonetary Transactions" (New York, 1973).

DEPRECIATION, FEDERAL INCOME TAX, AND NET INCOME

On property purchased *prior to January 1, 1981,* companies could elect to use any of the depreciation methods for federal income tax purposes regardless of which depreciation method they used for their financial statements.

Most companies elected the accelerated depreciation methods (declining-balance, sum-of-the-year's-digits) for income tax purposes because these methods charge more depreciation expense in the early years of an asset's life than the straight-line method and result in lower income taxes in those years.

Assume that a company paying federal income taxes at the rate of 40 percent has purchased a truck for $1,000 with an estimated life of five years and a salvage value of $100. Since 40 percent of each dollar of income must be paid as income taxes, each dollar of expense that is deductible from taxable revenue will reduce federal income taxes by 40 cents. A depreciation tax benefit can be calculated in each year of the useful life of the asset by multiplying .40 times the depreciation that is reported for tax purposes. A comparison of the straight-line method to the sum-of-the-year's-digits method and a computation of the tax benefit is shown in Illustration 7–3.

ILLUSTRATION 7–3

	Depreciation Tax Benefit		
Year	Straight-Line Method	Sum-of-the-Years' Digits	Difference
1981	.40 × $180 = $ 72	.40 × $300 = $120	$ 48
1982	.40 × 180 = 72	.40 × 240 = 96	24
1983	.40 × 180 = 72	.40 × 180 = 72	–0–
1984	.40 × 180 = 72	.40 × 120 = 48	(24)
1985	.40 × 180 = 72	.40 × 60 = 24	(48)
	$360	$360	$–0–

Over the five-year asset life, the total tax benefit from both depreciation methods is $360. The cash savings from the depreciation income tax deduction occurs sooner under the sum-of-the-years'-digits method, and it is this time factor that is the incentive for firms to use an accelerated depreciation method for tax purposes. Accelerated depreciation and the resulting deferral of income taxes are used by the U.S. government as an instrument of economic policy to encourage investment in plant and equipment. Many companies use an accelerated depreciation method for tax purposes while using the straight-line method for their financial statements.

a dollar today is worth more than a dollar tomorrow

ACRS depreciation method

One of the objectives of the Economic Recovery Tax Act of 1981 was to stimulate investment by allowing faster write-offs of the cost of depreciable assets. The accelerated cost recovery system (ACRS) portion of the act prescribes accelerated rates of depreciation for new and used tangible depreciable property placed in service after January 1, 1981.

The cost of the property under ACRS is recovered (depreciated) over 3, 5, 10, or 15 years depending on its classification. Autos and trucks are considered 3-year ACRS property, practically all equipment is 5-year ACRS property, real estate with an average life of 12.5 years is classified as 10-year ACRS property, and the majority of real estate, which has an average life of more than 12.5 years, is considered 15-year ACRS property.

The depreciation charges approximate the results of using 150 percent declining-balance with a switch to the straight-line or sum-of-the-years'-digits method in the year that provides the fastest write-off.

ACRS rates for 3-year, 5-year, and 10-year property placed in service after January 1, 1981.[2]

Year of Ownership	3-year	5-year	10-year
1	25%	15%	8%
2	38	22	14
3	37	21	12
4		21	10
5		21	10
6			10
7			9
8			9
9			9
10			9
Total	100%	100%	100%

ACRS assumes that the fixed assets do not have a salvage value and employs the half-year convention. The half-year convention requires the deduction of 50 percent of the first year's depreciation

[2] The Tax Equity and Fiscal Responsibility Act of 1982 abolished increases in these rates, which, under the 1981 act, were scheduled to become effective in 1985.

in the year the fixed asset is placed in service regardless of whether that is on January 1 or December 31 of that year. For example, *first-year* depreciation for a five-year ACRS asset is 15 percent (150% × 20% (straight-line rate)/2). No ACRS depreciation is allowed in the year of disposition of tangible (non-real estate) property.

Comparison of ACRS and straight-line depreciation

For financial statement purposes a company may substitute the half-year convention for actual monthly use of the asset as long as it does it on a consistent basis.

Assume that Kay Corporation purchases a machine for $24,000 on December 1, 1981. The machine has an estimated useful life of eight years and is not expected to have any salvage value when it is retired in 1989.

Kay's federal income tax rate for 1981–89 is expected to be 46 percent.

Kay uses the straight-line method based on an estimated life of eight years and the half-year convention for its financial statements and uses ACRS for federal income tax purposes. The machine is classified as a five-year ACRS property.

	Financial Statement Depreciation	Federal Income Tax Depreciation		Difference	Tax Benefit*
1981 (½ × $3000)	$ 1,500	15%	$ 3,600	$ 2,100	$ 966.00
1982	3,000	22%	5,280	2,280	1,048.80
1983	3,000	21%	5,040	2,040	938.40
1984	3,000	21%	5,040	2,040	938.40
1985	3,000	21%	5,040	2,040	938.40
1986	3,000		–0–	(3,000)	(1,380.00)
1987	3,000		–0–	(3,000)	(1,380.00)
1988	3,000		–0–	(3,000)	(1,380.00)
1989 (½ × $3000)	1,500		–0–	(1,500)	(690.00)
	$24,000	100%	$24,000	$ –0–	$ –0–

* 46% × Difference.

Assume further that the Kay Corporation's book and taxable income for 1981 before depreciation and federal income taxes was $125,000 and that they own no other plant and equipment.

	Financial Statements	Federal Income Tax Return
Income before depreciation	$125,000	$125,000
Depreciation expense	1,500	3,600
	123,500	121,400
Income tax (46%)	56,810	55,844
Net income	$ 66,690	$ 65,556

Deferred income taxes

The journal entry on the books to record the income tax expense for 1981 is:

Income Tax Expense	56,810	
Deferred Income Tax		966
Income Tax Payable		55,844

Income tax expense on the financial statements is based on reported (straight-line depreciation in this case) income and not taxable income. This is consistent with the matching principle.

The difference between the income tax expense (straight-line method) shown on the financial statements and the actual tax liability (ACRS depreciation) on the tax return is reported on the balance sheet as deferred income taxes.

The deferred income tax account, which reconciles the income tax expense recorded on the books with the income tax payable to the federal government, is generally treated as a liability. This account represents the amount of tax benefits that should become payable in later years when depreciation expense under the ACRS method is less than depreciation expense under the straight-line method.

Many accountants disagree with the classification of deferred taxes as a liability. They argue that the deferred tax is not an actual obligation to pay the government and that in all likelihood the deferred portion of the tax will never be paid because of new deferrals created by the acquisition of new assets.

DEPRECIATION POLICY DECISIONS

For tax purposes management should select the depreciation method that results in the lowest income tax. This will generally be the ACRS accelerated method as long as the enterprise is earning income and investing in fixed assets.

For financial reporting purposes management will select a depreciation method that reflects their financial objectives. Management's financial reporting strategy will also be reflected in their choice of the estimated useful life of assets and decisions about capitalizing or expensing all gray area repairs.

Accelerated depreciation methods, short estimated useful lives of assets, and expensing all gray area repairs will result in lower net income in the earlier years than straight-line depreciation, longer estimated useful lives, and capitalizing all gray area repairs.

The depreciation method the company uses is disclosed in the footnotes to the financial statements.

An example of this type of disclosure taken from the 1981 annual report of the Dana Corporation is:

PROPERTIES AND DEPRECIATION
Depreciation is computed over the estimated useful lives of property, plant and equipment using primarily the straight-line method for financial reporting purposes and accelerated depreciation methods for federal income tax purposes.

General Electric Company, which has the reputation of using conservative accounting methods, made the following disclosure in its 1981 annual report.

PROPERTY, PLANT AND EQUIPMENT
Manufacturing plant and equipment includes the original cost of land, buildings, and equipment less depreciation, which is the estimated cost consumed by wear and obsolescence. An accelerated depreciation method, based principally on the sum-of-the-years'-digits formula, is used to record depreciation of the original cost of manufacturing plant and equipment in the U.S.

THE INVESTMENT TAX CREDIT

Since the Revenue Act of 1962 the investment tax credit has been used by the U.S. government as an instrument of economic policy to encourage investment in fixed assets, particularly productive facilities. The credit, which is calculated as a percentage of the cost of depreciable assets placed in service, is deducted directly from the business firm's income tax liability.

The investment tax credit is applied, dollar for dollar, against the first $25,000 of federal income tax liability, plus 90 percent (80 percent for years prior to 1982) of the tax liability in excess of $25,000. Unused investment tax credits may be carried back or forward to other taxable years.

The investment tax credit encourages investment because it reduces the cost of the investment by the amount of the tax credit. A company that purchases an asset for $100,000 and receives a 10 percent investment tax credit effectively pays $90,000, for the asset.

The Economic Recovery Act of 1981 defines property eligible for the investment tax credit as tangible property, other than real estate, used in connection with manufacturing or production and placed in service after December 30, 1980. The credit is 6 percent for three-year property and 10 percent for ACRS property in excess of three-years. The 1981 Tax Equity and Fiscal Responsibility Act provides for recapture of a portion of the investment tax credit if the property is disposed of prior to the three-year or five-year period. A 2 percent credit will be allowed for each full year's service the property is used. For example, a five-year property that received a credit equal to 10 percent of asset cost will have 4 percent of the asset cost recaptured if the property is disposed of after three years.

The 1982 Tax Equity and Fiscal Responsibility Act requires that the depreciable base (basis) of assets purchased commencing with 1983 be reduced by half of the investment tax credit. For example, if a company purchased a $30,000 asset (five-year ACRS) on January 1, 1983, its basis for federal income tax depreciation would be $28,500 ($30,000 − 3,000/2), and depreciation for 1983 would be $4,275 (15% × $28,500).

The investment tax credit and financial reports

There are two generally accepted methods for reporting the investment tax credit in the financial reports. It can be treated as a reduction in the federal income tax expense in the year the asset is placed in service (flow-through method), or it can be spread over the life of the asset that generated the credit (deferral method).

The flow-through method results in an increase in net income (decrease in income tax expense on the books) in the year the asset is placed in service. Advocates of the flow-through method subscribe to the theory that the company earns the investment tax credit when they purchase the fixed asset and that the credit is not related to the future use of the asset.

If the Kay Corporation had used the flow-through method of recording the investment tax credit on the $24,000 machine they purchased on December 1, 1981 and are depreciating over eight years for financial statement purposes, they would make the following income tax related journal entries on their books in 1981:

Income Tax Expense	56,810	
Deferred Income Tax		966
Income Tax Payable		55,844

To record income taxes for 1981 before recording
the investment tax credit.

Income Tax Payable	2,400	
Income Tax Expense		2,400

To record 1981 investment tax credit (10% ×
$24,000).

flow through

Treating the investment tax credit as a deferral results in the
following 1981 journal entries, which are based on the theory that
the investment tax credit is earned as the asset is used.

Income Tax Expense	56,810	
Deferred Income Tax		966
Income Tax Payable		55,844

To record income taxes for 1981 before recording
the investment tax credit.

deferral

Income Tax Payable	2,400	
Income Tax Expense		25
Deferred Investment Tax Credit		2,375

To record the investment tax credit for 1981 and
reduce income tax expense for the length of time
the asset was used in 1981 $\left(\dfrac{1\ \text{month}}{96\ \text{months}} \times \$2{,}400\right)$
and defer the balance to future years.

The journal entry for 1982 through 1988 would be:

Deferred Investment Tax Credit	300	
Income Tax Expense		300

To reduce income tax expense for 12/96 of the investment tax credit on the machine purchased in 1981.

The journal entry for 1989 would be:

Deferred Investment Tax Credit	275	
Income Tax Expense		275

To reduce income tax expense for 11/96 of the investment tax credit on the machine purchased in 1981.

It is important to note that regardless of whether the company
uses the flow-through or deferral method of reporting the investment tax credit on their financial statements, they will always de-

duct the full amount of the investment tax credit on their income tax returns in the year they place the asset in service.

The deferred investment tax credit is generally classified on the balance sheet as a noncurrent liability.

Management's choice of which investment tax credit method they use for financial reporting purposes is another indication of their overall financial reporting strategy.

General Electric Company made the following disclosures about their Investment Tax Credit in their 1981 annual report.

INVESTMENT TAX CREDIT
The investment tax credit is deferred and amortized as a reduction of the provision for taxes over the lives of the facilities to which the credit applies, rather than being "flowed through" to income in the year the asset is acquired.

PROVISION FOR INCOME TAXES
Investment credit amounted to $95 million in 1981, compared with $92 million in 1980 and $76 million in 1979. In 1981, $49 million was included in net earnings, compared with $36 million in 1980 and $31 million in 1979. At the end of 1981, the amount still deferred and to be included in net earnings in future years was $306 million.

NATURAL RESOURCES

Natural resources include long-lived assets, such as minerals, oil, and timber. Companies acquire natural resources in order to convert them into inventory and sell them. They are "wasting assets," and once used up, they cannot be replaced like plant and equipment.

In general, natural resources are recorded at cost when acquired. The conversion of the resource into inventory (barrels of oil, tons of coal, or feet of lumber) exhausts the cost of the wasting asset. The process of writing off the original cost of the resource to expense over the life of the asset is called depletion. The depletion method most commonly used is the units-of-production method. For example, if an oil company purchases an oil well for $15 million and it estimates the well contains 1.5 million barrels of oil, then the cost would be written off at the rate of $10 ($15,000,000/1,500,000) for each barrel of oil removed from the well.

Santa Fe Industries, Inc., made the following disclosure in the footnotes to their 1981 annual report, about the method they used to allocate the cost of their petroleum properties.

Depreciation and Depletion of Productive Petroleum Properties
Productive petroleum properties, consisting principally of tangible and intangible costs incurred in developing a property and costs of productive leasehold interests, are depreciated or depleted on a unit-

of-production method based on annual estimates of remaining proved developed reserves or proved reserves, as appropriate, for each defined property. Certain other petroleum properties are depreciated on a straight-line basis.

INTANGIBLE ASSETS

The distinguishing characteristics of intangible assets are that they generally lack physical substance and that there is some uncertainty about whether and when they will produce future benefits.

Examples of intangible assets are patents, trademarks, franchises, trade names, copyrights, goodwill, and organization costs. The difficulty with accounting for such intangible assets is in deciding whether the expenditures have future benefits and should be "capitalized" and the period of time over which the benefits should be allocated, or whether they have no future benefits and thus are expenses of the period. The allocation of the cost of intangible assets to future periods is called amortization.

Most intangibles have a limited term or existence, fixed by law or regulations or by their very nature. The cost of the intangible is amortized to expense over its useful (economic) life.

Assume the Kay Corporation purchased a patent with a cost of $70,000 on January 1, 1984. Management determined that the patent would only be useful in earning revenues over the next 7 years, despite the fact that the patent will not expire legally for 12 more years.

The journal entries for 1984 are:

```
Patent ...........................................  70,000
    Cash .........................................         70,000
    To record purchase of patent on January 1, 1984.

Amortization of Patent ...........................  10,000
    Patent .......................................         10,000
    To allocate 1/7 of the cost of the patent to expense
    for 1984.
```

There are other intangibles, such as goodwill, (discussed in detail in Chapter 11) trade names, and subscription lists, which may have no determinable term of existence. *Opinion No. 17* of the Accounting Principles Board requires that these intangibles be amortized over a period not to exceed 40 years.

In its 1981 annual report, Oshman Sporting Goods, Inc., made the following disclosure about the "Abercrombie and Fitch" trade name which they purchased.

Note C: Trade Name—On June 29, 1978, the Company entered into a licensing agreement with Abercrombie & Fitch Company, the First National Bank of Chicago and First Chicago International Banking Corporation for use of the name "Abercrombie & Fitch," trademarks, patents, and catalogs. The agreement provides for fifteen annual payments escalating from $25,000 to $175,000 (totaling $1,785,000), or 1% of annual sales associated with the trade name and trademarks, whichever is greater. If payments total $3,000,000 for the fifteen year period, ownership of the name, trademarks, and patents transfers to the Company. If payments during the fifteen year period are less than $3,000,000, the Company has the option to extend the agreement for an additional five years, at which time ownership of the name, trademarks, and patents would be transferred to the Company. For financial statement presentation, the minimum payments were capitalized at their discounted present value, using a 10% imputed interest rate (Note E), and included in other assets.

PROBLEMS AND CASES

7-1 Vantyke Printing Company

The Vantyke Printing Company was founded in 1936 by Charles Vantyke. The company printed scholarly books and journals and had a reputation as a high-quality printer.

In late 1984 John Draykin, the sales manager of a local printing company that specialized in color offset work, purchased Vantyke Printing from its founder. Draykin's strategy was to establish the company as a full-line printer. This would enable him to use the sales volume in scholarly books and journals as a base on which to build future sales in the more profitable color offset area.

In order to implement this strategy he had to make substantial capital expenditures.

Listed below are the transactions that arose from the implementation of Draykin's strategy. Prepare a journal entry for each of these transactions.

a. Sold two old Heidelberg presses he no longer needed for $11,000. These presses cost $15,000 each when they were purchased and were fully depreciated on the books and tax returns on the date of sale.

b. Purchased land and building in an adjacent town for $450,000. Borrowed $315,000 on a 9 percent, 25-year, first mortgage and $110,000 on a 12 percent, 5-year second mortgage. The balance of $25,000 was taken from the company's cash account. The town assessed the property for $270,000, (land, $54,000; and building, $216,000) for property tax purposes.

c. The cost of transporting and installing all the old equipment in the new plant amounted to $18,320.

d. Purchased a new four-color press from Karris Intertype. The invoice price of this press was $125,000. Vantyke paid Karris $122,500 because they were able to take advantage of the 2 percent discount that Karris offered. The Dijoa Trucking Company charged Vantyke $3,600 to deliver the press. Installation of the press was done by local tradespeople for $1,200.

e.   Prior to using the four-color press on actual jobs the company made test runs to make sure the printing was on register. Approximately 40 hours were spent on these test runs. The work crew that operated this press and did the test runs was paid $17 an hour ($8 for the lead printer and $4.50 for each of the two assistants). Draykin expected to charge his customers $40 an hour for all work done on this press.

f.   Traded in the 1981 delivery truck on a new larger truck at the Westfield Ford Company. Paid $5,000 plus the old truck for the new truck, which had a list (invoice) price of $9,000. The book value of the old truck on the date it was traded in was $3,200 (original cost of $6,000 less accumulated depreciation of $2,800). The Westfield Ford salesperson and Draykin agreed that the fair cash value of the old truck on the date of the trade-in was $2,600.

g.   Paid Jones Electrical Company $18,000 for replacing the wiring in the building with heavy duty wiring needed to operate the printing equipment.

h.   Paid $8,500 to overhaul a two-color press that had been purchased 10 years ago. The overhaul was done to increase the quality of the impressions, and it was not expected to change either the capacity or the useful life of the press. Prior to this time approximately $400 a year was spent on the maintenance of this press.

7-2   Cyprest Corporation

On January 2, 1984, the Cyprest Corporation purchased a delivery truck for $25,000. Service life is estimated to be five years, and the truck is not expected to have any salvage value at the end of the five years.

Required:

1.   Calculate annual depreciation on this truck for 1984 through 1988 using the following methods:

a.   Straight-line.
b.   Double-declining balance.
c.   Sum-of-the-years'-digits.
d.   ACRS tax method.

2.   Assume that on January 2, 1989, Cyprest, which used the straight-line depreciation method on its books, replaced the old truck with a new model with a list price of $38,000. The truck dealer granted Cyprest a trade-in allowance of $5,000 on the old truck even though both he and Mr. Cyprest agreed that the fair cash value of the 1984 truck was $2,000.

Make the journal entry to record the replacement of the old truck with the new one.

7-3 The Crossbar Company (A)

The Crossbar Company purchased a machine for $70,000 on September 30, 1981. The machine was expected to have a useful life of 10 years and an estimated salvage value of $10,000 at the end of the 10th year. For income tax purposes the machine is a five-year ACRS asset. Crossbar doesn't use the half-year convention to calculate depreciation for financial statement purposes.

Crossbar reports its income on a calendar year basis, and all of the depreciation taken in 1981 was included in products sold in 1981.

Crossbar's income for 1981 before the deduction of depreciation was $60,000, and their income tax rate was 40 percent.

Required:

1. Make the journal entry to record depreciation charges on Crossbar's books for the year ending December 31, 1981, assuming that Crossbar uses the:

a. Straight-line depreciation method.

b. Double-declining-balance depreciation method.

c. Sum-of-the-years'-digits depreciation method.

2. Calculate the ACRS depreciation expense Crossbar will report on its 1981 tax return.

3. Make the journal entry to record Crossbar's income tax expense for 1981. Assume that Crossbar used the straight-line method of depreciation on their books. For purposes of this question do not consider the investment tax credit.

4. Assume that Crossbar purchased the $70,000 machine on September 30, 1984, instead of September 30, 1981.

Calculate Crossbar's ACRS depreciation for 1984.

7-4 The Crossbar Company (B)
---

1. Make the journal entry to record Crossbar's investment tax credit in 1981 assuming that they used the flow-through method.

2. Make the entry to record Crossbar's investment tax credit in 1981 assuming that they used the deferral method.

3. Which method better measures net earnings for 1981?

4. Which method results in greater cash flow to Crossbar in 1981?

7-5   Aces Company, Inc.

Aces Company, Inc. purchased a machine for $111,111 on January 2, 1983. Since they received an investment tax credit of $11,111 (10 percent of $111,111), Aces considered their investment in the machine to be $100,000.

They expect this machine to generate an annual cash inflow (revenues minus expenses except depreciation) of $26,380 for the next five years. Jack Queen, Aces controller, says that this investment is expected to earn 10 percent annual return on investment based on the following calculation.

	Investment	Dep.	Cash Flow	Return on Investment at 10 Percent	Return of Investment
1983	$100,000	26,000	$26,380	$10,000	$16,380
1984	83,620	26,000	26,380	8,362	18,018
1985	65,602	20,000	26,380	6,560	19,820
1986	45,782	20,000	26,380	4,578	21,802
1987	23,980	20,000	26,380	2,398	23,982*

* Due to rounding.

He argues that the annuity depreciation method, which treats the return of investment as depreciation expense, is the most correct method as it measures the real (economic) reduction in the value of the machine for each period.

Required:

1. Calculate the return on investment (amount and percent) for each of the five years (1983–1987) assuming that Aces used the straight-line method of depreciation.

2. Why is the return *on* investment so much higher in 1986 using the straight-line method than the annuity method of depreciation?

3. Assume that you were hired as vice president–operations of Aces at the beginning of 1983 and that the major measure of your performance was return on investment (net income divided by assets). Would you prefer to use the annuity or the straight-line method of depreciation?

4. Assume that the company uses the straight-line method of depreciation and the vice president–operations has the opportunity in 1986 of replacing this machine with a new one that costs $200,000, has a five-year life, and is expected to generate annual cash flows of $63,956—approximately an 18 percent return on investment. Should he replace the machine? Do you think he will?

8

Long-term debt

Funds borrowed from outsiders that do not have to be paid back within one year or an operating cycle, whichever is longer, are classified as long-term debt.

Long-term debt, referred to as debt capital, and stockholders' equity, called equity capital, are the major components of an enterprise's long-term capital.

Management's objective in issuing long-term debt is to increase the stockholders' wealth. They expect to increase stockholders' wealth by earning more on the assets purchased with the debt capital than the cost (interest) they have to pay for it.

Long-term notes, bonds, and obligations under capital leases are the most common forms of long-term debt.

LONG-TERM NOTES PAYABLE (INTEREST-BEARING)

A long-term loan (long-term note payable) is usually made by an institutional lender, such as a bank or insurance company, for long-term enterprise purposes. Long-term lenders often impose restrictive covenants on the borrower to ensure that these term loans, which are often unsecured, are repaid. Common restrictive covenants required by lenders are that working capital is maintained at a certain level and that officers' salaries cannot be increased, dividends paid, additional borrowings made, or equipment purchased without the consent of the lender. If the loan is secured by the specific pledge of assets, it is called a mortgage loan (mortgage note payable). In the case of default (failure to make payments or violation of restrictive covenants) on a mortgage loan payable, the lender can foreclose, sell the mortgaged assets, and use the proceeds to retire the debt.

Assume that on January 1, 1984, the Santiago Corporation borrows $100,000 from the First National Bank of Texas. Loan terms require repayment of the principal (loan amount) in 10 equal annual installments with interest of 10 percent on the unpaid balance. The interest rate of 10 percent was established as a result of negotiations between the bank vice president and Santiago's chief financial officer. Items considered by the parties in deciding on the interest rate were current market interest rates, the financial condition of Santiago, the quality of Santiago's management, Santiago's bank balance, the future growth of Santiago, the opportunity for Santiago to borrow these funds from another bank at a lower rate of interest, and the bank's opportunity to loan these funds to other customers.

Entries made on Santiago's books for the first two years of the loan are:

January 1, 1984

Cash	100,000	
Notes Payable		100,000

To record at face value, 10-year, 10% term loan from FNB of Texas.

December 31, 1984

Interest Expense (10% of $100,000)	10,000	
Notes Payable	10,000	
Cash		20,000

To record payment of interest and principal, FNB of Texas loan.

December 31, 1985

Interest Expense (10% of $90,000)	9,000	
Notes Payable	10,000	
Cash		19,000

To record payment of interest and principal, FNB of Texas loan.

The payment schedule for the entire 10-year period is listed in Illustration 8–1.

ILLUSTRATION 8–1

	Interest Payment	Principal Payment	Loan Balance
1/1/84			$100,000
12/31/84	$10,000	$ 10,000	90,000
12/31/85	9,000	10,000	80,000
12/31/86	8,000	10,000	70,000
12/31/87	7,000	10,000	60,000
12/31/88	6,000	10,000	50,000
12/31/89	5,000	10,000	40,000
12/31/90	4,000	10,000	30,000
12/31/91	3,000	10,000	20,000
12/31/92	2,000	10,000	10,000
12/31/93	1,000	10,000	–0–
Total	$55,000	$100,000	

LONG-TERM NOTES PAYABLE (NONINTEREST-BEARING)

Generally accepted accounting principles recognize that there is an interest charge for the use of money borrowed regardless of the terms stipulated in the loan agreement.[1] Where the loan agreement does not stipulate an interest rate or indicates a rate substantially below the fair rate, it will be necessary to recalculate the transaction using an interest rate that is implicit in the transaction.

Assume the Santiago Company purchases a parcel of land from Texas Realtors on January 1, 1984, for $100,000. The agreement requires Santiago to make 10 annual payments of $10,000 on December 31 of each year to retire the debt. The contract is silent as to any interest payments.

Would the appropriate entry be:

Land.. 100,000
    Notes Payable............................. 100,000
Purchase of land from Texas Realtors.

Compare the liability of $100,000 with the liability of $100,000 for the 10-year, 10 percent loan from the First National Bank of Texas. That loan required payments of $155,000 ($100,000 principal and $55,000 interest) over the 10-year period. If the amounts repaid on two loans are substantially different, how can the liability on January 1, 1984, the date of the loan, be the same?

---

[1] AICPA, *Accounting Principles Board Opinion No. 21,* "Interest on Receivables and Payables (New York, August 1971).

Do you think $100,000 is the price Santiago would pay for the land if they could make a lump sum cash payment on January 1, 1984? If so, why would Texas Realtors allow them to make installment payments over a 10-year period? Certainly, Texas Realtors would rather receive $100,000 on January 1, 1984, than receive $10,000 at the end of each year for the next 10 years. It would give them the opportunity to earn interest on a larger sum for a longer period of time.

Given these facts, how can we determine the amount of the installment payments that should be allocated to the purchase price of the land and the amount that should be considered as interest?

APB Opinion 21 requires that we record the transaction at its equivalent cash price or if that is not determinable ". . . to approximate the rate which would have resulted if an independent borrower and an independent lender had negotiated a similar transaction under comparable terms and conditions with the option to pay the cash price upon purchase or to give a note for the amount of purchase which bears the prevailing rate of interest to maturity."

Let us assume that we cannot determine the equivalent cash price and that the rate of interest implicit in the transaction is 10 percent. The purchase price of the land and the amount of the liability would be the value today (present value) of all the installment payments at a 10 percent interest rate.

What is the present value (January 1, 1984) of the $10,000 paid on December 31, 1984? It is the amount on January 1, 1984, which at 10 percent interest will accumulate to $10,000 on December 31, 1984. The present value of $1 to be received one period from now at 10 percent is $.909.[2]

$$\$.909 + .10\,(\$.909) = \$1$$

The present value of the $10,000 to be received on December 31, 1984, is $9,090 (.909 × $10,000). The $9,090 on January 1, 1984, will accumulate to $10,000 on December 31, 1984, if it is invested at 10 percent.

What is the present value (January 1, 1984) of the $10,000 to be received on December 31, 1985? The present value of $1 to be received two periods from now at 10 percent is $.826.

---

[2] Tables for the present value of $1 and the present value of $1 received annually at the end of each period for n periods are printed at the end of this chapter. The formula for calculating the present value of $1 to be received in n periods at an interest rate of i is:

$$\frac{1}{(1+i)^n}$$

1/1/84   12/31/84   12/31/85

$.826 + .10 ($.826) = $.909
$.909 + .10 ($.909) = $1

The present value of the $10,000 to be received on December 31, 1985, is $8,260 (.826 × $10,000).

Illustration 8–2 lists the present value of $1 at 10 percent for 10 years and calculates the present value of all the note payments for each of the 10 years.

ILLUSTRATION 8–2

Period	Present Value of $1	Installment Payment	Present Value of Installment Payment
1	$ .909	$ 10,000	$ 9,090
2	.826	10,000	8,260
3	.751	10,000	7,510
4	.683	10,000	6,830
5	.621	10,000	6,210
6	.565	10,000	5,650
7	.513	10,000	5,130
8	.467	10,000	4,670
9	.424	10,000	4,240
10	.386	10,000	3,860
Total	$6.145	$100,000	$61,450

We can obtain the present value of all the installment payments using the present value of $1 table as we did in this calculation, or we could have referred to a table (like the one at the end of this chapter) that calculates the present value of $1 received annually at the end of each period for n periods.[3] The periodic payment or receipt of the same amount at regular intervals is called an annuity. An annuity in advance is one whose payments are made at the beginning of the period. An annuity in arrears is one where the payments are at the end of the period.

The present value of $1 received annually for 10 years at 10 percent is $6.145, which is the sum of all the time-adjusted present values over a 10-year period.

---

[3] The formula for calculating the present value of $1 received at the end of each period (annuity in arrears) for n periods is:

$$\frac{1 - \dfrac{1}{(1+i)^n}}{i}$$

The present value (January 1, 1984) of all the installment payments is $61,450 (6.145 × $10,000). This is the equivalent cash price of the land purchased by Santiago (sales price of Texas Realtors).

APB Opinion 21 requires the following journal entry on January 1, 1984, to record the purchase of the land.

Land   61,450
Unamortized Discount on Notes Payable   38,550
    Notes Payable   100,000
    To record purchase of land.

Unamortized Discount on Notes Payable is a contraliability account. For noninterest-bearing notes it is equal to the difference between the face amount of the note and the present value of the installment payments.

Disclosure of the note payable on the January 1, 1984, balance sheet would reflect the liability of $61,450 and appear as follows:

Notes payable (noninterest-bearing) $100,000
Less: Unamortized discount based on
    an interest rate of 10%   38,550
                                        $ 61,450

The journal entries for the installment payment on December 31, 1984, would be:

Notes Payable   10,000
    Cash   10,000
    To record 1984 installment payment.

Interest Expense (10% of $61,450)   6,145
    Unamortized Discount on Notes Payable   6,145
    To record 1984 interest based on imputed interest
    rate of 10%.

The general ledger accounts on December 31, 1984, reflect a liability of $57,595 ($90,000 − $32,405).

Notes Payable

10,000	100,000

**Unamortized Discount—
Notes Payable**

38,550	6,145

The December 31, 1984, balance sheet disclosure is

Notes payable (noninterest-bearing)	$90,000
Less: Unamortized discount based on imputed interest rate of 10%	32,405
	$57,595

The journal entries and general ledger accounts for the year ended December 31, 1985, reflect a liability of $53,355 ($80,000 − $26,645).

Notes Payable	10,000	
Cash		10,000
To record 1985 installment payment.		

Interest Expense (10% of $57,595)	5,760	
Unamortized Discount on Notes Payable		5,760
To record 1985 interest based on imputed interest rate of 10%.		

Notes Payable

10,000	100,000
10,000	

Unamortized Discount—Notes Payable

38,550	6,145
	5,760

The December 31, 1985, balance sheet disclosure is:

Notes payable (noninterest-bearing)	$80,000
Less: Unamortized discount based on an imputed interest rate of 10%	26,645
	$53,355

At the end of the 10-year period both the Notes Payable and the Unamortized Discount—Notes Payable accounts will have a zero balance (see Illustration 8–3).

The method we have used to amortize (write off) the discount is called the effective interest rate method.

ILLUSTRATION 8–3

	Pay-ment	Interest Expense (10 percent of liability)	Notes Payable	Unamortized Discount— Notes Payable	Balance Sheet Liability
1/1/84			$100,000	$38,550	$61,450
12/31/84	$10,000	$6,145	(10,000)	(6,145)	57,595
12/31/85	10,000	5,760	(10,000)	(5,760)	53,355
12/31/86	10,000	5,335	(10,000)	(5,335)	48,690
12/31/87	10,000	4,869	(10,000)	(4,869)	43,559
12/31/88	10,000	4,356	(10,000)	(4,356)	37,915
12/31/89	10,000	3,792	(10,000)	(3,792)	31,707
12/31/90	10,000	3,171	(10,000)	(3,171)	24,878
12/31/91	10,000	2,488	(10,000)	(2,488)	17,366
12/31/92	10,000	1,737	(10,000)	(1,737)	9,103
12/31/93	10,000	897*	(10,000)	(897)*	–0–

* Adjusted for differences in rounding to the nearest dollar.

BONDS

A bond is a formal contract containing promises (legal obligations) made by the issuing company or government agency (borrower) to the lender of the funds (bondholders). Most bonds promise to pay the amount borrowed (principal) at a future (maturity) date and to make periodic payments (interest) for the use of the money. Some bonds pay the total amount of interest and the principal in one lump sum on the maturity date, and others make installment payments of principal and interest during the life of the bond.

The borrower (issuing company) normally divides the total amount to be borrowed into denominations of $1,000 and sells them to the public through an investment bank. A trustee acts on behalf of the bondholders to make sure all covenants spelled out in the bond contract are fulfilled. The amount ($1,000) to be paid at maturity is called the par value or face amount of the bond. The interest rate stipulated on the bond, which determines the amount of the periodic interest payments, is called the coupon rate. Although bonds are normally issued in denominations of $1,000, they are quoted in the bond market in percentages based on 100. A $1,000 bond quoted at 108 has a market price of $1,080.

Bonds secured only by the general credit of the issuing company are called debentures. Mortgage bonds are secured by a lien on specific assets. Revenue bonds are secured by specific revenues set aside for the payment of the revenue bondholders. Convertible bonds are bonds that have the right to be converted into common stock at a specific price during some specified time interval.

The bond indenture (contract) specifies all the obligations and rights of the lender and the borrower.

Investors decide the prices at which bonds are sold by determining what they are willing to pay for the contractual cash flow promises (principal and coupon rate of interest) made by the bond issuer. The major ingredients in this decision are current money market (interest) rates and the issuer's financial condition.

During the last quarter of 1983 Santiago determines that they will need to borrow approximately $100,000 at the beginning of 1984. They decide to sell a 10-year, $100,000 bond issue on January 1, 1984. The coupon interest is fixed in late 1983 at an annual rate of 10 percent with the expectation that this will also be the yield (market) rate that investors will expect for this type of bond issue on January 1, 1984.

On January 1, 1984, investors agree to buy Santiago's bonds for $100,000. For purposes of this example we assume that there are no costs to issue the bonds.

These bonds will yield the investor 10 percent because the present value of the cash flows Santiago promises to pay bondholders (principal and coupon interest) is equal to 10 percent. If investors demanded a yield that was not the same as the 10 percent coupon rate, the proceeds would not be $100,000.

Present value of $10,000 a period
(annual coupon interest is 10%
of $100,000) for 10 annual periods*
($100,000 × 6.145) .... $ 61,450
Present value of $100,000 to be
paid in 10 years [principal (face
value) amount paid at maturity] at
10% ($100,000 × .3855) 38,550
$100,000

* We assume annual coupon interest payments in order to simplify the computations. Most bonds pay coupon interest on a semiannual basis.

The entries on Santiago's books for these bonds are:

January 1, 1984

Cash 100,000
    Bonds Payable 100,000
Issued 10-year, 10% bonds due 12/31/93.

Annually on December 31

Interest Expense	10,000	
Cash		10,000

To record annual interest expense (1984 through 1993).

December 31, 1993

Bonds Payable	100,000	
Cash		100,000

To record retirement of the bonds.

Bond discount

Suppose that on January 1, 1984, when Santiago was ready to issue their $100,000, 10-year, 10 percent coupon bonds, investors (bondbuyers) were demanding a 12 percent return on bonds of companies comparable to Santiago. The bondbuyers will pay (Santiago will receive) $88,700 because this is the present value of the cash flows at 12 percent.

The present value of $10,000 a period for 10 annual periods (annual coupon interest is 10% of $100,000) at 12% ($10,000 × 5.6502)	$56,502
The present value of $100,000 to be paid in 10 years (principal amount paid at maturity) at 12% ($100,000 × .32198).................	32,198
	$88,700

The $11,300 ($100,000 − $88,700) difference between the face amount of the bonds and the issue price is a bond discount. The bond discount represents the additional amount of interest that investors require to make this investment yield 12 percent. The investors will receive this $11,300 when the bonds mature in 10 years.

The *total* amount of interest that Santiago will pay on these bonds is the difference between what they receive from the bondholders on the issue date and what they actually pay out over the life of the bond.

Total payment:	
Annual coupon interest of $10,000 ($100,000 × 10%) × 10 years	$100,000
Repayment of face amount at maturity ...	100,000
	200,000
Issue price: (proceeds received by Santiago)	88,700
Interest expense for 10 years	$111,300

Whenever the market (effective yield) rate of interest is higher than the coupon rate, the borrower will receive less than the face amount of the bonds.

Bond premium

If the market rate of interest is lower than the coupon rate, the borrower will receive more than the face amount, and the difference will be a bond premium. If the Santiago bonds had been sold to yield 8 percent, the company would have received $113,420 on the issuance of the bonds resulting in a bond premium of $13,420.

The present value of $10,000 a period for 10 annual periods (annual coupon interest is 10% of $100,000) at 8% ($10,000 × 6.710)	$ 67,100
The present value of $100,000 to be paid in 10 years (principal amount paid at maturity) at 8% ($100,000 × .46320)	46,320
	$113,420

The *total* amount of interest that Santiago will pay on these bonds is $86,580.

Total payment:	
Annual coupon interest of $10,000 ($100,000 × 10%) × 10 years	$100,000
Repayment of face amount at maturity . . .	100,000
	200,000
Issue price: (proceeds received by Santiago)	113,420
Interest expense for 10 years	$ 86,580

The borrower's liability on the issue date is equal to the cash received from the sale of the bonds. In order to reflect the correct liability on the balance sheet, bond discount (a contra long-term liability account) is deducted from bonds payable at par value, and bond premium (an adjunct long-term liability account) is added to bonds payable at par value.

The balance sheet disclosures on January 1, 1984:

Bonds payable (10%, due December 31, 1993)	$100,000
Less: Unamortized bond discount . . .	11,300
	$ 88,700

Bonds payable (10%, due December 31, 1993)	$100,000
Add: Unamortized bond premium ...	13,420
	$113,420

BOND ISSUE COSTS

The costs to issue bonds (underwriters' fees, legal and accounting fees, printing costs, and so forth) are classified as an intangible asset on the balance sheet. They are charged to expense (amortized) on a straight-line basis over the life of the bond issue.

STRAIGHT-LINE AMORTIZATION OF BOND DISCOUNT AND BOND PREMIUM

The straight-line and the compound (effective) interest methods are the two methods most often used in amortizing bond discount and bond premium.

The annual journal entry for interest expense using the straight-line amortization method, assuming the 10 percent bonds were issued at an effective interest rate (yield to investors) of 12 percent is:

Annually on December 31

Interest Expense	11,130	
Unamortized Bond Discount		1,130
Cash		10,000
To record annual interest expense.		

The amount of the additional interest (bond discount) to make the 10 percent coupon rate bonds yield 12 percent is amortized on a straight-line basis ($11,300 ÷ 10). The interest expense is $11,130 each year, and the balance sheet liability (bonds payable minus bond discount) increases $1,130 each year until at the end of 10 years (before the principal payment) it is $100,000. The bond discount account decreases $1,130 each year and is zero on December 31, 1993.

The annual journal entry for interest expense using the straight-line amortization method assuming the 10 percent bonds were issued at an effective interest rate (yield to investors) of 8 percent are:

Annually on December 31

Interest Expense	8,658	
Unamortized Bond Premium	1,342	
Cash		10,000
To record annual interest expense.		

The reduction of the interest (bond premium) to make the 10 percent coupon rate bonds yield 8 percent is amortized on a straight-line basis ($13,420 ÷ 10). The interest expense is $8,658 each year, and the balance sheet liability decreases $1,342 each year until at the end of 10 years before the principal payment it is $100,000. The bond premium account decreases from $13,420 to zero.

Even though the straight-line method of amortization is often used in practice (primarily because it is computationally simple), it is not conceptually correct and cannot be used *(APB 21)* if the results are materially different from those which would be obtained using the compound (effective) interest method of bond amortization.

COMPOUND (EFFECTIVE) INTEREST RATE METHOD OF AMORTIZATION OF BOND DISCOUNT AND PREMIUM

The journal entry to record interest expense for 1984 using the compound (effective) interest method of amortization, assuming the 10 percent bonds were issued at an effective interest rate of 12 percent is:

December 31, 1984

Interest Expense (12% of $88,700)	10,644	
Unamortized Bond Discount		644
Cash		10,000
To record annual interest expense.		

The interest expense for any period is the effective interest rate times the outstanding liability. On January 1, 1984, the liability is $88,700, and the interest expense for 1984 is $10,644 (12 percent of $88,700). The amortization of bond discount of $644 ($10,644 − $10,000) increases the bond liability on December 31, 1984, to $89,344 ($88,700 + $644).

The interest expense for the year ended December 31, 1985, is $10,721 (12 percent of $89,344). The entry for December 31, 1985, is:

Interest Expense	10,721	
Unamortized Bond Discount		721
Cash		10,000
To record annual interest expense.		

The general ledger liability accounts on December 31, 1985, are:

Bonds Payable

	100,000

Unamortized Bond Discount

11,300	644
	721

The balance sheet disclosure on December 31, 1985, is:

Bonds payable (10%, due December 31, 1993)	$100,000
Less: Unamortized bond discount	9,935
	$ 90,065

At the end of the 10-year period, the bond discount account will be reduced to zero, and the balance sheet liability will increase to $100,000. Illustration 8–4 calculates the interest expense and the amortization of bond discount over the 10-year period using the compound interest method.

ILLUSTRATION 8–4

	Interest Expense	Coupon Payment	Bonds Payable	Bond Discount	Balance Sheet Liability
1/1/84			$100,000	$11,300	$ 88,700
12/31/84	$10,644	$10,000		(644)	89,344
12/31/85	10,721	10,000		(721)	90,065
12/31/86	10,808	10,000		(808)	90,873
12/31/87	10,905	10,000		(905)	91,778
12/31/88	11,013	10,000		(1,013)	92,791
12/31/89	11,135	10,000		(1,135)	93,926
12/31/90	11,271	10,000		(1,271)	95,197
12/31/91	11,424	10,000		(1,424)	96,621
12/31/92	11,594	10,000		(1,594)	98,215
12/31/93	11,785	10,000		(1,785)	100,000

When the compound interest method of amortization is used, the bond liability is always the present value of the future (interest and principal payments) cash flows.

The balance sheet liability always reflects the initial amount borrowed ($88,700) plus the portion of the total interest expense recognized to date (amortized bond discount) that will not be paid until the maturity date.

For example, on December 31, 1988, the liability on the balance sheet is:

Bonds payable		$100,000
Less: Bond discount ($11,300 − $4,091)......		7,209
		$ 92,791
The present value of $10,000 for five annual		
periods at 12% ($10,000 × 3.6048)		$ 36,048
The present value of $100,000 to be paid		
in five years at 12% ($100,000 × .56743)		56,743
		$ 92,791

The liability on December 31, 1988, is made up of $88,700 originally borrowed plus the amortized discount (additional interest expense) of $4,091 ($644 + $721 + $808 + $905 + $1,013).

If we had used the straight-line method of amortization, the liability on December 31, 1988, would have been $94,350 ($88,700 + $1,130 + $1,130 + $1,130 + $1,130 + $1,130), and the liability on December 31, 1988, would not reflect an effective interest rate of 12 percent.

Illustration 8–5 shows the calculation of interest expense, amortization of bond premium, and the balance sheet liability of the 10 percent bond issue until retirement assuming it was sold to yield 8 percent.

ILLUSTRATION 8–5

	Interest Expense	Coupon Payment	Bonds Payable	Bond Premium	Balance Sheet Liability
1/1/84			$100,000	$13,420	$113,420
12/31/84	$9,074	$10,000		(926)	112,494
12/31/85	9,000	10,000		(1,000)	111,494
12/31/86	8,920	10,000		(1,080)	110,414
12/31/87	8,833	10,000		(1,167)	109,247
12/31/88	8,740	10,000		(1,260)	107,987
12/31/89	8,639	10,000		(1,361)	106,626
12/31/90	8,530	10,000		(1,470)	105,156
12/31/91	8,413	10,000		(1,588)	103,566
12/31/92	8,285	10,000		(1,715)	101,853
12/31/93	8,147	10,000		(1,853)	100,000

The journal entries to record interest expense for the first two years of the bond issue:

Interest Expense (8% of $113,420) 9,074
Unamortized Bond Premium 926
   Cash 10,000
  To record 1984 interest.

Interest Expense (8% of $112,494) 9,000
Unamortized Bond Premium 1,000
   Cash 10,000
  To record 1985 interest.

BOND RETIREMENTS

Companies normally retire bonds by paying their face amount at maturity.

The journal entry to retire the bonds at maturity regardless of whether they were sold at par, a premium, or a discount (December 31, 1993) in the previous examples is:

Bonds Payable 100,000
  Cash 100,000
  To retire 10-year, 10% bonds.

Sinking-fund bonds have provisions that require the company to set aside enough cash or marketable securities during the life of the bond issue to ensure the payment of the face amount of the bond at maturity. Sinking fund cash and securities are listed in the noncurrent section of the balance sheet.

Serial bonds require payment of a certain portion of the bonds outstanding on an annual basis. The serial bonds retired each period are usually selected randomly.

Refunding bonds are bonds issued to replace another bond issue. The old bonds are retired with the cash received from the refunding bonds.

Companies can retire their bonds prior to maturity by evoking the call provision of callable bonds or by purchasing their bonds in the securities markets.

Callable bonds

Many bonds have a call provision that enables the company to retire or call the bonds prior to maturity. The redemption or call price usually includes a premium paid to bondholders for having their bonds called earlier than they had anticipated.

Assume that the company in Illustration 8–5 decides to call 40 percent of the bonds outstanding on December 31, 1987, and that the call price is 108.

The general ledger accounts on December 31, 1987, before the redemption are:

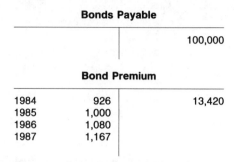

Bonds Payable

	100,000

Bond Premium

			13,420
1984	926		
1985	1,000		
1986	1,080		
1987	1,167		

The entry to call or redeem 40 percent of the bonds are:

Bonds Payable	40,000	
Unamortized Bond Premium (40% of $9,247)	3,699	
Gain on Bond Redemption		499
Cash ($40,000 × 108%)		43,200

To record redemption of $40,000 par value bonds.

In accordance with *FASB Statement 4* gains and losses on bond redemptions are reported net of income taxes as an extraordinary item on the income statement.[4]

Market purchases before maturity

Because bonds promise to pay stipulated amounts, the market price investors will be willing to pay for bonds at any time will fluctuate with the market rate of interest.

Assume that interest rates have moved upward in 1984 and 1985 and that on January 1, 1986, investors demand an 18 percent return on bonds similar to the ones in Illustration 8–4.

The market price of one of those $1,000 bonds on January 1, 1986, would reflect the 18 percent interest rate and sell for approximately $674.

The present value of the $100 interest payments (10% of $1,000) for 8 periods (1986–93) at 18% ($100 × 4.0776)	$408
The present value of $1,000 to be paid in 8 periods at 18% ($1,000 × .2660)	266
Total	$674

---
[4] FASB, *Statement of Financial Accounting Standards No. 4,* "Reporting Gains and Losses from Extinguishment of Debt" (Stamford, Conn., March 1975).

An investor purchasing this bond for $674 on January 1, 1986, would obtain an 18 percent yield to maturity on the investment. The bond sells at a high discount $326 ($1,000 − $674) from its face amount because the 18 percent market rate of interest is much higher than the 10 percent coupon rate. A decrease in interest rates increases the present value of the promises to pay interest and principal in the future and results in higher bond prices in the market. While fluctuations in interest rates after the bond issue date affect the market price of bonds, they do not affect the accounting for bonds by the issuer.

Assume further that the company in Illustration 8–4 decides to retire all their bonds on December 31, 1986.

The general ledger accounts before the redemption are:

Bonds Payable

	100,000

Unamortized Bond Discount

11,300	1984	644
	1985	721

The entry to record the purchase of the bonds is:

Bonds Payable	100,000	
Unamortized Bond Discount..................		9,935
Gain on Redemption		22,665
Cash		67,400

To record purchase of 10-year, 10% bonds.

During the 1970s and early 80s when interest rates soared a number of companies reacquired their bonds and reported large gains on redemption of these bonds. In some cases a substantial loss from operations was offset by a large gain on redemption of bonds.

Some companies, instead of redeeming their bonds for cash, exchanged newly issued common stock for their outstanding debt. The result of this transaction was to replace debt, which has stipulated payment requirements, with common stock, which does not. (Dividends on common stock are declared and paid only at the discretion of the board of directors.)

Gains and losses on redemption of debt

FASB 4 requires that gains and losses on redemption of debt be reported as an extraordinary item net of income taxes segregated from income from continuing operations. This disclosure enables readers of financial statements to make a better estimate of future earnings from continuing operations.

Western Union Corporation disclosed this type of transaction in their 1981 annual report as follows:

On the consolidated income statement:

Income from continuing operations before extraordinary item	$59,039,000
Extraordinary item (net of income taxes)......	10,567,000
Net income	$69,606,000

In the Financial Review section of the annual report:

> The extraordinary income recorded in 1981 was $10.6 million (net of related income taxes), or 66 cents per share which resulted from the exchange of 768,417 shares of newly issued common stock for $34.9 million principal amount of outstanding debentures.

BOND CONVERSION

Convertible bonds give bondholders the option of converting their bonds into common stock at a future date. This convertible feature gives the bondholder (investor) the opportunity to share in the growth (appreciation of the market price of the stock) of the company while maintaining a creditor (bond) position. The conversion feature usually enables the issuing company to sell the bonds in the market place at interest rates lower than interest rates of an equivalent issue without the conversion feature.

Assume that on January 1, 1978, the Yardley Corporation issues $1 million, 10 percent, 20-year convertible debentures for $920,000. The conversion option allows each $1,000 bond to be converted into 40 shares of common stock. On January 1, 1983, when the market price of Yardley common stock is $28, 30 percent of the bondholders decide to convert their bonds into common stock.

The relevant general ledger accounts on January 1, 1983, before conversion are:

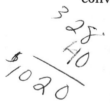

Convertible Bonds Payable

	1,000,000

Bond Discount*

80,000	1978	4,000
	1979	4,000
	1980	4,000
	1981	4,000
	1982	4,000

* Straight-line amortization.

The entry to record the conversion of 30 percent of the outstanding bonds is:

Bonds Payable	300,000	
Bond Discount		18,000
Common Stock		282,000

To convert $300,000 convertible bonds into
12,000 shares of common stock.

This method (which is preferred) is different than for a redemption because it ignores the market value of the stock on the date of conversion. It considers the convertible bond as a device to issue common stock and states the common stock at the amount received from the original convertible bond issue.

An alternative treatment is to consider the market value of the bonds to be their conversion value.

Bonds Payable	300,000	
Loss on Bond Conversion	54,000	
Bond Discount		18,000
Common Stock (12,000 shares at $28)		336,000

To convert $300,000 bonds into 12,000 shares of
common stock.

This method assumes that the common stock is sold at its market price and that the proceeds from the sale are used to redeem the convertible bonds.

LEASES

A lease is an agreement between the owner of an asset (lessor) and the user of the asset (lessee) in which the lessee pays the lessor for the right to use the asset.

Assume that on January 1, 1984, the Rogers Company leases an office copier from the SMD Corporation for 36 months. The lease provides cancellation rights on the part of either party with 30 days notice and does not contain any provision enabling Rogers to purchase the office copier either during or at the end of the lease period. Rogers agrees to pay SMD $100 at the end of each month with the first payment due January 31, 1984.

Monthly Entry on Rogers's Books

Rent (Lease) Expense	100	
Cash		100

To record one month's rental expense for the office copier.

Because the lease is cancellable and does not allow for the purchase of the office copier by Rogers, no asset or liability is recorded on Rogers's books on the date the lease is signed.

CAPITAL LEASES

Prior to 1976, in order to avoid recording either the fixed asset or the corresponding long-term liability on the balance sheet, many companies structured as leases what were actually purchases of fixed assets financed with long-term debt. To prevent this practice and to promulgate the idea of recording transactions in accordance with their economic substance, the Financial Accounting Standards Board on November 1976 issued *Statement 13,* "Accounting for Leases." This accounting standard applies to all companies that prepare their financial statements in accordance with generally accepted accounting principles.

FASB Statement 13 requires the capitalization (recording as assets) of all leases that are, in substance, purchases. These leases are defined as *capital leases.* All other leases are defined as *operating leases.* The lease payment in an operating lease is charged to rental expense as in the previous Rogers Company example.

According to *FASB 13,* if a noncancellable lease meets any of the following criteria, it is a capital lease:

1. Ownership is transferred to the lessee by the end of the lease.
2. There is a bargain purchase option that enables the lessee to purchase the leased property for a price less than its fair value on the option date.
3. The lease term is 75 percent or more of the leased property's estimated economic life.
4. The present value of the minimum lease payments is 90 percent or more of the fair value of the leased property (less the investment credit if retained by the lessor).

The method for calculating the liability for capital leases is the same as used in *APB 21* to calculate the liability for noninterest-bearing long-term notes payable.

The lease is recorded at the lower of the fair value of the leased property or the present value of the minimum lease payments. The interest rate to be used by the lessee is the interest rate implicit in the lease (probably known only to the lessor) or, if the implicit interest is not known, the lessee's incremental interest rate. The incremental interest rate is the rate the lessee company would pay if the funds were borrowed to purchase the asset and repaid over a period similar to the lease.

Assume that on January 1, 1984, the Santiago Corporation leases a large piece of equipment from the Roar Corporation. The terms of the lease require Santiago to pay $10,000 a year rental for 10 years and to pay all related insurance, maintenance, and property taxes. The fair value of the equipment on January 1, 1984, is estimated to be $68,000, and it is expected to have an economic life of 12 years.

The lease is a capital lease because the lease term is at least 75 percent (10 years/12 years = 83.3 percent) of the economic life of the machine. Santiago has to record the asset and the liability at the lower of the fair value of the equipment or the present value of the lease payments. Santiago's incremental interest rate is determined to be 10 percent, and the rate implicit in the lease is not known to them.

The present value of $10,000 a year at 10 percent for 10 years is $61,450. (See the calculation under noninterest-bearing long-term notes payable in the beginning of the chapter.) Because $61,450 is less than $68,000 the capital lease asset is recorded at $61,450.

The entry on January 1, 1984, is:

```
Capital Lease Asset ..............................  61,450
     Capital Lease Liability .......................           61,450
   To record 10-year lease at $10,000 per year.
```

Capital lease asset is classified on the balance sheet as a fixed asset, and capital lease liability is classified as a long-term liability.

December 31, 1984

```
Interest Expense (10% of $61,450) .................  6,145
Capital Lease Liability ..........................  3,855
     Cash ........................................           10,000
   To record lease payment for 1984.


Depreciation Expense—Capital Lease Asset.........  6,145
   Accumulated Depreciation—Capital
     Lease Asset ................................           6,145
   To record depreciation (10 years straight-line, 10%
   of $61,450).
```

The lessee has the same option for using the straight-line or an accelerated depreciation method for leased assets as for purchased assets. For leased assets the lessee also has the option of directly decreasing the value of the asset account rather than creating an accumulated depreciation account.

Insurance, Maintenance, Property Tax Expenses ...   xxxx
    Cash (Payables)   xxxx
To record expenses related to leased equipment.

December 31, 1985

Interest Expense (10% of $57,595)   5,760
Capital Lease Liability   4,240
    Cash   10,000
To record lease payment for 1980.

The amount of interest expense, which is calculated using the effective interest rate method, will decline each year because the liability is declining.

The allocation of the lease payments to interest expense and liability reduction for the entire 10-year period is shown in Illustration 8–6.

ILLUSTRATION 8–6

	Lease Payment	Interest	Principal Payment	Capital Lease Liability
1/1/84				$61,450
12/31/84	$10,000	$6,145	$3,855	57,595
12/31/85	10,000	5,760	4,240	53,355
12/31/86	10,000	5,335	4,665	48,690
12/31/87	10,000	4,869	5,131	43,559
12/31/88	10,000	4,356	5,644	37,915
12/31/89	10,000	3,792	6,208	31,707
12/31/90	10,000	3,171	6,829	24,878
12/31/91	10,000	2,488	7,512	17,366
12/31/92	10,000	1,737	8,263	9,103
12/31/93	10,000	897*	9,103	–0–

* Adjusted for differences in rounding to the nearest dollar.

FASB Statement 13's treatment for capital leases results in increasing both assets (the lease is capitalized) and the amount of debt outstanding and has a direct impact on three ratios often used by financial analysts: the ratio of debt to equity (debt/equity ratio), the ratio of net income to assets (rate of return on total assets), and the ratio of income before interest and income taxes to interest payments (times interest earned).

PROBLEMS AND CASES

8–1 Lucky, Mr. Lucky: An accounting vignette

Mr. Lucky: Hey, Jim, I won the lottery! The state lottery commission told me I'm an instant millionaire—before taxes, of course.

Jim Financier: That's great, Lucky! When do you get it?

Lucky: I get $50,000 tomorrow and $50,000 a year for the next 19 years; 20 years at $50,000 per year—a cool million bucks.

Jim: Wait a second, Lucky. You didn't win a million dollars. If you did they would be giving you a million dollars tomorrow.

Lucky: You mean the lottery commission misled me and I am not an instant millionaire?

Required:

1. Is Mr. Lucky an instant millionaire before income taxes?

2. Would you rather have $1 million now than $50,000 a year for 20 years? Than $100,000 a year for 20 years? Would you rather have $600,000 now than $100,000 a year for almost 20 years? Explain. *present value either greater*

8–2 Present value and bonds*

9999.99
6,209.06

3790.79
379079

sum of one & two

1. What is the most you would be willing to pay today for the privilege of receiving $10,000 five years from now? Assume you could earn 10 percent per year return on your money. *use table one*

2. What is the most you would be willing to pay today for the privilege of receiving $1,000 at the end of each of the next five years? Assume you could earn 10 percent per year return on the money.

3. What is the most you would be willing to pay for a $10,000 face value, 10 percent annual coupon rate bond with a five-year maturity? Assume you could earn 10 percent per year return on your money in an alternative investment. What is the present value of the $10,000 you would receive in five years? What is the present value of the five $1,000 annual interest payments?

4. Suppose you could earn 15 percent per year on an alternative invest-

---

* Tables for the present value of $1 and present value of $1 received at the end of each period for *n* periods are shown on pages 202 and 203. Calculators with financial functions may also be used to calculate the present value of $1, present value of $1 per period, future value of $1, and so forth. Bond tables that calculate bond prices (interest and maturity promises) are also published (see Problem 8–3).

ment. Now how much would you be willing to pay for the $10,000, five-year bond with a 10 percent annual coupon rate?

5.   Suppose a corporation issued this $10,000 bond, which yields 15 percent, for $8,324.

 a. What is the corporation's liability at the date of issue? Explain why it isn't $10,000.

 b. Make the journal entry to record the bond.

 c. Make the journal entry for the first year's interest payment assuming (1) straight-line amortization of bond discount and (2) effective-interest rate method amortization of bond discount.

 d. Explain why the liability at the end of the first year is not the same as at the beginning of the year.

 e. What is the *total* amount of interest that the corporation will pay on this $10,000 bond?

8–3   MPB Corporation

MPB Corporation issued $1 million of 8 percent, 20-year bonds to yield 9 percent on January 1, 1985. The 4 percent coupon is payable semiannually on July 1 and January 1. It uses the effective interest method of amortization of bond discount and premium.

Refer to the bond table (Exhibit 1) and answer the following questions.

Required:

1.   Make the journal entry on MPB's books to record the sale of the bonds. Assume no underwriting costs for purposes of this problem.

2.   Make the journal entries to record interest expense on June 30 and December 31, 1985.

3.   Five years later the effective interest rate on bonds of this type had increased to 10.5 percent. Calculate the market value of the MPB bonds on December 31, 1989.

4.   As an investor in MPB Corporation's bonds would you prefer to have market rates of interest rise or decline? Why?

5.   Make the journal entry to retire the bonds on December 31, 2004.

EXHIBIT 1. Bond Values in Percent of Par: 8 Percent Semiannual Coupons

Market Yield (percent per year compounded semiannually)	Years to Maturity							
	½	5	10	15	19½	20	30	40
5.0	101.463	113.128	123.384	131.396	137.096	137.654	146.363	151.678
5.5	101.217	110.800	119.034	125.312	129.675	130.098	136.528	140.266
6.0	100.971	108.530	114.877	119.600	122.808	123.115	127.676	130.201
6.5	100.726	106.317	110.905	114.236	116.448	116.656	119.690	121.291
7.0	100.483	104.158	107.106	109.196	110.551	110.678	112.472	113.374
7.1	100.435	103.733	106.367	108.225	109.424	109.536	111.113	111.898
7.2	100.386	103.310	105.634	107.266	108.314	108411	109.780	110.455
7.3	100.338	102.889	104.908	106.318	107.220	107.303	108.473	109.044
7.4	100.289	102.470	104.188	105.382	106.142	106.212	107.191	107.665
7.5	100.241	102.053	103.474	104.457	105.080	105.138	105.934	106.316
7.6	100.193	101.638	102.767	103.544	104.034	104.079	104.702	104.997
7.7	100.144	101.226	102.066	102.642	103.003	103.036	103.492	103.706
7.8	100.096	100.815	101.371	101.750	101.987	102.009	102.306	102.444
7.9	100.048	100.407	100.683	100.870	100.986	100.997	101.142	101.209
8.0	100	100	100	100	100	100	100	100
8.1	99.9519	99.5955	99.3235	99.1406	99.0279	99.0177	98.8794	98.8170
8.2	99.9039	99.1929	98.6529	98.2916	98.0699	98.0498	97.7798	97.6589
8.3	99.8560	98.7924	97.9882	97.4528	97.1257	97.0962	96.7006	96.5253
8.4	99.8081	98.3938	97.3294	96.6240	96.1951	96.1566	95.6414	95.4152
8.5	99.7602	97.9973	96.6764	95.8052	95.2780	95.2307	94.6018	94.3282
8.6	99.7124	97.6027	96.0291	94.9962	94.3739	94.3183	93.5812	93.2636
8.7	99.6646	97.2100	95.3875	94.1969	93.4829	93.4191	92.5792	92.2208
8.8	99.6169	96.8193	94.7514	93.4071	92.6045	92.5331	91.5955	91.1992
8.9	99.5692	96.4305	94.1210	92.6266	91.7387	91.6598	90.6295	90.1982
9.0	99.5215	96.0436	93.4960	91.8555	90.8851	90.7992	89.6810	89.2173
9.5	99.2840	94.1378	90.4520	88.1347	86.7949	86.6777	85.1858	84.5961
10.0	99.0476	92.2783	87.5378	84.6275	82.9830	82.8409	81.0707	80.4035
10.5	98.8123	90.4639	84.7472	81.3201	79.4271	79.2656	77.2656	76.5876
11.0	98.5782	88.6935	82.0744	78.1994	76.1070	75.9308	73.8252	73.1036

8–4 Expanso Corporation (A)

Mr. Jasper, president of Expanso Corporation, a rapidly expanding company, negotiates an agreement with Standard Insurance Company under which the insurance company is to lend Expanso $1 million on a 12 percent basis. The insurance company offers Expanso three options as to the method of repayment. The effective rate of interest for each option is 6 percent per half year.

Option 1—Expanso to receive $1 million now; Expanso to pay 6 percent interest at the end of each six months for 20 years and to pay $1 million at maturity 20 years hence.

Option 2—Expanso to receive $1 million now; Expanso to pay $10,-285,717.94 at the end of 20 years and to make no other payments of interest or principal during the 20-year term of the loan ($1 at 6 percent will accumulate to $10.28571794 at the end of 40 periods).

Option 3—Expanso to receive $1 million now; Expanso to pay $66,461.54 at the end of each six months for 20 years and to make no other payments of interest or principal during or at the end of the 20-year period (the present value of $.06646154 per period for 40 periods at 6 percent is $1).

Required:

1. Jasper asks you to make the following computations for each option.

 a. The amount of the liability at the date of the loan.

 b. The amount of interest expense for the first year.

 c. The total interest expense for the entire 20-year period.

 d. The cash flow (inward and outward) for the first year.

 e. The cash flow (inward and outward) for year 2 and year 20.

2. Which option should Mr. Jasper take? Why?

8–5   Expanso Corporation (B)

After reviewing the three options in Expanso A, the controller of Expanso suggests an entirely different arrangement. He says that what Expanso wants is not money as such but a method of paying the $1 million purchase price of a new papermaking machine that has just been installed. He suggests that the Standard Insurance Company buy the papermaking machine and lease it to Expanso for 20 years for $66,461.54, rent to be paid at the end of each six months.

The Standard Insurance Company agrees with the controller and purchases the papermaker on January 1, 1984, and immediately leases it to Expanso at the terms suggested by Expanso's controller. The economic life of the papermaker is determined to be 25 years, and Expanso's incremental interest rate is 12 percent per annum (compounded semiannually).

Required:

1. Make the journal entry to record the lease agreement on January 1, 1984. (See requirements under *FASB Statement 13.*)

2. Make the entry to record the lease payments on June 30, 1984, and December 31, 1984.

3. Make the entry to record 1984 straight-line depreciation expense on the books.*

---

* The leased asset is usually amortized or depreciated over the life of the lease unless the lease provides for a transfer of ownership or contains a bargain purchase option.

4. Is it more advantageous for Expanso to lease the papermaker from Standard Insurance or to borrow from Standard in accordance with option 2 and buy the papermaker?

8-6 Town of Grenoble*

The Town of Grenoble is planning to issue $1 million par value of bonds. The market (effective) rate will be determined by market conditions at the time that the issue is floated, but the nominal or coupon rate is to be fixed by town officials in consultation with the underwriters.

At the beginning of May 1984 the town officials and the underwriters agreed that a coupon rate of 6 percent (3 percent semiannually) was appropriate, and they proceeded to have bonds printed in $1,000 denominations with 20 coupons of $30 attached to each bond.

At the time the bonds were actually issued on June 1, 1984, the market rate of interest rose above 6 percent for commitments of this type, and the bonds were sold at a price to yield investors 7 percent per annum (compounded semiannually). The underwriter who handled the issue charged a fee of 2 percent of par value to cover all costs involved in putting out the issue.

Interest Tables and Facts

Bonds authorized: $1,000,000. Date: June 1, 1984.

Term: 10 years. Interest payable: June 1 and December 1.

Present value of $1 payable at the end of 20 periods with interest at:

3.00% .... $.5536758
3.50% .... .5025659

Present value of $1 per period for 20 periods with interest at:

3.00% $14.8774749
3.50% 14.2124033

Required:

1. Prepare the journal entry on the Town of Grenoble books to record the issue of the bonds on June 1, 1984.

2. Prepare the journal entry on December 1, 1984, to accrue and pay interest. Use both the straight-line and compound interest methods of amortization.

3. Prepare the journal entry to accrue interest on December 31, 1984. (Town of Grenoble reports on a calendar year basis.) Use both the straight-line and compound interest methods of amortization.

---

* Interest on municipal bonds is exempt from federal income taxes.

8-7 General Motors Acceptance Corporation discount notes due July 1, 1991

Refer to the announcement (tombstone ad) for the sale of the GMAC discount notes that appeared in the June 25, 1981, edition of *The Wall Street Journal* and answer the following questions:

Required:

1. What is the present value of $1,000 to be paid at the end of 20 periods at an interest rate of 7.125 percent?

2. Why would GMAC sell a note with a face value of $1,000 for $252.45?

3. Make the July 1, 1981, journal entry on GMAC's books for the amount that they received from the underwriters. For purposes of this entry assume no underwriting or issue costs.

4. Make the December 31, 1981, journal entry to record interest expense.

5. How much interest will GMAC be required to pay on these notes every six months? Over the 10-year period?

6. How much would GMAC have received from the underwriters if the notes that were issued on July 1, 1981, were not discount notes and required payment of a semiannual coupon of 7.125 percent as well as $1,000 per note on maturity? Assume that these notes were sold to yield 14.25 percent compounded semiannually (assume no note issue costs). How much interest will GMAC be required to pay on these notes every six months? Over the 10-year period?

8-8 IBM notes—issued October 1, 1979*

On October 1, 1979, a meeting was held in the conference room of the investment banker Salomon Brothers. Present at the meeting were representatives of Salomon Brothers and Merrill Lynch, another investment banker, and financial executives of International Business Machines (IBM).

The purpose of the meeting was to price an IBM offering of $500 million, seven-year notes with a coupon rate of 9½ percent (4.75 percent semiannually) and $500 million of 25-year debentures that bore a coupon rate of 9⅜ percent (4.6875 percent semiannually).

The IBM notes and bond issue were rated triple A (the highest rating) by both Standard & Poor's and Moody's and would be considered prime corporate paper. U.S. Treasury issues of comparable maturities are usually used as a key benchmark in pricing prime corporate paper.

---

* This case relies heavily on the article, "The Bomb Dropped on Wall Street," by Walter Guzzardi, Jr., published in the November 19, 1979, issue of *Fortune* magazine.

$750,000,000

General Motors Acceptance Corporation
Discount Notes Due July 1, 1991

There will be no periodic payment of interest on the Notes. The Price shown below results in
an annual yield to maturity of 14.25%, compounded on a semiannual basis.

Price 25.245% and Accrued Amortization

Copies of the prospectus may be obtained in any State from only such of the
undersigned as may legally offer these Securities in compliance
with the securities laws of such State.

MORGAN STANLEY & CO.
Incorporated

THE FIRST BOSTON CORPORATION   GOLDMAN, SACHS & CO.   LEHMAN BROTHERS KUHN LOEB
Incorporated

MERRILL LYNCH WHITE WELD CAPITAL MARKETS GROUP   SALOMON BROTHERS
Merrill Lynch, Pierce, Fenner & Smith Incorporated

BACHE HALSEY STUART SHIELDS   BEAR, STEARNS & CO.   BLYTH EASTMAN PAINE WEBBER
Incorporated   *Incorporated*

DILLON, READ & CO. INC.   DONALDSON, LUFKIN & JENRETTE   DREXEL BURNHAM LAMBERT
Securities Corporation   *Incorporated*

E. F. HUTTON & COMPANY INC.   KIDDER, PEABODY & CO.   LAZARD FRERES & CO.
Incorporated

L. F. ROTHSCHILD, UNTERBERG, TOWBIN   SHEARSON LOEB RHOADES INC.   SMITH BARNEY, HARRIS UPHAM & CO.
Incorporated

WARBURG PARIBAS BECKER   WERTHEIM & CO., INC.   DEAN WITTER REYNOLDS INC.
Incorporated

ATLANTIC CAPITAL   BASLE SECURITIES CORPORATION   BATEMAN EICHLER, HILL RICHARDS
Corporation   *Incorporated*

WILLIAM BLAIR & COMPANY   J. C. BRADFORD & CO.   ALEX. BROWN & SONS

A. G. EDWARDS & SONS, INC.   LADENBURG, THALMANN & CO. INC.   McDONALD & COMPANY

MOSELEY, HALLGARTEN, ESTABROOK & WEEDEN INC.   OPPENHEIMER & CO., INC.

PRESCOTT, BALL & TURBEN   RAUSCHER PIERCE REFSNES, INC.

THE ROBINSON-HUMPHREY COMPANY, INC.   ROTAN MOSLE INC.   THOMSON McKINNON SECURITIES INC.

TUCKER, ANTHONY & R. L. DAY, INC.   WHEAT, FIRST SECURITIES, INC.

June 25, 1981

Salomon Brothers, as the leader of the underwriting, wanted to price the bond and note issues so that they would both sell quickly and give IBM the lowest possible interest cost. Their immediate concern was that on October 1, 1979, interest rates were rising, the value of the dollar was declining, the value of gold was increasing, and bond and stock prices were falling.

After much negotiation the underwriters and IBM agreed at 12:40 P.M. on a yield to investors (interest cost to IBM) of seven basis points (a basis point is 1/100 of a percent) above U.S. Treasury notes for the IBM note and 12 basis points above U.S. Treasury bonds for the IBM debentures. The effective interest (yield) rates for the notes was 9.62 percent (4.81 percent semiannually) and 9.41 percent (4.705 percent semiannually) for the debentures.

The price to buyers on a note was set at $994 per $1,000 note with $987.75 of that amount going to IBM. The difference of $6.25 went to the underwriting syndicate for selling the issue ($1.25 went to Salomon and Merrill Lynch as managers of the issue, $1.25 to each underwriter, and $3.75 was paid as a selling concession to the sellers of the note).

Required:

1. Make the journal entry on IBM's books to record the proceeds they received from the underwriters on the sale of the $500 million, seven-year notes.

2. Make the journal entry on IBM's books to record the first six months interest expense and amortization of note issue costs. IBM used the straight-line method to amortize note issue costs ($6.25 per $1,000 note) and the compound (effective) interest method to amortize note discount. (For purposes of this journal entry disregard the fact that IBM reports on a calendar year basis and would have to make an adjusting entry on December 31, 1979. You should also assume that the first coupon interest payment will be made one day after your entry.)

3. During the next two days interest rates rose (four-year U.S. Treasury notes sold to yield 9.79 percent on October 3), and on Monday, October 8, the Federal Reserve Board introduced strong antiinflationary measures which resulted in large increases in interest rates.

On Wednesday, October 10, the underwriting syndicate was no longer able to sell the IBM notes and bonds at the original yield rates. The syndicate was disbanded, and the bonds were allowed to sell at the market price. The market price of the notes fell about $5 each, and the yield rose to approximately 9.9 percent. By November 1, the notes were selling for approximately 92⅜ ($923.75 per bond).

a. What journal entry should IBM make on their books on November 1 to reflect the 92⅜ note price?

b. What journal entry would an investor make to reflect the purchase of $10,000 face amount of notes on November 1, 1979, at 92⅜ plus accrued interest? (On November 1, 1979, there was one month's accrued interest (⅙ of $47.50) that the buyer of a $1,000 note had to pay the seller in addition to the market price of the note.)

8–9   Seitz, Incorporated

On December 31, 1983, the Seitz Corporation issued 10 percent subordinated debenture (unsecured) bonds with a face (par) value of $6 million and a maturity date of December 31, 1991. The coupon interest of 10 percent is paid semiannually (5 percent) on July 1 and January 1.

Listed below is the long-term debt section of the balance sheet and the related footnotes.

Long-term debt consists of the following:

Note payable to bank due in monthly installments of $6,180, including interest, to December 31, 1989	$2,949,140
10 percent subordinated debenture (with conversion privilege) due December 31, 1991	6,000,000
Less: Unamortized bond discount	(200,000)
	$8,749,140

Footnotes on long-term debt:

The note payable to the bank has an interest rate of 8¼ percent and is secured by inventory, property, and equipment, by the unlimited guarantee of T. Seitz and R. Seitz and by the assignment of life insurance policies on the lives of those individuals (face value $1,750,000 each).

The 10 percent subordinated debentures are subordinated (come after) in payment to any debt to any financial institution engaged in the business of lending money and may be converted at any time prior to December 31, 1990, into the company's common stock at the rate of one share of stock for each $25 of unpaid principal amount of the debentures. The company has agreed to reserve and keep available, out of authorized but unissued common stock or common stock held in the treasury, the full number of shares of common stock issuable upon the conversion of all outstanding debentures.

The 10 percent subordinated debentures are also redeemable, at Seitz's option, at any time until maturity at a price of $102 per bond.

The company had agreed that so long as the debentures are outstanding, it will not declare or pay any dividends.

On December 31, 1985, bonds having a face value of $1 million were converted into common stock.

On December 31, 1986, bonds having a face value of $400,000 were redeemed. The redeemed bonds were retired immediately.

Required:

1.   Make the journal entry to record the issue of the 10 percent subordinated debenture bonds on December 31, 1983.

2.   Record the journal entries for interest expense on the 10 percent subordinated debentures for 1984 (assume straight-line amortization of bond discount).

3.   Make the journal entry on December 31, 1985, to reflect the conversion of bonds to common stock.

4.   Make the journal entry to record the retirement of the 10 percent subordinated debenture bonds on December 31, 1986.

TABLE 8–1. Present Value of $1

(n) Periods	2%	2½%	3%	4%	5%	6%	8%	9%	10%	12%	15%	(n) Periods
1	.98039	.97561	.97087	.96154	.95238	.94340	.92593	.91743	.90909	.89286	.86957	1
2	.96117	.95181	.94260	.92456	.90703	.89000	.85734	.84168	.82645	.79719	.75614	2
3	.94232	.92860	.91514	.88900	.86384	.83962	.79383	.77218	.75132	.71178	.65752	3
4	.92385	.90595	.88849	.85480	.82270	.79209	.73503	.70843	.68301	.63552	.57175	4
5	.90573	.88385	.86261	.82193	.78353	.74726	.68058	.64993	.62092	.56743	.49718	5
6	.88797	.86230	.83748	.79031	.74622	.70496	.63017	.59627	.56447	.50663	.43233	6
7	.87056	.84127	.81309	.75992	.71068	.66506	.58349	.54703	.51316	.45235	.37594	7
8	.85349	.82075	.78941	.73069	.67684	.62741	.54027	.50187	.46651	.40388	.32690	8
9	.83676	.80073	.76642	.70259	.64461	.59190	.50025	.46043	.42410	.36061	.28426	9
10	.82035	.78120	.74409	.67556	.61391	.55839	.46319	.42241	.38554	.32197	.24719	10
11	.80426	.76214	.72242	.64958	.58468	.52679	.42888	.38753	.35049	.28748	.21494	11
12	.78849	.74356	.70138	.62460	.55684	.49697	.39711	.35554	.31863	.25668	.18691	12
13	.77303	.72542	.68095	.60057	.53032	.46884	.36770	.32618	.28966	.22917	.16253	13
14	.75788	.70773	.66112	.57748	.50507	.44230	.34046	.29925	.26333	.20462	.14133	14
15	.74301	.69047	.64186	.55526	.48102	.41727	.31524	.27454	.23939	.18270	.12289	15
16	.72845	.67362	.62317	.53391	.45811	.39365	.29189	.25187	.21763	.16312	.10687	16
17	.71416	.65720	.60502	.51337	.43630	.37136	.27027	.23107	.19785	.14564	.09293	17
18	.70016	.64117	.58739	.49363	.41552	.35034	.25025	.21199	.17986	.13004	.08081	18
19	.68643	.62553	.57029	.47464	.39573	.33051	.23171	.19449	.16351	.11611	.07027	19
20	.67297	.61027	.55368	.45639	.37689	.31180	.21455	.17843	.14864	.10367	.06110	20
21	.65978	.59539	.53755	.43883	.35894	.29416	.19866	.16370	.13513	.09256	.05313	21
22	.64684	.58086	.52189	.42196	.34185	.27751	.18394	.15018	.12285	.08264	.04620	22
23	.63416	.56670	.50669	.40573	.32557	.26180	.17032	.13778	.11168	.07379	.04017	23
24	.62172	.55288	.49193	.39012	.31007	.24698	.15770	.12641	.10153	.06588	.03493	24
25	.60953	.53939	.47761	.37512	.29530	.23300	.14602	.11597	.09230	.05882	.03038	25
26	.59758	.52623	.46369	.36069	.28124	.21981	.13520	.10639	.08391	.05252	.02642	26
27	.58586	.51340	.45019	.34682	.26785	.20737	.12519	.09761	.07628	.04689	.02297	27
28	.57437	.50088	.43708	.33348	.25509	.19563	.11591	.08955	.06934	.04187	.01997	28
29	.56311	.48866	.42435	.32065	.24295	.18456	.10733	.08216	.06304	.03738	.01737	29
30	.55207	.47674	.41199	.30832	.23138	.17411	.09938	.07537	.05731	.03338	.01510	30
31	.54125	.46511	.39999	.29646	.22036	.16425	.09202	.06915	.05210	.02980	.01313	31
32	.53063	.45377	.38834	.28506	.20987	.15496	.08520	.06344	.04736	.02661	.01142	32
33	.52023	.44270	.37703	.27409	.19987	.14619	.07889	.05820	.04306	.02376	.00993	33
34	.51003	.43191	.36604	.26355	.19035	.13791	.07305	.05340	.03914	.02121	.00864	34
35	.50003	.42137	.35538	.25342	.18129	.13011	.06763	.04899	.03558	.01894	.00751	35
36	.49022	.41109	.34503	.24367	.17266	.12274	.06262	.04494	.03235	.01691	.00653	36
37	.48061	.40107	.33498	.23430	.16444	.11579	.05799	.04123	.02941	.01510	.00568	37
38	.47119	.39128	.32523	.22529	.15661	.10924	.05369	.03783	.02674	.01348	.00494	38
39	.46195	.38174	.31575	.21662	.14915	.10306	.04971	.03470	.02430	.01204	.00429	39
40	.45289	.37243	.30656	.20829	.14205	.09722	.04603	.03184	.02210	.01075	.00373	40

TABLE 8–2.   Present Value of $1 Received at the End of Each Period for *n* periods (annuity in arrears)

(n) Periods	2%	2½%	3%	4%	5%	6%	8%	9%	10%	12%	15%	(n) Periods
1	.98039	.97561	.97087	.96154	.95238	.94340	.92593	.91743	.90909	.89286	.86957	1
2	1.94156	1.92742	1.91347	1.88609	1.85941	1.83339	1.78326	1.75911	1.73554	1.69005	1.62571	2
3	2.88388	2.85602	2.82861	2.77509	2.72325	2.67301	2.57710	2.53130	2.48685	2.40183	2.28323	3
4	3.80773	3.76197	3.71710	3.62990	3.54595	3.46511	3.31213	3.23972	3.16986	3.03735	2.85498	4
5	4.71346	4.64583	4.57971	4.45182	4.32948	4.21236	3.99271	3.88965	3.79079	3.60478	3.35216	5
6	5.60143	5.50813	5.41719	5.24214	5.07569	4.91732	4.62288	4.48592	4.35526	4.11141	3.78448	6
7	6.47199	6.34939	6.23028	6.00205	5.78637	5.58238	5.20637	5.03295	4.86842	4.56376	4.16042	7
8	7.32548	7.17014	7.01969	6.73274	6.46321	6.20979	5.74664	5.53482	5.33493	4.96764	4.48732	8
9	8.16224	7.97087	7.78611	7.43533	7.10782	6.80169	6.24689	5.99525	5.75902	5.32825	4.77158	9
10	8.98259	8.75206	8.53020	8.11090	7.72173	7.36009	6.71008	6.41766	6.14457	5.65022	5.01877	10
11	9.78685	9.51421	9.25262	8.76048	8.30641	7.88687	7.13896	6.80519	6.49506	5.93770	5.23371	11
12	10.57534	10.25776	9.95400	9.38507	8.86325	8.38384	7.53608	7.16073	6.81369	6.19437	5.42062	12
13	11.34837	10.98319	10.63496	9.98565	9.39357	8.85268	7.90378	7.48690	7.10336	6.42355	5.58315	13
14	12.10625	11.69091	11.29607	10.56312	9.89864	9.29498	8.24424	7.78615	7.36669	6.62817	5.72448	14
15	12.84926	12.38138	11.93794	11.11839	10.37966	9.71225	8.55948	8.06069	7.60608	6.81086	5.84737	15
16	13.57771	13.05500	12.56110	11.65230	10.83777	10.10590	8.85137	8.31256	7.82371	6.97399	5.95424	16
17	14.29187	13.71220	13.16612	12.16567	11.27407	10.47726	9.12164	8.54363	8.02155	7.11963	6.04716	17
18	14.99203	14.35336	13.75351	12.65930	11.68959	10.82760	9.37189	8.75563	8.20141	7.24967	6.12797	18
19	15.67846	14.97889	14.32380	13.13394	12.08532	11.15812	9.60360	8.95012	8.36492	7.36578	6.19823	19
20	16.35143	15.58916	14.87747	13.59033	12.46221	11.46992	9.81815	9.12855	8.51356	7.46944	6.25933	20
21	17.01121	16.18455	15.41502	14.02916	12.82115	11.76408	10.01680	9.29224	8.64869	7.56200	6.31246	21
22	17.65805	16.76541	15.93692	14.45112	13.16300	12.04158	10.20074	9.44243	8.77154	7.64465	6.35866	22
23	18.29220	17.33211	16.44361	14.85684	13.48857	12.30338	10.37106	9.58021	8.88322	7.71843	6.39884	23
24	18.91393	17.88499	16.93554	15.24696	13.79864	12.55036	10.52876	9.70661	8.98474	7.78432	6.43377	24
25	19.52346	18.42438	17.41315	15.62208	14.09394	12.78336	10.67478	9.82258	9.07704	7.84314	6.46415	25
26	20.12104	18.95061	17.87684	15.98277	14.37519	13.00317	10.80998	9.92897	9.16095	7.89566	6.49056	26
27	20.70690	19.46401	18.32703	16.32959	14.64303	13.21053	10.93516	10.02658	9.23722	7.94255	6.51353	27
28	21.28127	19.96489	18.76411	16.66306	14.89813	13.40616	11.05108	10.11613	9.30657	7.98442	6.53351	28
29	21.84438	20.45355	19.18845	16.98371	15.14107	13.59072	11.15841	10.19828	9.36961	8.02181	6.55088	29
30	22.39646	20.93029	19.60044	17.29203	15.37245	13.76483	11.25778	10.27365	9.42691	8.05518	6.56598	30
31	22.93770	21.39541	20.00043	17.58849	15.59281	13.92909	11.34980	10.34280	9.47901	8.08499	6.57911	31
32	23.46833	21.84918	20.38877	17.87355	15.80268	14.08404	11.43500	10.40624	9.52638	8.11159	6.59053	32
33	23.98856	22.29188	20.76579	18.14765	16.00255	14.23023	11.51389	10.46444	9.56943	8.13535	6.60046	33
34	24.49859	22.72379	21.13184	18.41120	16.19290	14.36814	11.58693	10.51784	9.60858	8.15656	6.60910	34
35	24.99862	23.14516	21.48722	18.66461	16.37419	14.49825	11.65457	10.56682	9.64416	8.17550	6.61661	35
36	25.48884	23.55625	21.83225	18.90828	16.54685	14.62099	11.71719	10.61176	9.67651	8.19241	6.62314	36
37	25.96945	23.95732	22.16724	19.14258	16.71129	14.73678	11.77518	10.65299	9.70592	8.20751	6.62882	37
38	26.44064	24.34860	22.49246	19.36786	16.86786	14.84602	11.82887	10.69482	9.73265	8.22099	6.63375	38
39	26.90259	24.73034	22.80822	19.58448	17.01704	14.94907	11.87858	10.72552	9.75697	8.23303	6.63805	39
40	27.35548	25.10278	23.11477	19.79277	17.15909	15.04630	11.92461	10.75736	9.77905	8.24378	6.64178	40

9

Owners' equity

Owners' equity is the long-term (equity) capital provided by the owners of an enterprise. Unlike long-term debt there is usually no legal requirement that a company either repay the capital contributed by owners or pay them for its use. Owners' equity is made up of two major sources: (1) the permanent capital contributed (provided) by the owners and (2) earnings retained in the enterprise.

In a proprietorship, permanent capital is combined with earnings and withdrawals of the owners in a single owner's equity account called Proprietor's Capital. Capital contributions, withdrawals (drawings), and net income or loss are all entered into the partners' capital accounts.

Corporations, which are legal entities separate from their owners, are required by state law to segregate amounts contributed as capital by their owners (stockholders) from their retained earnings. The state grants the corporation the right to exist and function within broad guidelines, which are spelled out in the corporation's articles of incorporation and bylaws filed with the secretary of state. The state also authorizes the right to issue capital stock. The method by which capital stock may be sold to the public is regulated by both the state and federal (Securities Exchange Commission) governments.

COMMON STOCK

The ownership capital stock of a corporation is called common stock. The common stockholders have voting rights and elect the board of directors of the corporation. The board of directors is responsible for the management of the corporation and hires the corporate officers to run it.

The entry to record the issue of 1,000 shares of common stock for $10,000 is:

```
Cash .......................................... 10,000
    Common Stock (Capital Contributed
        by Common Stockholders) ...................        10,000
    To record the issue of 1,000 shares of common
    stock at $10 per share.
```

Par value

It has been the custom in accounting and law to assign a par value to stock. This par value is indicated in the certificate of incorporation filed with the secretary of state.

Assume that the 1,000 shares of common stock in the preceding example has a par value of $8. The journal entry that recognizes the par value is:

```
Cash .......................................... 10,000
    Common Stock ...............................        8,000
    Paid-in Capital—Excess over
        Par Value .................................        2,000
    To record the issue of 1,000 shares at $8 par value
    stock.
```

If a corporation issues its stock in exchange for assets other than cash or for personal services rendered to the corporation or to settle a corporate liability, the transaction should be recorded on the books at the fair market value of the assets or personal services received or liabilities paid. For example, assume the company issued 2,000 shares of its $8 par value common stock to an inventor for a patent and the fair market value of the patent at the date of issue is estimated to be $20,000. The journal entry is:

Patent	20,000	
Common Stock		16,000
Paid-in Capital—Excess over Par Value		4,000

To record issue of 2,000 shares of $8 par value common stock for patent.

The fair market value of an asset can be determined by an appraisal or the market value (on the stock exchange) of the stock issued in exchange for the asset.[1]

There is no necessary relationship between the par value and the amount received upon issuance of the common stock. The only significance of par value is that it represents the minimum amount that must be legally contributed by the shareholders.

It is common procedure to indicate on the balance sheet the number of shares of stock authorized, as well as the number of shares issued and outstanding, with excess over par value entered in a paid-in capital account.

Common stock—par value $8 per share (authorized 3,000 shares: issued and outstanding 1,000 shares) $8,000
Paid-in capital—excess over par value 2,000

No-par value stock

When some states enacted franchise taxes based on par value, there was a switch to the issuance of no-par (zero) value stock. The logical entry for the issuance of 1,000 shares of no-par value stock for $10,000 should be:

| Cash | 10,000 | |
| Common Stock | | 10,000 |

To record the issue of 1,000 shares of no-par value stock at $10 a share.

In most cases, however, a stated value is arbitrarily assigned to no-par value stock, and the accounting procedure followed is the same as for par value stock.

Underwriting

Corporations often utilize the services of an investment banking firm (underwriter) in selling large issues of stock. The underwriter,

[1] AICPA, *Accounting Principles Board Opinion No. 29,* "Accounting for Nonmonetary Transactions" (New York, September, 1973).

in conjunction with corporate executives, sets the price at which the stock will be sold to the public, deducts an agreed-upon fee for accepting the risk involved in selling the issue and for sales effort, and remits the balance to the issuing corporation on the date of the sale. Essentially the underwriter buys the stock from the corporation and sells it to the public. For more speculative stock issues the underwriter only agrees to use their "best efforts" in selling the issue. The corporation records the stock issue at the amount received from the underwriter. For example, if a stock was issued for $12 a share and the underwriter's fee was $1.50 a share, the corporation would record the issue at $10.50 a share.

PREFERRED STOCK

Preferred stock is another type of capital stock. It does not usually have the ownership rights of the common stock, but it usually has the first claim on dividends and a preference over common stock on liquidation. The exact rights of each type of preferred stock (also common stock) can be obtained only by reading the contract (small print on stock certificate) between the corporation and its stockholders.

Typical rights and terms of preferred stock are:

1. The first right to dividends if they are declared. The amount of the dividend is usually stated on the stock certificate.
2. The cumulative right, which requires that all preferred dividends including those passed in prior years must be paid prior to the declaration of any common stock dividends.
3. Preference over common stockholders in case of liquidation.
4. Many preferred stocks have a call provision. They may be retired at the option of the corporation at a price set in the contract. For example, a $100 par value, cumulative preferred stock paying a $6 annual dividend might be callable at $105.

Other features sometimes found in preferred stocks are:

1. The convertible feature that allows the preferred stockholders to convert their preferred stock to common stock sometime in the future. Convertible preferred stockholders will usually exercise the conversion privilege if the market value of the common stock rises above the conversion price.
2. The participating feature, which allows preferred stockholders some participation in the earnings of the corporation over and above the fixed preferred dividend rate.
3. The redemption feature gives the preferred stockholders the option of having their preferred shares redeemed at certain

prices on certain dates. *SFAS 47,* "Disclosure of Long-Term Obligations," issued by the FASB in March 1981, requires disclosure of all redemption requirements including redemption dates and prices. Redeemable preferred stock with a mandatory redemption requirement has many of the characteristics of debt and is disclosed as a separate (non-shareholders' equity) item on the balance sheet.

In 1981 the Liquid Air Corporation made the following disclosure about its redeemable preferred stock.

> *Note G—Redeemable Preferred Stock*—Redeemable preferred stock is redeemable from and after December 31, 1986, at par plus a 5.5% premium and accumulated dividends. The premium declines each year thereafter by .25% and in any event the Company must redeem any remaining shares on July 1, 2012. The holders of the preferred shares do not have voting rights except in the event of dividend arrearages for four quarters in which case they may appoint two directors. A total of 375,000 common shares are reserved for conversion of the preferred shares.

The corporation will determine, based on an analysis of financial market conditions, which features it needs to include in order to sell a new issue of preferred stock.

Sale of preferred stock

The entry to record the sale of 100 shares of the corporation's $100 par value, $6, cumulative preferred stock at $110 a share is:

```
Cash .............................................. 11,000
      Preferred Stock .............................         10,000
      Preferred Stock—Premium (Excess
      over Par Value) ..............................          1,000
      To record the issuance of 100 shares of the $100
      par value, $6 preferred at $110.
```

Even though the account Paid-in Capital—Excess over Par Value is more descriptive and informative, it has been the custom to use the account Preferred Stock—Premium for preferred issues. If less than par value is received, the account has been called Preferred Stock—Discount.

Any arrearages (passed dividends) on cumulative preferred stock should be disclosed in the footnotes to the financial statements.

Balance sheet format

The balance sheet after issuing 1,000 shares of common stock at $10 per share and 100 shares of the $6 preferred stock is:

Stockholders' (Shareholders') equity

Preferred stockholders' equity:
Preferred stock—$6, cumulative $100
    par value: (authorized 1,000 shares:
    issued and outstanding 100 shares) $10,000
Premium on preferred stock 1,000 $11,000

Common stockholders' equity:
Common stock—par value $8 per share
    (authorized 3,000 shares: issued
    and outstanding 1,000 shares) 8,000
Paid-in capital—excess over par value   2,000   10,000

    Total stockholders' (shareholders')
      equity $21,000

TREASURY STOCK

In order to obtain stock for stock option plans,[2] for employee purchase plans, for purchases of other corporations, and for other corporate purposes, such as increasing earnings per share by reducing the number of shares outstanding, corporations repurchase their own stock. This reacquisition of a company's stock (treasury stock) is a decrease in both the assets (cash) and the stockholders' equity (common stock) of a corporation.

If the corporation purchased 100 shares of its $8 par value stock for $15 (market value at date of purchase) a share, the entry using the cost method would be:

Treasury Stock 1,500
    Cash   1,500
    To record the purchase of 100 shares of the corporation's stock at $15.

Another acceptable method for recording purchases of treasury stock is to record it at par value with any excess over par being prorated to paid-in capital based on an original issue price and retained earnings. This method is rarely used in practice.

The treasury stock has no voting or dividend rights and is not included in the computation of earnings per share. It is the same as unissued stock except that it has been issued once and is being held for ultimate reissue (it is *issued but not outstanding* stock). It is a reduction in stockholders' equity and is not an asset of the corporation.

---

[2] As an incentive, many companies offer key employees options to purchase a specified amount of common stock at specified prices in the future. When the option is exercised, the corporation makes an entry treating it as an issue of common stock at the option price.

The balance sheet presentation would be:

> Common stock—par value $8 per share
> (authorized 3,000 shares: issued
> 1,000 shares of which 100 are in
> the treasury .... $ 8,000
> Paid-in capital—excess over par value 2,000
>
>   10,000
> Less: Common stock held in the treasury
> (at cost, 100 shares) 1,500
>   Total .... $ 8,500

If the treasury stock is reissued at a later date for $16, the entry is:

Cash	1,600	
Treasury Stock		1,500
Paid-in Capital—Treasury Stock		
Transactions		100

To record the sale of 100 shares of treasury stock for $16 a share.

If the treasury stock is reissued at a price less than its purchase price, the difference should be charged to Paid-in Capital—Treasury Stock Transactions if this account exists. If not, the entry should be made to Retained Earnings. In no case should the difference between the cost of the treasury stock and the proceeds on the reissue be recorded on the income statement. The company has not earned income, it has issued common stock.

If the purpose in reacquiring stock is to reduce the total number of shares outstanding, the stock should be formally cancelled and not kept in the treasury. The entry would be:

Common Stock	800	
Paid-in Capital—Excess over Par Value	200	
Retained Earnings	500	
Cash		1,500

To record the purchase at $15 and the retirement of the 100 shares of common stock.

RETAINED EARNINGS

Retained earnings is the portion of stockholders' equity derived from earnings. In its simplest form, it should consist of earnings accumulated since the inception of the company less cash dividends declared (earnings returned to the stockholders). If there have been losses over the years, and liabilities plus capital contributed by stockholders exceed total assets, this account is called Deficit (Negative Retained Earnings). Retained earnings, formerly called earned surplus, is not a tangible item but is part of the stockholders' claim against assets.

CASH DIVIDENDS

Cash dividends represent a distribution to the stockholders. They result in a decrease in stockholders' equity (retained earnings) and a decrease in assets (cash). Many states require that a corporation have retained earnings (earnings in excess of the original investment) in order to declare cash dividends. In addition to retained earnings, a corporation must also have cash in order to pay a cash dividend.

Dividends become a legal liability at the time the board of directors declares the dividend (declaration date). If a dividend of $1 was declared on 20,000 shares of common stock, the entry made on the date of declaration would be:

```
Retained Earnings .............................   20,000
    Dividends Payable ..........................             20,000
    To record declaration of $1 dividend on outstand-
    ing common stock.
```

The declaration states that the dividend will be paid to all stockholders who own the stock on a specific date (record date). The dividend is declared on December 15, 1984, to be paid on January 2, 1985, to stockholders of record on December 28, 1984.

On January 2, 1985, when the dividend is paid, the entry is:

```
Dividends Payable .............................   20,000
    Cash .......................................             20,000
    To record payment of cash dividends declared De-
    cember 15, 1984.
```

Dividends based on capital contributed (common stock plus paid-in capital) rather than retained earnings are called liquidating dividends because they are considered to be a return of the stockholders' investment and not paid out of earnings. Corporations should disclose to their stockholders that the liquidating dividend is being paid "out of capital" and not out of retained earnings so that they are not misled about corporate profitability.

For example, the Wehr Corporation made the following disclosure to its stockholders.

On January 5, 1982 your Board of Directors approved a plan of "Partial Liquidation." The adopted "Plan" calls for the distribution of the proceeds from the sale of the Continental Air Filters Division. The resultant capital distributions are expected to be paid to shareholders during 1982 and 1983.

STOCK DIVIDENDS

A stock dividend (dividend paid in stock) is a pro rata distribution of a corporation's stock to its stockholders. The payment of a stock dividend does not result in a change in corporate assets or in aggregate stockholders' equity. The journal entry required to record stock dividends results in converting a portion of retained earnings into permanent capital.

Assume that the market price of the corporation's common stock is $20 on the date it declares and pays a stock dividend of 5 percent on its 10,000 outstanding shares of $10 par value common stock. The required entry is:

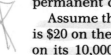

Retained Earnings (500 Shares at $20)	10,000	
Common Stock—Par Value		5,000
Paid-in Capital—Excess over Par Value		5,000

To record a 5% stock dividend.

This entry, which is required by GAAP, formally transfers a portion of earnings retained by the company to permanent capital. To label this transaction a "dividend" is considered by many accountants and analysts to be a deceptive practice.

Shareholders have exactly the same percentage interest in a corporation *after* a stock dividend as they did *before* the stock dividend. In the above example, a shareholder who owned 1,000 shares of stock before the stock dividend had a 10 percent 1,000/10,000, ownership interest in the corporation. After the stock dividend it is still a 10 percent, 1,050/10,500, interest in the corporation. Generally the market price of the stock declines in proportion to the additional shares issued. Stock dividends are not taxable for income tax purposes because they do not represent a distribution of income.

In most cases, companies that issue stock dividends do so because they want to conserve cash and still give the stockholders *something.* They could accomplish the same thing by indicating to investors that it is the policy of the company to reinvest its earnings and not pay cash dividends.

STOCK SPLITS

A stock split is the issuance of additional shares of stock to the current stockholders at no cost. There is no change in assets or in aggregate shareholders' equity. The only change is in the number of shares outstanding.

If a corporation declares a two-for-one split when it has 100,000 common shares ($10 par value) outstanding, it will issue 200,000 new shares of common stock and retire the 100,000 old shares. If it is a par value stock, the par value will usually be changed to accommodate the split. No accounting entry is necessary for a stock split when the par value is changed to accommodate the split because there has been no change in the shareholders' equity. This is inconsistent with the accounting treatment of stock dividends, which are essentially the same as stock splits.

The stockholders have two times as many shares ($5 par value) but the same percentage of ownership after the split as they had before the split. If the company decides to keep the same par value after the split they will have to make a journal entry to increase the Common Stock account to bring it up to the par value.

In our example the entry would be:

Paid-in Capital—Excess over Par Value 1,000,000
    Common Stock (100,000 × $10)   1,000,000
      To record two-for-one stock split.

In cases where the company does not have enough paid-in capital the debit should be to retained earnings. If the market price of the stock before the split was $50, it should be $25 after the split.

Corporations often declare stock splits because they believe they can obtain wider distribution of their stock at a lower market price.

APPROPRIATION OF RETAINED EARNINGS

State laws and business contracts often require the restriction of retained earnings so that it is not available for the declaration of dividends. For example, an agreement with the bondholders requires that $100,000 of retained earnings must be restricted until the bonds are retired.

An entry disclosing this fact could be made as follows:

Retained Earnings 100,000
    Retained Earnings Restricted
    (Appropriated) for Payment
      of Bondholders   100,000
      To record appropriation of retained earnings.

Upon retirement of the bonds an entry would be made to reverse the above entry since the appropriation is no longer necessary.

Retained Earnings Restricted (Appropriated)
  for Payment of Bondholders.................. 100,000
    Retained Earnings 100,000
To return to unappropriated retained earnings
the amount appropriated for retirement of
bonds.

The same disclosure could be obtained by a footnote to the financial statements instead of a journal entry. For example:

The agreement with the bondholders requires that $100,000 of retained earnings must be restricted until the payment of the bonds in 1984. Unrestricted retained earnings available for the payment of dividends amounted to $1 million.

Readers of the financial statements should be aware that this disclosure indicates that retained earnings are restricted as a base for the payment of dividends. It does not indicate that the corporation has adequate cash to retire the bonds.

FINANCIAL DISCLOSURE

There are many and diverse ways of classifying the effects of transactions on the stockholders' equity section. The important consideration in analyzing these financial transactions should be whether they effect permanent capital or earnings.

The balance sheet presentation of the stockholders' equity section should include full disclosure of how all major changes in the stockholders' equity accounts are reflected. This may be done in the body of the statement, in separate schedules, or in the footnotes to the financial statements.

An acceptable balance sheet format for the stockholders' equity section is shown in Illustration 9–1.

In addition to the income statement and balance sheet, the financial statements will also include a statement of the changes in retained earnings for the year. (See Illustration 9–2.)

ILLUSTRATION 9–1

Stockholders' Equity

Preferred stockholders' equity:
  Preferred stock—$6 cumulative $100
    par value (authorized 1,000 shares:
    issued and outstanding 100 shares)
    (Note 1) $10,000
  Premium on preferred stock 1,000
      Total 11,000
Common stockholders' equity:
  Common stock—par value $8 per share
    (authorized 3,000 shares: issued
    1,000 shares of which 100 are in
    the treasury) 8,000
  Paid-in capital—excess over par value 2,000
                                                               10,000
  Retained earnings (Note 2) 25,000
      Total 35,000
  Less: Common stock held in the treasury
    (at cost, 100 shares) 1,500
      Total 33,500
      Total stockholders' equity $44,500

Notes to Financial Statements:

Note 1: The preferred stock may be called at a price of $105 beginning July 1, 1989. There are no preferred dividends in arrears.

Note 2: Under the terms of an agreement with bondholders, $12,000 of the retained earnings is unavailable for dividend declaration, and $1,500 of retained earnings, equal to the cost of the treasury stock, is restricted in accordance with state statues.

ILLUSTRATION 9–2

XYZ CORPORATION
Statement of Retained Earnings
Fiscal Year Ended June 30, 1986

Balance July 1985 .... $1,000,000
  Add: Net income for the fiscal year
    ended June 30, 1986 300,000
                                        1,300,000
  Less: Dividends declared on common
    stock at $2 per share 200,000
Balance June 30, 1986 .... $1,100,000

BOOK VALUE OF A SHARE OF COMMON STOCK

The book value of a share of common stock is calculated by dividing common stockholders' equity by the number of common shares outstanding. If there is any preferred stock outstanding, any portion of the retained earnings that belongs to the preferred stockholders (cumulative preferred dividends in arrears) must be deducted before calculating the book value of common stockholders.

The book value per share of the common stock in Illustration 9–1 is:

$$\frac{\text{Common stockholders' equity}}{\text{Common shares outstanding}} = \frac{\$33,500}{900} = \$37.22$$

MARKET PRICE OF A SHARE OF COMMON STOCK

The market price of a share of common stock is the amount for which it can be sold (usually on a securities exchange) and should be equal to the present value of the company's expected future cash flow to stockholders divided by the number of shares outstanding. Market value may or may not bear a relationship to book value.

EARNINGS PER (COMMON) SHARE

One of the measures most widely used by investors is earnings per share (EPS). Investors relate the earnings per share and the dividends per share to per share market price as part of the process they use in deciding whether to purchase a security.

For companies with simple capital structures the calculation of earnings per share of common stock is:

$$\frac{\text{Net Income} - \text{Preferred Dividends}}{\text{Weighted Average of Common Shares Outstanding}}$$

Assume the following information for the Hudnut Corporation for 1985:

Preferred stock—$8 cumulative $100
  par value (authorized 5,000 shares:
  issued and outstanding 2,000 shares) ... $200,000
Common stock—par value $10 per share
  (authorized 100,000 shares: issued
  and outstanding 80,000 shares*) 800,000
Paid-in capital—excess over par value 160,000
Retained earnings (not including 1985's
  net income) 280,000
Net income—1985 166,000

   * 60,000 of these shares were issued prior to January 1, 1985,
and 20,000 were issued on April 1, 1985.

$$\text{Earnings per common share} = \frac{\$166,000 - \$8(2,000)}{(60,000 \times 1/4) + (80,000 \times 3/4)}$$

$$= \frac{150,000}{75,000}$$

$$= \$2.00$$

The net income of $166,000 less the $16,000 preferred dividend represents the amount earned by the common stockholders.

Weighted average of common shares outstanding

The weighted average of common shares outstanding for the year is 75,000 shares; 60,000 shares for the first three months of the year and 80,000 shares for the period April 1 to December 31, 1985.

In calculating the weighted average of common shares outstanding stock dividends and stock splits should be treated retroactively as if they have always been outstanding.

For example, assume the following facts for the Jones Corporation for 1985.

Net income $220,000
No preferred stock outstanding
Common stock outstanding, January 1, 1985, 100,000 shares
10 percent stock dividend on March 31, 1985
No other issues or retirement of common stock in 1985

$$\text{Earnings per share for 1985} = \frac{\$220,000}{110,000} = \$2.00$$

The 10,000 common shares paid as a dividend are treated as if they were outstanding all year because they represent a pro rata distribution to all the common stockholders. One share of the January 1, 1985, common stock is now 1.1 shares, and $2.20 ($220,000/

100,000) earnings per share on the old stock is equivalent to $2 a share on the new stock.

The calculation of earnings per share becomes more difficult as a firm's capital structure becomes more complex. In the mid-1960s, a wave of business mergers financed by convertible debt or convertible preferred stock focused attention on the EPS computation. In May 1969, the Accounting Principles Board issued *Opinion 15,* which provided guidelines for complex situations and considered the effect of convertible securities on EPS computations. *APB Opinion 15* requires two types of EPS data to be disclosed in the financial statements.

Primary earnings per share

Calculation is based on the weighted average of outstanding common shares and common stock equivalents (CSE). CSEs are those securities that are in substance equivalent to common shares and have the effect of diluting earnings. An example would be convertible bonds that are *likely* to be converted to common stock.

Fully diluted earnings per share

An EPS pro forma (as if) presentation will "reflect the dilution of earnings per share that would have occurred if all contingent issuances of common stock that would individually reduce earnings per share had taken place." For example, a convertible bond that is *not* expected to be converted to common stock is included in the calculation of fully diluted earnings per share but not in the calculation of primary earnings per share.

PROBLEMS AND CASES

 ## 9–1 P. R. Corporation

P. R. CORPORATION
Shareholders' Equity
December 31, 1984

Capital stock:	
Preferred, $6, $100 par value, authorized 350,000 shares, issued 275,000 shares	$27,500,000
Common, par value $10, authorized 2.5 million shares, issued 1.5 million shares	15,000,000
Additional paid-in capital on common stock	900,000
Retained earnings	6,100,000
Total shareholders' equity	$49,500,000

During 1984 the following transactions occurred:

Jan. 1   The P. R. Company sold 100,000 shares of common stock at $14 a share. The proceeds of the stock sale were received in cash.

25   The P. R. Company declared and paid its quarterly cash dividends: $1.50 on the preferred stock and $.10 on the common stock outstanding.

March 15   A 5 percent common stock dividend was declared and distributed to the common stockholders. (Each shareholder received one share for each 20 shares owned.) The market price of the P. R. Company on March 15, 1984, was $14.50.

April 25   The P. R. Company declared and paid its quarterly cash dividend: $1.50 on the preferred stock and $.10 on the common stock outstanding.

May 1   The P. R. Company purchased 5,000 shares of the company's common stock at $15 a share on the American Stock Exchange. This stock was to be held as treasury stock.

31   The P. R. Company purchased and retired 1,000 shares of its preferred stock at $110 per share.

July 25   The P. R. Company declared and paid its quarterly cash dividends: $1.50 on the preferred stock and $.10 on the common stock outstanding.

Aug. 29   The board of directors appropriated $4 million of retained earnings for plant expansion.

Oct. 25   The P. R. Company declared and paid its quarterly cash dividends: $1.50 on the preferred stock and $.10 on the common stock outstanding.

Nov. 18   The common stock was split two for one. The new stock had a par value of $5.

Required:

1.   Prepare journal entries to record each of the above transactions.

2.   Present the shareholders' equity section of the balance sheet as it would appear on December 31, 1984. The net income for the year ended December 31, 1984, was $4 million.

3.   Calculate the book value per share of common stock on December 31, 1984.

4.   Calculate the earnings per share on common stock for the year ended December 31, 1984.

9–2   Rexo Corporation

The shareholders' equity section of Rexo Corporation on December 31, 1984, was:

Shareholders' Equity

Common stock—$5 par value (authorized 7,000,000 shares issued 5,559,500 shares of which 9,500 are in the treasury)	$27,797,500
Paid-in capital	10,960,500
Retained earnings	55,389,500
	94,147,500
Less: Common stock held in the treasury (at cost, 9,500 shares)	153,500
Total shareholders' equity	$93,994,000

Additional information:

a. On March 31, 1985, when the market price of its common stock was $20, Rexo declared and issued a 10 percent stock dividend.

b. For the year ended December 31, 1985, Rexo earned a net income of $5,000,000 and declared and paid cash dividends of $2,390,585.

c. On December 31, 1985, Rexo declared and issued a two-for-one stock split. Rexo changed the par value of the new common stock to $2.50.

Required:

1. Make the journal entry to record the stock dividend.

2. Make the journal entry to record the cash dividends.

3. Make the journal entry to record the stock split.

4. Calculate book value per share on December 31, 1985.

5. Calculate earnings per share for the year ended December 31, 1985.

9–3 General Electric

The stockholders' equity section of the General Electric Corporation on December 31, 1981, and 1980 is shown below:

	$ Millions	
	1981	1980
Common stock ($2.50 par value; 251,500,000 shares authorized; 231,463,949 shares issued 1981 and 1980)	$ 579	$ 579
Amounts received for stock in excess of par value	657	659
Retained earnings	8,088	7,151
	9,324	8,389
Deduct common stock held in treasury (at cost)*	(196)	(189)
Total shareowners' equity	$9,128	$8,200

* 3,703,000 shares on 12/31/81 and 3,699,000 shares on 12/31/80.

Required:

1. Calculate the book value per share of General Electric's common stock on December 31, 1981, and December 31, 1980.

2. General Electric suffered a $2 million loss on their 1981 disposition of treasury stock. This $2 million loss on the treasury stock, which cost $169 million, was charged (debited) to Amount Received for Stock in Excess of Par Value.

a. Why didn't GE consider the loss on disposition of treasury stock to be an expense on the income statement?

b. Make the journal entry to record General Electric's *purchases* of treasury stock in 1981.

3. What accounted for the increase in General Electric's book value from December 31, 1980, to December 31, 1981?

4. Explain why General Electric's book value per share on December 31, 1981, is so much lower than its market price range (53⅛ to 60 per share) for the fourth quarter of 1981.

5. Where does General Electric's $8,088 million in retained earnings come from? Is it cash? If not, what and where is it?

9–4   Zero Corporation

The Zero Corporation designs and manufactures a wide variety of specialized enclosures, cooling equipment, and other metal and plastic products, primarily for the electronics industry.

Their consolidated shareholders' equity section for the year ended March 31, 1982, is listed below:

	Outstanding shares	Common stock*	Additional paid-in capital	Retained earnings	Total
Balance at March 31, 1981	2,959,309	$2,959,000	$ 6,319,000	$19,291,000	$28,569,000
Five-for-four stock split (including $40,000 in cash paid in lieu of fractional shares)	750,372	750,000	(750,000)	(40,000)	(40,000)
Net income for the year				7,431,000	7,431,000
Cash dividends declared—$.46 per share				(1,729,000)	(1,729,000)
Sale of common stock	250,000	250,000	4,888,000		5,138,000
Exercise of stock options	49,514	50,000	370,000		420,000
Balance at March 31, 1982	4,009,195	$4,009,000	$10,827,000	$24,953,000	$39,789,000

* Rounded to the nearest $000. Par value is $1.

Required:

1. Make the journal entry to record the five-for-four stock split. Why do you think this entry is at the par value of $1 instead of Zero's market price of approximately $25 on the date the stock split was declared? What's the difference between a five-for-four stock split and a 25 percent stock dividend?

2. Make the journal entry to record the declaration of the cash dividends.

3. Make the journal entry to record the sale of common stock.

4. Make the journal entry to record the exercising of the stock options.

9–5 Flower Industries, Inc.

The following schedule and footnote appeared in the annual report of Flower Industries, a specialty foods company producing baked foods, snack foods, and frozen convenience foods.

FLOWER INDUSTRIES, INC.
Consolidated Statement of Changes in Common Stockholders' Equity
(Amounts in Thousands except Number of Shares)

	Common Stock				Treasury Stock	
	Number of shares	Par value	Capital in excess of par value	Retained earnings	Number of shares	Cost
Balances at June 30, 1979	6,245,061	3,903	10,465	47,300	250,690	1,682
Purchases of treasury stock					41,383	435
Exercise of employee stock options				(166)	(61,513)	(442)
Net income for the year				10,247		
Dividends paid:						
$3.00 per Class A preferred share				(28)		
$4.00 per Class B preferred share				(44)		
$5.50 per Class E preferred share				(101)		
$.47 per common share ($.625 par value)				(2,823)		
Balances at June 28, 1980	6,245,061	3,903	10,465	54,385	230,560	1,675

Convertible Subordinated Notes: The convertible subordinated notes due December 8, 1992, bear interest at 6.5% per annum. The notes are payable in annual instalments of $575,000 commencing December 8, 1980, and are convertible at the option of the holders at any time into shares of common stock at a conversion price of $10. Subject to this conversion right, the Company has the right to prepay all or part of the notes prior to scheduled maturity and has the right of first refusal to purchase any of the notes or common stock previously issued upon conversion. In August 1980, the holders exercised their right of conversion of $575,000 of the notes and acquired 57,500 shares of the Company's common stock.

Required:

1. Make journal entries to record the following transactions for the fiscal year ended June 28, 1980:

a. The declaration and payment of the preferred and common dividends.

b. The purchase of treasury stock.

c. The exercising of employee stock options (employees pay the company the option price of the stock at the date the option is granted).

2. Make the journal entry to record the conversion of the $575,000 of convertible subordinated notes in August 1980. Do you think the market price of Flower's common stock was higher or lower than $10 in August 1980?

9–6 The case of disguised debt

A number of companies have recently issued a preferred stock which must be repurchased by the company within a stated time period. The companies are often required to make annual (sinking fund) deposits with a trustee to ensure that they have adequate cash to redeem the preferred stock. This redeemable preferred stock also provides for a stated dividend to be paid periodically. Many companies have utilized this type of stock instead of cash in connection with the buyout of all of the shares of another corporation.

The Securities and Exchange Commission (SEC), the federal regulatory body that prescribes certain reporting conventions for public companies, recently proposed to change the rules governing how such redeemable preferred stock is presented on financial statements "to give a better picture of the capital structure of companies." Specifically, the proposal would require companies to classify all stock into three categories:

a. Preferred shares that must be redeemed.

b. Preferred shares that can't or may be redeemed at the option of the company.

c. Common stock.

Required:

1. What is the rationale underlying the SEC proposal?

2. Do you agree with the proposal?

3. Are there steps that should be taken beyond merely restating the equity section of the balance sheet to further reflect the different nature of this type of preferred stock?

9-7 Purcell, Inc.

Purcell, Inc., planned to add to its existing manufacturing capacity. Its proposed expansion will require $8 million of new long-term capital. The creation of the additional manufacturing capacity would increase pretax net income (before deducting additional interest in the event bonds are issued) to $3.9 million from its present annual level of $2.1 million.

The funds needed could be obtained by issuing 20-year bonds at par with a coupon rate of 10 percent or by issuing common stock at its current market price of $10. The company's relevant balance sheet information is:

Long-term debt	–0–
Common stock, authorized 2.5 million shares, issued and outstanding— 1 million shares, $5 par value	$5,000,000
Additional paid-in capital	1,200,000
Retained earnings	2,300,000

Required:

1. Calculate the net income per share if the funds to expand manufacturing capacity are obtained by issuing the long-term bonds. Assume a tax rate of 46 percent.

2. Calculate the net income per share if these funds are obtained by issuing common stock.

3. Which type of financing should present short-term creditors favor? Why?

4. Which type of financing should present common stockholders favor? Why?

10

Intercorporate investments and business combinations

Many corporations try to increase their profitability by investing in the common stock of other corporations. These investments can be either short-term or long-term in nature depending on the intention of corporate management at the time they make the investment.

A corporation's short-term or temporary investment objective is to earn a return on cash not immediately needed for current operations.

A corporation's long-term investment objective depends on whether they are a passive or active investor.

Passive, noncontrol investors are interested in obtaining dividends and selling the common stock at a profit. The amount of stock acquired is usually not large enough to enable the investor to have a significant influence over the affairs of the investee corporation.

Active investors are interested in obtaining control over another corporation in order to increase the efficiency of their present operations (purchasing another company in the same line of business), to gain access to raw material sources, distribution services, or markets (purchasing a company that increases their control of vertical operations from the raw material to the sale of the product), or to diversify risk (purchasing a company in a different business).

When one corporation purchases all or part of the common stock of another corporation it raises the accounting issue of what is the most appropriate method to disclose the implications of this investment on the financial statements. If the intention of the corporation is to invest excess cash on a temporary basis, the investment will be recorded as a marketable security in the current asset section of the balance sheet. If it is a long-term investment, the method of recording it will depend primarily on the percentage of ownership acquired and the relationship between the acquiring (investor, parent) corporation and the acquired (investee, subsidiary) corporation.

Customarily the *cost method* is used for recording long-term investments when the ownership interest is less than 20 percent and the *equity method* when the ownership interest is 20 to 50 percent. The *consolidation method,* which results in the preparation of *consolidated annual statements,* is generally required when there is an ownership interest greater than 50 percent.

COST METHOD

Generally accepted accounting principles presume that a less than 20 percent ownership interest is not adequate to significantly influence the operating and financial policies of another corporation.

A corporation that has a long-term investment of less than 20 percent of another corporation's common stock is considered a passive, noncontrol investor and uses the cost method to record the investment. The investment is recorded at cost, and dividends are recognized as revenue when they are declared.

On January 1, 1984, the Vegetable Corporation purchases 8,000 of the Carrot Corporation's 80,000 outstanding common shares at $10 per share.

The journal entry on Vegetable Corporation's books is:

Investment (in Carrot Corporation) 80,000
    Cash 80,000
    To record purchase of 8,000 shares of Carrot Corporation.

No journal entry is necessary on Carrot's books as the only thing that has changed for them is the name of the stockholders, not the number of shares outstanding.

Carrot's net income for 1984 is $52,000, and on December 31, 1984, they declare an annual cash dividend of 12 cents per share.

Under the cost method Vegetable will recognize revenue in 1984 equal to their pro rata share of Carrot's *dividend.*

The entry on Vegetable Corporation's books is:

```
Dividends Receivable .................................  960
    Dividend Income (Revenue) .......................        960
    To record as income the dividend ($.12 × 8,000 shares)
    declared by Carrot Corporation.
```

On February 14, 1985, when the dividend is paid the entry is:

```
Cash ..................................................  960
    Dividend Receivable ..............................        960
    To record receipt of a dividend from Carrot Corporation.
```

The common stock of all investee corporations listed on a national securities exchange (marketable equity security) must be reported on the balance sheet at the lower of cost or market on a portfolio basis.

The accounting for noncurrent marketable equity securities is exactly the same as for current marketable equity securities (see Chapter 5) except that the unrealized loss or gain on noncurrent marketable equity securities account is not treated as a deduction or increase in current net income but is reflected in the stockholders' equity section of the balance sheet in the same manner as treasury stock. An example for a hypothetical company is shown below:

Stockholders' equity:	
Common stock	$ 500,000
Paid-in capital	250,000
Retained earnings	250,000
Total	1,000,000
Less: Unrealized loss on noncurrent	
marketable equity securities	82,000
Total stockholders' equity	$ 918,000

EQUITY METHOD

A company that owns 20 to 50 percent of another company's common stock is presumed to have the ability to exercise significant influence over that company's operating and financial policies.[1]

---

[1] AICPA, *Accounting Principles Board Opinion No. 19,* "The Equity Method of Accounting for Investments in Common Stock" (New York, March 1971).

The equity method assumes that the investor corporation has significant influence over the financial operations of the investee corporation and requires the investor corporation to accrue its pro rata share of the investee corporation's net income in the accounting period in which it is earned. If significant influence exists with less than 20 percent ownership, the investor corporation should use the equity method in preference to the cost method. If the investor corporation can prove that it does not have significant influence over the investee corporation, even though it owns more than 20 percent, it may use the cost method.

On January 1, 1984, Orange Corporation purchases 40 percent (20,000 shares) of Green Corporation's common stock for $200,000. The entry in Orange Corporation's books is:

Investment in Unconsolidated Affiliate 200,000
   Cash 200,000
   To record purchase of 20,000 shares of Green
   Corporation.

Green Corporation's net income for the year ended December 31, 1984, is $25,000.

The entry on Orange Corporation's books to accrue their 40 percent share of the net income is:

Investment in Unconsolidated Affiliate 10,000
   Equity in Net Earnings of Unconsolidated
    Affiliates* 10,000
   To record as income for the year ended December
   31, 1984, our share (40%) of Green Corporation's
   net income.

* This entry assumes that Green's book value was $500,000 (40% of $500,000 = $200,000) on the date Orange purchased the 20,000 shares of common stock. If the investor's purchase price is higher than the investee's book value, the difference is depreciated (difference attributable to excess of fair value over book value of fixed assets) and/or amortized (difference attributable to excess of purchase price over net assets at fair value) and charged to equity in net earnings of unconsolidated affiliate. The equity method also requires an adjustment to current year's earnings and the investment account for any intercompany transactions between Orange and Green.

On January 31, 1985, Green Corporation declares a dividend of $10,000. Orange makes the following entry.

Dividend Receivable 4,000
   Investment in Unconsolidated Affiliate 4,000
   To record declaration of dividend by Green Corporation.

The Orange Corporation reduces its investment account because the dividend represents a return of a portion of its investment.

On March 10, 1985, when the dividend is paid:

Cash 4,000
     Dividend Receivable   4,000
To record receipt of dividend from Green Corporation.

The equity method journal entries, which are based on the investor corporation having significant influence on the investee's financial policies, are in accordance with the accrual method of accounting. They record the income on the investor corporation's books in the accounting period in which the income is earned by the investee corporation.

The general ledger accounts in Orange's books for its 40 percent investment in Green would appear as follows:

Investment in Unconsolidated Affiliate				Equity in Net Earnings of Unconsolidated Affiliates	
(a)	200,000	(c)	4,000	(b)	10,000
(b)	10,000				

Cash			
(d)	4,000	(a)	200,000

Dividend Receivable			
(c)	4,000	(d)	4,000

The Equity in Net Earnings of Unconsolidated Affiliates is often classified on the income statement as other income.

Burndy Corporations' 1981 consolidated statement of earnings (page 230) reflects this treatment.

Readers of financial statements should understand that although the equity in net earnings of unconsolidated affiliates increases net earnings, it does not increase working capital or cash flow from operations. The investor company's cash flow is only increased by the amount of cash dividends it is paid by the investee corporation.

Burndy Corporation's 1981 calculation of working capital from operations on their statement of changes in financial position (the subject of Chapter 11) illustrates this adjustment.

Investment in Unconsolidated Affiliates is classified as a noncurrent asset on the balance sheet of the investor. The account will always reflect the cost of the investment plus (minus if a deficit) the investor corporation's pro rata share of the investee corpora-

BURNDY CORPORATION AND SUBSIDIARY COMPANIES
Consolidated Statement of Earnings
(Dollars in thousands except per share data)
Year Ended December 31, 1981

Net sales	$256,764
Cost of sales	150,393
Gross income	106,371
Selling, general, and administrative expenses	60,654
Operating income	45,717
Interest expense—net	(3,515)
Nonrecurring gain on sale of assets	11,895
Earnings before income taxes and equity in net earnings of unconsolidated affiliates	54,097
Income taxes	24,008
Earnings before equity in net earnings of unconsolidated affiliates	30,089
Equity in net earnings of unconsolidated affiliates	2,750
Net earnings	$ 32,839
Net earnings per share	$ 2.64

Statement of Changes in Financial Position

Sources of Working Capital:
Operations:

Net earnings	$32,839
Items not requiring an outlay of working capital:	
Depreciation and amortization of property, plant and equipment	9,444
Other amortization	487
Deferred income taxes	(147)
Deferred retirement	194
Gain on sale of assets	(8,140)
Equity in net earnings of unconsolidated affiliates	(2,750)
Working capital provided from operations	31,927

tion's retained earnings since the date of acquisition, adjusted, if necessary, for profits on intercompany transactions and amortization or depreciation on the excess investment cost over investee's book value.

CONSOLIDATION METHOD

If a corporation owns more than 50 percent of the common stock of any other corporation(s) it will ordinarily use the *consolidation method.*

This method requires that the financial statements be prepared as if the parent (investor) corporation and the subsidiary (investee) corporation(s) were a single economic entity. It disregards the fact that each of the corporations in this group affiliated through common ownership is a separate legal entity and prepares its own financial statements. The parent corporation reports the investment in the subsidiary on *its* financial statements using the equity method.

Generally accepted accounting principles assume that consolidated financial statements provide better disclosure of the operations controlled by the parent corporation than separate financial statements prepared for each corporation.

The parent corporation is not required to use the consolidation method if it does not provide better disclosure even if the parent owns more than 50 percent of the subsidiary. Foreign subsidiaries and domestic subsidiaries operating under the Federal Bankruptcy Act or under a consent decree of the Federal Trade Commission (legal restrictions) are often not consolidated for these reasons. Consolidation is also not required where the asset and liability structure of the subsidiary is significantly different in nature from that of the parent. An example would be a finance corporation that is a subsidiary of a manufacturing corporation. In all of these cases, where the subsidiary is not consolidated, the parent corporation will report its investment using the equity method.

PREPARATION OF CONSOLIDATED FINANCIAL STATEMENTS

The consolidation process consists of combining the general ledger accounts of the parent and all the consolidated subsidiaries, eliminating intercompany accounts and transactions, recording the difference between the purchase price paid for a subsidiary and its book value at date of purchase, indicating the minority (less than 50 percent) interest of the stockholders in the subsidiary corporations, and making all other necessary adjustments in order to prepare a consolidated balance sheet, consolidated income statement, and consolidated statement of changes in financial position.

The consolidation elimination and adjusting entries are only recorded on the worksheets used to prepare consolidated financial statements. They are not recorded on the books and records of the affiliated companies, which are separate accounting and legal entities.

CONSOLIDATED BALANCE SHEET

In order to illustrate the procedure for preparing a consolidated balance sheet let us assume that Orange Corporation purchased

ILLUSTRATION 10–1

ORANGE CORPORATION
Worksheet—Consolidated Balance Sheet
December 31, 1985

Accounts	Individual Company Statements		Combined Balance Sheet	Eliminations		Consolidated Balance Sheet
	Orange	Red		Debit	Credit	
Cash	100	20	120			120
Accounts receivable	54	35	89		(1) 10	79
Notes receivable	40	—	40		(2) 40	—
Inventory	100	85	185			185
Investment in Green Corporation	206	—	206			206
Investment in Red Corporation	100	—	100		(3) 100	—
Fixed assets (net of accumulated depreciation)	300	90	390			390
	900	230	1,130			980
Accounts payable	50	45	95	(1) 10		85
Notes payable	—	40	40	(2) 40		—
Other current liabilities	40	10	50			50
Long-term liabilities	110	35	145			145
Common stock	300	70	370	(3) 70		300
Retained earnings	400	30	430	(3) 30		400
	900	230	1,130	150	150	980

all the common stock of the Red Corporation on December 31, 1985, for $100.

The procedure for preparing a consolidated balance sheet on December 31, 1985, would be as follows:

A. List the balance sheet accounts of each company on a worksheet and combine them. (See Illustration 10–1.)

B. Eliminate intercompany accounts and transactions.

1. Our analysis reveals that on December 31, 1985, Red Corporation owes Orange Corporation $10 for merchandise it purchased on credit. The appropriate elimination on the consolidated worksheet is:

    Accounts Payable (Red Corporation) 10
        Accounts Receivable (Orange Corporation)   10
    To eliminate intercompany account.

The result of this elimination is to reduce the combined accounts receivable of $89 to $79, the amount the *consolidated entity* is owed by customers. The consolidated accounts payable are reduced from the combined total of $95 to $85, the amount owed to outside creditors.

2. The note receivable represents a loan by Orange Corporation to Red Corporation. The appropriate elimination entry is:

    Notes Payable (Red Corporation).......................... 40
        Notes Receivable (Orange Corporation)   40
    To eliminate intercompany loan.

The consolidated balance sheet will not reflect this note as it is an intercompany item. The *consolidated entity* has neither a note receivable nor a note payable.

C. Eliminate parent corporation's investment in the subsidiary corporation and allocate excess of purchase price over book value to fixed assets and goodwill.

    Common Stock (Red Corporation) 70
    Retained Earnings (Red Corporation) 30
        Investment in Red Corporation
            (Orange Corporation)   100
    To eliminate investment in Red Corporation.

The impact of this entry, which assumes that the fair market value of Red's net assets equals their book value, is the same as if the subsidiary corporation were *merged* into the parent corporation and no longer existed as a separate entity.

Suppose the parent company pays more for the subsidiary company than its book value. How should this excess of purchase price over book value be classified on the consolidated balance sheet? Generally accepted accounting principles require that the acquiring corporation *first* allocate any excess of fair value of assets over book value to identifiable assets and then assign any remaining balance to Goodwill (Excess of Purchase Price over Fair Value of Net Assets).[2]

---

[2] AICPA, *Accounting Principles Board Opinion No. 16,* "Business Combinations" (New York, August 1970).

If a parent company purchases the net assets of a subsidiary company for less than fair market value (bargain purchase or because the expected future earnings justify a lower price), GAAP requires that the assets be reduced to the amount actually paid for them. Any residual amount, after the noncurrent assets are written down to zero, is recorded as *negative goodwill* (excess of fair value of net assets over purchase price).

Assume that Orange Corporation paid $125 instead of $100 for Red Corporation's common stock on December 31, 1985. This is $25 more than Red's net assets or book value of $100 (assets of $230 minus liabilities of $130) on December 31, 1985.

The entry on *Orange's books* on December 31, 1985 is:

Investment in Red Corporation 125
   Cash 125
  To record purchase of all the common stock of Red Corporation.

The entry that is made for consolidated statement purposes will have to allocate this $25 to a consolidated balance sheet account when the $125 investment in Red Corporation is eliminated.

Assume that an appraisal indicates that the fixed assets of Red Corporation have a fair value of $105 ($15 more than their book value of $90) and the market value of Red's other assets are approximately equal to their book value.

The journal entry to be made in preparation of the consolidated balance sheet on December 31, 1985, is:

Fixed Assets 15
Excess of Purchase Price over Fair
   Value of Net Assets (Goodwill) 10
Common Stock (Red Corporation) 70
Retained Earnings (Red Corporation) 30
   Investment in Red Corporation
     (Orange Corporation) 125
  To eliminate investment in Red Corporation.

The $15 increase in fixed assets appears *on the consolidated balance sheet,* and the depreciation expense relating to it is recorded *on the consolidated income statement.* The $10 excess of purchasing price over fair value of net assets is recorded on the consolidated balance sheet and is amortized over a period that should not exceed 40 years.[3]

---

[3] AICPA, *Accounting Principles Board Opinion No. 17,* "Intangible Assets" (New York, August 1970).

No adjustment is made to consolidate the Green Corporation as Orange Corporation owns 40 percent of the common stock of the Green Corporation and reports it on the *consolidated balance sheet* using the equity method.

D. Record the Minority Interest in Consolidated Subsidiary.

Suppose the parent company purchases less than 100 percent ownership in the subsidiary company. How should the minority ownership in the subsidiary company be treated on the consolidated balance sheet?

The objective of consolidated financial statements is to report on all activities *controlled* by the parent corporation. Assets and liabilities of subsidiaries are combined, after eliminating intercompany accounts, as if they were 100 percent owned by the parent corporation, and the minority ownership interest in the subsidiary is treated as a claim against the consolidated entity.

Assume now that Orange Corporation pays $100 for 80 percent of the outstanding common stock of the Red Corporation on December 31, 1985.

The elimination entry for Orange's 80 percent investment in Red would be:

Common Stock (80% × $70) 56
Retained Earnings (80% × $30).......................... 24
Goodwill* 20
    Investment in Red Corporation 100
    To eliminate investment in Red Corporation.

    * This entry assumes that the $20 excess of purchase price over book value [$100 − .80 ($230 − $130)] could not be allocated to any identifiable tangible assets and is allocated to goodwill.

Orange's consolidated balance sheet must now reflect the fact that 20 percent of Red is owned by outsiders (the minority stockholders of Red who are not part of the consolidated entity).

The journal entry to reflect the minority interest is:

Common Stock (Red Corporation) 14
Retained Earnings (Red Corporation) 6
    Minority Interest in Consolidated Subsidiary 20
    To record the minority interest in Red Corporation.

The effect of this entry is to show that minority stockholders have a claim of $20 against the consolidated entity.

Since there is a disagreement as to whether it should be considered a liability or equity account, the account, Minority Interest

---

ILLUSTRATION 10–2

ORANGE CORPORATION
Worksheet—Consolidated Balance Sheet
December 31, 1985

Accounts	Orange	Red	Combined Balance Sheet	Debit	Credit	Consolidated Balance Sheet
Cash	100	20	120			120
Accounts receivable	54	35	89		(1) 10	79
Notes receivable	40	—	40		(2) 40	—
Inventory	100	85	185			185
Investment in Green Corporation	206	—	206			206
Investment in Red Corporation	100	—	100		(4) 100	—
Goodwill				(4) 20		20
Fixed assets (net of accumulated depreciation)	300	90	390			390
	900	230	1,130			1,000
Accounts payable	50	45	95	(1) 10		85
Notes payable	—	40	40	(2) 40		—
Other current liabilities	40	10	50			50
Long-term liabilities	110	35	145			145
Minority interest					(3) 20	20
Common stock	300	70	370	(3) 14 (4) 56		300
Retained earnings	400	30	430	(3) 6 (4) 24		400
	900	230	1,130	170	170	1,000

in Consolidated Subsidiary, is usually classified on the consolidated balance sheet between the liability and equity sections.

The consolidated worksheet and consolidated balance sheet for the Orange Corporation on December 31, 1985, assuming they acquired 80 percent of the common stock of Red Corporation for $100 on December 31, 1985, are shown in Illustration 10–2 and Illustration 10–3.

CONSOLIDATED INCOME STATEMENT

The preparation of the consolidated income statement requires combining the income statement accounts of the parent and subsidiaries, eliminating all intercompany accounts and transactions,

ILLUSTRATION 10–3

ORANGE CORPORATION
Consolidated Balance Sheet
December 31, 1985

Assets

Current assets:
Cash	$ 120
Accounts receivable	79
Inventory	185
Total current assets	384
Investment in nonconsolidated affiliate	206
Fixed assets (net of accumulated depreciation)	390
Other assets:	
Excess of purchase price over fair value of net assets	20
Total assets	$1,000

Liabilities and Stockholders' Equity

Current liabilities:
Accounts payable	$ 85
Other current liabilities	50
Total current liabilities	135
Long-term liabilities	145
Total liabilities	280
Minority interest in consolidated subsidiary	20
Stockholders' equity:	
Common stock	300
Retained earnings	400
Total stockholders' equity	700
Total liabilities and stockholders' equity	$1,000

recording any additional depreciation on the adjustment of assets to fair value, and amortizing goodwill and adjusting the net income of the subsidiaries to reflect the minority stockholders interest.

In order to illustrate the method for preparing a consolidated income statement, assume that Orange Corporation purchased 80 percent of the common stock of Red Corporation for $100 on *December 31, 1985.*

The procedure for preparing Orange's consolidated income statement for *1986* would be as follows:[4]

---

[4] In practice both the consolidated income statement and consolidated balance sheet would be prepared at the same time. In our example we illustrate only the portion of the worksheet used to prepare Orange's consolidated income statement for 1986. The worksheet for Orange's 1985 balance sheet was shown earlier in this chapter.

ILLUSTRATION 10–4

ORANGE CORPORATION
Worksheet—Consolidated Statement of Income
For the Year Ended December 31, 1986

	Individual Company Statements		Combined Income Statements	Adjustments and Eliminations		Consolidated Statement of Income
	Orange	Red		Debit	Credit	
Sales	1,300	600	1,900	(1) 350		1,550
Cost of sales	700	355	1,055		(1) 350	705
Gross margin	600	245	845			845
Selling and administrative expenses	266	185	451			451
Amortization of goodwill				(3) 1		1
Interest expense	11	10	21		(2) 3	18
Interest income	3		3	(2) 3		
Equity in income of Green Corporation	22		22			22
Equity in income of Red Corporation	20		20	(4) 20		
Minority interest in Red Corporation's net income				(5) 5		5
Net income before income taxes	368	50	418			392
Income taxes	163	25	188			188
Net income	205	25	230			204

List the income statement accounts of both companies and combine them. See Illustration 10–4.

1. Eliminate intercompany sales and cost of sales.

Orange sold merchandise which cost it $175 to Red for $350. Red sold this same merchandise to its customers for $750.

The consolidated entity should report sales (to Red's customers) of $750 and cost of sales (Orange's cost) of $175.

The elimination entry is:

Sales (Orange Corporation) 350
    Cost of Sales (Red
        Corporation) 350
  To eliminate intercompany sales.

If Red had not sold all the inventory it purchased from Orange as of the balance sheet date, an adjusting entry to eliminate the intercompany profit in inventory would be made.

2. Eliminate intercompany interest.

Orange's $3 interest income and $3 of Red's interest expense relate to Red's $30 note payable to Orange.

Interest Income (Orange) 3
    Interest Expense (Red)   3
    To eliminate intercompany interest.

As a result of the above entry the consolidated income statement will only reflect the $18 interest expense to outsiders.

3. Amortize goodwill.

The $20 excess of purchase price over book value paid by Orange for 80 percent of Red's common stock is all assumed to be allocated to goodwill. Orange has chosen to amortize the goodwill over a 20-year period.

Amortization of Goodwill 1
    Goodwill   1
    To record amortization of goodwill on purchase of Red Corporation's common stock over a 20-year period.

4. Eliminate equity in income of Red Corporation account.

Orange Corporation records their investment in Red Corporation on its books using the equity method.

On December 31, 1986, Orange would have made the following entry on their book to accrue their pro rata share of Red's 1986 earnings.

Investment in Red Corporation 20
    Equity in Income of Red
        Corporation   20
    To accrue pro rata share of Red's income for 1986 (80% of $25).

For consolidated statement purposes the entry is:

Equity in Income of Red Corporation 20
    Investment in Red Corporation   20
    To eliminate Orange's share of Red's earnings recorded using the equity method.

ILLUSTRATION 10–5

ORANGE CORPORATION
Consolidated Statement of Income
For the Year Ended December 31, 1986

Sales	$1,550
Cost of sales	705
Gross margin	845
Expenses:	
Selling and administrative expenses	451
Amortization of goodwill	1
Interest expense	18
Total expenses	470
	375
Other income:	
Equity in unconsolidated affiliate	
(Green Corporation)	22
	397
Income tax	188
	209
Less: Minority interest in consolidated subsidiary's earnings	5
Net income	$ 204

Because Red's sales and expenses are included in the consolidated income statement, its net income would be double-counted if this entry was not made.

5. To record the minority stockholders' (Red Corporation) interest in net income for 1986.

Minority Interest in Red
   Corporation's Net Income 5
    Minority Interest in
      Subsidiary Corporation 5
To record the expense for the minority interest in 1986 income.

Only $20, 80 percent of Red Corporation's net income of $25, belongs to the consolidated company. The remaining $5, 20 percent, belongs to the minority stockholders of the Red Corporation and reduces the income of the consolidated entity.

The consolidated income statement for Orange Corporation for 1986 which is prepared from the consolidated worksheet is shown in Illustration 10–5.

CONSOLIDATED STATEMENT OF CHANGES IN FINANCIAL POSITION

Amortization of goodwill and minority interest in consolidated subsidiary's earnings are accounts that reduce net income but don't consume cash or working capital. The offsetting credits are to the nonworking capital accounts, Goodwill and Minority Interest in Subsidiary Corporation. The balances in these accounts would have to be added back to net income to determine working capital or cash flow from operations using the method that adjusts net income to cash flow or working capital from operations (see Chapter 11).

A consolidated statement of changes in financial position can be prepared from the consolidated balance sheets and consolidated income statement using the techniques described in Chapter 11.

Disclosure of principles of consolidation

The notes to the consolidated financial statements will disclose the details of the parent corporation's consolidation policy.

In the summary of significant accounting policies section of their 1981 annual report General Electric made the following disclosure:

BASIS OF CONSOLIDATION

The financial statements consolidate the accounts of the parent General Electric Company and those of all majority-owned and controlled companies ("affiliated companies"), except finance companies whose operations are not similar to those of the consolidated group. All significant transactions among the parent and affiliated companies are eliminated from the consolidated statements.

The nonconsolidated finance companies are included in the statement of financial position under investments and are valued at equity plus advances. In addition, companies in which GE and/or its consolidated affiliates own 20% or 50% of the voting stock ("associated companies") are included under investments, valued at the appropriate share of equity plus advances. After tax-earnings of nonconsolidated finance companies and associated companies are included in the statement of earnings under other income.

A nonconsolidated uranium mining company (see note 11) is also included under investments and is valued at lower of cost or equity, plus advances.

Summary

Consolidated financial statements are prepared for *economic* rather than *legal* entities and do not purport to show the financial results of any of the individual corporations (legal entities) in the consolidated group. Present and potential creditors of the parent and subsidiary corporations have an interest in their liquidity and profitability, not that of the consolidated entity (unless the parent is guaranteeing the subsidiary's debts). Similarly, investors (minority stockholders) in a subsidiary corporation look to its earnings and cash flows as a source of potential dividends.

To be well informed, the reader of the consolidated financial statements should also consult the financial statements of each individual corporation in the consolidated group.

BUSINESS COMBINATIONS

Accounting Principles Board Opinion 16, "Business Combinations," states:

> A business combination occurs when a corporation and one or more incorporated or unincorporated businesses are brought together into one accounting entity. The single entity carries on the activities of the previously separate, independent enterprises.

If one company *acquires* the assets or voting common stock of another company, the business combination is a purchase.

If there is *no acquisition* but a merger of common interests with only the voting common stock of one company being exchanged for at least 90 percent of the voting common stock of another company and the transaction meets all of the other criteria listed in *APB Opinion 16,* the business combination is called a *a pooling of interests.*

Purchase method

The purchase method, which was used in Orange Corporation's acquisition of Red Corporation, records the acquisition at its cost to the acquiring corporation. Any excess of cost over the book value of the net assets of the acquired company is first assigned to the assets (fair value) purchased and then to goodwill. The earnings of the two companies are combined commencing with the date of acquisition.

Pooling of interests method

The pooling of interests method assumes that the two corporations who have exchanged their common stock have combined (pooled their resources) into *one continuing entity* and that no purchase (acquisition) of one corporation by the other has taken place.

In that the pooling of interests method assumes continuing ownership, there is no revaluation of assets and equities as there is in the purchase method. The book values of the assets and equities of the two corporations are added together and become the balance sheet of the continuing entity. The earnings of the two corporations are combined commencing with the first day of the year in which the exchange of stock takes place. For example, if two corporations, both of whom report on a calendar year basis, exchange their common stock on November 1, 1984, and the exchange qualifies as a pooling of interests, they will combine their earnings as if they had been together on January 1, 1984.

To illustrate the difference in the consolidated financial statements using the purchase and pooling of interests methods, assume the following balance sheets for the Jeanne Corporation (Illustration 10–6) and Marie Corporation (Illustration 10–7).

ILLUSTRATION 10–6

JEANNE CORPORATION
Balance Sheet
December 31, 1984

Assets

Current assets	$ 5,000
Fixed assets (net of accumulated depreciation)	7,900
Total assets	$12,900

Equities

Current liabilities	$ 2,900
Stockholders' equity:	
Common stock—par value $5	5,000
Paid-in capital—excess over par value	900
Retained earnings	4,100
Total stockholders' equity	10,000
Total equities	$12,900

Example of purchase method

On January 1, 1985, the Jeanne Corporation purchased all the common stock of the Marie Corporation (from Marie Corporation stockholders) for $5,000 in cash. The entry on Jeanne's books to record this transaction (purchase method) is:

Investment in Marie Corporation 5,000

Cash 5,000

To record acquisition of all of the outstanding common stock of Marie Corporation.

ILLUSTRATION 10–7

MARIE CORPORATION
Balance Sheet
December 31, 1984

Assets

Current assets	$ 900
Fixed assets (net of accumulated depreciation)	800
Total assets	$1,700

Equities

Current liabilities	$ 210
Stockholders' equity:	
Common Stock—par value $1	300
Paid-in capital—excess over par value	100
Retained earnings	1,090
Total stockholders' equity	1,490
Total equities	$1,700

If Jeanne had issued its own common stock instead of cash to the Marie stockholders, the purchase price would be the number of shares issued times the market price at the date of issue.

Assume Jeanne issued 200 shares of their $5 par value stock to Marie stockholders and that the market value on January 1, 1985, was $25 per share.

The entry would be:

Investment in Marie Corporation 5,000

Common Stock—$5 Par Value 1,000

Paid-in Capital (Excess over Par Value) 4,000

To record the acquisition of the Marie Corporation for 200 shares of $5 par value common stock.

The worksheet for the preparation of the consolidated balance sheet on January 1, 1985 (assume Marie is to continue as a separate legal entity and is not liquidated), after the acquisition has been recorded on Jeanne's books would be:

JEANNE CORPORATION
Worksheet for Consolidated Balance Sheet
January 1, 1985

	Jeanne	Marie	Combined	Elimination	Consolidated Balance Sheet
Assets					
Current assets	$ 5,000	$ 900	$ 5,900		$ 5,900
Investment in Marie	5,000		5,000	(5,000)	—
Fixed assets (net)	7,900	800	8,700	2,510	11,210
Goodwill				1,000	1,000
	$17,900	$1,700	$19,600		$18,110
Liabilities and Stockholders' Equity					
Current liabilities	$ 2,900	$ 210	$ 3,110		$ 3,110
Common stock	6,000	300	6,300	(300)	6,000
Paid-in capital	4,900	100	5,000	(100)	4,900
Retained earnings	4,100	1,090	5,190	(1,090)	4,100
	$17,900	$1,700	$19,600		$18,110

The elimination entry shown above for the investment on the consolidated worksheet assumes that the $3,510 (5,000 − 1,490) excess of fair market value over book value of Marie ($1,700 − $210) is to be allocated $2,510 to fixed assets (the fair market value of the fixed assets was determined by an appraisal) and $1,000 to goodwill.

The appropriate elimination entry is:

```
Common Stock ......................................    300
Paid-in Capital ....................................    100
Retained Earnings .................................  1,090
Goodwill ...........................................  1,000
Fixed Assets .......................................  2,510
    Investment in Marie Corporation ...............            5,000
```
To eliminate the investment in Marie Corporation.

The *consolidated balance sheet* reflects the amount paid for the assets acquired and eliminates the stockholders' equity of the acquired company as of the date of acquisition. Consolidated net income after the acquisition will be reduced by the depreciation expense on the increased valuation ($2,510) of the fixed assets and the amortization of the goodwill ($1,000).

Example of pooling of interests method

Assume that on January 1, 1985, Jeanne issued 200 shares of its $5 par value common stock to Marie stockholders in exchange for all of Marie's common stock, and this business combination is recorded as a *pooling of interests*. The journal entry to record the issuance of stock on Jeanne's books is:

Investment in Marie Corporation	1,490	
Common Stock—Par Value $5		1,000
Paid-in Capital (Excess over Par)		490

To record exchange of 200 shares of our common stock for all the common stock of Marie Corporation (Marie's book value is $1,700 − $210).

Because the business combination is a pooling of interests and is not a purchase, Jeanne will record the investment on its books at an amount equal to Marie's book value.

The worksheet for the preparation of the consolidated balance sheet on January 1, 1985, after this business combination has been recorded on Jeanne's books, would be:

JEANNE CORPORATION
Worksheet for Consolidated Balance Sheet
January 1, 1985

	Jeanne	Marie	Combined	Elimination	Consolidated Balance Sheet
Current assets	$ 5,000	$ 900	$ 5,900		$ 5,900
Investment in Marie Corporation	1,490		1,490	(1,490)	
Fixed assets (net)	7,900	800	8,700		8,700
	$14,390	$1,700	$16,090		14,600
Current liabilities	$ 2,900	210	$ 3,110		$ 3,110
Common stock	6,000	300	6,300	(300)	6,000
Paid-in capital	1,390	100	1,490	(1,190)	300
Retained earnings	4,100	1,090	5,190		5,190
	$14,390	$1,700	$16,090		$14,600

The common stock ($300) of Marie is eliminated with the remainder of Marie's book value ($1,190) being offset against the pooled ($1,490) Paid-in Capital—Excess over Par. The method of eliminating the book value of the pooled company is to first offset the par or stated value of common stock of the pooled company and then the combined (pooled) Paid-in Capital account with any remaining residual charged to the Pooled Retained Earnings account.

Comparison of purchase and pooling of interests consolidated financial statements

An examination of the two consolidated balance sheets (purchase and pooling of interests) indicates that assets are $3,510 ($18,110 − $14,600) higher using the purchase method. The allocation of this additional asset cost to future periods (depreciation expense and amortization of goodwill) will result in lower reported earnings using the purchase method than the pooling of interests method.

The pooling of interests method also creates the opportunity to obtain "instant earnings" for the consolidated entity by selling at a much higher market value some of the assets that have been recorded at book value. For example, the sale of Marie's fixed assets by the consolidated entity on January 2, 1985, at their market value would result in "instant earnings" of $2,510. Separate disclosure is required on the financial statements if the profit or loss on disposal of pooled assets is material and occurs within two years of the consummation of the business combination.

It is also possible for the issuing (dominant) company to create earnings and increase earnings per share by combining at the end of the year with a company that has current earnings and a ratio of market price to earnings which is lower than theirs.

These opportunities to increase reported earnings by treating what is really an acquisition as a pooling of interest resulted in many abuses and led to the issuing of *APB 16* in August 1970. *APB 16 requires* that the pooling of interest method be used to account for *business combinations* when all 12 specific criteria of the opinion are met. These criteria relate primarily to the independence and autonomy of the companies prior to the business combination and the requirement that at least 90 percent of a company's voting common stock be exchanged for the voting common stock of the other company pursuant to a plan to be completed within one year. All business combinations that do not meet all the criteria of *APB 16* must be treated as purchases.

The purpose of the opinion was to eliminate alternative accounting procedures for business combinations and to try to establish criteria that will allow the pooling of interests method to be used only when there is a bona fide merger of interest into one continuing entity.

DISCLOSURE ON THE FINANCIAL STATEMENTS OF PURCHASE AND POOLING OF INTERESTS METHODS

The notes to the financial statements will disclose whether a business combination is recorded using the purchase or the pooling of interests method. If the pooling of interests method is used, restatement of earnings for prior periods is required. If the purchase method is used, no restatement of prior periods is required, which makes it more difficult to evaluate the earnings trend for the business combination from the consolidated statements.

Some examples of this type of disclosure (purchase and pooling of interests) quoted from published financial statements are:

MERRILL LYNCH AND COMPANY, INC.—1981
AMIC Corporation
On February 14, 1979, the Corporation acquired all of the outstanding common stock of AMIC Corporation ("AMIC") for approximately $90 million in cash and unsecured promissory notes maturing in three equal installments. The first installment was paid on March 1, 1980 and the remaining installments are due on March 1, 1981 and March 1, 1982, with interest payable at 8¾% per annum. The excess of the purchase price over the fair market value of the net assets acquired, in an amount of approximately $48 million, is being amortized over forty years. Since this acquisition was accounted for as a purchase, the results of operations of AMIC have been included in the consolidated financial statements from the date of acquisition.

GOULD, INC.—1980
Note B: Mergers, Acquisitions and Dispositions
In December 1980, the Company issued 5,880,822 shares of Common Stock in exchange for all of the outstanding shares of Systems Engineering Laboratories, Incorporated (SYSTEMS), which designs, manufactures, markets and services medium-scale, high-speed digital computer systems and related products. The merger was accounted for as a pooling of interests and the accompanying consolidated financial statements have been restated to include the accounts of SYSTEMS for 1980 and prior years. The separate results of operations of SYSTEMS which have been included in the consolidated statements of earnings are as follows (in thousands):

Year Ended December 31	1980	1979	1978
Net Sales	$89,099	$71,008	$61,610
Net earnings	$ 6,501	$ 4,476	$ 5,409

In addition, the Company and SYSTEMS incurred ancillary costs of the merger of approximately $2,700,000 ($.08 per share) which were charged to earnings during the year ended December 31, 1980.

Summary

Whether a business combination is treated as a pooling of interests or a purchase is determined by the guidelines established in *APB Opinion 16*. If the business combination is *structured* to conform to *APB 16* criteria for pooling of interests, it will probably result in higher current and future earnings and understated assets. The pooling of interests method does not record the net assets of the acquired company at their fair market value (understated assets) and therefore does not reduce future earnings by the amortization of acquired goodwill or the depreciation on the increased cost of the fixed assets acquired. Future earnings can also be enhanced under the pooling of interests method if acquired assets (recorded at net book value) are sold for their fair market value.[5] Net income in the year of acquisition will also be higher assuming a pooling of interests as earnings of the acquired company are picked up as of the first day of the year that the acquisition takes place rather than the date of the acquisition as is required in the purchase. Return on investment (net income divided by total assets) will also usually be higher using the pooling of interests method rather than the purchase method because net income will be higher and total assets will be lower. In the unusual case where there is substantial negative goodwill and the pooling of interests method would report lower earnings than the purchase method, the transaction would probably be structured as a purchase.

PROBLEMS AND CASES

10-1 Flemister Corporation

On January 1, 1985, the Flemister Corporation made the following acquisitions of common stock of other companies. All of these acquisitions were classified by Flemister as long-term investments.

Company	Number of Shares	Acquisition Cost (per share)	Percent of Ownership	Market Price per Share on December 31, 1985	Traded
Allis-Chalmers, Inc.	5,000	$36	Less than 1%	$37	NYSE*
Amax, Inc.	5,000	52	Less than 1%	48	NYSE
GATX, Inc.	5,000	40	Less than 1%	38	NYSE
Vyquest, Inc.	450,000	8	20%	8½	OTC†

* NYSE = New York Stock Exchange.
† OTC = Over-the-counter.

[5] If the combined companies intended to dispose of a *significant* part of these assets (except for duplicate facilities and excess capacity) within two years after the combination date, the business combination would not qualify for pooling of interests treatment.

Required:

1. Make the journal entry to record the acquisition of Allis-Chalmers, Amax, and GATX.

2. Make the journal entry at the end of 1985, if necessary, to account for the fact that the market value of Allis-Chalmers, Amax, and GATX has changed.

3. Assume that Vyquest had a net income of $1,000,000 and declared and paid dividends of $350,000 in 1985. Make all the entries on Flemister's books for 1985 to account for this investment using the equity method.

4. Assume that Flemister amortizes goodwill arising from acquisitions over 20 years and that the book value of Vyquest's net assets on January 1, 1985, was $16,100,000. This amount was also equal to the fair value of Vyquest's net assets. Does Flemister have to make any additional journal entries based on this information? If so, make the appropriate entry or entries.

10–2   Robert Corporation

Listed below are the December 31, 1985, balance sheets of the Robert Corporation and its 80 percent owned subsidiary the Shaw Corporation.

	Robert	Shaw
Assets		
Cash	$ 1,580	$1,390
Accounts receivable	8,650	1,500
Dividends receivable	300	—
Inventories	12,500	2,500
Notes receivable	2,000	—
Investment in Shaw Corporation	3,200	—
Plant, property, and equipment		
(net of accumulated depreciation)	14,600	4,450
Total assets	$42,830	$9,840
Equities		
Accounts payable	$11,010	$2,640
Dividends payable	—	300
Income taxes payable	3,500	900
Notes payable	—	2,000
Common stock	20,000	2,000
Retained earnings	8,320	2,000
Total equities	$42,830	$9,840

Additional information:

a. $1,800 of Robert's accounts receivable are due from Shaw Corporation.

b. Robert's $2,000 note receivable is a four-year, 10 percent note from the Shaw Corporation.

c. The $300 dividend receivable is the annual dividend declared by Shaw Corporation on December 31, 1985.

d. The Robert Corporation purchased 80 percent of the common stock of the Shaw Corporation in 1983. On the date of acquisition Shaw's common stock account was $2,000 and its retained earnings were $1,000. Goodwill is amortized over 20 years.

Required:

Prepare a consolidated balance sheet on December 31, 1985.

10–3 General Motors

Refer to the 1978 financial statements of General Motors Corporation and related footnotes and answer the following questions:

Required:

1. What method did General Motors (GM) use to report their investment in General Motors Acceptance Corporation (GMAC) on their consolidated balance sheet?

2. Identify the items that were responsible for the increase in the Investment in GMAC account.

3. Assume that GM had reported their investment in GMAC using the cost method.

a. How much larger or smaller would GM's earned on common stock for 1978 have been?

b. What would be the amount in the Investment in GMAC account on December 31, 1978?

c. Do you think the cost method provides better disclosure than the equity method?

4. Assume GM accounted for its investment in GMAC using the consolidation method instead of the equity method.

a. How much larger or smaller would GM's earned on common stock for 1978 have been?

b. How much more or less would the *total assets* be?

c. How much more or less would the long-term debt (payable after one year) be?

5. Calculate the ratio of earned on common stock to total assets using:

a. Equity method.

b. Consolidation method.

6. Calculate the ratio of earned on common stock to common stockholders' equity (stockholders' equity minus preferred stock) using:

a. Equity method.

b. Consolidation method.

7. Calculate the ratio of long-term debt to long-term debt plus stock-holders' equity using:

a. Equity method.

b. Consolidation method.

8. Which method provides the best disclosure, the equity or the consolidation method?

GENERAL MOTORS CORPORATION
Statement of Consolidated Income*
For the Years Ended December 31, 1978, and 1977
(dollars in millions except per share amounts)

	1978	1977
Net sales	$63,221.1	$54,961.3
Equity in earnings of nonconsolidated subsidiaries and associates (dividends received amounted to $123.7 in 1978 and $110.3 in 1977)	253.0	222.1
Other income less income deductions—net	(141.4)	54.9
Total	$63,332.7	$55,238.3
Costs and expenses		
Cost of sales and other operating charges, exclusive of items listed below	51,275.7	44,427.9
Selling, general, and administrative expenses	2,255.8	1,997.3
Depreciation of real estate, plants, and equipment	1,180.6	974.0
Amortization of special tools	1,855.7	1,406.4
Provision for the Bonus Plan	168.4	161.0
United States, foreign, and other income taxes	3,088.5	2,934.2
Total	$59,824.7	$51,900.8
Net income	3,508.0	3,337.5
Dividends on preferred stocks	12.9	12.9
Earned on common stock	$ 3,495.1	$ 3,324.6
Average number of shares of common stock outstanding (in millions)	285.5	286.1
Earned per share of common stock	$12.24	$11.62

* References should be made to Notes to Financial Statements.
Certain amounts for 1977 have been reclassified to conform with classifications for 1978.

GENERAL MOTORS CORPORATION
Consolidated Balance Sheet*
December 31, 1978, and 1977
(dollars in millions)

	1978	1977
Assets		
Current assets:		
Cash	$ 177.3	$ 293.4
United States Government and other marketable securities and time deposits—at cost, which approximates market:		
Held for payment of income taxes	791.3	715.3
Other	3,086.2	2,231.3
Accounts and notes receivable (Note 7)	5,638.7	4,681.1
Inventories	7,576.7	7,175.7
Prepaid expenses	729.3	860.4
Total current assets	$17,999.5	$15,957.2
Investments and miscellaneous assets (Note 8)	2,812.1	2,351.7
Common stock held for the incentive program	181.1	146.5
Property		
Real estate, plants, and equipment	22,052.0	19,860.9
Less accumulated depreciation	13,438.8	12,679.4
Net real estate, plants, and equipment	8,613.2	7,181.5
Special tools—less amortization	992.4	1,021.4
Total property	$ 9,605.6	$ 8,202.9
Total assets	$30,598.3	$26,658.3
Liabilities and Stockholders' Equity		
Current liabilities:		
Accounts, drafts, and loans payable	$ 4,612.4	$ 3,719.1
United States, foreign, and other income taxes payable	944.8	887.5
Accrued liabilities	4,493.4	3,720.3
Total current liabilities	$10,050.6	$ 8,326.9
Long-term debt—less unamortized discount	978.9	1,068.2
Other liabilities	1,384.4	1,023.5
Deferred investment tax credits	519.9	368.2
Other deferred credits	94.6	104.6
Stockholders' equity:		
Preferred stock ($5.00 series, $183.6; $3.75 series, $100.0)	283.6	283.6
Common stock	480.1	479.5
Capital surplus (principally additional paid-in capital)	792.0	772.1
Net income retained for use in the business	16,014.2	14,231.7
Total stockholders' equity	$17,569.9	$15,766.9
Total liabilities and stockholders' equity	$30,598.3	$26,658.3

* Reference should be made to Notes to Financial Statements.

GENERAL MOTORS CORPORATION
Statement of Changes in Consolidated Financial Position*
For the Years Ended December 31, 1978, and 1977
(dollars in millions)

	1978	1977
Source of Funds		
Net income	$3,508.0	$3,337.5
Depreciation of real estate, plants, and equipment	1,180.6	974.0
Amortization of special tools	1,855.7	1,406.4
Deferred income taxes, undistributed earnings of nonconsolidated subsidiaries and associates, etc.—net	(4.6)	(157.9)
Total current operations	6,479.7	5,560.0
Proceeds from issuance of long-term debt	111.9	130.7
Proceeds from disposals of property—net	125.5	110.7
Proceeds from sale of newly issued common stock	20.5	1.9
Other—net	273.8	120.8
Total	$7,011.4	$5,924.1
Application of Funds		
Dividends paid to stockholders	1,725.5	1,957.7
Expenditures for real estate, plants, and equipment	2,737.8	1,870.9
Expenditures for special tools	1,826.7	1,775.8
Investments in nonconsolidated subsidiaries and associates	201.6	139.5
Retirement of long-term debt	201.2	106.5
Total	$6,692.8	$5,850.4
Increase in working capital	318.6	73.7
Working capital at beginning of the year	7,630.3	7,556.6
Working capital at end of the year	$7,948.9	$7,630.3
Increase (decrease) in Working Capital by Element		
Cash, marketable securities, and time deposits	$ 814.8	($1,384.9)
Accountsand notes receivable	957.6	722.0
Inventories	401.0	847.9
Prepaid expenses	(131.1)	299.6
Accounts, drafts, and loans payable	(893.3)	(651.7)
United States, foreign, and other income taxes payable	(57.3)	764.0
Accrued liabilities	(773.1)	(523.2)
Increase in working capital	$ 318.6	$ 73.7

* Reference should be made to Notes to Financial Statements.

NOTES TO FINANCIAL STATEMENTS:

Note 1. Significant Accounting Policies

Principles of Consolidation. The consolidated financial statements include the accounts of the corporation and all domestic and foreign subsidiaries which are more than 50 percent owned and engaged principally in manufacturing or wholesale marketing of General Motors products. General Motors' share of earnings or losses of nonconsolidated subsidiaries and of associates in which at least 20 percent of the voting securities is owned is generally included in consolidated income under the equity method of accounting. Intercompany items and transactions between companies included in the consolidation are eliminated, and unrealized intercompany profits on sales to nonconsolidated subsidiaries and to associates are deferred.

Income Taxes. Investment tax credits are deducted in determining taxes estimated to be payable currently and are deferred and amortized over the lives of the related assets. The tax effects of timing differences between pretax accounting income and taxable income (principally related to depreciation, sales, and product allowances, undistributed earnings of subsidiaries and associates, and benefit plans expense) are deferred, except that the tax effects of certain expenses charged to income prior to 1968 have not been deferred but are recognized in income taxes provided at the time such expenses become allowable deductions for tax purposes. Provisions are made for estimated U.S. and foreign taxes, less available tax credits and deductions, which may be incurred on remittance of the corporation's share of subsidiaries' and associates' undistributed earnings included in the consolidated financial statements.

Inventories. Inventories are stated generally at cost, which is not in excess of market. The cost of substantially all domestic inventories was determined by the last-in, first-out (Lifo) method, which was adopted in 1976. If the first-in, first-out (Fifo) method of inventory valuation had been used by the corporation for U.S. inventories, it is estimated they would be $1,097.7 million higher at December 31, 1978, compared with $697.3 million higher at December 31, 1977. The cost of inventories outside the United States was determined generally by the Fifo or the average cost method.

Property, Depreciation, and Amortization. Property is stated at cost. Maintenance, repairs, rearrangement expenses, and renewals and betterments which do not enhance the value or increase the basic productive capacity of the assets are charged to costs and expenses as incurred.

Depreciation is provided on groups of property using, with minor exceptions, an accelerated method which accumulates depreciation of approximately two thirds of the depreciable cost during the first half of the estimated lives of the property. The annual group rates of depreciation are as follows:

Classification of Property	Annual Group Rates (percent)
Land improvements	5
Buildings	3½
Machinery and equipment	8⅓ (average)
Furniture and office equipment	6 (average)

Expenditures for special tools are amortized, with the amortization applied directly to the asset account, over short periods of time because the utility value of the tools is radically affected by frequent changes in the design of the functional components and appearance of the product. Replacement of special tools for reasons other than changes in products is charged directly to cost of sales.

Product-Related Expenses. Expenditures for advertising and sales promotion and for other product-related expenses are charged to costs and expenses as incurred; provisions for estimated costs related to product warranty are made at the time the products are sold.

Expenditures for research and development are charged to expenses as incurred and amounted to $1,633.1 million in 1978 and $1,451.4 million in 1977.

Foreign Exchange. All exchange and translation activity is included in cost of sales and amounted to a gain of $62.7 million in 1978 and a loss of $47.6 million in 1977.

Note 7. Accounts and Notes Receivable (dollars in millions)

	1978	1977
GMAC and subsidiaries (relating to current wholesale financing of sales of GM products, etc.)	$2,893.5	$2,496.6
Other trade and sundry receivables (less allowances)	2,745.2	2,184.5
Total	$5,638.7	$4,681.1

Note 8. Investments and Miscellaneous Assets (dollars in millions)

	1978	1977
Nonconsolidated subsidiaries:		
GMAC and subsidiaries (Note 9)	$2,005.8	$1,688.2
Dealerships (retail companies)	113.5	110.4
Other domestic and foreign subsidiaries	60.9	53.8
Associates (interests in overseas companies)	95.6	92.6
Other investments and miscellaneous assets —at cost (less allowances)	536.3	406.7
Total	$2,812.1	$2,351.7

Note 9. General Motors Acceptance Corporation and Subsidiaries Condensed Consolidated Balance Sheet (dollars in millions)—

	1978	1977
Cash	$ 484.5	$ 342.3
Marketable securities (market value, 1978—$579.4; 1977—$574.6)	552.5	532.7
Finance receivables (including installments maturing after one year: 1978—$10,343.0; 1977—$8,150.3; less unearned income: 1978—$1,977.8; 1977—$1,530.8; and allowance for financing losses: 1978—$216.9; 1977—$177.6)	25,622.7	22,582.6
Insurance receivables	45.0	36.8
Unamortized debt expense	42.2	41.3
Other assets	156.5	105.0
Total assets	$26,903.4	$23,640.7

	1978	1977
Notes, loans, and debentures payable within one year (less unamortized discount)	$12,058.4	$10,480.0
Accounts payable and other liabilities		
General Motors Corporation and affiliated companies	$ 2,893.5	$ 2,496.6
Other	1,105.8	899.2
Total accounts payable and other liabilities	$ 3,999.3	$ 3,395.8
Notes, loans, and debentures payable after one year (maturing prior to 2009—less unamortized discount)	7,165.3	6,602.1
Subordinated indebtedness payable after one year (maturing prior to 1998—less unamortized discount)	1,674.6	1,474.6
Total liabilities	$24,897.6	$21,952.5
Stockholder's equity:		
Preferred stock, $100 par value (authorized and outstanding, 1,100,000 shares):		
6 percent cumulative	$ 75.0	$ 75.0
7¼ percent cumulative	35.0	35.0
Common stock, $100 par value (authorized and outstanding, 1978—9,650,000 shares; 1977—7,650,000 shares)	965.0	765.0
Net income retained for use in the business:		
Balance at beginning of the year	$ 813.2	$ 709.8
Net income	229.6	205.4
Total	$ 1,042.8	$ 915.2
Cash dividends	112.0	102.0
Balance at end of the year	$ 930.8	$ 813.2
Total stockholder's equity	$ 2,005.8	$ 1,688.2
Total liabilities and stockholder's equity	$26,903.4	$23,640.7

10–4 NL Industries, Inc. (A)

Refer to the NL Industries, Inc., consolidated financial statements and Note 2 and answer the following questions:

Required:

1. Make the journal entry on *NL Industries books* to record the purchase of Sperry-Sun, Inc., in April 1981. Assume the book value of Sperry-Sun's net assets is approximately equal to the fair value of these assets.

2. Where does NL Industries investment of $252,340,000 in Sperry-Sun, Inc., appear on NL Industries, Inc., consolidated balance sheet?

3. Make the consolidation journal entry for 1981 to record amortization of the excess of purchase price over the fair value of Sperry-Sun, Inc.'s assets acquired by NL Industries, Inc.

258

4. Why is the entry in (3) only made for consolidation purposes?

5. How do you think NL Industries calculated that interest expenses would have been $7,530,000 higher in 1981 and $19,540,000 higher in 1980 if they had acquired Sperry-Sun, Inc., as of January 1, 1980? Is this disclosure useful to the reader of the financial statements?

NL INDUSTRIES, INC.
Consolidated Statement of Income and Retained Earnings
(in thousands, except per share amounts)

Years Ended December 31	1981	Per Share of Common Stock	1980	Per Share of Common Stock	1979	Per Share of Common Stock
Revenues:						
Net sales	$2,463,828		$1,811,497		$1,465,404	
Equity in partially-owned companies (Note 4)	51,034		33,443		16,855	
Other income (loss), net ..	21,802		(3,673)		(623)	
	2,536,664		1,841,267		1,481,636	
Costs and expenses:						
Cost of goods sold	1,469,058		1,132,851		940,787	
Selling, general and administrative	491,786		415,291		338,596	
Interest	65,177		41,947		48,858	
Minority interest	6,174		4,565		2,869	
	2,032,195		1,594,654		1,331,110	
Income before items shown below	504,469		246,613		150,526	
Provision for income taxes ..	194,243		88,219		56,888	
Income from continuing operations	310,226	4.61	158,394	2.33	93,638	1.36
Discontinued operations:						
Income from discontinued operations, net of income taxes—$8,908,000, $8,604,000 and $20,617,000 in 1981, 1980 and 1979, respectively	5,757		9,279		27,407	
(Loss) from disposal of discontinued operations, net of $28,227,000 income tax benefit	—		—		(35,359)	
Income before cumulative effect of accounting change	315,983		167,673		85,686	
Cumulative effect of accounting change............	—		—		26,257	
Net income	315,983	4.69	167,673	2.47	111,943	1.64

NL INDUSTRIES, INC. (*continued*)

Years Ended December 31	1981		1980		1979	
Retained earnings at beginning of year	$ 761,814		$ 641,447		$ 573,224	
Less dividends paid: Common: 1981, $.825 per share; 1980, $.65 per common share; 1979, $.60 per common share	54,802		42,993		39,407	
Preferred	4,313		4,313		4,313	
Retained earnings at end of year	$1,018,682		$ 761,814		$ 641,447	
Pro-Forma Information: Income from continuing operations (Pro-Forma) .	310,226	4.61	158,394	2.33	93,638	1.36
Net income (Pro-Forma)	315,983	4.69	167,673	2.47	85,686	1.24

NL INDUSTRIES, INC.
Consolidated Balance Sheet
(in thousands)

December 31	1981	1980
Assets		
Current assets:		
Cash and equivalents	$ 26,732	$ 27,375
Accounts and notes receivable less allowance of $9,776,000 in 1981 and $7,001,000 in 1980	459,877	370,735
Inventories	393,758	337,474
Prepaid expenses	12,469	9,770
Total current assets	892,836	745,354
Investments—Unconsolidated partially-owned companies, at equity, and other investments, at cost	124,151	142,699
Property, plant, and equipment, at cost, less accumulated depreciation and depletion of $465,728,000 in 1981 and $381,852,000 in 1980	895,851	655,143
Net assets of discontinued operations	145,152	147,776
Other assets (Note 2)	240,480	58,375
	$2,298,470	$1,749,347
Liabilities		
Current liabilities:		
Loans payable (primarily banks)	$ 32,158	$ 77,294
Accounts payable	119,096	96,599
Accrued liabilities	208,727	153,725
Taxes on income	107,949	68,180
Total current liabilities	467,930	395,798

NL INDUSTRIES, INC. (*continued*)

December 31	1981	1980
Long-term debt	$ 498,979	$ 303,419
Deferred taxes on income	80,852	62,731
Other liabilities	21,654	22,367
Minority interest	15,251	11,992
Preferred stock, stated value $100; shares issued—		
500,000	50,000	50,000
Common Shareholders' Equity (Note 2):		
Common stock, par value $1.25; shares authorized 150,000,000:		
Shares issued—1981, 66,454,715; 1980, 66,268,462	83,068	82,836
Capital surplus	62,054	58,390
Retained earnings	1,018,682	761,814
	1,163,804	903,040
	$2,298,470	$1,749,347

NL INDUSTRIES, INC.
Consolidated Statement of Changes in Financial Position
(in thousands)

Years Ended December 31	1981	1980	1979
Source of Funds:			
Income from continuing operations, net of taxes	$310,226	$158,394	$ 93,638
Items not requiring the use of funds:			
Depreciation and amortization	98,401	69,326	67,437
Deferred income taxes	15,939	9,803	20,362
Equity in income of partially-owned companies, net of dividends received	21,000	(29,924)	9,068
Minority interest in income of majority-owned companies, net of dividends received	3,259	3,492	2,859
Funds provided from continuing operations	448,825	211,091	193,364
Disposal of fixed assets	23,647	13,857	23,390
Long-term borrowings, net	195,560	(59,535)	(73,260)
Proceeds from issuance of common stock	3,896	3,426	2,075
Discontinued operations:			
Proceeds from sale	6,381	60,000	110,000
Other (loss on sale, capital expenditures, depreciation, deferred taxes, etc.)	4,182	21,420	8,736
	682,491	250,259	264,305
Application of Funds:			
Acquisitions (Note 2):			
Property, plant, and equipment (net)	49,653	2,138	7,657
Intangibles and other noncurrent assets	191,728	2,272	6,991
Fair market value of common shares issued	—	(1,825)	(9,228)
	241,381	2,585	5,420

NL INDUSTRIES, INC. (*continued*)

Years Ended December 31	1981	1980	1979
Dividends:			
Common stock	$ 54,802	$ 42,993	$ 39,407
Preferred stock	4,313	4,313	4,313
Capital expenditures	293,924	180,447	140,832
Investments, net	2,452	4,968	432
(Increase) decrease in other liabilities	713	(125)	(2,553)
Other	9,556	6,946	2,184
	607,141	242,127	190,035
Increase in working capital	$ 75,350	$ 8,132	$ 74,270
Details of the above increases are as follows:			
Cash and equivalents:			
For payment of Well Service acquisition	$ —	$ —	$ (74,436)
Other	(643)	562	(6,267)
Accounts and notes receivable	89,142	55,490	47,192
Inventories	56,284	50,495	36,137
Prepaid expenses	2,699	1,459	34
	147,482	108,006	2,660
Loans payable:			
Due on Well Service acquisition	—	—	74,436
Other	45,136	(34,073)	27,900
Accounts payable and accrued liabilities	(77,499)	(61,196)	(16,068)
Taxes on Income	(39,769)	(4,605)	(14,658)
	(72,132)	(99,874)	71,610
	$ 75,350	$ 8,132	$ 74,270

Note 2

Acquisitions

In April 1981, the Company acquired Sperry-Sun, Inc. for cash in the amount of $252,340,000. This acquisition has been accounted for as a purchase and, accordingly, the results of operations since date of purchase have been included for 1981. Had this acquisition occurred as of January 1, 1980, the effect of Sperry-Sun, Inc.'s sales and earnings would not have been significant in relation to the Company's sales and earnings, however, interest expense, net of income taxes, would have increased $7,530,000 and $19,540,000 in 1981 and 1980, respectively. The excess of the total purchase price over the fair value of the assets acquired totalled $136,830,000 and is being amortized to income over a period of 40 years.

10–5 A. J. Johnson, Inc.

"To purchase or to pool—that is the question"

The following conversation took place on July 8, 1984, between Martha Cummings, vice president of finance, and Robert Sterling, controller for A. J. Johnson, Inc.

Cummings: Bob, I just heard from A. J. (A. J. Johnson, president of A. J. Johnson, Inc.) regarding the negotiations with Research Products, Inc. Research (a privately owned company) has agreed to accept our take-over bid. The price is $7 million. Their common stockholders will tender all their common stock in exchange for approximately 100,000 shares of our common stock provided our current price of $70 a share holds up through December 31, 1984, which is our tentative closing date. If the price of our stock drops below $70, we will have to issue additional stock to make up any price differential. We have the option at the closing of substituting cash for up to 11 percent of the $7 million.

A. J. asked me whether we should record the acquisition as a purchase or a pool (pooling of interest) and let her know later in the week. Her present intention is to run Research as a separate entity rather than to merge it into A. J. Johnson, Inc. I'd like you to prepare an analysis and recommendation for me by tomorrow morning.

You should look at our file on the proposed acquisition, which is on my desk. It contains pro forma (as if) balance sheets for both companies as of December 31, 1984 (Exhibit 1), and projected income and reconciliation of retained earnings statements for 1984 (Exhibit 2), and a memo written by A. J. (Exhibit 3) on what she considers the underlying value of Research's assets.

EXHIBIT 1

A. J. JOHNSON, INC., AND RESEARCH PRODUCTS, INC.
Summary Pro Forma Balance Sheets
December 31, 1984
(000s)

	A. J. Johnson*	Research Products
Assets		
Current assets	$ 8,272	$1,350
Buildings and equipment (net of depreciation)	7,500	1,500
Patents	—	520
Total assets	$15,772	$3,370
Equities		
Current liabilities	$ 1,000	$ 140
Common stock—$10 par value	4,000	—
Common stock—no par value	—	1,000†
Paid-in capital (excess paid in over par value)	3,300	1,500
Retained earnings	7,472	730
Total equities	$15,772	$3,370

* Does not include acquisition of Research Products, Inc.
† 150,000 shares issued and outstanding.

EXHIBIT 2

A. J. JOHNSON, INC., AND RESEARCH PRODUCTS, INC.
Projected Income Statements and Reconciliation of Retained Earnings
For Year Ended December 31, 1984
(000s)

	A. J. Johnson*	Research Products
Sales	$60,000	$10,500
Expenses:		
Cost of goods sold	43,500	4,300
Depreciation	400	92
Amortization of patents	—	88
Selling and general administrative expenses	10,000	1,200
Total expenses	53,900	5,680
Income (loss before income taxes	6,100	4,820
Income taxes	2,928	2,314
Net income	3,172	2,506
Retained earnings (deficit)— 1/1/84	4,300	(1,776)
Retained earnings 12/31/84	$ 7,472	$ 730

* Does not include any income attributable to the acquisition of Research Products, Inc. There are no intracompany transactions projected for 1984.

EXHIBIT 3

From: A. J. Johnson, Inc., President   July 5, 1984

To: Board of Directors

Re: Purchase of Research Products, Inc.

My analysis of Research indicates that, with the exception of the patents, the net book value of their assets on December 31, 1984, will be about equal to their fair market value. We estimate that as of December 31, 1984, the patents will have a market value of $3 million. At that point they will have a legal and economic life of 10 years. In fact, my strategy is to sell approximately one half of the patents early in 1985 for $1.5 million, which should more than offset our projected decrease in earnings for 1985. The remaining excess of $1.29 million of purchase price over fair market value should be allocated to goodwill. If we structure the deal as a purchase, we'll amortize the goodwill over a 20-year period.

Required:

Prepare the analysis requested by Martha Cummings, assuming the closing takes place on December 31, 1984, and that A. J. Johnson, Inc.'s common is $70 on that date. It should include:

1. Pro forma consolidated balance sheet on December 31, 1984, assuming the acquisition is treated

a. As a pooling of interest.

b. As a purchase.*

2. Projected consolidated income statement for 1984, assuming the acquisition is treated

a. As a pooling of interest.

b. As a purchase.*

3. Calculate 1984 pro forma earnings per share for the consolidated entity, assuming the acquisition is treated

a. As a pooling of interest.

b. As a purchase.*

4. What would be the impact on 1985 earnings per share of the sale on January 21, 1985, of one half of the patents for $1.5 million, assuming that the acquisition is treated

a. As a pooling of interest (assume amortization of patents of $88,000 per year).

b. As a purchase (amortization based on economic life at date of purchase).

5. Which method do you recommend?

---

* Treatment as a purchase assumes cash is paid for 11 percent of the $7 million purchase price and 89,000 shares of A. J. Johnson, Inc., are issued for the balance of the $7 million.

11

Statement of changes in financial position

The statement of changes in financial position, sometimes called a funds statement, reports the financing and investing activities of an enterprise and the changes in its financial position during an accounting period.

APB Opinion 19 requires that this statement be included as an integral part of an enterprise's financial statements. It states:[1]

> . . . . information concerning the financing and investing activities of a business enterprise and the changes in its financial position for a period is essential for financial statement users, particularly owners and creditors, in making economic decisions. When financial statements purporting to present both financial positions (balance sheet) and results of operations (statement of income and retained earnings) are issued, a statement summarizing changes in financial position should also be presented as a basic financial statement for each period for which an income statement is presented.

---

[1] AICPA, *Accounting Principles Board Opinion No. 19,* "Reporting Changes in Financial Position" (New York, September 1971).

The statement of changes in financial position explains how an enterprise obtains its resources (source of funds) and how it invests these resources (use of funds). It is essentially a statement of resource flows and answers such questions as: How much in funds were generated from operations? From outside financing? From sale of assets and from other resources? Were the funds generated from operations adequate to finance the enterprise's operating cycle? Pay dividends? Make capital expenditures?

Funds are usually defined either as working capital (current assets minus current liabilities) or cash. In practice most firms use the broader definition of funds, working capital, in order to emphasize managements longer-term (nonworking capital) decisions.

For example, the collection of an accounts receivable would not be listed as a source or use of funds when funds are defined as working capital because there is no change in working capital: the decline in the working capital item, accounts receivable, is offset by an increase of an equal amount in the working capital item, cash. When funds are defined as cash, the collection of accounts receivable would be listed as a source of funds because the decline in a nonfunds item, accounts receivable, is offset by an increase in a funds item, cash.

Major sources of an enterprise's working capital are operations, sale of fixed assets, long-term borrowing, and the issue of capital stock.

Major uses of working capital are capital expenditures, retirement of long-term debt, purchase of capital stock, and the payment of dividends.

MAJOR SOURCES OF WORKING CAPITAL

1. Operations

An enterprise's operations generally are its largest source of working capital. If working capital consumed by expenses is greater than working capital generated from revenues, funds from operations is a *use* rather than a *source* of funds. Working capital from operations is not the same figure as net income from operations because there are expenses, such as depreciation, depletion, amortization, and loss on sale of fixed assets, which do not use working capital, as well as revenues, such as undistributed earnings of subsidiaries and gain on sale of fixed assets, which do not provide working capital.

Listed below is the income statement of the Texas Bookstore, Inc., for the year ended December 31, 1984.

TEXAS BOOKSTORE, INC.
Statement of Income
For the Year Ended December 31, 1984

Sales		$100,000
Cost of sales		60,000
Gross margin		40,000
Expenses:		
Wages and salaries	$15,500	
Rent	3,600	
Depreciation expense	2,880	
Amortization of copyright	1,800	
Selling and administrative expenses	10,120	33,900
Income before income taxes		6,100
Income taxes		1,000
Net income		$ 5,100
Working capital from operations:		
Working capital (accounts receivable, cash) received from sales		$100,000
Less working capital consumed by expenses:		
Cost of sales (inventory)	60,000	
Wages and salaries (cash or wages payable)	15,500	
Rent (cash or rent payable)	3,600	
Selling and administrative expenses (cash or accounts payable)	10,120	
Income taxes (income tax payable or cash)	550*	89,770
Total working capital from operations		$ 10,230

* $450 of Texas Bookstore's income tax expense is a long-term deferral because income tax depreciation (ACRS) is greater than financial statement (straight-line) depreciation.

Neither depreciation expense, amortization of copyright, or the long-term deferral of income taxes is part of the calculation of working capital. The offsetting credit in the depreciation expense entry is Accumulated Depreciation, a contra fixed asset (nonworking capital) account. Similarly, the credit in the entry to amortize the copyright is to the intangible asset (nonworking capital) account, Copyright.

The entry to record income tax expense is:

Income Tax Expense	1,000	
Income Tax Payable		550
Deferred Income Taxes		450

Only $550 is a reduction in working capital, it increases a current liability, and $450 is a long-term deferral (nonworking capital account).

Another method of *calculating* working capital from operations, which is often used in practice, is to start with net income as reported and add back any expenses that do not reduce working capital and subtract any revenues that do not increase working capital. For Texas Bookstore the calculation is:

see previous page

Net income	$ 5,100
Add back expenses not requiring an outlay of working capital:	
Depreciation	2,880
Amortization of copyright	1,800
Deferred income taxes	450
	5,130
	$10,230

Unfortunately, this reporting procedure has created one of the most misunderstood concepts in financial analysis, the idea that depreciation expense is a source of working capital because it is added back to net income to calculate working capital from operations. Texas Bookstore, Inc.'s only source of *working capital from operations* is the $100,000 increase in accounts receivable or cash from the sales for the year ended December 31, 1984.

2. Sale of noncurrent assets

The sale of fixed assets results in an increase in working capital (cash, accounts receivable) equal to the net proceeds received from the sale.

3. Long-term borrowing

An increase in long-term borrowing will result in an increase in working capital to the extent of the net proceeds borrowed. Short-term borrowing is not an increase in working capital because it increases the current liability, notes payable, as well as the current asset, cash, and results in no change in working capital.

4. Issue of capital stock

If the enterprise issues capital stock it will increase working capital by an amount equivalent to the net proceeds received.

MAJOR USES OF WORKING CAPITAL

1. Capital expenditures

Capital expenditures are one of the major uses of an enterprises working capital. Typical capital expenditures are those for land, buildings, equipment, investments in other companies, patents, etc. The decrease in working capital is measured by the amount of the capital expenditures.

2. Retirement of long-term debt

The decrease in the long-term debt account is usually attributable to either a cash payment or the transfer to current liabilities of the current installment of the long-term debt due within one year of the balance sheet date. The cash payment reduces working capital by decreasing the current asset, cash. The transfer of the current installment long-term debt decreases working capital by increasing the current liability, current installment of long-term debt due within one year.

3. Purchase of capital stock

When a company purchases its own capital stock either for the treasury or retirement, it is a use of working capital because it decreases cash.

4. Payment of cash dividends

The payment of cash dividends is a major use of working capital. The dividends are a use of working capital when they are declared because the current liability, dividends payable, is increased and working capital is decreased.

Stock dividends do not use working capital. They represent an increase in one shareholders' equity (nonworking capital) account and a decrease in another shareholders' equity account.

ALL RESOURCES CONCEPT OF STATEMENT OF CHANGES IN FINANCIAL POSITION

In order to meet its objectives of disclosing all significant financing and investing activities of the enterprise, this statement will have to report certain transactions that do not *directly* affect working capital. For example, the Samson Company issues $1,000,000 in common stock in exchange for property. The entry on Samson's books is:

Property	1,000,000	
Common Stock		1,000,000

There is no entry to a working capital item, and this transaction would not appear on the statement of changes in financial position if it is viewed in its narrowest sense. The broader interpretation of this transaction by the Accounting Principles Board in *Opinion 19* requires that it be reflected on the statement of changes in financial position. The substance of the transaction is an issue of common stock for cash (source of working capital) and an expenditure of the cash for the property (use of working capital). Other financing and investing transactions that do not directly affect working capital and that would be included in the statement are the conversion of long-term debt or preferred stock to common stock and the acquisition or disposal of property for long-term debt, prefered or common stock.

SCHEDULE OF WORKING CAPITAL ACCOUNTS

In addition to listing the sources and uses of working capital the statement of changes in financial position will also include a schedule detailing the changes in all working capital accounts.

The statement of changes in financial position for the XYZ Corporation for the fiscal year ended June 30, 1984, is an illustration of an appropriate format for this statement (See Illustration 11–1).

This statement reveals that the XYZ Corporation generated working capital of $2,440,000 in 1984. Of this amount, $2,270,000 came from operations, $120,000 from an increase in long-term debt, and $50,000 from collection of a long-term note receivable. The XYZ Corporation used this $2,440,000 to purchase $878,000 of property, plant, and equipment, declare cash dividends of $536,000, retire long-term debt of $330,000, purchase treasury stock in the amount of $31,000, and increase its working capital by $665,000. The changes in the individual working capital accounts totaling $665,000 are shown in the bottom portion of the statement. The most significant changes in these working capital accounts are the $449,000 increase in accounts receivable, the $1,206,000 increase in inventories, and the $750,000 increase in notes payable to banks.

METHOD OF PREPARING A STATEMENT OF CHANGES IN FINANCIAL POSITION

The statement of changes in financial position is prepared from information obtained from the statement of income and reconciliation of retained earnings, the comparative balance sheets, and other financial information.

ILLUSTRATION 11–1

XYZ CORPORATION
Statement of Changes in Financial Condition
Fiscal Year Ended June 30, 1984

Sources of working capital:
Net income	$1,460,000
Add expenses not requiring working capital:	
Depreciation and amortization	810,000
Total from operations	2,270,000
Increase in long-term debt	120,000
Decrease in long-term note receivable	50,000
Total sources of working capital	2,440,000

Uses of working capital:
Additions to property, plant, and equipment	878,000
Cash dividends declared	536,000
Payment of long-term debt	330,000
Purchase of treasury stock	31,000
Total uses of working capital	1,775,000
Increase in working capital	$ 665,000

Changes in components of working capital:
Cash and treasury bills	$ (67,000)*
Accounts receivable	449,000
Inventories	1,206,000
Prepaid expenses	27,000
Notes payable to bank	(750,000)
Accounts payable	(96,000)
Accrued and other liabilities	(73,000)
Accrued federal and state income taxes	(94,000)
Current portion of long-term debt	63,000
Increase in working capital	$ 665,000

* Figures in parentheses represent *decreases in working capital.*

In preparing the statement of changes in financial position, we use the same journal entry method of analyzing transactions and adjustments as we did in preparing the balance sheet and income statement. The only difference is that our emphasis is on the effect of each entry on working capital. If the entry increases or decreases working capital, it becomes part of our statement of changes in financial position and is recorded in the *working capital summary* at the bottom of the worksheet.

The comparative balance sheets and statement of income and reconciliation of retained earnings of the Roberts Corporation for the years ended December 31, 1984, and December 31, 1985, are shown in Illustration 11–2 and Illustration 11–3.

ILLUSTRATION 11–2

THE ROBERTS CORPORATION
Comparative Balance Sheets
December 31, 1984, and 1985

	1985	1984
Assets		
Current assets:		
Cash	$ 60,000	$ 50,000
Accounts receivable	40,000	35,000
Inventory	50,000	55,000
Prepayments	10,000	8,000
Total current assets	160,000	148,000
Fixed assets	40,000	45,000
Less: Accumulated depreciation	20,000	15,000
Total fixed assets	20,000	30,000
Total assets	$180,000	$178,000
Equities		
Current liabilities:		
Accounts payable	$ 32,500	$ 43,000
Income tax payable	7,500	5,000
Total current liabilities	40,000	48,000
Bonds payable	45,000	50,000
Total liabilities	85,000	98,000
Stockholders' equity:		
Common stock	75,000	70,000
Retained earnings	20,000	10,000
Total stockholders' equity	95,000	80,000
Total equities	$180,000	$178,000

Worksheet

A six-column worksheet can be used to obtain the information necessary to prepare the statement of changes in financial position.

The first two columns are for the balance sheet accounts at the beginning of the year, and the last two columns are for the balance sheet accounts at the end of the year. The two middle columns are for transactions. The lower half of the worksheet will contain statement of changes in working capital entries only.

Calculate the working capital (current assets minus current liabilities) from the December 31, 1984, and December 31, 1985, balance sheets and put these figures on the worksheet (Illustration 11–4). Then insert all other balance sheet (nonworking capital items) accounts on the worksheet. Foot (add) the worksheet to make sure it is in balance.

ILLUSTRATION 11–3

THE ROBERTS CORPORATION
Statement of Income and Reconciliation of Retained Earnings
For the Year Ended December 31, 1985

Sales		$140,000
Expenses:		
Operating expenses (except depreciation)	$105,000	
Depreciation	10,000	115,000
		25,000
Provision for federal income taxes		7,500
		17,500
Gain on sale of fixed assets*		2,500
Net income		20,000
Retained earnings—January 1, 1985		10,000
		30,000
Deduct:		
Cash dividend	5,000	
Stock dividend	5,000	10,000
Retained earnings—December 31, 1985		$ 20,000

* The company sold fixed assets with an original cost of $8,000 on December 31, 1985.

Start with the income statement and record journal entries as they occur. Post all entries that affect any current asset or current liability account in the working capital summary.

1. Sales for the year, $140,000:

Accounts Receivable/Cash 140,000
    Sales 140,000

The increase in accounts receivable/cash increases capital and is recorded in the working capital summary. The sales (revenue account) is part of the computation of the net income for the year, which has been closed to retained earnings.

Entry (1) on the working capital statement worksheet (Illustration 11–4) is:

Working Capital from Operations 140,000
    Retained Earnings 140,000

2. Operating expenses for the year, $105,000:[2]

---

[2] For purposes of this problem all operating expenses are assumed to be uses of working capital. In practice a number of expenses (classified as operating expenses), such as the long-term deferred portion of income taxes or the portion of interest expense that represents amortization of bond discount, are not uses of working capital.

ILLUSTRATION 11–4

THE ROBERTS CORPORATION
Worksheet for Statement of Changes in Financial Position
Year Ended December 31, 1985
(Funds Defined as Working Capital)

	December 31, 1984		Transactions		December 31, 1985	
	Debit	Credit	Debit	Credit	Debit	Credit
Working capital	100,000		(10) 20,000	(5) 8,000	120,000	
Fixed assets	45,000		(9) 3,000		40,000	
Accumulated depreciation		15,000	(5) 5,000	(3) 10,000		20,000
Bonds payable		50,000	(8) 5,000			45,000
Common stock		70,000		(7) 5,000		75,000
Retained earnings		10,000	(2) 105,000			20,000
			(3) 10,000			
			(4) 7,500	(1) 140,000		
			(6) 5,000	(5) 2,500		
			(7) 5,000			
	145,000	145,000			160,000	160,000

	Working Capital Summary	
	Increase	Decrease
Working capital from operations:		
Sales	(1) 140,000	
Operating expenses		(2) 105,000
Income tax		(4) 7,500
Financial and other effects:		
Proceeds on sale of fixed assets	(5) 5,500	
Paid dividends		(6) 5,000
Retired bonds		(8) 5,000
Purchased fixed assets		(9) 3,000
	145,500	125,500
Increase in working capital		(10) 20,000
	145,500	145,000

Operating Expenses 105,000
    Accounts Payable, Inventory,
       Prepayments, etc. 105,000

The increases in payables or decrease in inventory and prepayments is a reduction in working capital.

The operating expenses are a decrease in net income and are reflected in the December 31, 1985, retained earnings account. The entry for the worksheet is:

```
Retained Earnings ............................  105,000
    Working Capital from Operations ...........        105,000
```

3. Depreciation Expense, $10,000:

```
Depreciation Expense..........................   10,000
    Accumulated Depreciation .................        10,000
```

The depreciation expense is a decrease in net income and is reflected in retained earnings. The credit is to accumulated depreciation, which is not a working capital item. The entry for the worksheet is:

```
Retained Earnings ..............................   10,000
    Accumulated Depreciation ...........................        10,000
```

4. Federal Income Tax, $7,500:

```
Federal Income Tax Expense.......................   7,500
    Federal Income Tax Payable ...................        7,500
```

The income tax expense reduces net income and is reflected in retained earnings. The payable increases current liabilities (decreases working capital). The entry for the worksheet is:

```
Retained Earnings ................................   7,500
    Working Capital from Operations...............        7,500
```

5. Gain on Sale of Fixed Assets, $2,500:

The company sold fixed assets costing $8,000 and realized a gain of $2,500. To make the entry we have to deduce both the accumulated depreciation on the $8,000 fixed asset sold and the cash received on the sale. Analysis of the Accumulated Depreciation account reveals that the balance at the beginning of the year was $15,000 and that depreciation for the year was $10,000. The balance at the end of the year, assuming no further transactions, should be $25,000. The actual balance is $20,000, so some transactions must have occurred to reduce the balance by $5,000 to $20,000. The most logical explanation (we know only one asset with a cost of $8,000 was sold) is that this $5,000 is the accumulated depreciation on the fixed asset sold. The journal entry for the sale of the fixed asset is:

```
Cash ..............................................   5,500
Accumulated Depreciation ........................   5,000
    Fixed Assets....................................        8,000
    Gain on Sale ...................................        2,500
```

The cash figure is derived from the other three figures. Since cash is a working capital item, it will go in the working capital summary as proceeds from sale of fixed assets. The Gain on Sale, a revenue account, is an increase in net income and retained earnings. The worksheet entry is:

Working Capital from Sale of Fixed Assets	5,500	
Accumulated Depreciation	5,000	
Fixed Assets.....................................		8,000
Retained Earnings		2,500

An analysis of retained earnings reveals additional information:

6. Paid a Cash Dividend, $5,000:

Retained Earnings	5,000	
Cash/Dividends Payable.........................		5,000

The decrease in cash or increase in dividends payable is a decrease in working capital. The worksheet entry is:

Retained Earnings	5,000	
Working Capital Used to		
Pay Cash Dividends		5,000

7. Paid a Stock Dividend, $5,000:

Retained Earnings	5,000	
Common Stock		5,000

Since there is no effect on working capital, the entry is recorded in the upper portion of the worksheet.

The Retained Earnings account had a beginning balance of $10,000 and an ending balance of $20,000. Increases for the year amounted to $142,500 and decreases to $132,500, which explains the charge of $10,000 in the Retained Earnings account. The increase in the capital stock account from $70,000 to $75,000 is a result of the $5,000 stock dividend.

The procedure to be followed now is to search for any hidden transactions that might affect working capital. Start by analyzing all the other balance sheet accounts on the worksheet.

8. Retired Bonds, $5,000:

The bonds payable account has a decrease of $5,000 for the year. The most logical explanation for this change would be the retirement of bonds.

Bonds Payable	5,000	
Cash		5,000

On the worksheet:

Bonds Payable	5,000	
Working Capital Used to Retire Bonds		5,000

9. Purchased Fixed Assets, $3,000:

The Fixed Assets account had a beginning balance of $45,000; it decreased $8,000 because of the sale of a fixed asset, reducing it to $37,000. At the end of the period it was $40,000. The most logical explanation for the $3,000 increase in this account is the purchase of fixed assets, which would result in a $3,000 decrease in working capital.

Fixed Assets	3,000	
Cash/Accounts Payable		3,000

The worksheet entry is:

Fixed Assets	3,000	
Working Capital Used to		
Purchase Fixed Assets		3,000

We have now explained all the differences in the nonworking capital accounts. If we have proceeded correctly, the increase or decrease in working capital should agree with the balance in the working capital summary. See journal entry 10 recorded directly on the worksheet.

We can now prepare a statement of changes in financial position from the bottom half of the worksheet. This formal statement also includes the changes in each working capital account.

ROBERTS CORPORATION
Statement of Changes in Financial Position
For the Year Ended December 31, 1985

Source of working capital:		
Operations	$ 27,500	
Sale of fixed assets	5,500	$ 33,000
Uses of working capital:		
Paid dividends	5,000	
Retired bonds	5,000	
Purchased fixed assets	3,000	13,000
Increase in working capital		$ 20,000
Changes in components of working capital:		
Cash..		$ 10,000
Accounts receivable		5,000
Inventory		(5,000)
Prepayments..		2,000
Accounts payable		10,500
Income tax payable		(2,500)
Increase in working capital		$ 20,000

(Other possible formats for the *working capital from operations* portion of the statement are:)

Working capital from operations:

Sales:		$140,000
Operating expenses	105,000	
Federal income tax	7,500	112,500
Working capital from operations		$ 27,500

Working capital from operations:

Net income	$ 20,000
Add back expenses which do not require an outflow of working capital—Depreciation	10,000
Deduct revenues which did not provide working capital	30,000
gain on sale of fixed assets	2,500
Working capital from operations	$ 27,500

FUNDS DEFINED AS CASH

Creditors and investors often focus on cash rather than working capital in assessing an enterprise's liquidity (ability to meet current obligations) and in estimating its future financial strength.

Short-term creditors need to assess the enterprise's ability to generate enough cash to pay its current obligations.

Long-term creditors are concerned with the ability of an enterprise to make interest payments and retire debt principal.

Equity investors focus on the present value of the cash flows they will receive (cash dividends plus the sale price of the capital stock) in the future in determining the price they will pay for a security.

Creditors' and investors' ability to predict the enterprise's capacity to generate enough cash to finance investment and growth and pay dividends is enhanced by a statement of changes in financial position that defines funds as cash.

If funds are defined as cash instead of as working capital, the changes in all the working capital accounts, such as accounts receivable, inventories, accounts payable, and accrued expenses, will be listed separately in the statement of changes in financial position.

Assume that the Roberts Corporation defined funds as cash instead of working capital. The worksheet to prepare the statement of changes in financial position would start with cash and list accounts receivable, inventory, prepayments, accounts payable, and income tax payable as separate items (see Illustration 11–5).

The first nine entries on this worksheet are exactly the same as in Illustration 11–4 where funds are defined as working capital.

Entries 10 through 15 adjust working capital from operations to cash from operations by analyzing the change in each working

ILLUSTRATION 11–5

THE ROBERTS CORPORATION
Worksheet for Statement of Changes in Financial Position
Year Ended December 31, 1985
(funds defined as cash)

	December 31, 1984		Transactions		December 31, 1985	
	Debit	Credit	Debit	Credit	Debit	Credit
Cash	50,000		(15) 10,000		60,000	
Accounts receivable	35,000		(10) 5,000		40,000	
Inventory	55,000			(11) 5,000	50,000	
Prepayments	8,000		(12) 2,000		10,000	
Fixed assets	45,000		(9) 3,000	(5) 8,000	40,000	
Accumulated depreciation		15,000	(5) 5,000	(3) 10,000		20,000
Accounts payable		43,000	(13) 10,500			32,500
Income tax payable		5,000		(14) 2,500		7,500
Bonds payable		50,000	(8) 5,000			45,000
Common stock		70,000		(7) 5,000		75,000
Retained earnings		10,000	(2) 105,000	(1) 140,000		20,000
			(3) 10,000	(5) 2,500		
			(4) 7,500			
			(6) 5,000			
			(7) 5,000			
	193,000	193,000			200,000	200,000

	Working Capital Summary	
	Increase	Decrease
Cash from operations:		
Sales	(1) 140,000	
Cost of goods sold		(2) 105,000
Income tax		(4) 7,500
Increase in accounts receivable		(10) 5,000
Decrease in inventory	(11) 5,000	
Increase in prepayments		(12) 2,000
Decrease in accounts payable		(13) 10,500
Increase in income tax payable	(14) 2,500	
Financial and other effects:		
Proceeds on sale of fixed assets	(5) 5,500	
Paid dividends		(6) 5,000
Retired bonds		(8) 5,000
Purchased fixed assets		(9) 3,000
	153,000	143,000
Increase in cash		(15) 10,000
	153,000	153,000

capital account. These adjustments essentially are adjustments from the accrual to the cash basis method of accounting.

10. Increase in Accounts Receivable, $5,000:

Accounts Receivable 5,000
    Cash from Operations 5,000

This entry is made to adjust sales on account to cash collected from customers.

> Beginning Accounts Receivable + Sales − Cash Receipts from Customers
>
> = Ending Accounts Receivable

Cash Receipts from Customers = Beginning Accounts Receivable + Sales − Ending Accounts Receivable

$$= \$35,000 + \$140,000 - \$40,000$$

$$= \$135,000$$

11. Decrease in inventory, $5,000:

Cash from Operations 5,000
    Inventory 5,000

A decrease in inventory means that $5,000 in operating expenses (cost of goods sold) came from inventory purchased in a previous period that was not paid for in this period. Cost of goods sold will be $5,000 lower on a cash from operations basis than on a working capital from operations basis because of this adjustment.

12. Increase in prepayments, $2,000:

Prepayments 2,000
    Cash from Operations 2,000

This increase in prepayments is a use of cash. The cash expenditure for prepayments will be $2,000 larger than the expense recorded on the income statement.

13. Decrease in accounts payable, $10,500:

Accounts Payable 10,500
    Cash from Operations 10,500

The decrease in accounts payable, all of which is assumed to relate to operating expenses, is a use of cash.

14.

Cash from Operations	2,500	
Income Tax Payable		2,500

The increase in the income tax liability is a source of cash because the $5,000 cash expenditure for income taxes in 1985 is $2,500 less than the $7,500 income tax expense on the income statement.

ILLUSTRATION 11–6

ROBERTS CORPORATION
Statement of Changes in Financial Position
For the Year Ended December 31, 1985
(funds defined as cash)

Sources of cash:	
From operations:	
Sales	$140,000
Cash basis adjustments:	
Increase in accounts receivable	(5,000)
Cash inflow from sales	135,000
Operating expenses..	105,000
Cash basis adjustments:	
Decrease in inventory	(5,000)
Increase in prepayments	2,000
Decrease in accounts payable	10,500
Cash outflow for operating expenses	112,500
Income tax expense	7,500
Cash basis adjustments:	
Increase in income taxes payable.......................	(2,500)
Cash outflow for income taxes	5,000
Cash outflow for operating expenses	
and income taxes	117,500
Cash from operations	17,500
Sale of fixed assets	5,500
Total sources of cash	$ 23,000
Uses of cash:	
Paid dividends	$ 5,000
Retired bonds	5,000
Purchased fixed assets	3,000
Total uses of cash..	$ 13,000
Increase in cash..	$ 10,000

Income Tax Payable				Income Tax Expense	
(2)	5,000		5,000	(1)	7,500
		(1)	7,500		

Cash		
	(2)	5,000

The statement of changes in financial position (Illustration 11–6) with funds defined as cash indicates that the Roberts Corporation generated $17,500 cash from operations and had a cash increase of $10,000 (journal entry 15) in 1985.

Another format used by companies that define funds as cash is to calculate funds from operations based on a working capital definition and treat the changes in each working capital item as a separate line item.

The Wehr Corporation's 1981 consolidated changes in financial position is an example of this format.

CASH FLOW ANALYSIS

Cash from operations is probably more useful than working capital from operations in assessing a firm's liquidity and ability to pay cash dividends.

Companies with growing receivables and inventories will be unable to meet their current obligations and pay dividends unless they are able to generate cash flow from operations.

An analysis of the cash flows of the W. T. Grant Company from 1966 to 1973 would have indicated increasing receivables and inventories and negative cash flows from operations over the same period of time that the company was reporting net income. The inability of the company to generate adequate cash flows from operations to meet its current obligations resulted in its bankruptcy.

Investors should estimate future cash dividends based on the ability of the company to generate enough cash from operations to maintain growth and still pay dividends.

Kidder, Peabody and Company, an investment banking firm, suggests that investors calculate distributable and discretionary cash flows in making an assessment of a company's potential dividend paying ability and of its future growth.[3]

---

[3] Richard Greene, "Are More Chryslers in the Offing?", *Forbes,* February 2, 1981. Case 11–6 is based on this article.

WEHR CORPORATION AND SUBSIDIARIES
Consolidated Changes in Financial Position

	Year Ended December 31		
	1981	1980	1979
CASH AND TEMPORARY INVESTMENTS—			
Beginning of year	$ 1,496	$11,539	$11,368
SOURCES OF CASH:			
Operations:			
Net earnings	3,489	752	1,697
Items not affecting cash:			
Depreciation	2,910	2,477	2,531
Amortization	343	109	34
Deferred income taxes	575	(20)	(208)
Write-off of goodwill	656		
Funds provided from operations	7,973	3,318	4,054
Acquisition of Thermotron:			
Long-term debt assumed		1,897	
Long-term debt issued		5,650	
Property, plant and equipment acquired		(4,915)	
Trademarks, patents, leasehold interests, engineering drawings and other assets acquired		(2,235)	
Net assets of division sold	1,844		
Decrease in accounts receivable	1,327		
Decrease in inventories	1,698		
Increase in accounts payable	155	1,787	
Increase in other current liabilities		3,030	
Additions to long-term debt	1,090		643
Other—net	824	1,577	156
Total cash provided	14,911	10,109	4,853
USES OF CASH:			
Cash dividends paid	540	720	675
Increase in accounts receivable		7,152	754
Increase in inventories		7,009	503
Increase in other current assets		476	7
Increase in marketable securities	736	1,426	
Additions to property, plant and equipment	1,449	1,639	1,491
Decrease in accounts payable			821
Decrease in other current liabilities	1,381		
Payments and current maturities on long-term debt	1,850	1,730	431
Total cash used	5,956	20,152	4,682
Net change in cash for the year	8,955	(10,043)	171
CASH AND TEMPORARY INVESTMENTS—			
End of year	$10,451	$ 1,496	$11,539

They define distributable cash flow as cash flow from operations minus the current cost of replacing the company's assets. The current cost of replacing the company's assets is calculated as the current year's depreciation adjusted for inflation.

They argue that it is only after making provisions for maintaining its assets that a company should consider paying dividends.

Discretionary cash flow is distributable cash flow minus dividends. It is the amount available for future growth.

USES OF THE STATEMENT OF CHANGES IN FINANCIAL POSITION

The statement of changes in financial position indicates the strategy the firm has used in obtaining and employing its resources. Management's current decisions about the sources and uses of their resources are probably the best predictor of what they will do in the future. This statement can therefore be very useful in estimating the policy the firm will follow for dividend payments, capital expenditures, and financing by debt and equity.

When funds are defined as cash this statement can also be useful in assessing a company's liquidity.

PROBLEMS AND CASES

 11-1 Joycelita Corporation

JOYCELITA CORPORATION
Income Statement
For the Year Ended December 31, 1984

Sales		$200,000
Cost of goods sold*		140,000
Gross profit		60,000
Other expenses:		
Selling, general, and administrative†	$25,500	
Loss on sale of truck	1,800	27,300
		32,700
Other income:		
Equity in net earnings of unconsolidated subsidiary‡		5,650
		38,350
Income Taxes (40% × $32,700)		13,080
Net income		$ 25,270

　* Includes straight-line depreciation of $16,000. ACRS depreciation taken on the income tax return was $22,000.
　† Includes bad debt expense of $6,300.
　‡ Joycelita owns 35 percent of the common stock of Jones Corporation, which did not pay any dividends in 1984.

Required:

Calculate Joycelita's *funds from operations.* For purposes of this problem funds are defined as working capital.

 SSC Corporation

Comparative balance sheets of the SSC Corporation as of December 31, 1985, and December 31, 1984, an income statement, and a statement of changes in stockholders' equity for the year ended December 31, 1985, are shown below.

SSC CORPORATION
Comparative Balance Sheets
(000s)

	Dec. 31, 1985	Dec. 31, 1984
Assets		
Current assets:		
Cash	$ 230	$ 319
Accounts receivable	2,388	1,616
Inventories	2,492	1,449
Prepaid expenses	62	78
Total current assets	5,172	3,462
Fixed assets:		
Property, plant, and equipment, at cost:		
Land	186	94
Buildings	968	570
Machinery and equipment	865	583
	2,019	1,247
Less: Accumulated depreciation	528	416
Total fixed assets	1,491	831
Excess of purchase price over net assets of companies acquired	1,224	1,227
Total assets	$7,887	$5,520
Equities		
Current liabilities:		
Notes payable—current portion	$1,118	$ 628
Accounts payable	880	417
Accrued liabilities	963	532
Total current liabilities	2,961	1,577
Notes payable after one year	314	291
Total liabilities	3,275	1,868
Stockholders' equity:		
Common stock	22	25
Paid-in capital	2,426	2,916
Retained earnings	2,164	711
Total stockholders' equity	4,612	3,652
Total equities	$7,887	$5,520

SSC CORPORATION
Statement of Income
For the Year Ended December 31, 1985

Sales	$11,988
Cost and expenses:	
Cost of sales*	$ 5,280
Selling and administrative†	4,428
Interest	93
	$ 9,801
	$ 2,187
Other income:	
Gain on sale of equipment‡	19
Income before income taxes	$ 2,206
Provision for income taxes	753
Net income	$ 1,453

* Includes depreciation of $126.
† Includes amortization of goodwill of $3.
‡ The only equipment sold in 1985 was fully depreciated.

SSC CORPORATION
Statement of Changes in Stockholders' Equity
For the Year Ended December 31, 1985

	Common Stock	Paid-in Capital	Retained Earnings (deficit)
Balance, January 1, 1985	$25	$2,916	$ 711
Repurchase of common stock	(3)	(490)	
Net income			1,453
Balance, December 31, 1985	$22	$2,426	$2,164

Required:

1. Prepare a statement of changes in financial position worksheet. Assume funds are defined as working capital. Make sure you cross-reference each entry on the worksheet.

2. Prepare a statement of changes in financial position for the year ended December 31, 1985.

11–3 General Electric (A)

Refer to General Electric's statement of changes in financial position and answer the questions that follow the statement.

GENERAL ELECTRIC COMPANY AND CONSOLIDATED AFFILIATES
Statement of Changes in Financial Position

For the Years Ended December 31 (In millions)	1981	1980	1979
Source of funds From operations:			
Net earnings	$1,652	$1,514	$1,409
Depreciation, depletion and amortization	882	707	624
Investment tax credit deferred—net	46	56	45
Income tax timing difference	33	63	(37)
Earnings retained by nonconsolidated finance affiliates	(27)	(22)	(17)
Minority interest in earnings of consolidated affiliates	46	21	29
	2,632	2,339	2,053
Increase in long-term borrowings	160	122	50
Disposition of treasury shares	169	136	148
Increase in current liabilities other than short-term borrowings	1,064	498	786
Other—net	(78)	143	101
Total source of funds	3,947	3,238	3,138
Application of funds Additions to property, plant and equipment	2,025	1,948	1,262
Dividends declared on common stock	715	670	624
Increase in investments	87	129	281
Reduction in long-term borrowings	101	69	97
Purchase of treasury shares	176	145	156
Increase in current receivables	533	692	358
Increase in inventories	118	182	158
Total application of funds	3,755	3,835	2,936
Net change Net change in cash, marketable securities and short-term borrowings	$ 192	$ (597)	$ 202
Analysis of net change Increase (decrease) in cash and marketable securities	$ 270	$ (375)	$ 113
Decrease (increase) in short-term borrowings	(78)	(222)	89
Increase (decrease) in net liquid assets	$ 192	$ (597)	$ 202

Required:

1. How does General Electric define funds?

2. Why does General Electric add depreciation, depletion, and amortization to net earnings to obtain funds from operations?

3. Explain why General Electric subtracts earnings retained by nonconsolidated finance affiliates from net earnings to obtain funds from operations.

4. What do you think caused the income tax timing differences? Why are they added back to net earnings to obtain funds from operations?

5. What was the offsetting credit to the $46 million debit to minority

interest in earnings of consolidated affiliates? Why is this amount added to net income to obtain funds from operations?

6. How much did General Electric's working capital increase (decrease) in 1981?

7. Based on GE's statement of changes in financial position would you be concerned about GE's ability to pay cash dividends in the future?

11–4 Fort Howard Paper Company

Fort Howard Paper Company manufactures toilet tissue, paper towels, windshield towels, disposable wipers, boxed facial tissue, paper napkins, place mats, tray covers, doilies, coasters, and guest towels. These products are distributed through a nationwide network of wholesalers who serve the industrial, institutional, commercial, food service, lodging, and automotive aftermarkets.

FORT HOWARD PAPER COMPANY
Consolidated Statement of Earnings and Retained Earnings
For the Year Ended December 31, 1981
($000, except per share data)

	1981
Net sales	$471,261
Cost of sales	285,497
Selling, general, and administrative	42,863
Earnings from operations	142,901
Interest expense	(4,042)
Other income, primarily interest	12,181
Earnings before income taxes	151,040
Provision for income taxes	67,990
Net earnings	$ 83,050
Net earnings per share	$ 3.08
Retained earnings—Beginning of year	$292,785
Net earnings	83,050

	Per Share			
	1981	1980	1979	
Dividends declared on common stock	$.93	$.77½	$.64½	(25,041)
Two-for-one stock split				—
Retained earnings—End of year				$350,794

FORT HOWARD PAPER COMPANY
Consolidated Balance Sheets
($000)

December 31	1981	1980
Assets		
Current assets:		
Cash and short-term investments	$117,419	$ 46,286
Receivables, less allowance for doubtful accounts		
of $650 in 1981 and 1980	29,500	30,828
Inventories	76,471	67,182
Total current assets	223,390	144,296
Investments held for plant expansion	—	25,000
Property, plant, and equipment	479,450	435,391
Less: Accumulated depreciation	128,372	102,472
Total property, plant, and equipment	351,078	332,919
Other assets	6,247	6,733
Total assets	$580,715	$508,948
Liabilities and shareholders' equity		
Current liabilities:		
Accounts payable	$ 17,878	$ 18,368
Current portion of long-term debt	16,329	15,243
Income taxes	16,689	3,721
Other liabilities	40,619	35,565
Total current liabilities	91,515	72,897
Long-term debt	49,849	65,751
Deferred income taxes	49,496	35,546
Shareholders' equity:		
Preferred stock	—	—
Common stock	43,286	43,351
Retained earnings	350,794	292,785
Treasury stock	(4,225)	(1,382)
Total shareholders' equity	389,855	334,754
Total liabilities and shareholders' equity	$580,715	$508,948

Additional information:

a. During 1981 fully depreciated equipment with a cost of $1,507,000 was retired. There was no salvage value. No other sales or retirements of property, plant, and equipment were made.

b. Proceeds from long-term debt issued in 1981 was $427,000.

c. 112,000 shares of common stock were purchased at a cost of $4,021,000 and classified as treasury stock; 35,000 shares of treasury stock were issued to employees in 1981 as incentive bonuses.

d. Assume the decrease in the common stock account represents the purchase and retirement of approximately 1,850 shares of common stock. Fort Howard's common stock account represents the total capital contributed (par value of $1 plus paid-in capital) by shareholders.

Required:

1. Prepare a statement of changes in financial position worksheet. Assume funds are defined as working capital.

2. Prepare a statement of changes in financial position for the year ended December 31, 1981.

3. What does this statement tell us about the way Fort Howard finances its capital expenditures?

11–5   Red-Hots Corporation

Red-Hots Corporation is a Sarasota-based operator and franchiser of snack bars. Since its inception the company has located its fast-food outlets exclusively in the enclosed, air-conditioned malls of major regional shopping centers. Stores were designed to provide quick, convenient, and economical snack service for shoppers in high traffic areas. The company actively cultivated a reputation of cleanliness, courtesy, and efficiency for its stores.

In 1982, Walter O'Connell purchased 125,000 shares of Red-Hot Corporation's common stock at a price of $287,500. He had been extremely impressed by the energy and creativity of the company's management and by the bright growth prospects for the stores.

In the next three years, O'Connell's investment judgment seemed to be vindicated as the corporation proceeded to fulfill his high growth expectations. By the middle of 1985, the value of O'Connell's investment had more than doubled.

The performance of the Red-Hots Corporation had been particularly good in the fiscal year ending July 31, 1985. The number of snack bars increased to 71, an increase of 45 percent over the year before. Twenty were company-owned, 46 franchised, and 5 joint ventures. In addition, another 15 company-owned stores were under construction. During the period, net income before taxes jumped 48 percent to $235,000 in 1985, from $159,000 in 1984. Total assets climbed 52 percent to $1,901,000 in 1985, from $1,252,000 in 1984 (see Exhibits 1 and 2).

EXHIBIT 1

THE RED–HOTS CORPORATION AND SUBSIDIARIES
Consolidated Balance Sheets
July 31, 1985, and 1984

	1985	1984
Assets		
Current assets:		
Cash	$ 297,000	$ 248,000
Due from franchises	401,000	223,000
Miscellaneous receivables	31,000	55,000
Inventory	23,000	14,000
Prepaid expenses	31,000	27,000
Total current assets	783,000	567,000
Long-term assets:		
Land	190,000	12,000
Building and improvements	66,000	66,000
Equipment and furniture	432,000	352,000
Leasehold improvements	420,000	220,000
	1,108,000	650,000
Less: Accumulated depreciation	(169,000)	(124,000)
	939,000	526,000
Marketable securities	6,000	—
Investments in joint ventures	92,000	79,000
Investments in subsidiary	44,000	44,000
Other assets	37,000	36,000
Total assets	$1,901,000	$1,252,000
Liabilities and Stockholders' Equity		
Current liabilities:		
Notes and mortgages payable (current portion)	$ 147,000	$ 116,000
Accounts payable	270,000	86,000
Accrued expenses	46,000	36,000
Accrued income taxes	82,000	40,000
Reserve for loss on lease settlements	15,000	2,000
Other current liabilities	82,000	102,000
Total current liabilities	642,000	382,000
Long-term liabilities:		
Notes and mortgages payable	354,000	148,000
Deposits from franchises	42,000	22,000
Deferred franchise fees	85,000	51,000
Total long-term liabilities	481,000	221,000
Stockholders' equity:		
Common stock ($.10 par value, authorized 1,000,000 shares, issued 490,000 shares)	49,000	49,000
Paid-in surplus	462,000	462,000
Retained earnings	267,000	138,000
Total stockholders' equity	778,000	649,000
Total liabilities and equity	$1,901,000	$1,252,000

EXHIBIT 2

THE RED–HOTS CORPORATION AND SUBSIDIARIES
Consolidated Statement of Income
Fiscal Year Ended July 31, 1985

Income from operations:	
Sales of food and beverages	$1,601,000
Less: Cost of goods sold	554,000
Gross profit from operations	1,047,000
Other income:	
Sales of franchises	194,000
Franchise royalties	154,000
Gross income	1,395,000
Expenses:	
Selling, general, and administrative expenses (includes depreciation of $50,000 and amortization of leasehold improvements of $11,000)	1,125,000
Provision for loss on lease settlements	35,000
Net income before taxes	235,000
Provision for income taxes	106,000
Net income after taxes	$ 129,000

O'Connell, however, was worried. His optimism had been tempered by several recent cases in which aggressive "go-go" companies had succumbed to too rapid growth. These companies had placed excessive reliance on external financing in years of profit and growth, and subsequently encountered difficulty in meeting debt repayments and obtaining new loans when a bad year occurred.

O'Connell feared that the Red-Hots Corporation might fit such a pattern. He was particularly concerned with the 140 percent increase in company borrowings, from $148,000 in 1984 to $354,000 in 1985. In addition, working capital had declined by $44,000.

Owing 25 percent of the company's outstanding stock, O'Connell had considerable influence on management. He communicated his anxiety to Leonard Ross, the president of the company, who attempted to show O'Connell that the company was pursuing a prudent growth policy. He contended that the company was generating over half its cash needs internally and that the sharp increase in the company's debt account was due to the purchase of 2.75 acres of unimproved land in Sarasota County, Florida, which the company planned to hold as an investment.

Required:

1. As the company's accountant, prepare a statement of changes in financial position for 1985. Also provide a written analysis of the statement, keeping in mind Ross's contention that the company generates over half of its cash needs internally.

2. If you were Ross, what other facts would you present to convince O'Connell that you are a prudent manager?

3. If you were O'Connell, what would you do? Would you sell your stock? Why or why not?

11-6 General Electric (B)

Read Richard Greene's 1981 *Forbes* article "Are More Chryslers in the Offing?" and refer to General Electric's 1981 statement of changes in financial position (Case 11–3). Then complete the following requirements.

Required:

1. Calculate General Electric's net earnings per share for 1981 and 1980. Average number of shares outstanding in 1981 and 1980 were 231,460,000.

2. Calculate General Electric's cash flow per share from operations for 1981 and 1980. For purposes of this calculation use General Electric's definition of funds (net liquid assets) as cash.

3. Explain the difference between the net earnings and the cash (net liquid assets) flow figures.

4. Using the Kidder, Peabody definitions, calculate General Electric's distributable and discretionary cash flow for 1981. General Electric's historical cost depreciation, depletion, and amortization of $882 million was equivalent to $1,297 million adjusted for general inflation. Current cost (adjusted for specific price changes) depreciation was $1,294 million.*

5. Would you advocate disclosing cash flow per share, discretionary cash flow, and distributable cash flow in the annual financial reports of all companies?

ARE MORE CHRYSLERS IN THE OFFING?

We're probably coming to an end of what could be called "The Time of the Bottom Line." For a long time now most corporate attention has been focused on the profit-and-loss statement, on earnings per share. But a company can show very nice earnings per share and still go bankrupt. Penn Central is only one example. Chrysler Corp. showed a huge profit in 1976. A mask of profitability can easily be superimposed upon a mess of insolvency.

When the truth is suddenly forced on the public—as it was with W. T. Grant, Penn Central and Chrysler—investors naturally ask: Why couldn't

(continued)

---

*Supplementary information, effect of changing prices, *General Electric 1981 Annual Report,* p. 37.

we see this coming before it was upon us? With all the facts and figures churned out by these companies, where was the truth?

The answer is that it was there all along, in the form of cash flow information, but these numbers have been virtually hidden in the attic. Although many bankers, security analysts and company managements have been scrutinizing cash flow information for years, the investors have concentrated primarily on the seemingly all-important earnings per share figure. That's unfortunate. Cash flow analysis can show an investor what a company is really doing—where the cash is coming from and where it is going in inflation-adjusted terms. Most important, it's the only accurate indication of whether a company is growing or—as many of the FORBES 500 currently are—shrinking.

"It's an unfortunate situation that's developed in this country. We've been entirely too earnings-per-share conscious," says Tom Thorsen, chief financial officer of General Electric. "The ball game ultimately is generation of cash."

Harold William, chairman of the Securities & Exchange Commission, was even more emphatic: "If I had to make a forced choice between having earnings information and having cash flow information, today I would take the cash flow information."

The simple truth is this: In times of high inflation, earnings figures become less and less meaningful. Why? Mainly because inflation throws depreciation charges—and hence the earnings figures themselves—thoroughly out of line. As the cost of replacing plant and equipment soars in an inflated economy, depreciating historical cost produces less meaningful results, especially for capital-intensive companies.

If borrowing were less traumatic, the problem wouldn't be so painful. In the past, if a company didn't have sufficient internal cash flow it would simply go to the banks for a few million. But with the prime rate around 20%, borrowing money for growth is slow suicide. How many investments have a sure return of better than 20%? Anything less than that is a losing proposition.

Inflation isn't the only problem with earnings figures. Some companies, especially retailers like Sears and J. C. Penney, have millions of dollars in receivables that have been booked as revenues even though no cash came in. Unfortunately, they may not see any cash from those receivables for years. In a severe recession, as a large number of people default on their debts, they may not see the cash at all.

Other companies, like Borg-Warner, Teledyne, and Sun Chemical, use another device. They book earnings from firms in which they have equity investments of between 20% and 50% (FORBES, Mar. 31, 1980). They never actually get that money. They never actually spend that money. All they do with it is report it. If you want to know how meaningless this is, try claiming as income the proportionate undistributed profits of companies you happen to own stock in. Your share, say, of IBM's undistributed profits, or General Electric's. A banker would throw you out, and with good reason. But companies do it and get away with it.

(continued)

Even more significant, companies' depreciation schedules vary enormously. Although the trend is toward faster depreciation, there are still a fair number of firms that don't want to punish earnings that way. So, they keep their depreciation nice and slow and earnings nice and high. This is a perfect formula for earnings success if you don't mind rusting plants, inferior R&D and yesterday's technology.

All of this adds up to some rather jarring differences between the picture of a company as seen through earnings analysis and the status of a firm discovered through attention to cash flow.

Take a look, for example, at Dow Chemical and Union Carbide, two giant chemical companies. Over the four years from 1976 to 1979, Dow showed earnings totaling about $2.5 billion. Over the same period, Union Carbide reported cumulative earnings of $1.8 billion. It would appear that both firms were robust moneymakers in the same league.

But take a step further and look at cash flow. Kidder, Peabody & Co. did this, and although Kidder's methodology is a bit controversial, the question is a matter of degree—not direction. Kidder came up with a number called discretionary cash flow. That's the figure representing how much money a firm has left to grow with—after taking out the amount necessary to maintain its property, plant, and equipment and after dividends. Companies don't really set aside money to replace equipment, but ultimately they have to put out that cash—and it's not going toward growth.

Dow's discretionary cash flow is at a healthy level, with $924 million over the four-year period. But Union Carbide has a different story: negative discretionary cash flow of $663 million. That means, according to Kidder, UC was paying dividends for that whole period of time with borrowed money. It was, in effect, cannibalizing its capital structure to keep the stock price up. That's not a healthy habit. But it's common among the kind of huge firms you'd think would know better. Kidder's list only begins with U.S. Steel, Bethlehem Steel, American Can, Goodyear and Inco.

Union Carbide's comptroller, Louis G. Peloubet, admits that the company was headed in the wrong direction, but claims it had done an about-face. "When I came here five years ago," he says, "the whole emphasis was on the profit-and-loss statement. We moved it from there to the balance sheet and now to cash flow. All our managers are looking at cash flow, both from a liquidity standpoint and from the point of view of capital investment. They didn't even have that information three years ago." True. In fact, Carbide has upped its capital spending 60% over the past three years.

How did big, supposedly well-run businesses ever let themselves get in this kind of a bind?

One of the reasons for ignoring cash flow is that everyone thinks it's something different. The term is used so often that its meaning has been blurred. But, from a technical standpoint, it is derived simply by subtracting the expense of doing business from the cash brought in. It does *not* take depreciation into account. That's because depreciation is only a paper transaction. You can charge off $10 million against your plant this year—but you still have that $10 million to spend anywhere you please.

(continued)

Cash flow is not simply earnings plus depreciation, however. That's only half the story. Cash flow also takes into account changes in inventories, accounts receivable, and accounts payable. After all, when money is tied up in inventories, it can't be used to pay bills. So when inventories go up, cash flow goes down. On the other hand, when a firm has fewer receivables and more payables, it has more cash. And vice versa.

That kind of information can be invaluable in providing early warning signals that something is going wrong in a company. According to James Largay and Clyde Stickney, accounting professors at Lehigh and Dartmouth universities, respectively, in some cases this information can practically hand you a crystal ball. They use W. T. Grant as an example. "The problems that brought Grant into bankruptcy and ultimately liquidation did not develop overnight," they write. "Whereas traditional ratio analysis of Grant's financial statements would not have revealed the existence of many of the company's problems until 1970 or 1971, careful analysis of its cash flows would have revealed impending doom as much as a decade before the collapse."

Hindsight is always 20–20, but the professors are persuasive. Grant's earnings held steady until 1973, when its stock was still selling for as high as 20 times earnings. But its cash flow from operations was in the red as far back as 1966, only surfacing into the black two years out of the subsequent eight. The company ultimately choked to death on its inventories. Investors who saw that coming were able to get out in time.

Unfortunately, there is a misconception that cash flow need only be used to analyze borderline cases like Grant's. In fact, such analysis can lead to a fuller understanding of any company no matter how successful or stable.

Look at Savin Corp., the $357 million copy machine manufacturer. Last year the company's earnings were down by $4 million, to $28 million. Only a 12% drop; not bad in a recession right?

But Savin is a leader in providing cogent cash flow information, and last year that information was of particular interest. Although the red flags that pop up don't point to catastrophe at Savin, they do make the investor aware of potentially significant problems.

The first flag shows up in inventories: up $31 million from 1979. That's $31 million less the company has to spend than it had last year. The reason for the increase is unclear. Maybe sales are slowing and the firm is overproducing. It could even be a planned buildup for an expected surge in sales. The numbers themselves offer no explanation—but they send you hunting for one.

The next worrisome item is the increase in accounts and royalties receivable: up $34 million. The problem here is fairly clear. People are paying more slowly, preferring to use Savin's money rather than their own. Again, not a catastrophe, but the kind of thing that could really hurt a company if it continues.

Throw in some changes in payables, depreciation and deferred accounts and you come up with net cash flow from operations of $6 million, down

(continued)

from $30 million in 1979. That's a much bigger drop than in reported earnings. Says the firm's senior vice president for finance, Daniel L. Gotthilf, "The question is what happens this year and next year—you can't judge cash flow by any single year or quarter."

Gotthilf is right. What's more, when you look a little farther down the cash flow statement you discover that the firm laid out $51 million for capital expenditures and $21 million for an acquisition. Those are good signs. This is not a company that is putting off investment because times are hard. Still, the problem of receivables and inventories cannot be ignored. Future quarterly reports will have to be carefully scrutinized to make sure the company is taking action.

Even General Electric, widely regarded as one of the best-managed companies around, only recently woke up to cash flow analysis.

According to GE's internally circulated bible on cash flow, written in 1976, "Up until a few years ago, cash planning in the General Electric Company was pretty much of an unheard art because we had a very favorable cash situation. As a result, little long-term planning was done in the company other than in the treasury. We, of course, went through the exercise each year of developing figures for the long-range budget. However, most of the figures were based on some overall predetermined ratio to sales, and we never really got into in-depth cash planning."

As a result, the document continued: "GE Co.'s liquidity has declined to a level that could impare its triple-A bond rating."

In 1976 GE launched a massive program in which every corporate officer was forced to pay close attention to every element of cash flow: depreciation, receivables, payables, and inventories—everything.

The program has been a smashing success, with the company keeping well over $1 billion in cash that otherwise would have been sitting unproductive in such items as inventories and receivables. When money is wasted like that, it sends a company to the death market. That's no fun.

But if cash flow is so internally vital to companies—and so externally valuable to investors—why don't we get the information in annual reports? The closest thing we have now is the statement of changes in financial position. But that focuses on an almost meaningless item: working capital. Working capital is of so little use to investors that many accountants have fought to have the statement completely redesigned.

The Financial Accounting Standards Board has recently issued an impressive discussion memorandum on cash flow and liquidity that addresses many of these problems. As a discussion draft it makes no proposals, but rather suggests possibilities for disclosure to investors. Still, the FASB's message is clear: Cash flow information is necessary. Unfortunately, as with all FASB projects, it could be several years before we'll see this reflected in annual reports. But the demand for the information may be irresistible. A recent FASB survey of 415 executives, analysts and academics revealed that 67% thought cash flow information was "highly important"—while no more than 49% said the same thing about earnings per share.

(continued)

As a first step, the SEC has required that 1980 annual reports include a discussion by management of any unusual cash flow problems, and of the steps being taken to remedy them. As for the possibility of anything more concrete in the near future, Williams pointed out the problems the SEC had getting disclosure of inflation-adjusted earnings numbers. "The corporate community didn't like it because they wouldn't look as good, and the accountants didn't like it because it wasn't measurable and might get them into areas that they were uncomfortable with. I expect that the problems will be similar."

The truth is we are simply relearning lessons of the past. "The Romans only knew about cash flow," says Fred Tepperman of Arthur Young and Co. "But then we got sophisticated, learned about accrual and forgot about cash." He's not knocking accrual, he's only saying it's not the same as cash. (One of our more colorful captains of industry puts it slightly differently. "There are," he quips, "two kinds of money, cash and the other kind. I'll take cash every time.")

According to Lloyd Heath, a professor of accounting at the University of Washington and the author of a much-praised 1978 monograph on liquidity, "In the early part of this century, accountants were very concerned with cash flow—with the needs of short-term creditors. But beginning in the 1930s, with the passage of the Securities Acts, the accountants began to shift their attention away from this. There was a sort of backlash. They didn't want to be dictated to by the commercial banks or short-term creditors. They had found a new interest in earnings. And they not only de-emphasized cash flow, but they seemed to completely ignore it."

"It's not that cash flow is new to accountants," says Heath. "They should have seen it all along, but they were blinded because they thought the measurement of earnings was the beginning and the end, the alpha and omega of accounting."

But you can't ignore the rain when it's pouring through your roof, and the destructive inflation of recent years has forced accountants to take note. However, on their way to presenting some kind of unified cash flow information, they have run into a crucial question: How do you determine how much money a company needs to maintain its plant and equipment, without any growth? You need to answer this question before you can come up with a distributable (or "free") cash flow figure—the figure that tells you how much money the company *really* has control over to spend on dividends or growth.

This is a slippery one. Companies are constantly expanding and contracting operations in response to market conditions. What's more, new technology can slash a company's cost of upgrading its assets. So pinning down the exact point at which maintenance—or need for maintenance—ends and growth begins can be nearly impossible.

The FASB offers one solution in its *Statement 33,* which adjusts earnings for inflation. They recalculate depreciation using replacement costs rather

(continued)

than historical costs. That's probably the best figure at the disposal of the average investor.

However, Barre Littel and Robert Levine, the analysts who developed Kidder, Peabody's cash flow system, argue that the FASB numbers can understate the amount it costs to keep plant and equipment up to snuff. Here's why: Let's say a firm has two factories. One is depreciated at $1 million a year. The other is fully depreciated. The company needs both plants to continue in business. Under the FASB's system, the plant depreciated at $1 million a year would be assigned a new depreciation figure to account for inflation. However, the plant that was fully off the books could stay off the books. Kidder's analysts say that plant, too, should be assigned a new depreciation figure. It makes sense. It's precisely those old, fully depreciated plants that are most in need of replacement—at a cost much greater than their historical costs.

The numbers Kidder has come up with make much of U.S. industry look shaky. While some critics argue that Kidder has gone too far and make things look worse than they are, even if Kidder is near the truth, that's reason to examine your investment portfolio carefully.

When you see companies like GM, Sears, International Harvester and Du Pont with negative cash flows, it's time to reevaluate the way you look at all companies. Especially with the market turning back to blue chips, the time is now for investors to look at these cash flow figures.

Emphasizing earnings while ignoring cash flow actually rewards companies for putting off needed capital investment. The smaller the depreciation charge, the higher the earnings. In turn, higher earnings produce better stock prices. Finally, the stock price is often reflected in a fatter paycheck for the CEO. Is that one important reason for the notoriously low level of capital spending in the U.S.? CEOs are only human.

Of course, total reliance on cash flow information could be equally dangerous. Any capital investment turns cash into plant and hurts cash flow in the short term. Cash flow figures are only valuable when looked at over a number of quarters or years. As Bryan Carsberg, an FASB expert on cash flow, says, "Asking which one is better, cash flow or earnings, is like asking which you should cut out, your heart or your lungs."

Ideally, investors will start looking at—and annuals will start showing—earnings information and cash flow information side by side. The earnings information will show how well the company is doing at making money. The cash flow information will show how real that money is.

A vice president of a major international bank wrinkles his forehead and strokes his jaw as he says, "Sure, cash flow information will be here in a relatively few years. What worries me is how many companies will have gone under by then."

Source: Richard Greene, *Forbes,* February 2, 1981. Reprinted by permission.

12

Financial reporting and changing prices

Generally accepted accounting principles require financial statements to be prepared using the historical cost model. In accordance with this model assets are recorded at their acquisition cost measured in dollars. Dollars of different dates are considered to be the same, and no adjustments are made to the historical cost financial statements to reflect changes in the purchasing power of the dollar caused by an increase (inflation) or decrease (deflation) in the general price level.

The purchasing power of the dollar is the reciprocal of the general price index. As the general price index increases, the purchasing power of the dollar declines. For example, if the general price index rises from 100 at the end of year 1 to 110 at the end of year 2, the purchasing power of the dollar will have declined from $1 (100/100) to 90.9 cents (100/110).

The more severe the changes in the general price level, the greater will be the change in the purchasing power of the dollar and the more likely financial statements prepared using the historical cost model (which assumes all dollars are the same) will be misleading.

Constant-dollar (general price level) accounting restates histori- cal cost financial statements in a common measuring unit (unit of purchasing power) in order to correct for the impact of general inflation or deflation on the financial statements.

Financial statements that do not consider increases or decreases in the *specific prices* of assets may also be misleading. The prices of specific assets may fluctuate for reasons other than changes in the general price level. Technology and changes in supply and de- mand may even cause the prices of specific assets to move inversely to the general price level. For example, over the past decade, when the general price level rose significantly, the price of computers decreased rather than increased.

Historical cost financial statements fail to record specific price changes of assets and do not reflect management's decision to hold rather than to sell assets. When assets are sold the gains or losses from holding the assets in prior periods are reflected in the *current* income statement. Unrealized gains or losses (increases or de- creases in the specific prices of assets held) are not recognized in the periods in which they occur.

Current cost accounting adjusts historical cost financial state- ments for specific price changes. The current cost balance sheet reflects current values, and the income statement reflects the cur- rent cost of assets consumed in operations and the effects of unreal- ized gains and losses due to the increase or decrease in the specific prices of assets held during the period.

CONSTANT–DOLLAR (GENERAL PRICE LEVEL) ACCOUNTING

The objective of constant-dollar accounting is to restate the his- torical cost values of conventional accrual accounting in a common measuring unit and to calculate the purchasing power gain or loss on the enterprise's monetary position. All accounts are translated into constant (same unit of general purchasing power) dollars using a general price level index.

A general price level index is used to measure the general pur- chasing power of the dollar at different points in time. Two such indices are the consumer price index (CPI) and the gross national product implicit price deflator (GNPIPD). The CPI tracks the price level of a basket of goods and services purchased by a typical con- sumer. The GNPIPD tracks the price level of all goods and services making up the GNP.

The constant dollar chosen as the common measuring unit is either the current balance sheet dollar (end-of-year price index) or the average dollar for the year (average price index).

The only difference between historical cost and constant-dollar financial statements is the unit of measure. Historical cost financial statements use the dollar, which fluctuates in purchasing power during periods of changing prices. Constant-dollar financial statements use the same unit of purchasing power.

Constant-dollar financial statements derived from the historical cost financial statements are objective, comparable, and verifiable.

Restatement of financial statements in constant dollars

Assume that Bailey's Drug Store had the following historical cost balance sheet and income statement in a year in which the CPI rose from 100 to 110.

Balance sheet

Bailey's has decided to use the balance sheet (end-of-year) dollar as the constant dollar and the CPI as a measure of the general price level.

BAILEY'S DRUG STORE
Balance Sheet
December 31, 19x1

Assets		Equities	
Current assets:		Current liabilities:	
Cash	$ 30,000	Accounts payable	$ 15,000
Accounts receivable	45,000		
Inventory	100,000		
Total current assets	175,000		
Fixed assets:		Shareholders' equity:	
Equipment	100,000	Common stock	150,000
Less: Accumulated		Retained earnings	60,000
Depreciation	50,000	Total shareholders'	
Total fixed assets	50,000	equity	210,000
Total assets	$225,000	Total equities	$225,000

BAILEY'S DRUG STORE
Statement of Income
Year Ended December 31, 19x1

Sales	$400,000
Cost of goods sold	320,000
Gross profit	80,000
Depreciation	5,000
Other expenses	55,000
Total expenses	60,000
Net income	$ 20,000

Net monetary assets. Bailey's monetary assets and monetary liabilities do not have to be restated as they are already stated in dollars as of the balance sheet date (end-of-year price index). *Monetary assets* are cash and fixed obligations to receive cash, such as accounts receivable and notes receivable. *Monetary liabilities* are fixed obligations to pay cash, such as accounts payable and long-term debt. Net monetary assets are monetary assets minus monetary liabilities.

Inventory. Inventory is not a monetary asset since it is neither an obligation to pay or to receive cash. Bailey's beginning inventory of $60,000 was purchased in a prior year when the CPI was 88. This year's inventory purchases of $360,000 were made evenly throughout the year when the CPI was 105. Bailey uses the LIFO cost flow assumption.

	Historical Cost		Constant Dollars
Ending inventory	$ 60,000 $\times$	$\frac{110}{88}$	$ 75,000
	40,000 $\times$	$\frac{110}{105}$	41,905
	$100,000		$116,905

Equipment. The equipment was acquired 10 years ago at a cost of $100,000 when the CPI was 50. The equipment has no salvage value and is being depreciated on a straight-line basis over 20 years.

	Historical Cost		Constant Dollars
Equipment	$100,000 $\times$	$\frac{110}{50}$	$220,000
Accumulated depreciation	50,000 $\times$	$\frac{110}{50}$	110,000
	$ 50,000		$110,000

Common stock. Common stock was issued when the company started 10 years ago and the CPI was 50.

	Historical Cost		Constant Dollars
Common stock	$150,000 $\times$	$\frac{110}{50}$	$330,000

Retained earnings. The Constant-Dollar Retained Earnings account is obtained by subtracting all the constant-dollar liability and stockholder equity accounts from the constant-dollar asset accounts. The Retained Earnings account will reflect all the prior years' earnings minus dividends expressed in constant dollars.

A comparison of the balance sheets indicates that in constant dollars Bailey's has suffered a deficit of $43,095 from the date it started business until the balance sheet date rather than the $60,000 increase in retained earnings reported in the historical cost financial statements.

	Historical Cost	Constant Dollars
Assets		
Current assets:		
Cash	$ 30,000	$ 30,000
Accounts Receivable	45,000	45,000
Inventory	100,000	116,905
Total current assets	175,000	191,905
Fixed assets:		
Equipment	100,000	220,000
Less: Accumulated depreciation	50,000	110,000
Total fixed assets	50,000	110,000
Total assets	$225,000	$301,905
Equities		
Current liabilities:		
Accounts payable	$ 15,000	$ 15,000
Shareholders' equity:		
Common stock	150,000	330,000
Retained earnings (deficit)	60,000	(43,095)
Total shareholders' equity	210,000	286,905
Total equities	$225,000	$301,905

Income statement

Sales and other expenses. Bailey's sales and other expenses, such as salaries and wages and rent, are assumed to occur evenly throughout the year at a CPI of 105 [(100 + 110)/2].

	Historical Cost	Constant Dollars
Sales	$400,000 $\times \frac{110}{105}$	$419,048
Other expenses	$ 55,000 $\times \frac{110}{105}$	$ 57,619

If the average dollar had been chosen as the constant dollar no adjustment for sales or other expenses would have been necessary because the sales and other expenses occurred evenly throughout the year at the average price index for the year.

Cost of sales

	Historical Cost			Constant Dollars
Beginning inventory	$ 60,000	×	$\frac{110}{88}$	$ 75,000
Purchases	360,000	×	$\frac{110}{105}$	377,143
	420,000			452,143
Ending inventory (see balance sheet)	100,000			116,905
Cost of goods sold	$320,000			$335,238

(handwritten margin note: see inventory section on p. 303)

Because Bailey's uses the LIFO cost flow method the $320,000 historical cost of goods sold comes from the purchases made during the year at the average price index, and the difference in cost of goods sold of $15,238 ($335,238 − $320,000) is $320,000 (110/105 − 110/110).

If Bailey's had used the FIFO inventory cost flow method the distortion would have been greater because the $60,000 in the beginning inventory, which has a constant-dollar cost of $75,000, would have been sold first.

Depreciation—equipment

	Historical Cost	Constant Dollars
100,000 × 1/20	$5,000	
220,000 × 1/20		$11,000

Depreciation is the major understated expense in the historical cost income statement because the equipment was purchased with dollars that had 2.2 (110/50) times the purchasing power of the constant dollar.

Purchasing power loss or gain on net monetary assets. When the general price level rises, a company loses purchasing power on all the monetary assets it holds because the monetary assets will purchase fewer goods and services.

Companies with monetary liabilities in excess of monetary assets will gain purchasing power during an inflationary period. They will pay off their debt with "cheaper" dollars.

Purchasing power gains on debt should be considered when figuring a firm's real cost of borrowing money. If purchasing power gains on debt equal the reported historical cost interest expense for the period, both the company and its creditors agreed to interest rates which just offset the general rise in prices over the period. The creditors would probably be upset over such an outcome because their expectation at the beginning of the period was that they would earn interest in excess of rises in the general price level. If interest expense exceeds the purchasing power gain on debt for the period, the company paid more than the general price level inflation rate in interest, and the creditors of the company "earned more" than the inflation rate.

Assume that Bailey's net monetary assets (Cash + Accounts receivable − Accounts payable) at the beginning of the year were $40,000 and the increase of $20,000 to $60,000 ($30,000 + $45,000 − $15,000) at the end of the year occurred evenly throughout the year. The purchasing power loss on the net monetary assets held are:

The $40,000 held for the entire year suffers a purchasing power loss of (110/100 − 110/110) $40,000	$4,000
The $20,000 increase that occurred evenly throughout the year suffers a loss of (110/105 − 110/110) $20,000	952
	$4,952

ILLUSTRATION 12–1. **Comparative Income Statements**

	Historical Cost	Constant Dollars
Sales.................	$400,000 × $\frac{110}{105}$	$419,048
Cost of goods sold......	320,000 (see calculation	335,238
Gross profit	80,000	83,810
Depreciation	5,000 × $\frac{110}{50}$	11,000
Other expenses	55,000 × $\frac{110}{105}$	57,619
	60,000	68,619
		15,191
Loss of purchasing power on net monetary assets		4,952
Net income	$ 20,000	$ 10,239

The comparative income statements (Illustration 12–1) show that in constant (end-of-year) dollars Bailey's net income is $10,239 as compared to the $20,000 net income figure reported on the historical cost income statement.

If companies do not adjust their income statements for changes in the purchasing power of the measuring unit (the dollar), their net income figures will not be an accurate measure of the results of operations. This is particularly true for companies that have a large fixed-asset base, do not use the LIFO inventory cost flow assumption, and have a large net monetary position.

CURRENT COST ACCOUNTING (SPECIFIC PRICE CHANGES)

This method of measurement emphasizes specific price changes of assets rather than price changes caused by general inflation (constant-dollar accounting). It records individual assets at the cost to replace them as of the current balance sheet date.

Balance sheet

The two major methods for obtaining specific price change adjusted asset values are *current cost* and *current replacement cost.* The current cost approach values assets at the current cost to produce an *identical asset,* whether or not an identical asset would actually ever be used to replace the current one. The current replacement cost approach values assets at the current cost of replacing the *existing productive capacity* of the asset.

Consider the current valuation of a steel mill in operation since 1960. The *current cost* of the mill is an estimate of the cost to construct a mill identical in all respects to the existing mill, even though the existing mill is technologically outdated and would probably never be replaced with a new mill of the same type. The *current replacement cost* valuation would first develop an estimate of the capacity of the existing mill and then determine the cost to build a new mill of similar capacity based on new technology. In the current balance sheet both the current cost and current replacement cost of the new mill would be adjusted for approximately 25 years of straight-line depreciation. If technology is not changing, current cost and current replacement cost valuations are likely to be almost identical. In the steel industry, where technology has changed dramatically over the past 25 years, the valuation under the two methods would be substantially different.

Current cost and current replacement cost are subjective estimates of value that are difficult to verify. For example, it is particularly difficult to determine the current cost of a specially designed asset. The lack of objectivity and verifiability are cited as the reason that current cost financial statements have not been readily accepted by the financial community.

Income statement

Current cost revenues are the same as historical cost revenues. Current cost expenses are stated at the cost of replacing the asset at the moment in time it is consumed in the generation of revenue. Suppose an item in inventory acquired one year ago for $25 is sold for $75. At the time of the sale, price lists show that it would cost $45 to obtain an identical item for inventory. The current cost of goods sold is $45. The current operating income realized on the sale is $30 ($75 − $45). Historical cost income is $50 ($75 − $25). The $20 difference in income results because the current cost of inventory has gone up by $20.

Holding gains

The difference between the current cost of an asset (for example, $45 inventory item) and the historical cost of an asset ($25 inventory item) is a *holding gain.* The holding gain or loss on the item in inventory is realized when the item is sold.

The current cost method attempts to decompose historical cost income into two components, current operating income and realized holding gains.

Historical Cost		Current Cost	
Revenue	$75	Revenue	$75
Cost of goods sold	25	Cost of goods sold	45
Net income	$50	Current operating income	30
		Realized holding gain	20
		Realized income	$50

Current operating income is the difference between historical cost revenue (which equals current cost revenue) and current cost expenses. Realized holding gains measure the holding gains present in the assets used up or sold during the period. Current operating income (distributable income) is an informative measure of income. If the firm wishes to maintain operations at its current level and replenish its inventory at current cost, no more than $30 should be paid out in taxes and dividends.

Current cost depreciation expense is also likely to exceed historical cost depreciation expense since current costs of assets are likely to exceed historical costs of assets. Suppose Company X acquired an asset five years ago at a cost of $1,000. The asset has a 10-year life, zero salvage value, and is being depreciated on a straight-line basis. Historical cost depreciation is $100. If the current value of a net asset in similar condition is $3,000, current cost depreciation expense will be $300 for the period.

In addition to realized holding gains, current cost methods usually propose that the unrealized holding gains of the period (changes in current values from the beginning of the period to the end of the period for assets not sold) be reported. In the preceding inventory example, if the item was not sold, the $20 would be reported as an unrealized rather than realized holding gain of the period.

Current costs and financial analysis

Current cost statements are generally viewed as providing a better economic measure of the success of operations in a period than historical cost or constant-dollar financial statements because they focus on the specific price changes affecting the enterprise. The rate of return on investment can be computed using current operating income in the numerator and current cost or current replacement cost of assets in the denominator. Unlike the standard rate of return measure (historical cost income/book value of assets), this measure is independent of realized holding gains and obsolete asset values and is comparable across time and across firms.

SFAS 33, "FINANCIAL REPORTING AND CHANGING PRICES"

In October 1979 the FASB issued *Statement 33,* "Financial Reporting and Changing Prices," to address the effects of inflation on the financial statements of larger companies.

The FASB requires companies with inventories and gross fixed assets exceeding $125 million or with a book value of total assets in excess of $1 billion to provide supplementary financial statement information about the effects of inflation on their operations and financial postion. Both constant-dollar and specific price change information is required. This requirement is intended to help readers assess the performance, the status of operating capability, and the future cash flows of an enterprise.

The consumer price index is to be used for restatement to constant dollars because it is published monthly and is better understood than other alternative indices, such as the GNP implicit price deflator.

SFAS 33 allows the use of either the end-of-year or average price index to determine constant dollars if the financial statements are comprehensively restated.

The average dollar for the year must be used if the company complies only with the minimum requirements (restatement of inventory, property, plant, equipment, cost of goods sold, depreciation, and amortization) of this accounting standard.

The FASB defines current cost as the current cost of acquiring the same service potential (indicated by operating costs and physical output capacity) embodied by the asset owned. Current costs may be determined by applying specialized indexes to the historical cost of assets, by obtaining readily available current purchase prices of some standard assets, or by any other method appropriate to the circumstances.

SFAS 33 requires the restatement of certain historical cost information, namely inventories, property and equipment, cost of goods sold, and depreciation and amortization expense, and the calculation of income from continued operations using both the constant and current-dollar approaches . It also requires the calculation and separate disclosure of the purchasing power gain or loss on net monetary assets or liabilities and current cost holding gains or losses on inventory and property and equipment.

Cash dividends and market prices per common share are reported as adjusted for changes in the general price level, which enables readers to focus on real changes in dividend payments and market prices.

Example of *SFAS 33* disclosure

In their 1981 annual report Tandy Corporation made the following *Statement 33* disclosure, which includes an excellent explanation of the manner in which the various accounts are converted to constant dollars and current costs and the significance of these adjustments in measuring the company's operating results.

SUPPLEMENTARY FINANCIAL DATA ADJUSTED FOR THE EFFECTS OF CHANGING PRICES (Unaudited)

Tandy Corporation's financial statements are prepared in accordance with generally accepted accounting principles, which include the concept of historical cost. Under this concept, transactions are recorded and reported in units of purchasing power at the entry date of such assets, liabilities, revenues and expenses. As a result of the effects of inflation, historical

(continued)

cost financial statements are reported in dollars representing a variety of purchasing power.

In an attempt to remedy this situation, the Financial Accounting Standards Board issued Statement of Financial Accounting Standards No. 33 entitled "Financial Reporting and Changing Prices." Statement No. 33 requires disclosure of selected data under two different sets of assumptions—constant dollar and current cost.

Constant dollar disclosures require adjustment of inventories; property, plant and equipment; cost of products sold; and depreciation expense. These are adjusted to equal units of purchasing power through the application of the Consumer Price Index—All Urban Consumers. The methods used in computation are the same as those in the historical cost financial statements. Other items of revenue and expense are assumed to have occurred proportionately throughout the year and are therefore already stated in average 1981 dollars.

Current cost disclosures also require adjustment of inventories; property, plant and equipment; cost of products sold; and depreciation expense. This method is based on the assumption that Tandy Corporation would replace its entire inventory and facilities with identical assets at fiscal year end. The primary purpose, however, is to show the effect of changes in specific prices related to a given company's operations. This effect may be greater or less than the effect of changes in general purchasing power depending on the specific industry in which a company is conducting business. In the case of Tandy Corporation, the effect of changes in specific prices has less of an impact on net income than changes in general purchasing power. This is due in large part to the technological advances made in the electronics industry. Tandy has been able to utilize these technological advances to reduce or control manufacturing costs of many self-manufactured items. Therefore, prices to the consumer have increased only nominally in recent years while the Company has been able to retain adequate gross margins. These advances have also allowed the Company's outside vendors to maintain their products at price levels that have allowed Tandy to increase or retain gross margins at satisfactory levels. The computation of current cost data was accomplished through the use of internally and externally generated indices using similar methods as those in the historical cost financial statements.

As required by Statement No. 33, both constant-dollar and current cost net income are before holding gains or losses. During periods of inflation monetary assets such as cash and receivables are reduced in value through a decrease in purchasing power. Monetary liabilities, however, experience a gain in value since they will be liquidated in dollars of decreased purchasing power. Because of Tandy Corporation's net monetary liability position a holding gain has resulted for fiscal years 1981 and 1980. A holding gain was also experienced due to the increase in current costs of inventories and property and equipment held during the last two fiscal years. These

(continued)

increases in current costs, however, did not rise as rapidly as the general price level.

Adjusted pretax earnings under both methods were below those reported in the primary financial statements. Statement No. 33 provided that income tax expense should not be restated since income taxes are determined and payable on the basis of historical income. As a result, the effective income tax rates were 56.5% under the constant dollar method and 52.8% under the current cost method compared to 47.1% in the primary financial statements.

TANDY CORPORATION AND SUBSIDIARIES
Consolidated Statement of Income Adjusted for Changing Prices (Unaudited)
(In thousands, except per share amounts)

	Year Ended June 30, 1981		
	As Reported in the Primary Statements	Adjusted for General Inflation	Adjusted for Changes in Specific Prices (Current Costs)
Net Sales	$1,691,373	$1,691,373	$1,691,373
Other income	15,697	15,697	15,697
	1,707,070	1,707,070	1,707,070
Costs and expenses:			
Cost of products sold	701,777	748,096	726,932
Selling, general, and administrative	645,934	645,934	645,934
Depreciation and amortization	23,288	30,235	32,907
Interest expense, net of interest income	15,454	15,454	15,454
	1,386,453	1,439,719	1,421,227
Income before income taxes	320,617	267,351	285,843
Provision for income taxes	151,015	151,015	151,015
Net income	$ 169,602	$ 116,336	$ 134,828
Net income per average common share	$1.65	$1.13	$1.31
Stockholders' equity at year-end	$ 571,863	$ 626,934	$ 622,017
Purchasing power gain from holding net monetary liabilities during the year		$ 21,361	$ 21,361
Inventories and property and equipment held during the year*:			
Effect of increase in general price level			$ 66,640
Effect of increase in specific prices (current costs)			35,337
Excess of general price level increase over specific price level increase			$ 31,303

 * At June 30, 1981, the current cost of inventory was $513,455,000 (historical amount—$513,709,000), and the current cost of property and equipment, net of accumulated depreciation, was $269,049,000 (historical amount—$190,429,000).

(continued)

TANDY CORPORATION AND SUBSIDIARIES
Comparison of Selected Supplemental Financial Data (Unaudited)
(In thousands, except per share and index amounts)
(Per share amounts restated for two-for-one stock splits in May 1981, December 1980 and June 1978)
(Amounts adjusted for general inflation and specific price changes are in average 1981 dollars)

| | *Year Ended June 30* | | | | |
	1981	*1980*	*1979*	*1978*	*1977*
Net Sales:					
As reported	$1,691,373	$1,384,637	$1,215,483	$1,059,324	$ 949,267
Adjusted for general inflation	$1,691,373	$1,544,174	$1,536,531	$1,464,758	$1,400,682
Income from continuing operations:					
As reported	$ 169,602	$ 112,235	$ 83,229	$ 66,146	$ 71,819
Adjusted for general inflation	$ 116,336	$ 57,066			
Adjusted for specific price changes .	$ 134,828	$ 91,943			
Income from continuing operations per average common share and common share equivalent:					
As reported	$ 1.65	$ 1.12	.81	$ .69	$ .54
Adjusted for general inflation	$ 1.13	$ .58			
Adjusted for specific price changes .	$ 1.31	$ .92			
Excess of general price level increase over specific price level increase ...	$ 31,303	$ 51,923			
Purchasing power gain from holding net monetary liabilities during the year	$ 21,361	48,696			
Net assets at year end:					
As reported	$ 571,863	$ 283,125			
Adjusted for general inflation	$ 626,934	$ 373,095			
Adjusted for specific price changes .	$ 622,017	$ 377,994			
Total assets (as reported)	$ 936,545	$ 710,298	$ 609,589	$ 553,455	$ 474,675
Total long-term liabilities (as reported) .	$ 160,902	$ 258,456	$ 263,383	$ 268,338	$ 156,931
Cash dividends per common share ...	None	None	None	None	None
Market price per common share at year end:					
Historical	$ 30.88	$ 10.38	$ 5.34	$ 5.55	$ 3.48
Adjusted for general inflation	$ 29.52	$ 10.87	$ 6.40	$ 7.37	$ 4.97
Average consumer price index	259.4	232.6	205.2	187.6	175.8

SUMMARY

The general price level and specific price changes disclosures required by *SFAS 33* are useful in assessing the impact of changing prices on an enterprise's operations and financial position.

The general price level disclosure makes it possible to determine whether the firm has maintained its capital (assets minus liabilities) and earned a profit in terms of constant (units of the same amount of purchasing power) dollars. Some accountants assert that the computation of net income should also include the purchasing power gains or losses from holding net monetary assets or liabilities. For example, they would report Tandy's net income adjusted for general inflation as $137,697 ($116,336 + $21,361) or $1.34 per average common share.

Specific price change disclosure makes it possible to determine whether the firm has earned a profit after it maintains its current productive capacity. Current cost net income is the difference between revenues and the current cost of assets consumed in operations.

PROBLEMS AND CASES

12–1   The Inflatable Company (A)

THE INFLATABLE COMPANY
Balance Sheets
December 31, 1985, and 1984
($000)

	1984	1985
Assets		
Cash	–0–	$10,000
Inventories	$10,000	6,000
Fixed assets (net of depreciation)	20,000	18,000
Total assets	$30,000	$34,000
Equities		
Accounts payable	$ 6,000	$ 7,000
Common stock	20,000	20,000
Retained earnings	4,000	7,000
Total equities	$30,000	$34,000

THE INFLATABLE COMPANY
Income Statement
For the Year Ended December 31, 1985

Sales............................		$15,000
Cost of goods sold................	8,000	
Depreciation	2,000	10,000
Income before taxes		5,000
Income taxes		2,000
Net income		$ 3,000

Additional information:

a. The December 31, 1984, inventory of 5,000 units was purchased on that date.
b. All the fixed assets were purchased and the common stock was issued on January 1, 1974.
c. The Inflatable Company uses the FIFO inventory cost flow method.
d. All the transactions, including the purchase of 2,000 units of inventory, occurred evenly thoughout 1985.
e. General price level indices assumed for purposes of this problem are:

January	1, 1974	75
December 31, 1984		120
Average	1985	130
December 31, 1985		138

Required:

1. Prepare a December 31, 1985, balance sheet expressed in average 1985 constant dollars.

2. Prepare a 1985 income statement expressed in average 1985 constant dollars. Be sure to include the unrealized purchasing power gain or loss on net monetary assets.

12–2 Toledo Edison

TOLEDO EDISON
Balance Sheet
December 31, 1974

	Traditional Historical Cost Accounting	General Price-Level Accounting*
	(Thousands of Dollars)	
ASSETS		
Property, plant, and equipment:		
In service	$438,639	$747,442
Less: Accumulated provision for depreciation	116,062	202,806
	$322,577	$544,636
Construction work in progress	276,157	315,853
	$598,734	$860,489
Current assets	41,179	41,373
Investments and other	15,070	17,049
Total assets	$654,983	$918,911
LIABILITIES		
Capitalization:		
Common stock equity:		
Common stock	$ 40,801	$ 75,668
Premium on capital stock	60,216	79,086
Earnings reinvested	76,279	140,823
	$177,296	$295,577
Cumulative preferred stock	81,000	81,000
Long-term debt	299,172	299,172
Accumulated inflation effect from financing sources other than common stock equity	—	145,345
	$557,468	$821,094
Current liabilities:		
Short-term notes payable	$ 38,500	$ 38,500
Other current liabilities	43,981	44,283
	$ 82,481	$ 82,783
Accumulated provision for deferred taxes and other	$ 15,034	$ 15,034
Total liabilities	$654,983	$918,911

COMPARATIVE RATE OF RETURN RATIOS

Return on Net Plant Investment (Year End Basis)	9%	5%
Return on Common Stock Equity (Year End Basis)	11%	6%

* General price-level values based on current purchasing power of the dollar as of December 31, 1974.

The notes on the following pages are an integral part of these statements.

TOLEDO EDISON
Results of Operations
For the Year Ended December 31, 1974

	Traditional Historical Cost Accounting	General Price-level Accounting
	(Thousands of Dollars)	
Operating revenues	$147,794	$154,317
Operating expenses:		
Depreciation provisions	$ 13,089	$ 23,181
Less: Amortization of inflation effect from financing sources other than common stock equity	—	5,417
	$ 13,089	$ 17,764
Taxes	13,863	14,193
Other operating expenses	91,562	95,637
Total operating expenses	$118,514	$127,594
Operating income	$ 29,281	$ 26,723
Other income:		
Allowance for funds used during construction	$ 15,886	$ 16,587
Price-level loss from other monetary items	—	(85)
Other income and deductions (net)	387	404
Total other income	$ 16,273	$ 16,906
Income before interest charges	$ 45,554	$ 43,629
Interest charges	20,904	21,846
Net income	$ 24,650	$ 21,783
Preferred stock monthly dividends accrued . . .	4,964	5,183
Earnings on common stock	$ 19,686	$ 16,600

EARNINGS REINVESTED
For the Year Ended December 31, 1974

Balance, beginning of year	$ 71,096	$139,336
Add: Net income	$ 24,650	$ 21,783
Deduct:		
Preferred stock quarterly dividends declared	5,147	5,363
Common stock cash dividends declared	14,320	14,933
Earnings reinvested during the year	$ 5,183	$ 1,487
Balance, end of year	$ 76,279	$140,823

Notes to General Price-Level Financial Statement Study, December 31, 1974:

1: Results of Operations—The comparative price-level values of all items, except those detailed below, represent the amounts recorded in our traditional historical cost statement, which amounts generally occurred ratably throughout the year, converted to year-end 1974 purchasing power. This conversion was accomplished through the use of the Gross National Product Implicit Price Deflator (GNP Deflator) as Recommended in the FASB exposure draft. No federal income tax benefits for any inflation adjustment are reflected since current tax law does not allow any consideration for the erosion of capital which exists during inflationary periods.

The significant items in the Results of Operations Statement which are exceptions to the general explanation above are "price-level loss from other monetary items" (see first two paragraphs of Note 3) and the following:

Depreciation Provisions—The 1974 depreciation provision was determined by applying the same average depreciation rate used in the historical cost financial statements (3.3 percent) to the average plant in service which has been price-level adjusted to December 31, 1974. Such a provision reflects the actual year-end purchasing power applicable to current operations.

Amortization of Inflation Effect from Financing Sources Other Than Common Stock Equity— Partially offsetting the impact of inflation on current depreciation, the "accumulated inflation effect from financing sources, other than common stock equity" is being amortized into income at the same rate as the overall composite rate (3.3 percent) being used to determine the annual depreciation provision for property, plant, and equipment. In our opinion, treating the sources of property investment on the same basis as the property it finances results in a realistic presentation for evaluating the overall impact of inflation.

2: Earnings Reinvested—The 1974 beginning balance of earnings reinvested as converted to year-end 1974 purchasing power, represents historical cost earnings reinvested along with the net impact of restating the 1973 balance sheet from historical cost to year-end 1974 purchasing power through the use of the GNP Deflator. The amounts for 1974 preferred, and common dividends declared, are the historical cost amounts converted to year-end 1974 purchasing power.

3: Balance Sheet—In developing the comparative price-level values, the nature (i.e., monetary or nonmonetary) of each asset and liability was determined based on the criteria set forth in the FASB exposure draft. Assets and liabilities are considered "monetary" if their amounts are fixed in terms of dollars regardless of changes in general price-level.

Excluding the major "nonmonetary" items, such as property, plant, equipment, and common stock equity items, most of the other asset and liability accounts have been identified as "monetary." These accounts in the traditional historical cost statement are stated in dollars of current purchasing power. Consequently, although not apparent in every instance because of consolidations with minor nomonetary items, the value of these monetary items remains at the same amounts on the comparative price-level statements. During 1974 the net impact of inflation on holding these monetary items resulted in the price-level loss, as reported in the income statement. This price-level loss was determined as the difference between the historical value of the monetary items and the year-end 1974 purchasing power value of both the beginning of year balances and the net changes in these items which occurred ratably throughout the year.

The major items classified as nonmonetary assets and liabilities consist of earnings reinvested (see Note 2) and the following.

Property, Plant, and Equipment—The actual amounts of property, plant, and equipment in service, as shown in the company's historical cost balance sheet at the end of 1974, were analyzed using property records of surviving plant by vintage year. The continuing property records of the company classify the investment in facilities by the year they were placed in service. Therefore, to more closely determine the year expenditures were made, the year-to-year changes in the construction work-in-progress account (excluding the ending balance) were netted with the vintage year values of surviving plant in service. The results of this approach, representing amounts expended for property each year, were then restated to year-end 1974 purchasing power. The amounts invested in construction work-in-progress at the end of 1974 were vintaged and also restated to year-end 1974 purchasing power.

Accumulated Provision for Depreciation—The beginning 1974 comparative price-level reserve was established at the same percentage relationship to price-level plant in service as that which existed on the historical cost basis at December 31, 1973. This approach was used as the most logical and supportable alternative to the ideal approach as outlined in the FASB exposure draft. In establishing the starting point for beginning a restatement of the accumulated provision for depreciation for 1974, the ideal approach would have required us to have analyzed in detail the transactions against the accumulated reserve for each prior year. Such an approach under a composite depreciation method would be an extremely extensive and costly undertaking and require substantial time and effort. Several alternative methods were considered, but the results (i.e. providing lower ratios of reserve for depreciation to plant-in-service than being experienced on a historical basis) appeared to require further reveiw and consideration.

Common Stock and Premium on Capital Stock—The values of common stock and premium on capital stock on the comparative price-level statement were computed by restating the historical costs amounts, based on the year invested, to year-end 1974 purchasing power.

Accumulated Inflation Effect from Financing Sources Other Than Common Stock Equity— Debt financing through the issuance of first mortgage bonds, short-term notes and other obligations and funds secured through the issuance of preferred stock have been identified as "monetary" items (see first paragraph of Note 3). However, since these items comprise some of the sources of funds invested in property, plant, and equipment, they have been treated on a basis consistent with the property financed. The approach used was to restate the historical cost amounts for these sources, based on the year of investment, to year-end 1974 purchasing power. The excess amounts over historical cost are identified as the "accumulated inflation effect from financing sources other than common stock equity." A portion of this accumulated inflation effect, equivalent to the percentage of reserve for depreciation to the plant in service, was credited to earnings reinvested at the beginning of the year. (See Note 1 for current year amortization.)

Required:

1.   The president of the Toledo Edison Company feels that heavily capitalized industries such as electric utilities should be allowed depreciation on the replacement cost of fixed assets to reflect the value of plant investment "used up." Do you agree? Would the replacement cost depreciation for 1974 be $23,181? (See results of operations.)

2.   Which figures more fairly present the results of operations for the year ended December 31, 1974.

3.   Do you think federal income taxes should be based on general price-level accounting net income rather than on historical cost net income?

4.   Are the stockholders earning a fair rate of return on their investment? If not, should utility rates be raised?

5.   Do you think the general price-level accounting figures are as easily understood by investors as the historical cost figures?

12–3   Worthington Industries, Inc.

Worthington Industries, Inc., is a diversified manufacturing company in the metal and plastic fields.

Refer to the company's *SFAS 33* "Financial Reporting and Changing

Prices" supplementary disclosure in their 1981 annual report and answer the following questions:

1. Explain what causes the differences in the historical cost, constant-dollar, and current cost net earnings figures.

2. Explain why the income taxes figure is the same for each of the three different methods even though earnings from operations is different.

3. What does the company mean when they state that the impact of inflation was borne by our creditors.

4. If the purchasing power gain on holding net monetary liabilities of $7,252 is added to constant dollar net earnings of $16,292, the total of $23,544 exceeds historical cost net earnings of $22,891. Does this mean that Worthington has successfully coped with general price inflation for the fiscal year ended May 31, 1981?

5. Do you agree with the company's conclusion that the *FASB 33* disclosure demonstrates that changes must be made in current depreciation practices and tax rates if business is to remain healthy in the face of rising inflation?

Note L: Supplementary financial data and the effects of changing prices (unaudited)—

In 1979, the Financial Accounting Standards Board (FASB) issued statement No. 33 "Financial Reporting and Changing Prices." This statement, which is experimental in nature, requires certain financial data be restated to reflect the impact of inflation. Under the FASB guidelines, the effect of inflation is to be measured in general terms (constant dollars) and using the Company's more specific prices (current cost). The impact of these computations is provided in the following supplemental financial data.

The measurement selected for developing the effect of general inflation is the Consumer Price Index–All Urban Consumers (CPI-U). Under this method, the financial data is presented in dollars having the same general purchasing power; i.e., if the inflation rate increases 10 percent from one year to the next, 10 percent more dollars are needed to acquire the same goods and services.

For current cost data, adjustments were made in the prices of specific goods and services used by the Company. This method reflects the varying rates of inflation that have taken place in the goods and services actually consumed by the Company. The effect of this change was largely developed through the use of selected price indices.

Under the FASB 33 guidelines, the value of inventories, property, plant and equipment were adjusted in these calculations. This necessarily impacts cost of goods sold and depreciation expense. In addition, net monetary liabilities were converted to average-for-the-year constant dollars for inclusion in the computation of net assets. The income tax provision has not been adjusted to reflect the reduced earnings, thereby creating a substantially higher effective tax rate.

Under both the constant dollar and current cost methods, income from continuing operations is lower than that developed under historic accounting rules. Cost of goods sold is higher as it reflects the higher cost of raw materials being used. The higher depreciation expense is caused by the shortcomings of current allowable depreciation methods which amortize historic costs over a longer period of time without contemplating the rising cost of capital equipment.

A beneficial effect of inflation on the Company's financial position is the net purchasing power gain from holding net monetary liabilities. This gain arises because the Company held liabilities which were recorded in historic dollars, but which were repaid in subsequent inflated dollars. When this gain is compared with the decrease in net earnings, it becomes apparent the impact of inflation has been borne by our creditors.

The increase in the specific prices of inventories, property, plant and equipment is greater than the increase in the general price level, principally because the specific indices used to obtain the current cost of major segments of our machinery and equipment increased more than the CPI-U.

Although earnings have been eroded by inflation, the Company is attempting to minimize these rising costs by carefully monitoring its pricing and by improving its manufacturing facilities and techniques. Clearly, the data demonstrates the changes that must be made in current

WORTHINGTON INDUSTRIES, INC.
Comparison of Selected Data Adjusted for the Effects of Changing Prices
For the Years Ended May 31, 1981
(all data is expressed in average fiscal year 1981 dollars)
(Dollars in thousands, except per share amounts)

	1981	1980	1979	1978	1977
Net sales and revenues					
Historical	$428,144	$286,417	$278,154	$191,501	$148,597
Constant dollar	428,144	320,538	351,827	264,302	218,815
Net earnings					
Historical	$ 22,891				
Constant dollar	16,292				
Current cost	16,801				
Earnings per share					
Historical	$ 1.85				
Constant dollar	1.32				
Current cost	1.36				
Purchasing power gain	$ 7,252				
Excess of increase in specific prices over increase in general price level of inventories and property	$ 103				
Net assets at year end					
Historical	$101,022				
Constant dollar	128,429				
Current cost	131,263				
Dividends delcared per share					
Historical	$ .54	$ .48	$ .36	$ .22	$ .13
Constant dollar	$ .54	$ .53	$ .45	$ .30	$ .19
Market price per share at year end					
Historical	$ 22.37	$ 15.12	$ 20.25	$ 20.00	$ 6.59
Constant dollar	21.45	15.89	24.34	26.64	9.39
Average consumer price index for all urban consumers	257.4	230.0	203.5	186.5	174.8

depreciation practices and tax rates if business is to remain healthy in the face of the rising inflation.

Each of the methods used in this presentation inherently involves the use of assumptions, approximations and estimates. Therefore, the resulting measurement must be cautiously viewed in that context and not as precise indicators of the effects of inflation. This data is most meaningful when used for identifying trends and relationships.

WORTHINGTON INDUSTRIES, INC.
Consolidated Statement of Earnings Adjusted for the Effects of Changing Prices
Year Ended May 31, 1981
(Dollars in thousands)

	Historical Cost	Constant Dollar	Current Cost
Net sales and revenues	$428,144	$428,144	$428,144
Cost of products sold	336,389	340,843	340,128
Depreciation expense	9,581	11,726	11,932
Other operating expenses	32,829	32,829	32,829
Interest expense	7,608	7,608	7,608
Earnings From Operations	41,737	35,138	35,647
Income taxes	18,846	18,846	18,846
Net Earnings	$ 22,891	$ 16,292	$ 16,801
Effective Income Tax Rate	45.2%	53.6%	52.9%
Purchasing power gain from holding net monetary liabilities during the year		$ 7,252	$ 7,252
Increase in the specific prices of inventories, property, plant and equipment held during the years			$ 17,245
Less effect of increase in general price level			$ 17,142
Excess of increase in specific prices over increase in general price level			$ 103

Note: At May 31, 1981, current cost of inventory was $55,244 (historical amount—$53,838) and current cost of property, plant and equipment, net of accumulated depreciation, was $139,200 (historical amount—$113,496).

12–4 Dayco Corporation

Dayco Corporation manufactures rubber and plastic component parts for nearly every industry in the United States.

Refer to Note M, Effects of Changing Prices, from Dayco's 1981 annual report and answer the following questions:

1. Which income statement, historical cost, adjusted for general inflation, or adjusted for changes in specific prices, best measures Dayco's results of operations for 1981?

2.   Explain how this supplementary changing prices disclosure would enable a present or potential Dayco shareholder or creditor to estimate future earnings and cash flow.

Note M: Effects of changing prices

In recent years, inflation has impacted the financial statements of many U.S. companies to a significant degree. Financial statements traditionally have reported transactions in historical dollars of varying degrees of purchasing power. This method does not adequately measure the effects of inflation. For example, investments in property, plant and equipment made over an extended period of time are aggregated as though the dollars from these periods were common units of measurement. Depreciation of these prior period costs is deducted from current period revenues and does not reflect the current cost of assets consumed.

The accompanying Statement of Income and Selected Financial Data and Five Year Comparison of Selected Supplementary Financial Data were prepared in accordance with the experimental guidelines established by the Financial Accounting Standards Board. These guidelines were established to provide some estimate of the impact of general inflation and specific changing prices on the traditional financial statements. However, the FASB has imposed certain assumptions in making these calculations such that their worth is highly questionable.

Constant-Dollar Data—Constant dollar data represent historical cost financial information stated in 1981 average dollars to reflect the impact of general inflation. The historical cost has been adjusted to eliminate the changes in the general purchasing power of the dollar and is based on the Consumer Price Index.

Current Cost Data—Current cost data adjust historical cost to reflect changes in specific prices of resources in order to express their measurement and consumption in terms of current replacement cost rather than historical amounts to acquire them.

Inventories and Cost of Sales—Inventories have been calculated using the FIFO method of costing inventories. Such amounts were adjusted to reflect replacement costs, depreciation, and the approximate time lag in recognizing price changes. Since the Corporation employs the LIFO method of accounting for inventories, the adjustment to cost of sales is relatively small (less than 1% of historical cost of sales).

Property, Plant, and Equipment—Land has been valued based on estimates of local market value. All other property, plant, and equipment was valued by using an industry construction index appropriately applied by year of asset acquisition. The amounts do not reflect any economic benefits of new and different technology.

Depreciation Expense—Depreciation expense had been computed for the current cost of productive capacity by using approximately the same methods and depreciable life assumptions as in the historical financial statements.

Purchasing Power Gain—During periods of high inflation, the holding of monetary assets (e.g. cash and receivables) results in a loss of general purchasing power, since these assets will purchase fewer goods and services. Conversely, holders of liabilities benefit during such periods because less purchasing power will be required to satisfy their obligations. Since monetary liabilities at year end were greater than monetary assets, an unrealized purchasing power gain is shown.

Review of Information—Earnings on a constant-dollar and current cost basis are significantly lower, primarily owing to higher depreciation expense. Because the Corporation principally used the LIFO method of accounting for inventories, the adjustment to cost of goods sold is not significant since current costs are reflected in the historical cost financial statements.

(continued on page 325)

324

DAYCO CORPORATION
Statement of Income and Selected Financial Data Adjusted for Changing Prices

(Amounts in thousands except per share amounts)	As Reported in the Primary Statements 1981	Adjust for General Inflation 1981	Adjusted for Changes in Specific Prices (current costs) 1981	1980
Net sales	$786,957	$786,957	$786,957	$794,555
Cost of goods sold[a]	593,323	596,900	596,900	606,956
Depreciation expense	14,356	21,882	23,479	22,194
Selling, general, and administrative expenses[a]	149,159	149,159	149,159	148,241
All other—net	17,754	17,754	17,754	12,953
Earnings from continuing operations before income taxes	12,365	1,262	(335)	4,211
Provision for income taxes[b]	3,322	3,322	3,322	3,376
Net earnings from continuing operations before extraordinary item	$ 9,043	$ (2,060)	$ (3,657)	$ 835
Primary earnings per share before extraordinary item	$ 1.53	$ (.38)	$ (.66)	$ .12
Net assets at year end	$140,688	$271,504	$266,434	$267,049
Gain from decline in purchasing power of net amounts owed		$ 15,166	$ 15,166	$ 17,266
Effect of increase in general price level[c]			$ 39,223	$ 44,866
Increase in specific prices (current cost) of inventories and property, plant and equipment held during the year			35,359	32,335
Excess of increase in the general price level over increase in specific prices			$ 3,864	$ 12,531

[a] Excluding depreciation expense.

[b] No adjustment has been made to the provision for income taxes. The effect is to increase the effective tax rate from 27% (26% in 1980) as reported in the primary statements, to 263% in the 1981 constant dollar calculation and resulted in taxing a loss from continuing operations in the 1981 current cost calculation (effective rate of 80% for 1980 current cost).

[c] At October 31, 1981, the current cost of inventory was $178,064,000 ($157,628,000 in 1980) and the cost of property, plant and equipment, net of accumulated depreciation, was $231,945,000 ($204,812,000 in 1980).

Both the constant-dollar and current cost methods assume the entire replacement of the existing production capacity at the current cost at each year end. Obviously, replacement of existing property, plant and equipment would not take place all at once. Further, any replacement would entail the latest technology so as to minimize all operating costs, including depreciation. It should also be noted that the methods prohibit assuming any increases in product prices. Certainly such replacement would not take place if our investment could not be recovered in the market place.

The provision for income taxes has not been reduced because inflationary increases in costs are not deductible for income tax purposes. The substantially higher effective tax rate under both constant-dollar and current cost calculations is evidence of the impact of inflation on taxes. The result of this impact is to reduce funds available for increasing and replacing production facilities and providing returns to shareholders.

It should be noted that the information provided by the constant-dollar and current cost analysis is not a reliable predictor of future cash flows. Future cash flows can be influenced by improved technology and increased productivity and, therefore, cannot be assessed solely by evaluating existing assets.

DAYCO CORPORATION
Five-Year Comparison of Selected Supplementary Financial Data Adjusted for the Effects of Changing Prices
(In average 1981 dollars)

(Amounts in thousands, except per share amounts)	1981	1980	1979	1978	1977
Net sales	$786,957	$794,555	$931,892	$910,014	$856,943
Net earnings from continuing operations:[a]					
In constant dollars	$ (2,060)	$ (969)			
In current cost	$ (3,657)	$ 835			
Earnings per common share[a]					
In constant dollars	$ (.38)	$ (.21)			
In current cost	$ (.66)	$ .12			
Dividends per share of common stock	$ .056	$ .621	$ .623	$ .577	$ .567
Net assets at year end[a]					
In constant dollars	$271,504	$274,870			
In current cost	$266,434	$267,049			
Gain from decline in purchasing power of net amounts owed[a]	$ 15,166	$ 17,266			
Excess of increase in general price over increase in specific prices[a]	$ 3,864	$ 12,531			
Market price per share of common stock at year end	$ 13	$ 13⅞	$ 16⅞	$ 16¾	$ 18⅞
Average consumer price index	268.4	242.0	213.1	192.6	179.6

[a] Constant dollar and current cost information for years prior to 1980 is not readily determinable.

13

The income statement: A closer look

Events of an unusual (nonroutine) nature that affect owners' equity require special accounting treatment. Prior period adjustments, extraordinary items, and discontinued operations are examples of such unusual events. Special accounting treatment is also required when enterprises change their methods of accounting for particular types of events or report income for federal tax purposes different than reported financial statement income.

Proper disclosure of unusual (nonroutine) events and changes in accounting method is based on the accounting profession's current answers to two very general questions: Should the income statement include the effects of all events that increase or decrease owners' equity during the accounting period with the exception of dividend distributions and capital transactions? This is a question of inclusion. How should we disclose the effects of these events in a particular income statement? This is a question of format.

Investors can best estimate the future results and cash flows of an enterprise if the nature and amount of income generated by unusual (nonroutine) events is reported separately from income from continuing (normal) operations.

THE ALL-INCLUSIVE VIEW OF THE INCOME STATEMENT

The following paragraph was excerpted from the litigation footnote of Georgia-Pacific Corporation's 1980 annual report.

> The corporation, along with numerous other manufacturers of corrugated containers, has been named as a defendant in a number of treble damage civil antitrust actions alleging a conspiracy to fix the prices of corrugated containers. Many of these actions were consolidated into a class action in the United States District Court for the Southern District of Texas at Houston, Texas. On April 2, 1980, the corporation and two other defendant manufacturers entered into a settlement agreement with the named representatives of the class, which is subject to court approval, under which the three settling defendants will be dismissed from the class action in exchange for a payment to the class totaling $3 million. There remain against the corporation nine actions in which the plaintiffs opted out of the class proceedings. Management believes and trial counsel concurs that the maximum liability, if any, in the opt-out actions would not have in the aggregate a material adverse effect on the financial position of the corporation.

Suppose Georgia-Pacific's accountants agree that $1,500,000 represents their likely damages from these antitrust actions. How should they record the $1,500,000 on the books? The $1,500,000 should be credited to a liability account, but what account should be debited? Since the settlement agreement was made in 1980 one possible alternative is to show a loss in the 1980 income statement. The journal entry would be:

Loss from Lawsuit 1,500,000
    Liability for Damages 1,500,000

The other possible alternative is not to show any of the $1,500,000 loss in the 1980 income statement since the loss is a direct result of events that occurred in accounting periods prior to 1980. The only effect in the 1980 statements would be a reduction in the beginning balance of retained earnings. The 1980 journal entry using this alternative would be:

Retained Earnings 1,500,000
    Liability for Damanges 1,500,000

Georgia-Pacific's December 31, 1980, balance sheets would be identical under these alternative treatments since the loss appearing in the 1980 income statement under the first alternative would be closed to retained earnings at the end of 1980. The pretax income for 1980 would be $1,500,000 smaller under the first alternative.

The FASB requires that with few exceptions *all items of income and loss recognized during a period should be included in the income statement for the period.*[1] Georgia-Pacific must show the loss resulting from the antitrust action in its 1980 income statement. Losses, whether directly or indirectly related to events of the current period, affect the long-run profitability of the firm and are best brought to the attention of financial statement readers if they are completely and objectively disclosed in the income statement. This is an *all-inclusive view* of the income statement.

PRIOR PERIOD ADJUSTMENTS

The only items of income and loss that are treated as *prior period adjustments* and excluded from the income statement by making an entry directly to retained earnings are correction of errors found in prior statements, recognition of an income tax loss carry-forward acquired through purchase of a subsidiary,[2] and compliance with a FASB or APB statement or opinion dealing with the reporting of a change in accounting method that permits or requires such treatment.

Correction of errors

Errors may be mathematical in nature or result from the incorrect application of an accounting principle or misuse of information which existed at the time of statement preparation.

Suppose ABC Company forgot to include $2,000 of depreciation on office equipment as an expense in its 1981 income statement. The error is discovered in 1982, at which time the correcting entry would be:

Retained Earnings	2,000	
Accumulated Depreciation—		
Office Equipment		2,000

Compliance with accounting standards

The change from LIFO to some other cost flow assumption is disclosed as a prior period adjustment. Usually this adjustment is substantial, and showing it in the current income statement would severely distort income for the current period.

---

[1] FASB, *Statement of Financial Accounting Standards No. 16,* "Prior Period Adjustments" (Stamford, Conn., October 1977).

[2] Under certain circumstances, the Internal Revenue Service allows companies to carry back and forward losses of one year to another year.

Statement of Financial Accounting Standards 13, "Accounting for Leases," issued by the FASB in November 1976, requires companies to restate retained earnings as of January 1, 1976, as if the new methods of lease accounting had been in effect prior to 1976. Subsequent years' income statements are reported in conformity with the new methods. Changes in accounting methods must be described in a footnote to the financial statements.

In 1977 the annual report of TRW Incorporated contained the following footnote (Illustration 13–1) and statement of retained earnings (Illustration 13–2), which reflect the change in accounting methods for leases.

ILLUSTRATION 13–1

TRW INCORPORATED
Change in Accounting Method

In compliance with a recent pronouncement of the Financial Accounting Standards Board, the company in 1977 changed its method of accounting for certain leases in which it is the lessee. The new method, which requires that amounts related to lease agreements meeting the criteria for classification as capital leases be recorded as assets with the related lease obligations recorded as liabilities, has been applied retroactively to lease agreements in existence prior to January 1, 1977. Retained earnings at January 1, 1976, have been reduced by $8.1 million, and net earnings and earnings per share as previously reported for 1976 have been reduced by $.9 million and $.03, respectively.

ILLUSTRATION 13–2

TRW INCORPORATED
Statement of Changes in Consolidated Shareholders' Investment
($000)

	Years Ended December 31	
	1977	1976 (restated)
Retained earnings		
Balance at January 1, as previously reported	$650,183	$582,674
Retroactive adjustment for capitalizing leases	—	(8,050)
Balance at January 1, as restated	$650,183	$574,624
Net earnings	154,217	132,169
	$804,400	$706,793
Deduct dividends declared:		
Preference stock	17,522	17,966
Common stock	44,895	38,644
	$ 62,417	$ 56,610
Balance at December 31	$741,983	$650,183

EXTRAORDINARY ITEMS

Extraordinary items are an important class of items that are *disclosed separately* in the income statement after net income from operations. Any material item is an extraordinary item if it is *both unusual* in nature and *infrequent* in occurrence.[3] Losses resulting from earthquakes or expropriations would usually be considered extraordinary for U.S. firms because they are unusual and infrequent. However, flood damage suffered by a business located in the flood plain of a river is not extraordinary. The loss may be infrequent, but it is not unusual. Whether a particular gain or loss is extraordinary depends on a firm's individual operating environment. Items that are either infrequent but usual or frequent but unusual are disclosed as other income or other expense in the recurring revenue and expense section of the income statement. Only rarely do items meet both conditions for classification as an extraordinary item.

Sedco, Inc., considered a loss they suffered as a result of the revolution in Iran to be both unusual and infrequent and recorded it as an extraordinary loss. a summary of the income statement and the related footnote is shown in Illustration 13–3.

Other income

In 1981 the Burndy Corporation realized an $11,985,000 gain on the sale of assets. Although infrequent, sales of assets are not unusual. Burndy disclosed the sale as other income under the heading nonrecurring gain on sale of assets (Illustration 13–4).[4]

Premature retirement of debt

The FASB may also require extraordinary item presentation for items which are not both infrequent and unusual in order to highlight specific items that might otherwise be overlooked if listed as a component of operating income. Currently, utilized tax loss carry-forwards and gains and losses on premature retirement of debt are to be classified as extraordinary items. In the early 1970s corporate bonds outstanding generally had market values that were much less than their book values because interest rates had in-

---

[3] AICPA, *Accounting Principles Board Opinion No. 30*, "Reporting the Results of Operations" (New York, September 1973).

[4] This treatment is in accordance with the FASB's *Statement of Financial Accounting Concepts No. 3*, "Elements of Financial Statements of Business Enterprises," December 1980, which defines gains and losses as increases and decreases in equity from peripheral (not ongoing or central) operations of an enterprise. Statement of Financial Accounting Concepts are *not* GAAP but are considered as a conceptual framework in establishing GAAP.

ILLUSTRATION 13–3

SEDCO, INC., AND SUBSIDIARIES
Consolidated Income Statement
Year Ended June 30, 1979
($000)

Revenues	$255,037
Costs and Expenses	218,619
Income from Consolidated Operations before Income Taxes	36,418
Provision for Income Taxes on Consolidated Operations	9,529
Income from Consolidated Operations	26,889
Equity in Income (Loss) of Associated Companies, Net of Income Tax Effects	(588)
Income from Consolidated Operations and Associated Companies	26,301
Equity in Income of Iranian Operations, Net of Income Tax Effects (Note 4)	3,052
Income before Discontinued Operations and Extraordinary Item	29,353
Discontinued Operations, Net of Income Tax Effects:	
Income (Loss) from Operations	(17,490)
Extraordinary Item—Provision for Losses in Iran, Net of Income Tax Effects (Note 4)	(50,000)
Net Income (Loss)	$ (38,137)
Average Shares Outstanding	30,866
Income (Loss) per Share:	
Income before discontinued operations and extraordinary items	$ .95
Discontinued operations	(.57)
Extraordinary item	(1.62)
Net income (loss)	$ (1.24)

Note 4: Iranian Operations—Sedco has conducted contract drilling, pipeline construction, and ship repair operations in Iran through Iranian subsidiary and associated companies and Iranian branches of other subsidiary and associated companies. In December
1978 substantially all of these operations were disrupted during the revolution and
change of government in Iran, which disruption continues to the present time. In view
of the situation in Iran, Sedco, as of June 30, 1979, recorded a liability for its guarantee
of loans of an Iranian associated company and made a provision for losses in Iran of
$50,000,000 (after income tax effects of $9,190,000) to state its investments in those
entities at estimated realizable value.

creased since the time the bonds were issued. A company could
realize large gains by the early retirement of these bonds through
market purchases or exchange of a new issue of securities for these
bonds. Since such gains (or losses) aren't attributable to normal
operations the FASB decided to alert the readers of financial statements by requiring that the gains be disclosed as extraordinary
items.[5]

[5] FASB, *Statement of Financial Accounting Standards No. 4,* "Reporting Gains
and Losses from Extinguishment of Debt" (Stamford, Conn., March 1975).

ILLUSTRATION 13–4

BURNDY CORPORATION AND SUBSIDIARY COMPANIES
Consolidated Statements of Earnings
Year Ended December 31, 1981
($000, except per share data)

Net sales	$256,764
Cost of sales	150,393
Gross income	106,371
Selling, general, and administrative expense	60,654
Operating income	45,717
Interest expense—net	(3,515)
Nonrecurring gain on sale of assets	11,895
Earnings before income taxes and equity in net earnings of unconsolidated affiliates	54,097
Income taxes	24,008
Earnings before equity in net earnings of unconsolidated affiliates	30,089
Equity in net earnings of unconsolidated affiliates	2,750
Net earnings	$ 32,839
Net earnings per share	$2.64

In 1980 the General Host Corporation exchanged their 7% Subordinate Debentures with a book value of $47,735,000 for $37,741,000 principal amount 12¾% Convertible Subordinated Debentures resulting in an *extraordinary gain* of $7,141,000 net of income taxes and expenses (Illustration 13–5).

ACCOUNTING CHANGES

The FASB requires special disclosure (net of tax effects and after operating income) of several other items not meeting the unusual and infrequency criteria for classification as extraordinary items. The cumulative effects of changing from one generally accepted accounting principle to another generally accepted accounting principle (if not required or permitted by an FASB Statement, FASB Interpretation, or APB Opinion to be reported in some other manner) are to be shown in their entirety *in the income statement* of the period in which the switch occurs.

Ale Company acquired an asset with a useful life of four years

ILLUSTRATION 13–5

GENERAL HOST CORPORATION
Consolidated Statement of Income
(Dollars in thousands, except per share amounts)

	1980	1979	1978
Revenues:			
Sales of continuing operations	**$ 424,713**	$ 350,375	$ 298,780
Other income	**6,613**	9,986	2,162
	431,326	360,361	300,942
Costs and expenses:			
Cost of sales	**326,439**	281,216	244,222
Selling, general, and administrative	**63,982**	46,783	35,343
Depreciation and amortization	**7,956**	5,802	5,205
Interest and debt expense	**10,944**	10,731	11,436
Provision for uncollectible note			1,135
	409,321	344,532	297,341
Income from continuing operations before income taxes	**22,005**	15,829	3,601
Provision for income taxes	**10,589**	6,157	1,089
Income from continuing operations	**11,416**	9,672	2,512
Discontinued operations, after income taxes	**(18,142)**	10,565	(5,116)
Income (loss) before extraordinary gains	**(6,726)**	20,237	(2,604)
Extraordinary gains	**7,141**	9,233	
Net income (loss)	**$ 415**	$ 29,470	$ (2,604)
Primary earnings per share:			
Income from continuing operations	**$ 4.00**	$ 3.99	$ 1.44
Discontinued operations	**(6.36)**	4.36	(2.94)
Income (loss) before extraordinary gains	**(2.36)**	8.35	(1.50)
Extraordinary gains	**2.50**	3.81	
Net income (loss)	**$ .14**	$ 12.16	$ (1.50)
Fully diluted earnings per share:			
Income from continuing operations	**$ 3.48**	$ 3.24	$ 1.21
Discontinued operations		3.29	
Income before extraordinary gain		6.53	
Extraordinary gain		2.95	
Net income		$ 9.48	
Average shares outstanding	**2,851,622**	2,422,796	1,738,416
Fully diluted shares	**3,712,829**	3,212,091	3,205,320

Note 5: Extraordinary Gains—In 1980, the Company offered to exchange for each $100 principal amount of its outstanding 7% Subordinated Debentures, due February 1, 1994, $65 principal amount of 12¾% Convertible Subordinated Debentures, due June 15, 1999, which are convertible into common stock at $30 per share. $58,-063,000 principal amount of the 7% Debentures, with a carrying value of $47,735,000, after deducting original issue discount, were exchanged for $37,741,000 principal amount of 12¾% Debentures. This exchange resulted in an extraordinary gain on extinguishment of debt which amounted to $7,141,000, after deducting related expenses and $2,602,000 of income taxes.

and zero salvage value for $1,000. Ale used sum-of-the-years'-digits depreciation for the first two years (for both taxes and financial statements) resulting in depreciation expense of $400 (4/10 × $1,000) in year 1 and $300 (3/10 × $1,000) in year 2. At the start of the third year Ale and Ale's auditor agreed that a switch to straight-line depreciation would be appropriate for this particular asset. Straight-line depreciation would have resulted in a total of $500 in depreciation expense for the first two years. Therefore Ale reported $200 more depreciation expense (and less income) over the first two years than would have been shown if straight-line depreciation had been used. The pretax cumulative effect of the switch is $200. Assuming a 40 percent tax rate the switch should be disclosed in Ale's third-year income statement (along with a footnote explaining and justifying the change if necessary).

ALE COMPANY
Abbreviated Third-Year Income Statement

Net income from operations   xxx
Add: Cumulative effect on prior years
   of switch in method of depreciation
   (net of $80 tax effect) $120
Net income   xxx

Since Ale would have reported $200 more income during the first two years had it used straight-line depreciation, aftertax financial statement income would have been $120 more. The cumulative effect of the restatement of prior years' income due to the depreciation method switch is shown in the third year.

Prior to January 1, 1977, Mountain Fuel Supply Company (MFSC) reduced financial statement income tax expense by the amount of the investment tax credit earned during the period. Beginning in 1977 MFSC elected to defer investment tax credits in the financial statements equally over the useful life of the asset that generated the credit. This is a change from one generally accepted accounting principle (flow-through method) to another generally accepted accounting principle (deferral method) and was reported as in Illustration 13–6.

CHANGES IN ACCOUNTING ESTIMATES

There are many estimates inherent in the accounting process. Depreciation accounting relies on estimates of useful lives and future salvage values. Accounting for doubtful accounts relies on an estimate of future bad debts.

ILLUSTRATION 13–6

MOUNTAIN FUEL SUPPLY COMPANY AND SUBSIDIARIES
Consolidated Statements of Income
($000)

	Year Ended December 31	
	1978	1977
Income before federal income taxes and cumulative effect of change in accounting principle	$37,497	$40,701
Total federal income taxes	16,567	13,768
Income before cumulative effect of change in accounting principle	20,930	26,933
Cumulative effect to December 31, 1976, to defer investment tax credits on nonutility properties (Note B).......................................	—	1,688
Net income	$20,930	$25,245
Dividends on preferred stock	869	661
Income available to common stock	$20,061	$24,584

Note B: Changes in Accounting for Investment Tax Credits—The company elected to defer the investment tax credits for nonutility properties, beginning January 1, 1977. The cumulative effect of the change to December 31, 1976, of $1,688,000 ($.27 per share) was included as a reduction of net income in 1977. The effect of this change in 1977 was to decrease net income $878,000 ($.14 per share). The change will relate the investment tax credits to the estimated remaining lives of the respective properties.

Changes in estimates are not considered to be errors (treated as prior period adjustments) or changes in accounting principles (treated as cumulative effects of accounting changes). The proper accounting treatment of changes in estimates is current and prospective—the change in estimate is adjusted for in this and future periods.

Suppose XYZ Company acquired a piece of equipment two years ago at a cost of $500. The useful life is estimated to be five years, and the salvage value is zero. After two years of straight-line depreciation the net book value of the equipment is $300. At the beginning of the third year XYZ's accountants realize that the equipment has a remaining useful life of two rather than three years. The depreciation expense recognized in each of the subsequent two years will be $150 (300 ÷ 2). No adjustment to retained earnings is made at the time the estimate of the useful life is revised to correct for the underdepreciation of the first two years. The change in estimate is adjusted for in the current and future periods.

DISCONTINUED OPERATIONS

Firms that dispose of an entire segment of a business or an entire product line (discontinued operations) must disclose the gain or loss on the disposal in a fashion similar to the disclosure required for extraordinary items *(APB Opinion 30)*.

Gains on disposal of a discontinued operation are recognized on the disposal date, the date on which the sale is closed, or the date on which the property is abandoned. Losses anticipated on the date management commits itself to a formal disposal plan (measurement date) are recognized as of the measurement date. This is consistent with the principle of conservatism.

The results of the discontinued operations for the current accounting period are also disclosed separately. Deciding if a particular disposal qualifies for discontinued operations treatment is a complicated and subjective process. The assets and activities of a segment should be physically and operationally distinct from the other assets and activities of the business.

The General Host Corporation, whose income statement is shown in Illustration 10–5, considered the sale of the fresh and processed meat business segment by its wholly owned subsidiary, Cudahy Company, in 1980, the sale of its tourism business segment at Yellowstone National Park in 1979, the sale of its Allied Leather Company in 1978, and the sale of its Eddy Bakeries and Van DeKamp's Bakery Division in 1978 and 1979 to all qualify for discontinued operations treatment.

The following footnote explaining these transactions appeared in General Host's 1980 financial statement.

Note 3: Discontinued Operations—During 1980, the Company decided to discontinue the fresh and processed meat business segment of its wholly owned subsidiary, Cudahy Company, and established a $28,500,000 loss provision, consisting of $5,900,000 for estimated losses on disposal of assets and $22,600,000 for estimated employee termination costs (including pension and other retirement benefits), operating losses during phase-out periods and other closing costs. Of the $22,600,000, approximately $8,500,000 is included in accrued expenses and $14,100,000 is included in other liabilities and deferred credits in the balance sheet. After income taxes, the loss provision reduced income by $17,745,000 or $6.22 per share ($4.78 fully diluted).

Sales of these discontinued operations, amounting to $407,960,000 in 1980, $401,640,000 in 1979 and $346,577,000 in 1978, are eliminated in the consolidated statement of income and their operating results are included in discontinued operations. The Company expects to complete the disposal of the operating units which comprise this business segment by the end of 1982.

During 1979, the National Park Service, United States Department of the Interior, terminated the concession contract under which the Company's Yellowstone Park Company subsidiary operated tourist facilities in Yellowstone National Park, discontinuing the Company's tourism business segment. Yellowstone Park Company's interest in buildings and its equipment were sold to the United States of America for $19,900,000 and the inventories and other assets were sold to the successor concessioner for approximately their carrying values. After income taxes, these sales resulted in a gain of $8,274,000 or $3.42 per share ($2.58 fully diluted). Sales of discontinued Yellowstone Park Company operations, amounting to $16,405,000 in 1979 and $15,129,000 in 1978, are eliminated in the consolidated statement of income and its income is included in discontinued operations.

During 1978, the Company sold the Allied Leather Company operations which comprised its footwear and apparel materials business segment, and in 1978 and early 1979 sold its Eddy Bakeries and Van de Kamp's Bakery Divisions which comprised its bakery products business segment. Sales of these discontinued operations, amounting to $82,537,000 in 1978, are eliminated in the consolidated statement of income, and the losses of these operations are included in discontinued operations in 1978.

Operating results and gains or losses on disposals of these business segments are as follows:

| | Year Ended | | |
	Dec. 27, 1980	Dec. 29, 1979	Dec. 30, 1978
Operating income (losses) prior to disposals of businesses	$ (1,756)	$ 3,600	$ (501)
Gain from sale of Yellowstone Park Company assets		11,981	
Provisions for estimated losses on disposals of fresh and processed meat business segment in 1980 and footwear and apparel materials and bakery products business segments in 1978	(28,500)		(5,502)
	(30,256)	15,581	(6,003)
Less: Applicable income taxes	(12,114)	5,016	(887)
	$(18,142)	$10,565	$(5,116)

Uniroyal Incorporated closed and disposed of several individual facilities, none of which represented an entire segment of their business. Gains or losses on such disposals are shown as other income or other expense (similar to disclosure of unusual but frequently occurring items) in net income from operations in Illustration 13–7.

ILLUSTRATION 13–7

UNIROYAL, INC., AND SUBSIDIARY COMPANIES
Statements of Consolidated Income
($000)

	Fiscal Year Ended	
	January 1, 1978	January 2, 1977
Net sales	$2,581,927	$2,314,841
Cost of goods sold	2,071,802	1,847,127
Selling, administrative, and		
general expenses	399,850	390,596
Interest expense	49,810	44,083
(Gain) or loss on closed facilities	(3,826)	3,025
Other (income)—expense	309	(8,259)
Total costs and expenses	2,517,945	2,276,572
Income before income taxes	63,982	38,269
Federal and foreign income taxes	29,191	18,137
Net income	$ 34,791	$ 20,132

Gain or Loss on Closed Facilities—Operations in 1977 reflect a net pretax gain of $3,826,000 applicable to closed facilities. Included in this gain are the pretax profits of $4,124,000, recorded in the first quarter of 1977 applicable to the company's sale of its 51 percent interest in Latex Fiber Industries, Inc.

The fourth quarter of 1977 includes the effect of gains totaling $5,708,000 on the sale of certain properties; however, this gain was offset by additional provisions of $6,006,000 to cover the disposal of footwear operations in Naugatuck, Conn. and the planned closing of tire operations in Los Angeles, Calif. as well as adjustments to previous accruals to bring them in line with actual disposals or current estimates of the costs remaining to be incurred. The sale of facilities included a former manufacturing facility in Santa Ana, Calif. which for the last several years has been used only for warehousing and computer operations; a warehouse in Philadelphia, Pa. which was no longer required and had been subleased; the Fabric Fire Hose operations and equipment located in Sandy Hook, Conn. and the auto tube manufacturing facility in Indianapolis, Ind.

ACCOUNTING FOR INCOME TAXES

Taxable income may not be the same as income on the financial statements because the rules in the Internal Revenue Code for determining taxable income differ from the generally accepted accounting principles used to construct financial statement income.

Interperiod income tax allocation is the process of computing and accounting for the difference between taxes due the IRS and income tax expense reported in the financial statements in a particular accounting period.

Permanent differences

Some items considered to be revenues and expenses in determining accounting income are not ever considered to be revenues and expenses in computing taxable income.

Interest earned on most municipal securities and life insurance proceeds paid to a corporation upon the death of one of its officers are revenues included in accounting income but not included in taxable income. Fines a company pays for violation of pollution emission standards and amortization of goodwill are expenses in the financial statements but are not allowable deductions (expenses) in determining taxable income. The differences between taxable income and accounting income caused by such items are called permanent differences.

Permanent differences are also caused by items considered to be revenues or expenses for tax purposes but not for financial statement purposes.

Berly Corporation's 1984 taxable income is computed below:

Sales revenue	$5,000
Cost of goods sold	2,000
Gross margin	3,000
Interest expense	500
Taxable income	$2,500

Since Berly Corporation pays taxes to the IRS at the rate of 40 percent of taxable income, its 1984 income tax is $1,000 (.4 × $2,500).

Berly's 1984 income statement is shown below:

Sales revenue	$5,000
Cost of goods	2,000
Gross margin	3,000
Interest expense	500
Amortization of goodwill	500
Income before taxes	2,000
Income tax expense	1,000
Net income	$1,000

Except for amortization of goodwill all revenues and expenses are identical for tax and accounting purposes. Because amortization of goodwill will never be deductible for tax purposes, it creates a permanent difference between taxable income and accounting income. Income tax expense for financial statement purposes is computed after adjusting net income before taxes for all permanent differences and Berly's 1984 income tax expense on both the financial statements and income tax returns is 40 percent of $2,500.

Timing differences

Many transactions affect taxable income and accounting income in different accounting periods. These timing differences originate in one period and "turn around" in another period.

Sales on account, with the buyer agreeing to pay in several separate payments, are called installment sales. Installment sales usually are recognized as revenues for financial statement purposes in the period the sale is made. For tax purposes the revenue on installment sales may be recognized as the cash is collected. This creates a timing difference between taxable and accounting income.

Company Z sells $500 worth of merchandise (cost $280) for cash and $100 worth of merchandise (cost $20) under an installment purchase plan. Installments of $50 each will be received in 1982 and 1983. Company Z has no other revenues or expenses and pays income taxes amounting to 40 percent of taxable income. Assume that in both 1982 and 1983 Company Z makes no further installment sales, sells $700 of merchandise for cash (cost $500), and collects the installments due. Their taxable and accounting income for the three years will appear as follows:

COMPANY Z
Income Tax Returns

	1981	1982	1983
Revenues	$500	$750 (700 + 50)	$750 (700 + 50)
Cost of goods sold	280	510 (500 + 10)	510 (500 + 10)
Taxable income	220	240	240
Taxes	88 (.4 × $220)	96 (.4 × $240)	96 (.4 × $240)
Aftertax income	$132	$144	$144

COMPANY Z
Income Statements

	1981	1982	1983
Revenues	$600 (500 + 100)	$700	$700
Cost of goods sold	300 (280 + 20)	500	500
Income before taxes	300	200	200
Income tax expense	120 (.4 × $300)	80 (.4 × $200)	80 (.4 × $200)
Net income	$180	$120	$120

A timing difference of $80 ($300 pretax accounting income minus $220 taxable income) originates in 1981 and reverses itself in 1982 and 1983 when taxable income exceeds pretax accounting income by $40 ($240 − $200).

Timing differences also arise because firms may use different methods of depreciation for tax and accounting purposes, because rents collected in advance are included in taxable income before they are included in accounting income, and because estimated warranty costs appear as expenses earlier in accounting income than in taxable income. Many other items may also cause timing differences.

Deferred income taxes

Deferred income tax accounts are used to record the effects of all timing differences in an accounting period.

If a timing difference results in income tax expense that exceeds income taxes payable for the period, the difference is credited to the Deferred Income Tax account. In the previous installment sales example Company Z makes the following entry to record income tax expense, income taxes payable, and the effect due to the timing differences in 1981:

Income Tax Expense	120	
Income Taxes Payable		88
Deferred Income Taxes—Current		32

In 1982 and 1983 when the timing difference is reversed Company Z makes the following entry:

Deferred Income Taxes—Current	16	
Income Tax Expense	80	
Income Taxes Payable		96

The balance in the deferred income tax account at the end of 1983 is zero since the timing difference has been completely reversed.

If in 1982 and 1983 Company Z makes new installment sales at the 1981 rate, the tax and accounting income will be equal in 1983, and the deferred income tax account will still have a credit balance. The balance in Deferred Income Tax will remain as long as Company Z continues to make installment sales at or above the 1981 level.

Every timing difference must be accounted for as in the above example.[6] The tax rate in effect when the timing difference origi-

---

[6] *AICPA, Opinion No. 11,* "Accounting for Income Taxes" (New York, December 1967).

nates is used to compute the entry to the Deferred Tax account. The Deferred Tax account associated with a particular timing difference is classified as a short-term or long-term asset or liability depending on whether it has a debit or a credit balance and how the assets and liabilities related to the timing differences are classified. For instance, a Deferred Tax account originating because depreciation expense on the tax return exceeded the depreciation charge on the financial statements has a credit balance and is classified as a long-term liability (since depreciation relates to long-term assets).

Since permanent differences are never reversed, an accounting entry to deferred taxes is unnecessary.

Classification of deferred income taxes

Many accountants question the classification of deferred income taxes as a liability. They argue that only income taxes computed on taxable income have to be paid to the U.S. government and that deferred income taxes will never have to be paid by companies that continue to grow: make installment sales or purchase fixed assets at the same or higher rate than they did in prior years.

The consequence of recording deferred income taxes as expenses and liabilities on the income statement and balance sheet is addressed in a *Forbes article.*

MYTHICAL LIABILITIES

Companies must count deferred income taxes as liabilities, even though most of those taxes will probably never be paid. Result: Both income and net worth may be seriously understated. Assuming for the sake of simplicity that the 26 companies [page 343] would never pay *any* of their deferred taxes (not too unrealistic an assumption in most cases), we added 1980 deferred taxes (found in the income tax footnote) back into net income, and total deferred tax liabilities (from the balance sheet) into shareholders' equity. While perhaps a bit extreme, the resulting adjusted earnings and equity-per-share figures show how significant deferred tax distortions can be.

INCOME TAX DISCLOSURE

Investors and potential investors are concerned with the earnings and cash flows of a firm. In addition to the above deferred tax treatment of timing effects required by the FASB, the SEC requires disclosure of other tax information, which aids investors in their assessments of the value of a firm.

The SEC requires firms to report in the annual report filed with

Company	Total Deferred Income Taxes as of 12/31/80 ($ millions)	As Percent of Equity	1980 Earnings per Share		1980 Equity per Share	
			Reported	Adjusted	Reported	Adjusted
Grumman	$ 130	41.1	$ 2.35	$ 4.11	$20.40	$30.36
Coastal Corp	282	39.7	4.63	7.76	24.78	36.71
McDonnell Douglas	598†	39.5	3.65	3.98	38.18	53.27
Combustion Engineering	239	37.6	3.56	4.28	19.41	26.71
Murphy Oil	241	35.5	4.03	6.59	18.18	24.65
Union Pacific	897	31.7	4.22	5.77	29.54	38.89
Martin Marietta	330	29.9	7.55	10.85	44.27	57.51
Raytheon	385	29.5	6.80	8.71	31.41	40.67
The Williams Cos	270	28.0	5.07	6.86	35.30	45.17
General Dynamics	284	27.7	3.58	5.45	18.35	23.57
MAPCO	137	27.3	4.48	5.79	18.38	23.40
TRW	348	27.1	6.39	9.43	38.82	49.32
Air Products & Chemicals*	176	26.4	4.07	4.61	23.43	29.62
Anheuser-Busch	268	25.7	3.80	5.30	22.96	28.88
Atlantic Richfield	1,796	24.1	6.64	8.57	29.91	37.13
Marathon Oil	451	23.5	6.27	8.01	31.82	39.28
Georgia-Pacific	435	22.8	2.34	2.87	18.31	22.48
Occidental Petroleum	511†	22.4	8.82	10.88	25.49	31.84
Pennzoil	229	22.4	5.90	6.93	19.85	24.29
Conoco	999	21.8	9.52	na	45.53	51.80
National Steel	306	21.2	4.42	4.73	76.21	92.34
Diamond Shamrock	260	20.9	3.66	4.75	22.59	27.31
Tenneco	982	20.6	5.95	9.01	36.76	45.43
IC Industries	300	20.4	6.02	7.91	79.21	97.80
Cities Service	521	20.2	5.73	7.04	30.94	37.20
Mobil	2,633	20.1	15.40	18.04	61.51	73.90

* As of 9/30/80.
† Includes some taxes other than deferred.
na: Not available.
Sources: Dennis Beresford, Ernst & Whinney annual reports; *Forbes* estimates.

Forbes Magazine, January 18, 1982. "Rollover" by Jane Carmichael (Numbers Game Section). Reprinted by Permission © Forbes, Inc. 1982.

them (Form 10-K) the tax effects of timing differences of the current period, to disclose that portion of income tax expense currently payable, and to reconcile the statutory corporate tax rate with the effective tax rate shown in the financial statements.

The first two disclosures provide information about the necessary current cash flows required to discharge tax obligations. A reconciliation of the effective tax rate with the statutory rate makes investors aware of the abnormally high or low current rates. If temporary in nature, the tax rate might change materially in future periods, leading to a material increase or decrease in earnings and cash flow.

The footnote in Illustration 13–8, which is taken from the June 30, 1981, annual report of the Tandy Corporation, makes it possible to determine the cash outflows for income taxes for the past five years and to ascertain whether the effective tax rates are abnormally high or low.

In 1981 Tandy's income tax expense was $151,016; of this amount $1,888 ($151,016 − $149,128) was deferred for short and long-term timing differences. Tandy's effective tax rates are very close to the statutory rates and can be used for projecting future earnings and cash flows.

ILLUSTRATION 13–8. **Provision for Income Taxes**

The Company provides for income taxes on all items included in the consolidated statements of income regardless of the period when such items are reported for tax purposes. The components of pretax income and the related income tax expense for the five years ended June 30, 1981, are detailed in the following charts:

Components of Income before Income Taxes

(In thousands)	1981	1980	1979	1978	1977
United States	$285,089	$183,342	$146,827	$109,153	$133,309
Foreign	35,528	27,316	14,674	16,979	8,480
Total	$320,617	$210,658	$161,501	$126,132	$141,789

Income Tax Expense

(In thousands)	1981	1980	1979	1978	1977
Current:					
Federal	$122,678	$ 84,992	$64,858	$48,477	$52,168
State	10,568	6,552	5,147	3,959	6,898
Foreign	15,882	9,996	5,515	4,667	7,029
	149,128	101,540	75,520	57,103	66,095
Deferred:					
Federal	2,319	(1,223)	1,649	1,874	3,674
Foreign	(431)	(1,894)	1,103	1,009	201
Total income tax expense on continuing operations	$151,016	$ 98,423	$78,272	$59,986	$69,970
Effective tax rate on continuing operations	47.1%	46.7%	48.5%	47.6%	49.3%

ILLUSTRATION 13–8 *(concluded)*

Certain provisions of the income tax laws and regulations result in some income and expense items being recorded in one period for financial accounting purposes and in another period for income tax purposes. Such items, which are included in the provision for income taxes as deferred taxes, relate primarily to differences between tax and book depreciation, income from installment sales, and provisions for future losses; changes in intercompany profits in ending inventories not eliminated for tax purposes; taxes provided on net undistributed earnings of certain foreign subsidiaries not currently taxable in the United States; and unrealized gains or losses on foreign currency translation. The tax effect of each of these timing differences was less than 5 percent of the amount computed by multiplying pretax income from continuing operations for the year by the statutory tax rate. Management expects deferred taxes related to computer installment sales to increase as these sales grow.

The Company uses the "flow-through" method for investment tax credits whereby income taxes are reduced in the year an asset is placed in service by the amount of the investment credit.

The Company's statutory tax rate for fiscal years 1981 and 1980 was 46 percent. The fiscal 1979 rate was 47 percent, a weighted average rate of the 48 percent and 46 percent rates. The statutory tax rate for each of the two years ended June 30, 1978, was 48 percent. The effective tax rate differed from the statutory rate as shown in the following schedule:

(In thousands)	**1981**	1980	1979	1978	1977
Federal income tax at statutory rate ...	**$147,484**	$96,903	$75,905	$60,543	$68,059
Investment tax credit	**(2,992)**	(1,499)	(695)	(1,479)	(1,098)
State income taxes, less federal income tax benefit	**6,970**	4,418	3,430	2,657	4,190
Other, net	**(446)**	(1,399)	(368)	(1,735)	(1,181)
Total income tax expense on continuing operations	**$151,016**	$98,423	$78,272	$59,986	$69,970

PROBLEMS AND CASES

13–1 Zebo Corporation

ZEBO CORPORATION
Statement of Income
For the Year Ended December 1, 1984

Sales revenues	$750,000
Interest revenue (municipal bonds)	10,000
	760,000
Operating expenses (excluding depreciation)	450,000
Depreciation expense	130,000
	580,000
Income before income taxes	$180,000

Additional information:

a. Zebo's ACRS depreciation on its income tax return for 1984 was $185,000.

b. Zebo's income taxes for 1984 were calculated at the statutory tax rate of 46 percent.

Required:

1. Make the journal entry to record Zebo's income tax expense for 1984 (assume the income taxes will not be paid until 1985).

2. What was Zebo's effective income tax rate for financial statement purposes?

3. Reconcile Zebo's effective income tax rate for financial statement purposes with the statutory tax rate of 46 percent. Explain why the reduction in income taxes due to ACRS depreciation is not included in this reconciliation.

13-2 Dayco Corporation

Dayco Corporation and Subsidiaries Statement of
Consolidated Earnings

Year Ended October 31	**1981**	1980	1979
Net sales	**$786,957,000**	$716,402,000	$739,889,000
Other income—net	**3,774,000**	4,158,000	4,258,000
	790,731,000	720,560,000	744,147,000
Costs and expenses:			
Costs of sales	**605,737,000**	557,942,000	565,241,000
Selling, general, and administrative expenses	**151,101,000**	137,051,000	130,847,000
Interest expense net of interest income	**21,528,000**	13,881,000	11,725,000
	778,366,000	708,874,000	707,813,000
Earnings before income taxes and extraordinary item	**12,365,000**	11,686,000	36,334,000
Income taxes—	**3,322,000**	3,044,000	15,208,000
Earnings before extraordinary item	**9,043,000**	8,642,000	21,126,000
Extraordinary item net of tax— Note B	**(11,721,000)**	—	—
Net earnings (loss)	**$ (2,678,000)**	$ 8,642,000	$ 21,126,000
Earnings per common share Primary:			
Earnings before extraordinary item	**$1.53**	$1.51	$3.87
Extraordinary item	**(2.02)**	—	—
Net earnings (loss)	**$(.49)**	$1.51	$3.87

Note B: Extraordinary Loss—Subsequent to year-end the Corporation determined that an outside sales agent had made substantial misrepresentations in connection with orders submitted for certain export customers. This determination was made because of discrepancies discovered between orders presented by the agent and actual orders verified by the customers. As a result the Corporation determined that accounts receivable and prepaid expenses related to these orders should be written off. The nonrecurring write-off of these amounts gave rise to an extraordinary loss of $11,721,000 (net of taxes totaling $11,860,000, of which $11,412,000 were deferred taxes) or $2.02 per share. The Corporation has referred the matter to counsel.

Required:

1. What possible alternative method might Dayco have used to disclose this loss of $23,581,000 before taxes due to a sales agent's misrepresentation?

2. Do you think Dayco's treatment of the item as an extraordinary loss is better disclosure than the method you suggest in 1? Why?

13-3 Pennwalt Corporation (A), Unusual Expenses and Discontinued Operations

Pennwalt Corporation's business, principal products, and major markets were listed in their 1981 annual report.

BUSINESS:
Chemicals, health products, and precision equipment

PRINCIPAL PRODUCTS:

Chemicals:
Intermediates: organic sulfur chemicals, Lucidol® organic peroxides, Kynar® high performance plastics, Isotron® refrigerants and foaming agents and amines.
Specialties: products for metal processing; laundry chemicals; flour treatment; food industry sanitation; pesticides; corrosion engineering; post-harvest decay control chemicals and equipment; rubber chemicals; precision lubricants and gas odorants.
Commodities: chlorine, caustic soda, hydrofluoric acid, muriatic acid and chlorates.
Natural resources: fluorspar, salt, sodium sulfate, oil and natural gas.

Health:
Proprietary pharmaceutical: Desenex® and Cruex® antifungal agents; Allerest® hay fever remedy; Sinarest® sinus headache medicine; CaldeCORT® hydrocortisone cream; Caldesene® medicated powder; Fresh® deodorant and other over-the-counter products.
Ethical pharmaceutical: Zaroxolyn® diuretic and antihypertensive agent; Adapin® antianxiety and antidepressant agent; Ionamin® appetite suppressant; Tussionex® antitussive and others.
Jelenko: precious metal alloys, dental consumables and laboratory equipment.

Precision Equipment:
Sharples® centrifuges and Wallace & Tiernan® chemical feeders, chlorinators and measuring devices for use in the chemical industry, pollution control, and water and waste treatment. Stokes® high vacuum equipment, plastics molding machines and compacting presses, Merrill® packaging equipment. S.S. White™ flexible shafting & Airbrasive® equipment. API navigational aids.

MAJOR MARKETS:
Health (18%) of sales; Chemical Process Industry (25%); Agriculture & Food Processing (16%); Plastics (12%); Environmental Cleanup (9%).

In his letter to the shareholders, Edwin E. Tuttle, chairman of the board and chief executive officer of Pennwalt, explained the reasons for the divestitures made by the company in 1981. A portion of his comments is quoted below:

DIVESTITURES

In the first quarter of the year, we sold the CVI Division (cryogenic equipment) and announced the termination of the dyestuffs business of our subsidiary in Holland. Although CVI was profitable and well managed, this operation simply did not "fit" our future plans for the rest of the company. Then, at year-end, we announced our plans to shut down the company's chlor-caustic operation at the Calvert City, Kentucky, plant and to divest the entire S. S. White dental operation.

As we said at the time of this last announcement, we continue to believe that the potential for the business of S. S. White is good. However, the potential for profitable participation by Pennwalt is significantly greater in some of our other business areas. Therefore, in keeping with the philosophy outlined above, a redeployment of this S. S. White investment seemed desirable.

A similar line of reasoning led to the decision to shut down the chlor-caustic facility at our Calvert City, Kentucky plant. This particular manufacturing operation is relatively small, and the plant had reached the stage where a major infusion of capital would soon be required to properly maintain it. Again, it seemed more desirable to direct our available resources into the more promising leadership segments of the company.

I want to emphasize that we will continue to manufacture chlorine and caustic at our two plants in the Pacific Northwest and at Wyandotte, Michigan, . . .

Pennwalt's 1981 statement of consolidated earnings and footnotes relating to the divestures were as follows:

PENNWALT CORPORATION FINANCIAL STATEMENTS

Statement of Consolidated Earnings

	1981	1980	1979
	(Thousands of Dollars)		
Income			
Net sales	**$1,056,118**	$1,043,126	$938,418
Other net, including equity ($3,644,000, $2,559,000 and $2,675,000) in net earnings of nonconsolidated companies and $5,436,000 gain on Mexican stock sale in 1979	**3,365**	7,993	11,481
	1,059,483	1,051,119	949,899
Costs and expenses:			
Cost of goods sold	**728,828**	750,786	659,692
Selling and administrative	**199,117**	190,103	173,171
Research and development	**26,632**	24,483	22,326
Interest expense	**22,332**	23,134	19,216
	976,909	988,506	874,405
	82,574	62,613	75,494
Loss on chemical plant shutdown (Note 2) .	**21,452**	—	—
	61,122	62,613	75,494
Federal and other income taxes	**24,461**	23,053	29,485
Earnings from continuing operations	**36,661**	39,560	46,009
Discontinued operations net of income taxes (Note 3):			
Earnings (loss) from operations	**(670)**	3,731	3,988
Loss from disposal	**(10,691)**	—	—
Cumulative effect of change in accounting for investment credit ($1.57 per share) (Note 6)	**16,295**	—	—
Net earnings	**$ 41,595**	$ 43,291	$ 49,997
Earnings per common and common equivalent share:			
Earnings from continuing operations ..	**$ 3.55**	$ 3.84	$ 4.61
Net earnings	**$ 4.02**	$ 4.20	$ 5.01

Notes to consolidated financial statements:

Note 2: Loss on Chemical Plant Shutdown—In the fourth quarter pretax charges against income of $21,452,000 were made as a result of the decision to shut down the Company's chlor-caustic operation at its Calvert City, Kentucky, plant. The provision for federal and other income taxes has been reduced by $9,950,000 as a result of the write-off. The impact on 1981 earnings was $1.11 per share.

Note 3: Discontinued Operations—During the first quarter of 1981, the Company sold its CVI operations and shut down the Vondelingenplaat Dyestuffs operations. As of December 31, 1981, the Company decided to sell its S. S. White dental operations. Estimated proceeds from the sale of the dental operations are expected to be received in early 1982 and therefore have been reflected as a current asset at December 31, 1981.

Operating results of these discontinued operations have been reclassified in the statement of consolidated earnings as "Discontinued operations net of income taxes: Earnings (Loss) from operations." The effect thereof on earnings per share was a loss of $.07 and income of $.36 and $.40 per share of common stock for the years 1981, 1980 and 1979 respectively. Earnings were net of income taxes (tax credits) of $(1,411,000) in 1981, $138,000 in 1980, and $1,629,000 in 1979, which taxes reflect the impact of the 1979 United Kingdom stock relief legislation of $417,000 in 1981, $1,057,000 in 1980, and $466,000 in 1979. Net sales of discontinued operations aggregated $126,011,000 in 1981, $145,576,000 in 1980, and $140,885,000 in 1979. A provision of $1.03 per share ($13,691,000, less related income taxes of $3,000,000) was made in 1981 for the loss from disposal of discontinued operations.

At December 31, 1981, the estimated net realizable values of the remaining assets of discontinued operations are shown in the consolidated balance sheet captions "Outstanding from sale of discontinued operations" and "Net noncurrent assets of discontinued operations." The reported carrying values of the net assets of discontinued operations have been segregated as to net current assets and net noncurrent assets at December 31, 1980.

Required:

1. Do you agree with Pennwalt's treatment of the loss on the shutdown of the chemical plant as an unusual item (deduction from earnings) rather than a discontinued operation?

2. How much is the aftertax cost of the loss on shutdown of the chemical plant?

3. Explain the rationale for treating the sale of CVI, the shutdown of Vondelingenplaat Dyestuffs, and the sale of S. S. White dental operations as discontinued operations rather than as an unusual items deducted from current income.

4. What additional information does treatment as a discontinued operation give that a reduction in earnings from continuing operations for unusual items doesn't?

5. Does disclosure of discontinued operations in this manner make it easier for analysts to assess Pennwalt's future earnings and cash flows?

13-4 Pennwalt Corporation (B), Accounting Changes

Notes to consolidated financial statements:

Note 6: Investment Tax Credit—Effective January 1, 1981, the Company changed its method of accounting for the investment tax credit from the deferral to the flow-through method, which is the method utilized by most reporting companies. The effect of this change was to increase 1981 earnings by $728,000 ($.07 per share) applicable to the current year, and by $16,295,000 ($1.57 per share) for the cumulative effect of this accounting change applicable to prior years. Assuming the change were made retroactively, earnings on a pro-forma basis would increase by $2,852,000 ($.28 per share) in 1980 and $1,883,000 ($.19 per share) in 1979 as follows:

	1981	1980	1979
	(Thousands of Dollars)		
Pro-Forma:			
Net earnings	$25,300	$46,143	$51,880
Net earnings per share	$ 2.45	$ 4.48	$ 5.20
Actual:			
Net earnings	$41,594	$43,291	$49,997
Net earnings per share	$ 4.02	$ 4.20	$ 5.01

Required:

Refer to Pennwalt's Investment Tax Credit footnote and the 1981 Statement of Consolidated Earnings (See Pennwalt A) and answer the following questions:

1. What journal entry did Pennwalt make to record the cumulative effect of change in accounting for investment tax credit?

2. Why wasn't the $16,295,000 stated net of income taxes like discontinued operations?

3. How much did the change in the method that Pennwalt used for recording the investment tax credit increase cash flow in 1981?

4. Why do you think Pennwalt decided to change their method of handling the investment tax credit in 1981?

5. What earnings figure should an analyst interested in predicting Pennwalt's future earnings use for 1981?

13–5 LTV Corporation

Footnotes to financial statements are frequently difficult to read and interpret.

Required:

1. Read the footnotes to LTV's 1978 financial statements and indicate whether the disclosure is complete, informative, and in accordance with GAAP for each of the events listed on the 1978 and 1979 statement of consolidated operations as unusual items and accounting changes.

2. What other accounting changes aren't disclosed in the income statements?

THE LTV CORPORATION AND SUBSIDIARIES
Statement of Consolidated Operations
Years Ended December 31, 1978, and 1977
(in thousands except per share data)

	1978	1977
Sales	$5,260,537	$4,703,296
Other income	17,544	16,136
Total sales and other income	$5,278,081	$4,719,432
Operating costs and expenses:		
Cost of products sold	$4,885,989	$4,400,942
Depreciation	83,257	70,857
Selling, administrative, and general expenses	195,206	190,133
Unusual items	(16,721)	(3,129)
Interest and debt discount	105,694	99,617
Minority interest in subsidiaries	572	572
Total costs and expenses	$5,253,997	$4,758,992
Income (loss) from continuing operations before income taxes	$ 24,084	$ (39,560)
Federal, state and foreign income tax (charge) credit	(4,100)	4,000
Income (loss) from continuing operations	$ 19,984	$ (35,560)
Discontinued operations	6,500	(38,270)
Income (loss) before extraordinary items and accounting change	$ 26,484	$ (73,830)
Extraordinary items	—	20,674
Cumulative effect on prior years of accounting change	13,119	—
Net Income (loss)	$ 39,603	$ (53,156)
Income (loss) per share—primary:		
Continuing operations	$ 1.07	$ (2.63)
Discontinued operations	0.42	(2.65)
Before extraordinary items and accounting change	$ 1.49	$ (5.28)
Extraordinary items	—	1.43
Accounting change	0.84	—
Net income (loss)	$ 2.33	$ (3.85)
Income (loss) per share—assuming full dilution:		
Continuing operations	$ 1.09	$ (2.63)
Discontinued operations	0.33	(2.65)
Before extraordinary items and accounting change	$ 1.42	$ (5.28)
Extraordinary items	—	1.43
Accounting change	0.67	—
Net income (loss)	$ 2.09	$ (3.85)

Note B: Receivables and Inventories—Approximately $44,605,000 of total receivables at December 31, 1978, relate to long-term contracts, of which no material amount is due or billable after one year. Receivables have been reduced for allowances for possible losses of $6,202,000 at December 31, 1978 and $1,874,000 at December 31, 1977.

Inventories at December 31 include the following (in thousands):

	1978	1977
Products	$ 503,090	$226,665
Contracts in progress	121,179	146,743
Materials, purchased parts, and supplies	388,342	128,661
Unreimbursed costs and fees under		
cost-plus-fee contracts	15,174	15,247
	$1,027,785	$517,316
Less progress payments received	67,922	100,142
	$ 959,863	$417,174

Inventories by business segment at December 31, 1978 (in thousands), were:

Steel	$782,370
Aerospace	102,578
Meat and food processing	71,712
Shipping	3,203
	$959,863

At December 31, 1978, the excess of current cost over carrying value of inventories valued on the Lifo basis was approximately $352 million (1977—$319 million).

In 1978 the method of computing Lifo inventories was changed from the dollar value, single-pool method to the specific goods multiple-pool method. The company believes that the specific goods multiple-pool method is the prevalent method in the industry and is preferable to the method previously used. This change increased 1978 net income by $19 million ($1.22 per share). The liquidation of Lifo inventory quantities carried as though acquired at lower costs which prevailed in earlier years decreased cost of products sold by approximately $27 million in 1978, inclusive of the pretax effect ($21,055,000) of the change to the specific goods multiple-pool method.

Note C: Property, Plant, and Equipment—Property, plant, and equipment at cost is as follows (in thousands):

	1978	1977
Land and land improvements	$ 162,343	$ 54,285
Plants and equipment—steel manufacturing	2,422,112	2,101,162
Ocean shipping vessels and equipment	85,692	—
Equipment, furniture, and fixtures	131,027	129,906
Assets acquired under capitalized leases	115,218	108,894
Unexpected proceeds of pollution control bonds	41,211	17,542
Other	10,155	5,495
	$2,967,758	$2,417,284
Less allowances for depreciation	1,338,897	1,317,013
Net carrying value	$1,628,861	$1,100,271

The company adopted the policy in 1978 of charging steel mill roll costs, net of estimated salvage value, to operating expense over the estimated useful life of the roll ($9,019,000 amortization expense in 1978). Previously, such costs were charged to operating expense at the time the rolls were placed into service. The company believes the new method is preferable because it minimizes fluctuations in roll expense between periods. As a result of this change, 1978 results of operations include a pretax credit of $13,119,000 representing the unamortized cost of rolls in service at the beginning of 1978. The effect of this change on the results of operations for 1978, and on a pro forma basis for 1977, was immaterial.

Note D: Indebtedness and Dividend Restrictions—

	Average Effective Rate of Interest	Amounts (in thousands)	
		December 31, 1978	December 31, 1977
The LTV Corporation:			
5% Subordinated debentures due 1988	7.3%	$ 181,646	$ 181,646
7½% Subordinated debentures due 1993 and 1994	12.0	206,114	—
11% Subordinated debentures due 2000 and 2007	11.6	92,038	65,079
9¼% Sinking Fund debentures due 1997	11.6	75,000	75,000
Subsidiaries:			
6½% and 6¾% Subordinated debentures due 1988	10.2	63,899	67,500
6¾% Subordinated debentures due 1994	10.2	172,301	172,978
7⅞% and 8⅜% Sinking fund debentures due 1997	8.2	60,000	60,000
9½% Sinking fund debentures due 1984	9.5	14,374	15,972
3⅜% to 10½% Mortgage bonds due through 2005	9.1	498,482	320,190
5% Guaranteed convertible (Subordinated) debentures due 1988	5.0	68,973	70,950
4.20% to 8.30% U.S. government insured Merchant Marine Bonds due through 1991	9.5	47,447	—
6½% to 9% Pollution control obligations due 1983 through 2006	9.0	84,420	—
Notes payable to banks due 1979–83		144,550	76,550
Sundry mortgage and other notes		11,433	15,811
		$1,720,677	$1,121,676
Less current portion		28,646	10,586
		$1,692,031	$1,111,090
Less unamortized discount		171,937	77,919
Total consolidated long-term debt		$1,520,094	$1,033,171

Each share of Series B preferred stock is convertible into 2.3 shares of common stock and .3 shares of Series 1 participating preference stock. Holders of the Series B preferred stock are entitled to receive cumulative cash dividends annually of $2.60 per share, payable quarterly. In the event of liquidation, they would be entitled to receive $60 per share plus dividends accrued. The aggregate amount of such liquidation preference in excess of par value amounted to $245,901,000 at December 31, 1978. The Series B preferred stock may be redeemed at $30 per share plus accrued dividends.

Under an exchange offer of January 26, 1979, the company has offered to exchange, through May 11, 1979, two shares of Series B stock for each share of Series A stock.

Each share of Class AA special stock is convertible into common stock at ratios increasing from 1.45 shares on December 31, 1978, to 1.50 shares in 1979. The shares of special stock are entitled to annual cumulative stock dividends of 3 percent payable in special stock through 1992.

Each share of Series 1 participating preference stock is convertible into one share of common stock. Holders are entitled to receive cash dividends equal to 110 percent of any cash dividend declared on the common stock. In the event of liquidation, after any preference in distribution in respect to the preferred stock, the holders of the Series 1 participating preference stock would be entitled to receive $10 per share plus accrued dividends.

The holders of the common stock, the Series A and B preferred stock, and the Series 1 participating preference stock are entitled to one vote per share. The holders of the special stock are entitled to a number of votes equal to the number of common shares into which their stock is convertible.

Changes in capital surplus are (in thousands):

	1978	1977
Balance at beginning of year	$332,550	$321,080
Excess over par value of shares issued upon:		
Stock dividends on Class AA special stock	401	294
Exercise of stock options	—	73
Conversion of $5 Series A preferred	471	—
Acquisition of Lykes Corporation	158,453	—
Other issuances of common shares	1,887	11,113
Sundry (charges) credits	369	(10)
Balance at end of year	$494,131	$332,550

Changes in consolidated retained earnings are (in thousands):

	1978	1977
Balance at beginning of year, as previously reported		$67,788
Retroactive restatement for change in accounting for leases		(5,867)
Balance at beginning of year, as restated	$ 5,933	$ 61,921
Net income (loss)	39,603	(53,156)
Cash dividends on preferred stock	(5,029)	(2,524)
Stock dividends on special stock	(414)	(308)
Balance at end of year	$ 40,093	$ 5,933

Note H. Leases—During 1978, the company changed its method of accounting for leases to comply with *Statement of Financial Accounting Standards No. 13 (FAS 13)*. As a result, the assets and related obligations for property under capital leases have been recorded. The financial statements for 1977 have been restated with the result that the net loss for the year was increased by $3.2 million, due primarily to the cumulative effect of restating income in years prior to 1977, which reduced tax credits available in 1977 by $2.7 million. The effect of adopting *FAS 13* was not material to the results of operations in 1978.

Leased capital assets included in property and equipment are as follows (in thousands):

	December 31	
	1978	1977
Buildings	$ 43,146	$ 45,085
Plants and equipment—steel manufacturing	49,561	32,672
Equipment, furniture and fixtures	22,511	31,137
	$115,218	$108,894
Less accumulated depreciation	37,598	41,182
	$ 77,620	$ 67,712

Future minimum lease payments for capital leases together with the present value of net minimum lease payments at December 31, 1978, are (in thousands):

1979	$ 14,146
1980	13,089
1981	11,835
1982	10,163
1983	9,782
Later years	87,994
Total minimum lease payments	$147,009
Less amount representing interest	58,095
Present value of net minimum lease payments	$ 88,914
Less current portion	7,735
Long-term obligations under capital leases	$ 81,179

The charges to operations for the rental expense for all operating leases, less sublease rentals, was $26,608,000 in 1978 and $28,557,000 in 1977.

Future minimum operating lease commitments, exclusive of taxes and insurance, as of December 31, 1978, are as follows (in thousands):

1979	$ 18,209
1980	14,626
1981	11,620
1982	10,180
1983	9,399
Later years	41,466
	$105,500

Note I: Unusual Items, Discontinued Operations, and Extraordinary Items—
1. The unusual credit for 1978 of $16,721,000 is comprised of the net gain from the sale of the company's poultry, gelatin, and steel service center operations and the disposition of certain iron ore and coal mine properties. The unusual credit for 1977 of $3,129,000 is comprised of a credit resulting from the settlement of a legal claim, a charge relating to plant closings and consolidations, and a charge for a legal dispute relating to poultry operations.

2. In September 1977, LTV decided to discontinue its hotel, resort, inter-island passenger service, and steel conduit operations. In addition to the net operating losses of these operations a provision of $32 million was made to cover losses on disposition and costs and losses through date of disposition. The discontinued operations credit of $6.5 million in 1978 represents the portion of the loss provision recorded in 1977 which is no longer necessary.

3. Extraordinary items for the year 1977 include a $26,574,000 gain from early extinguishment of debt and a loss of $5,900,000 from a coal mine fire.

Note J: Estimated Liability for Plant Closing Costs—The statement of consolidated financial position at December 31, 1978, includes the remaining noncurrent provision of $196,099,000 for estimated costs relating to the closing of facilities by Lykes in 1977 and 1978.

13–6   Sears (A)

SEARS ROEBUCK, INC.
Statements of Income
($000)

	Year Ended January 31	
	1978	1977
Net sales	$17,224,033	$14,950,208
Cost of sales, buying, and occupancy expenses	11,172,965	9,399,491
Selling and administrative expenses	4,839,653	4,293,933
Operating income from sales and services	$ 1,211,415	$ 1,256,784
Other income	1,960	4,230
Equity in net income of Allstate Group:		
Allstate Insurance Company		
In accordance with prescribed standards,		
unrealized net increases in market value of		
marketable equity securities of $26,249 and		
$129,564 are not included in the determination		
of net income	395,104	195,314
Allstate Enterprises, Inc.	21,881	15,015
Total Allstate Group	$ 416,985	$ 210,329
Other unconsolidated subsidiaries and affiliates	57,048	42,568
	$ 474,033	$ 252,897
General Expenses		
Interest	353,131	270,122
Contribution to Employees' Profit Sharing Fund	140,276	114,455
Discontinued subsidiary loss	—	54,058
Income taxes (Note 8)		
Current operations	356,019	434,806
Benefit from disposition of subsidiary	—	(53,652)
	$ 849,426	$ 819,789
Net income	837,982	694,122
Per share (average shares 319,925 and 317,798)*	$2.62	$2.18

* Adjusted for two-for-one stock split effective May 27, 1977.

Note 8: Income Taxes—Federal and state income taxes on current operations include (in millions):

	Year Ended January 31	
	1978	1977
Current portion	$262	$341
Investment tax credit (flow-through method)	(16)	(13)
Deferred tax expense		
Current		
Installment sales	96	93
Receivable reserves	6	(8)
Maintenance agreement income	(8)	(11)
Supplemental pension costs	—	9
Other	(9)	(4)
Long-term:		
Depreciation	21	28
Other	4	—
Total deferred	$110	$107
Financial statement income tax provisions	$356	$435

The financial statement tax expense for 1977 and 1976 includes state income tax expense of $44 million ($12 million deferred) and $43 million ($11 million deferred), respectively. A reconciliation of effective rates, based upon income before taxes, equity in net income of unconsolidated subsidiaries, and the Belgian subsidiary loss with the statutory federal tax rate is:

	Year Ended January 31	
	1978	1977
Statutory federal income tax rate	48.0%	48.0%
State income taxes, net of federal income taxes	3.2	2.6
Investment tax credit (flow-through method)	(2.2)	(1.4)
Miscellaneous items	.5	.4
Effective income tax rate	49.5%	49.6%

SEARS ROEBUCK, INC.
Statements of Financial Position
($000)

	January 31	
	1978	1977
Assets		
Cash	$ 237,382	$ 223,112
Receivables	6,671,402	5,672,270
Inventories..	2,626,070	2,215,141
Prepaid advertising and other charges	106,821	90,445
Total current assets.................................	$ 9,641,675	$ 8,200,968
Investments:		
Allstate Insurance Company (cost $62,156 and		
$62,072)	1,735,382	1,433,945
Other investments and advances	822,788	695,368
	$ 2,558,170	$ 2,129,313
Property, plant, and equipment	2,534,841	2,487,790
Deferred charges	11,561	8,935
Total assets	$14,746,247	$12,827,006
Liabilities		
Short-term borrowings:		
Commercial paper	$ 2,586,051	$ 1,940,578
Banks	404,936	305,869
Agreements with bank trust departments	717,958	655,046
Current maturity of long-term debt	30,473	54,969
Accounts payable and accrued expenses	1,124,713	990,762
Unearned maintenance agreement income	276,969	242,143
Deferred income taxes	917,645	855,893
Total current liabilities	$ 6,058,745	$ 5,045,260
Deferred income taxes	173,139	154,959
Long-term debt..	1,990,295	1,706,099
Total liabilities	$ 8,222,179	$ 6,906,318
Shareholders' equity	$ 6,524,068	$ 5,920,688

Required:

1. What is Sears' pretax income for 1978? What percentage of pretax income is the $356 million of income taxes shown on the income statement? In Note 8 to their financial statements, Sears claims that their effective tax rate is 49.5 percent. Explain the difference.

2. If Sears were to report as income tax expense the amount of income taxes actually paid or payable (including the reduction caused by the investment tax credit), how much larger or smaller would their income for the year have been?

3. If Sears had reported income tax expense in every year equal to

income taxes paid or payable, how much larger or smaller would their shareholders' equity have been?

4. How much higher would actual income taxes have been if Sears used the same depreciation methods on both its financial statement and income tax returns? How much more or less would depreciation expense be in Sears' 1977 income statement?

14

Special topics (pensions, segment reporting, interim financial statements, and forecasts)

A pension plan is an agreement between a company and its employees for the purpose of providing retirement income to the employees.

The agreement specifies:

1. The types and amounts of benefits the employees are to receive upon retirement.
2. The required contributions to the plan by the employer and employee.
3. How and when employees become vested (obtain full control of their pension benefits).

Types of pension plans

There are two primary types of pension plans: *defined benefit* and *defined contribution*. The defined benefit plan pays a specified or determinable amount to the employee upon retirement. The amount, which is usually paid monthly, is calculated using a formula that reflects the employee's years of service, earnings, or a combination of years of service and earnings.

In defined contribution plans the employer agrees (the employee may also agree) to contribute a specified amount each year to a plan. The monthly pension benefits the employee ultimately receives depend upon the investment performance over time of the contributed amounts. There are no guaranteed benefit levels upon retirement as there are in a defined benefit plan.

Terminology

Pension plans may be *contributory* or *noncontributory*. Contributory plans require that both employer and employees make payments to the pension fund. In noncontributory plans payments are made only by the employer.

Pension plans, which are separate entities distinct from the corporation, are managed by a trustee called the pension plan administrator. The employer makes periodic cash payments to the trustee according to funding provisions specified by the plan. A pension plan is *fully funded* if the cash value of the pension fund is equal to (or exceeds) the present value of all expected future retirement obligations to be paid by the plan. Computation of the present value of all future pension funds is a very difficult actuarial task and is based on assumptions about employee turnover, investment performance of pension fund assets, employees future salary levels, and mortality rates.

Vested benefits are earned benefits that are not contingent on the employee's continuing to work for the employer. Under most pension plans, rights vest gradually until the employee becomes fully vested. For example, an employee may become 50 percent vested after five years service and receive an additional 10 percent vesting for each year's service beyond five years. At the end of 10 years of service the employee is fully vested. Rights to benefits earned by the employee's contribution to the plan (if any) are always fully vested.

Normal pension cost is the present value of all future benefits earned by employees in the current accounting period. *Past service cost* is the present value of all future benefits granted to employees for years of service prior to the inception of a pension plan. *Prior service cost* includes the obligation created by the initiation of the plan (past service cost) plus the obligation created by any subsequent amendments to the plan.

Federal pension law

The Employee Retirement Income Security Act of 1974 (ERISA, Pension Reform Act of 1974) was passed by Congress to regulate private sector pension plans. ERISA requires firms to fund normal pension costs as incurred, to fund past or prior service costs systematically over a period not to exceed 30 years, to cover employees without discrimination, and to guarantee minimum vesting (specified in the act) of benefits. It also requires the pension plan administrator to prepare audited financial statements for the pension plan.

ERISA protects employee benefits when a firm's pension plan is terminated and the pension fund is inadequate to insure payment of all earned benefits. It gives the government a claim against the assets of the enterprise (in addition to the pension fund assets) of up to 30 percent of the net worth (assets minus liabilities) of the company to ensure payment of the pension benefits.

ACCOUNTING FOR PENSIONS[1]

An enterprise's accounting for pension plans is concerned with the recognition of pension costs as expenses.

GAAP requires normal service costs of a period to be recorded as an expense of that period. Past or prior service costs are amortized and accrued as expenses over a period of 10 (minimum) to 40 (maximum) years.[2]

On January 1, 1985, Major, Inc., established a defined benefit, noncontributory employee pension fund with a major insurance company as trustee.

Normal costs

Actuarially computed current cost of benefits earned during the first year was $5,000. This amount is the present value of the future pension benefits earned by the employees this period. The December 31, 1985, journal entry to recognize this normal pension cost as an expense is:

Pension Expense (Normal Costs)	5,000	
Pension Liability		5,000
To accrue normal pension cost.		

---

[1] This section focuses on noncontributory, defined benefit plans, which are the most common private sector pension plans.

[2] AICPA, *Accounting Principles Board Opinion No. 8,* "Accounting for the Cost of Pension Plans" (New York, November 1966), FASB, *Statement of Financial Accounting Standards No. 36,* "Disclosure of Pension Information" (Stamford, Conn., May 1980).

Past service costs

Major's pension plan also granted retirement benefits for work performed by employees prior to January 1, 1985.

The insurance company, using a 6 percent interest rate assumption, estimates that the past service cost is $14,688. This is the amount of money which (given the actuarial assumptions of the insurance company) would have to be set aside on January 1, 1985, to guarantee that all the retroactively granted defined benefits could be paid as they came due. Major chooses to amortize past service cost as an *expense* systematically over the next three years (for computational efficiency we ignore the 10-year minimum accrual required by GAAP). The present value of $5,495 received at the end of each year for three years at 6 percent is $14,688.[3] The journal entry to accrue past service costs as an expense is:

```
Pension Expense (Past Service Costs) ...............   5,495
     Pension Liability ...............................            5,495
  To accrue past service costs.
```

Funding

The pension liability account now has a balance of $10,495 ($5,000 + $5,495). It will be reduced as the pension obligation is funded. Funding requirements are set by ERISA not GAAP. Suppose, as many corporations do, that Major, Inc., chooses to fund pension liabilities as they accrue. On December 31, 1985, Major makes a cash payment of $10,495 to the pension fund trustee. This completely eliminates the liability that was just recognized.

```
Pension Liability ..................................   10,495
     Cash ........................................            10,495
  To record payment of pension liability.
```

This cash payment discharges Major's pension liability for 1985. If the cash transfer to the fund trustee in the first year was less than $10,495, a pension liability for the difference between $10,495 and the amount transferred would appear on Major's balance sheet. If the cash transfer to the fund trustee was greater than $10,495, a pension asset account would appear on Major's 1985 balance sheet.

Although the cash payment of $10,495 discharged the accrued pension liability, the yet-to-be accrued portion of the past service obligation amounting to $10,074 (the present value of $5,495 for two periods at 6 percent), which is expected to be paid to retired employees in the future, *does not* appear as a liability on Major's

---

[3] The present value of $1, three years, 6 percent is $2.673 ($5,495 × $2.673 = $14,688).

December 31, 1985, balance sheet. This liability is disclosed as a footnote in Major's financial statements and as a liability in the financial statements of the pension plan, which is a separate accounting entity.[4]

Financial statement disclosure

SFAS 36 requires that an enterprise describe all of its pension plans, the employees covered, the funding policy, and the total pension cost for the period in a footnote to the financial statements. It also requires footnote disclosure of the actuarial present value of vested and nonvested benefits, the pension plans' net assets available to pay benefits, the rates of return used in the computations, and the date as of which the benefit information was determined. This information can be disclosed for each individual company pension plan or in the aggregate for all pension plans.

B. F. Goodrich's 1981 annual report contains the following footnote, which is in accordance with *SFAS 36*.

Pension expense, including amortization of prior service costs principally over thirty years, amounted to $59.3, $59.5 and $52.5 for the years ended December 31, 1981, 1980 and 1979, respectively. The increase in 1980 pension expense arises from improved benefits.

A summary of accumulated plan benefits and assets (principally as of January 1, 1981 and 1980) for Goodrich's domestic defined benefit plans is presented below:

	1981	1980
Actuarial present value of accumulated plan benefits:		
Vested	$549.3	$565.5
Nonvested	58.3	44.5
Total	$607.6	$610.0
Net assets available for plan benefits	$467.7	$380.9

The weighted average assumed rates of return (9% in 1981 and 8% in 1980) used to determine the actuarial present value of plan benefits are based on those published by the Pension Benefit Guaranty Corporation.

Goodrich's foreign pension plans are not required to report to certain U.S. governmental agencies under ERISA and do not otherwise determine the actuarial value of accumulated plan benefits or net assets available for benefits as calculated and disclosed above. For these plans, the actuarially computed value of vested benefits exceeded the total of the pension funds and balance sheet accruals by approximately $5.8 as of December 31, 1981.

---

[4] FASB, *SFAS No. 35*, "Accounting and Reporting by Defined Benefit Plan" (Stamford, Conn., March 1980), sets financial accounting and reporting standards for the annual financial statements of a defined benefit pension plan.

Many accountants believe that unfunded prior service costs should be recorded as a liability on the enterprise's balance sheet rather than disclosed as supplementary information in the footnotes to the financial statements.

They argue that the unfunded prior service costs meet all the criteria established for liabilities by the FASB in its *Statement of Financial Concepts No. 3,* issued in December 1980. The unfunded prior service costs are *present* obligations, which can be determined actuarially, to make future transfers of assets to the pension plan as a result of either work performed by employees in the past or supplementary amendments to the pension plan.

An April 1, 1983, discussion memorandum issued by the FASB suggests that unfunded prior service costs be recorded on the company's balance sheet as a liability.

SEGMENT REPORTING

Prior to 1976 consolidated financial statements of enterprises that operated in a number of different industries, had extensive foreign operations, and relied heavily on major customers did not contain detailed information about these activities.

For example, City Investing Corporation's domestic operations include the manufacture of heating and air conditioning units (Rheem Manufacturing), magazine printing (World Color Press), and the production of molded plastic products for the automobile and appliance industry (Alma Plastics). They also operate a budget motel chain (Motel 6), build single-family homes in the West and Southwest (Wood Bros. Homes), produce mobile homes (Guerdon Industries), and sell property and casualty insurance (City Home Corporation). They are involved in oil and gas exploration (Watson Oil Corporation) and have interests in oil reserves in the North Sea. Each of these markets differs in its supply, demand, and risk characteristics.

Without disclosure of the operating results and asset investments for each of City Investing's major industry lines, it is virtually impossible to predict their future earnings and cash flows.

SFAS 14

In response to the need for disaggregated financial information the FASB issued *SFAS 14,* "Financial Reporting for Segments of a Business Enterprise" in December 1976 and *Statement of Financial Accounting Standards No. 30,* "Disclosure of Information about Major Customers," in August 1979.

These accounting standards require that financial statements include information pertaining to operations in different industries (reportable segments) and markets, and disclose the names of certain major customers of the firm.

A particular segment is a reportable segment if any of the following conditions are met:

1. The segment revenues exceed 10 percent of the combined revenues of all segments.
2. The assets used exclusively in segment operations (identifiable assets) exceed 10 percent of the identifiable assets of all segments.
3. The operating profit (loss) of the segment exceeds 10 percent of the combined operating profits (losses) of all profitable (unprofitable) segments.

Although the 10 percent cutoff is somewhat arbitrary, the intent is to identify the major product lines that contribute to the firm's overall profitability. The determination of reportable segments is a subjective process because the grouping of individual products and services into the industry lines (segments) of a business is based on management's judgment.

In a footnote, in the body of the financial statements, or in a separate schedule in the annual report, companies must disclose the revenues (including intersegment sales) and operating profits of each reportable segment. Identifiable assets, depreciation, depletion and amortization expense, capital expenditures, and the effects of accounting changes must also be presented for each segment.

If the corporation uses the equity method to account for an unconsolidated subsidiary whose operations are vertically integrated with the operations of a reportable segment, the firm's equity in net income and investment in net assets of the subsidiary are reported with the segment data.

Results of foreign operations are to be disclosed in aggregate or geographically if revenues from foreign operations exceed 10 percent of consolidated revenues or if the identifiable assets of foreign operations exceed 10 percent of total assets.

Segment profitability data are useful in making year-to-year comparisons for each of the enterprise's major operations. When this material is used in conjunction with overall industry data, the reader of the statement can estimate the market share of the firm in particular industries. Combined with profitability information, the asset information is useful in computing rates of return.

Disclosure of any heavy dependence of revenues on a single customer is also very important to the readers of the statement so they can assess the probability that the customer will continue as a source of revenue in the future. *FASB 30* requires firms that derive 10 percent or more of their revenue from sales to a single customer (or group of customers under common control) to disclose this information with the segment data. For purposes of this disclosure the federal government, a state or local government, or a foreign government is considered to be an individual customer.

Example of *SFAS 14* disclosure

Anderson Clayton is a diversified food producer with major operations in the United States, Mexico, and Brazil. From the business segment disclosure in their 1981 annual report (see Illustration 14–1), it is possible to discern revenues, income (operating contribution), identifiable assets, capital expenditure, and depreciation of each of the company's major domestic and international business segments as well as of the insurance company subsidiary, which is reported on the equity basis for 1981, 1980, and 1979. The amount of intersegment sales that are recorded at market prices are listed separately so that the reader is able to determine Anderson Clayton's sales to outsiders. Corporate income and expenses, which can be arbitrarily assigned to the segments, are listed separately and deducted from the gross operating contribution in order to make

ILLUSTRATION 14–1. **Segment Information**

(In thousands of dollars)	1981	1980	1979
Consolidated sales:			
Domestic foods:			
Consumer and other	$ 420,879	$ 398,708	$ 363,494
Oilseed processing	362,368	385,055	269,651
Feeds and seed	76,245	89,476	83,948
Coffee	—	10,387	92,136
Total domestic foods	859,492	883,626	809,229
International foods:			
Consumer and other	292,458	262,936	251,404
Oilseed processing	511,613	384,691	298,408
Feeds and seed	245,257	199,470	157,666
Coffee	235,648	160,197	147,204
Total international	1,284,976	1,007,294	854,682
Total foods	2,144,468	1,890,920	1,663,911
Non-food (excluding insurance)	114,428	32,312	31,132
Total gross sales—consolidated	2,258,896	1,923,232	1,695,043
Deduct—intersegment sales	329,249	220,130	205,118
Net sales—consolidated	$1,929,647	$1,703,102	$1,489,925

ILLUSTRATION 14–1 *(continued)*

Intersegment sales are generally based on published or posted price lists the same as sales to unaffiliated persons. Export sales were $103,770,000, $150,266,000 and $109,887,000 for the years ended June 30, 1981, 1980 and 1979 respectively. The Company has no single customer that accounts for 10% or more of consolidated sales.

(In thousands of dollars)	1981	1980	1979
Consolidated operating contribution:			
Domestic foods:			
Consumer and other	$ 4,748	$ 12,387	$ 11,178
Oilseed processing	23,724	29,192	29,692
Feeds and seed	3,238	4,862	4,033
Coffee	(224)	63	(600)
Total domestic foods	31,486	46,504	44,303
International foods:			
Consumer and other	25,410	23,991	14,818
Oilseed processing	40,012	19,811	13,725
Feeds and seed	27,198	11,319	8,010
Coffee	(558)	792	875
Total international foods	92,062	55,913	37,428
Total foods	123,548	102,417	81,731
Non-food (excluding insurance)	18,361	2,368	5,929
Insurance—equity in income of insurance subsidiaries—before taxes:			
Property/casualty	9,139	14,893	16,029
Life	5,161	6,112	7,126
Total insurance	14,300	21,005	23,155
Corporate investment income—net	9,751	9,403	7,574
Total operating contribution	165,960	135,193	118,389
Deduct—corporate administrative expense	12,045	13,731	13,278
—interest expense	42,167	25,603	19,305
—translation loss from decline in foreign exchange rates	11,357	2,526	2,556
Income before taxes on income, minority interest and extraordinary items	100,391	93,333	83,250
Deduct—U.S. and foreign taxes on income	40,031	33,912	30,209
Income before minority interest and extraordinary items	60,360	59,421	53,041
Income applicable to minority interest	8,961	6,672	4,226
Income before extraordinary items	$ 51,399	$ 52,749	$ 48,815

it possible to assess the operating performance of each of the segments.

Anderson Clayton also reports its sales, operating contribution, and identifiable assets for each country in which it does business (see Illustration 14–2).

ILLUSTRATION 14–1 *(concluded)*

Identifiable translation loss from decline in foreign exchange rates has been allocated to segments.

(In thousands of dollars)	1981	1980	1979
Consolidated identifiable assets:			
Domestic foods			
Consumer and other	$100,269	$101,227	$ 96,153
Oilseed processing	115,779	142,295	127,317
Feeds and seed	17,347	38,973	51,764
Coffee	—	225	8,062
Total domestic foods	233,395	282,720	283,296
International foods:			
Consumer and other	78,329	81,553	70,018
Oilseed processing	168,291	152,797	95,319
Feeds and seed	77,488	73,451	45,029
Coffee	34,719	29,579	21,554
Total international foods	358,827	337,380	231,920
Total foods	592,222	620,100	515,216
Non-food (excluding insurance)	89,853	21,814	20,100
Investment in nonconsolidated insurance subsidiaries	112,816	103,171	86,998
Corporate	100,493	119,931	115,863
Consolidated assets	$895,384	$865,016	$738,177

Identifiable assets by segment are those assets used in the Company's operation in each line of business. Corporate assets are principally cash, marketable securities, and prepaid expenses.

(In thousands of dollars)	Capital Expenditures			Depreciation		
	1981	1980	1979	1981	1980	1979
Domestic foods:						
Consumer and other	$ 8,262	$ 7,412	$14,467	$ 4,776	$ 3,965	$ 3,546
Oilseed processing	12,856	8,948	8,311	4,115	3,508	3,616
Feeds and seed	1,510	2,826	4,350	1,162	1,543	1,512
Coffee	—	—	—	—	—	2
Total domestic foods	22,628	19,186	27,128	10,053	9,016	8,676
International foods:						
Consumer and other	8,927	3,347	1,287	1,739	1,506	1,424
Oilseed processing	3,920	2,359	1,429	2,116	2,095	1,944
Feeds and seed	1,704	886	1,120	1,137	1,042	931
Coffee	8	3	46	27	27	156
Total international foods	14,559	6,595	3,882	5,019	4,670	4,455
Total foods	37,187	25,781	31,010	15,072	13,686	13,131
Non-food	4,251	4,529	2,389	5,444	1,725	1,434
Total	$41,438	$30,310	$33,399	$20,516	$15,411	$14,565

ILLUSTRATION 14–2. **Geographic Area Information**

(In thousands of dollars)	1981	1980	1979
Consolidated sales to customers:			
United States	$ 973,920	$ 913,332	$ 840,361
Switzerland	290,193	193,658	158,264
Brazil	262,858	259,156	210,800
Mexico	402,676	336,956	280,500
	1,929,647	1,703,102	1,489,925
Transfers between geographic areas:			
United States	491	1,053	239
Switzerland	38,381	31,539	(102)
Brazil	237,962	138,259	158,001
Mexico	—	—	—
	276,834	170,851	158,138
	2,206,481	1,873,953	1,648.063
Eliminations	276,834	170,851	158,138
Net Consolidated Sales	$1,929,647	$1,703,102	$1,489,925

Transfers between geographic areas are generally based on published or posted price lists the same as sales to unaffiliated persons.

(In thousands of dollars)	1981	1980	1979
Operating contribution:			
United States	$ 73,898	$ 79,280	$ 80,961
Switzerland	(809)	(202)	1,003
Brazil	49,775	28,199	19,198
Mexico	43,096	27,916	17,227
Total Operating Contribution	$165,960	$135,193	$118,389

(In thousands of dollars)	1981	1980	1979
Identifiable assets:			
United States	$323,248	$306,101	$313,759
Switzerland	36,692	38,635	14,833
Brazil	188,071	203,704	138,336
Mexico	139,131	123,433	80,349
Total	687,142	671,873	547,277
Investment in nonconsolidated insurance subsidiaries	112,816	103,171	86,998
Corporate assets	95,426	89,972	103,902
Consolidated assets	$895,384	$865,016	$738,177

In its 1981 annual report the Dana Corporation made the following disclosure about sales to major customers.

Sales to Ford amounted to $318,753,000 in 1981, $365,600,000 in 1980 and $621,026,000 in 1979. Sales to General Motors amounted to $353,927,000 in 1981, $325,197,000 in 1980 and $413,982,000 in 1979. These sales were primarily from the Vehicular segment and approximated 25%, 27% and 37% of consolidated sales in 1981, 1980 and 1979 respectively.

This major customer disclosure is extremely important for the investor or analyst who is estimating Dana's future performance and the effect of decreased automobile sales on that performance.

INTERIM FINANCIAL REPORTS

Interim financial reports are reports that are prepared for periods of less than one year.

All companies whose stock is listed on the American and New York Stock Exchanges are required to send quarterly financial reports to their shareholders. These reports must contain at least a condensed income statement and earnings per share data with comparative figures for the corresponding period of the prior year and information about the seasonality of revenue, significant changes in estimates of income tax provisions, disposal of business segments, extraordinary, unusual, or infrequently occurring items, contingencies, changes in accounting principles, and any significant changes in financial position. An interim balance sheet and statement of changes in financial position are not required but are recommended by the FASB.[5]

Interim financial information provided on a timely basis is important both in assessing operating progress for the current period and as a basis for predicting income from operations for the entire year.

Each interim report should be viewed as an integral part of the annual report because in constructing the interim report it is necessary to anticipate the results of operations for the remainder of the year.

Readers of interim reports should be aware that they are more subjective than annual reports because some revenues and expenses of the interim period are estimated and are therefore more susceptible to manipulation than annual reports.

Items requiring special consideration in the preparation of interim reports include:

Operating costs

Operating costs incurred throughout the year must be allocated to interim periods. How should annual rent payments on a firm's

---

[5] AICPA, *APB Opinion* No. 28, "Interim Financial Reporting" (New York, May 1973), FASB, *SFAS No. 3,* "Reporting Accounting Changes in Interim Financial Statements" (Stamford, Conn. December 1974).

sales office be allocated to quarterly interim statements? Should each quarter reflect 25 percent of the rent payment as rent expense, or should rent payments be allocated to quarters on the basis of the percentage of quarterly revenue earned to total annual revenues earned? Either approach is acceptable. Costs (other than product costs or expenses directly related to revenues) may be expensed as incurred or allocated among interim periods using any reasonable basis. The difference in the quarterly net income can be significant for a company with a highly seasonal revenue pattern.

Income tax expense

Income tax expense for an interim period is based on the best estimate of the effective tax rate for the year. The annual effective rate depends on the types of income generated, investment and foreign tax credits earned, and tax loss carry-forwards utilized during the entire year.

LIFO inventories

Companies that expect to replace LIFO layers sold during an interim period by the end of the year should include the expected cost to replace the liquidated layers (not the historical cost of the liquidated layers) in cost of goods sold.

Accounting changes, unusual items, extraordinary items

All material unusual, infrequent, or extraordinary items are to be reported in their entirety in the interim period in which they occur. Changes in an accounting principle should be reported in the interim period in which the change occurs.

Interim financial reports

Assume that the Seattle Company, which sells a single product, has just completed operations for the first quarter of 1984. Operating data for the first quarter and estimates for the subsequent three quarters are shown in Illustration 14–3.

Additional facts.   Seattle uses the LIFO cost flow assumption. Beginning inventory consists of 40 units valued at $1 each. In the first quarter five units were purchased at a cost of $2 per unit. The replacement cost of inventory units is expected to remain at $2 per unit for the three subsequent quarters.

Seattle estimates its effective annual tax rate to be 40 percent.

During the first quarter Seattle realized an extraordinary loss of $10 (before taxes) on a premature retirement of debt.

Seattle's first-quarter interim income statement would be prepared in the following manner.

ILLUSTRATION 14–3

	Quarter				Total for year
	1	2	3	4	
Estimated sales revenue	$100 (10 units at $10) (actual)	$200 (20 units at $10)	$400 (40 units at $10)	$100 (10 units at $10)	$800
Estimated operating costs (excluding product costs) . .	$ 80 (actual)	$ 80	$ 80	$ 80	$320
Planned level of ending inventory (units)	35 (actual)	20	20	40	

Sales

Interim sales revenue is the amount of sales revenue realized during the quarter. Seattle Company's first quarter sales revenue is $100 (10 units at $10).

LIFO inventory

Seattle Company uses the LIFO cost flow method for inventory valuation. Beginning inventory was 40 units. The inventory level at the end of the first quarter dropped to 35 units (10 sold, 5 purchased), but expectations are that by the end of the fourth quarter inventory levels will again be 40 units.

If Seattle computes cost of goods for the first quarter in the conventional LIFO manner, the quarterly income statement will show a cost of goods sold equal to $15 (five units of currently purchased items at $2 per unit plus five units of inventory purchased previously at $1 per unit).

However, Seattle expects to replace the liquidated base of five units in its inventory by the end of the year at a cost of $2 per unit. On an annual basis they do not expect to use any of the inventory layer valued at $1 per unit. Based on this replacement assumption, interim cost of goods sold should be $20 (five units purchased in first quarter at $2 per unit plus five units expected to be purchased before year end at $2 per unit).

Operating costs

None of the operating costs of Seattle Company are directly related to the generation of sales revenue. Seattle Company allocates yearly operating costs to quarters in proportion to the percentage of estimated total yearly sales revenues earned during each quarter. Anticipated revenues for the year are $800. Revenues for the first quarter total $100, and total operating costs are estimated to be $320. Seattle allocates $40 ($\frac{1}{8} \times$ $320) of operating costs to the first quarter. An acceptable alternative would be to record operating expenses of $80 in each quarter.

Net income before taxes and extraordinary items is $40. The estimated annual tax rate of 40 percent is used to compute income tax expense of $16 (40 percent of $40) for the first quarter.

Extraordinary items are shown in their entirety in the quarter in which they are incurred. Seattle Company must show the $6 aftertax loss on premature retirement of debt in the first-quarter statement.

In addition, Seattle Company is required to disclose the seasonal nature of its business in a footnote to the quarterly statement of income (see Illustration 14–4).

ILLUSTRATION 14–4

SEATTLE COMPANY
Statement of Income
For the First Quarter of 1981*

Revenue (10 units at $10)	$100
Cost of goods sold	20
Gross margin	80
Operating expenses (1/8 × $320)	40
Net income before taxes and extraordinary item	40
Income tax expense (40% of $40)	16
Net income before extraordinary item	24
Extraordinary loss ($10 less tax effect of $4)†	6
Net income	$ 18

* Historically, sales for the four quarters have been in the approximate ratio 1:2:4:1. Expectations are that this ratio will continue.

† The extraordinary loss resulted from premature retirement of long-term debt during the first quarter.

Review by independent certified public accountants

Interim financial statements are not subject to detailed audits by independent certified public accountants. Interim statements are reviewed by CPAs, but no opinion regarding the financial statements taken as a whole is rendered.[6] Price Waterhouse and Company explained their review of United Technologies 1979 first quarter income in the accompanying letter:

To the Shareholders of
United Technologies Corporation

We have made a review of the consolidated summary of income of United Technologies Corporation and subsidiaries for the three-month periods ended March 31, 1979, and 1978 in accordance with standards established by the American Institute of Certified Public Accountants. We did not review the financial information for the three-month period ended March 31, 1979, relating to the company's investment in Carrier Corporation, which constituted approximately 12 percent of the consolidated assets at March 31, 1979, and is accounted for under the equity method.

A review of interim financial information consists principally of obtaining an understanding of the system for the preparation of interim financial information, applying analytical review procedures to financial data, and making inquiries of persons responsible for financial and accounting matters. It is substantially less in scope than an examination in accordance with generally accepted auditing standards, the objective of which is the expression of an opinion regarding the financial statements taken as a whole. Accordingly, we do not express such an opinion.

Based on our review, we are not aware of any material modifications that should be made to the accompanying consolidated summary of income for it to be in conformity with generally accepted accounting principles.

Hartford, Connecticut   Price Waterhouse & Co.
April 10, 1979

FORECASTS

Investors make decisions that are to a great extent based on the future performance of the enterprise. Supplemental information, such as earnings and cash flow projections, planned capital expenditures, financing plans, production and backlog information, is extremely useful to investors in making their forecasts of the company's future performance.

The two major problems inherent in the disclosure of supplemental or soft information of this type are the legal liability of the

---

[6] AICPA, *Statements on Auditing Standards No. 24*, "Review of Interim Financial Information" (New York, June 1979).

preparers and auditors of published financial forecasts that turn out to be incorrect and the development and adherence to standards for reporting supplemental financial information.

The SEC and FASB have indicated their support for the disclosure of supplemental information by addressing these two problems.

SEC

In June 1979 the SEC addressed the legal liability question. A rule covering all companies reporting to the SEC or filing registration statements with the SEC guarantees companies a "safe harbor" against fraud charges provided their disclosures are made in "good faith." Prior to this rule the burden of proof as to the fairness and reasonableness of the projections rested with the reporting company. Under the new rule any person or entity filing a complaint must prove the reporting company's intent to commit fraud.

This rule, which encourages (but does not require) disclosure of supplemental information, applies to all financial forecasts appearing as supplemental information to annual reports and 10-Ks.

FASB

Recognizing the need for more and better financial information, the FASB broadened its mission from that of setting standards (rule making) for financial statements to setting standards for financial reporting.

> Some useful information is better provided by financial statements and some is better provided, or can only be provided, by means of financial reporting other than financial statements.[7]

The FASB's statement on inflation accounting exemplifies this new mission. *FASB Statement 33* requires supplemental disclosure of current cost and constant-dollar information from some 1,350 of the largest U.S. corporations. This disclosure on the effects of inflation is not subject to audit although it is reviewed for reasonableness by the enterprises' independent certified public accountants.

Faced with an increasing demand by investors for supplemental financial and nonfinancial information, the SEC and FASB are moving in the direction of filling this need. It is likely that both bodies will require disclosure of supplemental information including earnings forecasts in the future.

---

[7] FASB, *Statement of Financial Accounting Concepts No. 1,* "Objectives of Financial Reporting by Business Enterprises" (Stamford, Conn., November 1978).

PROBLEMS AND CASES

14–1 Brush-Wellman, Inc.

The 1981 financial statements of Brush-Wellman, the world's major producer of beryllium-containing materials, contained the following footnote:

Note H: Pension Plans—The Company and certain of its subsidiaries have pension plans covering substantially all of their employees. Pension expense, including amortization of prior service costs over a thirty-year period, amounted to $3,130,000 for 1981, $2,573,000 for 1980 and $2,174,000 for 1979. Pension amendments and revised actuarial assumptions had the effect of increasing pension expense approximately $442,000 in 1981. It is the policy of the Company to fund currently the pension expense for each year. A comparison of accumulated plan benefits determined by consulting actuaries and plan net assets is presented below:

(Dollars in thousands)	June 1 1981	1980
Actuarial present value of accumulated plan benefits:		
Vested	$31,465	$26,646
Nonvested	3,716	2,763
	$35,181	$29,409
Net assets available for benefits at valuation date	$24,952	$20,474

The assumed rate of return used in determining the actuarial present value of accumulated plan benefits was 5½ percent.

Required:

1. Make the entry to record 1981 pension expense.

2. What is the rationale for amortizing prior service costs to future years instead of treating them as an expense of the current year like normal pension costs?

3. How much of Brush-Wellman's pension liability is unfunded?

4. Where does this unfunded liability appear on Brush-Wellman's financial statements.

14–2 Western Union Corporation

The following pension footnote was taken from Western Union's 1981 annual report.

Note B: Pension Plans—The Corporation has several pension plans, covering virtually all full-time employees. Contributions are made into pension trust funds in amounts determined by independent consulting actuaries to cover 100% of current service costs plus, for the Telegraph Company pension plan, commencing in 1973, amounts sufficient to fund prior service costs over 40 years. All costs are computed assuming a 6% rate of return on pension trust fund assets. Most payments to pensioners are made directly from the trust funds.

The cost of such plans was $39.5, $37.4 and $37.8 million in 1981, 1980 and 1979, respectively. Of such amounts $7.5, $7.4, and $9.6 million, respectively, were allocated to construction accounts as part of employee benefits; the remainder was charged to expense.

Pertinent data with respect to the plans as of January 1, 1981, the date of the most recent actuarial valuation, is set forth below:

Thousands

Actuarial present value	
of accumulated plan benefits:	
Vested	$265,683
Nonvested	15,499
Total	281,182
Market value of assets	127,144
Unfunded liabilities	$154,038

The actuarial present value of accumulated plan benefits was computed by independent consulting actuaries assuming a 9.1% rate of return. This rate is equivalent to the rate used by the Pension Benefit Guaranty Corporation to calculate annuity values.

Required:

1. Would you be concerned if you were due to receive a pension from Western Union starting in 1985?

2. Do you think vested benefits should have to be 100 percent funded?

3. When will Western Union have to pay the unfunded pension liability?

4. What's the justification for not requiring that this liability be shown on Western Union's balance sheet?

14–3 Inter Rim, Inc.

Inter Rim, Inc., wishes to present its senior corporate officials with quarterly net income figures which can be projected to obtain estimates of yearly net income.

Their plan is to allocate all fixed costs to quarters in proportion to the number of units expected to be sold in each quarter. The following formula is to be used to project annual net income from quarterly net income (and will be disclosed):

$$\text{Annual Net Income} = \frac{\text{Yearly Unit Sales}}{\text{Quarterly Units Sold}} (\text{Quarterly Net Income})$$

In addition the quarterly statement will contain the latest estimate of expected sales for the year.

	Estimated Data for Quarter			
	1	2	3	4
Sales price/unit	$5 (actual)	$6	$5	$8
Expected sales (units)	100,000 (actual)	300,000	200,000	400,000

Expected costs:
Variable manufacturing (unit)	$1
Fixed manufacturing (year)	$600,000
Variable selling (unit)	$2
Fixed selling (year)	$200,000

Note: *Fixed* manufacturing costs, like depreciation and factory rent, do not vary with the number of units manufactured. Variable manufacturing costs, like material and labor used to manufacture the product, vary with production.

Sales commissions, which vary with sales, are variable selling expenses. Sales salaries, which do not vary with sales, are fixed selling expenses.

Required:

1. Compute net income for the first quarter. The actual variable manufacturing cost is $1 per unit, the actual variable selling cost is $2 per unit, and management's best estimates of total sales and total fixed costs for the year are still 1 million units and $800,000, respectively (ignore income taxes).

2. Using the above formula, project annual net income. Compute "actual" net income assuming that actual costs were the same as expected costs. Why aren't projected and "actual" net income equal?

3. Can you suggest an alternative allocation of fixed costs to quarters and an alternative equation for projecting annual net income from quarterly net income? Will your procedure always work?

14-4 Varlen Corporation

Varlen Corporation is a diversified industrial metalworking company.

The industry segments disclosure in their annual report for the year ended January 31, 1982, indicates that they operate in five reportable segments.

Refer to this disclosure and answer the following questions.

Note 11: *Industry Segments*—Certain information (in thousands of dollars) relating to the Company's industry segments is as follows:

	Metal-Related Products	Railroad Products and Services	Tanks, Pressure Vessels, and Chemical Process Equipment	Industrial Fasteners	Other Industries	Consolidated
Fiscal year ended January 31, 1982:						
Net sales	$44,070	$47,360	$22,695	$9,076	$11,200	$134,401
Operating profit	7,178	10,217	1,621	1,126	1,568	$ 21,710
General corporate expenses, net						(932)
Interest expense						(3,367)
Income before federal income taxes						17,411
Identifiable assets	17,605	45,820	9,043	3,191	4,695	$ 80,354
Corporate assets						14,562*
Total assets as of January 31, 1982						$ 94,916
Depreciation	414	1,177	512	151	247	
Capital expenditures	453	6,986	785	116	252	
Fiscal year ended January 31, 1981:						
Net sales	$40,204	$38,676	$18,985	$7,489	$10,746	$116,100
Operating profit	4,942	8,007	2,069	902	1,347	$ 17,267
General corporate expenses, net						(843)
Interest expense						(2,094)
Income before federal income taxes						$ 14,330
Identifiable assets	16,270	22,981	7,311	3,293	6,860	$ 56,715
Corporate assets						13,410*
Total assets as of January 31, 1981						$ 70,125
Depreciation	380	732	230	133	292	
Capital expenditures	421	755	620	134	521	
Fiscal year ended January 31, 1980:						
Net sales	$43,915	$49,218	$21,866	$8,687	$10,576	$134,262
Operating profit	5,281	9,354	(531)	1,137	1,233	$ 16,474
General corporate expenses, net						(968)
Interest expense						(2,112)
Income before Federal income taxes						$ 13,394
Identifiable assets	19,310	22,055	9,383	3,567	5,971	$ 60,286
Corporate assets						7,604*
Total assets as of January 31, 1980						$ 67,890
Depreciation	356	550	375	117	337	
Capital expenditures	642	2,218	140	89	376	

* Assets of the Company's discontinued operations have been reclassified and included with corporate assets for each of the years presented above and aggregated approximately $1,904,000 at January 31, 1982.

Required:

1. Which industry segment was the most profitable in the fiscal year ended January 31, 1982? Was this segment more profitable than the consolidated company? Use the ratio of operating profit to sales to measure profitability.

2. Which industry segment earned the greatest return on investment for the fiscal year ended January 31, 1982? Did this industry segment have a greater return on investment than the consolidated company? Use the ratio of operating profit to identifiable assets to measure return on investment.

3. Why doesn't Varlen allocate general corporate expenses and interest expenses to the industry segments?

4. Is segment disclosure helpful in assessing future earnings and cash flows?

14–5 Pennzoil Company

Required:

Project net income for the fiscal year ending December 31, 1979. Explain how you arrived at your projection. Be sure to list all the assumptions you are making. What other quantitative or qualitative information would you require in order to improve your earnings forecast?

PENNZOIL COMPANY AND SUBSIDIARIES
Condensed Consolidated Statement of Income (unaudited)
(expressed in thousands, except per share amounts)

	Three Months Ended March 31	
	1979	1978
Revenues	$433,421	$336,176
Costs and expenses:		
Cost of goods sold and operating expenses	247,521	210,511
Selling, general, and administrative expenses	30,448	20,258
Depreciation, depletion, and amortization	53,545	44,295
Taxes, other than federal income	12,595	10,017
Interest charges, net	20,701	18,291
Interest capitalized	(3,472)	(2,519)
Federal income tax:		
Current	27,064	12,499
Deferred	1,436	1,092
Investment tax credit	(2,539)	(1,813)
Minority interest	(51)	(106)
	$387,248	$312,525
Net income	$ 46,173	$ 23,651
Dividends on preferred stock	1,219	1,300
Earnings available for common stock	$ 44,954	$ 22,351

PENNZOIL COMPANY AND SUBSIDIARIES
Consolidated Statement of Income
(expressed in thousands, except per share amounts)

	Year Ended December 31	
	1978	1977
Revenues	$1,553,108	$1,280,432
Costs and expenses		
Cost of goods sold and operating expenses	943,584	809,767
Selling, general, and administrative expenses	95,461	78,843
Depreciation, depletion, and amortization	209,798	155,058
Taxes, other than federal income	45,292	40,943
Interest charges, net.................................	78,962	66,133
Interest capitalized	(12,773)	(14,141)
Federal income tax		
Current...	63,508	46,064
Deferred	8,566	9,088
Investment tax credit	(7,400)	(9,083)
Minority interest	(57)	(2,630)
	$1,424,941	$1,180,042
Net Income...	$ 128,167	$ 100,390
Dividends on preferred stock	4,997	5,200
Earnings available for common	$ 123,170	$ 95,190

PENNZOIL COMPANY AND SUBSIDIARIES
Consolidated Balance Sheet
(expressed in thousands)

	December 31	
	1978	1977
Assets		
Current Assets:		
Cash	$ 18,194	$ 37,026
Temporary cash investments...........................	108,058	25,298
Trade accounts and notes receivable	270,575	221,751
Inventories:		
Crude oil, metals, sulphur, and potash	50,446	116,011
Manufactured products	47,799	49,290
Materials and supplies, at average cost	40,459	43,464
Other current assets	9,260	4,022
Total current assets.............................	$ 544,791	$ 496,862
Property, plant and equipment, at cost:		
Oil and gas production (including $144,749,000		
and $87,537,000 not being amortized in 1978,		
and 1977, respectively)—full cost method		
of accounting	1,935,812	1,644,488
Manufacturing and marketing	207,870	189,755
Mining	593,484	575,067
Other	66,927	68,633
	$2,804,093	$2,477,943

PENNZOIL BALANCE SHEET *(continued)*

	December 31	
Assets	*1978*	*1977*
Less—accumulated depreciation, depletion and amortization	$1,330,929	$1,139,071
	$1,473,164	$1,338,872
Excess of cost of predecessor company stock over underlying book value, being amortized	23,641	24,821
Other assets:		
Long-term receivables	22,133	26,165
Deferred charges	6,224	10,051
Other	13,217	15,631
	41,574	51,847
Total assets	$2,083,170	$1,912,402

Liabilities and Shareholders' Equity		
Current liabilities:		
Convertible subordinated debentures of Pennzoil Louisiana and Texas Offshore, Inc., due May, 1, 1979	$ 123,478	$ —
Sinking fund obligations and long-term debt due within one year	15,814	19,170
Notes payable	4,000	19,550
Accounts payable	211,531	162,922
Exploration and development advances payable	—	7,610
Taxes accrued	39,962	22,957
Interest accrued	14,644	9,813
Dividends declared	1,219	1,438
Other current liabilities	35,552	7,326
Total current liabilities	$ 446,200	$ 250,786
Long-term debt, less amount due within one year	764,000	681,541
Convertible subordinated debentures, 6%, due May 1, 1979, of Pennzoil Louisiana and Texas Offshore, Inc., less unamortized discount of $3,327,000	—	120,151
Exploration and development advances payable	14,939	20,402
Proceeds from sale of production payments	—	51,264
Deferred federal income tax	164,780	156,214
Deferred credits	27,807	17,517
Minority interest	1,355	1,393
	$1,419,081	$1,299,268
Commitments and contingencies		
Shareholders' equity:		
Capital stock	27,990	27,944
Additional capital	185,598	192,444
Retained earnings	450,501	392,746
Total shareholders' equity	$ 664,089	$ 613,134
	$2,083,170	$1,912,402

PENNZOIL COMPANY AND SUBSIDIARIES
Consolidated Statement of Changes in Financial Position
(expressed in thousands)

	Year Ended December 31	
	1978	1977
Financial resources provided by:		
Net income	$ 128,167	$100,390
Charges (credits) to income not requiring funds:		
Depreciation, depletion, and amortization	209,798	155,058
Deferred federal income tax	8,566	9,088
Interest capitalized	(12,773)	(14,141)
Minority interest	(57)	(2,630)
Funds provided from operations	$ 333,701	$247,765
Issuance of long-term debt	226,005	158,000
Decrease in long-term receivables	4,032	5,357
Sale of production payment	—	16,020
Noncash and other, net	10,930	8,010
Decrease in working capital	147,485	—
	$ 722,153	$435,152
Financial resources used for:		
Additions to property, plant, and equipment, excluding interest capitalized at $12,733,000 and $14,141,000	$ 331,317	$244,290
Dividends	70,412	60,693
Retirement of long-term debt	143,546	79,040
Reduction of exploration and development advances	5,463	12,356
Reduction of production payments	51,264	28,836
Reclassification of convertible subordinated debentures	120,151	—
Increase in working capital	—	9,937
	$ 722,153	$435,152
Increase (decrease) in working capital:		
Cash	$ (18,832)	$ (27,625)
Temporary cash investments	82,760	(13,472)
Receivables	48,824	31,539
Inventories	(67,056)	12,101
Materials and supplies	(3,005)	7,935
Other current assets	5,238	986
Convertible subordinated debentures	(123,478)	—
Current maturities of long-term debt	3,356	(8,711)
Notes payable	15,550	(18,000)
Accounts payable	(48,609)	(31,527)
Advances payable	7,610	(7,610)
Taxes accrued	(17,005)	64,231
Interest accrued	(4,831)	(50)
Dividends declared	219	14
Other current liabilities	(28,226)	126
	$(147,485)	$ 9,937

15

Introduction to financial statement analysis

Financial statement analysis is a process that uses financial statements and other information, such as industry averages, stock market prices, and economic indicators, to evaluate the economic condition of an enterprise and predict its future performance.

The method and emphasis of the financial statement analysis will depend on the particular decision the analyst has to make.

Short-term creditors and lenders are interested in the ability of the enterprise to pay its present and prospective current obligations. Their focus is on *liquidity*. Does the enterprise have enough liquid (cash or near cash) assets to pay its current liabilities? Will it generate adequate cash flow from operations to pay short-term obligation as they come due?

Long-term creditors want to make sure that future cash flows will be adequate to pay interest and debt principal. They tend to concentrate on the *long-term solvency* (ability to pay debts when due) as well as the liquidity of the enterprise. What is the relationship of cash flow generated from operations to debt service (interest and principal payments)? Is long-term debt such a large portion of the capital (debt plus equity) structure that there is a risk of default on debt service payments and possible insolvency of the enterprise?

Present and potential stockholders make investment decisions based on the total return they expect to receive on their investments. They define total return as cash dividends plus the difference between the sale and purchase prices of the security. They also want to assess the risk of obtaining the return on their investment so they can compare it with other investment opportunities. Their analysis is centered on *profitability* and *risk*. Will future profitability produce enough cash flow to pay obligations, maintain and expand the productive capacity of the enterprise, and pay cash dividends? How volatile and risky are the forecasted future profits (earnings) and cash flows?

Management uses financial analysis to evaluate their performance. They are particularly interested in measures of operational efficiency. Did we improve our profit margins over last year? What return did we earn on our assets? On stockholders' equity? How do our profit margins and return on assets and stockholders' equity compare with our budgeted objectives and with other firms in the industry?

Some other major users of financial statement analysis are government agencies such as the SEC and the Federal Trade Commission, who use it for regulatory purposes, and labor unions, who use it in the negotiation process.

Traditionally three general methods have been employed to interpret and evaluate financial statements. One method, working capital and cash flow analysis, was examined in Chapter 11 (Statement of Changes in Financial Position). The two other methods are financial ratio analysis and comparative financial statement analysis.

FINANCIAL RATIO AND COMPARATIVE FINANCIAL STATEMENT ANALYSIS

A ratio is the proportional relationship between one number and another. The analyst computes ratios of related financial statement items as part of the process of assessing the liquidity, solvency, profitability, and operating efficiency of the enterprise.

Comparative financial statement analysis involves the comparison of the ratios and individual financial statement items over time (time-series analysis), with the results of other enterprises in the industry (cross-sectional analysis), and often with a rule of thumb value based on the experience or feel of the analyst for the appropriate relationships.

Average ratios for companies in the same industry are published by many sources (Dun & Bradstreet, Robert Morris Associates, Moody's, Standard & Poor's). The use of industrywide averages includes all the difficulties associated with diverse accounting principles, plus the statistical problems arising when figures for many companies are averaged into one number.

The 1984 financial statements of the Ranth Manufacturing Cor-

ILLUSTRATION 15–1

RANTH MANUFACTURING CORPORATION
Comparative Balance Sheets
December 31, 1984, 1983, and 1982
($000)

	1984	1983	1982
Assets			
Current assets:			
Cash	$ 346	$ 414	$ 253
Accounts receivable (net of allowance)	3,891	3,442	4,280
Inventories	6,494	5,287	6,385
Prepaid expenses	303	276	268
Total current assets	11,034	9,419	11,186
Property and equipment, at cost:			
Land	1,154	1,154	1,154
Building and improvements	4,114	3,968	3,850
Machinery and equipment	7,266	6,724	5,601
	12,534	11,846	10,605
Accumulated depreciation	5,546	4,775	4,024
Total property and equipment	6,988	7,071	6,581
Total assets	$18,022	$16,490	$17,767
Equities			
Current liabilities:			
Notes payable	$ 950	$ 200	$ 1,250
Accounts payable—trade	1,092	1,139	2,481
Accrued expenses	959	806	810
Income taxes payable	454	359	269
Total current liabilities	3,455	2,504	4,810
Long-term debt	1,447	2,187	2,228
Total liabilities	4,902	4,691	7,038
Shareholders' equity:			
Common stock (625,000 shares outstanding)	6,443	6,443	6,443
Retained earnings	6,677	5,356	4,286
Total shareholders' equity	13,120	11,799	10,729
Total equities	$18,022	$16,490	$17,767

ILLUSTRATION 15–2

RANTH MANUFACTURING CORPORATION
Comparative Income Statements
For the Years Ended December 31, 1984, and 1983
($000)

	1984	1983
Net sales	$33,088	$28,216
Cost of goods sold*	26,872	23,253
Gross margin	6,216	4,963
Other expenses:		
Selling expenses	1,135	1,091
General and administrative expenses	2,000	1,208
Interest expense	272	358
Total	3,407	2,657
Income before income taxes	2,809	2,306
Provision for income taxes	1,388	1,136
Net income	$ 1,421	$ 1,170
Earnings per common share	$ 2.27	$ 1.87

Additional information:

  Cash dividends:
    1984 and 1983—16¢ per common share

  Market price of common stock
    12/31/84—$23.00
    12/31/83—$18.25

  * Includes depreciation of $771 in 1984 and $751 in 1983.

poration, which appear as Illustrations 15–1, 15–2, and 15–3, are used as the basis for illustrating financial ratio and comparative statement analysis.

LIQUIDITY (SHORT-TERM SOLVENCY) MEASURES

Short-term creditors and lenders often use the current ratio as one measure in evaluating the enterprise's ability to repay its short-term obligations.

$$\text{Current Ratio} = \frac{\text{Current Assets}}{\text{Current Liabilities}}$$

ILLUSTRATION 15–3

RANTH MANUFACTURING CORPORATION
Comparative Statements of Changes in Financial Position
For the Years Ended December 31, 1984, and 1983
($000)

	1984	1983
Sources of working capital:		
From operations:		
Net income	$1,421	$1,170
Add back expenses not requiring an outflow		
of working capital: Depreciation	771	751
	2,192	1,921
Uses of working capital:		
Payment of dividends	100	100
Purchase of building and improvements	146	118
Purchase of machinery and equipment	542	1,123
Retired long-term debt	740	41
	1,528	1,382
Increase in working capital	$ 664	$ 539
Changes in components in working capital:		
Cash	$ (68)	$ 161
Accounts receivable	449	(838)
Inventories	1,207	(1,098)
Prepaid expenses	27	8
Notes payable	(750)	1,050
Accounts payable—trade	47	1,342
Accrued expenses	(153)	4
Income taxes payable	(95)	(90)
	$ 664	$ 539

The current ratio indicates the amount of current assets available to cover the current liabilities on the balance sheet date. The current ratios for the Ranth Corporation are:

		Industry Averages*
December 31, 1984	$\frac{\$11,034}{\$3,455} = 3.19$ to 1	3.13 to 1
December 31, 1983	$\frac{\$9,419}{\$2,504} = 3.76$ to 1	3.50 to 1
December 31, 1982	$\frac{\$11,186}{\$4,810} = 2.33$ to 1	2.43 to 1

* Industry averages are assumed in this chapter for illustrative purposes.

Ranth's current ratio follows the trend of the industry and is substantially above the $2 of current assets for each $1 of current liabilities, which has often been the benchmark used by analysts for manufacturing companies.

Ranth's current ratio was probably lower at the end of 1982 because the recession that year resulted in high inventory levels due to lack of sales, a longer collection period for the receivables, and the need to finance these increases with short-term borrowing and an extension of the payment period for trade creditors. Ranth was apparently able to sell inventory and collect receivables faster in 1983 than in 1982 and used this increased cash flow to pay its short-term notes and other current liabilities; 1984 reflects a new buildup in receivables and inventories financed by an increase in current liabilities.

LIFO and the current ratio

For enterprises that use the LIFO cost flow method the balance sheet value for inventory will often reflect old rather than current costs. Old inventory costs have little significance for the analyst who is evaluating the enterprise's liquidity.

In calculating the current ratio for LIFO companies the historical cost balance sheet value for inventory should be adjusted to current cost, using *SFAS 33* information, or at least to FIFO.

Some analysts make this adjustment by increasing inventories by the full amount current cost exceeds LIFO cost (LIFO reserve). Others calculate it as the difference after income taxes. They say that on the sale of the inventory at current cost the enterprise earns a taxable profit (current cost minus LIFO cost) on which they have to pay income taxes and only the aftertax amount will be available to pay obligations.

Summary

The current ratio by itself is not adequate to evaluate enterprise liquidity because it does not consider the amount of accounts receivable and inventories in total current assets or the length of time it takes to convert these assets to cash. Nor does it relate amounts and flow of cash generated by the enterprise to the amount and timing of payments of current liabilities.

Acid-test (quick) ratio

The acid test ratio eliminates inventories and prepayments from the current ratio and compares the most liquid assets with current liabilities.

$$\text{Acid-Test Ratio} = \frac{\text{Cash} + \text{Marketable Securities} + \text{Net Receivables}}{\text{Current Liabilities}}$$

The acid-test ratios for Ranth are:

			Industry Averages
December 31, 1984	$\dfrac{\$346 + \$3,891}{\$3,455}$	= 1.23 to 1	1.30 to 1
December 31, 1983	$\dfrac{\$414 + \$3,442}{\$2,504}$	= 1.54 to 1	1.35 to 1
December 31, 1982	$\dfrac{\$253 + \$4,280}{\$4,810}$	= .94 to 1	1.12 to 1

It would appear from this ratio that Ranth should not have any trouble meeting its current obligations unless the collection period for receivables is longer than the maximum payment period for the current liabilities.

Accounts receivable turnover ratio

$$\text{Accounts Receivable Turnover Ratio} = \frac{\text{Net Credit Sales}}{\text{Average Accounts Receivable}}$$

The faster (larger the ratio) the turnover, the shorter the collection period for the accounts receivable. The shorter the collection period, the more liquid (nearer to cash) the accounts receivable and the more valid the use of the current and quick ratios.

The accounts receivable turnover ratios for Ranth are:

			Industry Average
1984	$\dfrac{\$33,088}{(\$3,891 + \$3,442)/2}$	= 9.02	8.25
1983	$\dfrac{\$28,216}{(\$3,442 + \$4,280)/2}$	= 7.31	6.85

The calculation of this ratio assumes that all the sales are credit sales and that there is no large seasonal pattern to the sales and the receivables. This assumption makes it acceptable to compute average accounts receivable by dividing the sum of the beginning plus the ending balance of accounts receivable by two.

Average accounts receivable collection period

A related, better understood ratio is the average account receivable collection period. It is obtained by dividing 365 days by the accounts receivable turnover ratio or by dividing credit sales by 365 to get average daily sales and dividing this figure into accounts receivable.

The average accounts receivable collection ratios for Ranth are:

		Industry Average
1984	$\frac{365}{9.02} = 40.5$ days	44.4 days
1983	$\frac{365}{7.31} = 49.9$ days	53.3 days

Ranth is turning over its accounts receivable and collecting them faster than the industry. This performance is favorable if it represents increased efficiency in collection of accounts receivable but could be unfavorable if the more rapid turnover is caused by a tight credit policy which could result in the future loss of profitable sales.

Inventory turnover ratio

The faster the inventory is sold, the sooner it will be converted to accounts receivable and result in cash available to pay current liabilities.

$$\text{Inventory Turnover} = \frac{\text{Cost of Goods Sold}}{\text{Average Inventory}}$$

Cost of goods sold is usually used rather than sales in this ratio so that both the numerator and denominator are stated at cost.

For Ranth the inventory turnover ratios are:

		Industry Average
1984	$\frac{\$26,872}{(\$6,494 + \$5,287)/2} = 4.56$	4.86
1983	$\frac{\$23,253}{(\$5,287 + \$6,385)/2} = 3.98$	4.20

The number of days of inventory a company has on hand can be determined by dividing 365 by the turnover ratio. The calculations for Ranth are:

		Industry Average
1984	365/4.56 = 80.0 days	75.1
1983	365/3.98 = 91.7 days	86.9

Ranth turned over its inventory faster and had fewer days of inventory on hand in 1984 than 1983 but did not turnover the inventory as fast or operate with as little inventory as the industry average in either year.

Further investigation is needed to determine whether the increase in the ratio was caused by efficient inventory management or a reduction in inventories below optimal inventory levels, which could ultimately result in lost sales.

A decreasing inventory turnover ratio could be a sign of slow-moving and obsolete inventory. For limited periods, however, a company may deliberately increase its inventory (resulting in a lower turnover ratio) to take advantage of lower unit prices on large purchases or to obtain a large supply of a particularly critical raw material. In computing the inventory turnover, current cost or FIFO not LIFO inventory values should be used.

One of the problems with the current and acid-test ratios as indicators of liquidity is that they are static (balance sheet) ratios and don't relate cash inflows to cash outflows during the period. Most banks require borrowers to prepare a cash flow statement, which compares budgeted cash receipts with cash disbursements, including the repayment of prospective loans and interest, for the period of time the loan is granted.

Defensive-interval and liquidity ratios

The analyst can use the defensive-interval and liquidity ratios to calculate the adequacy of cash flows to pay current liabilities.

$$\text{Defensive Interval Ratio} = \frac{\text{Cash} + \text{Marketable Securities} + \text{Net Receivables}}{\text{Daily Cash Operating Expenditures}}$$

Daily cash operating expenses are equal to historical income statement expenses (excluding noncash items) divided by 365.

The defensive-interval ratios for Ranth are:

1984 $$\frac{\$346 + \$3,891}{(\$26,872 + \$3,407 + \$1,388 - \$771)/365^*} = \frac{\$4,237}{\$84.65} = 50.05 \text{ days}$$

1983 $$\frac{\$414 + \$3,442}{(\$23,253 + \$2,657 + \$1,136 - \$751)/365^*} = \frac{\$3,856}{\$72.04} = 53.53 \text{ days}$$

* (Cost of goods sold + Other expenses + Provision for income taxes − Depreciation)/365 days.

This measure indicates that Ranth could operate for approximately 50 days without additional financing or new sales assuming the same level of cash operating expenditures in the future as there was in the past.

$$\text{Liquidity Ratio} = \frac{\text{Cash Flow from Operations}}{\text{Projected Daily Cash Operating Expenditures}}$$

We can determine Ranth's cash flow from operations (Illustration 15–4) from their statement of changes in financial position (Illustration 15–3). The projected daily cash operating expenditures for purposes of this problem are assumed to be the same as we used to calculate the defensive-interval ratio.

ILLUSTRATION 15–4

RANTH MANUFACTURING CORPORATION
Cash Flow from Operations
($000)

	1984	1983
Working capital from operations	$2,192	$1,921
Subtract increases and add decreases in current asset accounts:		
Accounts receivable	(449)	838
Inventories	(1,207)	1,098
Prepaid expenses	(27)	(8)
Add increases and subtract decreases in current liability accounts:		
Notes payable	750	(1,050)
Accounts payable—trade	(47)	(1,342)
Accrued expenses	153	(4)
Income taxes payable	95	90
Cash flow from operations	$1,460	$1,543

The liquidity ratios for Ranth are:

$$1984 \quad \frac{\$1,460}{\$84.65} = 17.25 \text{ days}$$

$$1983 \quad \frac{\$1,543}{\$72.04} = 21.42 \text{ days}$$

This ratio indicates the number of days projected cash expenditures are covered by cash flow from operations. Ranth's coverage has declined because of their increased investment in accounts receivable and inventories.

LONG-TERM SOLVENCY MEASURES

Two ratios to measure the long-run solvency of an enterprise are the debt-to-asset ratio and the debt-to-equity ratio.

$$\text{Debt-to-Asset Ratio} = \frac{\text{Total Liabilities}}{\text{Total Assets}}$$

$$\text{Debt-to-Equity Ratio} = \frac{\text{Long-Term Debt}}{\text{Shareholders' Equity}}$$

Other versions of the debt-to-equity ratio are:

$$\frac{\text{Total Liabilities}}{\text{Shareholders' Equity}} \quad \text{and} \quad \frac{\text{Long-Term Debt}}{\text{Long-Term Debt} + \text{Shareholders' Equity}}$$

The lower these ratios the more protection the creditors should have against insolvency. In calculating this ratio the analyst should take into consideration that the net realizable value of assets in liquidation may be significantly different than the historical cost balance sheet amounts and that some creditors may have a preferred position (mortgage on specific assets) in liquidation.

The classification and disclosure of deferred taxes, minority interest in consolidated subsidiary, redeemable preferred, stock and unfunded pension liability discussed in prior chapters can have a large impact on the debt-to-equity ratio.

Although deferred taxes are classified as a liability on the balance sheet many analysts include it as equity rather than debt in computing these ratios because there is no obligation to pay this amount to the government.

Minority interest in consolidated subsidiaries ordinarily is not included as debt or equity and has no effect on the debt-to-equity ratio.

Redeemable preferred stock should be included as debt in the calculation of these ratios.

Unfunded pension liability is not recorded as a liability by the enterprise and is not included in the debt-to-equity ratio.[1] Analysts should consider that the enterprise must fund this liability in the future and consider it in making their evaluation of the firm's long-term solvency.

The debt-to-asset ratios for Ranth are:

		Industry Average
1984	$\frac{\$4,902}{\$18,022} = 27.2\%$	37.9%
1983	$\frac{\$4,691}{\$16,490} = 28.4\%$	38.6%
1982	$\frac{\$7,038}{\$17,767} = 39.6\%$	42.1%

Ranth finances a smaller percentage of assets with liabilities than does the industry and has lowered this ratio since 1982. They would appear to have additional borrowing capability (debt capacity) because of their relatively low debt-to-asset ratio. Debt capacity is a function of both a low debt-to-asset ratio and the prospect of future earnings and cash flows. Companies such as utilities that have stable earnings can sustain higher debt-to-asset ratios than cyclical industrial companies that have volatile earnings.

The long-run solvency ratio most commonly used in financial analysis is:

$$\frac{\text{Long-Term Debt}}{\text{Shareholders' Equity}}$$

The larger this ratio and the more volatile an enterprise's earnings, the greater the risk of future insolvency.

---

[1] On April 1, 1983, the FASB issued a discussion memorandum which suggests that pension liabilities should be reported on the balance sheet as a liability.

For example, the decline in automobile sales, earnings, and cash flow from operations in the late 1970s and early 1980s almost resulted in the bankruptcy of the Chrysler Corporation, whose debt-to-equity ratio increased from 32 percent in 1972 to 100 percent in early 1980. But the same situation had almost no effect on the long-term solvency of General Motors, whose debt-to-equity ratio was only approximately 10 percent in early 1980.

For the most part, manufacturing firms prefer "not to owe more than they own." This old Wall Street adage suggests that a 50–50 balance (a long-term debt/shareholders' equity ratio of 1) would be the *outer limit* for the debt-to-equity ratio.

The debt-to-equity ratios for Ranth are:

			Industry Average
1984	$\dfrac{\$1,447}{\$13,120}$	= 11.0%	28.6%
1983	$\dfrac{\$2,187}{\$11,799}$	= 18.5%	30.5%
1982	$\dfrac{\$2,228}{\$10,729}$	= 20.8%	35.6%

Ranth has a much lower debt-to-equity ratio than the average firm in the industry and appears to have substantial long-term debt capacity.

TIMES-INTEREST-EARNED

This ratio computes the coverage of the interest charges.

$$\text{Times-Interest-Earned Ratio} = \frac{\text{Income before Taxes and Interest Charges (Expenses)}}{\text{Interest Charges}}$$

The higher the ratio the greater the safety margin that the interest payments will be made.

For Ranth the ratios are:

1984	$\dfrac{\$2,809 + \$272}{\$272}$	= 11.33 times
1983	$\dfrac{\$2,306 + \$358}{\$358}$	= 7.44 times

Ranth has increased its coverage in 1984 by both increasing its earnings and decreasing its debt.

A more useful version of this ratio considers that the interest will be paid with cash, not income.

$$\frac{\text{Cash Flow Provided from Operations before}}{\text{Income Taxes and Interest Charges}}$$
$$\frac{}{\text{Interest Charges}}$$

The calculation of these ratios are:[2]

$$1984 \quad \frac{\$1,460 + \$1,388 + \$272}{\$272} = 11.47 \text{ times}$$

$$1983 \quad \frac{\$1,543 + \$1,136 + \$358}{\$358} = 8.48 \text{ times}$$

If the long-term debt requires periodic principal payments this figure should be included in the denominator with the interest charges.

PROFITABILITY AND OPERATING EFFICIENCY MEASURES

Net profit margin on sales

The net profit margin or return on sales measures the percentage of profit earned on sales. The higher the ratio the more efficient the enterprise is in turning $1 of sales into $1 of profit.

The ratio is:

$$\frac{\text{Net Income}}{\text{Net Sales}}$$

The net profit margin ratios for Ranth are:

		Industry Average
1984	$\dfrac{\$1,421}{\$33,088} = 4.3\%$	4.6%
1983	$\dfrac{\$1,170}{\$28,216} = 4.1\%$	4.4%

---

[2] Cash flow from operations is calculated in Illustration 15–4. Income taxes and interest charges are reported on the comparative income statement, Illustration 15–2.

Percentage income statement

The expression of each of the expenses as a percentage of sales (see Illustration 15–5) is useful in identifying the reasons for changes in net income.

ILLUSTRATION 15–5

RANTH MANUFACTURING CORPORATION
Expenses and Net Income as a Percentage of Sales
Years Ended December 31, 1984, and 1983

	1984	1983
Net sales	100.0%	100.0%
Cost of goods sold	81.2	82.4
Gross margin	18.8	17.6
Selling expenses	3.4	3.8
General and administrative expenses	6.1	4.3
Interest expense	.8	1.3
	10.3	9.4
Income before income taxes	8.5	8.2
Provision for income taxes	4.2	4.0
Net income	4.3%	4.2%

This analysis indicates that although Ranth's net income as a percentage of sales was approximately the same in 1984 and in 1983, there were increases in their general and administrative expenses in 1984 which were offset by decreases in their cost of goods sold, selling expenses, and interest expense. Further analysis should be done to explain the increase in general and administrative expenses.

Net profit margin excluding financing costs

In order to emphasize operating efficiency analysts and management often eliminate the impact of borrowing when they calculate the net profit margin. They are interested in the operating margin excluding financing costs.

The calculation of Ranth's 1984 income before debt financing is shown below:

Income before interest and income taxes ($2,809 + $272)	$3,081
Income tax expense based on 49.4 percent $\left(\frac{\$1,388}{\$2,809}\right)$ tax rate	1,522
Income before debt financing	$1,559

Another way of making this calculation is to add aftertax interest expense [Interest expense × (1 − Tax rate)] to net income. The calculations for Ranth are:

Net income + Aftertax interest expense

1984 $1,421   + [(1 − .494) $272]   = $1,559

1983 $1,170   + [(1 − .493) $358]   = $1,352

The net profit margin ratio eliminating the interest expense on debt financing is:

$$\frac{\text{Net Income} + \text{Aftertax Interest Expense}}{\text{Sales}}$$

For Ranth the ratios are:

		Industry Average
1984	$\frac{\$1,559}{\$33,088} = 4.7\%$	4.9%
1983	$\frac{\$1,352}{\$28,216} = 4.8\%$	5.2%

Asset turnover ratio

This ratio measures the amount of sales generated by the average assets used during the year by the enterprise.

The asset turnover ratio, which is a function of the turnover ratios of the individual assets such as accounts receivable, inventory, and plant and equipment, is:

$$\frac{\text{Net Sales}}{\text{Average Total Assets}}$$

The higher this ratio, the more efficiently the enterprise is perceived to use its assets. A problem with this interpretation is that higher ratios can be obtained by using older assets with low book values. This could result in failure to replace these assets and in future operating inefficiency. Another problem is that a company using accelerated depreciation methods will have lower book values (denominator of the ratio) and a higher asset turnover ratio than an identical company that uses the straight-line method and not be any more efficient.

For Ranth the asset turnover ratios are:

		Industry Average
1984	$\dfrac{\$33,088}{(\$18,022 + \$16,490)/2} = 1.92$	1.71
1983	$\dfrac{\$28,216}{(\$16,490 + \$17,767)/2} = 1.65$	1.48

Rate of return on assets

Rate of return on assets or return on investment (ROI) measures the profitability of the enterprise. Separate ROIs using segment information for each line of business should be used for diversified companies. This ratio recognizes that profitability is a function of both the operating margin on sales and the amount of assets used to generate the sales. Companies with low operating margins, such as food operations and supermarkets, obtain satisfactory ROI's because they generate large sales volume from each dollar they have invested in assets (primarily inventory).

Conversely, jewelry stores and haute couture boutiques obtain a satisfactory ROI even though they have a relatively slow asset (inventory) turnover because they have high profit margins.

The ratio is:

$$\frac{\text{Net Income}}{\text{Net Sales}} \times \frac{\text{Net Sales}}{\text{Average Total Assets}} = \frac{\text{Net Income}}{\text{Total Average Assets}}$$

$$\text{Profit Margin} \times \text{Asset Turnover} = \text{Rate of Return on Assets}$$

For companies with debt financing the aftertax interest expense should be added back to net income. This adjustment allows the enterprise to measure the return on assets exclusive of whether they were financed by debt or equity.

The calculations for Ranth are:

		Industry Average
1984	$\dfrac{\$1,559}{\$33,088} \times \dfrac{\$33,088}{(\$18,022 + \$16,490)/2}$	
	$4.7\% \times 1.92 = 9.02\%$	8.38%

Industry Average

$$1983 \quad \frac{\$1,352}{\$28,216} \times \frac{\$28,216}{(\$16,490 + \$17,767)/2}$$

$$4.8\% \quad \times \quad 1.65 \quad = 7.92\% \quad \quad 7.70\%$$

Ranth's rate of return on assets improved in 1984 over 1983. The improvement was achieved in spite of a small decline in the net profit margin because of an increase in asset turnover. A higher asset turnover ratio was also the reason their rate of return was better than the industry average.

Analysts should use historical cost ROI measures with care particularly when predicting future results. Management may have adopted a short-term strategy of maximizing short-term ROI by not replacing older assets with newer more productive assets that penalize short-term ROI but increase ROI in the future.

Current cost ROI

Many analysts believe a better measure of an enterprise's return on assets (ROI) is

$$\frac{\text{Current Cost Net Income}}{\text{Current Cost of Assets (Specific Price Changes)}}$$

Current cost income reflects the current value of assets consumed (current cost of inventory sold and current cost depreciation). It recognizes unrealized holding gains which reduces the potential for management to manipulate net income by deciding when holding gains on inventory and other assets will be taken. And it separates out operating income from holding gains and therefore enables the analyst to make a more refined calculation of operating performance.

The current cost of assets represents the economic value of the assets used during the period to earn the current cost income. It eliminates the historical cost problems of assets purchased at different times and not adjusted for increases or decreases in the specific prices of assets.

This ratio, which can be calculated using *SFAS 33* disclosures, is a better economic measure of an enterprise's performance, and because it adjusts for holding gains and the timing of asset purchases, it enhances interfirm comparability.

LEVERAGE

Leverage, or "trading on the equity," is the financing of assets with debt or preferred stock in order to increase the return to common stockholders. As long as the return to the common stockholders is greater than the aftertax cost of interest or preferred dividends there will be a benefit to the common shareholders.

As the debt-to-equity ratio increases, the risk associated with the repayment of the debt increases as does the cost of borrowing. The cost of borrowing and the ability to generate cash flow from operations to repay debt service costs are major factors to be considered by firms in determining their level of financial leverage.

Financial leverage is often expressed as the ratio of

$$\frac{\text{Average Total Assets}}{\text{Average Common Stockholders' Equity}}$$

It is a measure of the amount of assets financed by the common stockholders. Financial leverage can be raised by increasing borrowing, repurchasing stock, or any substitution of debt for equity.

The financial leverage ratios for Ranth are:

		Industry Average
1984	$\dfrac{(\$18{,}022 + \$16{,}490)/2}{(\$13{,}120 + \$11{,}799)/2} = 1.38$	1.83
1983	$\dfrac{(\$16{,}490 + \$17{,}767)/2}{(\$11{,}799 + \$10{,}729)/2} = 1.52$	1.68

Ranth uses less financial leverage than the average industry enterprise.

Rate of return on common stockholders' equity

This ratio measures the return to the common stockholders.

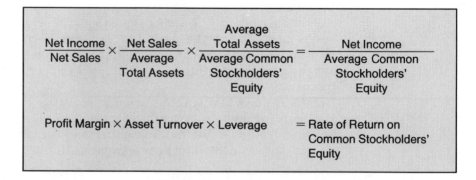

$$\frac{\text{Net Income}}{\text{Net Sales}} \times \frac{\text{Net Sales}}{\text{Average Total Assets}} \times \frac{\text{Average Total Assets}}{\text{Average Common Stockholders' Equity}} = \frac{\text{Net Income}}{\text{Average Common Stockholders' Equity}}$$

Profit Margin × Asset Turnover × Leverage = Rate of Return on Common Stockholders' Equity

If the company has preferred dividends they should be deducted from net income to get net income applicable to common stockholders.

The ratios for Ranth are:

$$1984 \quad \frac{\$1{,}421}{\$33{,}088} \times \frac{\$33{,}088}{(\$18{,}022+\$16{,}490)/2} \times \frac{(\$18{,}022+\$16{,}490)/2}{(\$13{,}120+\$11{,}799)/2} = \frac{\$1{,}421}{(\$13{,}120+\$11{,}799)/2}$$

1984	4.3% ×	1.92 ×	1.38 =	11.4%
Industry average	4.6% ×	1.71 ×	1.83 =	14.4%
1983	4.1% ×	1.65 ×	1.52 =	10.3%
Industry average	4.4% ×	1.48 ×	1.69 =	11.0%

Ranth has improved its rate of return on common stockholders' equity from 10.3 percent in 1983 to 11.4 percent in 1984. The improvement was primarily due to an increase in asset turnover from 1.65 to 1.92. The industry averages were higher than Ranth's in both 1983 and 1984. The average industry enterprise used more leverage than Ranth which enabled it to convert a lower rate of return on assets to a higher return on common stockholders' equity.

EARNINGS PER SHARE

The calculation of earnings per share (EPS) is explained in detail in Chapter 9. It is:

$$\frac{\text{Net Income} - \text{Preferred Dividends}}{\text{Weighted Average Number of Common Shares Outstanding}}$$

Earnings per share figures are disclosed on the face of the income statement; it is one of the measures most often used by analysts.

One of the problems with this statistic is that it doesn't measure profitability because it doesn't relate the earnings to assets used (ROI) or stockholders' equity (return on common stockholders' equity).

Another problem in using EPS as a profitability measure is that EPS can be raised by reducing the number of common shares outstanding and it fails to recognize that companies that retain more of their earnings and increase their asset base will increase their EPS even though their profit margins may be declining.

When comparing EPS over time the analyst should use *SFAS 33* disclosure, which adjusts earnings per share for the impact of inflation.

When using EPS to compare companies the analyst should recognize that GAAP allows companies a choice in computing their earnings and that some companies earnings may be of "higher quality" than others.

Companies with high-quality earnings have these characteristics:

1. A set of conservative accounting policies, consistently applied.
2. A stable stream of earnings.
3. Sales that quickly convert to cash after being reported.
4. An appropriate debt level.
5. Earnings that have not been inflated.

PRICE EARNINGS RATIO

The price-earnings (P/E) ratio is:

$$\frac{\text{Market Price per Share}}{\text{Earnings per Share}}$$

For Ranth the ratio is:

		Industry Average
1984	$\frac{\$23.00}{\$2.27} = 10.13$ to 1	9.62 to 1
1983	$\frac{\$18.25}{\$1.87} = 9.76$ to 1	8.76 to 1

Common stocks trade at price-earnings multiples largely determined by current earning power and expectation of potential earnings and cash flows. High technology common stocks, such as Hewlett Packard Corporation (P/E 17 to 1, June 1982) have higher P/E ratios than companies like American Telephone & Telegraph (P/E 6 to 1, June 1982) because they are perceived to have better earnings and cash flow growth potential. The ability to estimate future earnings and cash flows accurately is the mark of the successful analyst.

CAPITALIZATION RATIO

This ratio is a reciprocal of the price-earnings ratio and measures the relationship of earnings to the current market price of the stockholder's investment.

$$\frac{\text{Earnings per Share}}{\text{Market Price per Share}}$$

For Ranth the ratios are:

$$1984 \quad \frac{\$2.27}{\$23.00} = 9.9\%$$

$$1983 \quad \frac{\$1.87}{\$18.25} = 10.2\%$$

DIVIDEND YIELD RATIO

This ratio measures the cash return the investor will receive on the investment in one share of common stock.

The ratio is:

$$\frac{\text{Annual Cash Dividends per Share}}{\text{Market Price per Share}}$$

For Ranth the ratio is:

$$1984 \quad \frac{\$.16}{\$23.00} = .7\%$$

$$1983 \quad \frac{\$.16}{\$18.25} = .9\%$$

Ranth pays little out in dividends, preferring to retain its earnings for future growth. Investors who do not need current income should be indifferent to a low dividend payout as long as Ranth earns more on the funds retained in the business than they (investors) could earn in investing these funds (dividends) after paying income taxes on the dividend income.

USES OF FINANCIAL RATIO AND COMPARATIVE FINANCIAL STATEMENT ANALYSIS

Ratios are mechanical tools of analysis. Because of their statistical aura they are mistakenly viewed to be an end or a standard in themselves. One writer has suggested that ratios are like a thermometer. Beyond a certain range the thermometer reading indicates that something is wrong but not exactly what it is.

Ratios are useful within relevant ranges. If, for example, the current ratio is too low, a liquidity problem *may* exist. If the current ratio is too high, the indicator *may* be pointing to the inefficient use of current assets.

Ratio analysis takes on more meaning when several years of a business firm are studied or when intercompany comparisons are made. Ratios are helpful in pointing out trends; standing alone, any given ratio may be meaningless.

Sound business judgment is required in making comparisons and analyzing trends. For example, one firm may show a lower receivable turnover than its industry competitors. This may indicate the firm is guilty of lax credit policies, or the low ratio may be a reflection of a conscious management policy to compete for sales through liberal credit policies.

Industry characteristics also play an important role when analyzing businesses. For example, fast food companies are able to operate with current ratios of 1 to 1 because inventory turns over almost immediately and is sold for cash. Inventory for McDonald's Corporation, the fast-food company, should be considered a quick asset.

Analysts have also concerned themselves with the use of financial statement analysis in the development of models to make bank lending decisions, predict bankruptcy, and predict corporate earnings and growth rates in order to predict future stock prices.[3] The most successful predictors of bankruptcy, for example, are return on investment, debt-to-asset, and cash-flow-to-total-debt ratios. Almost without exception, troubled companies experience severe declines in ROI and cash flow and rely more heavily on debt financing.

PROBLEMS AND CASES

15-1 Russell Hodges Corporation

The condensed financial statements of the Russell Hodges Corporation (a manufacturer of hose clamps) for 1984 are:

---

[3] Development and composition of these models is beyond the scope of this text. Readers should refer to Baruch Lev, *Financial Statement Analysis: A New Approach* (Englewood Cliffs, N.J.: Prentice Hall, 1974), chapters 7–11.

RUSSELL HODGES CORPORATION
Comparative Balance Sheets
December 31, 1984, and 1983

	1984	1983
Assets		
Current assets:		
Cash	$ 30,000	$ 50,000
Accounts receivable	110,000	75,000
Inventories	620,000	445,000
Total current assets	760,000	570,000
Fixed assets:		
Property, plant, and equipment		
(net of accumulated depreciation) ..	836,000	750,000
Total assets	$1,596,000	$1,320,000
Equities		
Current liabilities:		
Accounts payable	$ 200,000	$ 150,000
Accrued expenses..................	26,000	20,000
Total current liabilities	226,000	170,000
Bonds payable	500,000	500,000
Total liabilities	726,000	670,000
Stockholders' equity		
Common stock.....................	500,000	400,000
Retained earnings	370,000	250,000
	870,000	650,000
Total equities	$1,596,000	$1,320,000

RUSSELL HODGES CORPORATION
Income Statement
For The Year Ended December 31, 1984

Sales.................................	$1,500,000
Cost of goods sold....................	1,050,000
Gross profit	450,000
Selling expenses	120,000
General and administrative expenses....	80,000
Interest expense	50,000
	250,000
Income before taxes	200,000
Income taxes (40 percent)	80,000
Net income	$ 120,000

Required:

1. Calculate the following 1984 financial ratios:

a. Current.

b. Acid-test.

c. Accounts receivable turnover and average accounts receivable collection period.

d. Inventory turnover.

e. Asset turnover.

f. Net profit margin.

g. Debt-to-equity.

h. Rate of return on assets.

i. Rate of return on common stockholders' equity.

2. Comment on the liquidity, long-term solvency, and profitability of Russell Hodges Corporation.

15–2 United Electron Corporation and Diode Manufacturing Corporation

Mr. James Gerber, a securities analyst with a well-known Wall Street firm, was studying the published annual reports of the United Electron Corporation and the Diode Manufacturing Corporation. Mr. Gerber specialized in the electronics industry and periodically issued comparative reports on various companies within the industry. His comments were highly regarded within the financial community and often created a flurry of activity among investment professionals and speculators.

Mr. Gerber has asked that you prepare a preliminary comparative report on United Electron Corporation and Diode Manufacturing Corporation for his review. The following condensed data was taken from the published statements of the two companies:

	($000)	
	United Electron Corporation	*Diode Manufacturing Corporation*
Sales	$19,500	$36,000
Cost of goods sold*	14,200	27,000
Selling, general, and administrative expenses*	2,800	6,000
Interest expense	400	200
Extraordinary losses (gain)	100	(400)
Income taxes	1,000	1,600
Quick assets	800	3,500
Inventories	2,700	6,000
Fixed assets	10,000	18,000
Accumulated depreciation	2,500	8,000
Investments	400	500
Other assets	600	5,000
Current liabilities	1,200	2,700
Long-term debt	4,250	2,200
Capital stock ($10 par value)	5,000	15,000
Retained earnings	1,550	5,100
Current market price per share	30	10
* Includes depreciation expense.	800	1,200

Required:

1. Draft the comparative report for Mr. Gerber, specifically commenting on each corporation's:

a. Liquidity.

b. Long-term solvency.

c. Profitability.

d. Financial leverage.

Use relevant financial ratios to support your analysis.

2. What additional information would you like to have before making an investment recommendation? Is this information readily available to investors?

15–3 General Electric

Refer to General Electric's Financial Highlights for the year ended December 31, 1980, and December 31, 1979.

GENERAL ELECTRIC
Financial Highlights
(dollar amounts in millions; per share amounts in dollars)

		1980	1979	Percent Increase
For the year:	Sales of products and services to customers	$24,959	$22,461	11%
	Other income	564	519	9
	Total revenues	25,523	22,980	11
	Net earnings applicable to common stock	1,514	1,409	7
At year-end:	Total capital invested	$10,447	$ 9,332	12%
	Share owners' equity	8,200	7,362	11
	Short-and long-term borrowings	2,093	1,818	15
Per share:	Net earnings	$ 6.65	$ 6.20	7%
	Dividends declared	2.95	2.75	7
	Share owners' equity—year-end	36.00	32.31	11
Measurements:	Operating margin as a percentage of sales	9.0%	9.5%	
	Effective income tax rate	38.4	39.9	
	Earnings as a percentage of sales	6.1	6.3	
	Percent earned on average total capital invested	17.3	17.6	
	Percent earned on average share owners' equity	19.5	20.2	
	Borrowings as a percentage of total capital invested	20.0	19.5	

Required:

1.   Explain the significance of each of these measurements in determining GE's financial success for the year.

a.   Operating margin as a percentage of sales.

b.   Effective income tax rate.

c.   Earnings as a percentage of sales.

d.   Percent earned on average total capital invested.

e.   Percent earned on average shareowners' equity.

2.   A spokesman for the industry indicated that percent earned on average total capital invested was a better measure of financial success than earnings per share. Do you agree?

3.   Explain why the percent earned on average shareowners' equity (19.5 percent) is higher than the percent earned on average total capital invested (17.3 percent).

4.   On page 30 of its annual report GE reported that earnings per share adjusted for current cost was $4.40. What would cause this figure to be so much lower than the $6.65 reported earnings per share?

15–4   Tribunal Printing Corporation

The Tribunal Printing Corporation was founded as a commercial printing business in New York City by Samuel J. Decker in 1935. While accepting almost any type of printing order, the company specialized in the production and printing of corporate annual reports. Over the years, the company has been very successful because of its quality printing and its ability to deliver orders on time to its major customers (nearby large, Manhatten-based corporations).

In 1982, Mr. Decker died unexpectedly, leaving his majority interest in the corporation to his son Michael. Michael Decker, employed at the time in his own venture capital firm, had been involved in the management of Tribunal on a part-time basis since graduating from college in 1968. Upon his father's death, he delegated complete operational responsibility to Peter Tedesco, who had joined the company as a managerial associate in 1975. Mr. Tedesco was given a three-year employment contract, which was renewable on December 31, 1985.

In mid-1985, Mr. Decker began to evaluate Tribunal's operational results to appraise the performance of Mr. Tedesco. As a basis for comparison, Mr. Decker obtained printing industry data for an average printing company. He believed that Tribunal's financial statements in 1984, as well as the 1984 industry data (See Exhibits 1 and 2) were representative of the financial statements of both the company and the industry for the past few years.

EXHIBIT 1

TRIBUNAL PRINTING CORPORATION
Condensed Comparative Income Statements
1984
($000)

	Tribunal Printing Corporation	Average Printing Industry Company
Sales	$2,091	$2,349
Cost of sales	1,388	1,588
Gross profit	703	761
Selling, general, and administrative Income from operations	526	602
	177	159
Interest income	(3)	(6)
Interest expense	31	15
Net income before tax	149	150
Income tax	46	46
Net income	103	104
Dividends	26	43
Addition to retained earnings	$ 77	$ 61

EXHIBIT 2

TRIBUNAL PRINTING CORPORATION
Condensed Comparative Balance Sheets
December 31, 1984
($000)

	Tribunal Printing Corp.		Average Printing Industry Company	
	1983	1984	1983	1984
Assets				
Current assets:				
Cash	$ 239	$ 301	$ 109	$ 71
Marketable securities	90	108	92	90
Accounts receivable	306	337	395	358
Inventory	196	264	244	291
Total current assets	831	1,010	840	810
Land	35	35	49	42
Buildings and equipment	1,090	1,111	1,218	1,358
Less: Accumulated depreciation	563	640	657	741
	527	471	561	617
Total assets	$1,393	$1,516	$1,450	$1,469

EXHIBIT 2 *(continued)*

	Tribunal Printing Corp.		Average Printing Industry Company	
	1983	1984	1983	1984
Equities				
Current liabilities:				
Notes payable to bank	$ 178	$ 180	$ 111	$ 92
Accounts payable........................	76	79	158	180
Due to finance companies	138	178	31	12
Taxes payable	39	40	48	44
Total current liabilities	431	477	348	328
Long-term debt...........................	—	—	140	118
Total liabilities	431	477	488	446
Shareholders' equity:				
Capital stock	300	300	320	320
Retained earnings	662	739	642	703
Total shareholders' equity	962	1,039	962	1,023
Total equities	$1,393	$1,516	$1,450	$1,469

Required:

1. Do you think Mr. Decker should renew Mr. Tedesco's contract? Use the data in the financial statements to support your position.

2. What additional financial information would be helpful to support your recommendation?

----------- **15–5 Tandy Corporation** -----------

Tandy Corporation and its principal division, Radio Shack, have gained a position as one of the world's leading distributors of technology to the individual consumer.

Tandy/Radio Shack currently distributes retail electronics to the world market through 5,147 company-owned retail stores, plus more than 3,000 dealer/franchise outlets. In number of outlets Radio Shack is the largest retail electronics chain in the world. Radio Shack stores carry a multitude of electronic products including antennas, radios, receivers, magnetic tape, speakers, turntables, telephones, security devices, public address systems, intercoms, calculators, electronic and scientific toys, games and kits, citizens band radios, scanners and electronic parts.

The Company's manufacturing capabilities are allowing Tandy to capitalize on the latest technological opportunities. This captive supply source allows quick reactions to changing market conditions. The 28 factories, 24 in the United States and 4 foreign plants, provide about 43% of the products included in the Radio Shack line. Many of the products manufactured by these plants, such as the TRS-80 Microcomputer, have special features unique to Radio Shack.

Tandy Corporation uses the following investment equation to report to shareholders on the investing in assets, measuring how efficiently those assets were employed, the financing of the assets and their attitude about shareholder returns.

June 30	Asset Turnover	×	Return on Sales	=	Return on Assets	×	Financial Leverage	=	Return on Equity
	$\frac{Sales}{Avg.\ Assets}$	×	$\frac{Net\ Income}{Sales}$	=	$\frac{Net\ Income}{Avg.\ Assets}$	×	$\frac{Avg.\ Assets}{Avg.\ Equity}$	=	$\frac{Net\ Income}{Avg.\ Equity}$
1973	1.34	×	4.4%	=	5.9%	×	2.06	=	12.1%
1974	1.47	×	3.6	=	5.3	×	2.41	=	12.8
1975	1.71	×	5.1	=	8.7	×	2.53	=	22.0
1976	2.04	×	8.7	=	17.7	×	2.18	=	38.7
1977	2.16	×	7.3	=	15.7	×	2.37	=	37.2
1978	2.06	×	6.2	=	12.8	×	3.39	=	43.6
1979	2.09	×	6.9	=	14.3	×	3.35	=	47.9
1980	2.10	×	8.1	=	17.0	×	2.69	=	45.7
1981	2.06	×	10.0	=	20.6	×	1.93	=	39.7

Required:

1. Asset turnover.

a. Explain what this ratio measures.

b. Approximately half of Tandy's total assets were invested in inventories in 1981 and 1982. Estimate Tandy's inventory turnover (Sales ÷ Average Inventory) for the fiscal year ended June 30, 1981. Is this a more important measure for Tandy than asset turnover?

c. Tandy indicated in their annual report that they were willing to accept lower asset turnover for a higher gross margin. Do you agree with this policy?

2. Return on sales.

a. Explain what the ratio measures.

b. Tandy's annual report contained the following statement: "On the operating side, we believe the gross margin level is the biggest factor in determining the net profit margin." Do you agree?

3. Return on assets.

a. Explain what this ratio measures.

b. What is the significance of the substantial increase in this ratio from 1973 to 1981?

    c. The following statement comes from Tandy's discussion of this ratio in the annual report: "Although new investments or acquisitions rarely have such returns (20.6 percent) initially, it is management's intention to reinvest Tandy's capital in those projects or areas which have a clear prospect of generating high real rates of return (above inflation) within a foreseeable time frame." Should the projected return-on-assets ratio be the criterion for deciding what asset investments to make in the future?

    4. Financial leverage.

a. Explain what this ratio measures.

b. What is the significance of the large decline in this ratio from 1980 to 1981?

    5. Return on equity.

a. Explain what this ratio measures.

b. What caused the decline in this ratio from 1980 to 1981?

c. Is this ratio more important than return on assets?

15–6 Rowan Companies, Inc.

Rowan Companies, Inc., founded in 1923, is an international petroleum service firm engaged in three businesses.

Offshore contract drilling for the worldwide petroleum industry and onshore drilling in domestic areas are conducted with a diversified complement of 14 deep-water jack-ups, 1 semisubmersible barge, 3 submersible barges, 1 self-contained platform-type rig, and 14 land rigs including 5 winterized rigs for arctic operations.

Charter and contract helicopter and fixed-wing aircraft service is conducted primarily in Alaska and the Gulf of Mexico with a fleet of 92 helicopters and 15 aircraft.

Finally, the firm is involved in oil and gas exploration and production principally as an investor in such properties.

Capital expansion commitments in years 1982–85 amount to about $700 million including 10 cantilever jack-ups and an Arctic land rig under construction or on order.

Required:

1. Using the 10-year financial review and the 1981 statement of changes in consolidated financial position, compare the company's 1981 performance with prior years. Consider important trends that have developed in the company over the past 10 years.

2. What business risks does Rowan face?

3. Insofar as past data is a reflection of future performance, what do you predict for Rowan in the future?

ROWAN COMPANIES, INC., AND SUBSIDIARIES
Statement of Changes in Consolidated Financial Position
For the Years Ended December 31, 1981, 1980, and 1979

	1981	1980	1979
		(in thousands)	
WORKING CAPITAL PROVIDED BY:			
Operations:			
Net income	$111,835	$ 71,166	$ 32,772
Items not requiring working capital:			
Depreciation, depletion and amortization	33,511	28,599	25,086
Book value of property sold	6,601	8,394	2,240
Deferred income taxes	32,498	13,911	7,941
Compensation expense	3,333	2,524	850
Total	187,778	124,594	68,889
Common stock issued under stock option plans ...	83	437	181
Common stock issued for conversion of securities .	222	73,699	
Long-term borrowings	29,000	191,250	40,400
Other—net	899	360	266
Total	217,982	390,340	109,736
WORKING CAPITAL APPLIED TO:			
Property additions	171,417	137,874	62,459
Reduction of long-term debt	18,197	203,050	45,524
Conversion of preferred stock	222	344	
Dividends paid or declared.....................	7,498	6,077	5,704
Other assets	6,382	(1,776)	768
Total	203,716	345,569	114,455
INCREASE (DECREASE) IN WORKING CAPITAL ...	$ 14,266	$ 44,771	$ (4,719)
CHANGES WITHIN WORKING CAPITAL:			
Increase (decrease) in current assets:			
Cash and short-term investments	$ 19,459	$ 27,040	(634)
Accounts receivable	20,724	12,710	8,504
Materials and supplies.......................	1,736	1,037	283
Prepaid expenses...........................	(356)	425	(186)
Decrease (increase) in current liabilities:			
Note payable	5,000	(5,000)	
Current maturities of long-term debt............	(9,693)	9,910	(2,536)
Accounts payable—trade	(6,264)	(144)	(2,580)
Accrued income taxes.......................	(9,326)	(2,052)	(5,413)
Other accruals	(7,014)	845	(2,157)
INCREASE (DECREASE) IN WORKING CAPITAL ...	$ 14,266	$ 44,771	$ (4,719)

ROWAN COMPANIES, INC., AND SUBSIDIARIES
Ten-Year Financial Review
($000, except per share amounts and ratios)

	1981	1980	1979	1978
OPERATIONS				
REVENUES:				
Drilling operations	$329,146	$225,045	$164,493	$115,941
Aircraft operations	39,829	30,119	24,121	19,568
Total	368,975	255,164	188,614	135,509
COSTS AND EXPENSES:				
Drilling operations	134,196	103,682	82,540	66,483
Aircraft operations	29,213	22,180	15,852	14,784
Depreciation, depletion and amortization	33,511	28,599	25,086	17,782
General and administrative	7,291	5,909	4,251	4,367
Total	204,211	160,370	127,729	103,416
INCOME FROM OPERATIONS	164,764	94,794	60,885	32,093
OTHER INCOME (EXPENSE):				
Interest expense	(19,573)	(16,509)	(14,876)	(9,922)
Less interest capitalized	11,993	7,215	438	816
Gain on disposals of property and equipment	7,400	11,688	3,106	5,267
Interest income	6,857	1,856	1,470	769
Other—net	949	2,520	438	100
Other income (expense)—net	7,626	6,770	(9,379)	(2,970)
EQUITY IN EARNINGS OF 50% OWNED COMPANIES .				2,013
INCOME BEFORE INCOME TAXES	172,390	101,564	51,506	31,136
PROVISION FOR INCOME TAXES	60,555	30,398	18,734	8,491
NET INCOME	$111,835	$ 71,166	$ 32,772	$ 22,645
PER SHARE OF COMMON STOCK				
Net income:				
Primary	$ 2.22	$ 1.49	$ .67	$ .48
Fully diluted	$ 2.08	$ 1.42	$ .67	$ .48
Cash dividends declared	$ .06	$ .034	$ .025	$ .02
FINANCIAL POSITION				
Working capital	$ 77,601	$ 63,335	$ 18,564	$ 23,316
Property and equipment—at cost:				
Drilling	491,182	358,305	283,723	266,632
Aircraft	69,005	44,414	31,470	27,207
Other	54,767	42,805	27,359	17,137
Construction in progress	36,619	52,210	30,587	4,748
Total—at cost	651,573	497,734	373,139	315,724
Property and equipment—net	503,049	371,468	270,595	235,013
Total assets	658,873	479,623	341,611	298,374
Investment in 50% owned companies				
Long-term debt	87,802	76,999	88,799	93,923
Redeemable preferred stock	47,434	47,656	48,000	48,000
Common stockholders' equity	394,194	283,699	140,349	111,887
Current ratio	2.23	2.78	1.48	1.88
Debt—common stockholders' equity	.22	.27	.63	.84
Book value per common share	$ 8.23	$ 5.98	$ 3.42	$ 2.75

1977	1976	1975	1974	1973	1972

$ 77,786	$ 58,718	$ 49,181	$24,649	$14,894	$15,261
21,822	15,152	15,555	12,821	5,572	4,332
99,608	73,870	64,736	37,470	20,466	19,593
49,134	35,093	31,771	15,477	10,480	10,708
14,419	10,999	11,014	6,796	3,425	2,364
11,030	8,917	6,357	4,115	3,535	3,429
1,880	1,366	1,560	1,051	784	777
76,463	56,375	50,702	27,439	18,224	17,278
23,145	17,495	14,034	10,031	2,242	2,315
(4,997)	(3,899)	(3,904)	(2,396)	(263)	(153)
550	334	1,182	781	4	
2,121	1,525	1,345	1,168	1,309	778
151	367	171	215	545	435
21	44	116	123	51	(62)
(2,154)	(1,629)	(1,090)	(109)	1,646	998
1,306	4,330	4,862	2,985	1,985	924
22,297	20,196	17,806	12,907	5,873	4,237
5,787	5,836	2,010	4,050	1,485	1,506
$ 16,510	$ 14,360	$ 15,796	$ 8,857	$ 4,388	$ 2,731
$ .40	$ .35	$ .40	$ .23	$ .12	$ .07
$ .40	$ .35	$ .40	$ .23	$ .12	$ .07
$ .015	$ .0125	$ .00875	$.00875	$.00875	$.00875
$ 6,957	$ 5,164	$ 6,939	$ 7,513	$ 6,801	$11,868
132,516	86,923	80,832	40,865	25,880	21,842
26,304	21,616	22,372	14,440	8,619	7,094
13,954	10,594	9,661	8,578	5,811	2,793
4,184	19,591		15,872	880	
176,958	138,724	112,865	79,755	41,190	31,729
131,695	102,538	83,385	55,882	20,836	13,441
183,387	142,710	122,609	83,439	43,226	36,915
20,709	20,653	17,243	11,008	10,129	6,450
57,362	44,750	41,593	28,328	1,935	563
91,847	74,878	60,285	43,802	34,782	30,142
1.32	1.41	1.52	2.00	2.77	4.21
.62	.60	.69	.65	.06	.02
$ 2.28	$ 1.90	$ 1.54	$ 1.14	$ .92	$ .81

16

Introduction to managerial accounting and absorption (full) costing

The objective of managerial accounting is to provide information that is useful to management in planning and controlling the operations of an organization.

Managerial accounting is often called internal accounting in contrast to financial accounting which provides information to external users of the financial statements. Because it is developed for internal users managerial accounting is not based on a set of generally accepted accounting principles.

Cost accounting, decision making, budgeting, control, and performance evaluation are among the major topics covered in managerial accounting.

COST ACCOUNTING

Cost accounting is concerned with the determination, allocation, and interpretation of costs.

Cost is broadly defined as the dollar measure of the resources consumed or foregone to obtain some good or service. A cost objective or cost object is the purpose for which management is measuring the costs. Examples of cost objects are products (one or many), departments, or activities. *Cost allocation* is the process of assigning costs to cost objects for purposes of inventory valuation, decision making, control, or performance evaluation.

DECISION MAKING

Managers are decision makers. They analyze alternative courses of action and select the one that benefits the organization most.

Costs are necessary inputs to many managerial decisions. Managerial accounting is concerned with the determination of costs relevant to particular decisions and the design of information systems to collect these costs.

Some typical managerial decisions are whether to purchase a new machine, whether to discontinue production and sale of a product, whether to make a product or buy it from some external source, and whether to accept incremental business.

BUDGETING AND CONTROL

Budgets are quantitative expressions of comprehensive corporate plans. Budgets summarize the expected outcomes of planned managerial actions during the coming period.

Budgeting also helps management to anticipate problems and reinforces management's understanding of the goals of the organization.

Managerial accounting is concerned with structuring the budget process and the budget document to best facilitate planning and control so as to maximize the probability of attaining corporate objectives.

PERFORMANCE EVALUATION

The methods used to evaluate and reward performance in an organization have a large impact on the way organizational decisions are made. Managerial accounting is concerned with the development of reports and techniques to measure and evaluate the performance of managers, departments, and divisions.

ABSORPTION COSTING

Absorption (full) costing is the process by which a portion of *all manufacturing costs* incurred in an accounting period are assigned to each unit of product produced in the period in order to value inventory and compute cost of goods sold.

Manufacturing costs include both direct product costs and factory overhead costs. Raw material and direct labor are *direct* product costs because they can be specifically traced to the manufacture of an individual product. Factory (manufacturing) overhead costs include all costs incurred in the manufacturing process that cannot be assigned directly to an individual product. Factory rent; the cost of light, heat, and power; factory wages paid to timekeepers and supervisors; and depreciation on machinery are examples of factory overhead costs.

Fixed factory overhead costs

Fixed factory overhead costs do not change as the output level of the factory varies over reasonable levels. Depreciation on manufacturing equipment, property taxes on the factory building, and the plant manager's salary are examples of fixed factory overhead costs.

Variable factory overhead costs

Variable factory overhead costs vary with changes in the output level of the factory. The amount and cost of lubricating oil consumed in a factory increases in a manner roughly proportional to the total output of the factory. The cost of the oil is a factory overhead cost rather than a direct product cost because of the difficulty (or impossibility) of assigning the oil consumed to a particular unit of output.

Selling, general, and administrative costs

Selling, general, and administrative costs may be allocated to cost objects at the discretion of management to facilitate decision making, control of operations, and evaluation of performance. However, selling and administrative costs are never part of the cost of the product manufactured. They are period costs not product costs and are expensed in the period when they are incurred.

The full factory costs (raw material, direct labor, and factory overhead) are assigned to each unit of output in an absorption (full) costing accounting system. Firms often use the full costs of products in setting selling prices. In the long run, in order to insure profitable operation, selling prices must cover *all* manufacturing, selling, and administrative costs of the firm.

JOB ORDER AND PROCESS COSTING SYSTEMS

The two major types of cost accounting systems used in practice are job order and process. *Job order* (job lot) *costing* is used to assign manufacturing costs to products that require different amounts of direct labor and raw material for each unit or group of units produced. For example, job order costing is used by a printer because the required amount of typesetting, paper, ink, and direct labor is different for each printing job. It is also used in the shipbuilding and construction industries. A consultant accounting for the cost of a particular project or a public accountant determining the cost of a particular audit engagement would also use job order costing. *Process costing* is used in industries producing large quantities of similar units or standardized products, such as plastics, chemicals, and petroleum. Each of the units produced is exactly alike and contains the same amount of direct labor and raw material.

In either process or job order costing the cost assigned to an individual item in inventory is an average cost to manufacture the item.

In process costing, the product is homogeneous, and the average cost is usually the average manufacturing cost *for the period,* which is equal to the total manufacturing cost of the period divided by the number of units produced during the period. It is computed *once* at the end of the period.

In job order costing the average is over the number of items *produced at one time.* It is the total cost to produce a batch of items divided by the number of items in the batch. In many instances the production process results in the development of accounting systems that are a composite of a process and a job order costing system.

Job lot (job order) costing

To illustrate the determination of the absorption (full) cost of a product using a job lot costing system we can use the data in Illustration 16–1 for the Aero Manufacturing Company. Aero Manufacturing, which began operations in 1984, produces electronic components for the aerospace industry. Because of their general applicability in the industry, components can be manufactured and held in inventory in anticipation of future sales.

Aero expects to produce many different products in the future and has installed a job lot costing system. Aero considers each electronic component to be an individual job for cost accounting purposes.

ILLUSTRATION 16–1

AERO MANUFACTURING
Manufacturing Cost Data for 1984*

Actual Direct Manufacturing Costs
(10,000 components produced)

Raw materials (*average* cost of $15 per component)	$150,000
Direct labor (*average* 5 direct labor hours per component at $6.50/hour)...............................	$325,000

Factory Overhead Costs

Beginning-of-year estimates for factory overhead costs:

Fixed factory overhead:		
Depreciation	$50,000	
Supervision	80,000	
Insurance	10,000	
Other	10,000	$150,000
Variable factory overhead (assuming 75,000 direct labor hours will be worked in 1984):		
Lubricants	37,500	
Miscellaneous supplies	18,750	56,250
Total estimated factory overhead		$206,250

Actual factory overhead costs:	
Fixed	$150,000
Variable (50,000 direct labor hours worked in 1984)...	38,500
Total	$188,500

* There are no work in process inventories at the end of 1984.

Aero's management uses the costs of the electronic components in its periodic assessment of the economic performance of its operations, in its annual performance review of operating management, and in making operating, investment, and pricing decisions throughout the year.

Direct product costs

Direct product costs for each component averaged $47.50 ($32.50 direct labor and $15.00 raw material). The 10,000 components produced in 1984 required $325,000 of direct labor and $150,000 of raw materials. These costs were listed on individual job tickets that accompanied the jobs through the manufacturing process.

Assume Aero Manufacturing has just completed the manufacture of one component, model TS47. This *particular* model required five direct labor-hours, which cost $6.50 an hour, and $15 of raw material to complete. The company made the following journal entry to allocate the cost of direct labor and raw material to the TS47 component.

Work in Process Inventory............................	47.50	
Raw Material Inventory		15.00
Wages Payable		32.50

Factory overhead cost

In addition to the cost of direct labor and raw material, each component worked on is assigned its fair share of factory overhead under the absorption costing method.

The Factory Overhead account is an asset account that temporarily collects factory overhead costs before their assignment to the inventory account, Work in Process.

Actual factory overhead costs are recorded as they are incurred during the period. For instance, Aero's payment of $1,500 for the annual fire insurance bill on the factory is recorded as:

Factory Overhead	1,500	
Cash		1,500

Factory overhead is assigned to individual components using the following process:

1. Estimate factory overhead costs for the year. Aero estimates these costs to be $206,250.
2. Choose a basis for allocating factory overhead to individual products. Selection of a basis is subjective. Are particular products worth more than others? If so, should more factory overhead be assigned to them? Is there more time spent making one product than another? Most companies use measures of the factory activity level, such as direct labor-hours or direct machine-hours, to allocate factory overhead costs. Aero uses direct labor-hours as a means of assigning factory overhead to finished product.
3. Estimate the expected level for the coming year of the activity base selected in 2. Aero estimates on January 1, 1984, that it will produce 15,000 components during the year. Since each unit of production (component) is expected to require five direct labor-hours on average to produce, the expected level of direct labor usage is 75,000 hours.

4. Compute an overhead allocation rate (OAR = Estimated factory overhead costs ÷ Estimated activity level).[1] The factory overhead allocation rate is based on estimates made at the beginning of the year because assignment of overhead to individual products takes place throughout the year before total actual factory overhead and direct labor-hours worked are known. The OAR for Aero Manufacturing is $2.75 per direct labor-hour ($206,250/ 75,000 direct labor-hours). This rate includes $2 ($150,000/ 75,000) of fixed factory overhead and $.75 ($56,250/75,000) of variable factory overhead and is allocated to the product every time a direct labor hour is worked.

5. Allocate the factory overhead to the product. The following journal entry allocates a portion of total factory overhead to the individual TS47 model which required five direct-labor hours to manufacture.

```
Work in Process Inventory ..........   13.75
      Factory Overhead  ..............             13.75 (5 hours at 2.75)
```

Transfer of the completed TS47 component to finished goods can now be made at its full unit cost of $61.25 ($15.00 raw material, $32.50 direct labor, and $13.75 factory overhead).

```
Finished Goods Inventory  ...........................   61.25
      Work in Process Inventory.......................             61.25
```

Factory overhead variances

During 1984 Aero produced 10,000 components. Actual factory overhead cost incurred was $188,500. Factory overhead was assigned to components on the basis of estimates (made at the beginning of the year) of the total factory overhead costs for the year and the total number of direct labor-hours for the year. Since 50,000 direct labor hours were actually worked during 1984 factory overhead assigned to (applied to, absorbed by) components amounted to $137,500 (50,000 hours at $2.75). At the end of 1984 the factory overhead account appeared as follows:

---

[1] The normal level of capacity, the average, expected, direct labor-hour usage over the next several years, may be also used as the estimated activity level instead of the next year's expected direct labor-hour usage. Using a long-run average of the activity level in the factory will smooth out factory overhead allocation rates (and therefore full unit costs) in cyclical industries.

Factory Overhead

(actual)	188,500	137,500*

* Transferred to Work in Process Inventory.

This $51,000 balance is called the total factory overhead variance. It represents the amount of actual factory overhead that was not applied to units produced and is called unabsorbed (underapplied) factory overhead. There is both a variable and fixed component of the $51,000 total factory overhead variance.

Variable factory overhead variance

Actual variable factory overhead is $38,500 and $37,500 (50,000 direct labor-hours at $.75) of variable factory overhead was allocated to components. The difference, $1,000 ($38,500 − $37,500), between actual variable factory overhead and allocated variable factory overhead is called the *variable factory overhead variance*. It represents the amount spent on variable overhead in excess of the planned expenditure.

Fixed factory overhead variance

Actual fixed factory overhead is $150,000, and only $100,000 (50,000 direct labor-hours at $2) of fixed factory overhead was allocated to components. The difference, $50,000 ($150,000 − $100,000), is called the *fixed factory overhead variance.*

The fixed factory overhead variance has two components. The *fixed factory overhead volume variance* is the difference between estimated (budgeted) fixed factory overhead, at the activity level used to calculate the overhead allocation rate, and the amount of fixed factory overhead allocated to production. The 1984 fixed factory overhead volume variance is $50,000. It is the difference between estimated (budgeted) fixed factory overhead of $150,000 and allocated fixed factory overhead of $100,000 (50,000 direct labor hours × $2). The *fixed factory overhead spending variance* of zero is the difference between estimated (budgeted) fixed factory overhead of $150,000 and actual fixed factory overhead of $150,000.

In practice, the total factory overhead variance is usually charged as an adjustment to cost of goods sold unless the amount is material in the calculation of net income. In 1984 the entry to adjust cost of goods sold for the $51,000 underabsorbed (underapplied) factory overhead is

Cost of Goods Sold—Adjustment for Factory
    Overhead Variance 51,000
       Factory Overhead   51,000

This journal entry reduces the end-of-period balance in the factory overhead account to zero and increases expense for the period by $51,000.

Variances and the income statement

Assume 9,000 of the 10,000 components produced at an average cost of $61.25 were sold at an average price of $115 per component in 1984. Cost of goods sold for 1984 would be $551,250 (9,000 components at $61.25 each) and finished goods inventory on December 31 would be $61,250 (1,000 components at $61.25 each).

The absorption (full) costing income statement for 1984 with the factory overhead variance charged to cost of goods sold appears in the first column of Illustration 16–2.

If production and sales levels are significantly different in any period, charging cost of goods sold with the entire factory overhead variance could lead to a material distortion in reported net income. If the change in net income is considered material, generally accepted accounting principles would require an allocation of the

ILLUSTRATION 16–2

AERO MANUFACTURING COMPANY
1984 Absorption Costing Income Statements
(produce 10,000 components, sell 9,000 components)

	Variance Charged to Cost of Goods Sold	Variance Prorated
Sales revenue (9,000 at $115)	$1,035,000	$1,035,000
Cost of goods sold...........................	551,250	551,250
Gross margin................................	483,750	483,750
Variable factory overhead variance............	(1,000)	(900)†
Fixed factory overhead volume variance	(50,000)	(45,000)†
Adjusted gross margin.......................	432,750	437,850
Variable selling expenses‡	90,000	90,000
Fixed selling expenses‡	100,000	100,000
	190,000	190,000
Net income	$ 242,750	$ 247,850
Ending inventory............................	$ 61,250*	$ 66,350†

* 1,000 components left in inventory at a cost to produce of $61,250.
† Total production is 10,000 modules of which 9,000 are sold. Therefore 9/10 of the factory overhead variance is attributed to cost of goods sold; 1/10 of the factory overhead variance is absorbed into inventory, which will be valued at $66,350 ($61,250 plus $5,100 of the factory overhead variance).
‡ Variable and fixed selling expenses are actual costs for the period.

factory overhead variance to Work in Process Inventory, Finished Goods Inventory, and Cost of Goods Sold in proportion to the amount of the activity level allocation base (direct labor-hours for Aero) in each account. In the Aero Company example there is no work in process inventory, 45,000 direct labor-hours were required to produce the components sold during 1984, and 5,000 direct labor-hours were required to produce the 1,000 components in ending finished goods inventory. The following journal entry prorates the factory overhead variance ($51,000) between cost of goods sold and finished goods inventory.

Cost of Goods Sold—Adjustment for Factory
   Overhead Variance 45,900
Finished Goods Inventory—Adjustment for
   Factory Overhead Variance 5,100
      Factory Overhead   51,000

Aero's 1984 absorption costing income statement, with proration of the factory overhead variance between cost of goods sold and finished goods inventory, is presented in the second column of Illustration 16–2. Income is $5,100 higher when the variance is prorated because $5,100 more cost ($66,350 versus $61,250) has been carried forward as an asset—rather than recorded as an expense (adjustment to cost of goods sold) in the 1984 income statement. If the $5,100 difference in incomes is considered material, Aero would be required to show $247,850 in income and $66,350 in finished goods inventory in its annual report to shareholders.

THE INFLUENCE OF THE LEVEL OF PRODUCTION ON INCOME

Because fixed factory overhead volume variances are treated as adjustments to cost of goods sold on the income statement, the level of production as well as the level of sales determines the amount of absorption costing net income.

Assume that Aero sold 9,000 components at an average price of $115 per component during 1984 and that Aero produced 18,000 instead of 10,000 average components during 1984.

The 18,000 components would require 90,000 direct labor-hours to produce (18,000 components × 5 direct labor-hours on average per component), and $180,000 (90,000 direct labor hours × $2 per direct labor-hour) of fixed factory overhead would be allocated to these components. The fixed factory overhead volume variance would be $30,000 ($180,000 allocated fixed factory overhead − $150,000 planned fixed factory overhead).

If the $30,000 overabsorbed fixed factory overhead volume variance is charged directly to cost of goods sold, net income for 1984 would be $322,750. This is $80,000 higher than the $242,750 net income when the 10,000 components were produced (Illustration 16–2). Since sales were 9,000 components in both cases, the difference is due entirely to the difference in production levels.

Absorption costing income (produce 18,000, sell 9,000)	$322,750
Absorption costing income (produce 10,000, sell 9,000)	242,750
Difference [(18,000 units − 10,000 units) × 5 direct labor × $2]	$ 80,000

In general the size of the variance and the adjustment to cost of goods is dependent on the level of production. If actual production levels (actual direct labor usage) exceed estimated production levels, (estimated direct labor usage), fixed factory overhead will be overabsorbed, and net income will be increased by the amount of the overabsorption. The opposite is true when actual production levels are below estimated production levels. Production level changes affect the allocation of fixed factory overhead, the fixed factory overhead volume variance, and ultimately the assignment of fixed factory overhead costs to inventory and to the income statement. *Absorption costing net income is dependent not only on the level of sales but also on the level of production.*

PROCESS COSTING

The Small Manufacturing Company produces a single standardized wooden crate. Small calculates its costs monthly using a process cost system. Small's production and cost data for the month of January are shown in Illustration 16–3.

Since each crate is the same Small determines its cost per crate by dividing the total material, direct labor, and factory overhead cost by the appropriate equivalent units of production.

Raw materials

Since raw materials are added at the beginning of the process, no additional raw materials had to be added during January to complete the 100 crates in the beginning work in process inventory. The 250 crates started and finished in January and the 50 crates in the ending work in process inventory are also complete as to raw materials.

Equivalent units of raw material added to production
  during January:
  Beginning work in process inventory ....   –0–
  Crates started and completed in January   250
  Ending work in process inventory   50
                                                     ─────
                                                     300
                                                     ═════

Raw material costs (January 1984) $1,170
Raw material cost per equivalent unit of
  production (crate) $1,170/300 .... $ 3.90
                                                   ═══════

ILLUSTRATION 16–3. **Data for Small Manufacturing Company (month of January)**

Beginning work in process inventory (100 half-completed crates)	$1,300
Direct manufacturing costs added to production in January:	
Raw materials*	$1,170
Labor (650 hours at $8.10)*	$5,265
Ending work in process inventory (50 half-completed crates)	?
Work performed during the period:	
Number of crates put into production in prior months but completed in January	100
Number of crates started and completed in January	250
Number of crates started and partially completed in January	50
Factory overhead allocation rate	$1/direct labor hour

* Direct materials are added at the beginning of the process. Direct labor and factory overhead are added uniformly throughout the process.

Direct labor

The number of direct labor-hours worked in January to complete the 100 crates in beginning work in process is *equivalent* to the number of direct labor-hours necessary to produce 50 entire crates (since direct labor is added uniformly throughout the process and only half of the total direct labor required to manufacture the crates was worked in January). The 250 crates started and finished in January contain the direct labor equivalent of 250 crates. The direct labor-hours worked to make the 50 half-completed crates in ending work in process is equivalent to the direct labor-hours needed to produce 25 complete crates.

Equivalent units of direct labor added to production during January:

Beginning work in process inventory	50 (100 × 50%)
Crates started and completed in January	250 (250 × 100%)
Ending work in process inventory...................................	25 (50 × 50%)
	325
Direct labor cost (January 1984)	$5,265
Direct labor cost per equivalent unit of production (crate) $5,265/325	$16.20

Factory overhead

On January 1, 1984, Small Manufacturing estimated that its factory overhead cost for the year would amount to $8,000 and that 8,000 direct labor-hours would be worked during the year. The factory overhead allocation rate is $1 ($8,000/8,000). Since 650 direct labor-hours were actually worked during January, $650 of factory overhead cost was allocated to January output. Since factory overhead is allocated on a direct labor-hour basis and is applied uniformly throughout the production process, it has the same equivalent unit calculation as direct labor.

Factory overhead will be allocated at the rate of $2 ($650/325) per equivalent unit of production.

The cost per equivalent unit computations are summarized below:

	Raw Materials	Direct Labor	Factory Overhead
Cost	$1,170	$5,265	$ 650
Equivalent units	300	325	325
Cost/equivalent unit	$ 3.90	$16.20	$2.00

Inventories

The following journal entry recorded January's actual manufacturing costs in the Work in Process account.

(1) Work in Process	7,085	
Raw Material Inventory		1,170
Wages Payable		5,265
Factory Overhead...........................		650

The initial 100 crates were valued in work in process at $1,300. Completion of these crates required 50 equivalent units of direct labor (at $16.20) and 50 equivalent units of factory overhead (at $2). There was no additional raw material added to these crates in January. The cost of these crates upon completion was $2,210 ($1,300 + 50 × $16.20 + 50 × $2.00). Transfer of these crates to finished goods inventory was recognized as follows:

(2) Finished Goods Inventory   2,210
      Work in Process   2,210

The 250 crates started and completed in January contain 250 equivalent units each of raw material, direct labor, and overhead. The cost of these crates is $5,525 (250 × $3.90 + 250 × $16.20 + 250 × $2.00). Transfer of these crates to finished goods inventory was recognized as follows:

(3) Finished Goods Inventory   5,525
      Work in Process   5,525

The 50 partially completed units in work in process contain 50 equivalent units of raw material and 25 equivalent units each of direct labor and factory overhead. These crates have a cost of $650 (50 × $3.90 + 25 × $16.20 + 25 × $2.00).

During January, Small sold 100 crates on account for $4,000. Small uses the FIFO flow assumption for finished goods inventory. The sale of these crates was recognized as follows:

(4) Accounts Receivable   4,000
      Sales Revenue   4,000

(5) Cost of Goods Sold   2,210
      Finished Goods Inventory   2,210

The above journal entries are summarized in Small's accounts as follows:

Raw Material Inventory				Work in Process			
		(1)	1,170	Beg. bal.	1,300	(2)	2,210
				(1)	7,085	(3)	5,525

Finished Goods				Factory Overhead			
(2)	2,210	(5)	2,210			(1)	650
(3)	5,525						

Wages Payable				Accounts Receivable			
		(1)	5,265	(4)	4,000		

Cost of Goods Sold				Sales			
(5)	2,210					(4)	4,000

The above example assumes a FIFO flow in the Work in Process Inventory account. Process costing may also be used with LIFO or average costing and in a multiple-department factory with transfers of goods between departments.

In process costing, as in job lot costing, any factory overhead variance will be charged to cost of goods sold (or prorated among work in process inventory, finished goods inventory, and cost of goods sold) at the end of the year.

FURTHER REMARKS

Generally accepted accounting principles require that absorption (full) costing be used to construct external reports to shareholders.

Because absorption costing income is dependent on production as well as sales levels, it can distort the true level of performance to external and internal users of financial reports. Users must recognize that the production level as well as the sales level affect net income for the period.

Care must also be taken when using absorption (full) costing income to measure the performance of or to determine the compensation paid to managers. For instance suppose the compensation of a divisional manager is linked to absorption (full) costing income and the manager is paid a bonus based on the amount of actual income in excess of some planned level of income. If the manager produces much in excess of planned production for the period, a large fixed factory overhead volume variance will result (much overabsorbed fixed factory overhead) and will be credited to cost of goods sold, raising income.

A cost accounting system should facilitate control of operations, planning, and decision making. The absorption costing system developed in this chapter, which values output using *actual* costs of production, is not as useful as a standard cost system based on what cost should be under normal conditions, in providing benchmarks for comparison to actual costs and in facilitating planning and decision making. In Chapter 17 the standard cost concept will be integrated into the absorption costing system.

Because they include both fixed and variable costs of production, full costs may not facilitate short-run decision making in a firm. Many short-run operating decisions are concerned primarily with variable costs of production. Suppose a machine with idle capacity can be used to produce either one unit of product A or one unit of product B. Product A and product B both have the same selling price. Since fixed costs do not change if either product A or product B is made, the product with the lowest variable cost of production and selling should be produced.

A cost accumulation and measurement system that distinguishes between variable costs, which change with the level of production, and fixed costs, which do not change with the level of production, is a useful aid to management. Such a system will be presented in Chapter 19, and its usefulness in short-run decision making will be discussed in Chapter 20.

One of the main difficulties in determining the absorption (full) cost of a product or activity is the manner in which indirect costs are allocated to the cost objective. Chapter 18 discusses the cost allocation process.

PROBLEMS AND CASES

16–1 Stone Manufacturing Company

The following incomplete general ledger accounts with beginning and ending balances and information relate to 1984 operations of the Stone Manufacturing Company.

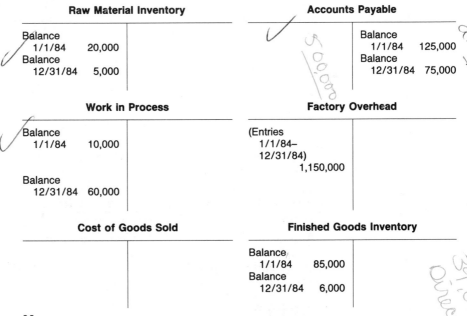

Raw Material Inventory				Accounts Payable	
Balance 1/1/84	20,000			Balance 1/1/84	125,000
Balance 12/31/84	5,000			Balance 12/31/84	75,000

Work in Process				Factory Overhead	
Balance 1/1/84	10,000			(Entries 1/1/84– 12/31/84)	1,150,000
Balance 12/31/84	60,000				

Cost of Goods Sold				Finished Goods Inventory	
				Balance 1/1/84	85,000
				Balance 12/31/84	6,000

Notes:

a. Factory overhead is applied using direct labor-hours. The application rate for 1984 is based on estimates of 200,000 direct labor-hours and $1,200,000 of factory overhead.

b. Accounts payable relates to purchases of raw materials only. All raw materials are purchased on account. Payments during the year amounted to $500,000.

c. 195,000 direct labor-hours were worked during the year. All direct labor is paid $5 per hour.

Required:

1. Determine raw material purchases for the year.

2. Determine the amount of raw materials put into production during 1984.

3. Determine the cost of goods completed and transferred to finished goods inventory.

4. Determine the amount of factory overhead applied to production during 1984.

5. Determine the amount of over- or underapplied factory overhead for the year.

6. Determine the cost of goods sold for 1984.

16–2 Technical Manufacturing

The Technical Manufacturing Company produces part 413 in a single-department factory. Technical uses a process costing system. The following information relates to the month of December.

Direct manufacturing costs added to production in December:

Raw material A	$6,750
Raw material B	$8,300
Labor (1,200 hours at $8)	$9,600

Work performed during December:

Number of part 413 started and completed in December	400
Number of part 413 started and partially completed in December	100

Factory overhead allocation rate	$.50 per direct labor $

Beginning work in process inventory	$0
Ending work in process inventory (100 part 413, ¼ complete with respect to direct labor input)	?

Raw material A is added at the beginning of the process, direct labor is added uniformly throughout the process, and raw material B is added after the part is 50 percent complete with respect to the addition of direct labor.

Required:

1. Calculate the total amount of cost debited to work in process for the month of December.

2. Calculate the cost per equivalent unit of production for the month of December.

3.   Calculate the ending work in process inventory balance as of December 31.

16–3   Seasonal Manufacturing Company

The Seasonal Manufacturing Company estimates fixed factory overhead costs for 1985 will total $1,600,000. The breakdown according to quarters is as follows:

	Quarter				
	1	2	3	4	Total
Estimated fixed factory over- head cost	$800,000	$200,000	$100,000	$500,000	$1,600,000

Seasonal allocates fixed factory overhead to production using direct labor-hours. Planned direct labor-hour usage by quarters is projected as follows:

	Quarter				
	1	2	3	4	Total
Direct labor hours............	40,000	40,000	40,000	40,000	160,000

The Seasonal Manufacturing Company has no beginning finished goods or work in process inventories at the beginning of 1985. There are no planned finished goods or work in process inventories at the end of any quarter in 1985.

Consider the following alternative ways of allocating fixed factory overhead to production during 1985:

Alternative 1: Compute a fixed factory overhead allocation rate based on the yearly estimates of fixed factory overhead cost and direct labor-hour usage.

Alternative 2: Use a different fixed factory overhead allocation rate in each quarter. The quarterly rate is determined by dividing estimated quarterly fixed factory overhead costs by quarterly direct labor-hour usage.

Assume that actual fixed factory overhead cost and direct labor hour usage is exactly as projected for each quarter. Under- or overallocated fixed factory overhead is carried forward in a balance sheet account at the end of the first three quarters and is closed to cost of goods sold at the end of the year.

Required:

1.   Will pretax income be higher or lower in the first quarter of 1985 if alternative 1 as opposed to alternative 2 is used to allocate fixed factory overhead? By how much?

2.   What is the cumulative amount of under- or overallocated fixed factory overhead at the end of the third quarter under each alternative?

3.   Which alternative will generate the largest total income for the year?

4.   Suppose fixed factory overhead costs are as previously estimated. Under what pattern of direct labor-hour usage will the net incomes computed using each alternative approach be identical?

5.   Suppose over- or underapplied fixed factory overhead is closed to cost of goods sold at the end of each quarter. By how much will the quarterly incomes differ under each alternative?

6.   What are the major advantages and drawbacks of each approach to fixed factory overhead allocation?

16-4   Kardboard Corporation

The Kardboard Corporation produces specialty cardboard boxes for packaging sensitive electronic components. All of the boxes are produced from five-square-foot pieces of cardboard acquired in bulk from a local paper mill.

The following information pertains to Kardboard's operations for the first quarter of 1984.

a.   Factory overhead is applied to production at the rate of $3 per direct labor-hour. Total factory overhead for the first quarter amounted to $40,000; $36,000 of factory overhead was applied to production during the quarter.

b.   Direct labor is paid $8 per hour, and indirect labor is paid $5 per hour. Accrued wages payable on January 1, 1984, amounted to $10,000; $130,000 of wages were paid in cash during the first quarter. Accrued wages payable on April 1, 1984, amounted to $20,000.

c.   On January 1, 1984, work in process and finished goods inventory were zero. No cardboard was purchased for raw materials inventory during the first quarter. All materials are added at the beginning of processing. Direct labor is worked uniformly throughout the process.

d.   The following information pertains to the three orders worked on during the first quarter.

Order No.	Size	Labor Completion (April 1)
697A	5,000 boxes	100%
707C	5,000 boxes	50%
432D	10,000 boxes	?

The direct labor and raw material necessary to produce a box is constant across all styles and sizes of boxes that Kardboard Corporation produces.

e.   Raw material inventory requirements:

Order No.	Inventory Issued	Inventory Balance (1/1/84 150,000 sq. ft. at $.50)
697A	25,000 sq. ft. at $.50	125,000 sq. ft. at $.50
707C	25,000 sq. ft. at ?	? *100,000*
432D	*50,000* ?	? *50,000*

f. The balance in finished goods inventory (order 697A) on April 1, 1984, is $57,500. Cost of goods sold has not yet been recorded.

Required:

1. What is the total labor cost applicable to production for the quarter?

2. What is the total direct labor cost for the quarter?

3. How many indirect labor-hours were worked during the quarter?

4. What is the best estimate of the dollar value of the raw materials charged to work in process for the quarter?

5. What is the April 1, 1984, balance in work in process?

6. How much of the $57,500 cost of order 697A in ending finished goods inventory is a direct labor cost? Raw material cost? Factory overhead cost?

7. What percent complete is order 432D? *who knows?*

16–5   Inventory cost allocation

The following information is taken from 1975 annual reports of the Hesston Corporation and the Lamson and Sessions Company.

HESSTON CORPORATION
Consolidated Statement of Income

	Years Ended September 30	
	1975	1974
Per share amounts:		
Earnings per common share—assuming no dilution:		
Income before cumulative effect of a change		
in accounting principle	$3.95	$4.15
Cumulative effect on prior years (to		
September 30, 1974) of a change in method		
of costing inventories	.65	
Net income	$4.60	$4.15
Earnings per common share—assuming full dilution:		
Income before cumulative effect of a change		
in accounting principle	$3.66	
Cumulative effect on prior years (to		
September 30, 1974) of a change in method		
of costing inventories	.57	
Net income	$4.23	
Pro forma amounts assuming the new inventory costing		
method is applied retroactively (Note 1):		
Net income	$8,275	$8,783

	Years Ended September 30	
	1975	1974
Earnings per common share:		
Assuming no dilution	$3.95	$4.42
Assuming full dilution	3.66	

Notes to Financial Statements:

Note 1: Change in method of costing inventories—In fiscal 1975, the Company changed its method of costing domestic inventories, pursuant to changes in Internal Revenue Service regulations, by expanding the composition of elements of overhead costs included in inventory. This change constitutes a refinement of the inventory costing procedure and more properly matches revenues and costs. The effect of the change in 1975 was to increase income before the cumulative effect of a change in accounting principle $821,000 ($.42 per share). The adjustment of $1,297,000 (after reduction for income taxes of $1,197,000), retroactively applying the new method, is included in net income of 1975. The pro forma amounts show the effect of retroactive application of the revised inventory costing, the change in provision for profit sharing that would have been made in 1974 had the new method been in effect, and related income taxes.

THE LAMSON AND SESSIONS COMPANY
Consolidated Statement of Earnings

	Year Ended December 31	
	1975	1974
Per share amounts (Note B):		
Earnings from continuing operations before cumulative effect of a change in accounting principle	$1.78	$6.18
Loss from discontinued operations	(.67)	(.74)
Cumulative effect on prior years (to December 31, 1974) of change in inventory costing method	1.14	–0–
Net earnings per common share	$2.25	$5.44

Notes to Financial Statements:

Note B: Inventories—Inventories in the consolidated statement of financial position are comprised of the following:

	December 31	
	1975	1974
Finished and in-process products	$16,978,126	$18,207,997
Raw materials	8,558,519	11,118,733
Manufacturing supplies	641,975	873,153
Total inventories	$26,178,620	$30,199,882

Effective January 1, 1975, the Company changed its method of inventory costing for both financial reporting and tax purposes to include certain costs in inventory that were previously accounted for as period costs. The Company believes the newly adopted method of inventory costing is a preferable alternative under generally accepted methods of accounting for inventories since it provides a better matching of revenues and expenses. The effect of this change was to increase inventory at December 31, 1975, by approximately $2,500,000 ($3,010,000 at December 31, 1974) and, in 1975, reduce earnings from continuing operations before cumulative effect of a change in accounting principle by approximately $253,000 ($.14 a share) and increase net earnings by approximately $1,757,000 ($1 a share).

Required:

The effect of the change in inventory costing method *increased* the income ($.42 per share) of the Hesston Corporation and *decreased* the income ($.14 per share) of the Lamson and Sessions Company. Explain what must have happened in each company to justify the increased or decreased income.

17

Manufacturing cost standards and production variances

STANDARDS

Standards are the yardsticks an organization uses to measure and control performance. They are prespecified costs and quantities that expedite planning and budgeting.

Unit price standards are target amounts to be paid for each unit of raw material and each hour of labor. Efficiency or usage standards specify the quantities of each type of raw material and category of labor expected to be consumed in the production of a unit of output. A minimum acceptable level of quality is implicit in all standards.

Aggregate cost standards or budgeted amounts are calculated for factory overhead, advertising, research and development, and other expenses.

Revenue standards reflect expected sales volume and anticipated selling prices per unit of output.

Standards are developed from price schedules (e.g., advertising and utility rate schedules), from engineering studies (e.g., time and motion studies), and from statistical studies of past accounting data.

442

Standards best motivate personnel to behave in a manner consistent with broad organizational goals when they are tight but reasonable, when employees participate in their establishment, and when employee rewards are tied to their success in achieving the standards. The standards should relate to an actual outcome that is controllable by the employee, and feedback on employee performance should be timely.

Standards are an integral part of the planning-budgeting-control system of an organization (see Illustration 17–1).

Once set, standards are used in the planning process for the coming period when the organization selects the course of action that comes closest to meeting organizational goals. The final agreed-upon plan is translated, using standards, into the master budget, a collection of pro forma schedules and financial statements reflecting expected performance and financial position of the organization during the coming period. Actual results are compared to budgeted results. Responsibility is assigned for differences, which, if significant, are investigated in an attempt to find their cause. These comparisons are likely to result in modifications to existing standards, and what is learned through the observation of actual results is likely to affect planning in the future.

MANUFACTURING COST STANDARDS

Standard manufacturing cost systems determine the "standard" amount each unit of product *should* cost. The *standard direct material cost* of a unit of output is the expected number of units of raw material necessary to produce the unit of output (standard raw material usage) times the expected price to be paid for a unit of raw material (standard raw material price). The *standard direct labor cost* of a unit of output is the expected number of hours of direct labor necessary to produce the unit of product (standard direct labor usage) times the expected wage (labor) rate to be paid production employees (standard direct labor wage rate). Fringe ben-

ILLUSTRATION 17–1. **The Accounting-Planning-Control System**

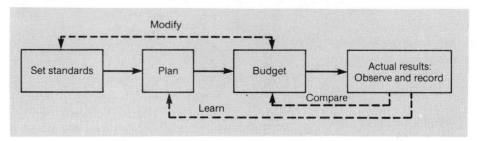

efits, such as payroll taxes, health insurance, and vacation pay, are usually included in the employees' wage rate.

The *standard factory overhead cost* of a unit of output is the factory overhead allocation rate times the standard number of allocation base units (often standard direct labor-hours) in a unit of product.

Factory overhead allocation—expected capacity

The standard (combined variable and fixed) factory overhead allocation rate is determined by dividing the total amount of estimated factory overhead for the coming year, at the expected or normal level of capacity, by the expected or normal level of capacity (measured in units of the allocation base). For example suppose total estimated factory overhead is to be allocated to the product using direct labor-hours. The *expected* level of capacity is the standard number of direct labor-hours required to produce *next year's* planned outputs. Assume the expected level of capacity is 5 million direct labor-hours and total estimated factory overhead is $10 million ($5 million variable + $5 million fixed). The factory overhead allocation rate will be $2 ($10 million/5 million) per direct labor-hour. If 5 million direct labor-hours are actually worked during the period, the entire $10 million (5 million × $2) will be allocated to production.

Factory overhead allocation—normal capacity

The *normal* level of capacity allocates factory overhead using a long-run average (usually five years) of the activity level in the factory. This method is often used in cyclical industries because it results in smoothing out factory overhead allocation rates. In the above example, if the normal level of capacity is 6,250,000 direct labor-hours and total estimated factory overhead is $11,250,000 ($6,250,000 variable + $5,000,000 fixed), the factory overhead allocation rate will be $1.80 ($11,250,000/6,250,000) per direct labor-hour. If 6,250,000 direct labor-hours are worked during the period, $11,250,000 (6,250,000 × $1.80) of factory overhead will be allocated to production.

The expected or normal capacity levels can be used to determine the factory overhead allocation rate in a standard absorption costing system.

If the production level in the factory is stable from year to year factory overhead allocation rates computed using expected or normal capacity are identical. If normal and expected capacity are not equal, then the factory overhead allocation rates will differ, and inventory values, cost of goods sold, and net incomes will be different under the two approaches.

PRODUCTION VARIANCES

The difference between standard costs and actual costs are called variances. An analysis of these variances is useful in isolating potential problems. For example, if actual material cost exceeds standard material cost of production the material variance could indicate that the company is paying more than the standard price for raw material, that there is careless use of raw material in the production process, that there is raw material spoilage, or that the material price and usage standards were developed incorrectly.

Example of a standard cost system

Kastings, Inc., is a manufacturer of molded ornamental pewter figurines, which it sells to major department stores across the country.

A standard cost system is a vital component of Kastings management control and evaluation system. Kastings management compares actual results to standards, calculates variances, investigates the causes of the variances, takes appropriate corrective actions, and assigns responsibility for the occurrence of the variances as part of their evaluation of personnel.

Kastings began operations on January 1, 1984, and uses a standard absorption (full) process cost system. The 1984 cost standards for a figurine are shown in Illustration 17–2.

The purchase price of raw material, pewter, is expected to average $5 per pound during the coming year. If *reasonable care* is exercised in processing, 1.2 pounds of pewter should be consumed in the production of one unit of output (figurine). Thus, the standard

ILLUSTRATION 17–2. **Kastings, Inc.: Cost Standards for 1984**

Input	$\left(\begin{array}{c}\text{Standard Price}\\\text{(Rate) per Unit}\\\text{of Input}\end{array}\right) \times$	$\left(\begin{array}{c}\text{Standard Usage}\\\text{of Input per}\\\text{Unit of Output}\end{array}\right) =$	$\left(\begin{array}{c}\text{Standard Cost}\\\text{of Input per}\\\text{Unit of Output}\end{array}\right)$
Raw material	$5/pound	1.2 pounds	$ 6
Direct labor	$8/hour	2 hours	16
Factory overhead	$1.50/direct labor-hour	2 hours	3
Standard full cost per unit			$25

cost of raw material per unit of output is $6 ($5 × 1.2 pounds). Similarly, if production is reasonably efficient two direct labor-hours should be used to produce a unit of output. The particular class of labor required is expected to cost $8 per hour. The standard direct labor cost per figurine is $16 ($8 × 2 hours).

Kastings allocates fixed and variable factory overhead to figurines using direct labor-hours. Management estimates that production over the next five years will average 5,000 figurines per year. The normal capacity of 10,000 direct labor-hours (5,000 figurines at two direct labor-hours) is used to compute the factory overhead allocation rate. At an output level of 5,000 figurines per year management estimates that the following factory overhead will be incurred.

Variable factory overhead (at 10,000 direct labor-hours)	$ 5,000
Fixed factory overhead	10,000
Total estimated factory overhead	$15,000

The factory overhead allocation rate, $1.50 per direct labor-hour, is obtained by dividing total estimated factory overhead, $15,000, by the normal capacity, 10,000 direct labor-hours. Standard factory overhead for one figurine is $3 ($1.50 × 2 hours).

The standard full cost per figurine is $25 ($6 + $16 + $3).

Kasting's actual production costs and output for 1984 are shown in Illustration 17–3.

ILLUSTRATION 17–3. **Kastings, Inc.: Actual 1984 Operating Data**

	Direct Inputs	
	Actual Unit Price (Rate)	Actual Total Usage
Labor	$7.80/hour	9,500 hours
Raw material	$5.10/pound	6,500 pounds

Actual Factory Overhead Costs	
Variable	$ 5,000
Fixed	10,200

The following information relates to 1984 operatons:
1. 50,000 pounds of pewter were purchased.
2. 3,000 figurines were started and completed.
3. 2,000 figurines were started but are only ¾ through processing by the end of 1984.

Kastings uses a standard process cost system. All raw material is added at the beginning of the process, and direct labor is added uniformly throughout the process. Since Kastings began operations in 1984 there were no beginning inventories.

RAW MATERIAL AND DIRECT LABOR PRODUCTION COST VARIANCES

Direct labor and raw material variances compare the actual direct labor and raw material costs for a period with the standard direct labor and material costs allowed for the *actual* level of output.

Raw material price variance

The *raw material price variance* is the difference between the standard and actual raw material prices times the amount of raw material purchased.

$$\text{Raw Material Price Variance} = \left(\begin{array}{c}\text{Actual Raw}\\\text{Material}\\\text{Price Per Unit}\end{array} - \begin{array}{c}\text{Standard Raw}\\\text{Material}\\\text{Price Per Unit}\end{array}\right) \times \left(\begin{array}{c}\text{Actual}\\\text{Material}\\\text{Purchased}\end{array}\right)$$

This variance depends on the amount of raw material purchased, not on the amount of raw material used in production.[1]

Kastings made raw material purchases of 50,000 pounds of pewter during 1984. The raw material price variance is

$$(\$5.10 - \$5)\,(50,000 \text{ pounds}) = \$5,000$$

This is an unfavorable variance because Kastings paid more for the material than the standard price. A variance is called *favorable* if net income is higher as a result of the variance and *unfavorable* if net income is lower as a result of the variance.

This unfavorable variance could be due to a poor performance by the purchasing department or because of a general increase in raw material prices. An analysis of this variance should consider that a favorable raw material price variance may be caused by the purchase of cheaper but poorer-quality materials, which could result in an unfavorable raw material usage variance.

---

[1] Less frequently the raw material price variance is defined as the difference between the standard and actual raw material prices times the amount of raw material put into production. If calculated in this manner the price variance is not appropriate for evaluating purchasing performance during the period.

Raw material usage variance

The *raw material usage variance* is the difference between the actual and standard amount of raw materials used to produce the actual level of output for the period times the standard raw material price per unit.

$$\text{Raw Material Usage Variance} = \left(\begin{array}{c}\text{Actual Raw Material Used}\end{array} - \begin{array}{c}\text{Standard Raw Material Allowed for Actual Output}\end{array}\right) \times \left(\begin{array}{c}\text{Standard Price per Unit of Raw Material}\end{array}\right)$$

Kastings worked on 5,000 figurines during 1984. Because raw material is added at the beginning of the process these figurines contain the raw material equivalent of 5,000 completed figurines. The standard raw material input allowed for actual output is 6,000 pounds (5,000 equivalent units at standard raw material input of 1.2 pounds).

Kastings's material usage variance is

$$(6,500 \text{ pounds} - 6,000 \text{ pounds}) (\$5/\text{pound}) = \$2,500$$

The material usage variance is unfavorable because Kastings used more materials than the standard allowed for the actual level of figurine production.

Direct labor rate variance

The *direct labor rate* (or *price*) *variance* is the product of the difference between the actual and standard direct labor cost and the actual number of direct labor hours worked during the period.

$$\text{Labor Rate Variance} = \left(\begin{array}{c}\text{Actual Wage Rate}\end{array} - \begin{array}{c}\text{Standard Wage Rate}\end{array}\right) \times \left(\begin{array}{c}\text{Actual Number of Direct Labor Hours}\end{array}\right)$$

Kastings's direct labor rate variance is

$$(\$7.80/\text{hour} - \$8/\text{hour}) (9,500 \text{ hours}) = -\$1,900$$

It is a favorable variance because the wage rate paid is less than the standard rate.

Labor rate variances may be caused by hiring workers for more or less than the standard rate during the period or they might be due to changes in wage rates. Production managers should not be held responsible for labor rate variances in the latter case unless they have the authority to set wage rates.

Direct labor usage variance

The *direct labor usage* (or *efficiency*) *variance* is the product of the difference between the actual direct labor-hours worked and the standard direct labor-hours allowed for the actual output of the period and the standard direct labor wage rate.

$$\text{Direct Labor Usage Variance} = \left(\begin{array}{c}\text{Actual Direct Labor-Hours Worked}\end{array} - \begin{array}{c}\text{Standard Direct Labor-Hours Allowed for Actual Output}\end{array}\right) \times \left(\begin{array}{c}\text{Standard Wage Rate}\end{array}\right)$$

The 5,000 figurines worked on during 1984 contained the direct labor equivalent of 4,500 completed figurines. The company started and completed 3,000 figurines and had 2,000 figurines ¾ finished in its inventory. Since labor is applied evenly throughout the process it is equivalent to producing 4,500 completed figurines (3,000 + ¾(2,000)). The standard direct labor input to actual output is 9,000 hours (4,500 equivalent units at standard input of two direct labor hours).

Kastings's direct labor usage variance is

$$(9,500 \text{ hours} - 9,000 \text{ hours})\,(\$8/\text{hour}) = \$4,000$$

This is an unfavorable variance because Kastings actually used more direct labor-hours to produce the year's output than the standard direct labor-hours allowed.

Production managers can usually control the direct labor-hours worked to achieve the level of output for the period, and the direct labor usage variance is generally a good measure of their effectiveness.

Interpretation of direct labor variances

Variances have to be interpreted with care. Favorable variances are not necessarily associated with actions that are beneficial to the organization, nor is the direct labor rate variance necessarily independent of the direct labor efficiency variance. In the Kastings example it is quite possible that the $1,900 favorable labor rate variance is the result of hiring cheaper, less-skilled labor requiring more direct labor-hours per unit of output and thus causing the $4,000 unfavorable labor usage variance.

Unfavorable labor rate and usage variances can be caused by company policy that requires the temporary transfer of higher-priced, less-skilled (in the particular production technique) workers to another production department rather than lay them off when activity slows down in their own department. This transfer may have a favorable long-term effect on the company but produces short-term unfavorable labor variances that the production manager cannot control. Variances merely indicate actions or areas in need of investigation.

FACTORY OVERHEAD VARIANCES

Techniques used to control departmental factory overhead costs differ from techniques used to control direct product costs. Unlike direct product costs, variable and fixed overhead costs have multiple components such as rent and depreciation, which, by definition, are not directly traceable to output. This is the reason why factory overhead cost is allocated to product using some base such as direct labor-hours.

Variable factory overhead variance

The *total variable factory overhead variance* is the difference between actual variable factory overhead cost and the amount of variable factory overhead allocated to product.

$$\begin{pmatrix} \text{Variable} \\ \text{Factory} \\ \text{Overhead} \\ \text{Variance} \end{pmatrix} = \begin{pmatrix} \text{Actual} \\ \text{Variable} \\ \text{Factory Over-} \\ \text{head Cost} \end{pmatrix} - \begin{pmatrix} \text{Standard Direct} \\ \text{Labor-Hours} \\ \text{Allowed for} \\ \text{Actual Output} \end{pmatrix} \times \begin{pmatrix} \text{Variable} \\ \text{Factory} \\ \text{Overhead} \\ \text{Allocation} \\ \text{Rate} \end{pmatrix}$$

The total variable factory overhead variance is equal to the amount of under- or overabsorbed variable factory overhead. For Kastings the variable factory overhead allocation rate is $.50 per standard direct labor hour ($5,000/10,000 hours). Kastings' variable factory overhead variance is

$$\$5,000 - (9,000 \text{ hours})(\$.50/\text{hour}) = \$500$$

ILLUSTRATION 17–4. **Analysis of Variable Overhead Cost**

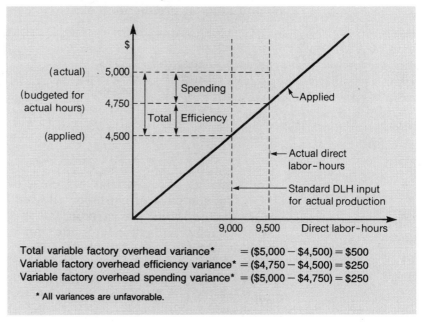

Total variable factory overhead variance*   = ($5,000 − $4,500) = $500
Variable factory overhead efficiency variance* = ($4,750 − $4,500) = $250
Variable factory overhead spending variance* = ($5,000 − $4,750) = $250

  * All variances are unfavorable.

This is an unfavorable variance because not all of the actual variable factory overhead has been allocated to product. It has two primary causes: actual direct labor-hours worked may not equal the standard direct labor-hours allowed for the actual output; and more or less than the standard variable factory overhead allowed for the actual number of direct labor-hours worked may have been spent for variable factory overhead.

The total variable factory overhead variance is graphically presented in Illustration 17–4. Variable overhead cost is allocated to output on the basis of the number of *standard* direct labor-hours in the output.

The total variable factor overhead variance is usually broken down into an efficiency and a spending variance in order to assign responsibility for its occurrence.

Variable factory overhead efficiency variance

The *variable factory overhead efficiency variance* is the difference between the amount of variable factory overhead that should have been incurred for the actual number of direct labor-hours worked and the amount of variable factory overhead that was allocated to units of production.

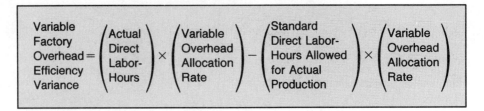

For Kastings, actual variable factory overhead cost for 1984 is $5,000. The standard direct labor allowed for actual production is 9,000 hours, and since the variable factory overhead allocation rate is $.50 for each direct labor-hour, the standard variable factory overhead cost allowed for actual production (variable factory overhead allocated to production) is $4,500 (9,000 hours × $.50). The standard variable factory overhead cost allowed (budgeted) for the actual number of direct labor hours worked is $4,750 (9,500 hours at $.50).

Kastings's variable factory overhead efficiency variance is

$$(9,500 \text{ hours}) (\$.50/\text{hour}) - (9,000 \text{ hours}) (\$.50/\text{hour}) = \$250$$

This is an unfavorable variance because more than the standard number of direct labor-hours for the actual output were worked in 1984.

If direct labor-hours cause variable factory overhead this variance is a dollar measure of how efficiencies or inefficiencies in the utilization of direct labor-hours during the period affected variable factory overhead costs. It is usually the responsibility of the production manager who determines the level of direct labor utilization for the period.

The variable factory overhead efficiency variance is graphically presented in Illustration 17–4.

Variable factory overhead spending variance

The *variable factory overhead spending variance* is the difference between actual variable factory overhead cost and the amount of variable overhead cost that should have been incurred for the actual number of direct labor hours worked.

$$\begin{pmatrix} \text{Variable Factory} \\ \text{Overhead} \\ \text{Spending} \\ \text{Variance} \end{pmatrix} = \begin{pmatrix} \text{Actual} \\ \text{Variable} \\ \text{Factory} \\ \text{Overhead} \end{pmatrix} - \begin{pmatrix} \text{Actual Direct} \\ \text{Labor-Hours} \end{pmatrix} \times \begin{pmatrix} \text{Variable} \\ \text{Overhead} \\ \text{Allocation} \\ \text{Rate} \end{pmatrix}$$

Kastings's variable factory overhead spending variance is

$$\$5,000 - (9,500 \text{ hours}) (\$.50/\text{hour}) = \$250$$

This is an unfavorable variance because Kastings paid more than expected for variable factory overhead considering that 9,500 direct labor-hours were worked (see Illustration 17–4).

To the extent that variable factory overhead cost is a composite of costs (i.e., direct labor is not the sole cause of variable factory overhead cost), the variable factory overhead spending variance is really a combined price and efficiency variance. For example, if machine hours also cause variable factory overhead costs and if variable factory overhead cost is allocated on the basis of direct labor-hours, a large, unfavorable, variable overhead spending variance could result from an excessive number of machine hours being used during the period (usage) with each machine-hour causing variable overhead at a higher or lower than normal rate (price). For this reason it is difficult to assign responsibility for variable overhead spending and efficiency variances, and frequently only the total variable factory overhead variance is computed.

Fixed factory overhead variance

The *fixed factory overhead variance* is the difference between actual fixed factory overhead cost and the amount of fixed factory overhead allocated to product.

$$\begin{pmatrix} \text{Fixed} \\ \text{Factory} \\ \text{Overhead} \\ \text{Variance} \end{pmatrix} = \begin{pmatrix} \text{Actual} \\ \text{Fixed} \\ \text{Factory} \\ \text{Overhead} \end{pmatrix} - \begin{pmatrix} \text{Standard} \\ \text{Direct Labor-} \\ \text{Hours Allowed for} \\ \text{Actual Production} \end{pmatrix} \times \begin{pmatrix} \text{Fixed} \\ \text{Overhead} \\ \text{Allocation} \\ \text{Rate} \end{pmatrix}$$

For Kastings the fixed factory overhead allocation rate is $1 per direct labor-hour ($10,000/10,000 hours), and the fixed overhead variance is

$$\$10,200 - (9,000 \text{ hours}) (\$1/\text{hour}) = \$1,200$$

This represents the amount of underabsorbed fixed factory overhead and is an unfavorable variance.

The fixed factory overhead variance is graphically presented in Illustration 17–5. Budgeted fixed factory overhead is a straight line parallel to the labor-hour axis since, by definition, fixed overhead cost does not vary with output. In standard absorption costing systems fixed overhead is applied on the basis of *standard* direct labor inputs (or some other reasonable basis) to production. Applied (allocated) fixed overhead cost is a line through the origin with slope equal to the fixed overhead allocation rate.

ILLUSTRATION 17–5. **Analysis of Fixed Factory Overhead Cost**

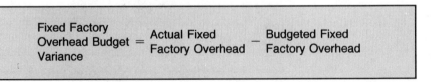

Fixed factory overhead total variance* = $1,200
Fixed factory overhead volume variance* = $1,000
Fixed factory overhead budget variance* = $ 200

* All variances are unfavorable.

Fixed factory overhead budget variance

The *fixed factory overhead budget variance* is the difference between actual and planned (budgeted) fixed factory overhead cost.

$$\text{Fixed Factory Overhead Budget Variance} = \text{Actual Fixed Factory Overhead} - \text{Budgeted Fixed Factory Overhead}$$

Kastings's fixed factory overhead budget variance is

$$\$10,200 - \$10,000 = \$200$$

This is an unfavorable variance because actual fixed factory overhead cost exceeded fixed factory overhead cost that was planned (budgeted) at the beginning of the year (see Illustration 17–5).

Frequently fixed overhead budget variances are likely to be small since many of the components of fixed factory overhead costs are easily estimated (e.g., factory depreciation for the period) and are truly fixed.

Fixed factory overhead volume variance

The *fixed factory overhead volume variance* is the difference between planned (budgeted) fixed factory overhead and applied fixed factory overhead.

Fixed Factory Overhead Volume Variance	=	Budgeted Fixed Factory Overhead	−	(Standard Direct Labor-Hours Allowed for Actual Production)	×	(Fixed Overhead Allocation Rate)

Kastings's fixed factory overhead volume variance is

$$\$10,000 - (9,000 \text{ hours}) (\$1/\text{hour}) = \$1,000$$

If the standard direct labor input to actual production for the period is less than the normal direct labor-hour input, an unfavorable volume variance will result as in Kastings (see Illustration 17–5). A favorable volume variance results when the standard direct labor input to actual production exceeds normal levels.

Generally it is difficult to attach a meaningful interpretation to the volume variance other than to say it is a measure of how close actual volume came to expected or normal volume. If unfavorable, it is viewed as the cost of operating the facility at less than normal capacity (if normal capacity is chosen as an attainable efficient capacity).

STANDARD COST SYSTEMS AND FINANCIAL STATEMENTS

In a standard full (absorption) cost system each unit produced is inventoried at its full standard cost of production. Any discrepancies between actual and standard costs are collected in temporary variance accounts, which are usually closed to cost of goods sold at the end of the year if they are not material.

Kastings's journal entries for 1984, which include all the standard cost entries, are listed below.

Kastings began operations on January 1, 1984. Common stock was sold for $1 million cash on that day.

Cash	1,000,000	
Common Stock		1,000,000

The following transactions took place during 1984.

(1) Kastings purchased 50,000 pounds of pewter on account. Total cost was $255,000 (50,000 pounds at $5.10). Raw material is inventoried at standard cost, and the price variance is computed immediately. This enables Kastings to develop rapid feedback on deviations from standard prices, which is desirable for planning and control. The journal entry is:

Raw Material Inventory (50,000 at $5)	250,000	
Raw Material Price Variance (50,000 at $.10)	5,000	
Accounts Payable		255,000

(2) During 1984 the stockroom issued the standard raw material equivalent of 5,000 units of output (6,000 pounds). The stockroom also issued 500 additional pounds to replace raw material destroyed during processing. A total of 6,500 pounds of pewter was transferred from raw materials inventory to work in process. The following journal entry records the material input at standard and recognizes the raw material usage variance.

Work in Process (5,000 × 1.2 at $5)	30,000	
Raw Material Usage Variance (500 at $5)..........	2,500	
Raw Material Inventory (6,500 at $5)		32,500

(3) Direct labor is added uniformly during processing of the figurine. Three thousand figurines were completed, and 2,000 figurines were ¾ through processing at the end of the period; 9,500 direct labor-hours were worked, and the actual wage rate was $7.80 per hour.

The standard direct labor input per figurine is two hours, and the total standard equivalent direct labor for the work performed during 1984 is 9,000 hours (4,500 equivalent units at two hours). The standard cost of this standard input is $72,000 (9,000 at $8).

The following journal entry records the direct labor input to work in process at standard, recognizes wages payable (9,500 hours at $7.80), and tabulates the direct labor price and usage variances.

Work in Process (9,000 at $8)	72,000	
Direct Labor Usage Variance (500 at $8)...........	4,000	
Wages Payable (9,500 at $7.80)		74,100
Direct Labor Price Variance (9,500 at $.20)		1,900

(4) Variable and fixed factory overhead are allocated to units produced using predetermined allocation rates and the standard direct labor input to figurines. The standard direct labor input to work for the year is 9,000 hours. The variable and fixed overhead allocation rates are $.50 and $1 per direct labor-hour, respectively. The following journal entry assigns the standard amount of factory overhead cost to Work in Process.

Work in Process	13,500	
Variable Factory Overhead (9,000 at $.50).......		4,500
Fixed Factory Overhead (9,000 at $1.00)		9,000

(5) Actual fixed factory overhead amounted to $10,200 in 1984. Variable overhead amounted to $5,000, and $10,000 of the total was paid in cash. The remaining $5,200 was credited to accounts payable.

Variable Factory Overhead	5,000	
Fixed Factory Overhead	10,200	
Accounts Payable		5,200
Cash		10,000

(6) Kastings analyzes the factory overhead accounts and computes overhead variances. The variable factory overhead efficiency variance is $250 unfavorable. The variable overhead spending variance is also $250 unfavorable. The fixed factory overhead volume and budget variances are $1,000 unfavorable and $200 unfavorable, respectively.

Variable Factory Overhead Spending Variance	250	
Variable Factory Overhead Efficiency Variance	250	
Fixed Factory Overhead Volume Variance	1,000	
Fixed Factory Overhead Budget Variance	200	
Variable Factory Overhead		500
Fixed Factory Overhead		1,200

The balances in both the fixed and variable overhead accounts are zero after this entry.

(7) The 3,000 completed figurines were transferred to Finished Goods at the standard full cost of $25 per unit.

Finished Goods Inventory	75,000	
Work in Process (3,000 at $25)		75,000

After this entry the balance in Work in Process is $40,500 (30,000 + 72,000 + 13,500 − 75,000).

Standard Cost of Ending Inventory (2,000 partially completed figurines: ¾ processed)

	Raw Material (Pewter)	Direct Labor	Variable Factory Overhead	Fixed Factory Overhead
Equivalent units in ending inventory	2,000	1,500	1,500	1,500
Standard cost per equivalent unit	$ 6	$ 16	$ 1	$ 2
Standard cost in ending inventory	$12,000	$24,000	$1,500	$3,000
Total standard cost in ending inventory	$40,500 ($12,000 + $24,000 + $1,500 + $3,000)			

(8) Kastings sold 2,500 figurines for $60 each on account. The following journal entry records the receivable and the sales revenue.

Accounts Receivable	150,000	
Sales Revenue (2,500 at $60)		150,000

(9) Cost of goods sold at standard is recognized by the following journal entry:

Cost of Goods Sold	62,500	
Finished Goods Inventory (2,500 at $25)		62,500

(10) Selling and administrative expenses amounted to $9,800 for the year. They were paid in cash.

Selling and Administrative Expense	9,800	
Cash		9,800

(11) Accounts receivable in the amount of $45,000 were collected during the year. No provision is required for bad debts. The journal entry to record this is:

Cash	45,000	
Accounts Receivable		45,000

(12) Kastings paid $50,000 in wages and $100,000 of accounts payable in cash during the year.

Wages Payable	50,000	
Accounts Payable	100,000	
Cash		150,000

(13) Kastings prepares its income statement for fiscal 1984 (see Illustration 17–7), closes all temporary accounts to Retained Earnings, and prepares a balance sheet as of December 31, 1984 (see Illustration 17–7). The closing entry is as follows:

Sales Revenue	150,000	
Direct Labor Price Variance	1,900	
Cost of Goods Sold		62,500
Selling and Administrative		
Expenses		9,800
Raw Material Price Variance		5,000
Raw Material Usage Variance................		2,500
Direct Labor Usage Variance................		4,000
Variable Overhead Spending		
Variance		250
Variable Overhead Efficiency		
Variance		250
Fixed Overhead Volume		
Variance		1,000
Fixed Overhead Budget		
Variance		200
Retained Earnings		66,400

The full set of T-accounts with a complete posting of all transactions is contained in Illustration 17–6.

Kastings, Inc., reports $66,400 in pretax income (Illustration 17–7) for the year ending December 31, 1984. The sales revenue of $150,000 (2,500 figurines at $60) relates to items sold during the year. Consistent with the matching principle cost of goods sold is the inventory carrying value of the 2,500 figurines sold during the year (2,500 at $25). Since Kastings uses a standard costing system, cost of goods sold consists of the standard production costs of the items sold. Contrary to the matching principle the production cost variances appear in the income statement of the period in which the variances were generated. This period may or may not coincide with the period of sale of the items that generated the production variances. This is another example of how production, in addition to sales, affects reported absorption costing income.

If standard costing production variances are material in amount they should be prorated between inventories and cost of goods sold.

ILLUSTRATION 17-6. Kastings, Inc.: T-Accounts ($00)

Assets

Cash

	10,000	(5)	100
(11)	450	(10)	98
		(12)	1,500
	8,752		

Accounts Receivable

(8)	1,500	(11)	450
	1,050		

Finished Goods Inventory

(7)	750	(9)	625
	125		

Raw Material Inventory

(1)	2,500	(2)	325
	2,175		

Work in Process

(2)	300	(7)	750
(3)	720		
(4)	135		
	405		

Liabilities

Accounts Payable

(12)	1,000	(1)	2,550
		(5)	52
			1,602

Common Stock

			10,000
			10,000

Wages Payable

(12)	500	(3)	741
			241

Retained Earnings

(13)	50	(13)	19
(13)	25	(13)	1,500
(13)	40		
(13)	625		
(13)	98		
(13)	2.5		
(13)	2.5		
(13)	10		
(13)	2		
			664

Temporary Accounts

Variable Overhead

(5)	50	(4)	45
		(6)	5

Fixed Overhead

(5)	102	(4)	90
		(6)	12

Selling & Administrative Expenses

(10)	98	(13)	98

Raw Materials—Usage Variance

(2)	25	(13)	25

Direct Labor—Usage Variance

(3)	40	(13)	40

Cost of Goods Sold

(9)	625	(13)	625

Raw Materials—Price Variance

(1)	50	(13)	50

Direct Labor—Price Variance

(3)	19	(13)	19

Sales Revenue

(13)	1,500	(8)	1,500

Variable Overhead Spending Variance

(6)	2.5	(13)	2.5

Variable Overhead Efficiency Variance

(6)	2.5	(13)	2.5

Fixed Overhead—Volume Variance

(6)	10	(13)	10

Fixed Overhead—Budget Variance

(6)	2	(13)	2

ILLUSTRATION 17–7

KASTINGS, INC.
Balance Sheet
As of December 31, 1984
($00)

Assets		Equities	
Cash	$ 8,752	Accounts payable	$ 1,602
Accounts receivable	1,050	Wages payable	241
Raw material inventory	2,175	Common stock	10,000
Work in process inventory	405	Retained earnings	664
Finished goods inventory	125		
Total assets	$12,507	Total equities	$12,507

KASTINGS, Inc.
Income Statement
For Year Ended December 31, 1984
($00)

Sales revenue	$1,500
Cost of goods sold	625
Gross margin	875
Production cost variances:	
Material price	(50)
Material usage	(25)
Labor rate	19
Labor usage	(40)
Variable overhead spending	(2.5)
Variable overhead efficiency	(2.5)
Fixed overhead volume	(10)
Fixed overhead budget	(2)
	(113)
Adjusted gross margin	762
Selling and administrative expense	98
Pretax income	$ 664*

* For purposes of this illustration, we have ignored income taxes.

Large variances are likely to arise in standard costing systems based on theoretical, difficult-to-achieve standards rather than reasonably attainable standards (as in Kastings) since it is very likely that the theoretical standards will not be met. If standards do not anticipate price inflation or learning in the production process, large variances are also likely to result. Learning refers to improved efficiency in the utilization of direct labor which often occurs in certain complex, repetitive tasks. For example the direct labor input in the production of each successive airframe of a particular model airplane produced is likely to decrease because of learning.

SUMMARY

Standard absorption (full) costing provides uniform cost valuations for similar items produced during an accounting period. Standards provide the basis for assigning responsibility for efficient or inefficient operating performance. Typically price and usage variances are computed for direct product costs, spending and efficiency variances for variable factory overhead costs, and spending and volume variances for fixed factory overhead costs. These decompositions of total variances are useful in explaining why a particular variance occurred and who in the organization was responsible for the variance.

Raw material price variances should be computed when raw materials are purchased. Other direct product usage and price variances are likely to be computed weekly or monthly, and factory overhead variances are likely to be computed monthly, quarterly, and annually.

Standards are usually adjusted annually. Since price standards are likely to reflect anticipated price changes for the coming year, quarterly reports are likely to contain price variances. In the first quarter favorable price variances are expected (prices paid are likely to be lower than standards, which reflect higher prices later in the year), while unfavorable price variances are usually expected in the third and fourth quarter reports.

Many variants of the basic standard costing system developed in this chapter exist in practice, but all are based on using a standard measure as a means of improving control and planning for the business firm.

PROBLEMS AND CASES

17-1 Clearone

The Industrial Chemicals Department of Chemco, Inc., produces a single product, which the company markets under the trade name Clearone. The amount of year-end work in process in the Industrial Chemicals Department is never significant.

Standard costs of producing a finished pound of Clearone for the coming year are shown below:

Standard Cost of Clearone per Pound

Direct material (1½ pounds at 20¢ per pound)	$ .30
Direct labor (1/10 hour at $4.50 per hour)	45
Factory overhead (1/10 hour at $4.50 per hour)	.45
Standard full cost per pound	$1.20

Factory Overhead Budget (normal capacity of 24,000 direct labor hours)

Budgeted fixed factory overhead	$ 60,000
Budgeted variable factory overhead	48,000
	$108,000
Normal capacity (direct labor hours)	24,000
Factory overhead allocation rate per	
direct labor-hour .... $	4.50

Actual results for the Industrial Chemicals Department for a recent year are as follows:

Direct material used (264,000 pounds at $.22)	$ 58,080
Direct labor worked (18,000 hours at $4.40)	79,200
Actual factory overhead:	
Fixed $61,200	
Variable 33,600	94,800
Total production costs	$232,080
Actual pounds of Clearone produced	168,000

Chemco, Inc., uses a standard absorption costing system in each of its departments.

Required:

1. Compute the following:

a. Standard cost of production for the year.
b. Actual cost of production for the year.
c. Direct material usage variance.
d. Direct material price variance.
e. Direct labor usage variance.
f. Direct labor price variance.
g. Fixed factory overhead budget variance.
h. Fixed factory overhead volume variance.
i. Variable factory overhead spending variance.
j. Variable factory overhead efficiency variance.

2. Label each of the above variances as favorable or unfavorable and give a brief explanation of its possible cause.

3. At the beginning of the year there wasn't any Clearone inventory in the finished goods warehouse. On December 31 of the current year 20,000 pounds of Clearone were in the warehouse. The work in process inventory of Clearone on both dates was negligible.

a. If all production cost variances are closed to cost of goods sold, what is the value of the 20,000 pounds of Clearone in ending finished goods inventory? $20,000 \times 1.2 = 24,000$
b. If all production cost variances are prorated to finished goods inventory and cost of goods sold on the basis of the number of standard direct labor hours in each, then what is the value of the 20,000 pounds of Clearone in ending finished goods inventory?

17-2 Kay Company

The Kay Company manufactures Alegite from material Z. All the work on Alegite is done in department X. The Company uses a standard cost system, and work in process inventories are not significant.

Standard Cost per Unit of Alegite

Material Z (5 pounds at $.20)	$ 1.00
Direct labor (2 hours at $6.00)	12.00
Factory overhead ($2 per direct labor-hour)	4.00
Standard full cost per unit	$17.00

Actual Production Data (March 1985)

Units of Alegite produced	4,300
Material Z used in production	22,000 pounds at $ .21
Direct labor used	9,000 hours at $5.80
Actual factory overhead	$19,000
Material Z purchased	32,000 pounds at $ .21

Department X—Annual Estimates of Factory Overhead

Fixed factory overhead	$ 84,000
Variable factory overhead (at normal capacity)	156,000
	$240,000
Normal capacity (direct labor-hours)	120,000
Factory overhead allocation rate	$2/direct labor-hour

Required:

1. Compute the following for the month of March.
   a. Standard cost of Alegite produced.
   b. Material Z price variance.
   c. Material Z usage variance.
   d. Labor price (rate) variance.
   e. Labor usage variance.
   f. Under- or overapplied factory overhead.

2. What would be the amount of under- or overapplied factory overhead for March if Kay Company had used the expected direct labor usage of 96,000 direct labor-hours (instead of normal) to compute the factory overhead allocation rate? (First compute the new allocation rate based on expected direct labor usage.)

17-3 Stake House Restaurant*

The Stake House Restaurant uses a standard cost system to control entrée costs. The entrée items (steak, lobster, chicken, etc.) account for about 80 percent of Stake House's food costs but only comprise about 20 percent of all food items needed to operate.

Three variances form the basis of Stake House's entree cost control program. The *purchase price* variance equals the quantity purchased times the difference between the actual price per unit and the standard price per unit of each entrée item.

The *yield variance,* computed for bulk meats (e.g., sirloin butts, tenderloin strips, etc.) processed during the period equals the difference between the standard value of the preprocessed meat and the standard value of the processed meat—the yield that results from cutting the meat.

The *use variance* is the difference between the standard values of the physical and book ending inventories.

Required:

1. Purchases of entrée items for a recent month are summarized below:

Item	Quantity Purchased (pounds)	Actual Total Price	Standard Total Price
Bulk sirloin	810.7 11.01	$1,429.82	$1,418.81
Prime rib	434.5 − 30.41	1,086.25	1,116.66
6-ounce chicken	192.0 1.22	135.62	134.40
Lamb chops	117.5 − 14.10	467.65	481.75
Crab	200.0 28.00	588.00	550.00

a. What is the standard price of a pound of crab?

b. Compute the purchase price variances for all items.

c. How would you decide which of the purchase price variances are significant? *How big a percent of the standard price the var. was*

d. Why does Stake House management compute purchase price variances?

2. During a recent month Stake House meat cutters processed 2,246.7 pounds of bulk sirloin. The cutting results are summarized below. Standard prices of individual outputs are based on the relative market values of the individual outputs and the yield of each output that should be obtained by a competent meat cutter processing an average piece of bulk sirloin.

Input—Preprocessed meat:

Item	Pounds	Standard Price of Input
Bulk sirloin	2,246.7	$3,931.73

* Based on the article, "Benefits from Standard Costing in the Restaurant Industry," by Matthew J. Mullett, *Management Accounting,* September 1978.

sum of output at standard price 3931.73 (handwritten)

Output—Processed meat:

Bulk sirloin 2246.7 (handwritten)

Item	Pounds		Standard Price of Output
6-ounce sirloin	211.0	*11.0*	$ 11.44
8-ounce sirloin	1,750.0	*1,750*	2,187.50
12-ounce sirloin	707.0	*707*	1,343.30
16-ounce sirloin	68.0		170.00
Hamburger	152.7	*2526.0*	122.18
Kabob	127.6		255.20

28163 (handwritten)

a. What is the standard price of bulk sirloin? Of 12-ounce sirloin? Of hamburger?

b. Compute the yield variance for the month.

c. Why is the yield variance computed?

3. The end-of-month inventory results for several items are shown below.

Item	Physical Ending Inventory (pounds)		Physical Ending Inventory (standard cost)	Book Ending Inventory (pounds)
Bulk hamburger	20.0	*80*	$ 16.00	34.0
Bulk crab	21.5	*2.7*	59.13	20.5
Bulk lobster	87.0		648.15	93.0
11-ounce salmon	9.0	*1.34*	12.05	10.0

34 x .80 - 1 for (handwritten)

a. Compute the use variance for each of the four items.

b. Explain the significance of each of the four use variances.

17–4 DeMayo Manufacturing

The DeMayo Manufacturing Company has recently installed a standard absorption costing system. The following budget formula was used to project DeMayo's 1984 factory overhead: $2,500,000 per year plus $6 per direct labor-hour. The standard combined fixed and variable factory overhead allocation rate for 1984, based on normal capacity, is $11.

Required:

1. What is DeMayo's normal capacity?

2. DeMayo Manufacturing produces and sells a single product for $250 per unit. The standard full cost per unit is $144 [four direct labor hours at $10 plus $60 direct material cost plus $44 of allocated factory overhead (four direct labor hours at $11)]. All expenses, other than costs of goods sold, are projected to be $5 million for 1984.

DeMayo Manufacturing has no current or anticipated work in process or raw material inventories and uses the LIFO flow assumption for finished goods inventory. DeMayo expects to produce 105,000 units and to sell 100,000 units during 1984. Construct an absorption costing 1984 pro forma income statement for DeMayo Manufacturing.

3.   Actual factory overhead for 1984 was as follows: $2,550,000 fixed; $2,480,000 variable. Direct labor-hours for 1984 were: 420,000 actual direct labor-hours worked; 400,000 standard direct labor-hours allowed for 1984 actual output. Compute the variable factory overhead efficiency and spending variances and the fixed factory overhead budget and volume variances for 1984. Enumerate the likely causes of these variances.

17-5   Rockingham Company

The Rockingham Company set up the following standards for their product.

Raw material A—10 pounds per unit, $1 per pound.
Direct labor:
   Machining—2 hours per unit, $3 per hour.
   Assembly—4 hours per unit, $2 per hour.
Factory (production) overhead is allocated on a per unit of production basis. The *yearly* overhead budget is:

	Machining	Assembly	Total
Fixed cost $4	$144,000	$ 36,000	$180,000 $5
Variable costs $4	144,000 $3	108,000	252,000 $7
	$288,000	$144,000	$432,000
Practical plant capacity (normal or standard volume) units of product	36,000	36,000	

All inventories are carried at standard cost. The following additional data are given for the *month* of *January:*

Raw material A purchased: 25,000 pounds at $1.01 per pound.

Raw material A used: 22,000 pounds.

Actual direct labor costs:

Machining labor—$2.90 per hour	$11,890	4,100
Assembly labor—$2.00 per hour	17,000	8,500
	$28,890	

Actual factory overhead costs:

Machining	$20,800	10,400
Assembly	11,500	28 2875
	$32,300	

January production was 2,000 units. January sales were 2,500 units.

Required:

Compute the following variances for January. Indicate whether the variances are favorable or unfavorable. (Show your computations.)

1. Material price variance.
2. Material usage variance.
3. Labor rate variances.
a. Machining.
b. Assembly.
4. Labor efficiency (time) variances.
a. Machining.
b. Assembly.
5. Fixed factory overhead volume variances.
a. Machining.
b. Assembly.
6. Spending (budget) variances.
a. Machining.
b. Assembly.
7. Calculate the standard cost of one unit of product.

17–6 Random Space Company

Engineers of the Random Space Company have been working for several months on a device to be used in moon rockets. After studying the company's plans and examining a mock-up of the device, the National Aeronautics and Space Administration (NASA) has placed an initial order for 32 units, work to begin on January 2. Experience with initial orders for other devices of the same general type indicates that an 80 percent learning or improvement curve will be appropriate. Both Random and NASA accept this rate as a basis for estimating costs and scheduling deliveries.

The best estimate that can be made in advance of actual production is that 1,000 hours of direct labor will be required to complete the first unit. An 80 percent learning or improvement curve implies that each time the quantity of production is doubled, the *cumulative average* direct labor-hours needed to complete all of the production will be 80 percent of the average direct labor-hours needed to complete the quantity that was doubled. Therefore, Random Space expects that the second unit will be produced after a total of 1,600 (.8 × 2,000) direct labor-hours have been worked. The average time to produce the first unit is 1,000 direct labor-hours and the average time to produce the first two units is 800 (1,600/2).

Since special skills are required, the Random Space Company plans to have all work on the order done by six men who work eight hours each working day. Overtime will be authorized only to meet emergencies. NASA wants the 32 units delivered as soon as possible. No additional units will be ordered this year, but prospects for future contracts will be improved if deliveries are prompt and on schedule. Working days and available hours of the six men are shown in the table below.

Month	Workdays	Per Month	Cumulative	Units to Be Delivered
January	22	1,056	1,056	_____
February	19	912	1,968	_____
March	23	1,104	3,072	_____
April	22	1,056	4,128	_____
May	23	1,104	5,232	_____
June	21	1,008	6,240	_____
July	22	1,056	7,296	_____
August	15	720	8,016	_____
September	23	1,104	9,120	_____
October	21	1,008	10,128	_____
November	22	1,056	11,184	_____
December	20	960	12,144	_____

Required:

1. What schedule of deliveries would it be reasonable for the Random Space Company to promise? Using the information in the above table, determine the number of units you would expect the Random Space Company to deliver each month in filling the initial order for 32 units. (Assume for ease of computation that every time production is doubled it requires an equal number of direct labor-hours to produce each unit in the last half of total production. For example, it takes 1,600 hours to produce two units and 2,560 hours to produce four units. Therefore, it takes 960 hours (2,560 − 1,600) to produce the third and fourth units. The time to produce individual units in the next batches of 4, 8, and 16 units is similarly computed.)

2. The selling price per unit is $12,000. The first unit produced is expected to cost $18,000 to produce (1,000 direct labor hours at $8 per hour, 1,000 direct labor hours at $2 per hour of allocated factory overhead, $8,000 raw material cost). The raw material cost is expected to remain at $8,000 per unit. The $2 per direct labor-hour of allocated factory overhead is equally split between variable and fixed factory overhead.

Explain carefully how you would compute Random Space Company's profit for the first quarter. Random has always used a standard absorption costing system. Standards are set once a year at the beginning of the year. Make a recommendation on how the direct labor standard per unit should be set. What should be done with any direct labor variance at the end of the quarter?

17-7 Standard Manufacturing

The Standard Company produces steel tool chests which are sold to several major retail hardware store chains. Standard Company uses a standard cost system and annually revises the standards for its single product. The standard costs for 1984 follow:

Raw material (4 lbs. at $1.20)	$ 4.80
Direct labor (2 hours at $6)	12.00
Factory overhead ($4 per direct labor hour)	8.00
Standard full cost per tool chest	$24.80

Upon receipt of raw material the Standard Company debits raw material inventory at standard cost. Work in process inventory is based on standard quantities and rates, and finished goods inventory is valued at the standard full cost per tool chest, $24.80. All production variance accounts are closed to cost of goods sold at the end of the year. Standard Company uses the LIFO inventory flow assumption for all inventories.

The following information relates to 1984 operations.

Estimated Factory Overhead

Fixed	$440,000
Variable (at normal capacity)	440,000
	$880,000
Normal capacity (direct labor-hours)	220,000
Factory overhead allocation rate	$4/direct labor-hour

Actual Factory Overhead

Fixed	$445,000
Variable	489,450
Total	$934,450

1984 Production Results

Standard direct labor in actual production (250,000 hours)	$1,500,000
Standard raw material in actual production (500,000 pounds)	600,000
Standard factory overhead in actual production (250,000 hours)	1,000,000
Standard cost of actual production	$3,100,000

Actual direct labor: 251,000 hours worked at a cost of $1,480,900.

Actual raw material used: 490,000 pounds.

Actual raw material purchases: 700,000 pounds at a cost of $875,000.

Cash Receipts and Disbursements

Receipts:
  Collection of accounts receivable
  and cash sales $3,010,000

Disbursements:
  Raw material purchases . . . . $ 860,000
  Wages   1,520,000
  Factory overhead   940,000
    Total disbursements $3,320,000

Additional information:

a. Sales for the year: 100,000 tool chests at $30.

b. Transfer from work in process to finished goods inventory: 120,000 tool chests.

c. $50,000 of fixed factory overhead is depreciation. All other factory overhead is paid in cash or is credited to short-term payables.

Required:

1. Prepare journal entries to record all of the above information. Set up as many variance accounts as possible.

2. Prepare Standard Company's 1984 income statement (ignore taxes).

3. Prepare an end-of-year balance sheet. The January 1, 1984, balance sheet accounts were as follows:

	Debit	Credit
Raw materials inventory	$ 50,000	
Work in process inventory	20,000	
Finished goods inventory	120,000	
All other assets	490,000	
Short-term payables		$120,000
Long-term liabilities		200,000
Shareholders equity		360,000
	$680,000	$680,000

18

Cost allocation

One of the most difficult problems in cost accounting is the allocation of indirect costs to cost objects.

A cost object or cost objective can be a department, program, activity, one unit of output (manufactured product), or 10,000 units of output. Management determines the cost object by deciding the purpose for which they are measuring the costs. For example, management might want to know the cost of a particular activity in order to decide whether it is operating efficiently and should be continued.

Some specific cost allocation problems are: How much indirect factory overhead should each unit of product contain? If two or more products are made from the same process how much of these joint costs should be assigned to each product? How should the cost of a maintenance department, which provides service, be allocated to production departments, which produce finished goods?

There are no specific rules governing the allocation of these indirect costs to cost objects. Management decides how these costs will be allocated using the general rule that each cost object should bear its "fair share" of the indirect costs.[1]

For example, the Aero Manufacturing Company (Chapter 16) determined that indirect factory overhead costs should be allocated to components on the basis of direct labor hours and that this allocation method would result in each component bearing its fair share of the total indirect factory overhead.

COST POOLS, ALLOCATION RULES, AND COST OBJECTS

Costs are collected in cost pools and assigned to cost objects using a cost allocation rule.

Cost may be pooled (collected) according to function (e.g., manufacturing, selling) physical aspects (e.g., labor type, raw material type), or behavior (e.g., fixed, variable). Generally cost objects should be defined before costs are pooled (collected). That is, the intended uses of cost data should dictate the number and location of cost pools. For instance, the fixed and variable costs of an activity are frequently collected in separate pools because it is important to distinguish between variable and fixed costs in decision making.

For example, in a hospital all costs of operating the hospital must eventually be allocated to various categories of patients in order to determine the patient's bill for the services received. Initially some costs are pooled according to type of service (e.g., housekeeping) and then allocated to some intermediate cost object, a department utilizing the service (e.g., nursing), on the basis of the number of hours of the service consumed. The costs now accumulated in the intermediate cost objects (e.g., nursing) will then be allocated to the final cost objects, individual patients, using measures of the relative intensity of the nursing care required by a patient and the length of stay of the patient.

Allocation of variable costs

Whenever possible the allocation of costs to cost objects should be made on the basis of the cost object's relative usage of that variable which seems to "cause" the cost. For example, if the variable costs of a maintenance department rise in proportion to the number of direct labor-hours worked by maintenance employees, then variable maintenance costs should be allocated to departments served on the basis of the relative amounts of maintenance hours used

---

[1] The United States government has guidelines that specify how indirect costs are allocated to its contracts. Many commercial cost-plus contracts also specify how indirect costs are to be calculated in arriving at the cost of the contract.

by the departments. As it becomes more difficult to identify a cause and effect relationship between cost pools and cost objects, the assignment of costs to objects becomes more arbitrary and therefore less useful in decision making, performance evaluation, and control. In the extreme, costs may be allocated to cost objects on the relative ability of the cost objects to bear the additional costs. Such allocations are not usually justifiable.

Allocation of fixed costs

Fixed costs of activities may be allocated to users on the basis of the *relative* amount of the total capacity available to the user, not on the basis of some measure of consumption of the activity by the user. This is justified on the basis that the level of fixed cost is primarily determined by the size of the activity, which in turn depends on the "basic capacity to serve" available to each user. For example, the output capacity of an internal power generation department is largely determined by the long-run average peak power needs of each of the departments it serves. The fixed costs of the power department are allocated to user departments using relative long-run average peak power needs, not short-run relative usage.

Combined overhead allocation rate

In practice one combined rate, which includes both variable and fixed overhead, is often used for departmental cost allocations. Factory overhead allocation rates are usually determined using yearly (at a minimum) cost and allocation base data. Rates determined on an annual basis should result in more stable product costs because of the "lumpy" nature of many indirect product costs (the costs are not incurred uniformly throughout the year) and the seasonal nature of production in many industries. For example, heating costs are only incurred in winter months in northern climates. Even if all fixed factory overhead costs are incurred uniformly throughout the year, seasonal production patterns will cause variation in monthly or quarterly factory overhead allocation rates. Suppose direct labor hours are used to allocate fixed factory overhead, which totals $100,000 per quarter, to the manufactured product. Suppose direct labor usage is planned to be 100,000, 50,000, 200,000, and 400,000 hours in each of the next four quarters, respectively. Quarterly fixed factory overhead allocation rates would be $1, $2, $.50, and $.25, respectively. An item requiring one direct labor-hour to produce would absorb $1 of fixed factory overhead in the first quarter. An identical item produced in the fourth quarter would absorb only $.25 of fixed factory overhead.

Factory overhead rates may also vary across production departments and across different categories of costs within a particular department. The end result of cost allocation for absorption costing purposes should be individual product costs that reflect the relative costs of the scarce resources consumed in the production of each product.

Example of cost allocation

The fixed cost of operating a warehouse, which serves two production departments, is estimated to be $200,000 for the coming year. The variable cost of warehouse operation, primarily labor, is estimated to be $150,000 for the coming year. Production department 1 requires three quarters of the total warehouse floor space because of high set-up costs that necessitate large production runs and high inventories. Two thirds of the warehouse labor is associated with the movement of the output of production department 2 in and out of the warehouse.

A fair allocation of warehouse costs to production departments is as follows: allocate $150,000 (¾ of the total fixed cost) of the fixed warehouse cost to production department 1 and $50,000 (¼ of the total fixed cost) to production department 2; allocate $50,000 (⅓ of the total variable cost) to production department 1 and $100,000 (⅔ of the total variable cost) to production department 2.

The above example illustrates that manufacturing costs may be allocated to intermediate cost objects (production departments in the example) before being allocated to the output of some department. The $200,000 ($150,000 + $50,000) warehouse cost allocated to production department 1 is a component of that department's manufacturing overhead and will be allocated to its output (products). The $150,000 ($50,000 + $100,000) warehouse cost allocated to production department 2 will subsequently be allocated to the output of that department.

The allocation of joint product costs and service department costs are examples of complicated cost allocation problems. The cost objects of joint product cost allocations are products, while the cost objects of service department cost allocations are production departments.

JOINT PRODUCT COSTS: ALLOCATION

Joint products[2] are simultaneously produced from common inputs. The inputs are jointly processed at a cost of C_J until they

---

[2] By-products are products of a joint process with little sales value in comparison to the major joint products. Scrap, in contrast to by-products, has almost no sales value at all. Net realizable values (sales prices less costs to complete the sales) of by-products and scrap are deducted from the cost of goods sold of the major joint products in determining net income.

become distinguishable as individual items. The point at which the products obtain an individual identity is known as the *split point* (see Illustration 18–1).

The processing of crude oil into regular gasoline, heating oil, and heavy viscosity oils is an example of joint processing. The outputs become distinguishable only after considerable processing of the raw crude. Kerosene is generally considered to be a by-product of gasoline production because the sales value of the amount of kerosene produced is minor in comparison to the amount of the gasoline produced.

Absorption costing requires that the joint cost, C_J, be allocated to products at the point they become identifiable. There are at least two conventional allocation procedures to accomplish this. The first relies on *physical measures* of the joint outputs to make the allocation, and the second is based on the *sales value* of the joint products.

Physical measures of output

Suppose there are two joint products each of which can be conveniently measured in terms of a common unit (gallons, pounds, feet, etc.). Let X_1 denote the number of units of product 1 and X_2 denote the number of units of product 2 that result from processing a common input at a cost of C_J. Total joint product output is $X_1 + X_2$ common units using a physical measure. C_J is allocated in proportion to the relative amount of product outputs as measured by the common unit.

	Allocated to:	
Joint Cost	Product 1	Product 2
C_J	$\left(\dfrac{X_1}{X_1 + X_2}\right)C_J$	$\left(\dfrac{X_2}{X_1 + X_2}\right)C_J$

For example, suppose a joint chemical process produces 1,000 gallons of chemical A and 3,000 gallons of chemical B at a cost of $12,000. Using gallons as the common measure of output results in the following allocation.

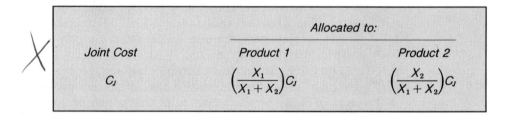

	Allocated to:	
Joint Cost	Chemical A	Chemical B
$12,000	$\left(\dfrac{1,000}{1,000 + 3,000}\right)\$12,000 = \$3,000$	$\left(\dfrac{3,000}{1,000 + 3,000}\right)\$12,000 = \$9,000$

ILLUSTRATION 18–1. **Joint Costs**

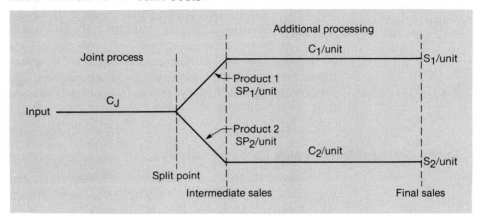

Relative sales value of output

Let SP_1 and SP_2 denote selling prices per unit of the joint products at the split point. If SP_1 and SP_2 are known, the *relative sales value* of the outputs can be used to allocate the joint cost. Again X_1 and X_2 denote the number of units of product 1 and product 2, respectively. This method results in the following allocation.

	Allocated to:	
Joint Cost	Product 1	Product 2
C_J	$\left(\dfrac{SP_1X_1}{SP_1X_1 + SP_2X_2}\right)C_J$	$\left(\dfrac{SP_2X_2}{SP_1X_1 + SP_2X_2}\right)C_J$

In the previous joint chemical process example, suppose chemical A can be sold at the split point for $1 a gallon and chemical B can be sold for $3 a gallon. The relative sales value cost allocation is as follows:

	Allocated to:	
Joint Cost	Chemical A	Chemical B
$12,000	$\left(\dfrac{\$1(1,000)}{\$1(1,000) + \$3(3000)}\right)\$12,000 = \$1,200$	$\left(\dfrac{\$3(3,000)}{\$1(1,000) + \$3(3,000)}\right)\$12,000 = \$10,800$

This allocation might be preferred to the physical measure allocation because chemical B, with its relatively high sales value, can bear more of the joint cost. If selling costs are significant in comparison to the split point selling prices, SP_1 and SP_2, or if the costs to complete the sales differ significantly across products, net realizable values may be used in the above cost allocation process instead of the split point selling prices. Net realizable value is equal to the sales price less all costs to complete the sale. All of the allocation procedures are arbitrary, and management chooses the method they find most useful in decision making.

Approximate relative sales value of output

Frequently the joint products represent intermediate products that are processed further before sale (See Illustration 18–1). Additional processing of products 1 and 2 cost C_1 per unit and C_2 per unit, respectively. The processed products can be sold for S_1 per unit and S_2 per unit. The relative sales value method could still be used to assign the joint cost to products 1 and 2 if the intermediate sales prices SP_1 and SP_2 are known. If they are not known the *approximate relative sales value method* may be used. The approximate sales value of product 1 at the split point is $S_1 X_1 - C_1 X_1 = SP_1'$, the final sales value of the further-processed product 1 minus the additional processing costs. This computation implicitly assumes that no value other than costs is added by the additional processing. The approximate sales value of product 2 at the split point is $S_2 X_2 - C_2 X_2 = SP_2'$. In general the approximate relative sales value method results in the following allocation.

	Allocated to:	
Joint Cost	Product 1	Product 2
C_J	$\left(\dfrac{SP_1'}{SP_1' + SP_2'}\right)C_J$	$\left(\dfrac{SP_2'}{SP_1' + SP_2'}\right)C_J$

Suppose in the chemical example that the sales prices at the split point are unknown, that additional processing of chemical A costs $1 a gallon and results in a product that can be sold for $4 a gallon, and additional processing of chemical B costs $2 a gallon and results in a product that can be sold for $5 a gallon. Then

$$SP_1' = \$4(1,000) - \$1(1,000) = \$3,000$$
$$SP_2' = \$5(3,000) - \$2(3,000) = \$9,000$$

The approximate relative sales value allocation is given by:

	Allocated to:	
Joint Cost	Chemical A	Chemical B
$12,000	$\left(\dfrac{\$3,000}{\$3,000 + \$9,000}\right)\$12,000 = \$3,000$	$\left(\dfrac{\$9,000}{\$3,000 + \$9,000}\right)\$12,000 = \$9,000$

Any of the above three allocation procedures can be readily extended to more than two joint products.

JOINT PRODUCT COSTS: DECISION MAKING

Absorption costing requires that joint costs be allocated to products for purposes of inventory valuation. However, allocated joint costs should be ignored in production decisions involving joint products.

The objective of most private sector decision making is to maximize wealth as measured by cash flow (as opposed to accounting income). Any choice between two actions should be based on an analysis of the total cash flows associated with each of the actions. Alternatively, an analysis of the incremental (differential) cash flows can be made. Incremental cash flows are cash inflows and cash outflows which will differ under each of the actions being considered. The production decisions we will consider now are short-term decisions since they affect cash flows in only the current period.

Suppose products 1 and 2 have emerged from a joint process. Consider the decision whether to process product 1 further. At the split point, C_J is a *sunk cost*—an irrevocable decision has been made to incur the cash outflow. Thus C_J, or any allocation of C_J, is not an incremental cash flow with respect to the decision to further process product 1. If product 1 is processed further it can be sold for S_1 per unit. However the additional processing will cost C_1 per unit, and the right to sell the product at the split point for SP_1 per unit will be lost. The incremental cash flow from further processing will be positive as long as

$$S_1 > C_1 + SP_1$$

Equivalently,

$$S_1 - C_1 > SP_1$$

Generally, the opportunity cost, O_1, of using capacity for additional processing should also be considered. An opportunity cost (opportunity cash flow) is the amount of cash foregone by using an asset one way instead of its next best alternative use. Further processing should be done as long as

$$S_1 > C_1 + SP_1 + O_1$$

The incremental cash inflow, S_1, should exceed the sum of the incremental processing cost, C_1, the forgone split point revenue, SP_1, and the cash inflow foregone because capacity is not being used to produce something else, O_1.

In the previous joint product chemical example, consider the decision to process chemical A further. Recall $SP_1 = \$1$, $C_1 = \$1$, and $S_1 = \$4$. Assume also that there is no alternative use for the facility if chemical A is not processed further, $O_1 = \$0$. The correct decision is to process further since

$$\$4 > \$1 + \$1 + \$0$$

If a gallon of A is sold at the split point \$1 will be received from the sale. If the gallon is processed further for \$1 it can be sold for \$4, and the net cash inflow will be \$3 instead of \$1. The company will be better off by \$2 for every gallon of A that is processed further.

Now suppose if additional processing is not done the company can rent the time it takes to process one gallon of A in the facility for \$5. Then

$$\$4 < \$1 + \$1 + \$5$$

and it would not be beneficial to process further. The company will be better off by \$3 (\$6 from selling at split point and renting capacity versus \$3 net inflow from further processing) if A is not processed further and the facility is rented.

The joint cost or any arbitrary allocation of the joint cost to products is not relevant to the process-further decision.

SERVICE DEPARTMENT COSTS: ALLOCATION

Service departments provide support for departments directly involved in production. Maintenance departments, computer centers, cafeterias, and internal power generation departments provide essential services to production departments and other service departments without being directly involved in production.

Inventory valuation and income determination under GAAP require the allocation of service department costs to production departments and ultimately to products. This allocation also is necessary to determine the total cost of a cost center and its output, which is useful in pricing the output and in computing "cost plus" reimbursements. Such allocations may affect the behavior of departmental managers and the quality of their decision making. We will illustrate these problems with examples.

Example of service department cost allocations

Business Products, Inc. (BPI), produces steel desks and filing cabinets in two separate production departments. An internal power generation department provides all of BPI's electrical needs, and a repair and maintenance department does routine repair and maintenance work throughout the company. During 1984 the following costs were incurred in each of these two service departments.

Power Generation Department

Fixed costs:		
Salaries	$30,000	
Depreciation—equipment	5,000	$35,000
Variable costs:		
Oil	18,000	
Miscellaneous	2,000	20,000
Total cost of power generation		$55,000

Repair and Maintenance Department

Fixed costs:		
Salaries	$25,000	
Depreciation—equipment	4,000	$29,000
Variable costs:		
Labor	30,000	
Materials	5,000	35,000
Total costs of repair and maintenance		$64,000

The costs collected in the power generation and repair and maintenance departments (cost pools) are to be allocated to the desk and cabinet production departments (cost objects) according to some allocation rule. The allocation rule is expressed in terms of an allocation base, usually a variable that measures the output of each service department. The allocation base may differ for variable and fixed costs in the same service department.

Fixed costs

BPI uses long-run relative peak demands for power to allocate fixed power department costs to the cabinet and desk production departments. Because the cabinet and desk departments are approximately the same size and have equal, long-run peak power demands measured in kilowatt hours, each is allocated half of the fixed cost of power generation.

BPI management believes that the more complex operations in the desk production department will, in the long run, require approximately three times more maintenance and repair work than will the cabinet production department. BPI allocates ¾ of the fixed cost of the maintenance and repair department to desk production and ¼ to cabinet production.

The following table summarizes BPI's allocation of fixed service department costs to production departments.

| | | Allocated to: | |
	Fixed Costs	Desk Production	Cabinet Production
Power			
Department	$35,000	$17,500	$17,500
Repair and			
Maintenance			
Department	29,000	21,750	7,250
		$39,250	$24,750

The following journal entry transfers the fixed service department costs, which are collected in overhead (asset) accounts in the individual service departments, to manufacturing overhead accounts of the individual production departments.

Fixed Manufacturing Overhead (Cabinets)	24,750	
Fixed Manufacturing Overhead (Desks)	39,250	
Fixed Overhead (Power)		35,000
Fixed Overhead (Repair and Maintenance)		29,000

Variable costs

BPI uses short-run relative usage of kilowatt hours to allocate the variable costs of the power generation department to departments consuming power. Variable repair and maintenance costs are allocated to departments according to the relative number of repair and maintenance labor-hours they use.

The following table summarizes the variable costs to be allocated from service departments to production departments and shows the relative consumption of the service department outputs by department.

		Fraction of Total Output of Service Department Used by:			
Service Department	Variable Cost	Power	Repair	Desks	Cabinets
Power	$20,000	–0–	.10	.45	.45
Repair	35,000	.20	–0–	.50	.30

Direct allocation method

The *direct allocation method* is a simple, often-used method to allocate variable service department costs to production departments. It completely ignores service rendered by one service department to another and allocates variable service department costs to production departments in proportion to the relative amounts of the outputs of the service departments consumed by each production department.

Since the desk and cabinet departments consumed equal numbers of kilowatt hours during 1984, under the direct method each will be allocated $10,000 [(45/(45 + 45)) × $20,000].

Desk production will be allocated $21,875 [(50/(50 + 30)) × $35,000], and cabinet production will be allocated $13,125 [(30/(50 + 30)) × $35,000] of variable repair and maintenance costs.

Power Department	Repair Department	Desks	Cabinets
$ 20,000	$ 35,000		
(20,000)		$10,000	$10,000
	(35,000)	21,875	13,125
–0–	–0–	$31,875	$23,125

Power and repair totals are zero since all costs have been allocated out of the power department and the repair department. Of the total $55,000 variable service department cost, $31,875 has been allocated to desk production and $23,125 to cabinet production.

The following journal entry transfers the variable service department costs, which have been collected in overhead (asset) accounts in the individual service departments, to manufacturing overhead accounts of the individual production departments.

Variable Manufacturing Overhead (Cabinets) 23,125
Variable Manufacturing Overhead (Desks) 31,875
    Variable Overhead (Power).................... 20,000
    Variable Overhead (Repair and Maintenance) . 35,000

After this journal entry, $71,125 ($31,875 variable + $39,250 fixed) of service department costs have been allocated to the desk department and $47,875 ($23,125 variable + $24,750 fixed) to the cabinet department.

The $71,125 is a component of the desk department manufacturing overhead that is to be allocated to desk production during 1984. The $47,875 is a component of the cabinet department manufacturing overhead that will be allocated to cabinets produced during 1984.

Step-down allocation method

An alternative method of variable service department cost allocation, the *step-down allocation* method, recognizes some of the interaction among service departments. It begins by allocating costs from one service department (usually, but not always, the service department that provides the largest fraction of its output to other service departments) to the remaining service and production departments. Once costs have been allocated from a service department, that service department is no longer considered in future allocation computations.

In the example assume the repair department allocation is first (20 percent of its output goes to the power department, while only 10 percent of the output of the power department goes to the repair department). The $35,000 variable repair and maintenance costs are allocated $7,000 (.2 × $35,000) to the power department, $17,500 (.5 × $35,000) to desk production, and $10,500 (.3 × $35,000) to cabinet production. After the allocation from the repair department $27,000 ($20,000 + $7,000) is associated with the power department. This amount is allocated equally [(45/(45 + 45))$27,000 = $13,500] to desks and cabinets. This allocation is summarized in the following table.

Power Department	Repair Department	Desks	Cabinets
$ 20,000	$ 35,000		
7,000	(35,000)	$17,500	$10,500
(27,000)		13,500	13,500
–0–	–0–	$31,000	$24,000

The step-down allocation method for variable service department costs results in the allocation of $70,250 ($31,000 variable + $39,250 fixed) of service department costs to the desk department and $48,750 ($24,000 variable + $24,750 fixed) to the cabinet department.

The step down method allocates $875 more service department costs to the cabinet department ($48,750 under direct allocation versus $47,875 under step-down allocation) and $875 less service department costs to the desk department ($71,125 under direct allocation versus $70,250 under step-down allocation) than the direct allocation method.

The method of service department cost allocation affects the amount of departmental manufacturing overhead in the desk and cabinet departments. Since all departmental manufacturing overhead is allocated to departmental output, the unit cost of production of desks and chairs depends on which service department cost allocation method is used.

Other rules for ordering the allocation sequence would lead to different final cost allocations to desks and cabinets. If costs had first been allocated from the power department, the following would result:

Power Department	Repair Department	Desks	Cabinets
$ 20,000	$ 35,000		
(20,000)	2,000	$ 9,000	$ 9,000
	(37,000)	23,125	13,875
–0–	–0–	$32,125	$22,875

Reciprocal allocation method

A third method of allocating variable service department costs to production departments, the *reciprocal allocation method,* recognizes all interactions among service departments and simultaneously determines all cost allocations by solving a system of linear equations. In our example let A_1 and A_2 denote the total cost to be allocated *from* the power department and the repair department, respectively. A_1 consists of the variable cost to the power department plus any costs allocated to it from the repair department. A_2 is similarly defined. Algebraically this can be stated as:

$$A_1 = \$20,000 + .2A_2$$
$$A_2 = \$35,000 + .1A_1$$

Since the power department uses 20 percent of the output of the repair department, it will be allocated 20 percent of the variable costs to be allocated from the repair department. Therefore $20,000 + .2A_2$ must be allocated from the power department. Similar reasoning indicates that $35,000 + .1A_1$ must be allocated from the repair department. The solution to the above two equations in two unknowns is computed as follows:

Substitute the expression for A_1 into the expression for A_2. This results in:

$$A_2 = \$35,000 + .1\ (\$20,000 + .2A_2)$$
$$= \$35,000 + \$2,000 + .02A_2$$
$$.98A_2 = \$37,000$$
$$A_2 = (\$37,000)/(.98)$$
$$= \$37,755$$

Now substitute $A_2 = \$37,755$ into the expression for A_1 to obtain a value for A_1.

$$A_1 = \$20,000 + .2\ (\$37,755)$$
$$= \$20,000 + \$7,551$$
$$= \$27,551$$

The solution to the above two equations is $A_1 = \$27,551$ and $A_2 = \$37,755$. The $27,551 to be allocated from the power department is allocated 10 percent to the repair department, 45 percent to desk production, and 45 percent to cabinet production. The $37,755 to be allocated from the repair department is allocated 20 percent to the power department, 50 percent to desk production, and 30 percent to cabinet production. The allocation is summarized below.

Power Department	Repair Department	Desks	Cabinets
$ 20,000	$ 35,000		
(27,551)	2,755	$12,398	$12,398
7,551	(37,755)	18,878	11,326
–0–	–0–	$31,276	$23,724

Notice that after all allocations are made there are no costs associated with either service department. As in every other approach to variable service department cost allocation, the total variable costs allocated to all production departments ($55,000 in the example) equals the sum of the variable costs in all the service departments.

Depending on which allocation method is used, direct, step-down, or reciprocal, the allocation of costs to the desk department and the cabinet department and the relative costs of desks and cabinets will be different.

The fairness, equity, and logic of arbitrary cost allocation are sometimes questioned. The perception that costs are allocated unfairly can result in serious behavioral and morale problems.

SERVICE DEPARTMENT COSTS: DECISION MAKING

The reciprocal allocation method is the best method to use if the allocated variable service department costs are to be used in decision making. It is the fairest method to use if total manufacturing cost is used as a measure of a production manager's performance.

Future cash flows should be used in making decisions. Future cash flows are frequently projected from historical costs, collected in an accounting system. Variable service department cost allocations under the reciprocal method are the most relevant allocations for projecting the future cost of providing service. In the following example we assume that service department costs do not change over time.

Suppose the current output of the power department is 300,000 kilowatt hours. Using the reciprocal method, desk production is allocated $12,398 for the 135,000 (45 percent of 300,000) kilowatt hours it consumes. From the desk department's perspective the variable cost per kilowatt hour is $.092 ($12,398/135,000). Suppose the manager of desk production is given the authority to contract with outside suppliers of power for small amounts of power. If the external price of a unit of power is less than $.092 per kilowatt hour, the manager would save *departmental* costs by contracting for outside service. This is only desirable from the *firm's* viewpoint, however, if the true internal cost of producing an additional kilowatt hour is $.092 or greater. In general it is true that if the reciprocal method is used to allocate variable costs from service departments then the allocated costs per unit will equal the true incremental economic costs of internal production of the units of service. We will illustrate this in our example.

Suppose the power department is eliminated entirely. The variable costs in the power department, $20,000, will no longer be incurred. Since the power department consumes 20 percent of the output of the repair department, the variable costs in the repair department should also decrease by 20 percent ($7,000 = .2($35,000)) since its output can be cut back by 20 percent. Therefore $27,000 ($20,000 + $7,000) of internal variable costs will be saved if the power department is closed. In order to maintain the same production levels in the desk and cabinet departments we must decide on how many kilowatt hours of power to purchase from external sources. Even though the current output of the power department is 300,000 kilowatt hours only 294,000 kilowatt hours of power will have to be purchased from external sources. The logic is as follows: the desk and cabinet departments will still each require 135,000 kilowatt hours of power. The repair department currently consumes 30,000 kilowatt hours of power, but if the power department closed, then demands for the output of the repair department will decrease by 20 percent, and the repair department will require 24,000 (80 percent of $30,000) kilowatt hours of power. If purchased externally 294,000 kilowatt hours (135,000 + 135,000 + 24,000) will be needed. Since $27,000 in costs would be eliminated by the purchase of 294,000 kilowatt hours from external sources, the incremental cost per kilowatt hour is $.092 ($27,000/294,000). This is precisely the allocated cost per unit under the reciprocal method.

The above analysis is a justification for using the reciprocal cost allocations in decisions to purchase small incremental numbers of kilowatts from external sources. Of course, if all power needs could be purchased externally, then BPI would be willing to pay in excess of $.092 per kilowatt hour. If the power department was shut down, then some fixed costs of power generation would also likely be eliminated.

In addition, if the reciprocal method is used to allocate variable costs, the allocations to individual production departments will be independent of the services consumed by other production departments. This is true because production departments, under reciprocal cost allocation, are always charged for the true economic cost per units of service produced during the period.

PROBLEMS AND CASES

18–1 Auto Body Shop Cost Allocation

A typical automobile dealership is usually concerned with six operations: new car sales, used car sales, vehicle service, vehicle body repair, replacement parts sales, and vehicle leasing and rental.

In order to appraise departmental and managerial performance, an income statement is constructed for each of the six above-mentioned operations (cost objectives). This requires that overhead costs of the dealership be allocated to individual operations.

Several overhead costs of a particular dealership, for the year ending December 31, 1985, are given below:

Overhead Cost	Total Dealership Cost
Real estate taxes	$30,000
Building insurance	6,000
Heat, light, and power	50,000
Legal and auditing	8,000
Telephone and telegraph	20,000
Owner's salary	45,000

The following facts relate to the dealership and the body shop operation of the dealership for the year ending December 31, 1985:

	Dealership	Body Shop
Sales	$8,000,000	$700,000
Size of facilities	200,000 square feet	60,000 square feet
Direct labor cost	$600,000	$200,000
Direct labor-hours	100,000	25,000

There is no way to directly trace any of the above six overhead costs to any of the individual dealership operations.

Required:

Suppose that the gross profit of the body shop, before considering any of the above six overhead costs, is $200,000. Develop and justify cost allocation rules to assign the six overhead costs to the various dealership operations. What is the pretax profit of the body shop?

Cost allocation rules and pretax profit of the body shop should be determined using only the information given above. Indicate any additional information that you would like to have in order to make the cost allocations "fairer" and the pretax body shop income a better measure of the success of the body shop operations for the year.

Would you use the body shop income statement to determine if body shop operations are successful and should be continued?

18–2 Yankee Rolling Pin

Yankee Rolling Pin Company is a small New England firm that manufactures wooden rolling pins and wooden shelving from red oak. The oak is purchased from a local saw mill for $.75 per board foot.

Each board foot of red oak is processed on a series of lathes to yield two rolling pins and three pounds of shavings. The lathes are rented on a yearly basis for $10,000 and process 10 board feet of oak per hour. It costs $3.50 per hour to operate the lathes. The unfinished rolling pins are sanded and varnished at a cost of $.20 per rolling pin. The shavings are mixed with chemicals and compressed into boards to be sold as shelving. Every five pounds of shavings yields two shelves. The chemical and pressure treatment costs $.10 per pound of shavings.

Yankee Rolling Pin processes 20,000 board feet of oak in a year. Rolling pins are sold for $1.20 each, and shelves are sold for $.80 each. Yankee has no beginning or planned ending inventories.

Required:

1. What is the amount of joint cost to be allocated to rolling pins and shelves (shavings)?

2. Suppose each rolling pin weighs one pound. Allocate the joint cost to rolling pins and shavings on the basis of weight.

3. What is Yankee Rolling Pin Company's anticipated net income for the year?

4. How many board feet of red oak must be processed in order to just break even (net income equal to zero)?

18–3 Thrift-Shops*

Thrift-Shops, Inc., operates a chain of three food stores in a state that recently enacted legislation permitting municipalities within the state to levy an income tax on corporations operating within their respective municipalities. The legislation establishes a uniform tax rate the municipalities may levy, and regulations provide that the tax is to be computed on income derived within the taxing municipality after a reasonable and consistent allocation of general overhead expenses. General overhead expenses have not been allocated to individual stores previously and include warehouse, general office, advertising, and delivery expenses.

Each of the municipalities in which Thrift-Shops, Inc., operates a store has levied the corporate income tax as provided by state legislation, and management is considering two plans for allocating general overhead expenses to the stores. The 1984 operating results before general overhead and taxes for each store were as follows:

---

* Material from Uniform CPA Examination Questions and Unofficial Answers, © May 1970 by the American Institute of Certified Public Accountants, Inc., is adapted with permission.

	Store			
	Asheville	Burns	Clinton	Total
Sales, net	$416,000	$353,600	$270,400	$1,040,000
Less cost of sales	215,700	183,300	140,200	539,200
Gross margin	200,300	$170,300	$130,200	$ 500,800
Less local operating expenses:				
Fixed	60,800	48,750	50,200	159,750
Variable	54,700	64,220	27,448	146,368
Total	115,500	112,970	77,648	306,118
Income before general overhead and taxes	$ 84,800	$ 57,330	$ 52,552	$ 194,682

General overhead expenses in 1984:		
Warehousing and delivery expenses:		
Warehouse depreciation	$ 20,000	
Warehouse operations	30,000	
Delivery expenses	40,000	$ 90,000
Central office expenses:		
Advertising	18,000	
Central office salaries	37,000	
Other central office expenses	28,000	83,000
Total general overhead		$173,000

Additional information includes the following:

a. One fifth of the warehouse space is used to house the central office, and depreciation on this space is included in other central office expenses. Warehouse operating expenses vary with quantity of merchandise sold.

b. Delivery expenses vary with distance and number of deliveries. The distances from the warehouse to each store and the number of deliveries made in 1984 were as follows:

Store	Miles	Number of Deliveries
Asheville	120	140
Burns	200	64
Clinton	100	104

c. All advertising is prepared by the central office and is distributed in the areas in which stores are located.

d. As each store was opened, the fixed portion of central office salaries increased $7,000, and other central office expenses increased $2,500. Basic fixed central office salaries amount to $10,000, and basic fixed other central office expenses amount to $12,000. The remainder of central office salaries and the remainder of other central office expenses vary with sales.

Required:

1. For each of the following plans for allocating general overhead expenses, compute the income of each store that would be subject to the municipal levy on corporation income:

Plan 1: Allocate all general overhead expenses on the basis of sales volume.

Plan 2: First, allocate central office salaries and other central office expenses evenly to warehouse operations and each store. Second, allocate the resulting warehouse operations expense, warehouse depreciation, and advertising to each store on the basis of sales volume. Third, allocate delivery expenses to each store on the basis of delivery miles times number of deliveries.

2. How would the individual municipalities react to each of the above allocations?

3. How would the managers of the individual stores react to each of the above plans if their yearly bonuses were computed as a percentage of their individual store's income? Give arguments that each manager might make for or against a particular allocation.

18–4 Reston, Inc.

Reston, Inc., generates its own electric power and charges the two large producing departments, A and B, at the standard rate of 4 cents per kilowatt hour for the actual amount used each month as shown by departmental meters. The actual cost of producing electricity seldom varies by more than ½ cent from the standard. The foreman for department B, although he considers 4 cents a reasonable standard for the power plant, claims that the total charge against his department is too high. He bases his case on the fact that the load factors in the two departments are very different. Department B's load is nearly constant during all hours of plant operation. Department A's load, however, is quite irregular due to the intermittent operation of three large machines. Three, two, one, or none of these machines may be in operation at any given time. The power plant therefore has to have a large "spinning reserve" to meet the demands of these machines. This means not only that the power plant has to be relatively large, but also that additional variable costs have to be incurred to keep generators spinning with very light loads when two or more machines in department A are off.

The foreman of department B shows that his department could purchase power from the local utility for about 3 cents a kilowatt hour.

Power Plant Costs for April

	Planned*		Actual
Fixed costs	$120,000		$119,000
Variable costs	80,000	(at .016 per kwh)	83,000
	$200,000		$202,000

* Planned April output is 5,000,000 kilowatt hours (2,500,000 kilowatt hours in each department).

Metered Consumption of Kilowatt Hours in April

Department A......	2,600,000
Department B......	2,400,000
	5,000,000

Hourly Demand for Kilowatt Hours during April

	Maximum	Average*	Minimum
Department A	44,000	15,476	5,000
Department B	16,000	14,286	13,000
Combined	58,000	29,762	20,000

* Average demand equals metered consumption divided by hours of operation. There were 168 hours (21 days at 8 hours) of operation in April.

Required:

Using the above data show how you would allocate the power costs for April to departments A and B. The relative maximum hourly power demands for April are typical of the relative maximum demands for every month. The production departments are "charged" for power on a weekly basis. Therefore your allocation rule should depend on planned power consumption and production for the month. Be sure to specify how the departments will be charged for any end-of-month variances. Show actual calculations and give reasons for your conclusions.

18–5 Acme Company

One division of the Acme Company consists of two production departments, P_1 and P_2, and two service departments, a power generation department, S_1, and a maintenance department, S_2. In February the power generation department incurred $30,000 in direct variable costs. Variable direct costs of the maintenance department are $20,000 for the month.

The output of the power department is measured in kilowatt hours (kwh), and the output of the maintenance department is measured in labor-hours.

The following table shows how the output of each service department was used.

Service Department	Variable Direct Costs	Users of Service				Total Output
		S_1	S_2	P_1	P_2	
Power	$30,000	—	180,000	210,000	210,000	600,000 kwh
Maintenance	$20,000	1,200	—	1,400	1,400	4,000 hrs.

Required:

1. Allocate the service department costs to production departments using the direct allocation method.

2. Allocate the service department costs to production departments using the step-down allocation method.

3. Allocate the service department costs to production departments using the reciprocal allocation method.

4. In addition to the variable costs of power generation traceable to the power department, there is $50,000 monthly fixed charge for renting the generator. Under the current rental agreement Acme can break the rental contract at the end of any month without penalty.

Acme has just been offered the opportunity to purchase all of its necessary power requirements from an outside power producer. Acme management is scheduled to attend a meeting to discuss the price of outside power within the next week. What is the maximum price per kilowatt hour that Acme should pay for outside power? (Be sure to list any assumptions you make.)

18–6 Wastewater Treatment Costs Allocation*

It would seem that a reasonably fair method of charging residential and industrial customers for the costs of wastewater collection and treatment could be developed and administered without much difficulty.

Civil engineers have identified the components of the cost of wastewater treatment as:

1. Cost of biochemical oxygen demand (BOD) expressed in pounds per day.

2. Cost of removing a pound of suspended solids.

---

* Excerpted from R. L. Blamey, "Setting Sewage Treatment User Charge Rates: A Cost/Benefit Approach," *Management Accounting,* December 1978, pp. 32–36, with permission.

3. Cost of removing a pound of phosphorus.

4. Cost of moving 1,000 cubic feet of liquid through the system.

The first three factors concern the strength of the wastewater, and the fourth pertains to volume. To measure strength requires sophisticated tests of effluent. Such tests usually are performed only on industrial customers. To measure volume, the easiest and most common method—although not the most exact one—is to assume it equals the customer's water use.

In the case of wet industries and other industrial users where strengths and components of strength vary, a combination of charges for volume (usually measured at the in-plant water source) and strength (usually determined by laboratory tests) is a reasonable basis of charge. Inflow can be a problem here, too, unless it is effectively policed or the volume of wastewater is metered.

The problem often lies in finding agreement as to just what costs the different classes of users should pay for—and whether some costs should be recovered at all from users. Unfortunately, this problem sometimes doesn't surface until the users (usually local wet industries, such as leather tanneries and cheese factories) realize that their sewerage cost is about to increase by 400 percent or more.

Costs of a wastewater collection and treatment system can be organized into these categories:

Costs attributable to excess capacity. Normally, wastewater treatment plants are built to handle load requirements 20 or more years from date of construction. If the engineers can define excess capacity and if a cost can be attributed to it, that cost might not be charged to present users, who receive no benefit from unused capacity; but instead deferred through long-term refinancing of debt service on excess capacity. There is some authoritative support for charging such debt service to property in the form of an ad valorem tax.

Costs attributable to infiltration and inflow. Inflow adds to both the cost of capacity and to operating and maintenance costs associated with volume. Since this water is basically rain water or subsurface ground water, costs of strength treatment are nil.

Cost attributable to administrative and office activities. Administrative and clerical services for billing, personnel management expenses, general insurance, building heat, communications, custodial and employee education and training might be charged on either a fixed or variable (full absorption) basis.

All other costs. These costs would be, ideally and logically, those attributed to handling the volume and strength of effluent contributed to the system. Accordingly, they would be distributed to the four strength and volume costs listed at the beginning of this article.

Assume that Small City, USA, sewage treatment costs for next year are budgeted as follows:

Categories of Cost	Variable	Fixed	Total
Debt service cost, associated with excess capacity		$ 350,000	$ 350,000
Infiltration and inflow costs:			
Debt service		150,000	150,000
Operating and maintenance		140,000	140,000
Administration and office overhead costs		360,000	360,000
Sewage volume and strength costs	$1,000,000		1,000,000
Total costs	$1,000,000	$1,000,000	$2,000,000

Assume also that the city's engineering firm was able to identify and measure the volume and strength likely to be contributed from the various classes of users. For simplicity, the volume/strength factor will be referred to as V/S units. In the real world it would be identified and measured in terms of the four cost factors (BOD, etc.) mentioned earlier.

Assume that Small City, USA, has the following user census profile.

User Class	Number of Users	Volume/Strength (V/S) Units per Year
Wet industry	3	80,000
Commercial and dry industry	150	50,000
Residential	9,847	120,000
Total	10,000	250,000

Required:

1. Suppose that Small City, USA, charges for wastewater treatment as follows: Total budgeted sewage treatment costs for next year are divided by the estimated number of V/S units for the year to obtain a charge per V/S unit (similar to finding a factory overhead allocation rate). Using this method of charging for wastewater treatment, determine the total user charge for each user class in Small City. Is this a fair approach? Explain. What are likely reactions of different user classes to this approach?

2.   An alternate wastewater charging scheme has been proposed. Determine a charge per V/S unit for the budgeted variable costs of treatment, recover the $500,000 in debt service costs through an ad valorem (based on value) property tax, and allocate the remaining $500,000 in fixed costs equally to each of the 10,000 users. Determine the total user charge for each user class in Small City. Is this a "fairer" approach than the above? How are users likely to react to this approach? Which approach do you think Small City should prefer? Why?

18–7   Patient Costs*

The hospital industry has been paid historically for services by medicare, medicaid, and sometimes Blue Cross on a cost-per-day-basis and by commercial insurance companies on a charge basis. While these methods often may seem to bear some resemblance to cost of services, rarely do they actually measure the resources utilized by a particular patient or a group of patients. There is increased interest in an approach that does this. It has been kindled by the hope for lowering costs for payors, and since the federal government, through its agencies, is the largest of these groups, it has shown keen interest.

The most widely known system of this kind is called Diagnostic Related Group (DRG). It categorizes a patient by the particular diagnosis or disease. In addition to the particular diagnosis, the classification system might also consider secondary diagnosis, operative procedure, or age to refine patient classification. The ability to classify and quantify case mix through the use of DRGs was developed by the Center for Health Service Research of Yale University. The 383 DRGs are formed by subdividing 83 major diagnostic categories into disease groupings that have similar resource consumption patterns as measured by length of stay. An example of a particular DRG is Disease of Vascular System with Surgery with Age Greater than 50 years. Three other DRGs deal with the vascular system, but they consider a secondary diagnosis or the presence or absence of a surgical procedure. Once the patient has been classified in a particular DRG, the next step is to accumulate the resources utilized. Several items are required, including a uniform bill, cost data, and some allocation statistics.

The uniform bill would contain the information associated with the patient's diagnostic data plus certain financial and statistical data. Common diagnostic data would be the length of the patient's stay, any operative procedures, services such as lab and x-ray, discharge diagnosis, and other

---

* Excerpted from M. F. Gleason, "DRG: Another Way to Reimburse Costs," *Management Focus,* November–December 1979, p. 23. Reprinted from *Management Focus* magazine, copyright November 1979 by Peat, Marwick, Mitchell & Co., New York City.

related medical facts regarding the patient's stay. The financial, and statistical data take the form of charges for services or the specific number of tests or procedures. Using this, together with the cost and various allocation statistics, we can determine the cost per case. The cost information relates to the actual costs incurred in running a particular department, such as housekeeping. The allocation statistics are used as a basis for distributing the cost of a specific department to departments receiving that service. For example, hours of service might be used as an allocation basis to distribute the costs of housekeeping to the departments utilizing the service.

As it is evident that nursing is directly related to patient care, it would seem impossible to segregate the cost applicable to a particular patient. However, a few nursing studies completed across the country attempt to give nursing weights to each DRG. One such study has a fixed intensity of service for each DRG in addition to a variable portion which is dependent upon the length of stay. The fixed intensity was based upon certain valuations of nursing time spent. These nursing weights are considered resource measurements. As an example DRG number 38 might have a fixed intensity of five while DRG number 43 might have an intensity of seven. These weights, both fixed and variable portions, are accumulated in total. The total weights for all patients are divided into the nursing costs to develop a factor, which is used in conjunction with the nursing weights to develop the cost consumed for a patient in a specific DRG.

Suppose, in a particular hospital, nursing costs and resource units are as follows:

Total nursing costs $3,000,000
Total nursing resource units...... 300,000

The allocation of housekeeping is slightly more complicated as it affects the nursing areas, the ancillary departments, and those indirectly related to patient care. Initially, housekeeping costs are allocated to departments utilizing housekeeping services. The costs that have been distributed to nursing areas are allocated to a particular patient's DRG based on standard weights for each day of the stay.

In the hypothetical hospital assume housekeeping costs allocated to nursing areas and the number of standard housekeeping units are as follows:

Housekeeping costs for patient care...... $300,000
Patient care housekeeping units 60,000

The housekeeping costs assigned to ancillary departments are allocated to the DRG based on patient ancillary service charges or statistics, whichever is used.

The hypothetical hospital has one ancillary department, a laboratory. The total laboratory costs (direct plus allocated) and the total relative value units (used to assign laboratory costs to patients) are as follows:

Direct costs .... $ 970,000
Housekeeping allocation 30,000
Total $1,000,000
Relative value unit (statistical) 1,000,000

Accounting costs are an expense of doing business but are not directly related to patient care and therefore might best be allocated evenly among all patients on admission.

Direct accounting costs	$290,000
Housekeeping allocation......	10,000
Total	$300,000
Total admissions	10,000

Required:

Patient DRG, number 43, has just been discharged. Determine the costs of providing these services to this patient who has consumed 13 nursing resource units, 5.5 housekeeping units, and 143 relative value units of laboratory service. Is this a fair measure of the "true cost" to provide these services to this patient? Would it be fair to base patient charges (and to bill medicaid and medicare) on the above allocated costs?

19

The contribution approach to net income: Variable costing and break-even analysis

Cost behavior is not readily apparent from absorption (full) costing income statements because full unit costs are composites of both variable and fixed manufacturing costs. Variable costing is an alternative costing method that highlights the contribution margin (selling price minus variable costs) of the units sold and the difference between variable and fixed costs.

VARIABLE COSTING

In variable costing, units produced are valued at the variable cost to produce them. Fixed factory overhead is treated as an expense in the accounting period in which it is incurred, rather than treated as a cost of units produced as it is in absorption costing.

Since fixed factory overhead costs are not averaged over differential numbers of units produced in each period, variable costing income is dependent on sales volume and is independent of fluctuations in the production level. There is no fixed factory overhead volume variance in the variable costing income statement because all of the fixed factory overhead is charged to expense.

ILLUSTRATION 19–1.   Sample Variable Costing Income Statement

Sales		$20,500,000
Less variable costs:		
Manufacturing	$8,020,000	
Selling	1,500,000	
General and administrative	380,000	9,900,000
Contribution margin		10,600,000
Less fixed costs:		
Manufacturing	6,627,000	
Selling	2,285,000	
General and administrative	1,149,000	10,061,000
Pretax income		$ 539,000

Variable costing is used primarily for internal decision making and is not allowable for either the preparation of external financial statements (GAAP) or to determine income taxable by the federal government.

An example of a variable costing income statement is shown in Illustration 19–1.

Variable costing: Example

To illustrate the valuation of inventory and calculation of net income using variable costing we can use data for the Aero Manufacturing Company, shown in Illustration 19–2. Aero Manufacturing began operations in 1984 and manufactures electronic components for the aerospace industry. The data in Illustration 19–2 are indentical to the Chapter 16 data, which were used to construct Aero Manufacturing's absorption (full) costing income statement.

Comparison of variable costing and absorption costing

Illustration 19–3 presents both the variable costing and absorption costing income statements for Aero Manufacturing Company.

A comparison of these income statements shows that the only substantive difference between absorption and variable costing income is the treatment of fixed factory overhead costs. This difference is reflected in three income statement line items: cost of goods sold, fixed factory overhead, and fixed factory overhead volume variance. Variable cost of goods sold is $461,250 (9,000 units sold at $51.25). Absorption cost of goods sold, which includes fixed factory overhead of $10 per unit, is $551,250. The difference is $90,000 (9,000 units × 5 direct labor-hours × $2 per direct labor-hour) of

ILLUSTRATION 19–2. **Aero Manufacturing: Manufacturing Cost Data for 1984 (no beginning or ending work in process inventories)**

Actual Direct Manufacturing Costs
10,000 Components Produced

Raw materials (average cost of $15 per component)	$150,000
Direct labor (average 5 direct labor-hours per component at $6.50/hour)	$325,000

Factory Overhead Costs

Beginning-of-year estimates for factory overhead costs:

Fixed factory overhead:		
Depreciation	$50,000	
Supervision	80,000	
Insurance	10,000	
Other	10,000	$150,000
Variable factory overhead (assuming 75,000 direct labor-hours will be worked in 1984):		
Lubricants	37,500	
Miscellaneous supplies	18,750	56,250
Total estimated factory overhead		$206,250

Factory overhead allocation rates:	
Fixed ($150,000/75,000 direct labor-hours)	$2/dlh
Variable ($56,250/75,000 direct labor-hours)	$.75/dlh
Actual factory overhead costs:	
Fixed	$150,000
Variable (50,000 direct labor-hours worked in 1984)	38,500
Total	$188,500

Average Absorption Cost per Unit

Raw materials	$15.00
Direct labor (5 hours at $6.50 on average)	32.50
Fixed factory overhead (5 hours at $2.)	10.00
Variable factory overhead (5 hours at $.75)	3.75
Total	$61.25

fixed factory overhead in absorption costing cost of goods sold but not in variable costing cost of goods sold.

There is no $50,000 fixed overhead volume variance in the variable costing statement. Instead Aero's entire fixed factory overhead for the year, $150,000, is expensed. The variable factory overhead spending variance appears in both statements, and the fixed and variable selling expenses also are identical (in both approaches selling expenses equal the actual costs incurred during the period).

ILLUSTRATION 19–3. **Aero Manufacturing: A Comparison of Variable Costing and Absorption (Full) Costing Incomes for 1984**

	Variable Costing	Absorption Costing
Sales revenue		
(9,000 at $115)	$1,035,000	$1,035,000
Cost of goods sold	461,250 (9,000 at $51.25)	551,250 (9,000 at $61.25)
Gross margin	573,750	483,750
Variable factory overhead variance	(1,000)	(1,000)
Fixed factory overhead volume variance		(50,000)
Adjusted gross margin	572,750	432,750
Fixed factory overhead	150,000	–0–
Fixed selling expenses	100,000	100,000
Variable selling expenses (9,000 at $10)	90,000	90,000
Pretax net income	$ 232,750	$ 242,750
Ending inventory	$ 51,250 (1,000 at $51.25)	$ 61,250 (1,000 at $61.25)

(handwritten notes: "included freight", "because we don't include any f.o+. this related to no variance their in all expense under")

The difference in net income computed using absorption (full) and variable costing is due only to the different amounts of fixed factory overhead in the two income statements. Illustration 19–4 reconciles absorption costing and variable costing incomes and ending inventory values for Aero Manufacturing.

Contribution margin and the contribution format income statement _____

An alternative format for the variable costing income statement is presented in Illustration 19–5.

This format, which focuses on the difference between all variable and all fixed costs (including selling and administrative), is frequently called a contribution income statement. The difference between sales revenue and all variable expenses (including variable selling expense and allocated variable factory overhead) is called the contribution margin. For a single product firm the unit contribution margin is the contribution margin divided by the number of units sold. The average unit contribution margin for Aero Manufacturing's products is $53.75 ($115 selling price less $15 direct material costs, $32.50 direct labor costs, $3.75 variable factory overhead, and $10 variable selling costs). The total contribution margin is $483,750 (9,000 × $53.75) for the 9,000 units sold. After adjusting for the varia-

ILLUSTRATION 19–4. **Reconciliation of Absorption Costing Income with Variable Costing Income**

Absorption costing fixed factory overhead:	
In cost of goods sold (9,000 at $10)	$ 90,000
Fixed factory overhead volume variance	50,000
Total fixed factory overhead in 1984	
income statement	140,000
Variable costing fixed factory overhead:	
Actual fixed factory overhead in 1984	
income statement	150,000
Difference	(10,000)
Absorption costing pretax net income	242,750
Variable costing pretax net income	$232,750
Ending inventories:	
Ending inventory value: Absorption costing	$ 61,250
Less: Fixed costs in ending inventory (1,000 at $10)	10,000
Ending inventory value: Variable costing	$ 51,250

ble factory overhead variance, actual fixed costs are subtracted from the adjusted contribution margin to obtain pretax net income of $232,750.

Unit contribution margin measures the contribution the sale of

ILLUSTRATION 19–5

Aero Manufacturing Company	
Variable Costing Income Statement (Contribution Format)	
Sales revenue (9,000 at $115)	$1,035,000
Less variable costs:	
Raw materials (9,000 at $15)	135,000
Direct labor (9,000 at $32.50)	292,500
Standard variable factory overhead (9,000 at $3.75)	33,750
Variable selling (9,000 at $10)	90,000
Contribution margin	483,750
Variable factory overhead variance	1,000
Adjusted contribution margin	482,750
Less fixed costs:	
Factory overhead	150,000
Selling	100,000
Pretax net income	$ 232,750
Ending inventory (1,000 at $51.25)	$ 51,250

an individual unit makes to covering fixed costs and generating income.

Variable costing and decision making

The contribution format for variable costing heightens management's awareness of relevant-cost classifications and patterns of cost behavior. Most important, profit (net income) is primarily determined by sales rather than by sales and production as in absorption (full) costing.

Although unit variable costs and contribution margins are useful in short-term decision making, the manager should be aware that unit variable costs of production understate the long-run average cost of producing a unit. They do not include the fixed costs of production, which certainly must be incurred if goods are to be manufactured and which must be covered by selling prices in the long run if the firm is to remain in business.

Sales equal production

If sales equal production and costs are stable *through time* net income under absorption (full) and variable costing should be the same. The fixed factory overhead in the units sold plus the fixed factory overhead volume variance which is charged on the absorption (full) costing income statement will be equal to actual fixed cost which is charged on the variable costing income statement.

Assume in the Aero Manufacturing example that both production and sales were 9,000 components in 1984. Illustration 19–6 demonstrates that absorption (full) costing pretax income will be $232,750 which is equal to variable costing pretax income when 9,000 units are sold (Illustration 19–3).

ILLUSTRATION 19–6

Aero Manufacturing Company Absorption Costing Income Statement (production and sales equal 9,000 components)	
Sale revenue (9,000 at $115)	$1,035,000
Cost of goods sold (9,000 at $61.25)	551,250
Gross margin	483,750
Variable factory overhead variance	(1,000)
Fixed factory overhead volume variance	(60,000)
Adjusted gross margin	442,750
Variable selling (9,000 at $10)	90,000
Fixed selling	100,000
Pretax net income	$ 232,750
Ending inventory	$ –0–

The reason income is the same is that the total fixed factory overhead cost is the same in both statements.

Absorption costing:

Fixed factory overhead in cost of goods sold (9,000 at $10)	$ 90,000
Fixed factory overhead volume variance (underabsorbed fixed factory overhead)	60,000
Fixed factory overhead in absorption costing income	$150,000

Variable costing:

Actual fixed factory overhead in variable costing income	$150,000

if you spend more than you allocate then you are under absorbing the cost.

Actual and estimated fixed factory overhead is $150,000. Allocated fixed factory overhead is $90,000 (9,000 components × 5 direct labor-hours per component × $2 allocated fixed factory overhead per direct labor-hour). The fixed factory overhead volume variance, representing underabsorbed fixed factory overhead is $60,000 ($150,000 − 9,000 units at $10).

If prices are reasonably stable and inventory levels are relatively constant (production approximates sales), then variable costing income is a good approximation to absorption (full) costing income. The variable costing income statement in contribution format makes apparent the effects of various managerial actions on reported income. For example, if production equals sales and Aero was to produce and sell one more component in 1984, the expected increase in variable costing income is $53.75, the unit contribution margin. Because it is very unlikely that additional fixed costs would be incurred for the production of only one more unit, absorption (full) costing income will probably also increase $53.75.

BREAK-EVEN ANALYSIS

fixed = f. FOH, f. selling, f. admin.

Many firms are interested in how many units they must sell in a period in order to cover *all* their fixed costs of the period and break even. A company's fixed costs include fixed factory overhead costs, fixed selling costs, and fixed administrative cost. The break-even point (BEP) is the level of sales that generates neither a profit nor a loss. The unit contribution margin is the key to computing the BEP.

Let p = Selling price per unit ($115)
v = Total variable cost per unit ($61.25)
F = Total fixed costs per period ($250,000)
x = Number of units sold in a period

The break-even point is expressed algebraically as:

selling price - Total [handwritten]

$$(p - v)x = F \text{ (Contribution margin at BEP equals fixed costs)}$$

$$BEP = x = \frac{F}{(p - v)}$$

Total Fixed costs/per. [handwritten]

Selling price - total var.cost/unit [handwritten]

The break-even point for Aero Manufacturing is approximately 4,651 units. It is equal to fixed (manufacturing and selling) costs of \$250,000 divided by the unit contribution margin of \$53.75. The break-even point can also be expressed in terms of dollars of sales required to break even (BEPs).

$$BEPs = (BEP)p = \frac{Fp}{(p - v)} = \frac{F}{\dfrac{(p - v)}{p}}$$

$(p - v)/p$ is called the contribution margin ratio, the portion of every sales dollar that goes to covering fixed costs. Aero Company's contribution margin ratio is \$53.75/\$115 ≈ .4674. If every sales dollar contributes 46.74 cents toward covering overhead, it will take \$250,000/.4674 ≈ \$534,874 total sales dollars (4,651 components at \$115) to cover \$250,000 in fixed costs in addition to all variable costs and just break even.

Let π denote variable costing income. The contribution margin, the break-even point, and variable costing income are related according to the following equation:

$$\pi = px - vx - F = (p - v)x - F$$
$$= \$115x - \$61.25x - \$250,000$$
$$= \$53.75x - \$250,000$$

x = # of units sold per period. [handwritten]

The above profit equation is called a cost-volume-profit (CVP) model since it relates sales volume and costs to profits; $p - v$ is the unit contribution margin, and $(p - v)x$ is the total contribution margin. Profits will be positive as long as the total contribution covers (is at least as large or exceeds) fixed costs. When $\pi = 0$, $(p - v)x$ equals F, and the break-even point is reached.

Illustration 19–7 is a graphical representation of the CVP model. In the upper portion Aero Manufacturing Company's expenses (costs) and revenues are plotted individually. Profit at any particular level is measured as the vertical distance (parallel to the \$ axis)

508

ILLUSTRATION 19–7. **Break-Even Chart (Cost-Volume-Profit Graph)**

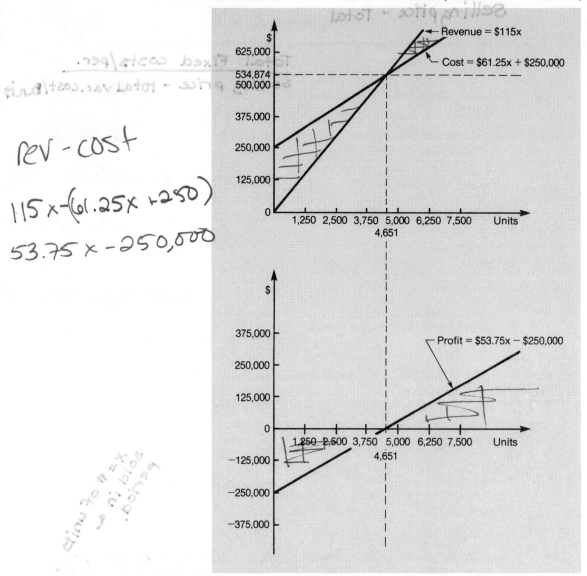

between the revenue line and the cost line. At a sales level of 1,000 units revenues are $115,000, total costs are $311,250 ($61,250 + $250,000), and a loss of $196,250 results. At any sales level where the cost curve is below the revenue curve Aero would experience a profit. The BEP is the intersection of the revenue and cost lines in the upper portion of Illustration 19–7 and the intersection of the profit line with the sales axis in the lower portion.

Frequently the profit equation is plotted directly (revenues and costs are not shown separately) making it easier to read what profit levels will be for given sales levels. See the lower portion of the chart.

Cost volume profit model and decision making

The CVP model is a compact expression that generates abbreviated variable costing income statements for any sales level assuming total fixed costs and variable costs per unit do not change. The CVP model variable costing statements are not actual income statements. They represent expectations about income if everything occurs as planned. The following examples illustrate the usefulness of the CVP model as a managerial tool.

Example: Sales necessary for a given profit level. At what sales level will Aero generate profits of $300,000? Illustration 19–7 can be used to find that a sales level of approximately 10,233 components generates $300,000 profit. Algebraically the basic CVP equation can be used.

$$\$300,000 = \$53.75x - \$250,000$$

$$x = \frac{\$300,000 + \$250,000}{\$53.75 \text{ per component}} = 10,233 \text{ components}$$

$$\left(\text{In general: } x = \frac{F + \text{Desired profit}}{(p - v)} \right)$$

Example: Cost changes. Suppose Aero Manufacturing's fixed costs per period increase from $250,000 to $300,000 due to an increase in property taxes. Market conditions will not permit the selling price to be raised above the current $115 per unit. What will Aero's variable cost have to decrease to in order to maintain a profit level of $232,750? From the basic equation: Profit $= (p - v)x - F$. Therefore:

$$\$232,750 = (\$115 - v)\,(9,000) - \$300,000$$

$$\frac{\$532,750}{9,000} = \$115 - v$$

$$v = \$55.81$$

Aero must introduce cost-cutting measures that reduce variable costs by $5.44 per unit from their current $61.25 per unit level in order to maintain profit levels at $232,750 per year.

Break-even points and future cash flows

The objective of a firm's management is to maximize the wealth of the firm (subject to socially acceptable behavior, of course). Wealth is generally measured by cash flow, and managers therefore should choose among alternatives on the basis of their effects on future cash flows, not on their effects on future reported accounting net income. Variable costing income statements make it easier for managers to focus on the cash flow effects of alternatives when making several common short-run decisions. Management also estimates cash flow from operations to plan their long- and short-term financing needs.

Noncash expenses

Since the focus should be on cash flows in decision making, adjustments must usually be made to variable costing income statements so that net income corresponds to net cash inflow. Depreciation on the factory, a noncash expense, requires such an adjustment. Assume that all items listed on the variable costing income statement correspond to cash flows of the period with the exception of depreciation.

The graphs in Illustration 19–7 and the previous break-even computations are based on variable costing income and not cash flows. For instance, if 4,651 units are produced and sold net income will be zero but there will be a net cash inflow of $50,000 for the year because depreciation does not correspond to a cash outflow in the period.

The break-even point for cash flow for Aero Manufacturing is approximately 3,721 units. It is equal to fixed cost of $200,000 ($250,000 fixed costs minus $50,000 depreciation, which is not a cash flow) divided by the unit contribution margin of $53.75. The BEP in terms of dollars of sales is $427,915 (3,721 units at $115). If x represents the number of units produced and sold during the period, the equation for *net cash flow* for the period is:

$$\text{Cash flow} = \$53.75x - \$200,000$$

If $x = 4,651$ units, the accounting income BEP, then net cash flow will be $50,000 ($53.75 × 4,651 − $200,000).

Example: Incremental business.   Aero Manufacturing has the opportunity to sell one more unit in 1984 at a reduced sales price of $80. Is Aero better off if it sells this 9,001st unit?

Cost of producing 9,000 units $= \$61.25(9,000) + \$200,000 = \$751,250$

Cost of producing 9,001 units $= \$61.25(9,001) + \$200,000 = \$751,311.25$

The incremental cash outflow to produce and sell one more unit is $61.25, which also is the variable cost of production and selling. Since Aero receives $80 for selling the unit, it will be better off. An alternative approach is to note that the unit contribution margin for the additional unit is $80 − $61.25 = $18.75, which is positive. Aero will be better off producing and selling the unit since it contributes $18.75 to covering fixed costs (which haven't changed) and increasing cash flow.

Assumptions made in break-even analysis

Break-even computations are valid only if several crucial assumptions are satisfied. One of these assumptions is that the fixed costs in the break-even chart are equal to the fixed costs in the absorption costing income statement. Since this is only true when production equals sales, the break-even analysis assumes that production equals sales during the period.

If inventory levels change (production does not equal sales) from the beginning to the end of the period, absorption and variable costing incomes will not be equal, and a cost-volume-profit analysis can give misleading results.

If inventory levels change, the equation for net cash flow is also invalid since it ignores the cash outflow required to produce modules added to inventory.

Other assumptions underlying the CVP model include the following. Efficiency of personnel and machines over all levels of operation is constant; variable costs are linear and stable and fixed costs unchanging over the full range of operations being considered; and the firm produces a single product or multiple products in a predetermined ratio.

If the above assumptions are reasonably valid the CVP model can be used to *describe* the profit and cash flow behavior of a firm and generate valuable insights that assist profit planning and decision making. Its usefulness is usually limited to analyzing small changes in p, v, x, or F. Large assumed changes in model parameters (particularly the sales level, x) are likely to invalidate the model's assumptions. For instance, output probably cannot be tripled without incurring additional fixed costs. The basic CVP model has been extended to multiple product settings and to allow for uncertainty in the variable or fixed cost components of the model. These extensions are beyond the scope of this chapter.

PROBLEMS AND CASES

19-1 Eysen Manufacturing

The Eysen Manufacturing Company produces a single product, which it sells for $20 per unit. In 1984 the actual variable manufacturing costs amounted to $5 per unit. Fixed factory overhead is allocated to units produced at the rate of $6 per unit (two direct labor hours per unit at $3 per direct labor-hour). The $3 allocation rate is based on estimated fixed factory overhead cost of $600,000 for the year and 200,000 direct labor-hours of work for the year.

Variable selling and administrative costs amount to $4 per unit sold. Actual fixed factory overhead cost for the year was $600,000. On average it took two direct labor-hours to produce a unit in 1984. Eysen Manufacturing never has work in process inventories. Beginning finished goods inventory was 10,000 units, and the ending 1984 finished goods inventory consisted of 20,000 units. Sales amounted to 70,000 units for the year. Eysen Manufacturing uses LIFO for finished goods inventory. Fixed selling and administrative costs amounted to $100,000 during 1984.

Any fixed factory overhead variance is written off to cost of goods sold at the end of the year.

Required:

1. Prepare an income statement for the year as it would appear under absorption costing.

2. Prepare an income statement for the year as it would appear under variable costing (prepare this statement in two different formats).

3. Explain the difference in net income as calculated in (1) and (2).

19-2 Jensen Company

The Jensen Company operates under a full cost system. Manufacturing variances are never deferred but are reported each month as gains or losses on the income statement. Selling and administrative expenses are treated as period costs.

The company's budgeted monthly sales volume, production, and costs for a normal month are as follows:

Sales (400,000 units at $3)		$1,200,000
Cost of goods sold:		
Raw material		200,000
Direct labor		400,000
Factory overhead:		
Variable		100,000
Nonvariable		200,000
Total cost of goods sold		900,000
Expenses:		
Selling expense ($40,000 + $.20 per unit sold)		120,000
General and administrative expense		
($30,000 + $.10 per unit sold)		70,000
Total selling and administrative		
expense		190,000
Total expenses		1,090,000
Pretax net income		$ 110,000

In May, sales soared to 500,000 units while production fell to only 200,000 units. The president of the company, Mr. Watts, who had risen to his present position through the sales department, was expecting a nice fat profit for May due to the exceptionally high volume of sales. On June 6, the controller presented the May income statement. Mr. Watts was shocked when he saw that the net income was only $55,000, which was less than half the amount budgeted for a normal month.

Required:

1. Calculate the net income Mr. Watts expected (based on the budget) for the month of May.

2. Explain the difference between the net income Mr. Watts expected and actual net income.

3. What net income would have been reported if the Jensen Company used the variable costing system in May?

19–3 Big Time Manufacturing

The Big Time Manufacturing Company recently hired (January 1, 1984) a new chief executive to assume start-up responsibility (marketing strategy, advertising, production levels, and so forth) for its new operations. In addition to a generous salary, the new executive officer is to be given a bonus amounting to 20 percent of net income from operations (before income taxes or the bonus) computed using GAAP.

Big Time sells its single product for $6 per unit. The estimated production level for the year, 50,000 units, is used to allocate the estimated fixed manufacturing overhead cost ($150,000) to units of final product [allocation rate is equal to $3 ($150,000/50,000) per unit produced].

On December 31, 1984, the results of operations for the year are collected:

Sales	40,000 units
Production	60,000 units
Fixed costs:	
Manufacturing overhead	$150,000
Selling	$ 70,000
Variable costs (per unit):	
Manufacturing	$1.00
Selling	$ .70

Required:

1. What is the amount of the bonus the new officer earned in 1984?

2. Calculate income before bonus and income taxes for 1984 using the variable costing method. Why does it differ from the absorption costing income figure computed in (1) above? Did the officer "deserve" the bonus?

3. Assume sales continue at a level of 40,000 units a year and costs do not change. What is your assessment of the success of Big Time's operations? Which of the two income statements (variable costing or absorption costing) presents an income figure consistent with your assessment?

4. Would your evaluation of the executive's performance change if you knew that sales would increase to 80,000 units next year? Why?

19–4 VEXatious Corporation

The VEXatious Corporation assembles product X from two components, V and E. The company is divided into three departments called V, E, and X after the products they make. Departments V and E transfer all of their outputs to department X. All of the output of department X is sold to outside customers.

In December detailed plans for the next calendar year are prepared, and the prices at which department X will be billed for components V and E are set (these prices are called transfer prices). Transfer prices are not changed during the year. A selling price for the finished product X is also set. This price may vary somewhat as market conditions change, but the company tries to maintain its set price.

The plan for 1985, prepared in December 1984, calls for the manufacture and sale of 12,000 units of X.

The same plan on a per-unit basis follows. (Each figure in the plan for the year is divided by 12,000.) None of the departments have any beginning raw material, work in process, or finished product inventories, and no ending inventories are planned.

The company's sales are seasonal, with a high plateau in November and December. In 1985 sales are expected to be 800 units of X a month

Plan for 1985

	Dept. V	Dept. E	Dept. X	Consolidated
Variable production costs*	$ 48,000	$144,000	$ 48,000	$240,000
Nonvariable production costs	24,000	96,000	60,000	180,000
Transfer price— Component V	—	—	108,000	—
Transfer price— Component E	—	—	288,000	—
Variable selling and administrative expenses	12,000	24,000	24,000	60,000
Nonvariable selling and administrative expenses	12,000	12,000	36,000	60,000
Net profit	12,000	12,000	36,000	60,000
Budgeted sales (and transfers)	$108,000	$288,000	$600,000	$600,000

* Exclusive of transfers.

Planned Costs and Prices per Unit—1985

	Dept. V	Dept. E	Dept. X	Consolidated
Variable production costs*	$4	$12	$ 4	$20
Nonvariable production costs	2	8	5	15
Transfer price—Component V	—	—	9	—
Transfer price—Component E	—	—	24	—
Variable selling and administrative expenses	1	2	2	5
Nonvariable selling and administrative expenses	1	1	3	5
Net profit	1	1	3	5
Sales (transfer) price	$9	$24	$50	$50

* Exclusive of transfers.

for each of the 10 months, January through October, and 2,000 units each in November and December. Departments E and X can easily adjust output to shipments, even up to 2,000 units a month, but irregular production is very costly in department V. The manager of V therefore accepts the 1985 budget as authority for producing 1,000 units a month throughout the year.

Each manager has correctly computed the break-even point for his department viewed as an independent entity. These break-even points are:

For V, 9,000 units a year or 750 a month.

For E, 10,800 units a year or 900 a month.

For X, 8,727 units a year or 727 a month.

Required:

1. What is the break-even point for the company as a whole?

2. What net profit will department V show for each of the first 10 months

during which it produces 1,000 units and "sells" 800 units to department X if it uses absorption costing? Variable costing?

3.   Assume now that each department produces 1,000 units a month during 1985. Sales are 800 units a month for 10 months and 2,000 units a month in November and December. What net profit would be shown for June and for December if the company uses absorption costing? Variable costing?

4.   There is a rumor among employees that the company earns all of its profit for the year in the last two months. Is this true? Explain.

5.   Suppose all company costs, with the exception of $50,000 in nonvariable production costs representing depreciation, are paid in cash and that all sales of X to outside customers are cash sales. What will the cash flow from operations be if VEXatious produces and sells exactly the break-even point number of units computed in 1? How many units of X must be sold to have a zero net cash flow from operations (break-even point cash flow)?

19–5   Kadok Corporation

The Kadok Corporation manufactures three grades of cameras, which are sold to a distributor in 1,000-unit lots. The agreement with the distributor provides that Kadok must supply the following *minimum* quantities of each grade of camera at the price indicated per camera:

Grade	Minimum Quantity	Price
A	20,000	$20
B	10,000	18
C	5,000	17

In addition, the distributor agrees to purchase, *in 1,000-camera lots,* any other cameras of these types that Kadok wants to supply. However, the price per camera within each given grade falls by 20 cents for each 1,000-unit lot taken. (e.g., the price per camera in the 21st 1,000-unit lot of A will be $19.80). All cameras produced by Kadok must be sold to the distributor.

In the coming year, Kadok expects to pay $4 per hour to its workers. In addition, fixed costs of $200,000 and variable overhead costs of 50 percent of direct labor cost will be incurred. Materials and labor per camera will be as follows:

Grade	Materials	Labor
A	$12.00	$2
B	3.60	4
C	3.00	4

Since Kadok had a similar contract last year, there are no beginning inventories, and no cameras are expected to be on hand or in process at the end of the year. Kadok's plant has a capacity of 38,500 direct labor-hours for the coming year.

Required:

1. What is the unit contribution margin for each grade of camera? What is the contribution margin per direct labor-hour in each grade of camera?

2. What is the total contribution margin at the minimum quantity?

3. Assuming Kadok seeks to maximize profit, prepare a schedule showing the number of each grade of camera that will be supplied and the sequence in which they will be supplied (up to full capacity) to the distributor during the coming year. What profit should Kadok expect for the coming year?

4. Assume that quantities below the minimum quantities are supplied in the ratio of 4:2:1 for A, B, and C, respectively, and that quantities above the minimum are supplied in the sequence determined in 3 above. What is the break-even point for Kadok expressed in terms of direct labor-hours? (For this computation only, ignore the provision that cameras must be supplied in 1,000-unit lots.)

19–6 Chrysler Corporation* ───────────────────────

CHICAGO—A sharply lower break-even point should help Chrysler Corporation earn a profit from operations in 1982, a company executive told analysts here.

Robert S. Miller, Jr., executive vice president, finance, said Chrysler will break even if it ships 1,244,000 vehicles in 1982, while in 1981 the company's theoretical break-even point stood at 1,413,000 units. Chrysler actually shipped 1,283,000 units last year.

The lower break-even point assumes Chrysler's cost-cutting programs, including cutbacks in rebates and other marketing outlays, succeed in 1982 as budgeted. The company also must sell more optional features on cars to meet the lower expected break-even point, Mr. Miller said.

A company forecast that it will sell 1,399,000 units this year—predicated on an economic upturn in the second half—means Chrysler will operate solidly in the black for the year if the break-even point is lowered as planned, Mr. Miller added. Chrysler chairman, Lee A. Iacocca, previously has forecast an operating profit in 1982.

Mr. Miller said Chrysler expects U.S. auto shipments in the first quarter to total an annual rate of 9 million vehicles and to fall in the second quarter to an annual rate of 7.9 million. Widespread price rebates have resulted in sales in the first quarter at the expense of the second quarter, he said.

Chrysler's 1981 loss totaled $475.6 million on sales of $10.82 billion.

* Reprinted by permission of *The Wall Street Journal,* © Dow Jones & Company, Inc. March 10, 1982. All rights reserved.

Required:

Use the chart below in conjunction with the information in the preceding Journal article to answer the following questions.

Total Contribution Margin

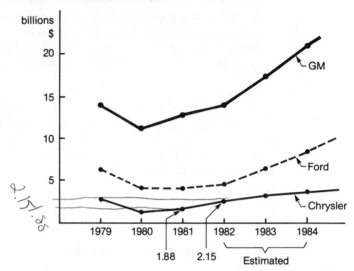

Source: *Business Week,* June 21, 1982, p. 82. Reprinted with permission.

1. What is Chrysler's average unit contribution margin per vehicle in 1982? In 1981?

2. What are Chrysler's fixed costs in 1982? In 1981?

3. What was Chrysler's average variable cost per vehicle in 1981? The average 1981 sales price per vehicle?

4. What is Chrysler's 1982 budgeted profit? Given Chrysler's 1982 budgeted sales level what would budgeted profits have been if all costs and revenues in 1982 were identical to those in 1981? If the budgeted sales level for 1982 is met do Chrysler's cost-cutting measures seem successful?

5. Do the above computations deal with breaking even in terms of cash flows or accounting income? Are they the same? (Explain.)

6. Suppose Chrysler allocates fixed factory overhead costs on a unit-of-production basis and that they charge over- or underapplied overhead to income for the year. Assuming all fixed costs are manufacturing costs (no fixed administrative or selling) and the normal level is the budgeted sales level for 1982. What is Chrysler's fixed overhead allocation rate for 1982? Suppose, contrary to actual fact, that Chrysler has no cars in 1982 beginning inventory. Suppose also that Chrysler sells (ships to dealers) 1,244,000 vehicles in 1982. How many cars would Chrysler have to *produce* during 1982 to still show the budgeted accounting profit computed in (4)?

19-7 Seductive Cologne

Seductive Cologne Company has for a number of years employed a standard variable costing method of reporting income. Seductive's new comptroller questioned the desirability of using the variable costing method. Seductive's president replied that the firm's erratic production schedule and its relatively stable sales make a full (absorption) costing method of reporting income undesirable. To prove his point he has asked the comptroller to compare the results of the two methods of reporting income for the same periods.

Required:

1. Exhibit 1 shows income statements figured using the variable costing method for the months of February and March 1984. Using the same sales figures, prepare income statements using the full costing method for the same two months. Assume that normal (standard volume) capacity is 12,000 ounces per month and that production was 4,000 ounces in February and 15,000 ounces in March.

EXHIBIT 1. **Variable Costing**

	February		March	
Sales, $2.25 per ounce	11,500 ounces	$25,875	12,000 ounces	$27,000
Cost of goods sold at standard:				
Variable costs of $1 per ounce	11,500 ounces	11,500	12,000 ounces	12,000
Standard gross margin		14,375		15,000
Production cost variances:				
Material	$(150)		$(200)	
Labor	200		(150)	
Production overhead spending	25	75	(100)	(450)
Actual gross margin		14,450		14,550
Sales and administrative expenses		1,400		1,500
Fixed production overhead		7,800		7,800
		9,200		9,300
Income before taxes		$ 5,250		$ 5,250

2. Assume that Seductive's February 1, 1984, inventory consisted of 10,000 ounces. Calculate the February 1, 1984, and March 31, 1984, inventory values using both the variable cost and the full cost methods (show your calculations). Is it a coincidence that the difference in the combined *income before taxes* for February and March using the variable and full costing methods is equal to the difference in the changes in the inventory values from February 1 to March 31 under the two methods? Explain.

20

Short-term decision making

Managers analyze alternative courses of action and select the one that benefits the organization most. Private, for-profit organizations try to maximize cash inflows, and the benefit is usually expressed in terms of the amounts and timing of the cash inflows and outflows associated with an action. Public or not-for-profit organizations generally seek to provide a given level of service (output) for minimal cash outflows or to maximize some measure of output or effectiveness for a given cash outflow. In all instances an analysis must be made of the anticipated cash flows that result from actions.

Let a denote an action and C_1, C_2, . . . C_n the cash flows that result in the next n periods (usually years) if action a is taken (C_1 denotes the cash flow—positive or negative—in the current period, C_2 denotes the cash flow in the next immediate period, etc). Any choice between two actions, a and a', should be based on an analysis of the cash flows C_1, C_2, . . . C_n and C_1', C_2', . . . C_n' associated with each of the actions. Equivalently an analysis of the *incremental* (differential) cash flows C_1-C_1', C_2-C_2', . . . C_n-C_n' can be made.

The decision to select action *a* or *a'* depends on both the magnitude and arrangement of the cash flows (incremental cash flows) through time. A decision problem is considered to be *short term* (short run) if the optimal choice among the alternative actions being considered can be found by focusing on the cash flows of the current period. Since all cash flows occur in the same period the short-run decision to select action *a* or *a'* involves a comparison of the magnitudes of the cash flows under each action. Examples of short-term decisions include the *process further* decision introduced in the material on joint cost allocation, the *make or buy* decision discussed in the context of the service department cost allocation problem, and decisions whether to *continue or drop a product*.

Long-term decision problems such as capital investments, which consider cash flows in multiple periods are considered in the next chapter.

NONQUANTITATIVE FACTORS IN DECISION MAKING

The first phase of an analysis of alternative courses of action selects those actions with favorable cash flows. A second, equally important phase considers the effects implementation of each of the actions is likely to have on employees, managers, and competitors. How will implementation of a particular action affect the culture of the organization? Will employee morale be lowered? Will productivity be decreased? Will personnel be motivated to produce quality products? How will competitors respond to various actions?

Actions with favorable cash flows should be implemented only if, in management's judgment, the cash flow benefits of the action are not outweighed by more subjective factors.

ACCRUAL ACCOUNTING AND CASH FLOWS

Decision making is future oriented and requires *estimates* of the effects on *future* cash flows of proposed management actions. Future cash flows are often projected from the historical cost financial statements, which are based on the accrual system of accounting. Since the objective of historical cost financial statements is to measure the economic performance of an organization they are only indirectly concerned with cash flow.

In the income statement, revenues in an accounting period may not correspond to receipts (cash inflows) in the same period nor expenses to expenditures (cash outflows). Revenues are recorded when the earnings process is complete and an exchange has taken place, not when the receipt of cash takes place. For example, the sale of merchandise on account results in an increase in accounts receivable not in cash. Expenses are all costs (not immediate cash outflows) incurred in the generation of revenues. For example, that portion of cost of goods sold that represents inventory purchased for cash in a prior period is an expense but not a cash outflow in the current period. Decision makers must "see through" accrual numbers to obtain information about cash flows.

Not all cash flow estimates are obtained from the accounting system. In particular, accounting systems rarely generate information about opportunity costs. An *opportunity cost* (opportunity cash flow) is the amount of cash foregone by using an asset one way instead of in its next best alternative way. Suppose you keep $1 in your pocket for one year as opposed to putting it in the bank and earning 10 percent interest. The opportunity cost of keeping it in your pocket is $.10 for the year. Estimates of opportunity costs must be obtained from outside the accounting system.

INCOME TAXES AND CASH FLOWS

The aggregate cash outflow a business must make for income taxes is a function of income tax rates and the tax law, which stipulates the manner in which revenues and expenses are included in taxable income. Income taxes are a major cash outflow that must be considered in decision making.

Illustration 20–1 summarizes the aftertax cash flows associated with four general categories of revenues and expenses that are included in the computation of taxable income.

Revenues increase taxable income and income taxes. If a revenue in an accounting period is accompanied by a cash inflow in the period, the amount of the inflow is reduced by the increased outflow for income taxes. For example, a firm making a *cash* sale for $100 ($R = \$100$) and paying income taxes at a 46 percent rate ($t = .46$)

ILLUSTRATION 20–1. **Taxable Revenues and Expenses: Aftertax Cash Flow**

Item	Pretax Cash Flow	Tax Effect	Aftertax Cash Flow
Revenue (R): (cash receipt)	R	$-tR$	$R - tR = (1 - t)R$
Revenue (R): (no cash receipt)	O	$-tR$	$-tR$
Expense (E): (cash expenditure)	$-E$	tE	$-E + tE = -(1 - t)E$
Expense (E): (no cash expenditure)	O	tE	tE

has a net cash inflow of $54 $((1-t)R)$ after income taxes are considered.

Some revenues are not directly accompanied by cash inflows but still increase cash outflows for income taxes. Suppose a firm sells a fixed asset with a net book value of $100 for $300 cash. At a 46 percent tax rate the $200 gain on the sale (revenue) results in a $92 cash outflow $(-tR = -.46(\$200))$ for income taxes. Net cash inflow from the sale is $208 ($300 − $92). It is equal to the total proceeds from the sale of the fixed asset (not revenue) less the outflow for income taxes.

Expenses decrease taxable income and income taxes. If an expense in an accounting period is accompanied by a cash outflow in the same period, the amount of the outflow is reduced by the decreased outflow for taxes. For example, a $500 cash expenditure for wage expense results in a net cash outflow of $270 ($500(1 − .46)) if the tax rate is 46 percent. The tax savings of $230 (.46 × $500) represents the amount by which the tax liability would increase if the $500 wage expense wasn't a deduction on the income tax return.

Several expenses are not directly accompanied by cash outflows but still shield (lower) income and reduce cash outflows for income taxes. Depreciation is the prime example. If the tax rate is 46 percent, then $1,000 in depreciation expense will decrease the cash outflow for income taxes by $460 (.46($1,000) = tE).

The following examples illustrate how to solve several short-term decision problems.

EXAMPLE: INCREMENTAL BUSINESS

A tire manufacturer has the capacity to produce 200,000 steel-belted radial tires per year. They currently expect to produce 150,000 tires per year and sell them for $15 per tire; 150,000 units per year is also the normal activity level used to determine the fixed factory overhead allocation rate. At this level of output the *average* cost to produce and sell a tire is $11. The average cost consists of:

Variable manufacturing cost (raw materials, direct labor, variable factory overhead)	$ 2
Fixed factory overhead	5
Variable selling cost	1
Fixed selling cost	3
Total	$11

no

A major discount department store has indicated a desire to purchase 30,000 tires (this would be in addition to the current 150,000 sales level) of varying sizes for $8 per tire. No sales commission would have to be paid on this order. Should the tire manufacturer produce and sell 30,000 tires to the discount department store?

Incremental cash inflows

If the tire manufacturer produces and sells the additional 30,000 tires, it will result in an incremental cash inflow of $240,000 (30,000 at $8) before considering taxes.

Incremental cash outflows

don't have to change these tires w/ FixFOH or Fixed selling costs.

The manufacture of 30,000 additional tires will require an incremental cash outflow of $2 per tire to pay for the required raw materials, direct labor, and variable factory overhead. The total incremental variable manufacturing cash outflow is $60,000 (30,000 at $2). Assuming that no additional fixed factory overhead cost will be incurred if 30,000 additional tires are produced, fixed factory overhead costs will remain at $750,000 (150,000 × $5). There will not be any incremental cash outflow for fixed factory overhead.

Similarly, fixed selling costs are expected to remain unchanged, and since no sales commission will be paid on the incremental order for 30,000 tires, no incremental cash outflow for variable selling costs will result.

The total incremental cash outflow to produce the 30,000 tires will be $60,000. Since the incremental cash inflow ($240,000) exceeds the incremental cash outflow ($60,000) the tire manufacturer will be better off before taxes by $180,000 ($240,000 − $60,000) if the incremental business is accepted. If the tax rate is 40 percent, the aftertax net benefit to the tire manufacturer will be $108,000 (.6 × $180,000).

Of course, the implications of the current sale on future business would also have to be considered. Is the discount department store likely to purchase additional tires in the future? Will the sale of these tires for $8 per tire impair the company's ability to sell tires through regular channels at $15 per tire?

INCREMENTAL FIXED COSTS

Regardless of whether a cost is considered fixed or variable it should be included in the analysis if it is incremental to the decision. In the previous example suppose production of 30,000 additional tires requires the addition of another full-time quality inspector at a cash outflow of $25,000 for the year. The inspector's salary, a fixed factory overhead cost, will be an incremental cash outflow of producing the 30,000 additional tires.

The total incremental cash outflow to produce the 30,000 additional tires will be $85,000 ($60,000 + $25,000). In this case the tires should still be produced, since the net pretax cash inflow will be $155,000 ($240,000 − $85,000) and result in a net cash inflow after taxes of $93,000 (.6 × $155,000).

EXAMPLE: RENT ADDITIONAL CAPACITY

Suppose the order from the discount store is for 70,000 tires at $8 per tire. In order to produce an additional 20,000 tires (the order specifies all 70,000 tires must be shipped) the tire manufacturer can do either one of two things: rent capacity to produce the additional 20,000 tires at a rental cost of $60,000 or not supply 20,000 tires to their regular customers.

Assume that the variable manufacturing cost per tire will also be $2 if produced in the rented capacity, and because the rented capacity is in the same building no additional supervisors will have to be hired, and fixed factory overhead will remain at $750,000.

Should the manufacturer reject the order for 70,000 additional tires, accept the order and rent additional capacity, or accept the order and supply its regular customers with 20,000 fewer tires this year?

The following alternatives should be examined:

Do nothing

If the order is rejected, incremental cash flow will be zero.

Accept order and rent capacity

If the order is accepted and additional capacity is rented there will be an incremental cash inflow of $560,000 (70,000 tires at $8).

There will be an incremental cash outflow of $140,000 (70,000 at $2) for variable production costs and an incremental cash outflow of $60,000 for rent. The net pretax cash inflow is $360,000 ($560,000 − $140,000 − $60,000). After income taxes the net cash inflow is $216,000 (.6 × $360,000).

Accept order and do not rent

If the order is accepted and 20,000 fewer tires are sold to regular customers, the manufacturer will produce 200,000 tires.

The cash inflow from the sale of the 70,000 tires to the discount department store will be $560,000 (70,000 at $8). Cash outflow for variable production costs will be $140,000 (70,000 at $2). There are no incremental fixed or variable selling costs.

The foregone cash inflow (opportunity cost) from the sale of 20,000 tires to regular customers is $240,000. (Each tire generates a $15 cash inflow upon sale and requires cash outflows of $2 for variable production costs and $1 for variable selling costs. ($240,000 = 20,000 × ($15 − $2 − $1)).

The net pretax inflow that results, if the order is accepted and sales to regular customers are reduced, is $180,000 ($560,000 − $140,000 − $240,000). After income taxes the net cash inflow is $108,000 (.6 × $180,000).

The alternative that results in the largest aftertax net cash inflow is to accept the order for 70,000 additional tires and rent additional capacity to produce 20,000 tires ($216,000 > $108,000).

COMPREHENSIVE EXAMPLE: DROPPING A PRODUCT

In the December 1983 management meeting of the Tripro Company, a manufacturer of three products for the automobile industry, it was suggested that, because of the projected loss for product B, production and sales of product B be discontinued.

In order to decide whether to drop product B management calculated all the incremental cash outflows and cash inflows associated with this action.

As part of their analysis Tripro's management prepared the 1984 projected (pro forma) income statement shown in Illustration 20–2.

Sales revenue

All of Tripro's sales are cash sales. If product B is dropped, Tripro will lose sales and cash inflow of $6,273,000 (Illustration 20–2). Since these sales revenues would be taxed at Tripro's income tax rate of 30 percent the net cash loss will be $4,391,100 = .7($6,273,000).[1]

Benefit	Cost	
—	$4,391,100 = .7($6,273,000)	Lost sales revenue

---

[1] Throughout this chapter we assume that all cash inflows and outflows, including the cash flow effects of taxes, occur at the same point in time. If cash flows occur at different points in time (e.g., cash is received now but is taxed one year later or sales are made on account and are to be collected in the next accounting period), discounting will be necessary to make the flows comparable.

ILLUSTRATION 20-2

TRIPRO COMPANY
Pro Forma Income Statement
Year Ended December 31, 1984
($000)

	A	B	C	Total
Net sales revenue	$11,875	$6,273	$14,400	$32,548
Cost of goods sold (Note 1)	7,790	5,986	12,960	26,736
Gross margin	4,085	287	1,440	5,812
Planned fixed factory overhead volume variance	(14)	(1)	(5)	(20)
Adjusted gross margin	4,099	288	1,445	5,832
Operating expenses:				
Telephone	120	90	82	292
Personnel	210	210	210	630
Rent	300	300	300	900
Sales commissions	238	125	288	651
Administrative costs	401	212	487	1,100
Pretax income	2,830	(649)	78	2,259
Income tax (credit) (Note 2)	849	(195)	24	678
Net income	$ 1,981	$ (454)	$ 54	$ 1,581

Notes:

(1) See Illustration 20-3 for standard costs and revenues, estimates of expense items, for the calculation of sales, cost of goods sold, and the planned fixed factory overhead volume variance.

(2) For arithmetic convenience the federal income tax rate is assumed to be 30 percent of pretax income. Taxable and financial statement income are identical. This rate is used in the determination of individual product income. The resulting tax expense is negative (a credit) in those cases where pretax product income is a loss. Gains and losses on the sale of assets are also taxed at the 30 percent ordinary income rate. All taxes on 1984 income will be paid in 1984.

Cost of goods sold and inventories

There are no planned beginning inventories of either product A, B, or C. Ending inventory of products B and C is budgeted at zero. The ending inventory of product A is planned at 40,000 units.

There are no beginning raw material inventories needed to produce A or C. Exactly enough of the raw materials needed to produce A (990,000 pounds: 950,000 units for sale at 1 pound; 40,000 units for inventory at 1 pound) and C (300,000 pounds: 1,200,000 units at ¼ pound) will be purchased. Raw material for the production of B will not be purchased. There is currently 205,000 pounds of this raw material in inventory (exactly enough to produce 410,000 units of B). It was purchased early in 1983 for $1 per pound. If not used, it can be disposed of for 80 cents per pound.

Fixed factory overhead is allocated to product using direct labor-hours. The $2 per direct hour fixed overhead allocation rate, based on normal direct labor-hour usage, is derived in Illustration 20–3. If B is not produced, *all* fixed factory overhead costs will still be incurred, and the fixed overhead allocation rate *will not* be revised.

Direct labor, variable overhead, and raw material purchases for products A and C will be paid for in cash. All fixed factory overhead, with the exception of depreciation, is paid in cash.

ILLUSTRATION 20–3

TRIPRO COMPANY
Standard Manufacturing Costs and Revenues

	A	B	C
Selling price	$12.50	$15.30	$12.00
Direct labor	5.00 (1 hour)	10.00 (2 hours)	7.50 (1½ hours)
Raw material	1.00 (1 pound)	.50 (½ pound)	.25 (¼ pound)
Variable overhead ...	.20	.10	.05
Fixed overhead	2.00	4.00	3.00
Full cost per unit	8.20	14.60	10.80

TRIPRO COMPANY
Sales Revenue and Cost of Goods Sold

	A	B	C
Budgeted unit sales	950,000	410,000	1,200,000
Sales revenue (budgeted unit sales × selling price)	$11,875,000	$6,273,000	$14,400,000
Cost of goods sold (budgeted unit sales × full unit cost)	$ 7,790,000	$5,986,000	$12,960,000
Ending inventory	$ 328,000 (40,000 at $8.20)	–0–	–0–

TRIPRO COMPANY
Fixed Overhead Allocation Rate and Planned Overabsorbed Fixed Factory Overhead

Budgeted fixed factory overhead costs:	
Depreciation	$2,600,000
Salaries—management	4,000,000
Other	600,000
Total fixed overhead	$7,200,000

ILLUSTRATION 20–3 *(concluded)*

Normal direct labor usage	3,600,000 hours
Fixed overhead allocation rate	$2/dlh ($7,200,000/3,600,000)
Budgeted direct labor usage:	
Product A (990,000 units at 1 dlh)	990,000
Product B (410,000 units at 2 dlh)	820,000
Product C (1,200,000 units at 1½ dlh)	1,800,000
Total planned direct labor usage (hours)	3,610,000
Total allocated fixed overhead at planned direct labor usage	$7,220,000 (3,610,000 at $2)
Planned fixed overhead volume variance (overabsorbed overhead)	$ 20,000

Raw material cost

The analysis of raw material costs must take into account the beginning inventory of raw material used to produce B. If B is not produced, cash flow *will not* be reduced by $205,000 (410,000 units at $.50 or 205,000 pounds at $1) because the expenditure for raw materials was made in 1983. The raw material cost is a sunk cost and is not relevant to the decision to drop B. However, if B is not produced, the raw material used to produce B can be sold for $164,000 (205,000 pounds at $.80). The $164,000 received from the sale of inventory does not increase taxable income, and there is no tax effect. The *loss* on the sale of inventory, $41,000 ($205,000 − $164,000), will reduce taxable income and result in a tax saving of $12,300 (.3 × $41,000). This $12,300 tax savings plus the $164,000 in cash received from the sale of the inventory results in a cash inflow of $176,300.

There is one other raw material cost associated with not producing B. Even though the $205,000 cash expenditure for raw material was made in a prior period, it appears in the 1984 income statement as part of cost of goods sold and has the effect of reducing taxable income in 1984. This tax shield of .3($205,000) is lost if B is not produced.

Benefit	Cost	
$176,300 = $164,000 + .3($41,000)	—	Sale of inventory at loss
—	$61,500 = .3($205,000)	Lost tax shield

Direct labor cost

If product B is dropped, the direct labor cost of $10 per unit will be saved, resulting in total direct labor savings of $4,100,000 (410,000 units at $10). Considering taxes the net benefit is .7($4,100,000).

Benefit	Cost	
$2,870,000 = .7($4,100,000)	—	Direct labor cost savings

Variable overhead

If product B is dropped, variable overhead will be reduced by $41,000 (410,000 units at $.10). Considering taxes the net benefit of this reduction is .7($41,000).

Benefit	Cost	
$28,700 = .7($41,000)	—	Reduced variable overhead

Fixed factory overhead

If B is not produced, total fixed factory overhead *will not decrease,* and the allocation rate based on normal volume will not change. If B is not produced, the amount of fixed factory overhead put into inventory will not change. Therefore, the amount of fixed factory overhead in the 1984 income statement will not change (all unallocated fixed factory overhead originally allocated to B will appear in the fixed overhead volume variance instead of in cost of goods sold), and there will not be an incremental tax effect associated with fixed overhead.

Telephone costs

All telephone costs are paid for in cash as incurred. In Illustration 20–2, long distance telephone charges are identified and assigned to the product that generated them. The remainder of the telephone bill, representing basic service at a cost of $180,000, was allocated equally to each of the three products. If product B is dropped, the basic service cost will not change.

Cash outflows for telephone usage will drop $30,000 if B is no longer produced. The telephone operating expense for product B is currently $90,000, but $60,000 of this total is an allocated share of the $180,000 basic service charge that will not change if B is not produced. Therefore, only $30,000 ($90,000 − $60,000) in long distance calls made in conjunction with producing and selling product B will be eliminated. Expenses reduce taxable income, and the net benefit in telephone costs if product B is dropped is .7($30,000).

Benefit	Cost	
$21,000 = .7($30,000)	—	Reduced telephone cost

Personnel cost

This is a cash expenditure for warehouse clerks. It is allocated equally among the three products. The cost will remain at $630,000 even if B is not produced.

Rent

This $900,000 cost, paid in cash, is for leasing the warehouse and administrative offices next year. Since the lease has already been signed this cost will not change even if B is not produced. It is allocated equally among the three products. Under the conditions of the lease Tripro has the right to sublet space. It is estimated that if B is not produced, warehouse space will be available to sublet for $200,000 for the year.

If B is not produced, Tripro will sublease, and this will result in a $200,000 cash inflow to Tripro which will be taxed at 30 percent. The net benefit to Tripro from subleasing is .7($200,000).

Benefit	Cost	
$140,000 = .7($200,000)	—	Net inflow from sublease

Sales commissions

Sales commissions at the rate of 2 percent of the net sales revenue for each product are paid in cash and are directly assignable to products.

The $125,000 expenditure for sales commissions on product B sales will be saved if B is not produced. Considering the loss of the tax shield on this expense Tripro is .7($125,000) better off.

Benefit	Cost	
$87,500 = .7($125,000)	—	Reduced sales commissions

Administrative cost

Administrative costs, $1,100,000 paid in cash, will be incurred in their entirety regardless of whether or not B is produced. Administrative costs are allocated to products on the basis of relative net sales revenue [e.g., $401,000 = ($11,875,000/$32,548,000) ($1,100,000)].

Conclusion

The analysis of incremental cash flows summarized in Illustration 20–4 indicates that product B should not be dropped since the cost, net cash outflow of $4,452,600, exceeds the benefit, net cash inflow of $3,323,500, by $1,129,100 if it is dropped. The $454,000 product B loss (Illustration 20–2), which led to speculation that product B should be eliminated, is the result of cost allocations to product B. Eliminating product B will not eliminate these allocated costs.

ILLUSTRATION 20–4

TRIPRO COMPANY
Summary of Cost and Benefits of
Dropping Product B
($000)

	Net Cost	Net Benefit
Sales revenue	$4,391.1	
Inventory: sale		$ 176.30
Inventory: lost tax shield	61.5	
Direct labor		2,870.00
Variable overhead		28.70
Telephone cost		21.00
Lease		140.00
Sales commissions		87.50
Total	$4,452.6	$3,323.50

CONSTRAINED SHORT-TERM DECISIONS

Management of the Durable Manufacturing Company must decide on the number of toasters, irons, and mixers it will produce and sell next year.

The following table lists the maximum number of each item which can be produced and sold, the number of machine-hours required to produce one unit of each item, and the unit contribution margin for each item.

	Products		
	Toasters	Irons	Mixers
Maximum sales	475,000	205,000	600,000
Machine-hours per unit	1	½	¼
Unit contribution margin	$6.00	$4.50	$4.00

Because each product has a positive contribution margin (contributes something to covering fixed costs and making a profit), Durable's management would like to produce and sell the maximum amounts of each of the three products. A total of 727,500 machine-hours is necessary to produce 475,000 toasters, 205,000 irons, and 600,000 mixers.

475,000 toasters at 1 hour	475,000
205,000 irons at ½ hour	102,500
600,000 mixers at ¼ hour	150,000
Total hours required	727,500

The production manager has just informed Durable's top management that there has been a delay of one year in the installation of new machinery and that for the coming year only 500,000 machine-hours are available to produce toasters, irons, and mixers.

There are no inventories of toasters, irons, or mixers. All the direct labor and raw materials necessary to produce any of the three products can be purchased as needed. How many toasters, irons, and mixers should Durable produce next year?

Should Durable produce 475,000 toasters (since it has the highest unit contribution margin) and use the remaining 25,000 machine hours to produce irons (since it has the second highest unit contribution margin)? The 25,000 machine-hours can be used to produce 50,000 irons, since each iron requires ½ hour of machine time. The total contribution of 475,000 toasters and 50,000 irons is $3,075,000.

475,000 toasters at $6.00	$2,850,000
50,000 irons at $4.50	225,000
Total contribution	$3,075,000

Is this the maximum possible total contribution that can be obtained from 500,000 machine-hours? The answer is no. If a constrained resource is consumed in the process of production, then the most preferred product (from a contribution viewpoint) is the one with the highest contribution margin per unit of scarce resource. The following computation shows that mixers are most preferred, followed by irons, and then toasters.

	Toasters	*Irons*	*Mixers*
Contribution/machine-hour	($6.00)/(1) = $6.00	($4.50)/(.50) = $9.00	($4.00)/(.25) = $16.00

The maximum number of irons and mixers can be produced since only 252,500 hours (600,000 at ¼ hour + 205,000 at ½ hour) will be consumed. The remaining 247,500 hours can be used to produce 247,500 toasters. This production plan results in a total contribution of $4,807,500.

247,500 toasters at $6.00	$1,485,000
205,000 irons at $4.50	922,500
600,000 mixers at $4.00	2,400,000
Total contribution	$4,807,500

This is considerably in excess of the $3,075,000 total contribution if 475,000 toasters and 50,000 irons are produced.

Linear programming

The above constrained decision problem can be formulated as a linear programming problem. Let x_A, x_B, and x_C denote the number of units of production of toasters, irons, and mixers, respectively. Durable seeks to maximize the total contribution, $6.00x_A + 4.50x_B + 4.00x_C$, from its production plan while recognizing there are limitations on the amounts of each product they can sell and on the number of machine hours they may use in production.

$$\text{Maximize } 6.00x_A + 4.50x_B + 4.00x_C$$
$$\text{Subject to}$$
$$1x_A + \tfrac{1}{2}x_B + \tfrac{1}{4}x_C \leq 500,000 \quad (1)$$
$$x_A \qquad\qquad\qquad \leq 475,000 \quad (2)$$
$$x_B \qquad\qquad \leq 205,000 \quad (3)$$
$$x_C \leq 600,000 \quad (4)$$
$$x_A, x_B, x_C \qquad \geq \qquad 0 \quad (5)$$

As stated, the objective is to maximize the total contribution margin. Constraint (1) limits the amount of available machine time to 500,000 hours. The left-hand side represents the total amount of machine time consumed if x_A, x_B, and x_C are produced. Constraints (2), (3), and (4) limit sales and production to the maximum demands, while constraint (5) ensures that Durable will not produce negative amounts. The above formulation can be readily generalized to include additional constraints on scarce resources and is easily solved using standard available computer programs.

PROBLEMS AND CASES

20–1 Tire Manufacturer

1. The following questions relate to the Incremental Business example in the chapter.
a. Compute the tire manufacturers total profit if 150,000 tires are produced.
b. Compute the tire manufacturers total profit if the 30,000 additional tires are sold to the discount department store.
c. Compare the profits computed in *(a)* and *(b)*. How does this difference compare to the incremental benefit computed in the chapter?

2. The following questions relate to the Rent Additional Capacity example in the chapter.
a. Compute the tire manufacturers total profit if the order for the 70,000 tires is accepted and additional capacity is rented.
b. Compute the total profit if the order is accepted but additional capacity is not rented.
c. Compare the profits computed in *(a)* and *(b)* with the profit computed in (1*a*). Which alternative is best?

20–2 Ace Automotive

Ace Automotive, Inc., consists of three separate departments; new car sales, used car sales, and customer service. For the first six months of 1984 Ace Automotive was profitable, generating aftertax net income equal to 5.2 percent of net sales. However, the service department income statement showed that its gross profit was insufficient to cover the department's operating expenses.

The president of Ace Automotive suggests that perhaps service and repair operations should be discontinued. You are asked to prepare a report on the president's suggestion for presentation at the next monthly management meeting.

Required:

1. Suppose that the first six months' results are typical of future results and that discontinuance of the service department will not affect new or used car sales. Should Ace Automotive close the service department? (Be very specific about any assumptions you make in your analysis.)

2. What other information would aid you in making the above decision?

ACE AUTOMOTIVE
Service Department Income Statement
Six Months Ended June 30, 1984

Service revenue	$351,928
Cost of service work	262,377
Gross profit	89,551
Other operating expenses:	
Department manager's office	10,202
Rent (Note 1)	23,498
Utilities (Note 2)	4,320
Inventory taxes and insurance	25,113
Interest expense (Note 3)	15,000
Administrative cost (Note 4)	21,639
Total operating expenses	99,772
Net loss before tax credit	(10,221)
Income tax (credit at 45%)	(4,599)
Net income (loss) (Note 5)	$ (5,622)

Notes:

(1) Rent is allocated to departments on the basis of square footage occupied. Ace Automotive has signed a 20-year lease for the facilities. The service department occupies 42 percent of all square footage.

(2) Each department has its own electric meter, and the service department was directly billed for $1,432 in the first six months of 1984. The remaining utility cost is primarily for heat and is allocated to departments on the basis of square footage occupied.

(3) Interest expense is allocated on the basis of average inventory value. The purpose of this allocation is to encourage managers not to carry excessive inventories. Actual interest expense is about 20 percent of total allocated interest expense.

(4) Administrative costs are allocated to departments on the basis of departmental revenues.

(5) All items on the service department income statement correspond to cash flows in the six-month period ended June 30, 1984.

20-3 Ocean Company*

Your client, Ocean Company, manufactures and sells three different products—Ex, Why, and Zee. Projected income statements (and statements of taxable income) by product line for the year ended December 31, 1984, are presented below:

* Material from Uniform CPA Examination Questions and Unofficial Answers, copyright © May 1975 by the American Institute of Certified Public Accountants, Inc., is reprinted with permission.

(handwritten margin notes:) some parts of Ex have to be redistributed why ?

(handwritten left margin note:) wouldn't have to pay those expenses but you also lose your revenue.

	Ex	Why	Zee	Total
Unit sales	100,000	500,000	125,000	725,000
Revenues	$925,000	$1,000,000	$575,000	$2,500,000
Variable cost of units sold	285,000	350,000	150,000	785,000
Fixed cost of units sold	304,200	289,000	166,800	760,000
Gross margin	335,800	361,000	258,200	955,000
Variable general and adminis-				
trative (G&A) expenses	270,000	200,000	80,000	550,000
Fixed G&A expenses	125,800	136,000	78,200	340,000
Income (loss) before tax	$ (60,000)	$ 25,000	$100,000	$ 65,000

Production costs are similar for all three products. The fixed G&A expenses are allocated to products in proportion to revenues. The fixed cost of units sold is allocated to products by various allocation bases, such as square feet for factory rent, machine-hours for repairs, etc.

Ocean management is concerned about the loss for product Ex and is considering the following course of action.

Ocean would discontine the manufacture of product Ex. Selling prices of products Why and Zee would remain constant. Management expects that product Zee production and revenues would increase by 50 percent. Some of the present machinery devoted to product Ex could be sold at scrap value, which equals its removal cost. The removal of this machinery would reduce fixed costs allocated to product Ex by $30,000 per year. The remaining fixed costs allocated to product Ex include $155,000 (cash out-flow) of rent expense per year. The space previously used for product Ex can be rented to an outside organization for $157,500 (cash inflow) per year. There are never any beginning or ending raw material, work in pro-cess, or finished goods inventories in the Ocean Company. Ocean pays taxes at the rate of 50 percent of pretax income. All revenues and variable ex-penses correspond to cash flows during the year.

Required:

Should Ocean discontinue the manufacture of product Ex?

20–4   Twopro Manufacturing

The Twopro Manufacturing Company produces two products, A and B, in two departments. A detailed analysis of the cost structure of Twopro is underway, and the following monthly data has already been gathered (all costs are cash flows in a given period).

Indirect Cost	Components	
	Fixed	Variable
Central administration	$8,000	
Production administration	$2,000	+ .20 per direct labor-hour worked in either department
Marketing	$ 500	+ $2 per unit of A + $3 per unit of B
Overhead—production department 1	$ 800	+ $1.20 per direct labor-hour worked in department 1
Overhead—production department 2	$1,000	+ $2.30 per direct labor-hour worked in department 2
Power*	$ 700	+ $.04 per kilowatt hour + .002 maintenance units per kilowatt hour
Maintenance	$ 400	+ $6 per maintenance unit + 60 kwh per maintenance unit

* Every time a kilowatt hour of power is produced, the direct variable cost in the power department is $.04. In addition, .002 maintenance units are consumed. If C_m is the cost of a unit of maintenance, then the total cost of producing P kilowatt hours of power is $700 + $.04 P + $.002 PC_m$.

Product Statistics

	Product A	Product B
Selling price	$150	$200
Direct material cost	$ 30	$ 25
Direct labor required in department 1	1 hour	1 hour
Direct labor required in department 2	1 hour	2 hours

Production Department Statistics

	Department 1	Department 2
Direct labor cost per hour	$ 10	$12
Power consumption per direct labor-hour	9 kwh	25 kwh
Maintenance consumption per direct labor-hour	.1 unit	.2 units

Required:

1. Determine the incremental costs of producing one unit of A and one unit of B. (In the analysis of power and maintenance costs a review of the reciprocal allocation method for service department costs, Chapter 18, might be helpful.)

2. Determine the pretax profit of producing and selling 200 units of A and 100 units of B in a month. (Twopro never has monthly ending inventories.)

20–5 The Family Car

The following hypothetical data refers to the cost of operating the family car for one year.

1857.60

Fuel (720 gallons at 1.29)	$ 928.80
Lubricating oil and additives....................	50.00
Chassis lubrications	18.50
Inspections and maintenance	35.00
Washing and polishing	47.50
Licenses, city and state	40.00
Garage rent...................................	402.50
Public liability and property damage insurance	290.00
Depreciation ($10,000 − $2,000) ÷ 4=...........	2,000.00
Personal property taxes (valuation $2,000)	158.00
Total	$3,970.30

Per mile, for 14,400 miles, 27.57 cents

only need to consider the costs that will be incurred in the future if you take the trip

Required:

1. What will it cost to take a business trip of 1,000 miles in your car? You want to be able to compare this cost to roundtrip airfare to the same destination. Be sure to list assumptions you make.

2. You are considering acquiring a second car with cost and mileage characteristics identical to those of the above car. If the second car is acquired, the total mileage driven in both cars in a typical year will increase to 21,600 miles. By how much will the annual cost of operating both cars increase above $3,970.30?

3. By how much will your cash flow increase if you give up ownership of the car?

20–6 Tripro Company

Using the information in this chapter construct a 1984 pro forma income statement for the Tripro Company under the assumption that product B is dropped. Use this income statement and the income statement in Illustration 20–2, which assumes products A, B, and C are produced, to analyze the total cash flow under each of the alternatives. Complete the following table, which assumes that Tripro will begin 1984 with a cash balance of $2,000,000.

| | Alternative ($000) | | |
	Produce A, B, and C	Produce A and C	Difference
Beginning cash balance	$2,000	$2,000	—
Additions:			
Sales revenues			
Rent income			
Sales of inventory			
Subtractions:			
Fixed factory overhead			
Direct labor			
Raw material			
Variable overhead			
Telephone			
Personnel			
Rent			
Sales commissions			
Administrative costs			
Taxes			
Ending cash balance			

21

Capital budgeting

In a *capital budgeting* (capital investment) problem, management must decide if it is beneficial to make a cash outflow in the current year in return for net cash inflows in future years.

Examples of capital investment problems include the equipment replacement problem (whether a current expenditure on a new machine is justified by future savings in operating costs), the new product introduction problem (whether current expenditures for research and development, advertising, and equipment generate sufficient future net cash inflows from the production and sale of the product), and the lease-or-buy decision (whether it is cheaper to lease or purchase facilities).

Criteria for capital investment opportunities

The criteria for accepting or rejecting capital investment opportunities should focus on *incremental cash flows,* recognize the *time value of money,* and consider how *risky* the proposed project is in comparison to other investments the firm has made.

Money has time value; a dollar received today is worth more than a dollar received in the future. Cash flows in different periods are made comparable by determining their present value (discounting the cash flows). The appropriate discount rate for capital budgeting decisions is $1/(1 + r)$, where r is the opportunity cost of capital,[1] the rate of return an investor expects to earn on investments involving risk equal to the *risk of the project under consideration*. The value of an asset to an investor is equal to the stream of cash inflows the asset will generate discounted at the opportunity cost of capital.

A firm has the opportunity to purchase a new machine for $100,000. The machine is expected to save $50,000 in aftertax cash outlays for production costs in each of the next four years. Investments similar to this one are expected to yield 16 percent after taxes.

The present value[2] of the $50,000 annual incremental cash inflows that are expected to result from the purchase of the machine is:

$$\$139,909 = \frac{\$50,000}{(1.16)} + \frac{\$50,000}{(1.16)^2} + \frac{\$50,000}{(1.16)^3} + \frac{\$50,000}{(1.16)^4}$$

Since the present value ($139,909) of the incremental future cash inflows at 16 percent exceeds the $100,000 cost of the machine, the machine should be purchased. This investment opportunity has a *net present* value of $39,909 ($139,909 − $100,000).

Net present value

Net present value is the sum of the discounted future cash flows an asset is expected to generate minus the cash outflow to acquire the asset. Investment projects with positive net present values should be undertaken unless there are important qualitative considerations, not directly reflected in the cash flows, that would argue against accepting the project.

Net present value computed at an appropriate discount rate considers the time value of money, the magnitudes of projected cash flows, and the riskiness of the project. Because it considers all of the above factors, *net present value is the correct criterion for making capital investment decisions*.

---

[1] In this text we will assume that the opportunity cost of capital is given. See any introductory corporate finance text for a discussion of methods used to estimate this rate.

[2] See Chapter 8 for a discussion of present value.

DISCOUNT RATES AND CASH FLOWS

Nominal rates of return (interest rates) depend on inflation rates and investor expectations of a real return on their investment. For instance, suppose an investor has the opportunity to invest $100 at 16 percent interest for one year. Sixteen percent is the nominal (stated) rate of interest. Suppose the investor expects inflation to be 10 percent over the next year. If the investment is made the investor will receive $116 at the end of one year. Because of a general inflation of 10 percent, $100 at the beginning of the year is equivalent to $110 ($110 $\times$ 1.10) at the end of the year, and $110 represents a return of the original $100 investment in year-end dollars. The remaining $6 ($116 $-$ $110) is a real return to the investor. It represents expected compensation for the use of the invested dollar. The real rate of return is a function of the riskiness of the investment. The greater the risk, the higher the expected real return. You would expect the real return on a loan to a person setting up a new business to be higher than the real return on a U.S. Treasury bill, which has very little risk of not being repaid.

In capital budgeting problems (net present value computations) nominal interest rates should be used to discount anticipated nominal cash flows, or real rates should be used to discount anticipated real cash flows. *Never* discount real flows using nominal rates, or vice versa. Since interest rates are usually stated by investors in nominal terms it is simpler to project future cash flows in nominal terms.

INCOME TAXES AND CASH FLOWS

The aggregate cash outflow a business must make for income taxes is an important consideration in capital budgeting problems. Depreciation tax shields, tax credits on the purchase cost of tangible personal property, and tax credits on incremental research and development expenditures are important tax benefits made available to businesses under current tax laws.

Depreciation tax shield

The depreciation tax shield in any year is the amount of depreciation expense in taxable income times the tax rate. The depreciation expense is not a cash outflow, but it does reduce taxable income and saves cash outflow for income taxes. In a given period the depreciation tax shield increases with increasing depreciation expense and higher tax rates. Depreciation tax shields reduce cash outflows for income taxes and have the same effect as a cash inflow for a business firm with taxable income.

Small Retailers, Inc.'s statement of taxable income is as follows:

Sales revenue	$400,000
Cost of goods sold	200,000
Gross margin	200,000
Less:	
Depreciation on store	50,000
Miscellaneous expenses	40,000
Taxable income	110,000
Income tax (at 40%)	44,000
Net income	$ 66,000

If depreciation on the store was not a deductible expense for tax purposes Small Retailers, Inc.'s taxable income would be:

Sales revenue	$400,000
Cost of goods sold	200,000
Gross margin	200,000
Less: Miscellaneous expenses	40,000
Taxable income	160,000
Income tax (at 40%)	64,000
Net income	$ 96,000

Small Retailers, Inc., would have to pay $64,000 in income taxes if depreciation on the store was not an expense for tax purposes. Small Retailers saves $20,000 in cash outflow for taxes because it is able to include depreciation expense of $50,000 in computing taxable income. This $20,000 cash savings for taxes is the benefit of a $50,000 depreciation tax shield. It is equal to the tax rate (40 percent) times the depreciation expense ($50,000).

The present value of a depreciation tax shield over the life of an asset depends on the cost of the asset, the pattern of depreciation over the life of the asset, the discount rate used to compute the present value, and the income tax rate. The present value of a depreciation tax shield measures the savings in cash outflows for taxes over the depreciable life of the asset in current dollars.

The depreciable cost basis of purchased property and current allowable patterns of depreciation for income tax purposes are determined by the accelerated cost recovery system (ACRS) portion of the Economic Recovery Tax Act of 1981 and by the Tax Equity and Fiscal Responsibility Act of 1982. Property is depreciated over

3, 5, 10, or 15 years depending on how it is classified at rates prescribed by ACRS.[3]

The present value of a depreciation tax shield is often a substantial determinant of the size and sign of the net present value of a potential investment. Income tax laws that permit accelerated depreciation increase the net present values of potential investments to business firms. The expectation by the government is that accelerated depreciation will spur economic activity because the additional tax shield increases net present value and makes more projects favorable (positive net present values) from a firm's viewpoint.

Example

Suppose an asset purchased in 1984, with a depreciable cost basis of $100,000, is in the three-year investment class under the accelerated cost recovery system. The percentages of the cost base allowed as depreciation over the next three years are 25 percent, 38 percent, and 37 percent. Depreciation will be $25,000, $38,000, and $37,000 in tax years 1984, 1985, and 1986, respectively.

Assuming the opportunity cost of capital is 15 percent for investments of similar risk, the present value of the accelerated cost recovery depreciation tax shield when the tax rate is 40 percent is $29,920 (see Illustration 21–1).

ILLUSTRATION 21–1. **Present Value of Accelerated Cost Recovery Depreciation Tax Shield**

	1984	1985	1986
Depreciation	$25,000	$38,000	$37,000
Tax shield	$10,000(.4 × $25,000)	$15,200(.4 × $38,000)	$14,800(.4 × $37,000)
Discount factor (at 15%)....	.8696	.7561	.6575
Present value	$ 8,696	$11,493	$ 9,731
Total present value	$29,920($8,696 + $11,493 + $9,731)		

As an option to accelerated cost recovery depreciation, the Economic Recovery Tax Act of 1981 allows straight-line depreciation of assets for income tax purposes. Businesses will usually select the accelerated cost recovery depreciation option because, given a total cost to depreciate, the net present value of an accelerated depreciation tax shield is larger than the net present value of a slower, straight-line depreciation shield. Under special circum-

---

[3] See the appendix to this chapter for classification of assets and depreciation (recovery) rates specified by the ERTA of 1981. The TEFRA of 1982 specifies how to compute the depreciable cost basis of purchased personal property.

stances, such as companies with losses in the investment year and anticipated changes in future income tax rates, it may be economically beneficial to elect the straight-line option.

Investment tax credit[4]

The Economic Recovery Tax Act of 1981 and the Tax Equity and Fiscal Responsibility Act of 1982 also provide for an investment tax credit when a firm purchases tangible personal property (property used in connection with manufacturing or production). Unlike depreciation, which is deducted in calculating taxable income, the investment tax credit reduces the firm's income tax. The amount of the credit is 6 percent of the purchase cost for three-year ACRS property and 10 percent for all other qualified property.

The investment tax credit encourages investment because it effectively reduces the acquisition cost of the asset. For example, a $100,000 piece of equipment qualifying for a 10 percent investment tax credit effectively costs $90,000 because the firm acquiring such an asset is able to reduce the amount of income taxes it must pay by $10,000. If the company makes the investment at the beginning of the tax year, it will not receive the benefit of the investment tax credit until the end of the year when it files its tax return. In making the net present value calculation under these circumstances, the firm should discount the investment tax credit from the date the tax return is filed to the investment date.

Under TEFRA the depreciable cost basis of a qualified asset purchased after December 31, 1982, is equal to the acquisition cost of the asset less half of any associated investment tax credit. For example, a $100,000 piece of equipment qualifying for a 10 percent investment tax credit will have a depreciation cost basis of $95,000 ($100,000 − .5 × $10,000).

Research and development tax credit

The Economic Recovery Tax Act of 1981 also allows a 25 percent tax credit for incremental qualified research and development expenditures. Wages paid to employees involved in research and development, supplies purchased for research and development purposes, and payments to others for property used in research and development (e.g., a leased computer) exceeding the average of research and development expenditures in the prior three-year period qualify for the credit.

For example, suppose a company with an average expenditure of $200,000 per year for research and development personnel wages

---

[4] See Chapter 7 for additional discussion of the investment tax credit.

in the years 1981 through 1983 hires additional researchers in 1984, increasing their total research and development wage expenditure to $300,000 in 1984. The company will be allowed a research and development tax credit of $25,000 (25% of $300,000 − $200,000).

The tax credit has no effect on the amount of research and development cost which can be expensed for tax purposes in any year.

SUMMARY OF THE CAPITAL BUDGETING PROCESS

A first step in solving capital investment problems is to determine the cost of the investment and the estimated incremental cash flows to be received from making the investment. These incremental cash flows are then discounted using the opportunity cost of capital, a rate that reflects the riskiness of the investment under consideration. The net present value of the investment is the present value of all the future incremental cash flows less the cash outflow for the initial investment. Investments with positive net present values are tentatively accepted; those with negative net present values are tentatively rejected. The final decision to accept or reject will also consider all important qualitative considerations that cannot be quantified and are not included in the net present value analysis.

EXAMPLE: EQUIPMENT REPLACEMENT

The Uniprod Company manufactures a single product, a standard circuit board, which it sells to electronics manufacturers. A single machine is used in Uniprod's manufacturing process. Late in 1983 Uniprod's management became aware of a new machine, equal in capacity to their current machine but capable of automating several operations currently done manually.

Uniprod's management has collected the following information relevant to the decision to purchase the new machine.

1. The old machine was acquired six years ago at a cost of $960,000. The old machine has an estimated life of eight years and is not expected to have any salvage value on retirement. It is being depreciated using sum-of-the-years'-digits depreciation and has a net book value of $80,000 at the end of 1983.

Although it will be fully depreciated in two more years it is expected to remain economically functional through 1987. It could be sold at the end of 1983 for $40,000, which would result in a loss on the sale of $40,000 ($80,000 − $40,000) that would reduce 1983 taxable income.

2. The acquisition cost of the new machine is $824,742. The new machine is assumed to have a three-year ACRS life and qualify

for a 6 percent investment tax credit. A three year ACRS life and 6 percent investment tax credit are used in this example for computational ease. In practice the machine would qualify for a five-year ACRS life and 10 percent investment tax credit. Uniprod would use the new machine through 1987, at which time it is expected that it could be disposed of for $100,000.

3. The new machine has identical production capacity to the old machine, is projected to cut direct labor costs by 50 percent, and would require that certain key managers be retrained during 1984 and 1985 at a tax-deductible cost of $50,000 per year.

4. Sales of circuit boards are projected at 100,000 units per year in 1984 through 1986. The needs of a major customer will increase sales to 180,000 units in 1987.

Uniprod Company uses the LIFO cost flow inventory method for finished goods and raw material inventories.

Production is expected to equal sales in every year, and exactly enough raw materials needed for production will be purchased each year.

5. The direct labor cost of producing a circuit board in 1984 is estimated to be $5 if the old machine is retained ($2.50 if the new machine is purchased). Under existing labor contracts these costs will rise by 12 percent per year through 1987. Direct labor costs are paid as incurred.

6. Uniprod's aftertax opportunity cost of capital for similar machinery is 16 percent.

7. Uniprod expects to pay income taxes at a 40 percent rate in all years.

8. Beginning in 1988 all cash inflows and outflows are expected to be identical whether or not the new machine is purchased. The old machine, if retained, is expected to wear out at the end of 1987, and the new machine, if purchased, is expected to be salvaged at the end of 1987.

In order to decide whether or not to purchase the new machine, Uniprod's management calculated all the incremental cash outflows and cash inflows associated with this action.

Net acquisition cost of new machine

The $824,742 cash outflow to purchase the new machine will be reduced by the investment tax credit, the proceeds from the sale of the old machine, and the tax shield provided by the loss on the sale of the old machine.

The 6 percent investment tax credit on the new machine reduces cash outflows for taxes in 1983 by $49,485 (.06 × $824,742).

The old machine will be sold for $40,000 in cash. Because the old machine has a book value of $80,000, its sale will generate a $40,000 loss ($80,000 book value − $40,000 proceeds from sale) for tax purposes. The loss shields $40,000 of 1983 income from taxes and reduces cash outflow for taxes in 1983 by $16,000 (.4 × $40,000).

The net cash outflow to purchase the new machine is $719,257.

Purchase price of new machine	$824,742
Less:	
Investment tax credit	49,485
Proceeds from sale of old machine	40,000
Tax shield on loss from sale	16,000
Total	105,485
Net acquisition cost of new machine	$719,257

Direct labor costs

In 1984, if the new machine is purchased, cash outflows for direct labor costs will be reduced by $250,000 (100,000 units at a savings of $2.50 per unit). The direct labor cost savings on the 100,000 units produced in 1985 will rise by 12 percent to $280,000 and by an additional 12 percent to $313,600 in 1986. In 1987, production will increase to 180,000 circuit boards, and direct labor cost savings will be $632,218 ($2.50 × (1.12)³ × 180,000).

Direct labor cost is a product cost that becomes a tax shield when the circuit boards are sold. In every year from 1984 through 1987 production of circuit boards is equal to sales of circuit boards, and the direct labor cost savings in every year will increase income in the same year. Increased cash outflows for income taxes equal to 40 percent of the direct labor cost savings in every year will result.

	1984	1985	1986	1987
Direct labor cost savings	$250,000	$280,000	$313,600	$632,218
Increased taxes (at 40%)	100,000	112,000	125,440	252,887
Net direct labor cost savings	$150,000	$168,000	$188,160	$379,331

Depreciation tax shield

Depreciation, like direct labor, is a product cost that does not become a tax shield until the product is sold. Under ACRS the cost basis of the new machine is the original cost of the machine minus half of the associated investment tax credit. The original cost is $824,742, and the applicable 6 percent investment tax credit is $49,485. The cost basis for income tax purposes of the new machine is $800,000 ($824,742 − (½)$49,485). The ACRS percentages of this cost recoverable as depreciation over the next three years are 25 percent, 38 percent, and 37 percent, respectively.

The old machine has a remaining useful life of two years at the end of 1983. Sum-of-the-years'-digits depreciation in 1984 will be ($\frac{2}{36}$) of $960,000 and ($\frac{1}{36}$) of $960,000 in 1985.

If the new machine is purchased, the old machine will be sold, and the depreciation on the old machine will no longer be a component of taxable income. The following table shows the benefit from the incremental depreciation if the new machine is purchased.

	1984	1985	1986
Depreciation on new machine	$200,000 (.25 × $800,000)	$304,000 (.38 × $800,000)	$296,000 (.37 × $800,000)
Depreciation on old machine	53,333 (($\frac{2}{36}$) × $960,000)	26,667 (($\frac{1}{36}$) × $960,000)	–0–
Incremental depreciation	146,667	277,333	296,000
Tax shield of incremental depreciation (at 40%)	$58,667	$110,933	$118,400

Salvage value of new machine

The only other expected net incremental cash inflow to result from purchasing the new machine is the inflow that results when the new machine is sold for $100,000 in 1987. Since the book value will be zero in 1987 the gain on sale of the machine will be $100,000. This will increase taxes[5] by $40,000 (.4 × $100,000), and the net proceeds from the sale will be $60,000 ($100,000 proceeds from sale less $40,000 taxes).

[5] Losses resulting from the disposition of equipment are treated as ordinary expenses. Portions of gains resulting from the disposition of equipment are sometimes treated as capital gains and taxed at lower-than-ordinary income tax rates. In this problem we assume the gain is taxed at the ordinary tax rate.

Training costs

The $50,000 expenditures for management training in 1984 and 1985 are additional incremental cash outflows associated with the purchase of the new machine. Since the training costs reduce taxable income, the cash outflow after income taxes is $30,000 (.6 × $50,000).

Conclusion

The analysis of incremental cash flows summarized in Illustration 21–2 indicates that the new machine should be purchased.

The incremental cash inflows, discounted at Uniprod's after tax cost of capital, 16 percent, have a present value of $778,092. The

ILLUSTRATION 21–2. **Uniprod Company: Summary of incremental benefits of new machine**

	1984	1985	1986	1987
Benefits:				
Direct labor savings	$250,000	$280,000	$313,600	$632,218
Increased taxes (at 40%)	100,000	112,000	125,440	252,887
Net direct labor cost savings	150,000	168,000	188,160	379,331
Increased depreciation	146,667	277,333	296,000	—
Depreciation tax shield (at 40%)	58,667	110,933	118,400	—
Disposal of new machine				100,000
Tax on gain from disposal				40,000
Net disposal gain				60,000
Cash benefits of purchase	208,667	278,933	306,560	439,331
Costs:				
Training costs	50,000	50,000		
Tax savings	20,000	20,000		
Net training costs	30,000	30,000		
Net benefit (cash inflow)	$178,667	$248,933	$306,560	$439,331
Discount factor (at 16%)	.8621	.7432	.6407	.5523
Present value	$154,029	$185,007	$196,413	$242,643
Sum of present value of benefits (1984–1987)	$778,092			
Less: Net acquisition cost	719,257			
Net present value	$ 58,835			

present value of the initial investment in the new machine is $719,257, and the present value of the future incremental cash flows less the initial investment, is $58,835 ($778,092 − $719,257). *Because the net present value is positive* Uniprod Company should purchase the new machine, assuming there are no apparent qualitative factors to offset the positive net present value.

CHANGING INVENTORY LEVELS AND OVERHEAD ALLOCATION RATES AND ESTIMATING CASH FLOWS

If finished goods, work in process, or raw material inventories fluctuate over time, or if factory overhead allocation rates change over time, all production costs will not appear in the statement of taxable income in the same year that they are incurred. Under these conditions it is more difficult than previously illustrated to estimate cash flows in capital budgeting problems.

Unless these changes are extreme, the change in the net present value won't be that great. Recognizing that the projected cash flows are usually rough estimates of what will occur and that qualitative factors will also be considered in the decision to accept or reject the project, it is frequently quicker, less computationally demanding, and just as useful for decision-making purposes, to solve the problem assuming constant inventory levels and overhead allocation rates.

ALTERNATIVES TO NET PRESENT VALUE

Net present value is the best investment criterion for project selection. It factors the time value of money, the magnitudes of projected cash flows, and the riskiness of the project into the evaluation of the project. We consider alternatives to the net present value criterion and indicate why they may lead to incorrect decisions.

Payback period

The payback period of an investment is the length of time it takes for cumulative projected cash inflows to equal the initial investment. The net initial investment for the machine in the Uniprod example was $719,257. The cash inflow from the investment was $178,667 in the first year (see Illustration 21–2 for cash flows) and $248,933 in year 2. Cumulative inflow for the first two years was $427,600 ($178,667 + $248,933), which is less than the initial $719,257 investment. The payback period is therefore greater than two years. In year 3 the cash inflow was $306,560, and the cumulative cash inflow for the three years was $734,160. Since $734,160 exceeds $719,257 the payback period is somewhere between two and three years. Assuming uniform cash flows throughout the third year the payback period is about 2.95 years ($719,257 is about .95 of the way between $427,600 and $734,160).

If Uniprod uses two years as a payback period cutoff for capital investment decisions, then the new machine will not be purchased. If Uniprod arbitrarily selects three years as a cutoff, the new machine will be purchased.

The payback period cutoff for investment selection is an arbitrarily specified rule that ignores the time value of money and all cash flows beyond some time period. It should not be used for capital budgeting.

The folly of the payback rule is readily illustrated by simple examples. Suppose a company uses two years as a cutoff payback period for capital budgeting. Consider two investments.

	Cash Flow in Year			
Investment	0	1	2	3
A	−$1	$.50	$.50	–0–
B	−$1	–0–	–0–	$10

Project A, for an initial investment of $1, returns $.50 in both years 1 and 2 and nothing thereafter. Project B, for an initial investment of $1, returns nothing in years 1 or 2 and $10 in year 3. Project A will be selected since it has a payback period of two years, and project B will be rejected because it has a payback period beyond two years.

Discounted payback, a generalization of simple payback, includes the time value of money. In the Uniprod Company example the discounted cash inflows for the first three years are $154,029, $185,007, and $196,413, respectively (see Illustration 21–2). Total discounted cash inflow for the three years is $535,449—less than the initial investment of $719,257. Since cumulative discounted cash inflow over four years is $778,092, ($535,449 + $242,643), the discounted payback period is between three and four years—approximately 3.76 years if cash inflows occur uniformly throughout the year. As an investment criterion, discounted payback, like simple payback, is an arbitrary rule that ignores cash inflows occurring after the cutoff date. It should not be used for capital budgeting.

Accounting rate of return

The accounting rate of return is usually defined as the average projected accounting net income (including depreciation and taxes) over the life of the project divided by the average book value of the investment over the project's life. It is also often called return on assets (ROA) or return on investment (ROI).

On January 1, 1980 (prior to 1981 ERTA), Transpo Company invested $30,000 in an asset that was expected to generate pretax cash inflows of $30,000, $15,000, and $10,000 in each of the next three years, respectively. At that time Transpo used sum-of-the-years'-digits depreciation for tax purposes and a 20 percent opportunity cost of capital to evaluate investments of this type. The following aftertax cash flows resulted.

	Year		
	1	2	3
Taxable income before depreciation	$30,000	$15,000	$10,000
Depreciation	15,000	10,000	5,000
Taxable income	15,000	5,000	5,000
Income tax (at 50%).......................	7,500	2,500	2,500
Cash flow (taxable income before depreciation − income tax)	$22,500	$12,500	$ 7,500

The net present value of the above investment, when the opportunity cost of capital is 20 percent, is $1,771.

$$NPV = -30,000 + \frac{\$22,500}{(1.2)} + \frac{\$12,500}{(1.2)^2} + \frac{\$7,500}{(1.2)^3} = \$1,771$$

Assuming straight-line depreciation for book purposes, the above investment was expected to result in the following sequence of accounting incomes.

	Year		
	1	2	3
Income before depreciation and taxes	$30,000	$15,000	$10,000
Depreciation	10,000	10,000	10,000
Pretax income	20,000	5,000	–0–
Income tax (at 50%)	10,000	2,500	–0–
Net income	$10,000	$ 2,500	$ –0–

The averaged projected accounting income was $4,166 ($12,500/3). The average projected book value of investment over the three years was $15,000 (the asset value declines at a uniform rate from $30,000 to $0 over three years). The accounting rate of return for this project was 27.78 percent ($4,166/$15,000). Using either net present value or accounting rate of return this investment will be made.

Now suppose the above $30,000 asset was expected to generate pretax cash flows of $15,000, $10,000, and $30,000 in each of the next three years (same cash flows as previously, except different ordering through time).

	Year		
	1	2	3
Taxable income before depreciation	$15,000	$10,000	$30,000
Depreciation	15,000	10,000	5,000
Taxable income	–0–	–0–	25,000
Income tax (at 50%)	–0–	–0–	12,500
Cash flow (taxable income before depreciation – income tax)	$15,000	$10,000	$17,500

The net present value of this investment when the opportunity cost of capital is 20 percent is −$428.

$$\text{NPV} = -30,000 + \frac{15,000}{(1.2)} + \frac{10,000}{(1.2)^2} + \frac{17,500}{(1.2)^3} = -\$428$$

	Year		
	1	2	3
Accounting income before depreciation and taxes	$15,000	$10,000	$30,000
Depreciation	10,000	10,000	10,000
Pretax income	5,000	–0–	20,000
Income tax (at 50%).............................	2,500	–0–	10,000
Net income.....................................	$ 2,500	$ –0–	$10,000

Since the average accounting income and book value of investment are identical to those in the previous example, the accounting rate of return will again be 27.78 ($4,166/$12,500) percent.

The accounting rate of return is identical for the above two investments, one that has a positive net present value and should be accepted and another that has a negative net present value and should be rejected.

Accounting rate of return should not be used to make capital budgeting decisions. It ignores the time value of money and project riskiness. It is based on accounting income rather than cash flows. It is an arbitrary rule without economic basis and can lead to incorrect capital investment decisions.

Internal rate of return

The internal rate of return is that discount rate that makes the net present value of an investment project zero. In the Uniprod Company example the internal rate of return, r, is the solution to the following equation:

$$0 = -\$719,257 + \frac{\$178,667}{(1+r)} + \frac{\$248,933}{(1+r)^2} + \frac{\$306,560}{(1+r)^3} + \frac{\$439,331}{(1+r)^4}$$

By trial and error the solution is determined to be $r = .194$. The internal rate of return is approximately 19.4 percent.

If the internal rate of return for a project exceeds the opportunity cost of capital, the project is accepted; if not, the project is rejected.

If all cash flows after the initial investment are positive, the investment under consideration is not part of a group of mutually exclusive projects (only one in the group will be selected), and the opportunity cost of capital doesn't change with time, then accepting only projects with internal rates of return in excess of the opportunity cost of capital is equivalent to accepting only projects with positive net present values.

If cash flows change sign over the life of the investment (there are net cash outflows in other than the year of initial investment) the equation that one would solve to obtain the internal rate of return may not have a unique solution.

INVESTMENT AND FINANCING DECISIONS

When investing and financing decisions are independent of each other the capital investment selection process does not consider how the investments are financed. In the Uniprod example we ignored how the purchase of the machine would be financed, assuming the purchase of that particular machine came from Uniprod's regular financing capacity.

In some instances the financing and investment decisions interact, and the interactions must be considered in decision making. Suppose in the Uniprod example the government would offer subsidized loans to purchasers of the type of equipment Uniprod is considering. If Uniprod decides to purchase the machine they will obtain a government loan of $500,000 bearing 4 percent interest, repayable in four equal annual payments of $137,740 ($500,000 is the present value at 4 percent of a four-year $137,740 annuity). Suppose that Uniprod currently pays interest at a rate of 8 percent on loans of this type. Illustration 21–3 computes the present value of the subsidized loan (shows the economic value of the loan to

Uniprod). At the time the equipment is purchased Uniprod will receive $500,000 in cash and then discharge this indebtedness over four years at the rate of $137,740 per year. Considering taxes saved on the interest and the fact that Uniprod is paying only 4 percent for what should be an 8 percent loan, the present value of all payments is only $438,680. Uniprod increases its net present value by $61,320 ($500,000 − $438,680) if the subsidized loan is taken. Considering the new machine and subsidized loan as a package Uniprod will have a net present value of $120,155 ($58,835, the net present value of the new machine, plus $61,320, the net present value of the subsidized financing) if the new machine is purchased.

ILLUSTRATION 21–3. **Present Value of the Cost of the Subsidized Loan (dollar amounts in 000s)**

		Year			
		1	2	3	4
(a)	Beginning indebtedness	$500.00	$382.26	$259.81	$132.46
(b)	Cash payment	$137.74	$137.74	$137.74	$137.74
(c)	Interest (.04(a))	$ 20.00	$ 15.29	$ 10.39	$ 5.30
(d)	Principal repayment ((b) − (c))	$117.74	$122.45	$127.35	$132.46
(e)	Ending indebtedness ((a) − (d))	$382.26	$259.81	$132.46	−0−
(f)	Tax shield on interest (.4(c))	$ 8.00	$ 6.12	$ 4.16	$ 2.12
(g)	Net cash outflow ((b) − (f))	$129.74	$131.62	$133.58	$135.62
	Present value factor at .08	.926	.857	.794	.735
	Present value	$120.14	$112.80	$106.06	$ 99.68
	Total present value	$438.68			

BUDGET CONSTRAINTS

A budget constraint limits the amount of capital available for investment. Many large corporations have almost unlimited access to money markets yet still impose budget constraints on capital investment. Frequently such constraints are imposed to slow rapid growth and represent a limit on available skilled personnel to manage projects rather than a limit on available capital.

If there is a budget constraint, project selection cannot be made solely on the basis of individual net present values. There is a complicated problem in selecting the package of projects that gives the highest net present value without exceeding available investment funds.

Suppose a company has a single budget constraint of $12. It is considering four projects with positive net present values. Each project generates only positive yearly cash inflows after the initial investment.

Project	Net Present Value		Initial Investment
A	$20		$10
B	5		3
C	19		8
D	3		2

If the project with the highest net present value is selected, A in the example, then the $2 in remaining funds can be invested in D. The combined net present value of A and D is $23. However the company will be better off by investing in B and C. Only $11 of the investment funds will be expended to obtain a combined net present value of $24.

Linear and integer programming are used to select optimal groups of projects when there are many projects and many constraints.

APPENDIX: ACCELERATED COST RECOVERY SYSTEM OVERVIEW

ILLUSTRATION 21A–1. **Classification of Property by Recovery Period**

Period of Recovery	Property Included
3-year	Autos, light trucks, equipment used in connection with research and experimentation, and personal property with an asset depreciation range (ADR)* midpoint life of four years or less.
5-year	Most other machinery and equipment, furniture and fixtures, single-purpose agricultural structures, and petroleum storage facilities.
10-year	Public utility property with an ADR midpoint life greater than 18 but not greater than 25 years, railroad tank cars, manufactured homes, and real property with an ADR midpoint life of 12.5 years or less.
15-year	Public utility property with an ADR midpoint life exceeding 25 years and real property with an ADR life of more than 12.5 years or with no ADR life.

* Asset depreciation ranges allowed under previous tax law.

ILLUSTRATION 21A–2. **Percentage of Cost of Recoverable as Depreciation Each Year**

Year of Recovery	Period of Recovery			
	3-year	5-year	10-year	15-year
1	25%	15%	8%	5%
2	38	22	14	10
3	37	21	12	9
4	—	21	10	8
5	—	21	10	7
6	—	—	10	7
7	—	—	9	6
8	—	—	9	6
9	—	—	9	6
10	—	—	9	6
11	—	—	—	6
12	—	—	—	6
13	—	—	—	6
14	—	—	—	6
15	—	—	—	6

Tax credits and depreciable basis of assets

Beginning in 1983

100 percent of the cost of the acquired asset *less* half of any associated investment, energy, or qualified rehabilitation credit is depreciated over the recovery period.

The reduction in the depreciable basis associated with the *investment* tax credit can be avoided by electing to reduce the ITC by 2 percentage points (from 10 percent to 8 percent or from 6 percent to 4 percent).

Investment tax credit limitation

Beginning in tax years after 1982 the maximum investment tax credit is $25,000 plus 90 percent of the tax liability in excess of $25,000.

PROBLEMS AND CASES

21-1 Big Investment Company

The Big Investment Company pays income taxes equal to 46 percent of taxable income. The relevant aftertax discount rate for all cash flows associated with Big Investment investments is 15 percent.

Required:

1. An asset is purchased for $500,000 cash. Under the ACRS system the cost of this asset, which qualifies for a 6 percent investment tax credit, is recoverable as depreciation over three years according to the following percentages: 25 percent, 38 percent, and 37 percent. What is the net present value of the asset (cost of the asset considering the investment tax credit and depreciation tax shield)?

2. Big Investment Company makes a $50,000 expenditure for qualified research and development (in excess of the company's three-year moving average R&D expenditure). What is the net cost of the $50,000 expenditure?

3. A $5,000 expenditure is made at the end of three successive years. The expenditure becomes part of the value of inventory, which will be sold at the end of the fourth year for $30,000 cash. What is the present value of this sequence of transactions?

4. Big Investment has the opportunity to acquire 100,000 pounds of raw material inventory for $100,000 from a competitor who is going out of business. If purchased, the raw material will not be used in production until three years from the date of purchase. If it isn't purchased now, the same raw material will be purchased in three years through normal channels for $160,000. If the material is purchased now, incremental warehousing costs will amount to $5,000 per year (a tax-deductible expense) for each of the next three years. Should the raw material be purchased from the bankrupt competitor?

21-2 Small Business Decision*

Although in most cases businesses are required to capitalize expenditures that will benefit future periods, one new provision in the Economic

---

* Excerpted with permission from Michael H. Morris and William D. Nichols, "The Decision to Expense Certain Capital Expenditures: 'Carrot' or 'Lemon' for the Small Business?" *Journal of Small Business Management,* July 1982, pp. 54–61.

Recovery Tax Act (ERTA) of 1981 gives businesses the option to expense a specific amount of these expenditures beginning in 1982.

The advantage to small businesses arises from the fact that the expense option allows for a write-off of the capital expenditure in the year of purchase. Since it has a maximum dollar amount, it is of limited value to large businesses. In addition, if the capital expenditures are small enough, small businesses may simplify their record keeping by avoiding depreciation computations altogether.

The Section 179 expense deduction, under ERTA of 1981, allows businesses to expense rather than capitalize limited amounts of qualifying expenditures. The dollar limitations on these expenditures are $5,000 for 1982 and 1983, $7,500 for 1984 and 1985, and $10,000 for 1986 and later. Qualifying expenditures include payments for recovery property purchased for use in a trade or business, which is also eligible for the investment tax credit (ITC).

Recovery property is depreciable tangible property that belongs to one of four cost recovery periods delineated by the Internal Revenue Code's new accelerated cost recovery system (ACRS).

In summary, a capital expenditure qualifies for the Section 179 expense deduction if it meets all the following conditions: (1) it is a payment for recovery property, (2) it is eligible for the ITC, (3) it is acquired by purchase, and (4) it is used in a trade or business. For payments that meet these conditions, the business must decide whether to expense or capitalize the expenditures.

(E)ven though this new provision was legislated with the small business in mind, taking advantage of it may yield adverse economic consequences to small businesses. That is, the "carrot" in the ERTA of 1981 for the small business is often a "lemon."

The Small Business Company, Inc., has just made an expenditure of $5,000 to obtain furniture and fixtures for its sales office. The furniture and fixtures are included in the five-year cost recovery period under the ACRS system and qualify for a 10 percent investment tax credit (the investment tax credit will be lost if Small Business decides to expense the cost of the furniture and fixtures).

Small Business Company pays income taxes at a 40 percent rate and uses an aftertax opportunity cost of capital of 8 percent for investment decisions.

Required:

1. Should Small Business Company expense or capitalize the cost of the furniture and fixtures?

2. Would the decision to capitalize or expense the cost of the furniture and fixtures change if only $3,000 had been expended to acquire them?

3. Given the 40 percent tax rate, at what opportunity cost of capital would Small Business be indifferent between expensing or capitalizing the cost of the furniture and fixtures?

21-3 CRR Company

The CRR Company is currently reviewing a project involving a net cash outflow of $100,000 for a new asset. The asset has a four-year useful life, qualifies for a 6 percent investment tax credit, and under ACRS guidelines the initial cost will be recovered over three years as depreciation according to the following percentages: 25 percent, 38 percent, and 37 percent.

CRR normally discounts cash flows at a 15 percent *nominal* rate. CRR estimates the following *real* pretax cash inflows will result if the new asset is acquired. CRR's tax rate is 40 percent.

	Real Cash Inflows for Period			
	1	2	3	4
Pretax cash inflows......	+35,000	+50,000	+20,000	+60,000

For example, at the end of period 1 the investment will generate a cash inflow equivalent to $35,000 *current* dollars; at the end of period 2 the cash inflow is equivalent to $50,000 current dollars, etc.

Inflation is projected at 10 percent per year.

Required:

1. What is the real discount rate?

2. Determine the net present value of the new asset by discounting real cash flows by the real discount rate.

3. Determine the net present value of the new asset by discounting nominal cash flows using the 15 percent nominal discount rate. How does this net present value compare to the net present value computed in 2?

21-4 West Publishing, Inc.

Mr. B. T. Wills, president of West Publishing, Inc., received the memorandum shown below concerning the desirability of purchasing a new bookbinder. Mr. Wills thought the memorandum generally covered the important issues and added that the machine would have to return at least 10 percent after taxes before it would be purchased.

West Publishing pays income taxes at the rate of 45 percent of net income.

Memorandum

To: Mr. B. T. Wills, President of West Publishing, Inc.

From: R. C. Randolph, Controller

Re: Replacement of Old Bookbinder

Listed below are the points to be considered in deciding whether to purchase a new book-binder:

1. It would eliminate the necessity of employing six men for 50 weeks a year who work 40 hours per week at an average wage of $4 per hour.
2. An extra 5,300 books could be produced and sold each year. The unit contribution margin on each additional book is $3. Lack of the present bookbinder's capacity is all that presently prevents this production.
3. The new machine should drastically reduce lost materials due to erratic behavior of the old machine. Estimated material savings are $42,000 per year.
4. Its list price is $695,000, and it will cost another $4,000 to install. The $4,000 installation cost will be expensed for tax purposes. The $695,000 cost of the new machine qualifies for a 10 percent investment tax credit and is recoverable as depreciation for tax purposes over the next five years according to the following percentages: 15 percent, 22 percent, 21 percent, 21 percent, and 21 percent.
5. Its useful life to us is estimated at 8 years, after which time its salvage value is expected to be $35,000.
6. We can sell our old machine for $104,000. Because its book value is $216,000, we incur a $112,000 loss.
7. The old machine allows us to charge off $27,000 straight-line depreciation expense against our 45 percent tax rate.
8. We can use the old machine at its present rate of efficiency for another eight years, although then it will be worthless.

Required:

1. Calculate the net present value of the new bookbinder. (Assume all of the above savings and benefits (items 1, 2, and 3 above) will be constant (0 inflation) over the next eight years. Also assume that West Publishing plans no changes in inventories over the next eight years).

2. What qualitative factors omitted in the net present value computation are relevant to the purchase decision?

3. What is the payback period if the new bookbinder is purchased?

4. What is the internal rate of return of the new bookbinder?

21–5 Uniprod Company

In the Uniprod Company equipment replacement example given earlier in the chapter, suppose that no more than 120,000 circuit boards, the normal level of capacity, can be produced in any year. Uniprod will no longer be able to meet the 1987 demand of 180,000 circuit boards with 1987 production.

Uniprod's planned production and inventory levels for the years 1984 through 1987 are modified to take this constraint into account. All other information is unchanged.

Sales of circuit boards are projected at 100,000 units per year in 1984 through 1986 and 180,000 units in 1987.

Uniprod Company uses the LIFO cost flow inventory method for finished goods and raw material inventories.

There are no beginning raw material, work in process, or finished goods inventories in 1984. No beginning or ending raw material or work in process inventories are planned through 1987. A *steady production* rate of 120,000 units per year from 1984 through 1987 will lead to a *gradual buildup of finished goods inventory* (60,000 units at the beginning of 1987), which will be sold in 1987.

The factory overhead allocation rate is computed every year by dividing the expected variable and fixed factory overhead costs for the year by the normal output of 120,000 circuit boards.

Required:

Compute the incremental cash inflows and cash outflows of purchasing the new machine. Should the new machine be purchased? What nonquantifiable factors would have to be considered in the decision?

21-6 General Electric Credit Corporation*

Although still linked in many peoples' minds with monthly payments on refrigerators and washing machines, General Electric Credit Corporation (GECC) has rapidly developed the capacity to come across with financing on a scale, and with a creative flair, that makes this subsidiary of General Electric Co. one of the largest, most aggressive—and, among competitors, sometimes resented—sources of capital for business.

GECC is pushing hard into all sorts of commercial and industrial financing, in which—thanks to immense tax advantages for its parent—it can sharply undercut the competition.

Since GECC's books are consolidated with its parent's for tax purposes, those tax benefits shave hundreds of millions of dollars a year off the total General Electric tax bill. Last year, GECC's considerable tax benefits, which included those purchased from others under the "safe harbor" provisions of the Economic Recovery Tax Act of 1981, slashed its parent's tax bill from $529 million to an almost token $50 million.

Tax advantages include the following: Owners of plant and equipment leased to others are entitled to investment tax credits, depreciation write-offs, and energy tax credits. The Windfall Profits Tax Act of 1980 grants energy tax credits, in addition to investment tax credits, to encourage investment in projects consistent with national energy policies [e.g., solar or wind energy property, recycling equipment, shale oil equipment, alternative (to oil) energy property]. Energy tax credits are available for the 1982–91 period if the following conditions are satisfied: all extensive engineering studies are complete before 1983, all construction permit applications are

---
*Excerpted with permission from "General Electric Credit: From Financing Home Appliances to an Aggressive Source of Funds for Industry," *Business Week*, August 30, 1982.

filed before 1983, and contracts to acquire or construct at least 50 percent of the qualifying project are signed before 1986.

Frequently lessees are unable to use the credits themselves because of low income or excess credits from other investments. GECC's banking competition is also at a disadvantage. The banks can make much less use of tax shelter, given their profit problems and holdings of tax-exempt municipal securities. What is more, loan problems have caused the rating agencies to downgrade debt issues of many bank holding companies, which tends to elevate their borrowing costs and hamper them in pricing loans competitively."

Required:

1.   Suppose company C has the opportunity to invest $100,000 in an asset that will reduce cash outflows for operating expenses by $41,667, $50,000, and $58,333 in each of the next three years, respectively. The cost of the asset is recoverable as depreciation for tax purposes over the next three years according to the following percentages: 25 percent, 38 percent, and 37 percent. Because of either low anticipated taxable income in the immediate future or sufficient tax credits from other investments which already offset the maximum taxes allowed, company C will not be able to use either the 6 percent investment tax credit or 10 percent energy tax credit that the equipment qualifies for. Company C has an aftertax opportunity cost of capital of 16 percent and pays income taxes at a 40 percent rate. Should company C invest in the new asset?

2.   Bank B, which can use both the investment and energy tax credits the above investment will generate, offers to lease the asset to company C for $44,000 to be paid at the end of each of the next three years. Bank B has an opportunity cost of capital of 18 percent and pays income taxes at a 40 percent rate. Bank B will retain ownership and depreciation rights to the asset. Show how these lease terms are favorable to both company C and bank B.

3.   Credit company D can also use both the investment and energy tax credits the above asset will generate. Credit company D has an opportunity cost of capital of 14 percent and pays income taxes at a 50 percent rate. What is the minimum lease payment (to be paid at the end of each of the next three years) that company D would accept from company C for the above asset?

───────────── **21–7   Southwestern Electric Power Company*** ─────────────

Electric utility rates are designed primarily to cover the cost of serving all customers. These costs, with the exception of return on equity, are taken from the utility's books, which must be kept in accordance with standards

* Excerpted with permission from L. W. Brewer, "Determining Revenue Requirements for Regulated Utilities," *Management Accounting,* September 1979, p. 41.

issued by various regulatory agencies. With some modifications that adapt the accounting system to the specific needs of the regulated industry, generally accepted accounting principles, as that term might be understood by the unregulated business sector, are followed.

Included in the cost to serve is a return to investors as well as operating costs incurred by the utility. Theoretically, when rates fail over time to reflect adequately the cost to serve, they are adjusted to restore service at cost. The result is that revenues likely to flow from an investment will depend on how the investment and related costs are accounted for in regulatory practice. This dependence of revenues on accounting cost recognition is important in distinguishing the investment analysis process in regulated firms from that of unregulated firms. Because the unregulated firm may charge what the market will bear, projects with the highest revenue for a given level of costs will be the most attractive. To the regulated electric utility, all projects with similar costs will produce similar revenues.

State-of-the-art methodology for investment analysis, such as the net present value method, attempts to identify the investment alternative that maximizes the wealth of the firm. Since the rate-making process sets charges on the basis of cost plus a fair return and no more, utility investment alternatives when examined under a wealth maximization criterion should be indistinguishable.

In addition to the neutrality of the net present value model, regulatory agencies require (and utilities recognize a duty to so provide) service at minimum cost. The penalty for not providing service at minimum cost is the potential disallowance of excessive expenditures in subsequent rate proceedings.

Because justification of utility investment is strongest when it demonstrates that the investment represents the minimum cost to the customer of obtaining necessary service, Southwestern Electric Power Company (SWEPCO) uses an approach similar to the one discussed in the next two sections for analyzing investments.

Exhibit 1 demonstrates the development of the revenue requirement for a hypothetical five-year investment using the following assumptions:

EXHIBIT 1. **Revenue Requirements for Hypothetical 5-Year Investment**

Line No.		Year 1	Year 2	Year 3	Year 4	Year 5
1	Operating expenses:					
2	Depreciation (straight-line)	$ 300.00	$ 300.00	$300.00	$300.00	$300.00
3	Maintenance	50.00	50.00	50.00	60.00	70.00
4	Insurance	8.00	8.00	8.00	8.00	8.00
5	Property taxes	10.00	8.00	6.00	5.00	5.00
6	Expense before income taxes	368.00	366.00	364.00	373.00	383.00
7	Income taxes	184.00	183.00	182.00	186.50	191.50
8	Investment tax credit	20.00	20.00	20.00	20.00	20.00
9	Net operating income	$ 164.00	$ 163.00	$162.00	$166.50	$171.50
10	Rate base (average)	$1,350.00	$1,050.00	$750.00	$450.00	$150.00
11	Deferred taxes (average)	50.00	125.00	150.00	125.00	50.00
12	Net rate base	1,300.00	925.00	600.00	325.00	100.00

EXHIBIT 1 *(concluded)*

Line No.		Year 1	Year 2	Year 3	Year 4	Year 5
13	Return on rate base	$ 108.55	$ 77.24	$ 50.10	$ 27.14	$ 8.35
14	Return requirements					
	(Line 9 + Line 13)	272.55	240.24	212.10	193.64	179.85
15	Revenue requirement					
	(Line 14 × 2)	545.10	480.48	424.20	387.28	359.70

a. An investment of $1,500 is required, and return on investment is at the marginal cost of capital as determined below, on the average amount of investment outstanding during the year.

b. The marginal cost of capital is 8.35 percent, determined as follows.

Component	Net- of-tax Cost*	Percent of Capital Structure	Component Cost
Debt	4.5%	50	2.25
Preferred	9 %	10	.90
Common	13 %	40	5.20
Total			8.35

* Assumed for purpose of this example only.

c. Depreciation is sum-of-the-years'-digits for tax purposes, straight-line for book purposes. Tax timing differences are normalized for book purposes by crediting deferred taxes to a reserve and drawing upon the reserve when tax depreciation is exceeded by book depreciation.

d. An investment tax credit of $100 is available on purchase of the asset.

e. The income tax rate is 50 percent.

Lines 2 through 5 in Exhibit 1 show expenses other than income taxes as they might occur on the books for regulatory purposes. Note that depreciation is at a straight-line rate. This is consistent with the normalization procedure discussed above. Line 7 shows income tax effects that would be allowed in a rate case and that result from the incurrence of the operating expenses shown in lines 2 through 5. Because of Internal Revenue Code requirements, investment tax credits do not reduce costs in the year received. The method of recovering these credits in rates is shown on line 8. They are flowed back ratably over the life of the asset. The effect of these operating account adjustments on net operating income (line 9) is a reduction of $164 in year 1. (Since net operating income is reduced by these expenses, rate relief must provide an additional $164.)

Line 10 represents the average investment outstanding for the year. This is offset by the deferred taxes generated from timing differences between book and tax depreciation. These amounts for year 1 are calculated as follows:

$$\text{Year 1: Average rate base} = \frac{\text{Beginning investment} + \text{Ending investment}}{2}$$

568

Where

Beginning investment = Prior year end investment

Ending investment = Beginning investment − Annual book depreciation

$$\frac{1{,}500 + 1{,}200}{2} = \$1{,}350$$

Year 1: Average deferred taxes $= \dfrac{\text{Beginning cumulative balance} + \text{Ending cumulative balance}}{2}$

Where:

Beginning cumulative balance = Prior year ending cumulative balance
Ending cumulative balance = (Tax depreciation − Straight-line) × Tax rate + Beginning cumulative balance

$$\frac{0 + (500 - 300).5}{2} = \$50$$

Line 13 reflects return needed on the additional net rate base at an 8.35 percent marginal cost of capital. The revenue requirements are shown on line 15, assuming a 50 percent income tax rate.

Required:

1. Assume that prior to making the investment, the utility income statement and rate base look like the following:

Revenues	$ 8,000.00
Depreciation	5,400.00*
Pretax income	2,600.00
Income tax	950.00
Net operating income	$ 1,650.00
Net rate base	$15,556.00
Return on net rate base	10.6%

* Tax depreciation is also $5,400.

Note that the assumed return on the rate base is 10.6 percent. Because the tax deductibility of interest is reflected in income tax expense (i.e., it reduces it), the 10.6 percent return is consistent with the 8.35 percent tax-adjusted return developed earlier. Show that the above income statement, when adjusted for the new investment, maintains the 10.6 percent return.

2. Suppose the customers' average cost of capital, 5 percent, is used to discount the above five-year revenue requirements (line 15 in Exhibit 1). What is the net present value?

3. Suppose SWEPCO has an alternative investment that will satisfy power needs the same as in the above example. This alternative investment

will have $445 per year in revenue requirements for each of the next five years. Should SWEPCO invest in this alternative investment or in the investment discussed above? Why?

21–8   Vantype Printing Company

The Vantype Printing Company is a printer and publisher of guide books and directories. The board of directors of the company has hired you as a consultant to determine the feasibility of accepting a proposal from a local outside printer to do Vantype's printing for the next five years.

The following information to be used in making the recommendation was obtained for you by your staff.

Annual Costs Based on Last Year's Volume

	Departments			
	Publishing	Printing	Shipping	Total
Salaries and wages	$275,000	$150,000	$25,000	$ 450,000
Telephone and telegraph ...	12,000	3,700	300	16,000
Materials and supplies	50,000	250,000	10,000	310,000
Occupancy costs	75,000	80,000	10,000	165,000
General and administrative ..	40,000	30,000	4,000	74,000
Depreciation	5,000	40,000	5,000	50,000
	$457,000	$553,700	$54,300	$1,065,000

Additional information:

a. A review of personnel requirements indicates that if printing is discontinued the publishing department will need one additional clerk at $4,000 per year to handle correspondence with the printer. Two layout men and a proofreader in the printing department will be retained at an aggregate annual cost of $17,000; other personnel in the printing department can be released. One mailing clerk, at $3,000, will be retained; others in the shipping department can be released. Employees whose employment was being terminated would immediately receive, on the average, three months' termination pay. The termination pay would be amortized on a straight-line basis over a five-year period on the company's books. It will be expensed immediately for tax purposes.

b. Long distance telephone and telegraph charges are identified and distributed to the responsible department. The remainder of the telephone bill, representing basic service at a cost of $4,000, was allocated in the ratio of 10 to publishing, 5 to printing, and 1 to shipping. The discontinuance of printing is not expected to have a material effect on the basic service cost.

c. Shipping materials and supplies consist of cartons, envelopes, and stamps. It is estimated that the cost of envelopes and stamps for mailing to an outside printer would be $3,000 per year.

d. If printing is discontinued, the company would retain its present building and could obtain a five-year sublet at an annual rental of $50,000 for a portion of the space now used for printing. Taxes, insurance, heat, light, and other occupancy costs would not be significantly affected.

e. One cost clerk would not be required ($6,000 per year) if printing is discontinued. Other general and administrative personnel would be retained.

f. Included in administrative expenses is interest expense on a 10 percent mortgage loan of $600,000. The mortgage is on the building.

g. Printing department inventory of paper and ink has a book value (which also approximates its net realizable value) of $25,000.

h. Printing and shipping room machinery having a net book value of $275,000 could be sold for $150,000 now. It was expected to have a salvage value of $50,000 five years from now. The company calculates its depreciation on original cost ($500,000) minus salvage value ($50,000) and uses a 10-year straight-line method for both financial reporting and tax returns.

i. The outside printer's proposal was $525,000 per year for a five-year contract with a printing volume equivalent to last year's level with a guarantee of no price increases.

j. The company estimated printing volume for the next five years would be approximately the same as it was for last year.

k. The company is in the 40 percent tax bracket and expects to be in this bracket for the next five years.

l. The company has been earning 12 percent (after tax) on its investment, and the board of directors consider this to be a satisfactory return.

Required:

Indicate whether you think Vantype Printing should accept the outside printer's proposal and subcontract its printing for the next five years. You should prepare a formal quantitative presentation to support your conclusion as well as a *brief* summary of all the nonquantitative factors you think should be considered.

21-9 Guilbran Boating

Guilbran Boating, a manufacturer of boats and marine equipment in southern Connecticut, is contemplating the manufacture and installation of boat docks. Equipment necessary for the production of the docks can be purchased for $100,000. Assume contrary to ACRS rules which would classify it as a five-year asset that the equipment qualifies for a 6 percent investment tax credit, has a four-year useful life, a zero salvage value, and will be depreciated over three years under the ACRS tax depreciation system (recovery percentages are 25 percent, 38 percent, and 37 percent).

Expected demand is 300 docks per year for the next four years. Guilbran Boating's tax rate is 40 percent, and Guilbran has ample income to offset any losses that may arise in any of the next four years from the boat dock business.

The vice president of manufacturing has assembled the following production cost estimates. Direct labor is paid at the rate of $4 per hour, and variable overhead amounts to 50 percent of direct labor costs. Direct materials will cost $1,000 per dock, and incremental fixed overhead (exclusive of depreciation) will require a cash outflow of $100,000 in each of the next four years if the docks are manufactured.

The completed docks will sell for $1,700 each. The manufacturing vice president learned from an old classmate, a vice president of a Florida boat dock manufacturer that had recently purchased a similar piece of equipment, that 6,810 direct labor-hours were required to produce the first 100 boat docks (68.10 direct labor-hours per dock).

Required:

1. On the basis of the above information demonstrate that Guilbran Boating should not purchase the new equipment. Guilbran requires an aftertax return of 15 percent on projects of equal risk. (Ignore the effects of inflation on costs in your computation.)

2. Having read the above report and your recommendation in 1, the new assistant controller, with several years of boat dock manufacturing experience behind her, became very upset. At the next general management meeting she argued that boat dock manufacturing involves a learning phenomena, which, if taken into account, might make the investment in new equipment favorable. She left you with the following explanation of learning curves and the instruction to redo the analysis in (1) considering the information.

The following is an expression for the average number of direct labor hours, Y, to produce X cumulative units of production if it takes 300 hours to produce the first dock and 80 percent learning is appropriate.

$$Y = 300 \, X^{-.322}$$

For example, when $X = 300$, then $Y = 47.81$ direct labor-hours. It takes an average of 47.81 direct labor-hours to produce each of the first 300 docks, a total direct labor usage of 14,343 hours (47.81 × 300). When $X = 600$, then $Y = 38.24$. The average number of direct labor-hours to produce each of the first 600 docks, 38.24 hours, is approximately 80 percent of the average number of direct labor-hours to produce each of the first 300 docks (38.24 = .8 × 47.81). It takes 8,601 (14,343 − 600 × 38.24) direct labor-hours to produce the second 300 docks. Should Guilbran Boating purchase the new equipment?

3. Assuming demand is not known for sure but will be equal for each of the next four years. What will demand have to be in order to break even (net present value of the investment equal to zero)?

22

Budgeting

Budgets are written documents that express management's consensus on the outcomes of planned actions during an accounting period. The *master budget,* the collection of schedules and plans describing the activities of an organization during a time period, results from a complex, iterative, interactive process involving all levels of management.

THE BUDGET PROCESS

The budget process of every organization is unique—it is determined by the organizational structure, the nature of its outputs, and how the master budget will be used in control and performance evaluation during and at the end of the period.

We will describe the budget process in a hypothetical, two-division, two-product manufacturing firm, PPM Company, and illustrate the basic components of a master budget. Illustration 22–1 contains a portion of the organizational chart of the PPM Company.

The operations of each division are coordinated by and are the

ILLUSTRATION 22–1. **Organizational Chart: PPM Company**

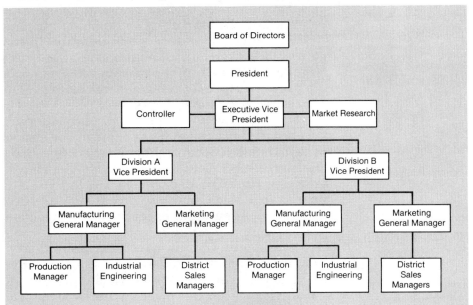

responsibility of a division vice president. Manufacturing general managers direct the production and industrial engineering functions in each division. Marketing general managers coordinate activities of the district sales managers in each division. The manufacturing and marketing general managers in each division report directly to the divisional vice presidents. An executive vice president coordinates divisional activities, plans financial strategy with the assistance of a corporate controller (determines cash levels, short- and long-term borrowing, new stock issues, etc.), and develops a formal statement of the general marketing climate in conjunction with the marketing research department (target market shares, advertising levels, etc).

PPM Company prepares annual budgets one fiscal year in advance of the date they will be used. PPM begins preparing the following year's budget in the month of July preceding the budget year that starts on January 1. Budgeting activity follows the organizational chart and usually begins with the formulation of a sales budget.

Preparing the sales budget

Projections of next year's sales levels are based on information about current sales levels, trends in industry sales volume and in the general economic climate, and target market shares. Sales levels also depend on the level of firm and industry advertising, pricing policies, and the marketing strategies of all competitors.

Sales projections can be made from the "bottom up" or the "top down." PPM Company combines aspects of both strategies as most large firms do. In July the district sales managers in all divisions are asked by the marketing general managers to provide preliminary estimates of next year's sales. District sales managers consider current sales levels, the quality of individual sales personnel, and knowledge about the plans of their major customers in projecting next years sales. Concurrently the executive vice president requests the marketing research department to independently formulate sales estimates. This department uses formal statistical approaches, such as regression analysis, to construct its sales estimates.[1]

Early in August the executive vice president, with sales projections from marketing research, meets with both of the divisional vice presidents, who by now have preliminary sales projections from their marketing general managers. The purpose of the meeting is to compare projections, isolate differences, and understand assumptions. After this meeting the divisional vice presidents meet with their marketing general managers and ask them to factor any new information into their projections. The executive vice president also allows marketing research to reconsider its projections. Early in September the executive and divisional vice presidents meet again to consider the revised sales estimates. Usually by this time both projections agree. If not, the budgets are sent back for revision, and additional meetings are held until consensus is reached.

Actual sales levels are compared to budgeted sales levels by division and district at the end of every fiscal year (December 31). Bonuses given to all sales personnel are dependent on their ability to meet or exceed sales budgets.

PPM Company believes that the above approach leads to realistic sales estimates for the coming year. The objective statistical approach guards against overly optimistic sales projections from dis-

---

[1] Regression analysis is a statistical technique for defining a straight line that best represents some data points. In sales estimation, for example, the data points could consist of past years' sales, advertising, expenditures, and gross national products (GNPs). After collecting past data, regression analysis could be used to estimate the three parameters, b_1, b_2, and b_3, in the following equation:

$$Sales = b_1 (advertising) + b_2 (GNP) + b_3$$

Planned advertising expenditures for next year and the government's projection of next year's GNP could then be inserted into the equation to obtain an estimate of sales for next year.

trict sales managers, while the input of sales personnel factors the human element and detailed information into the broader, mechanical approach of the marketing research department. The bonus system assures that all levels of sales personnel will strive to attain and exceed sales estimates (which are viewed as fair by all marketing personnel) for the year.

In the coming fiscal year PPM Company projects sales of 20,000 units of product A by division A and 10,000 units of product B by division B.

Preparing production and inventory budgets

Throughout the period the divisional industrial engineering departments develop and revise production cost and efficiency standards. Once divisional sales levels and revenues are set, divisional manufacturing general managers, in conjunction with their production managers, determine efficient production schedules for the next period. Short-term decision making begins in earnest at this point. Detailed information about the seasonal nature of next period's demand, the cost of holding inventory, the cost of setting up for various production runs, the cost of subcontracting, and technological constraints on machinery and personnel are considered. The result is a tentative production and inventory schedule for next period.

Illustration 22–2 contains various PPM Company cost, revenue, production, and inventory data for the coming fiscal year. We will focus on product A in division A.

Physical budget

The preliminary plan calls for a beginning finished goods inventory of 10,000 units, an ending level of 7,000 units, and expected sales of 20,000 units (see the sales budget in Illustration 22–3). The following computation demonstrates that a production level of 17,000 units of A is consistent with these inventory and sales figures.

Planned Beginning Inventory	+	Planned Production	−	Planned Ending Inventory	=	Planned Sales

10,000 units + 17,000 units − 7,000 units = 20,000 units

This computation is summarized in the production/inventory budget in Illustration 22–3.

ILLUSTRATION 22-2.   PPM Company Data

Standard production and selling costs

	Product A		Product B	
Raw material	$ 4	(2 lbs. at $2)	$ 4	(4 lbs. at $1)
Direct labor	6	(1 hr. at $6)	10	(2 hrs. at $5)
Variable overhead	5	($5/dlh)	8	(2 dlh at $4)
Fixed overhead	5	($5/dlh)	7	(2 dlh at $3.50)
Standard absorption cost	$20		$29	
Selling price	$30		$40	

Manufacturing overhead

	Division A		Division B	
Fixed				
Indirect labor	$20,000	(4,000 hrs. at $5)	$30,000	(6,000 hrs. at $5)
Depreciation	40,000		27,000	
Miscellaneous	25,000		20,000	
Total	$85,000		$77,000	
Variable/unit	$ 5		$ 8	

Estimated selling and administrative costs

	Division A	Division B	Corporate
Fixed selling	$30,000	$40,000	—
Variable selling	$4/unit	$3/unit	—
Administration	$20,000	$10,000	$50,000

Inventories

	Product A	Product B
Finished goods:		
Beginning inventory	10,000 units	5,000 units
	($200,000)	($145,000)
Planned ending inventory	7,000 units	6,000 units
Expected sales	20,000 units	10,000 units
Raw materials:		
Beginning inventory	–0–	2,000 pounds
Planned ending inventory	4,000 pounds	6,000 pounds

ILLUSTRATION 22–3. PPM Company: Division A Budgets (000s)

Physical Budgets

Sales

Product A	20 units

Production/Inventory

Planned ending inventory	7 units
Sales	20 units
Total requirements	27 units
Beginning inventory	10 units
Production	17 units

Raw Materials

Required for production	34 pounds
Planned ending inventory	4 pounds
Total requirements	38 pounds
Beginning inventory	0
Required purchases	38 pounds

Labor

Direct labor	17 hours
Indirect labor	4 hours

Cost Budgets

Raw Materials

Purchases	$ 76

Direct Labor

Requirements	$102

Manufacturing Overhead

Fixed:		
Indirect labor	$ 20	
Depreciation	40	
Miscellaneous	25	85
Variable:		
Miscellaneous		85
Total		$170

Selling and Administrative

Fixed selling	$ 30
Variable selling	80
Administrative	20
Total	$130

Inventory

Raw material:		
Ending inventory		$ 8
Finished goods:		
Beginning inventory		$200
Additions		340
Available for sale		540
Ending inventory		140
Cost of goods sold		$400

Pro Forma Income and Cash Flow

Pro Forma Income Statement

Sales	$600
Cost of goods sold	400
Gross margin	200
Selling	110
Administrative	20
Pretax divisional income	$ 70

Cash Flows

Outflows:	
Raw materials	$ 76
Direct labor	102
Indirect labor	20
Miscellaneous overhead	110
Selling	110
Administrative	20
Total	438
Inflows:	
Collection of prior period accounts receivables	200
Collection on current sales	350
Total	550
Net cash inflow	$112

Required purchases of raw materials to support the planned production of 17,000 units of A, considering the planned beginning and ending raw material inventory levels, are similarly computed. The standard input of raw material per unit of A is two pounds (Illustration 22–2). Production of 17,000 units of A will require 34,000 pounds of raw material.

Planned Beginning Inventory	+	Planned Purchases	−	Planned Ending Inventory	=	Planned Usage

$$0 \quad + 38{,}000 \text{ pounds} - 4{,}000 \text{ pounds} = 34{,}000 \text{ pounds}$$

This computation is summarized in the raw materials budget in Illustration 22–3.

Given that the standard direct labor input into a unit of A is 1 hour, 17,000 direct labor hours will be required to produce 17,000 units of A. Standard direct labor and raw material usage per unit of product allows for normal waste and inefficiency. The indirect labor requirement in division A is estimated to be 4,000 hours for the period (see Illustration 22–2). Labor requirements are summarized in the labor budget in Illustration 22–3.

Cost budgets

The quantities of inputs and outputs enumerated in the physical sales, production/inventory, raw materials, and labor budgets must be expressed in terms of dollars. The raw materials cost budget (Illustration 22–3) shows planned expenditures of $76,000 (38,000 pounds at a standard cost of $2 per pound). The direct labor cost budget expresses the 17,000 hour direct labor requirement in dollars (17,000 hours times the standard direct labor wage rate of $6 per hour or $102,000).

The manufacturing overhead cost budget (Illustration 22–3) contains the manufacturing general manager and divisional vice president's consensus assessment of fixed and variable manufacturing overhead for the coming year. Information the manufacturing general manager obtains from individual production managers is an important determinant of budgeted manufacturing overhead. Total budgeted variable overhead is the product of the planned production rate, 17,000 units, and the estimated variable manufacturing overhead cost per unit, $5.

Selling and administrative costs (Illustration 22–3) are joint estimates of the marketing general manager and divisional vice president. Total variable selling costs are the product of budgeted sales (20,000 units) and the estimated variable selling cost per unit ($4).

Inventory

The standard cost of a pound of raw material is $2. The 4,000 pounds in ending inventory are valued at $8,000. There is no work in process budget since no beginning or ending work in process inventories are planned for next year.

The standard cost of a unit of production is $20. It is comprised of a $4 raw material cost (two pounds at $2), a $6 direct labor cost (one hour at $6), an allocated variable manufacturing overhead cost of $5 (one unit at $5 or one direct labor-hour at $5), and an allocated fixed manufacturing overhead cost of $5 ($85,000 total fixed manufacturing overhead/17,000 units of production). The normal capacity is 17,000 units in division A and 11,000 units in division B.

Beginning finished goods inventory is valued at $200,000 (10,000 units at $20). Planned production will add $340,000 to finished goods inventory (17,000 units at $20), and the planned ending finished goods inventory is $140,000 (7,000 units at $20). This implies that budgeted cost of goods sold is $400,000. The inventory cost budget in Illustration 22–3 summarizes this computation.

Pro forma income and cash flow

The cost budgets are used to construct the budgeted (pro forma) divisional income statement in Illustration 22–3. Division A of the PPM Company anticipates pretax income of $70,000 based on a planned sales volume of 20,000 units for next year.

The cost budgets and assumptions about collections of accounts receivable are used to construct a statement of cash flow from operations. In division A of PPM Company all budgeted costs, with the exception of depreciation, are expected to result in cash outflows during the year. Assume current sales and collections of accounts receivable are expected to generate a cash inflow of $550,000 for the year. These cash flows are summarized in Illustration 22–3. Net cash inflow from operations is budgeted at $112,000 in division A.

Master operating budget

The budget for division B, presented in Illustration 22–4, is developed similarly. Divisional budgets are usually due in the executive vice president's office by mid-October preceding the budget year. The executive vice president and the controller's office consolidate the divisional budgets into the corporate master operating budget reproduced in Illustration 22–5.

ILLUSTRATION 22–4. PPM Company: Division B Budgets (000s)

Physical Budgets

Sales

Product B	10 units

Production/Inventory

Planned ending inventory	6 units
Sales	10 units
Total requirements	16 units
Beginning inventory	5 units
Production	11 units

Raw Materials

Required for production	44 pounds
Planned ending inventory	6 pounds
Total requirements	50 pounds
Beginning inventory	2 pounds
Required purchases	48 pounds

Labor

Direct labor	22 hours
Indirect labor	6 hours

Cost Budgets

Raw Materials

Purchase	$ 48

Direct Labor

Requirements	$110

Manufacturing Overhead

Fixed:	
Indirect labor	$ 30
Depreciation	27
Miscellaneous	20
	77
Variable:	
Miscellaneous	88
Total	$165

Selling and Administrative

Fixed selling	$ 40
Variable selling	30
Administrative	10
Total	$ 80

Inventory

Raw material:	
Ending inventory	$ 6
Finished goods:	
Beginning inventory	$145
Additions	319
Available for sale	464
Ending inventory	174
Cost of goods sold	$290

Pro Forma Income and Cash Flow

Pro Forma Income Statement

Sales	$400
Cost of goods sold	290
Gross margin	$110
Selling	70
Administrative	10
Pretax divisional income	30

Cash Flows

Outflows:	
Raw materials	$ 48
Direct labor	110
Indirect labor	30
Miscellaneous overhead	108
Selling	70
Administrative	10
Total	376
Inflows:	
Collection of prior period receivables	$ 60
Collection on current sales	275
	335
Net cash outflow	$ 41

ILLUSTRATION 22–5. PPM Company: Master Operating Budget (000s)

Raw Materials

Division A	$ 76
Division B	48
	$124

Direct Labor

Division A	102
Division B	110
	$212

Manufacturing Overhead

Fixed:	
Indirect labor	$ 50
Depreciation	67
Miscellaneous	45
	162
Variable:	
Miscellaneous	173
	$335

Selling and Administrative

Fixed selling	$ 70
Variable selling	110
Administrative: divisional	30
Administrative: corporate	50
	$260

Inventory

Raw material:		
Division A	$ 8	
Division B	6	
	$ 14	
Finished goods:		
Beginning inventory	$ 345	
Addition	659	
Available for sale	1,004	
Ending inventory	314	
Cost of goods sold	$ 690	

Pro Forma Income Statement

Sales	$1000	($600 + $400)
Cost of goods sold	690	($400 + $290)
Gross margin	310	($200 + $110)
Selling	180	($110 + $70)
Administration	80	($20 + $10 + $50)
Pretax income	$ 50	

Cash Requirements (operations)

Net cash inflows (outflows)	
Division B	$ (41)
Division A	112
Corporate	(50)
Net inflow from operations	$ 21

In the consolidation process the $50,000 cost of all activities planned for the coming year at the executive vice president (corporate) level is added to the budget. In addition any divisional revenues and costs associated with sales of one division to another division would have to be accounted for because sales revenue and cost of goods sold in the pro forma income statement relate only to a firm's transactions with external parties. This would involve adjustments to the revenue and inventory amounts. No such adjustments are necessary in PPM Company since all sales of products A and B are to external customers.

The executive vice president reviews the master operating budget for consistency with corporate goals. For example, the $50,000 pretax corporate income may not meet the president's and board of directors' expectations and have to be changed. The executive vice president would then send back the divisional budgets for adjustment, perhaps suggesting specific actions to division vice presidents (e.g., cut discretionary expenditures on advertising or research and development by $5,000 to bring them in line with other divisions, cut back on investment in inventory by 10 percent, etc.). This iterative process would continue until the executive vice president was satisfied that all corporate goals were met and the divisional vice presidents were satisfied that their divisional budgets were realistically attainable.

Budgeted cash flows and planned financing

In PPM Company, agreement on next year's budget generally is reached by late November.

PPM Company devotes the first few months of every year to capital investment decisions, reviewing its current long-term capital investments and deciding which new long-term capital investments should be made and how they should be financed. Typical capital investment decisions include: whether to replace current machinery with new, more costly, but more efficient machinery, whether to move operations to a new location, or whether to add a new product line.

PPM Company constructs a statement of budgeted cash flows and planned financing that combines the cash flow and financing effects of short-term (operations) and long-term (capital investments) budgeted activities (see Illustration 22–6).

PPM Company plans to begin the next fiscal year with $50,000 in cash. Budgeted operations will increase that amount by $21,000 (see Illustration 22–5). However PPM Company has committed itself to an $80,000 capital investment expenditure and must retire $20,000 in long-term debt during the coming year. To have an adequate reserve for any contingencies that may arise, PPM Company plans to have its cash balance remain above $45,000 during the year. In order to accomplish these plans, an additional $74,000 in new financing is required.

ILLUSTRATION 22–6. **PPM Company Budgeted Cash Flows, Planned Financing, and Debt Composition**

Beginning cash balance	$ 50,000
Add: Net inflow (outflow) from operations	21,000
Cash available before financing	71,000
Subtract:	
Net outflow for capital expenditures	80,000
Net outflow for retirement of long-term debt	20,000
Minimum cash balance desired	45,000
Required financing	$ 74,000
Beginning debt:	
Short-term	$ 20,000
Long-term	60,000
Total	80,000
Subtract: Planned retirement of long-term debt	20,000
Add: Planned increases in short-term financing	74,000
Ending debt:	
Short-term	94,000
Long-term	40,000
Total	$134,000

The bottom half of Illustration 22–6 shows the beginning composition of debt, the planned retirement of long-term debt, and the decision that all new financing will be short term. Total debt is expected to increase by $54,000 ($134,000 − $80,000) during the coming year.

Because adequate cash flow is vital to successful operations, in practice, cash budgets are usually made on a quarterly, monthly, weekly, and sometimes even daily basis.

THE BUDGET PROCESS: GENERAL COMMENTS

Budgeting is a dynamic, iterative, time-consuming process. Good budgeting facilitates interaction between managers at different levels and coordinates planning and decision making throughout the organization to ensure that corporate objectives are attained.

Interactive budgeting is the basis for *management by objective(s)* (MBO). MBO directly involves the person responsible for the achievement of certain objectives in the setting of these objectives. It is often used for precise objectives (profit targets) as well as for subjective goals. For example, a manager may be asked to strengthen the research and development effort in his division or to build employee morale in her department. During the budgeting process the other-than-profit objectives of all managers can be clarified. The budget process should make it clear to managers how they will be evaluated at the end of the budget year, and the budget document should serve as a constant reminder of what needs to be done.

Flexible budgets

A master budget is constructed ex ante. It is prepared before the budget period begins and is based on planned operations for the year. A *flexible budget* is constructed ex post. It is the master budget constructed for operations at the actual level (contrasted to planned or budgeted level) of operations.

Suppose a chemical company planned to produce 100,000 pounds of fertilizer during a year. During the year, farmers planted less than the anticipated acreage of certain crops, and only 80,000 pounds of the fertilizer was actually produced. The master budget lists the costs expected to be incurred if 100,000 pounds of the fertilizer are produced, whereas the flexible budget lists the costs expected to be incurred if 80,000 pounds are produced. Because actual production is 80,000 pounds, actual production costs should be compared to the flexible budget costs when evaluating the performance of production personnel.

Budgets usually cover a fiscal year, but any other time period can be used. Some organizations structure the budget process so that at the end of any quarter a budget for the subsequent 12 months is available. This is referred to as a *rolling budget* process.

There is no right way to budget. Whatever process best facilitates the attainment of organizational objectives is the preferred process (assuming reasonable cost).

ZBB AND PB

Zero-base budgeting (ZBB) and program budgeting (PB) are two general approaches to structuring the planning/budgeting process. These approaches are often used in organizations that have many conflicting objectives or objectives that are difficult to quantify.

Zero-base budgeting

Zero-base budgeting (ZBB) is a general approach to planning and budgeting. It seeks to create in budget process participants an awareness of organizational goals and available alternative means of attaining the goals. It forces managers to rank activities in order of preference. It is used in the private sector where the primary objective is profit maximization and in not-for-profit and governmental agencies where objectives are not as easily quantified.

ZBB begins with the identification of decision units, segments of the organization with significant decision-making or program responsibility. Decision units correspond to responsibility centers or groups of responsibility centers. Responsibility centers in organizations exercise control over an activity or cost. Managers of responsibility centers have control over how the activity is performed or the level of cost that is incurred. Responsibility centers will be discussed in detail in the next chapter.

In Illustration 22–7 there are three levels of decision units (responsibility centers), a lower level, middle level, and top level.

ILLUSTRATION 22–7. **Zero-Base Budgeting Ranking and Review Process**

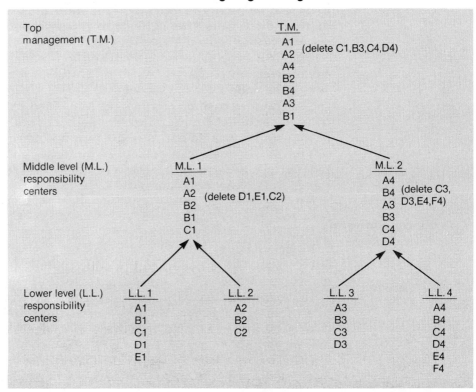

The manager of each decision unit ranks all of the unit's decision packages in order of preference. For example, in lower level responsibility center 3 in Illustration 22–7 there are four decision packages. A3 is the most preferred, and D3 is the least preferred. The ordering process requires that managers specify the objectives of the program or activity being ranked and relate the program's or activity's output to basic organizational objectives.

Managers at higher levels consolidate the proposals submitted to them by their subordinates, revising, deleting or adding decision packages while providing their own ordinal ranking. For example the middle level responsibility center manager 1 (Illustration 22–7) deletes programs D1, E1, and C2 from the budget. Of the remaining five activities, A1 is most preferred and C1 least preferred. The broader organizational perspective of higher level management should lead to a better coordinated and balanced set of activities being selected. Corporate objectives should be more closely met.

The difficulty is that higher level managers must combine different ordinal scales of lower level rankings. For instance, in Illustration 22–7 the M.L. 2 manager has no idea how much more preferred A4 is than B4 or if B3 is almost as preferred as A3. Furthermore, lower level managers can "game" the process by ranking an activity known to be highly favored by their immediate superior very low on their own scale. This is likely to gain acceptance in the budget for everything ranked above this activity.

The ZBB process terminates when top management selects its list of decision packages based on available resources and it becomes the budget for the subsequent period. Every activity appearing in the zero-base budget has been justified from the ground up (thus the name ZBB) regardless of whether or not it is a new activity or an activity carried out in many past accounting periods.

The ZBB process can consume immense amounts of management's time. Because of this cost a complete ZBB review of all activities is usually not done annually.

Program budgeting

Program budgeting (PB) or planning/programming/budgeting (PPB), like ZBB, attempts to integrate planning and budgeting in a formal process. PB is most often used to budget large projects with component activities spread across many responsibility centers in an organization. PB emphasizes the benefit/cost trade-offs of projects and associated activities—all budget requests are classified by activity.

Consider how to plan and budget for a new model automobile. Suppose the project is comprised of three major activities—research and development, promotion, and production—each carried out in different departments of the same division of an automobile manufacturer. Using PB each department would provide an estimate of the cost and benefit, for the current and several future periods, of engaging in its portion of the entire project. When the budget finally "filters up" to the divisional manager the cost and benefit of the entire project is available in isolation from all other divisional projects.

In PB it is frequently difficult to quantify the benefits of an activity. As the quantification of benefits becomes more subjective managers at higher levels in the organization are less likely to have confidence in the numbers.

The basic idea behind PB and ZBB is to overcome "line-item myopia," the danger in conventional budgeting schemes that budget items tend to get set at a fixed percentage above last year's levels. If budgeting systems are carefully designed to force interaction between managers at different levels, and if the process is iterative and flexible, then managers will think about where and why the money is being spent and the basic objective of the more formal ZBB and PB approaches will be met.

SUMMARY

The budget preparation process forces management to analyze alternative courses of action and to look to the future. This is an important benefit since management often tends to be myopic in its perspective, being more concerned with short-term operational problems than with longer-term planning.

Budgeting helps management to anticipate problems and reinforces management's understanding of the goals of the organization. Budgeting helps to coordinate all organizational activities. It uncovers bottlenecks and inconsistencies in current plans, providing a basis for revised plans. Budgeting motivates management to attain organizational goals and communicates decisions made in one segment of an organization to the rest of the organization.

The budget document is a control device since it reminds management of what needs to be accomplished during the period. It helps ensure that all organizational members and segments work toward the attainment of organizational goals. The budget is a convenient reference point for performance evaluation. Differences between actual and budgeted results can be analyzed to determine who or what is responsible for not meeting or for exceeding organizational expectations.

PROBLEMS AND CASES

22–1 A Manufacturing Company*

Required:

Complete the following profit and loss statement from the supporting sales, selling and shipping, general and administrative, and development engineering expense schedules.

A MANUFACTURING COMPANY
Profit and Loss Statement

	Amount		(Over) Under Budget	
	This Month	Year to Date	This Month	Year to Date
Net sales	$1,069,281	$3,977,542	$(18,006)	$(24,092)
Cost of sales (including variances)				
Gross profit on sales				
Expenses:				
Development engineering				
Selling and shipping				
General and administrative				
Total				
Profit from operations				
Other expenses (income):				
Interest expense	2,708	10,882	(8)	(82)
Other (net)	(3,420)	(18,640)	580	(2,640)
Total	(712)	(7,758)	588	(2,558)
Net profit before income taxes	154,744	571,141	18,200	9,761
Provision for income taxes	84,000	309,000	10,000	5,000
Net profit	$ 70,744	$ 262,141	$ 8,200	$ 4,761

---

*From AICPA, *Management Education Portfolio,* New York, 1970, with permission.

A MANUFACTURING COMPANY
Cost of Sales

	Amount		(Over) Under Budget	
	This Month	Year to Date	This Month	Year to Date
Production costs incurred at standard:				
Manufacturing overhead:				
Controllable factory costs	$139,079	$ 549,645	$ (4,466)	$ (5,963)
Costs not charged to departments	60,701	245,140	(51)	(540)
Transfers to other departments (net)	(8,735)	(34,705)	—	—
Variances (see below)	(5,754)	4,830	5,754	(4,830)
Total standard manufacturing overhead	185,291	764,910	1,237	(11,333)
Productive labor	110,365	457,922	2,335	(7,122)
Materials	419,837	1,817,091	19,513	(59,691)
Total standard costs incurred	715,493	3,039,923	23,085	(78,146)
Costs expensed or capitalized	(6,019)	(13,945)	3,263	2,561
Inventory (increase) or decrease	44,366	(192,189)	(44,946)	42,750
Standard cost of sales.....	753,840	2,833,789	(18,598)	(32,835)
Cost variances:				
Manufacturing overhead:				
Controllable factory costs	4,466	5.963	(4,466)	(5,963)
Costs not charged to departments	51	540	(51)	(540)
Volume variances	1,237	(11,333)	(1,237)	11,333
Total	5,754	(4,830)	(5,754)	4,830
Productive labor	1,951	14,583	(1,951)	(14,583)
Materials	(1,217)	(19,218)	1,217	19,218
Total cost variances	$ 6,488	$ (9,465)	$ (6,488)	$ 9,465

A MANUFACTURING COMPANY
Selling and Shipping Expenses (Vice President of Sales)

	Amount		(Over) Under Budget	
	This Month	Year to Date	This Month	Year to Date
Controllable costs:				
Sales vice president's office	$ 5,224	$ 21,152	$ (4)	$ (272)
Sales manager, Product A	17,320	62,204	(1,647)	(1,012)
Sales manager, Product B	14,475	56,220	(662)	32
Advertising department	30,489	106,227	(7,554)	(14,487)
Warehouse and shipping	12,224	51,463	35	(2,427)
Sales service department	7,219	25,273	(869)	127
Total	86,951	322,539	(10,701)	(18,039)
Transfers from other departments, net....................................	6,211	24,818	—	—

A MANUFACTURING COMPANY
General and Administrative Expenses

	Amount		(Over) Under Budget	
	This Month	*Year to Date*	*This Month*	*Year to Date*
Controllable costs:				
President's office	$15,511	$ 62,125	$ 314	$1,175
Secretary-treasurer's departments	12,895	48,652	(72)	2,610
Controller's departments	21,600	85,816	(211)	(257)
Total	50,006	196,593	31	3,528
Transfers from other departments, net ..	207	620	—	—

A MANUFACTURING COMPANY
Development Engineering Expenses

	Amount		(Over) Under Budget	
	This Month	*Year to Date*	*This Month*	*Year to Date*
Controllable costs:				
Chief product engineer's office	$3,665	$14,680	$ (75)	$ (320)
Drafting department	3,679	13,645	238	2,023
Model shop	1,885	7,673	(25)	(233)
Total	9,229	35,998	138	1,470
Transfers from other departments, net	2,317	9,267	—	—

22–2 Basic Manufacturing Company

The Basic Manufacturing Company produces and sells a single product. Basic is in the process of constructing next year's 1985, master budget. The following information has been collected.

Standard Production and Selling Costs

Raw material	$ 6.00	(3 pounds at $2)
Direct labor	6.00	(1 hour at $6)
Variable overhead	5.00	($5/dlh)
Fixed overhead	6.50	($6.50/dlh)
Standard absorption cost	$23.50	
Selling price	$50.00	

Manufacturing Overhead

Fixed:

Indirect labor	$ 20,000	(4,000 hours at $5)
Depreciation	50,000	
Miscellaneous	60,000	
	$130,000	
Variable/direct labor-hour	$ 5	

Estimated Selling and Administrative Costs

Fixed selling	$20,000
Variable selling	$3/unit
Administration	$20,000

Inventories

Finished goods:

Beginning inventory	5,000 units ($117,500)
Planned ending inventory	15,000 units
Expected sales...............................	10,000 units

Raw materials:

Beginning inventory	1,000 pounds (at $2)
Planned ending inventory	4,000 pounds (at $2)
Work in process.................................	None planned

Normal capacity is 20,000 direct labor-hours. Standard direct labor and raw material usage per unit of product allows for normal waste and inefficiency. There are no planned raw material and direct labor usage variances.

Required:

1. Prepare raw material, direct labor, manufacturing overhead, selling and administrative, and inventory cost budgets.

2. Prepare a 1985 pro forma income statement.

3. Assume normal capacity is 10,000 direct labor-hours instead of 20,000 direct labor-hours and that factory overhead variances are closed to cost of goods sold at year's end. Prepare a 1985 pro forma income statement.

22-3 The Overhead Tiger*

A consumer goods manufacturer in the Midlands recently faced a serious problem. Employing about 5,000 people in three factories, the company also had an administrative staff of 2,000 at its headquarters. Over the past five years, company costs had grown even faster than the retail price index.

---

* Excerpted from "Stopping the Overhead Tiger in its Tracks," *Management Today,* June 1981, pp. 33–44. Reprinted by permission.

Successive, across-the-board budget cuts failed to stem the ever-increasing rise in overheads. The traditional attempts to control expenditure seemed to have no real, long-lasting effect. What could management do to ensure productivity and the future health of the company, while containing costs?

Why this recent surge in overheads? Why are companies' management suddenly realising that overhead is eating up more and more of their budgets every year? Although the reasons for increased administrative costs are many, for medium and large firms the past five years show the following trends: (1) Creation of a great variety and number of new jobs at the highest levels of management, rather than an increase in line positions. (2) The increase in power of existing centralised functions, such as finance and planning, in decision making—and in their numbers as a proportion of the work force. (3) The burgeoning size of support functions, such as information systems and personnel. (4) The effect of automation in transferring costs from "direct variable" to "indirect fixed." (5) The need for more informational and central control to respond to local and government legislation.

These developments have removed overhead activities more and more from the demands for rationalisation of expenses that line functions must face. Overheads have become immune to traditional productivity measurements and budgetary monitoring. Cost increases often come about because cost factors are no longer under the control of the people who cause them. Lack of care and lack of knowledge can produce this situation, but so can a change in the structure of the organization. Many departments or divisions of the company incur charges that they cannot influence. They do not know how the costs are made up or what their justification is. The higher these charges, the stronger is their negative influence on the cost-consciousness of those who receive them, since a growing proportion of the latter's budgets are simply outside their control.

Although high costs in a particular department don't necessarily indicate inefficiency, their size relative to total costs can show the department's priority within the corporate structure. The higher the costs, the more attention should be paid to the efficient and effective allocation of people and money. But how do you judge whether the level of expenditure is right? There are several traditional approaches to evaluating and controlling budgets and allocation patterns.

One common way to judge the appropriateness of a specific overhead level is through intercompany comparison.

A more exact means to evaluate the necessity of a particular overhead cost is an in-depth analysis of a specific function or operation.

The final traditional way to contain overhead costs is by budgetary restrictions. Budgets can control costs on two levels: through cuts and through freezes on recruitment.

How, then, can a company rationally reduce or maintain overhead costs, while allocating people and money so that they are used to their fullest? The desirable results are fairly obvious. Every company would like to have speedy order processing, effective methods, an efficient finance department, a reduction in data processing and support costs, and the elimination of unnecessary tasks. But, though budget cuts have gratifying short-term effects, experience shows that "cost reduction by edict" cannot be maintained and often only results in delaying work that still has to be done. The basic structure of the activities and the organization—the root cause of the inefficient use of resources—remains unchanged. This is why a typical manufacturing company may go through three 10 percent across-the-board budget cuts in four years. Yet the same problem always returns.

Large organizations tend to operate like bureaucracies. Activities become rituals. Tasks are performed seriously and diligently, but without anyone having any idea of their original justification or present utility. For cost reduction or maintenance to be successful, it should be based on a philosophy—one which includes the following basic tenets: (1) A service can be judged only by its results; being active has no value in itself. (2) For every service, there must be a party who benefits in a way that is to the good of the firm. (3) Every service requires efforts: effort and benefit should be reasonably balanced. (4) The benefits of a service can best be judged by its receiver and its provider. (5) Alternative actions to determine the absolute level of overhead expenditure and how money can be allocated must be judged in terms of the total overhead.

Cost reduction is a detailed process, requiring management and staff commitment. Sometimes it may seem like an impossible task. But it can be done—and the rewards are real. The future profitability, and maybe even survival, of many manufacturing firms may depend on a rational evaluation of the overheads.

Required:

1. Enumerate weaknesses in the three traditional approaches to evaluating and controlling budgets and allocation patterns.

2. Discuss the difficulties in determining the proper level of expenditures for research and development, marketing, and advertising.

3. Managers in control of direct product costs are usually evaluated on the basis of variances—comparison of actual costs to standard costs. Is it reasonable to hold marketing, research and development, and advertising managers responsible for meeting their budgeted expenditures for the year? What sorts of problems will this kind of "control by variance" cause?

22-4 Tomlinson Retail*

Tomlinson Retail seeks your assistance to develop cash and other budget information for May, June, and July 1984. At April 30, 1984, the company had cash of $5,500, accounts receivable of $437,000, inventories of $309,400, and accounts payable of $133,055.

---

* Material from Uniform CPA Examination Questions and Unofficial Answers, copyright © May 1973 by the American Institute of Certified Public Accountants, Inc., is reprinted with permission.

The budget is to be based on the following assumptions:

I. Sales.
  (a) Each month's sales are billed on the last day of the month.
  (b) Customers are allowed a 3 percent discount if payment is made within 10 days after the billing date. Receivables are booked gross.
  (c) Sixty percent of the billings are collected within the discount period, 25 percent are collected by the end of the month, 9 percent are collected by the end of the second month, and 6 percent prove uncollectible.

II. Purchases.
  (a) Fifty-four percent of all purchases of material and selling, general, and administrative expenses are paid in the month purchased and the remainder in the following month.
  (b) Each month's units of ending inventory is equal to 130 percent of the next month's units of sales.
  (c) The cost of each unit of inventory is $20.
  (d) Selling, general, and administrative expenses, of which $2,000 is depreciation, are equal to 15 percent of the current month's sales.

Actual and projected sales are as follows:

1984	Dollars	Units
March	$354,000	11,800
April	363,000	12,100
May	357,000	11,900
June	342,000	11,400
July	360,000	12,000
August	366,000	12,200

Required:

Prepare a schedule of cash receipts and cash disbursements for the months of May, June, and July. Show supporting computations in good form.

22–5   The Clark Company*

The Clark Company has a contract with a labor union that guarantees a minimum wage of $500 per month to each direct labor employee having

* Material from Uniform CPA Examination Questions and Unofficial Answers, copyright © May 1970 by the American Institute of Certified Public Accountants, Inc., is reprinted with permission.

at least 12 years of service. One hundred employees currently qualify for coverage. All direct labor employees are paid $5 per hour.

The direct labor budget for 1985 was based on the annual usage of 400,000 hours of direct labor × $5, or a total of $2,000,000. Of this amount, $50,000 (100 employees × $500) per month (or $600,000 for the year) was regarded as fixed. Thus the budget for any given month was determined by the formula, $50,000 + $3.50 × direct labor hours worked.

Data on performance for the first three months of 1985 follow:

	January	February	March
Direct labor-hours worked	22,000	32,000	42,000
Direct labor costs budgeted	$127,000	$162,000	$197,000
Direct labor costs incurred	$110,000	$160,000	$210,000
Variance	$ 17,000F	$ 2,000F	$ 13,000U

F = Favorable.
U = Unfavorable.

The factory manager was perplexed by the results, which showed favorable variances when production was low and unfavorable variances when production was high, because he believed his control over labor costs was consistently good.

Required:

1. Why did the variances arise? Explain and illustrate using amounts and diagrams as necessary.

2. Does this direct labor budget provide a basis for controlling direct labor cost? Explain, indicating changes that might be made to improve control over direct labor cost and to facilitate performance evaluation of direct labor employees.

3. For inventory valuation purposes, how should per unit standard costs for direct labor be determined in a situation such as this? Explain, assuming that in some months fewer than 10,000 hours are expected to be utilized.

23

Performance evaluation and control

Control refers to actions undertaken to ensure that corporate objectives and plans embodied in the budget are met. Performance evaluations of managers and their use as incentives are basic components of a management control system because they affect managerial behavior and decision making.

EVALUATION CRITERIA

Ideally evaluations of managers should be based on what managers have control over, not on random phenomena or events controlled by other managers. The evaluation measure should motivate actions consistent with top management's objectives and should reflect the consequences current managerial effort and decision making are likely to have on future periods.

For example, as already indicated in our discussion of standards, the magnitude and favorability of departmental direct material and direct labor usage (efficiency) variances are the factors often used to gauge the performance of a departmental production manager.

Efficient utilization of direct materials and direct labor are the direct responsibility of and are controlled by the department manager. Efficiency variances are based on the flexible budget (the level at which the company is actually operating) rather than the master budget (the level at which they expected to operate at the beginning of the period). Forecast inaccuracies (differences between production costs at the master budgeted production level and actual production level), which are not under the control of the production manager, should be eliminated from the standard used to measure managerial efficiency.

Cost center

Methods of performance evaluation differ across responsibility center type. A *cost (expense) center* is an activity or organizational segment where management is responsible for cost incurred. Production departments are typically cost centers. One of the bases on which they are evaluated is their ability to meet cost standards. In addition to departments, cost centers can correspond to subdepartments, groups of machines or people performing similar functions, or entire divisions. A cost center is generally employed when division management can only control costs and cannot influence sales or investment.

Revenue centers

Managers of *revenue centers* have responsibility for the generation of revenues (sales responsibility) but do not have control over the costs of the items being sold. Revenue center managers (e.g., marketing managers) are usually evaluated on their ability to meet budgeted sales levels.

Profit centers

Profit center managers have responsibility for revenues and expenses. A division of a company is a profit center if the divisional manager is responsible for generating sales and controlling costs but is not responsible for investment decisions. Profit center net income is usually used as the main objective measure to evaluate, compare, and reward managers of profit centers.

Investment centers

The manager of an *investment center* has responsibility for both revenues and expenses as well as the level of investment in the activity. Investment centers are usually evaluated on measures that relate profit to the amount of the investment (profitability measures).

In an effective performance evaluation system the number and type of responsibility centers are determined by the goals of the organization. For example, a company that manufactures specialty items sold on a cost-plus basis will probably be primarily concerned with control of the sales function and have an evaluation system based on revenue and profit centers.

Once individual responsibility centers are defined care must be taken to allocate the proper (controllable) revenues, expenses, and investment to each responsibility center. This is a difficult process since many costs are common to more than one responsibility center, and responsibility centers are likely to interact with one another.

VARIANCE ANALYSIS: TOTAL PROFIT VARIANCE

Management by exception is the primary means of control in many organizations. Actual results are compared to planned results, and corrective actions are taken in those areas where actual outcomes deviate most from expectations. Variance analysis is the principal managerial accounting tool used in control by exception.

Variance analysis is used in performance evaluations and control of most responsibility centers. The objective of a variance analysis is to suggest possible reasons why, in the short run, actual profit differs from master budget profit.

Flexible budgets

The standard amount of cost allowed at a particular level of output is called the *flexibly budgeted cost* for that level of output. The flexibly budgeted cost of the actual level of output will differ from the planned or master budgeted cost prepared at the beginning of the period if the actual production level differs from the planned production level.

Cost centers are evaluated using variances that compare actual results to flexible budget numbers. It is important to use the flexible budget in cost center evaluations since cost center managers can only control usage and costs at the level of activity at which they operate, not at the level of production planned at the beginning of the year.

For example, assume at the beginning of the year that Kastings, Inc., planned to produce 6,000 figurines in 1984 and expected to use 7,200 pounds of raw material, pewter, since the standard amount of raw material allowed per figurine is 1.2 pounds. Suppose they actually used 6,500 pounds of pewter and produced 5,000 figurines. The flexible budget pewter usage at the actual level of figurine production is 6,000 pounds (5,000 × 1.2 pounds). Comparing the master budgeted 7,200 pounds with the 6,500 pounds actually used does not result in a variance that is useful to evaluate the efficiency of the production manager in using raw material. The 7,200 pounds relates to the 6,000 planned figurine production, not the 5,000 figurines that were actually produced during 1984.

A comparison of the 6,500 pounds of raw material actually used with the flexibly budgeted standard of 6,000 pounds develops a material usage variance of 500 pounds, which is useful in assessing the performance of the individual in charge of producing figurines.

Comparisons of flexible results to master budget figures can only be used in evaluating profit and investment center managers who make the initial sales projections in the master budget and have the responsibility of seeing they are met during the period.

Illustration 23–1 contains the master budget, flexible budget, and actual variable costing income statements for an accounting period of the Multi Company, a manufacturer of two consumer products, A and B. The company uses a standard variable costing system for purposes of internal control and performance evaluation. Master budget profit (MBP) and flexible budget profit (FBP) are based on the standards presented in Illustration 23–2. Actual profit (AP) for the period assumes the sales and revenue data in Illustration 23–3.

ILLUSTRATION 23–1

MULTI COMPANY
Variable Costing Income Statements
($000)

	Master Budget Profit (MBP)	Activity Level Variances	Flexible Budget Profit (FBP)	Operating Variances	Actual Profit (AP)
Sales revenue	$1,100	$30	$1,070	$20	$1,050
Less variable cost:					
Manufacturing	400	(20)	380	10	390
Selling	200		200	(10)	190
Contribution margin	500	10	490	20	470
Less fixed costs:					
Manufacturing	50		50		50
Selling	50		50	2	52
Income from operations	$ 400	$10	$ 390	$22	$ 368

ILLUSTRATION 23–2. **Budget Data for Multi Company**

Budgeted Standard Unit Contribution Margins

	Product A	Product B
Sales price	$7.00	$4.00
Direct labor....................	2.00 (½ hour at $4)	.50 (⅛ hour at $4)
Raw material	1.00 (1 pound at $1)	.50 (½ pound at $1)
Variable selling	1.00	1.00
Unit contribution margin	$3.00	$2.00

Budgeted Fixed Costs

Manufacturing	$50,000
Selling	$50,000

Budgeted Market Shares

	Forecast Industry Volume (units)	Budgeted Sales (units)	Budgeted Market Share
Product A	300,000	100,000	33⅓%
Product B	1,200,000	100,000	8⅓%
Total	1,500,000	200,000	13⅓%

ILLUSTRATION 23–3. **Multi Company Actual Sales Data**

	Actual Industry Volume (units)	Actual Sales (units)	Actual Selling Price per Unit	Actual Market Share
Product A	270,000	90,000	$6.90	33.33%
Product B	730,000	110,000	$3.90	15.07
Total	1,000,000	200,000	—	20%

Profit variance

The *total profit variance* is the difference between actual profit and master budget profit.

$$\text{Total Profit Variance} = AP - MBP$$

The total profit variance measures how close actual profit came to meeting profit expectations for the period. It may be used to evaluate the performance of the manager of the profit center.

The total profit variance for Multi Company is

$$-\$32,000 = \$368,000 - \$400,000$$
$$(U)$$

The total profit variance is considered to be unfavorable (U) because net income is less than planned. Any variance is considered to be favorable (F) if net income is higher than planned as a result of the variance and unfavorable (U) if net income is lower than planned as a result of the variance.

The object of a variance analysis is to determine possible causes of, and assign responsibility for, the total profit variance. The total profit can be broken up into an operating variance and a forecasting (sales volume) variance.

Sales volume variance

The *sales volume variance* is the difference between flexible budget profit and master budget profit.

> Sales Volume Variance = FBP − MBP

This variance measures (using standard costs and revenues) the effect on the period's profit due to deviations between actual and originally planned sales levels. Because both the flexible and master budgets are constructed from standards, changes in costs, prices, and operating efficiencies from those originally planned will not have an effect on the sales volume variance.

The sales volume variance is sometimes called a forecasting or activity level variance because it is the difference between the profit that would be projected with a perfect forecast of sales and the profit that was projected.

The sales volume variance is the responsibility of the chief sales or marketing executive and will help the profit center manager to interpret the total profit variance.

Multi Company's sales volume variance is:

$$-\$10,000 = \$390,000 - \$400,000$$
$$(U)$$

It is an unfavorable variance because the actual sales levels are *expected* to result in a lower profit than master budget profit.

The sales volume variance in a multiproduct firm has two primary determinants. The total quantity of items sold and the mix of items sold may differ from the assumed quantity and mix in the master budget.

602

Sales mix variance

The *sales mix variance* measures the effect on profit of a change in the average standard contribution margin from budget (which may change if the actual product mix differs from the master budget product mix).

$$\begin{array}{c}\text{Sales}\\\text{Mix}\\\text{Variance}\end{array}=\left(\begin{array}{c}\text{Actual Total}\\\text{Sales of All}\\\text{Products}\end{array}\right)\times\left(\begin{array}{c}\text{Actual Average}\\\text{Standard Unit}\\\text{Contribution Margin}\end{array}-\begin{array}{c}\text{Master Budget}\\\text{Average Standard}\\\text{Unit Contribution}\\\text{Margin}\end{array}\right)$$

The master budget average standard unit contribution margin for Multi Company can be computed from the budget information in Illustration 23–2. The unit contribution margins for the 100,000 units of budgeted sales of products A and B are $3 and $2, respectively. The master budget average standard unit contribution margin is:

$$\$2.50 = (100,000(\$3) + 100,000(\$2))/(100,000 + 100,000)$$

Actual sales of product A and B are 90,000 units and 110,000 units, respectively. The actual average standard unit contribution margin is

$$\$2.45 = (90,000(\$3) + 110,000(\$2))/(90,000 + 110,000)$$

Actual total sales of both products is 200,000 units. Multi Company's sales mix variance is:

$$-\$10,000 = (200,000)(\$2.45 - \$2.50)$$
$$(U)$$

The sales mix variance is unfavorable because the average standard unit contribution margin of an item sold was less than budget. Sales of product A, the high contribution item, were below budget by 10,000 units, while sales of product B, the low contribution item, exceeded budget by 10,000 units.

The sales mix variance is favorable when the average standard unit contribution margin on items sold exceeds the budgeted average standard contribution margin. This results when more high-contribution items or fewer low-contribution items are sold than originally planned.

The sales mix variance may be used in the performance evaluation of marketing personnel. In general, it indicates that increased sales of items with high individual unit contribution margins may be just as or more important in determining a firm's profit than rises in the aggregate sales level.

Sales quantity variance

The *sales quantity variance* measures the effect on profits of a change in the aggregate volume of units sold from budget *assuming the originally budgeted product mix is maintained*.

$$\text{Sales Quantity Variance} = \left(\begin{array}{c} \text{Actual Total} \\ \text{Sales of All} \\ \text{Products} \end{array} - \begin{array}{c} \text{Master Budget} \\ \text{Total Sales of} \\ \text{All Products} \end{array} \right) \times \left(\begin{array}{c} \text{Master Budget} \\ \text{Average Standard} \\ \text{Unit Contribution Margin} \end{array} \right)$$

Multi Company's sales quantity variance is:

$$0 = (200{,}000 - 200{,}000)\,(\$2.50)$$

The variance is zero because 200,000 total units were budgeted and 200,000 units were actually sold. In general the sales quantity variance will be favorable or unfavorable depending on whether actual aggregate sales are greater or less than master budget aggregate sales, respectively.

A firm's actual total sales volume is the product of the total industry sales volume and the firm's share of the market. Changes in industry volume or market share can affect the sales quantity variance.

Multi Company management budgets sales for a period by estimating total industry volume for the period and multiplying this figure by its expected share of the market. These estimates can be used to decompose the sales quantity variance into an industry volume variance and a market share variance. And this will help management *(a)* understand how market conditions affected profit and *(b)* isolate factors controllable by marketing managers from those that are not.

Industry volume variance

The *industry volume variance* measures the foregone or additional contribution margin (based on originally budgeted product mix and market share) due to contraction or expansion in the aggregate market for the firm's output.

$$\begin{array}{l} \text{Industry} \\ \text{Volume} \\ \text{Variance} \end{array} = \left(\begin{array}{l} \text{Actual} \\ \text{Industry} \\ \text{Volume} \end{array} - \begin{array}{l} \text{Master} \\ \text{Budget} \\ \text{Industry} \\ \text{Volume} \end{array} \right) \times \left(\begin{array}{l} \text{Master Budget} \\ \text{Market} \\ \text{Share} \end{array} \right) \times \left(\begin{array}{l} \text{Master Budget} \\ \text{Average Standard} \\ \text{Unit Contribution} \\ \text{Margin} \end{array} \right).$$

Multi Company's industry volume variance is (data from Illustrations 23–2 and 23–3).

$$-\$167,000 = (1,000,000 - 1,500,000)(.133)(\$2.5)$$
$$(U)$$

The industry volume variance is unfavorable because the markets in which Multi Company sells contracted by 33⅓ percent for the period (1.5 million units to 1 million units). A decline of this magnitude is expected to lower profits by $167,000 from the master budget amount.

Market share variance

The *market share variance* measures the foregone or additional profit, based on actual total market size and originally budgeted product mix, due to a decrease or an increase in a firm's aggregate market share.

$$\begin{array}{l} \text{Market} \\ \text{Share} \\ \text{Variance} \end{array} = \left(\begin{array}{l} \text{Actual} \\ \text{Industry} \\ \text{Volume} \end{array} \right) \times \left(\begin{array}{l} \text{Actual} \\ \text{Market} \\ \text{Share} \end{array} - \begin{array}{l} \text{Master Budget} \\ \text{Market} \\ \text{Share} \end{array} \right) \times \left(\begin{array}{l} \text{Master Budget} \\ \text{Average Standard} \\ \text{Unit Contribution} \\ \text{Margin} \end{array} \right)$$

Multi Company's market share variance is:

$$\$167,000 = (1,000,000)(.20 - .133)(\$2.50)$$
$$(F)$$

This is a favorable variance because Multi Company has raised its aggregate market share from the originally budgeted 13⅓ percent to 20 percent. This dramatic increase in aggregate market share is expected to increase profits by $167,000 from the master budgeted level.

Activity level variances summary

Illustration 23-4 summarizes the activity level variances for Multi Company, which help to explain why flexible budget profit is $10,000 lower than master budget profit. Although Multi Company sold the quantity of items expected (sales quantity variance is zero) the actual product mix consisted of more lower contribution margin items than anticipated (sales mix variance is $10,000 unfavorable).

Even though the sales quantity variance is zero, the expansion into industry volume and market share variances shows that Multi Company (marketing management in particular) has done remarkably well by capturing a dramatically increased share of a drastically lower aggregate market.

The sales mix, industry volume and market share variances could be analyzed further to highlight individual product effects on budgeted profit and to evaluate the performance of individual product (or product line) marketing managers.

ILLUSTRATION 23-4.   **Graphical Representation of Sales Volume Variance ($000)**

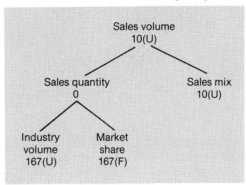

OPERATING VARIANCE

The *operating variance* is the difference between actual profit and flexible budget profit.

$$\text{Operating Variance} = AP - FBP$$

The operating variance measures the impact on profit resulting from actual costs and quantities being different from standard costs and quantities. For example, raw material inputs to product may have exceeded standard, direct labor could have been paid a lower than-anticipated wage rate, or per unit sales revenues may have exceeded expectations.

Multi Company's operating variance is:

$$-\$22{,}000 = (\$368{,}000 - \$390{,}000)$$
$$(U)$$

This is an unfavorable variance because actual profit was less than flexible budget profit. The operating variance is decomposed into component variances in order to explain why it occurred and to use it to evaluate the performance of operating personnel.

Revenue variance

The *revenue variance* is the difference between actual revenue and flexible budget revenue.

> Revenue Variance = Actual Revenue − Flexible Budget Revenue

Multi Company's revenue variance is:

$$-\$20{,}000 = ((90{,}000 \text{ units of A}) \times (\$6.90) + (110{,}000 \text{ units of B}) \times (\$3.90))$$
$$(U)$$
$$-((90{,}000 \text{ units of A}) \times (\$7.00) + (110{,}000 \text{ units of B}) \times (\$4.00))$$

This variance is unfavorable because all units of both product A and product B were sold for $.10 less than standard.

The revenue variance can be decomposed further to determine the deviations from flexibly budgeted profits due to individual product revenues. Individual product revenue variances are the product of the number of units sold and the difference between the actual and standard selling price per unit. For Multi Company the individual product revenue variances are:

Product A
Revenue $= -\$9{,}000 = (90{,}000 \text{ units})(\$6.90 - \$7.00)$
Variance $\quad$ (U)

Product B
Revenue $= -\$11{,}000 = (110{,}000 \text{ units})(\$3.90 - \$4.00)$
Variance $\quad$ (U)

Both variances are unfavorable since lower than standard selling prices decreased revenues below expectations for both products.

The revenue variance, in conjunction with the market share and sales mix variances, is used in the evaluation of marketing personnel performance.

An unfavorable revenue variance does not necessarily signal poor performance by marketing personnel. In Multi Company the lower than standard selling prices may have enabled the company to capture its much larger than anticipated share of the total market. This may have been a reasonable strategy in light of drastically reduced industry volume.

Variable manufacturing cost variance

The *variable manufacturing cost variance* is the difference between actual and flexible budget variable manufacturing costs.

$$
\begin{array}{ccc}
\text{Variable} & \text{Actual Variable} & \text{Flexible Budget} \\
\text{Manufacturing} = & \text{Manufacturing} - & \text{Variable Manufacturing} \\
\text{Cost Variance} & \text{Cost} & \text{Cost}
\end{array}
$$

This variance is a summary comparison of variable manufacturing cost to standard variable manufacturing cost and is likely to be of interest to higher levels of management concerned with production.

Multi Company's variable manufacturing cost variance is:

$$\$10,000 = \$390,000 - \$380,000$$
$$\text{(U)}$$

It is unfavorable because variable manufacturing costs exceeded the standard cost for the actual output.

The variable manufacturing cost variance can be broken down into aggregate raw material and direct labor variances. The *raw material* and *direct labor variances* are the differences between the actual and flexible budget raw material and direct labor costs, respectively.

In practice the raw material and direct labor variances are built up from individual product price and usage variances for raw materials and labor which would be computed at the departmental level in the plants where the products are produced. These variances have been defined and explained in Chapter 17.

Fixed manufacturing cost variance

The *fixed manufacturing cost variance* is the difference between actual and flexible budget fixed manufacturing costs. Multi Company's fixed manufacturing cost variance is:

$$0 = \$50,000 - \$50,000$$

Selling cost variances

The *variable selling cost variance* is the difference between actual variable selling cost and flexible budget variable selling cost.

$$
\begin{array}{c}
\text{Variable} \\
\text{Selling Cost} \\
\text{Variance}
\end{array}
=
\begin{array}{c}
\text{Actual} \\
\text{Variable} \\
\text{Selling} \\
\text{Cost}
\end{array}
-
\left(
\begin{array}{c}
\text{Actual Number} \\
\text{of Units} \\
\text{Sold}
\end{array}
\right)
\times
\left(
\begin{array}{c}
\text{Standard} \\
\text{Variable Selling} \\
\text{Cost per Unit}
\end{array}
\right).
$$

Multi Company's variable selling cost variance is:

$$-\$10,000 = \$190,000 - (200,000 \text{ units}) (\$1/\text{unit})$$
$$\text{(F)}$$

It is a favorable variance since actual variable selling costs were less than flexible budget variable selling costs.

The *fixed selling cost variance* is the difference between actual and flexible budget fixed selling costs.

$$
\begin{array}{c}
\text{Fixed} \\
\text{Selling Cost} \\
\text{Variance}
\end{array}
=
\begin{array}{c}
\text{Actual} \\
\text{Fixed Selling} \\
\text{Cost}
\end{array}
-
\begin{array}{c}
\text{Flexible} \\
\text{Budget Fixed} \\
\text{Selling Cost}
\end{array}
$$

For Multi Company this variance is $2,000 unfavorable.

$$\$2,000 = \$52,000 - \$50,000$$
$$\text{(U)}$$

Selling cost variances need to be interpreted with care. Selling costs are usually budgeted as a percentage of sales revenue. As sales revenues fall below expectations the prudent management action might be to spend more than budget on sales and marketing costs in an effort to spur sales. Such an action would generate unfavorable selling cost variances.

When sales commissions are a large component of variable sell-

ILLUSTRATION 23–5.   **Graphical Representation of Operating Variance ($000)**

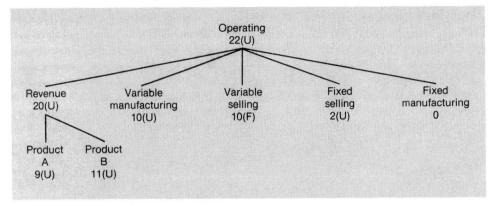

ing cost, variable selling cost variances are not usually significant.

Illustration 23–5 summarizes Multi Company's operating variances, which help to explain why actual profit is $22,000 lower than flexible budget profit.

VARIANCE ANALYSIS: SUMMARY

Actual profit in the period was $32,000 less than expected. Ten thousand dollars of this total was due to changes in the sales levels and product mix from initial expectations, while $22,000 resulted from increased costs of operations.

Actual aggregate sales were as planned (200,000 units) but the sales mix included a higher than planned percentage of low contribution margin product, which decreased profit $10,000 below expectations. The drop in overall industry volume was expected to decrease profits by $167,000 for the period, but Multi Company was able to exactly offset this by drastically increasing its market share.

In the aggregate, lower than standard selling prices decreased profit by $20,000. Production performance was also unfavorable by $2,000 overall. A $10,000 favorable variable selling variance was offset by a $10,000 unfavorable variable manufacturing cost variance.

VARIANCE ANALYSIS: REPORTS

The Multi Company example illustrates that variance analysis is a systematic attempt to explain why actual and master budgeted profits differ. A variance analysis, by isolating causes of deviations from expected results, helps management to better understand their organization and its environment and to insure that organizational goals are achieved.

The separation of the total profit variance into an operating variance and a sales volume variance is a key split in a variance analysis because the effects on profit of activity level changes from budget are separated from the effects of operational efficiencies and inefficiencies in the actual production and sales processes. The particular variances defined in the Multi Company example are not the only variances that could be computed. Product line, customer type, or geographic region variances could also be calculated.

It is unlikely that all variances computed will appear together in a single report. For example Illustration 23–6 contains a marketing variance report for Multi Company.

ILLUSTRATION 23–6

```
                    MULTI COMPANY
                   Marketing Variances
              Year Ended December 31, 1984
                        ($000)

Revenue variances:
    Product A .................    9 (U)
    Product B ................   11 (U)      20 (U)
Selling cost variances:
    Variable .................   10 (F)
    Fixed ....................    2 (U)       8 (F)
Industry volume variance .....              167 (U)
Market share variance ........              167 (F)
Sales mix variance ...........               10 (U)
Total marketing variance .....               22 (U)
```

In a report to the marketing vice president the individual product variances would likely be suppressed, whereas reports to product line managers would likely contain only information relevant to their particular products.

COMMENTS

This chapter emphasizes objective measures of performance. Subjective measures of performance, which are equally as important, must be made of managerial effectiveness. How are the manager's supervisory skills? Does the manager have the ability to motivate and train personnel? What is the quality of the output of the manager's department?

Subjective measures of performance are generally set during the budgeting process. As described in Chapter 22 an interactive budgeting process should be the basis for management by objective (MBO). MBO directly involves managers, who are held responsible for achieving an objective, in the definition and setting of the objective. MBO is a particularly useful process for seeing that subjective goals are defined and attained in an organization.

PROBLEMS AND CASES

23-1   Leisure Time Motors

Leisure Time Motors, Inc., is a regional manufacturer of mobile homes, mini mobile homes, and travel trailers. Substantial delivery costs of its finished vehicles limit distribution to approximately 135 locations within 600 miles of its plant in Cleveland, Ohio.

Leisure Time's mobile homes, approximately 14 feet wide and 50 feet long, are complete dwellings equipped with all necessary appliances and furnishings. A mini motor home is a light-duty truck chassis on which Leisure Time constructs a body. Travel trailers, 8 feet wide and 35 feet long, are designed to be towed behind trucks.

Mini motor homes and travel trailers are classified as recreational vehicles (as opposed to the large mobile homes). All three vehicles are produced using assembly line techniques.

The following information relates to the year ended December 31, 1984.

	Standard Unit Contribution Margins
Motor homes	$2,000
Mini mobile homes	$1,500
Travel trailers	$1,000

	Industry Volume (units)		Sales (units)	
	Forecast	Actual	Budgeted	Actual
Motor homes	120,000	100,000	900	800
Mini mobile homes . .	150,000	160,000	1,200	1,300
Travel trailers	400,000	450,000	2,000	2,150

Required:

Evaluate the success of Leisure Time Motors in meeting its master budgeted profit projection for 1984. Compute the sales volume variance, sales quantity variance, sales mix variance, industry volume variance, and the market share variance. What do these variances tell you about Leisure Time's success in selling its vehicles during 1984? What additional information would you require in addition to the information given above?

23-2 Winston Manufacturing

Winston Manufacturing Company, Inc., produces a single consumer product, which it sells to retailers. Because the model changes slightly every year, there are never any beginning or ending work in process or finished goods inventories. The following data relates to activities for the year ending December 31, 1985.

	Standard or Budgeted	Actual
Selling price per unit of final product	$77	$76
Direct material:		
Price per pound	$6	$5.90
Pounds per unit of final product	1.3	1.25
Direct labor:		
Price per hour	$10	$10.10
Hours per unit of final product.........	1.8	1.85
Manufacturing overhead:		
Fixed...............................	$400,000	$390,000
Variable per direct labor hour	$3	$2.90
General and administrative:		
Fixed...............................	$200,000	$205,000
Variable per unit of final product	$1	$1
Selling:		
Fixed...............................	$100,000	$ 98,000
Variable per unit of final product	$2	$1.90
Number of units produced and sold	100,000	110,000

There were no beginning raw materials inventory, and the Winston Manufacturing Company purchased 150,000 pounds of raw material during 1985. All variances appear in the actual income statement for the year.

Required:

1. Construct the variable costing income statement that was expected for 1985 (budgeted at the beginning of 1985).

2. Construct the actual variable costing income statement for 1985.

3. Factor the difference between budgeted and actual variable costing income into as many variances as possible given the above data. Provide likely interpretations for each of the variances. Assign responsibility for each of the variances.

23-3 Multi Company

The following information pertains to the Multi Company example in this chapter.

a. There are no beginning or ending work in process, finished goods, or raw material inventories.

b. The 90,000 units produced and sold of product A consumed 89,500 pounds of raw material and required 50,000 direct labor hours to produce. The actual wage rate was $4 per hour, and actual raw material cost was $.95 per pound.

c. The 110,000 units produced and sold of product B consumed 60,000 pounds of raw material and required 12,000 direct labor-hours to produce. Actual wage rates and raw material costs were similar to those for product A.

Required:

Use the above information and the information in the chapter to fill in the missing numbers in the decomposition of the $10,000 unfavorable variable manufacturing cost variance shown below (wherever a ? appears compute the variance and indicate if it is favorable or unfavorable). What do these variances tell you about Multi Company's operations for the year?

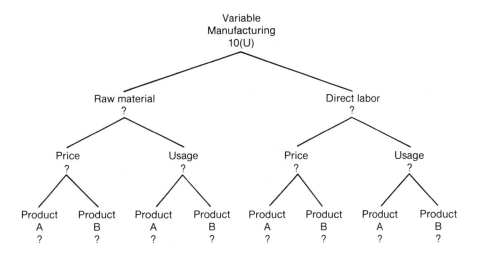

23-4   Wal-Mart*

From 78 outlets at the end of 1973, Wal-Mart has mushroomed into a chain of more than 500 mainly small-town stores located in 12 states, from Texas to South Carolina and Louisiana to Illinois. With no slowdown in sight, some experts predict that Wal-Mart will surpass K mart before the end of the decade as the nation's largest discounter.

* Excerpted from "Wal-Mart: The Model Discounter," *Dun's Business Month*, December 1982, pp. 60–61. Reprinted with the special permission of *Dun's Business Month* (formerly *Dun's Review*), December 1982, Copyright 1982, Dun & Bradstreet Publications Corporation.

Over the past five years, it has increased revenues and earnings per share at an annual compounded rate of 37.8 percent and 37 percent, respectively. This year, a lackluster one for retailers, analysts expect Wal-Mart's earnings to climb 41.6 percent to $117 million, or $1.77 per share, on a 41.7 percent increase in revenues to $3.4 billion.

Sam Walton, founder and chairman, attributes Wal-Mart's success partly to the grass roots management style he developed early on—a technique that emphasizes individual initiative and autonomy over close supervision. "Our philosophy is that management's role is simply to get the right people in the right places to do a job and then to encourage them to use their own inventiveness to accomplish the task at hand," he says.

Wal-Mart managers are required to meet with store personnel outside the workplace at least once a year to discuss the health and direction of the company and to gather suggestions on everything from merchandise selection to vacation policy; these are passed along to senior management. To reinforce the idea of self-motivation, all "associates"—the term "employee" has been banished from the Wal-Mart vocabulary—are eligible to share in corporate profits after a brief time with the company.

Although morale and productivity are key objectives of such a policy, the primary purpose is to encourage associates to keep their eyes on the bottom line. And as all company executives are quick to point out, Wal-Mart's tireless dedication to cost control is one of its greatest strengths. "Quite simply, our philosophy from the beginning has been to price as low as we can; and the lower our costs, the less we have to charge," says Jack Shewmaker, Wal-Mart's president and chief operating officer.

The heart of Wal-Mart's cost-control effort is a monthly financial statement prepared for each store that lists every expenditure charged against the store's account, from rent and taxes to paper clips and telephone tolls. District managers review these statements line by line with store managers, discussing ways to reduce controllable expenses. "These may be minor individually, but collectively they become major," Shewmaker explains. "This is a business of attending to details."

Another important cost advantage that separates Wal-Mart from the competition is in the purchase and distribution of merchandise. Instead of using outside jobbers and contract distributors, as do most discounters, Wal-Mart orders in bulk directly from suppliers and uses its own warehouses and fleet of delivery trucks. Store managers telephone their orders into a central computer once a week; the merchandise is shipped to the warehouse, where it is sorted by automated equipment onto the trucks and delivered to the stores. By ordering in bulk, Wal-Mart is able to negotiate lower prices than its competitors and is able to deliver it to stores at a much lower cost.

Not even senior executives are exempt from the cost-cutting pressures. Corporate offices are spartan and cramped. Such frugality allows Wal-Mart to spend only 2 percent of sales for general administrative expenses, less than most retailers can manage.

Wal-Mart gets the payoff from these low costs where it counts: low prices, which in turn generate customer loyalty. "Believe me," Shewmaker says, "customers know price and value. The housewives in our territory can tell you within pennies what a bottle of dishwashing liquid sells for, and if we can keep our prices lower than anyone else, the customer will spend less time worrying about shopping elsewhere."

Customer loyalty, Walton and Shewmaker believe, reduces the peaks and valleys in volume that drive labor costs through the roof. So to make sure that Wal-Mart maintains a consistent low-price image, they eschew the kind of rapid-fire promotional techniques common to the industry. While discounters features sales on selected merchandise once or twice a week to generate traffic, promotions are restricted to 13 a year at Wal-Mart stores.

Instead Wal-Mart tries to generate traffic through special events, such as the time the manager of the Jackson, Tennessee, store arranged for U.S. Army paratroopers to land in the Wal-Mart parking lot. "People want to go where they feel there is something happening," Shewmaker notes. "So we do a lot of in-store promotions that some people would refer to as being very hokey. We'll have dress-up Western days, when all of our associates will dress up with Western hats and blue jeans and cowboy belts. They have fun doing it, which contributes to their attitude and morale, and it rubs off on the customers."

Required:

1. What are Wal-Mart's general business objectives? What specifically must Wal-Mart do to have continuing success in the future?

2. Who determines the product mix in each of the stores?

3. Describe the type of responsibility centers Wal-Mart uses for its stores.

4. Do you think Wal-Mart's control system has contributed to its success? Explain.

23–5 Advanced Micro Devices*

Walter J. (Jerry) Sanders III is not the only chief executive who thinks of his business as a religion. But he is certainly one of the few to run it like an evangelist. The 45-year-old chairman and founder of Advanced Mirco Devices, Inc., uses imagery, symbolism, and fiery words as no other corporate leader to motivate employees, sell products, and influence people.

But no one, especially his competitors, takes Sanders or his fervor lightly. In the 12 years since he founded AMD, he has turned it into one of the fastest-growing, most aggressive companies in the semiconductor industry.

---

* Excerpted from "The Super Salesman at Advanced Micro Devices," *Dun's Business Month*, March 1982, pp. 49–51. Reprinted with the special permission of *Dun's Business Month* (formerly *Dun's Review),* March 1982, Copyright 1982, Dun & Bradstreet Publications Corporation.

In the five years through 1980, AMD's sales grew at a compound annual rate of 49 percent and earnings at 38 percent, matching the torrid tempo of Intel Corporation, long the industry's most profitable manufacturer. Only the effects of an industry-wide price-cutting rampage and heavy R&D expenditures held 1981 profits to $1.55 per share, a 6 percent gain.

"He was too late to market his own microprocessor, the revolutionary computer-on-a-chip developed by Intel, so he second-sourced Intel's device and a more powerful version designed by Zilog Corporation and spent the money on development of proprietary peripherals, the devices that link microprocessors to larger computers. With these products in hot demand, and with AMD's competence in engineering complex, large-scale integrated circuits reaching a degree surpassed only by Intel and Motorola, the company finally began to achieve the respect and acceptance Sanders had sought so long," comments analyst Stuart M. Johnson of Wertheim & Co.

Sanders has also refined his management style considerably. Stating that he thinks of himself as a leader rather than a manager, he now believes in inspiring his people to better performance and "tolerating more mistakes."

Sanders' colorful language and charismatic personality obviously appeal to his top staff, most of whom have remained with him from the start-up days. And he has stamped his brand on the rest of the company by a variety of decisions. Just below the top echelon, Sanders has created a series of profit and loss centers he calls managing directorates, a term he borrowed from European management parlance. Each is headed by a managing director—"my centurions," Sanders calls them—to whom he has delegated substantial autonomy to create their own teams and come up with innovative new products.

He also works hard to create an atmosphere in which all his employees enjoy their work. In recent times, he has thrown a $300,000 party for all and given away a house and Cadillacs as door prizes to workers, all in the interest of putting some "excitement" in their lives. In addition, he has been holding breakfast meetings with all employees hired since the semiconductor industry began to slump in April 1980 to assure them of their job security (unlike many of its competitors, AMD has not laid off any workers, and Sanders says he will not in the foreseeable future).

Required:

1. What factors determine the success of this high-technology company? What kinds of responsibility centers are appropriate for meeting the goals of a high-technology company? In general, contrast the high-technology system with a performance evaluation and control system that would be appropriate for a manufacturing firm in an established low-technology industry.

2. Comment on Sander's leadership style and the corporate culture he has created.

23-6 Penril*

Kenneth M. Miller, the 59-year-old chief executive of Rockville, Maryland's Penril Corporation has an impressive list of technological innovations to his credit. A pilot and engineer in the aircraft industry for many years, he developed the first automatic pilot for general aviation use, a life-saving automatic rudder control system to prevent airplanes from falling into a "graveyard" spiral, and the first solid-state automatic direction finder for planes.

Miller is also a conservative businessman with definite ideas about how to run a profitable company. And for the past decade, he has been applying these ideas to a unique kind of business: rebuilding money-losing or marginal operations acquired from larger companies.

Five years ago, for example, he visited Wells Benrus Corporation's Technipower Division, a Ridgefield, Connecticut, maker of electronic power supply units primarily for defense contractors. "I noticed that these power supply units, which weigh from 10 to 100 pounds, were being handled on an assembly line similar to one used to assemble watches," he recalls. "Jigs and fixtures used to hold the power supplies were inadequate. Workers were moving the items on rinky-dink wooden carts with casters or trying to carry them from place to place. The result was inefficient grunt work in which heavy items could drop on peoples' toes."

Wells Benrus was losing money on Technipower, but Miller felt he could turn it around by moving it to a new factory, setting up a progressive assembly line on bench rails, installing a standard cost system, and tightening purchasing controls to reduce inventory. Penril paid Wells Benrus $1.5 million for Technipower. It has not had a profitless quarter since.

Miller has turned around eight other similar situations, including a producer of test instruments to measure and analyze radio frequency and electromagnetic interference, bought from Fairchild for $323,000 in 1973; a line of modems, which permit computer signals to be sent over telephone lines, acquired from United Technologies for $2.2 million in 1979; a line of autotransformers and another of automatic line voltage regulators, purchased from Gen Rad, Inc., for $2.3 million in 1979. Each operation is run as a free-standing profit center, with its own purchasing, accounting, data-processing and other support departments.

Miller's brand of "hands-on" management centers on keeping close control over the cost of producing each product. This is done through a reporting system that originates at the purchasing department of each division. He believes that since a company in today's economic environment has little control over the prices it charges for its products, paying close attention to purchasing costs is the best way to figure profits. "We calculate

---

* Excerpted from "Turning Losers into Winners," *Dun's Business Month,* August 1982, p. 57. Reprinted with the special permission of *Dun's Business Month* (formerly *Dun's Review*), August 1982, Copyright 1982, Dun & Bradstreet Publications Corporation.

daily variances from standard costs as an early warning system," he says. "This way we can make decisions upstream about new suppliers or profit impact before it is too late."

The final control over the system is at headquarters, which runs a bank in effect, monitoring cash flow on a daily basis and shifting cash from division to division as necessary. With each division running its own show, Miller keeps the headquarters staff to a minimum—currently a total of 10.

Required:

1. What are Penril's general corporate objectives? What specific factors contribute to Penril's ability to meet its objectives?

2. What other variances besides cost variances would likely be a very important part of Penril's control system for production costs? Explain.

3. What kind of responsibility centers would you use to manage Penril's accounting and data processing departments?

23–7 Anheuser-Busch*

For Anheuser-Busch Cos., the World Series victory of its St. Louis Cardinals was the culmination of a banner year. After fending off a massive marketing push by Philip Morris' Miller Brewing Company to supplant it as the leading U.S. brewer, Anheuser-Busch actually increased its share of the market in 1982 from 30.3 percent to an estimated 32.7 percent.

Presiding over this performance is 45-year-old August A. Busch III, the fourth generation of the Busch family to run the 130-year-old company. Busch, who became chief executive officer in 1975 and chairman two years later, is credited with transforming Anheuser-Busch from a lumbering giant into a modern and efficient corporation, from a mere brewer into an aggressive marketing force, and from an authoritarian family business into a corporation dedicated to participative management.

He hired high-powered executives from General Mills and Procter & Gamble, set up joint work teams of merchandising, advertising, and planning people, and sponsored seminars for Anheuser-Busch's wholesalers to help them beef up sales. The company's advertising was also increased and refocused, with the result that it is now the biggest sponsor of sporting events in the United States.

More than anything else, though, it is Anheuser-Busch's operating efficiency that sets it apart from the rest of the industry. To meet the volume

* Excerpted from "Anheuser-Busch: The Once and Future King," *Dun's Business Month,* December 1982, pp. 48–49. Reprinted with the special permission of *Dun's Business Month* (formerly *Dun's Review*), December 1982, Copyright 1982, Dun & Bradstreet Publications Corporation.

increases expected from the marketing push, Busch launched an extensive expansion and modernization of its beer facilities, which boosted capacity 60 percent in five years at a cost of $1.8 billion. And through vertical integration to control the costs of materials, Anheuser-Busch's own facilities now supply 40 percent of its cans as well as a significant proportion of its malt and labeling needs. These efficiencies, plus its huge, modern distribution system—the best in the industry, analysts say—give Anheuser-Busch the highest profit per barrel of beer in the industry: $3.59.

The light-beer share of the market, currently 15 percent, is expected to increase to 25 to 30 percent in the next five years. Miller Brewing has 60 percent of the market against Anheuser-Busch's 28 percent, and Busch admits that Miller's being there first—since 1975—has given it a big advantage in the market.

Busch's goal is nothing less than to topple Miller from its Number One position. With Bud Light added to Natural Light and Michelob Light (introduced in 1977 and 1978, respectively), he notes, Anheuser-Busch has three light beers that are different in taste, price, and image. Armed with this variety, he believes, "We will gain the majority of that segment of the market over time, though not easily and not quickly. We will have more than 50 percent within this decade."

Industry analysts are skeptical that Busch can realize that goal. But they do expect Anheuser-Busch to become a strong Number Two in the light-beer market.

Anheuser-Busch is managed on three basic principles established by the chairman: planning, teamwork, and communications. In less able hands, such concepts might easily have become buzzwords. But Busch has insisted they be followed religiously, and they are strongly evident throughout the company.

The corporate planning process is continuous. Each subsidiary's annual budget is subject to approval and constant review by headquarter's nine-member policy committee, which also formulates a five-year plan of company goals and strategy.

Such detailed planning creates a predictable atmosphere in which to operate. In fact, according to Busch, the company's 1982 beer production is within 300,000 barrels of the amount planned for seven years ago. With production estimated at 59.3 million barrels, that is a remarkable 0.5 percent margin of error.

For a company the size of Anheuser-Busch, communications between management and operations are unusually close. Top-management teams visit all 18,000 company employees every year, and Busch makes contact with each employee every two years. The payoff has not been only vastly improved labor relations but increased productivity. Busch credits employee suggestions for the company's 7 percent year-to-year productivity increases over the last five years."

Required:

1.   What are Anheuser-Busch's general corporate objectives? What specific factors are necessary in order to achieve these objectives?

2. What type of responsibility center should the distribution system be? Can and malt production? Marketing?

3. Comment on Anheuser-Busch's planning and budgeting system.

4. What kind of responsibility center would you use to manage Anheuser-Busch's advertising function?

24

Decentralization and transfer pricing

In *centralized* organizations, resource allocation and utilization decisions are made in a single responsibility center. Organizations become *decentralized* as decision making responsibility is spread across many responsibility centers.

DECENTRALIZATION

The advantage of decentralization is that it can result in improved decision making because individual responsibility center managers better understand the problems confronting their centers and have access to more complete and timely information relevant to their solution than does corporate headquarters. Managers in decentralized firms who are responsible for the performance of their division are likely to experience increased job satisfaction and acquire decision-making skills that prepare them to assume even more responsible positions in the organization. Another benefit of decentralization is that highest levels of corporate management are able to focus on strategic and long-range planning because they do not have to make divisional operating decisions.

The risk in decentralization is that individual managers, left unsupervised, will take actions beneficial to their responsibility center but detrimental to the organization as a whole. Another disadvantage of decentralization is that it generally requires elaborate information-gathering and control mechanisms, which are more costly to operate than for highly centralized firms.

A *division* is a responsibility center with substantial decision-making authority in a decentralized firm. Divisional rewards and incentives should encourage divisional management to attain corporate goals, and performance evaluations made of divisional management should be consistent with these goals. Decentralization generally works best when divisions are independent of each other and when corporate management refrains from interfering in divisional operating decisions.

Transfer price objectives

The transfer of goods or services between two divisions in a decentralized firm is a common form of divisional dependency. The *transfer prices* of these goods and services, which are revenues of the selling divisions and costs of the purchasing divisions, should ensure an optimal economic allocation of firm resources and should lead to divisional actions that benefit the entire firm as well as the division. The transfer prices should also affect divisional profits in a manner that provides a meaningful basis for a performance evaluation of the division.

Transfer pricing example

We can illustrate the transfer pricing problem using the data in Illustration 24–1. The Brass Division of the Diversified Manufacturing Company currently has one ton of a special brass alloy in inventory that it can either sell to the gear division of Mista Machine Company, an external customer, for $500 or transfer to the Machine Division of its own company at a transfer price of T.

If the Brass Division sells the ton of brass alloy to Mista, incremental selling costs of $90 will be incurred and the Brass Division will have an incremental contribution of $410 ($500 − $90). If the transfer is made to the Machine Division of Diversified, the Machine Division will use the ton of brass alloy along with other inputs to produce a special machine mounting bracket, which it will sell to one of its external customers for $900. If the mounting bracket is produced the Machine Division will incur incremental produc-

ILLUSTRATION 24–1. **Transfer Pricing Example**

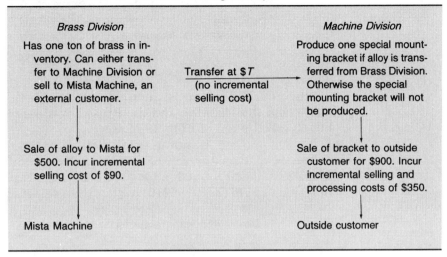

tion and selling costs of $350. If the ton of brass alloy is not transferred to the Machine Division then the mounting bracket will not be produced.

Now suppose the transfer price of the ton of brass alloy is $600. The Brass Division would prefer to transfer to the Machine Division rather than sell to Mista because it results in a $190 ($600 − $410) higher incremental contribution.

Brass Division Analysis

Action	Incremental Contribution
Sell alloy to Mista	$410 ($500 − $90)
Transfer alloy to Machine Division	$600

The cost of the ton of special brass alloy is a past cost incurred prior to making this decision. Costs resulting from irrevocable past decisions are called sunk costs and should be ignored when making current decisions.

The Machine Division prefers not to accept the transfer since it results in negative incremental contribution to it of $50. Incremental divisional revenue is $900 from the sale of the mounting bracket, and incremental costs amount to $950, the $350 incremental production and selling costs of the Machine Division plus the $600 cost of the ton of alloy transferred from the Brass Division.

Machine Division Analysis

Action	Incremental Contribution
Do nothing	–0–
Accept transfer of alloy and produce machine mounting	($50) = $900 − $350 − $600

Since each division is autonomous the Machine Division will not accept the transfer, and the Brass Division will have no option but to sell the ton of alloy to Mista.

For Diversified Manufacturing Company the optimal economic action is to transfer the alloy internally, produce the mounting bracket, and sell it outside for $900 because it results in a contribution that is $140 ($550 − $410) higher than selling the alloy to Mista.

Diversified Manufacturing

Action	Incremental Contribution
Sell alloy to Mista Machine	$410 ($500 − $90)
Transfer alloy and produce mounting bracket, which Machine Division sells for $900	$550 ($900 − $350)

Difficulty in setting transfer prices

The transfer price is a management technique to aid decision making and assist in performance evaluation in decentralized organizations.

In the above example if the transfer price is $600 the Brass Division will sell the alloy to Mista Machine for $500, and the Diversified Manufacturing Company will be worse off by $140 ($550 − $410).

Assuming that both divisions are interested in maximizing divisional profits, any transfer price in excess of $410 and less than $550 in the above example will result in both divisions favoring transfer, which is the optimal corporate economic action. The Brass Division should prefer to transfer as long as T (transfer price) is greater than $410, the incremental contribution from outside sale of the alloy. The Machine Division should accept the transfer as long as the incremental contribution from the sale of the special mounting bracket is positive, $900 − $350 − T is greater than zero.

Proper formulation of transfer pricing problems requires detailed knowledge of market conditions at the divisional level. A transfer price of $T = $500 (sale price to Mista Machine) in the Diversified Manufacturing Company example solves the *short-run*, corporate-wide, dollar profit maximization problem. It results in the Brass Division getting the market price it could get from an external customer, the Machine Division getting an incremental contribution of $50 ($900 − $350 − $500) which it would not otherwise get, and Diversified Manufacturing receiving an incremental contribution which is $140 higher than the alternative of not transferring the product internally.

Divisional decision making and transfer prices

Divisional managers should have the option of accepting short-term incremental gains or waiting for better returns in the future if their expectations of future market conditions lead them to believe such gains are possible. Any transfer pricing rule that forces managers to choose on the basis of short-run incremental profit can destroy divisional autonomy, forcing divisional managers to take actions they would not take on their own behalf, and lead to decisions that are not in the corporation's best interests in the long run.

A "solution" in the Diversified Manufacturing Company example was obtained only after a corporate-wide resource allocation problem was formulated and analyzed. If *corporate-wide* optimization problems have to be solved in order to determine transfer prices, then the corporation is effectively centralized. A true solution to the transfer pricing problem is a rule, *specified in advance* (ex ante), which generates prices for all possible transfers as opportunities occur, permits divisional managers to accept or reject transfers on the basis of the generated prices, and leads to actions consistent with corporate objectives.

In most practical settings it becomes difficult, if not impossible, to specify a transfer pricing rule which guarantees that autonomous divisions, acting in their own best interests, will simultaneously optimize corporate objectives. If both the markets for transferred products and final products sold by a firm are perfectly competitive, then such a rule is possible.

TRANSFER PRICING: PERFECT COMPETITION

In perfectly competitive markets, all firms produce a homogeneous product. The many identical buyers and sellers have perfect information about the market, are free to enter or leave the market, and act as if the price of the product is given.

If both the markets for transferred (intermediate) product and final product are perfectly competitive, then the transfer price should be set equal to the market price of the intermediate product. This will provide for an optimal allocation of firm resources and for an acceptable valuation of the transfer to both the buyer and seller divisions.

The transfer price can be viewed as a rule to allocate the total firm profit among the divisions. In general, because the transfer price may affect decision outcomes and profits, the transfer price may also determine the total firm profit.

In perfectly competitive markets, if transfers are made at market prices, autonomous divisions will make decisions resulting in maximum firm-wide profits. Divisions will initiate and accept transfers at market prices since no more favorable price terms are available in external transactions. In effect, perfect markets remove the dependencies among divisions when goods are transferred among divisions.[1]

TRANSFER PRICING: PRACTICE

There are three principal methods of pricing interdivisional transfers of goods and services in practice—market pricing, negotiated market pricing, and cost plus pricing.

Market pricing

Transfers of goods or services should be made at market prices in perfectly competitive settings. Market prices usually lead to fair performance evaluations and to optimal allocations of firms' resources. Unfortunately many markets are far from being perfectly competitive. Transferred goods and services may be relatively unique, there may be few buyers or sellers in the market, information may be imperfect, or the actions of a single buyer or seller may affect the market price of the goods. Even in perfectly competitive markets a transfer price less than market may be justified if selling or administrative costs can be saved because the sale is internal rather than external.

Negotiated market pricing

In imperfect markets divisional negotiation frequently determines whether interdivisional transfers take place and the prices associated with such transfers. In general the transfer price that makes the producing division indifferent between "transfer" and "no transfer" is the incremental cost to produce the transferred goods (usually the variable cost of production) plus the opportunity cost of transfer. In the case of capacity operations in the producing

---

[1] See the appendix to this chapter for an economic derivation of these results.

division, the opportunity cost of transfer is the contribution margin foregone on the goods that could be sold externally but that are displaced by production of the transferred goods. If the producing department has excess capacity this opportunity cost is zero.

Example

The Chemical Division of the Ace Manufacturing Company operates at full capacity and produces chemical A which has a variable manufacturing cost of $10 per ton. Chemical A is sold to the Acme Fertilizer Company for $21 per ton. Instead of producing a ton of chemical A, the Chemical Division can produce a ton of chemical B with a variable manufacturing cost of $12 per ton (using the same amount of capacity required to produce a ton of chemical A) and transfer it to the Plastics Division of its own company. A lower bound on the acceptable transfer price of a ton of chemical B from the Chemical Division's perspective is $23 ($12 + $11), the variable cost of producing a ton of chemical B plus the foregone contribution margin ($21 − $10) from the sale of a ton of chemical A. If the Chemical Division had excess capacity, the lower bound on the price it should consider for the transfer of chemical B to the Plastics Division is $12 (this price would just cover its variable costs). These are lower bounds on acceptable transfer prices to the Chemical Division (assuming there are no other current or future incremental economic effects to the Chemical Division) because in addition to those costs the Chemical Division is likely to insist on some contribution toward its profit.

In the above example the Chemical Division may still enter into transfers that do not result in the maximum possible profit for the Ace Manufacturing Company.

In determining the optimal corporate-wide action, the firm's (Ace's) opportunity cost of transfer and not the division's (Chemical's) opportunity cost, should be used in the analysis. For instance, it is quite possible if the transfer is made internally that a competitor, the Chemco Corporation, which was also attempting to sell the ton of chemical B to the Plastics Division of the Ace Manufacturing Company, may decrease the volume of its purchases of its own raw materials from the Chemical Division of Ace Manufacturing. This may result in lost profits, an opportunity cost. It is also possible that a sale, even an internal transfer, at a lower than normal markup can decrease future sales or increase costs of negotiating future sales with external customers.

Bids to supply the needed goods from external sources are brought to transfer price negotiations by purchasing divisions (departments), who have access to market information. Care is usually taken to solicit internal bids before disclosing bids from external sources. If the internal supplier is allowed to undercut external bids it will become impossible to obtain legitimate bids in the future. Internal suppliers are usually asked to submit one binding bid prior to learning the amount of external bids. At the risk of inefficient resource allocation, corporate-wide interests are frequently not represented in interdivisional transfer negotiations since corporate intervention might destroy the benefits the organization realizes from the decentralized structure.

Cost plus pricing

When no intermediate market for the transferred product exists (the product may be unique) *cost plus* transfer prices are often used. Cost may be the variable or full production cost of the producing division. The "plus" may be a contribution to divisional profit and overhead of the producing division in the variable cost case or a contribution to divisional profit of the producing division in the full cost case. A transfer at actual cost would not provide an incentive to the producing division. In all cases, standard costs should be used to determine transfer prices in order to encourage efficiency in production.

Cost-based transfers can lead to suboptimal firm-wide resource allocation decisions. Return to the Diversified Manufacturing Company example presented earlier in this chapter. Suppose that the ton of special brass alloy was produced at a standard variable cost of $300 and a standard full cost of $500 in the Brass Division. Suppose that because the standard variable cost of units produced is readily available, the transfer pricing rule is to transfer at standard variable cost of production plus 30 percent of the standard variable cost to cover fixed overhead and profit. Then the transfer price will be $390 ($300 + .3 × $300). At this price the Brass Division will sell to Mista Machine, the outside customer, which is not the most profitable alternative from the firm's viewpoint (Brass Division will transfer only if the transfer price exceeds $410).

Suppose instead that the transfer pricing rule is to transfer at the standard full cost of production plus 15 percent of the standard full cost to contribute to the profit of the Brass Division. Then the transfer price will be $575 ($500 + .15 × $500), and the Machine Division will be unwilling to accept the transfer. In general, it is impossible to know if a cost plus transfer pricing rule established ex ante will lead autonomous division managers to the best firm-wide decisions.

Summary

The opportunity cost of inefficient resource allocation decisions caused by improper transfer pricing is likely to be immaterial if interdivisional transfers are few in number and small in size. The benefits of decentralization will likely outweigh this cost. As the number of interdivisional interactions increases, it may become beneficial from the firm's viewpoint for central management to intercede in negotiations for transfers, which individually may have a significant impact on corporate profitability. When interdivisional dependencies are extensive, a centralized approach to decision making may be optimal.

Generally very little of a company's transfer pricing policies need be disclosed in its annual report. If a company is required to disclose segment information then a brief description of the transfer pricing mechanism for intersegmental transfers is also required.

TRANSFER PRICING IN MULTINATIONAL FIRMS[2]

Setting transfer prices to ensure an economic allocation of firm resources is more complex in multinational firms. Individual profit or investment centers may operate in countries with differing economic climates, tax laws, and restrictions on external funds transfers.

Low transfer prices on goods or services sent to divisions in countries with low tax rates may be part of a strategy to minimize overall corporate taxes. Artificially high transfer prices may facilitate flows of funds out of a country with tight restrictions on external funds transfers. Transfer prices may also be part of a strategy to shift funds between countries with more or less volatile exchange rates. Any such policies must be carried out within the limits of taxing agencies involved, and even then, the risks involved in the above strategies are manifold. Political risks of expropriation may increase, the IRS and equivalent foreign taxing agencies may impose penalties on adjustments to income resulting from arbitrarily high or low transfer prices, and divisional profits may no longer be valid measures of performance.

Section 482 of the Treasury Regulations empowers the Internal Revenue Service to adjust interdivisional transfer prices to reflect "true taxable income." If challenged on its transfer pricing mecha-

---

[2] The material in this section paraphrases S. S. Cowen, L. C. Phillips, and L. Stillabower, "Multinational Transfer Pricing," *Management Accounting,* January 1979, pp. 17–22. See this article for a more complete discussion.

nisms, the burden of proof of the reasonableness of the prices rests with the company. If unsuccessful in its defense, any reasonable reallocation of income by the IRS will stand.

The appropriateness of market-based transfer prices is recognized in the Treasury Regulations. "True taxable income" is meant to be income that results from "arm's-length" transactions. Thus companies selling the same products to external unrelated parties and to internal divisions located in other countries must use the outside selling price for the internal transfers. In the absence of market prices, cost plus prices are allowed. Section 482 imposes general restrictions on the size of the "plus" in such instances.

Because of the distortion in transfer prices (and therefore in divisional income) that can arise in attempting to minimize taxes or maximize funds flows between certain countries, a separate set of transfer prices for performance evaluation purposes may be used.

APPENDIX: TRANSFER PRICES UNDER PERFECT COMPETITION

Division A produces a product (product A) that can be sold in a perfectly competitive market or transferred to division B at a price of p per unit. Division A is indifferent between transferring to division B or selling outside the firm since its contribution is the same under each alternative. In Illustration 24A–1 MC_A is the marginal cost curve for division A. Marginal cost per unit of output (incremental cost per unit of output) increases as the level of output increases.

ILLUSTRATION 24A–1. **Transfer Pricing in Perfectly Competitive Markets**

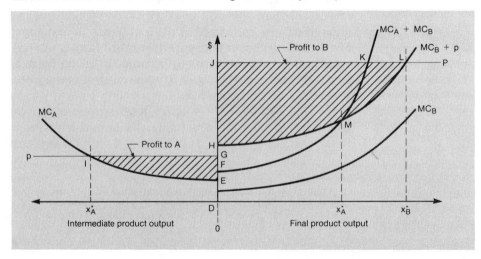

Division A's contribution will be maximized by producing x_A^* units, the level of output where the marginal cost of producing the x_A^*th unit is equal to its selling price, p. Any units produced and sold in excess of x_A^* will result in losses since the incremental cost of producing such units exceeds the incremental revenue from their sale. In Illustration 24A–1 total division A profit is the shaded area defined by *I–G–E*. Acting autonomously division A will produce x_A^* units, transfer to division B all that are requested, and sell any remaining units to customers outside the firm (without loss of generality, we will assume that division A produces less than division B demands and has no excess units to sell externally).

Division B produces a product that uses product A as an input. Division B is indifferent between purchasing this input externally or accepting a transfer from A since the cost per unit of product A will be p under each alternative.

In Illustration 24A–1 MC_B is the marginal cost curve of division B. MC_B includes all costs to division B except for the cost of product A. $MC_B + p$ is the marginal cost curve for division B if units of product A can be acquired externally or transferred internally at p per unit (for convenience we assume division B requires a single unit of product A for each unit of product B that it produces). Acting autonomously division B will produce x_B^* units to maximize its profits. This is the level of output where marginal (incremental) cost of production equals the selling price of P per unit of product B. Total division B profit is the shaded area defined by *H–L–J*.

Is it optimal from the firm's viewpoint to produce x_B^* units of product B? The firm's marginal cost curve for product B is given by F–M–L. Up to an output level of x_A^* it will be optimal to produce product A internally, and the marginal cost curve will be $MC_A + MC_B$. After that level it will be optimal for the firm to purchase product A from external sources at the market price of p per unit. The firm's marginal cost curve will be $MC_B + p$ for outputs of product B above x_A^* units. Thus the firm's optimal output of product B is determined by the intersection of the firm's marginal cost curve and the market price P. The intersection occurs at an output of x_B^*, precisely the level selected by division B when acting autonomously.

In the above example suppose division B is forced to accept transfers of product A at prices in excess of p per unit. Division B's marginal costs will increase and its optimal production level will fall below x_B^*. Division B will now have to be coerced to produce x_B^*. A transfer price less than p will lower division B's marginal costs and raise its optimal output beyond x_B^*. Again division B will have to be coerced to produce x_B^*. No coercion is necessary when transfers are at the market price.

Total profits to the firm are represented by the area F–M–L–J in Illustration 24A–1. Area F–M–H is equal to area I–E–G.

PROBLEMS AND CASES

24–1 Competitive Company

The Competitive Company has several divisions that produce a number of industrial products, all of which are sold in competitive markets. The Alpha Division of Competitive Company produces a subassembly for one of the company's products that is manufactured in the Beta Division. If Alpha decides to transfer the subassembly to Beta and Beta accepts (rather than purchasing one from a competitor), the transfer price will be the competitive market price.

The following data are well known:

Selling price of subassembly	$1,500
Variable cost to produce subassembly (in Alpha) ..	300
Selling price of final product	2,400
Variable cost to complete (in Beta)	1,100

Divisional managers are delegated profit responsibility and are given the authority to accept or reject internal transfers of materials at a transfer price equal to the market price, when available.

The manager of Beta Division argues that Alpha Division should be forced to transfer the subassembly at a price less than the market price. Beta Division will show a loss if the transfer is at market price (and therefore Beta won't accept the transfer), but the Competitive Company's profit on the final product would be increased by $1,000 if the transfer was made.

Required:

1. Justify the $1,000 profit if the subassembly is transferred. What is Beta's profit if the subassembly is transferred at market price?

2. Is the market price the appropriate transfer price? Explain.

3. Suppose Alpha has the capacity to produce 5,000 subassemblies in a month but only 4,000 can be sold in the competitive market at the stated market price. Additional sales would have to be made at a 30 percent discount below the regular competitive price. Should the last 1,000 subassemblies be sold outside or transferred to Beta? What is the appropriate transfer price? (Beta can sell unlimited units of final product without affecting the market price.)

24–2 Brass Company

Early in 1980 the Brass Company sold its two wholly owned subsidiaries: M P Corporation, a manufacturer of steel rods, to the Boston Company and A C Corporation, a manufacturer of forgings, to the Southeast Corporation.

One of the major customers for M P Corporation's steel rods was the affiliated A C Corporation. Subsequent to the sale the controller of the Boston Corporation found out that M P had been charging A C a premium above the price charged to unrelated customers for their steel rods.

On further investigation he determined that the amount of premium substantially changed the pro forma profits reflected in the financial statements prepared prior to the sale by Brass Company accountants. Boston Corporation relied on these financial statements in making their offer for the M P Corporation.

The table below indicates his computation of the net income (loss) adjusted for the transfer price premium.

Income (Loss) before Taxes

	Pro Forma*	Premium	Adjusted
1979	$(125,000)	$(635,000)	$(760,000)
1978	600,000	(595,000)	5,000
1977	(225,000)	(525,000)	(750,000)

* The figures are pro forma because they represent a calculation of the net income for each company based on an allocation of consolidated expenses. Brass Company's *actual* financial statements, on which an opinion was rendered, were prepared on a consolidated basis.

Boston Corporation sued the Brass Company because the pro forma financial statements did not disclose these transfer price premiums. They said that if they had known that the losses were of the magnitude reflected in the adjusted column, they would not have purchased the M P Corporation from the Brass Company.

Their argument was based on the fact that a reasonable person looking at the financial statements would not have expected a transfer price for the steel rods to be in excess of the prevailing market price, and they therefore assumed that the loss of sales to A C, which was no longer affiliated, would not have a material impact on profits because intercompany sales were only 5 percent of total sales.

The financial executives of the Brass Company indicated that it had always been their policy to have M P Corporation charge a premium over market price to A C Corporation for its steel rods. They said that this premium, which increased A C's cost for each forging, was necessary in order to get the A C sales force to sell the forgings at a price high enough to make a good profit.

Required:

If you were the judge and the transfer price was the only issue, would you award damages to Boston Corporation?

_____ **24–3 Multinational Manufacturing Company** _____

The Multinational Manufacturing Company consists of several domestic divisions and foreign affiliates. Divisional and affiliate managers are evaluated on their ability to meet target profit levels. Plants are evaluated as cost centers.

The standard material, direct labor, and variable factory overhead costs of component X, one of Multinational's products, are presented below. The component, produced in plant A, progresses through three departments (foundry, machining, and assembly) and has a standard variable cost of production of $12.85.

If the component is sent to plant B (in the same division as plant A) for final machining and assembly, an additional $6.10 in standard variable costs are incurred, raising the total standard variable cost of production to $18.95.

Components can be sold domestically for $15 per unit. If subjected to further processing in plant B, they can be sold for $35 as a finished product.

Domestic	(1) Standard Material	(2) Standard Labor	(3) Standard Variable Overhead at 120% of Labor	(4) Added Value	(5) Transfer from Previous Department	(6) Transfer to Next Department
Plant A—component:						
Foundry	$2.00	$3.00	$3.60	$8.60	—	$ 8.60
Machinery	.50	.50	.60	1.60	$ 8.60	10.20
Assembly	1.00	.75	.90	2.65	10.20	12.85
Plant B—finished product:						
Machining	.90	.80	.96	2.66	12.85	15.51
Assembly	3.00	.20	.24	3.44	15.51	18.95

Divisional and subsidiary managers have the authority to accept or reject internal transfers of products. Multinational Manufacturing Company determines transfer prices according to a system of markups. All production of a given plant in a division has the same markup factor. The total standard variable cost of a unit of production is "marked up" to allow the manufacturing division to recover administrative and fixed factory overhead costs. In the case of components the markup factor is 1.5, and the transfer price to the foreign affiliate is $19.275 ($12.85 × 1.5). For finished products the transfer price to foreign affiliates is $37.90 ($18.95 × 2). Multinational uses higher markup factors for finished products because management claims "manufacturing, engineering, and administrative costs should not be as high for a partially completed product as for a finished product."

Foreign Subsidiary	Component	Finished Product
Direct product cost	$12.85	$18.95
Markup factor	1.5	2.0
Transfer price to affiliate	19.275	37.90
Sale to customer	40.00	50.00
Gross margin to subsidiary before additional costs	20.725	12.10
Local value added	6.00	3.00
Markup factor (fixed overhead) . . .	5.055 (20% of $25.275)	7.58 (20% of $37.90)
Net profit to subsidiary	$ 9.67	$ 1.52

Required:

1. Comment on the merits and disadvantages of a system of transfer prices based on markups over standard variable costs of production.

2. Suppose plant B and the foreign affiliate are operating well below capacity. There is enough idle capacity in plant A to produce 10 more components. These 10 components could be sold to external customers or transferred to the foreign affiliate, or they could be transferred to plant B and then sold to external customers or transferred to the foreign affiliate. What is the optimal action from Multinational Company's viewpoint? What do you suppose will actually happen?

3. Suppose, in addition to what is assumed in (2), that the foreign affiliate can purchase components from a local manufacturer instead of from plant B for $30. Answer question (2).

24–4 First National Bank*

Bud Fowler, executive vice president (EVP)–retail of the First National Bank, was not looking forward to the Executive Committee's budget meeting. He knew what it would be like. An inquisition with the theme: "Why are retail profits lower than those of the rest of the bank?"

Last year's grilling was still a vivid memory. "Bud, those expenses of yours are getting mighty high, and any kind of steady profit growth still seems elusive. Can't you do anything about it? Why can't we do as well in retail as we did in 1974?" These remarks had come from the EVP–corpo-

---

* Excerpted from Bill Turner, "A Better Way to Measure Retail Banking Performance," *The Bankers Magazine,* November–December 1978. Reprinted by permission from *The Bankers Magazine,* Volume 161, Number 6, November–December 1978, Copyright 1978, Warren, Gorham and Lamont Inc., 210 South St., Boston, Mass. All Rights Reserved.

rate banking who, besides being the loudest critic, really spoke for the president and the others when it came to retail. Bud usually set goals that he believed were aggressive, but the others never saw them that way, so he always had trouble getting his programs adopted. This year would be no different. Reflecting on recent retail profits—relative to corporate, international, and even trust—the president and the other EVPs would no doubt once again challenge his aggressive and well-thought-out goals and plans for next year.

"Bottom-line" emphasis. Many retail executives have experienced this same kind of frustration, and many bank chief executive officers have struggled with the problem. As all concerned are beginning to realize, the use of a profit and loss statement for planning and measuring retail performance is at the heart of the problem. There are two fundamental reasons for this:

"Profitability" is dominated by uncontrollables.

The P&L statement does not focus on the funds generation role of retail.

As a result, the P&L is invalid as a tool for making operating decisions and evaluating managers at all levels of retail banking. Three factors put bottom-line results largely beyond management's control. The first and chief uncontrollable factor in any retail P&L is the "transfer" or "pool" rate. Most retail banking businesses raise substantially more funds than they use (i.e., deposits far exceed loans), and retail is properly credited for those net funds when its profits are calculated. The problem lies in the calculation of that credit: many bank managers endlessly debate the merits of alternative theories and methods of valuation, but most banks use a value based on external money market interest rates.

A second problem is that retail loan yields are fixed within a relatively narrow, low range by legislative rate ceilings or severe competition. This contrasts with flexible, variable pricing of corporate loans, which allows banks to maintain or at least influence the spread between corporate loan yields and the ever-changing external value of funds. Finally, rates that retail bankers can offer in bidding for new funds are often below market rates because they cannot pay interest on demand deposits and must keep interest on time deposits below Regulation Q ceilings.

As a result of these uncontrollables, retail profits can fluctuate dramatically over time without any change in the level or nature of the business or in management effectiveness. As a hypothetical but realistic illustration, Exhibit 1 shows pretax profits for a retail operation falling by 75 percent from 1974 to 1975, solely because of a drop in the market rate at which retail's net funds are valued.

An alternative measure of retail banking performance is the net cost of funds, NCF, defined as follows:

$$NCF = \frac{\text{Interest Expense} + \text{Operating Expenses} - \text{Fee Income} - \text{Interest Income}}{\text{Deposit Balances} - \text{Loans Outstanding}}$$

NCF is independent of the credit for net funds provided.

EXHIBIT 1.　**Impact of Market-Rate Changes on Reported Retail
Profit-and-Loss Performance**

	($ millions)		Uncontrollable
	1974	*1975*	*Factor*
Interest and fee income	$ 52.4	$52.4	Change in CD "transfer" rate: 10.3% to 6.4%
Credit for net funds provided	+93.7 (at 10.3%)	+58.2(at 6.4%)	
Total income	146.1	110.6	
Less interest and other expenses	−98.0	−98.0	
Net pretax profit	$ 48.1	$ 12.6	Reduces pretax profit by 74%

The following data reflects two years of operations of the retail banking activities of a large bank.

	($ millions)	
	1984	*1985*
Interest income	$ 47.9	$ 47.9
Fee income	4.5	4.5
Credit for net funds provided*	93.7	58.2
Interest expense	21.0	21.0
Operating expenses	73.9	73.9
Deposit balances	1,423.3	1,423.3
Loans outstanding	513.6	513.6

* At rate for large CDs of 10.3 percent in 1984 and 6.4 percent in 1985.

Required:

1.　Should managers of retail operations in banks strive for large or small values of NCF?

2.　Using the above data compute the net pretax profit and NCF for the years 1984 and 1985.

3.　Which of the measures computed in (1) better reflect the performance of retail operations in the bank during the two years?

4.　In general what are advantages of using NCF instead of pretax profit for performance evaluation? The disadvantages?

24–5　Scandia*

The Scandia Board Group (SBG) headquarters is in Malmo in Southern Sweden. SBG is based upon the Scandia Pulp Company (SPC), which is

* Excerpted with permission from D. H. Farmer and P. J. A. Herbert, "The Dilemmas of Transfer Pricing," *Journal of General Management,* Spring 1982.

FIGURE 1. **The Scandia Board Group Organization**

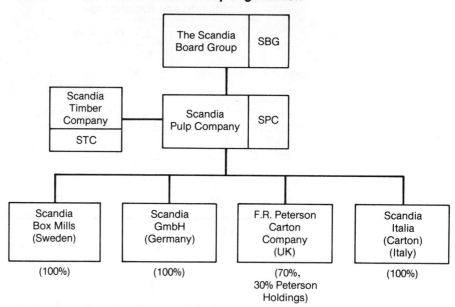

Note: The figures in parentheses represent the shareholding position related to to each company.

the "parent" of the group. The group consists of the Pulp Company (SPC), four converting companies, and a timber-growing concern. Figure 1 illustrates the organizational relationships.

The Group operates largely on a vertically integrated basis. All Scandia Timber output is purchased by the Pulp Company and represents some 60 percent of annual requirements. The remaining 40 percent is purchased from other growers. By tradition, since the formation of the group of converting companies in 1964, Scandia Pulp has supplied almost all corrugated board requirements to the four carton factories at an agreed rate. This rate has been subject to negotiation each year. However, in practice, the weight of the Pulp Company has been used by way of ensuring what the Group believes to be a "competitive yet fair contribution to Group profitability."

In November 1980, Dag Svennson, the SBG managing director, received an irate letter from the plant director of his German board mill. The letter complained of the behavior of the UK subsidiary in bidding for a Middle East contract where both companies had been competing with the other mills. The German complained that he had definite proof that the UK company had agreed to purchase board for the contract from an alternative UK source. This, he argued, was contrary to the Group arrangement where board should be purchased from the Pulp Company. Further, [he argued] that this was detrimental to Group profitability. "The result of this disloyal behavior," the German director continued, "was that there is a serious short-fall of business in my plant. If competition had been fair I should have obtained the business. How can I be held responsible for the profitability of my company when I follow Group policy and am penalized by the action of a fellow Group company?"

The German director had enclosed his selling price calculation, which was the basis for his contract bid. Svennson noted that the German included the agreed Group rate of £170 per ton for the corrugated board. He remembered the last round of discussions with the subsidiaries where this had been agreed.

Direct cost of finished board (ex. STC) was	£ 95.00
Contribution	£ 75.00
Total	£170.00 per ton

The contribution figure had been broken down to allow a "credit" to be attributed to the particular subsidiary.

The credit was designed to enable the Group to measure equitably the relative profitability of each of its operations—though it did not appear in the subsidiaries' profit and loss accounts. It had been calculated as follows:

Contribution	£75.00
Less: Freight (average)	£15.00
	£60.00
Less: Overhead directly attributable	£10.00
Profit "clawback" to subsidiary—central "credit"	£50.00

Svennson's telephone call to the United Kingdom following his consideration of the German letter confirmed that Tom Curtis, the UK plant director, had indeed purchased board from an outside source—at £100 per ton.

"You urged me to be competitive when you visited me at the beginning of the year," Curtis said. "You told me that it was my job to make this plant profitable. Clearly board represents the bulk of our prime cost, and quite frankly I believe I would have lost the contract had I gone in at the Group price."

Svennson rubbed his chin as he put the phone down. He had arranged for Curtis to visit him the next day, but he felt he was on a sticky wicket. Curtis had turned around the UK operation from heavy loss-maker into profit in 18 months. He was something of a corner-cutter, but he was good. Transfer pricing had always been a difficult topic, and Svennson felt that he had to be seen to be dealing with the situation fairly and firmly. Apart from the viewpoint of the German plant director, there was the Group's position to consider.

From the UK company's viewpoint, the Middle East contract had been extremely important. In effect, it would take up the equivalent of more than 20 percent of the plant's capacity for two thirds of the current year. The agreed selling price included a healthy contribution, and the guaranteed base-load was an attractive aspect. Despite the downturn in the UK economy, Curtis reckoned that the order would allow him to forecast a better profit and return on capital than the previous year.

Curtis was also concerned about satisfying the minority shareholder in his business. In addition, he wanted to encourage his management team, who had worked so hard with him to turn the business around. He believed that cash in the bank was far better than "notional" profits, and he was keen to use some of it for long overdue plant renovation.

Curtis believed that he could not be competitive at Group board rates. He was sure that he would have lost the Middle East order if he had bought his board from Group—even if only to the German plant—though that was highly improbable, he believed, for his sales manager had information which suggested that two other UK companies had quoted at around his price.

Finally, Curtis was reasonably confident that there was greater contribution in the variable figure than he had quoted. His waste allowance was also extremely generous. All in all, he thought that his true contribution could be between £60 and £65.

Baumann, the German plant manager, however, viewed the situation differently. He had lost a major order, due, he believed, to the unfair behavior of his UK colleague. If Curtis had negotiated according to the Group agreement, then Baumann felt the German plant would have had the order. Given the size of the order, Baumann had written his letter to Svennson at Group. The German plant director, while reluctantly having to accept the fact that the order was lost, felt that Group should deal with Curtis and ensure that the problem did not recur. Rules were rules, as far as he was concerned.

The third party in the triangle, Svennson at Group, had wider concerns. The motivation of his executives at the various national subsidiaries was an integral part of most of them. The case in hand highlighted several complicating aspects, not the least of which was the UK minority shareholder. On this point Svennson had been under pressure regarding what they termed "profits retained in Sweden." Up to that time he had managed to cloud that issue by pointing to an unofficial agreement with the Swedish Board Exporters Association. This required the company to sell board ex Sweden at a figure not below an agreed rate. The devaluation of the kroner had hardened that agreement, since it came at a time when there was a shortfall in demand for the material.

From the Group management viewpoint it was essential that a viable transfer pricing system was employed in the Group. Svennson had intended to do something about meeting this need for some time. The current arrangement had been a useful basis for working, up to now, but the present incident highlighted deficiencies.

Required:

1. Does the current method of pricing transfers lead to proper economic decisions and fair evaluations? (Be as specific as you can.)

2. What recommendations would you make for modifying the existing transfer pricing system?

24–6   Hospital Corporation of America*

Adding hospitals at a fast clip, both through acquisition and by building its own, HCA was a billion-dollar company by 1980 and this year is expected to amass revenues of $3.5 billion. The clear leader in the fast-growing hospital management industry, it now owns 212 hospitals in the United States and manages 150 others (a total of 52,000 beds). Humana, Inc., HCA's closest competitor, owns 88.

More than anything else, HCA's success is due to management's ability to develop—and stick to—a detailed blueprint for growth. Each step of its expansion has been planned and measured to ensure that the company does not take on more than it can absorb profitably. For example, it has set up very strict criteria on the type, size, and location of hospitals it buys or builds. And it has put financial limitations on growth by maintaining a 60:40 debt-to-equity ratio, the most conservative in the industry.

Group purchasing of everything from steel to scalpels saves cash. HCA also cuts costs by maintaining a central reimbursement office for processing medicare, which pays about 40 percent of all hospital bills, and other claims and a captive insurance company to cover malpractice risk.

In the actual running of the hospitals, HCA follows a highly decentralized policy that allows the hospital administrators to develop their own budgets and decide the types and prices of medical services they will provide. But a computer system measures administrators' performance relative to each other and also monitors how efficiently a hospital is utilizing its resources. "We let people take risks," Frist, HCA's CEO, says, "and then we find out if they're out of line."

Required:

Is HCA really a decentralized organization? Are all the hospitals autonomous? What is the nature of the interactions among the hospitals? Can you see any transfer pricing problems in this company? Are administrators really encouraged to take risks?

---

* Excerpted from "HCA: Champion in a New Growth Industry," *Dun's Business Month,* December 1982, pp. 52–53. Reprinted with the special permission of *Dun's Business Month* (formerly *Dun's Review*), December 1982, Copyright 1982, Dun & Bradstreet Publications Corporation.

25

Investment center performance evaluation

An investment center is a responsibility center in which management has the authority both to determine the level and composition of investments and to manage the investments once they are made. Investment centers are evaluated using measures of profitability that relate earnings (profits) of the center to its investment base (resources).

Investment centers are essentially self-contained businesses within a larger organization and usually correspond to divisions of a larger organization.

The economic mission of an investment center is to select projects which, given the center's cost of capital, have positive net present values and then to manage these projects to ensure that they result in maximum net cash inflows.

Ideally investment centers should use profitability measures that reflect economic values in their evaluations, and the rewards given to managers should motivate them to make both long- and short-term decisions in the best economic interest of the firm. Measuring the economic outcomes of decisions may be difficult because the historical cost accrual accounting data, frequently used to construct profitability measures, may not correctly capture the economics of the transactions they summarize.

PROFITABILITY: ECONOMIC MEASURES

Economic income, economic value, and economic depreciation, which relate to the net present value approach to capital budgeting, should be used to construct profitability measures for investment centers.

Economic income

Economic income in a period is the difference between cash flow and economic depreciation in the period.

$$\text{Economic Income} = \text{Cash Flow} - \text{Economic Depreciation}$$

Economic value

The economic value of an asset is the net present value of the cash flows the asset will generate over its useful life.

Economic depreciation

Economic depreciation of the asset in a period is the change in the asset's economic value from the beginning, NPV_B, to the end, NPV_E, of a period.

$$\text{Economic Depreciation} = NPV_B - NPV_E$$

Consider the following simple investment problem. A firm can acquire an asset with an economic life of four years for $191,627. The asset generates net cash inflows of $10,000, $125,000, $60,000, and $50,000 at the end of each of the next four years, respectively, and the firm's opportunity cost of capital is 10 percent per year. Since the net present value of the investment at 10 percent is zero it is an acceptable investment.

$$NPV = -\$191,627 + \frac{\$10,000}{(1.1)} + \frac{\$125,000}{(1.1)^2} + \frac{\$60,000}{(1.1)^3} + \frac{\$50,000}{(1.1)^4}$$

$$= -\$191,627 + \$9,091 + \$103,306 + \$45,079 + \$34,151$$

$$= 0$$

The economic value of the asset at time zero, the date the investment is made, is \$191,627, the present value of the four future cash flows.

Economic income and economic depreciation for each of the four years is as follows:

	Year				
	1	2	3	4	5
Present value of remaining cash flows (start of period) ...	\$191,627	\$200,789	\$95,867	\$45,455	–0–
Present value of remaining cash flows (end of period) ...	200,789	95,867	45,455	–0–	–0–
Economic depreciation	–9,162	104,922	50,412	45,455	–0–
Cash flow (end of year)........	10,000	125,000	60,000	50,000	–0–
Income	\$ 19,162	\$ 20,078	\$ 9,588	\$ 4,545	

Suppose the net cash inflow during the first year of investment is \$10,000, exactly what was expected. At the end of year 1 (the beginning of year 2) the net present value of the three remaining cash inflows is \$200,789 = (\$125,000/(1.1) + \$60,000/(1.1)^2 + \$50,000/(1.1)^3). This is the economic value of the asset at the beginning of year 2. Economic depreciation for the first year is the change in the economic value of the asset during the year and amounts to −\$9,162 (\$191,627 − \$200,789). In fact, the economic value of the asset has *appreciated* during the year. The first year's economic net income is then \$10,000 − (−\$9,162) = \$19,162.

An alternative approach to the computation of economic income is to note that the project has an internal rate of return of 10 percent and that \$191,627 is invested in the project at the beginning of year 1. Therefore, economic income in year 1 is (\$191,627)(.10) = \$19,162. Economic income for year 2 can be computed as (\$200,789) × (.10) = \$20,078. Economic income is similarly computed for years 3 and 4.

If actual cash flows differ from initial expectations, economic income is still equal to cash flow less economic depreciation, and economic depreciation is still $NPV_B - NPV_E$, where NPV_E is computed using updated estimates of remaining cash flows. In our example, we assume actual cash flows equal expected cash flows so that the economic rate of return is constant over time and can be contrasted with accounting rates of return.

Return on investment

Return on investment (ROI), the ratio of investment center (divisional, segment) income to divisional investment, is one measure of profitability.

$$\text{ROI} = \frac{\text{Divisional Income}}{\text{Divisional Investment}}$$

If divisional income is economic income and if divisional investment is the economic value of divisional assets, then ROI is the true economic return on investment. In the above example, in each year the ROI of the project (measuring the value of investment by its net present value at the beginning of the year) is exactly 10 percent ($19,162/$191,627 in year 1, $20,078/$200,789 in year 2, etc.), the internal rate of return on the project. The ROI of this project *will not* be 10 percent if the historical cost net income and historical cost value of investment are used instead of the economic income and economic value of investment.

esidual income

Residual income is an alternative measure of divisional profitability that charges the divisional manager for the use of assets at the division's opportunity cost of capital.

$$\text{Residual Income} = \text{Divisional Income} - (\text{Cost of Capital}) \times (\text{Divisional Investment})$$

In practice, since not all of the investments in the division are of equal risk, there will be more than one divisional opportunity cost of capital. The division manager will be charged for the use of an asset (inventory, plant and equipment, etc.) using a rate approximate for the risk of the asset. For purposes of simplicity a divisional cost of capital, which is a weighted average cost of divisional capital, is often used (weights equal the proportion of total investment in each group of equally risky assets). Residual income is zero if actual ROI is equal to the cost of capital, positive if ROI is in excess of the cost of capital, and negative otherwise.

In the previous example, where an asset was purchased for $191,627, suppose divisional investment is measured by its beginning-of-the-year economic value. Because the first year's economic income is $19,162 and the divisional opportunity cost of capital is 10 percent, residual income will be zero in the first year.

$$\text{Residual income} = \$19,162 - .10(\$191,627) = 0$$

If the first year's cash inflow was $12,000 instead of $10,000, the residual income would be $2,000.

$$\text{Residual income} = \$21,162 - .10(\$191,627) = \$2,000$$

The $2,000 represents a return on investment *in excess* of what is required by the 10 percent divisional opportunity cost of capital for assets of this particular type.

Maximizing residual income and ROI

If an investment center manager seeks to maximize residual income, then all projects with positive net present values will be accepted. If the manager seeks to maximize the investment center's ROI, then projects with positive net present values may be rejected.

Suppose the current ROI of a division is 13 percent and the divisional manager must decide whether or not to invest $191,627 in an asset that generates cash inflows of $12,000, $125,000, $60,000, and $50,000 in each of the next four years, respectively. The divisional opportunity cost of capital is 10 percent. The internal rate of return on this investment is approximately 10.4 percent. (Actual internal rate of return is 10.4114. The net present value of the cash flows at 10.4 percent is actually $191,678.)

$$NPV = -\$191,627 + \frac{\$12,000}{(1.104)} + \frac{\$125,000}{(1.104)^2} + \frac{\$60,000}{(1.104)^3} + \frac{\$50,000}{(1.104)^4}$$
$$= 0$$

If the divisional manager is evaluated on the basis of divisional ROI, the asset will not be purchased because the rate of return on this particular asset is only 10.4 percent and its purchase will reduce the 13 percent average ROI of the division. Since the project has a positive net present value at 10 percent, from the firm's viewpoint it should be purchased.

The residual incomes from this investment are expected to be positive, making it an acceptable investment from the perspective of a divisional manager seeking to maximize residual income.

	Year			
	1	*2*	*3*	*4*
Present value of remaining cash flows (start of period) ..	$191,627	$199,612	$95,371	$45,290
Present value of remaining cash flows (end of period) ..	199,612	95,371	45,290	–0–
Economic depreciation	–7,985	104,241	50,081	45,290
Cash flow (end of year)	12,000	125,000	60,000	50,000
Economic income	19,985	20,759	9,919	4,710
10% of present value of remaining cash inflows	19,163	19,961	9,537	4,529
Residual income	$ 822	$ 798	$ 382	$ 181

Comparison of residual income and ROI measures

A comparison of residual income and return on investment measures is shown in Illustration 25–1, which plots divisional income as a function of the level of capital investment. This graph assumes the division's initial investments were made in relatively low return projects deemed essential by management (e.g., pollution control equipment) and that all the remaining discretionary projects were ranked in order of their profitability. The most profitable projects rapidly increase divisional income. As total capital investment increases less profitable projects will probably be undertaken (the slope of the divisional income curve is decreasing) until finally projects with negative net present values remain (the divisional income curve turns down—the slope becomes negative).

A manager seeking to maximize ROI will invest P_1 dollars. The point of maximum return is determined by finding the line through the origin that touches the divisional income curve and has maximum slope. The slope of the line is the average return (divisional economic income/economic investment) on the investment of P_1 dollars.

A manager seeking to maximize residual income will invest P_2 dollars. The slope of the divisional income curve at P_2 is equal to r^*, the divisional opportunity cost of capital. A dollar of investment in excess of P_2 will return less than the incremental cost, r^*, of the dollar. Similarly, at any level of investment below P_2, residual income will be increased by investing more dollars because the increase in divisional income exceeds the increase in the cost of capital (the slope of the divisional income curve is greater than the cost of capital).

Every dollar of investment between P_1 and P_2 is in a project

ILLUSTRATION 25–1. **Residual Income and Return on Investment***

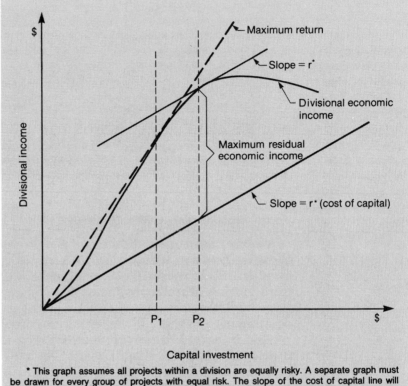

Capital investment

* This graph assumes all projects within a division are equally risky. A separate graph must be drawn for every group of projects with equal risk. The slope of the cost of capital line will be steeper for groups of more risky projects and less steep for groups of less risky projects. Alternatively, r^* in the above graph can be thought of as the weighted average divisional cost of capital.

with a positive net present value—the internal rate of return exceeds the cost of capital, r^*. From the firm's viewpoint these are favorable projects, and the division should invest in them. Even though these investments have positive net present values, a manager seeking to maximize ROI will not invest in them. These projects will reduce the division's ROI from what it is at an investment level of P_1.

Ideally measures of profitability, such as ROI and residual income, should be based on economic income, depreciation, and value of investment since these concepts are implicit in the net present value computations used to evaluate investments. Residual income is maximized by accepting all available projects with positive net present values and meets corporate objectives better than ROI, which is generally maximized by accepting only those projects with very high returns, ignoring other positive net present value projects with lower individual returns.

PROFITABILITY: ACCOUNTING MEASURES

Accounting income and depreciation usually differ from economic income and economic depreciation. The accounting book value of an asset is rarely equal to its economic value. Because of this, any computation of ROI and residual income using accounting income and book value of assets will not equal the economic ROI and residual income.

Comparing accounting and economic measures

Return to the simple investment problem defined earlier; $191,627 is invested in a project that returns $10,000, $125,000, $60,000, and $50,000 in years 1 through 4, respectively. The opportunity cost of capital is 10 percent. Suppose straight-line depreciation is used for accounting purposes, that gross margins equal to 20 percent of sales in all years are cash flows, and that depreciation is the only other expense.

The following table demonstrates what ROI and residual income will be over the life of the investment if *accounting* income and *accounting* book value of investment are used to construct these performance measures.

	Year			
	1	2	3	4
Sales revenue	$ 50,000	$625,000	$300,000	$250,000
Cost of goods sold	40,000	500,000	240,000	200,000
Gross margin	10,000	125,000	60,000	50,000
Depreciation	47,907	47,907	47,907	47,906
Net income	$ (37,907)	$ 77,093	$ 12,093	$ 2,094
Investment (beginning book value)	$ 191,627	$143,720	$ 95,813	$ 47,906
ROI (net income/investment)	(19.8%)	53.6%	12.6%	4.4%
Residual income (net income − (.10) × (investment))	$ (57,070)	$ 62,721	$ 2,512	$ (2,697)

For example, in year 3 accounting income is $12,093, and the beginning book value of investment[1] is $95,813 (the initial $191,627 investment less two years' straight-line depreciation at $47,907). ROI is 12.6 percent ($12,093/$95,813). Residual income is $2,512 ($12,093 − $9,581 (.10 × $95,813)). In none of the four years are the accounting-based ROI and residual income equal to the economic ROI of 10 percent and the residual income of 0.

Using an accelerated depreciation schedule in the above example will increase the disparity between economic and accounting profitability measures. Differences between accounting and economic depreciation are the primary reasons why accounting profitability measures do not agree with economic profitability measures. Other causes include the use of accrual accounting procedures, which recognize revenues and expenses in periods different than the corresponding cash receipt or expenditure, and inflation, which tends to affect revenues faster than costs.

Accounting profitability measures rely on historical costs. Economic profitability measures are future oriented. Each period, expected future cash flows are discounted to obtain a measure of economic value, which is the basis for computing depreciation. Since expectations are likely to change over time, even the total amount of economic depreciation relating to an investment is not likely to equal total accounting depreciation, which is based solely on the historical acquisition cost.

In general, historical cost accounting measures are likely to understate economic profitability for new projects and overstate economic profitability for older projects. Even if a firm has a portfolio of different-aged investments the accounting rate of return will only accidentally equal the economic rate of return.

PRACTICAL PROFITABILITY MEASURES

In practice, measures of profitability constructed from historical cost or from adjusted historical cost accounting numbers are often used to assess divisions as economic investments and to control and motivate divisional managers to attain corporate goals. The construction of these measures and their use in evaluations should recognize that they are imperfect substitutes for true economic measures.

Even though economic income, economic depreciation, and economic value accurately describe the net present value approach to capital investment, in practice these measures are rarely com-

---

[1] Alternatively, investment could be measured by the average of the beginning and ending book values.

puted. The computational burden to obtain them is considerable, and there are difficulties in projecting future cash flows and the opportunity cost of capital. Projected economic values are likely to change over time as estimates of future cash flows and opportunity costs of capital change. Economic value is less objective and verifiable than most accounting measures of value (e.g., historical cost).

Economic value is the norm against which practical, more objective, and verifiable measures of value should be measured.

Motivation and profitability measures

If used improperly, book measures of profitability can motivate improper managerial actions. Suppose the manager in charge of making the decision to accept or reject the earlier investment project ($191,627) is paid a bonus computed as a percentage of accounting income or accounting ROI. If the manager anticipates moving to another division in the company (or leaving the company) in the near future, there is no incentive to invest in the project even though it is desirable from the firm's viewpoint. If the project is accepted the manager's personal income will decrease (the bonus will decrease) because the new project will reduce accounting income by $37,907 (more if accelerated depreciation is used) in the first year of the project. Accounting ROI will also be lower than it would be if the project were not accepted (income is lower and investment is higher if the project is accepted).

Target ROI

Managers are best evaluated in comparison to prespecified divisional *target* ROIs, which recognize the risk, economic climate, and general potential for ROI of the division. Divisional target ROIs should be negotiated between divisional managers and superiors in the budgeting process. The budget process should make it clear to divisional managers that they will also be held accountable for meeting general divisional long-run objectives even if attainment of the long-run objectives leads to lower short-term performance measures.

Target accounting ROIs make sense when one considers that divisional management is in a continual state of flux. Current management is saddled with investments made by past managements and is likely to make decisions that will affect divisional performance for future management. A target value, rather than an absolute economic value, can often do more in the short run to motivate reasonable economic actions. Setting target ROIs can be difficult.

For instance, it may be insufficient to use projected accounting rates of return as targets because divisional management may still exceed these targets by dropping new projects with unfavorable consequences on accounting income and investment in the current period.

Alternatively, it is frequently argued that *managers* of investment centers are best evaluated on current profit, which they tend to control, than on divisional ROI, the denominator of which is likely to have been determined by previous management. This also motivates managers to do their best to ensure that expected or better than expected cash flows result from all current investment projects.

Residual income in practice

Residual income is infrequently used in practice. When it is used, however, different assets (e.g., inventory, plant and equipment, etc.) can be charged different rates of return, which reflect the risks of the assets, and the same asset can be charged identical rates across divisions. In addition some firms may have access to large amounts of capital but may still be unable to approach the optimum capital investment level (P_2 in Illustration 25–1) because they lack enough good managers to handle the number of investments necessary to achieve such a level.

Responsibility center profit report

Illustration 25–2 contains a hypothetical responsibility center profit report. Investment center (divisional) income is defined as the difference between revenues and expenses under divisional control. The controllable profit margin of $290 for center X should be used to evaluate the performance of center X's management. Those expenses not controllable by divisional management should be left out of the evaluations of individual investment center managers. If center X is being evaluated as an economic investment, then either the $270 center contribution to corporate expenses or the $250 center income before taxes is the appropriate number. Some corporate expenses are directly or indirectly (requiring a "reasonable" allocation) associated with the division as an investment and should be included in its evaluation as an economic investment.

Investment should consist of assets specific to the division. Again, the investment base for managerial evaluations should be limited to assets under managerial control. Total divisional assets and divisional income free of interest charges are favored if pure opera-

ILLUSTRATION 25–2. **Responsibility Center Profit Report**

CENTER X
Year Ended December 31, 1984
($000)

Revenues:	
External firm customers	$ 970
Sales to other divisions	210
Total revenues	1,180
Less controllable variable expenses:	
Direct product costs	600
Overhead	210
Total	810
Center controllable contribution margin	370
Less: Controllable fixed expenses	80
Center controllable profit margin	290
Less: Noncontrollable direct expense	20
Center contribution to corporate expenses	270
Less: Allocated corporate expenses	20
Income before taxes	$ 250
Divisional investment	$1,980
Divisional ROI ($250/$1,980)	12.63%

tional efficiency (financing considerations aside) is the main purpose of the evaluation.

Frequently investment is defined as divisional invested capital (total divisional assets minus divisional current liabilities) since one of the skills of good divisional management is to obtain "interest-free financing" in the form of current liabilities.

Investment might be defined as owners' equity if the investment center is a publicly traded corporation and the evaluator is a shareholder or security analyst.

Accounting profitability measures: Interpretation

The components of accounting profitability measures may be valued in several ways. Historical cost valuations are most often used because the financial accounting reporting system makes them readily available. Divisional ROIs based on historical costs frequently are not very useful in comparing performance across divisions. Assets acquired at different points in time, although functionally equivalent, may have drastically different historical cost valuations (even if gross book values are used). Managers in divisions with newer assets are at a disadvantage (high dollar measure of value of assets leads to low accounting ROI), and managers in divisions with older assets may be encouraged to delay replacement of assets (low dollar measure of value of assets leads to high accounting ROI) long after it becomes economically desirable to do so.

Current cost and ROI

Current financial reporting requirements make available (for most publicly traded large corporations) current cost and price level adjusted asset valuations and net incomes. Divisional ROIs computed using these numbers generally are more comparable than their historical cost equivalents. These comparisons tend to be more useful in evaluating divisions as economic investments or in deciding whether to be in a particular line or business, rather than in evaluating managerial performance. If used in evaluating performance, they would be subject to the same biases as historical cost measures, as indicated above, if the assets were acquired at different points in time.

Gross versus net book value

Another issue is whether to use gross or net book values of assets in the ROI denominator. Net book valuations, as previously indicated, tend to favor managers of divisions with older asset bases. For gross valuations the bias is reversed, and managers might be led to premature replacement of assets. Newer assets are likely to be more productive or have lower upkeep, resulting in higher income and therefore a higher ROI, since the denominator in the ROI will be identical for both the older and newer assets.

Graphical presentation of ROIs

Graphical presentation of the components of ROI frequently facilitates analysis of the divisions as economic investments. ROI can be expressed as the product of profit margin (net income/sales) and investment turnover (sales/invested capital). Illustration 25–3 displays divisional ROIs in a company where the corporate cost of capital (desired or target rate of return) is 16 percent. Any point on the line represents a combination of investment turnover and profit margin that corresponds to an ROI equal to 16 percent. Since divisional target ROIs may not be 16 percent (because of different risks of available investment alternatives), actual divisional ROIs should not necessarily lie on the line. If one point on the graph

ILLUSTRATION 25–3.   **Graphical Presentation of the Components of ROI**

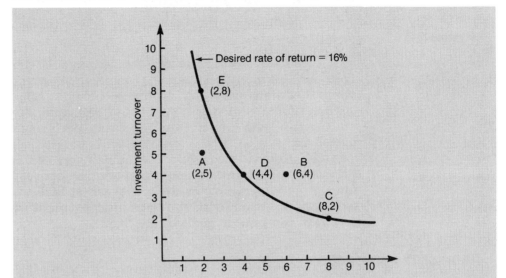

$$ROI^* = \frac{\text{Net income}}{\text{Invested capital}} = \frac{\text{Net income}}{\text{Sales}} \times \frac{\text{Sales}}{\text{Invested capital}} = (\text{Profit margin}) \times (\text{Investment turnover})$$

See Chapter 15 for a discussion of the decomposition of ROI into components.

corresponds to corporate ROI, its proximity to the line illustrates the company's success in meeting its ROI goal.

For instance division C, represented by the point (8,2) on the graph in Illustration 25–3, achieved a 16 percent return on investment with an 8 percent profit margin and an investment turnover of 2. Division B, the point (6,4) had a 24 percent return on investment. Its profit margin was only 6 percent, but it had an investment turnover of 4.

Generally such a presentation forces management to ask the right questions. For divisions with low investment turnover (e.g., division C) is better utilization of assets necessary? Are all assets productive? Is the turnover typical for the division's line of business? Are divisions with low profit margins (divisions A and E) selling products too cheaply? Are manufacturing or advertising costs too high?

Graphical presentation of the components of ROI helps direct management toward broad potential areas of improvement in divisional performance. It also illustrates how individual divisions contribute to corporate ROI.

The managers of the individual divisions should still be evaluated on their ability to meet the *budgeted* target returns, turnovers, and profit margins for their respective divisions.

SUMMARY

Theoretically, economic residual income is the performance measure that motivates managers to make optimal, firm-wide economic decisions. However economic income is a subjective and computationally unwieldly concept at best, and practicing managers usually settle for accounting-based performance evaluation measures.

Accounting ROIs, carefully used and understood, can be a powerful tool to ensure attainment of corporate objectives. In negotiation during the budget process divisional target ROIs should be set by managers familiar with the economic potential of the divisions and with the general goals of the firm.

PROBLEMS AND CASES*

25-1 The Cyclical Corporation

The Cyclical Corporation will acquire an asset with an economic life of four years for $191,627. The asset will generate cash inflows of $10,000, $125,000, $60,000, and $50,000 at the end of each of the next four years, respectively, and Cyclical's opportunity cost of capital is 10 percent. (Note: this asset is identical to the asset discussed in the text.)

Next year, when the above asset generates a cash inflow of $10,000, Cyclical Corporation will acquire another identical asset for $191,627. Cyclical will continue to purchase new assets for $191,627 at the rate of one per year until a total of six assets are purchased.

Required:

1. Compute the Cyclical Corporation's economic return on investment and economic residual income for the next nine years. Ignore taxes.

2. Compute the Cyclical Corporation's accounting return on investment and residual income for the next nine years assuming straight-line depreciation is used to compute accounting income, the net cash inflows represent gross margins equal to 20 percent of sales in all years, and depreciation is the only other expense. Ignore taxes.

3. Compare the results of (1) and (2). Describe the biases that exist when using accounting-based performance measures to approximate the

---

* Case 7–5 may be used as an introductory problem for this chapter.

economic measures. Is the bias different in the first three years after the initial purchase (year 0) than in years 4 through 6 or in years 7 through 9? Can you say anything in general about the direction of the bias when using accounting performance measures to approximate economic performance measures?

25-2　Mohasco Corporation

Mohasco Corporation's 1981 consolidated income statement and balance sheet, supplemental financial data adjusted for effects of changing prices, and industry segment data follow:

MOHASCO CORPORATION AND SUBSIDIARIES
Consolidated Statement of Earnings
Years Ended December 31, 1981, 1980, and 1979
($000, except per share data)

	1981	1980	1979
Net sales and other revenues	$640,336	745,213	747,100
Cost of sales..................................	477,695	580,663	584,167
Selling, administrative, and general expenses	123,843	142,439	132,903
	601,538	723,102	717,070
Operating income	38,798	22,111	30,030
Interest on indebtedness	15,564	18,612	16,634
	23,234	3,499	13,396
Other income (expenses)—Net	695	(3,105)	(1,716)
Earnings before income taxes and minority interest in subsidiary company	23,929	394	11,680
Provision for income taxes	8,725	2,510	3,930
Earnings (loss) before minority interest in subsidiary company	15,204	(2,116)	7,750
Minority interest in subsidiary company	—	41	21
Net earnings (loss)	$ 15,204	(2,157)	7,729
Net earnings (loss) per share of common stock	$ 2.30	(.34)	1.16

MOHASCO CORPORATION AND SUBSIDIARIES
Consolidated Balance Sheets
December 31, 1981, and 1980
($000)

	1981	1980
Assets		
Current assets:		
Cash	$ 4,415	$ 8,926
Accounts and notes receivable:		
Trade	101,205	116,697
Other	3,256	13,027
	104,461	129,724
Less: Allowance for discounts and doubtful accounts...................................	6,829	6,587
	97,632	123,137
Inventories......................................	89,628	114,864
Prepaid expenses................................	13,355	13,916
Total current assets	205,030	260,843
Rental furniture, at cost, less accumulated depreciation of $9,600,000 in 1981 and $8,704,000 in 1980	24,731	22,312
Property, plant, and equipment, at cost:		
Land	5,715	6,873
Buildings	62,264	70,792
Buildings capitalized under long-term leases	18,465	22,179
Machinery and equipment	137,661	152,785
Leasehold improvements	11,400	11,347
Construction in progress	8,913	5,533
	244,418	269,509
Less: Accumulated depreciation and amortization	128,562	136,566
	115,856	132,943
Other assets	6,751	5,671
Total assets	$352,368	$421,769
Liabilities and Equity		
Current liabilities:		
Notes payable—short-term	$ 10,500	$ 15,592
Current maturities of long-term debt.................	5,897	11,780
Accounts payable.................................	25,718	46,984
Accrued expenses	24,850	24,073
Federal, state, and foreign income taxes	3,635	2,195
Total current liabilities	70,600	100,624
Long-term debt, less current maturities:		
Senior notes	41,000	44,000
5% convertible debentures due 1987	20,000	20,000
Revolving credit notes.............................	1,038	45,000

Consolidated Balance Sheets *(concluded)*

	1981	1980
Liabilities and Equity		
Other notes	3,451	7,306
Capitalized lease obligations	4,114	7,208
	69,603	123,514
Deferred federal income taxes	5,496	6,567
Other liabilities	6,386	4,948
Minority interest in subsidiary company	—	990

Redeemable preferred stock:
Cumulative preferred, par value $100 per share:

	1981	1980
3½% series; authorized and issued 9,760 shares, less 1,388 and 1,098 shares in treasury in 1981 and 1980, respectively	837	866
4.20% series; authorized and issued 13,997 shares, less 2,550 and 2,050 shares in treasury in 1981 and 1980, respectively	1,145	1,195
	1,982	2,061

Common stock and other shareowners' equity:
Common stock, par value $5 per share. Authorized 12,500,000 shares;

	1981	1980
issued 6,673,454 and 6,666,239 shares in 1981 and 1980, respectively	33,367	33,331
Additional paid-in capital	33,070	32,995
Retained earnings	133,459	118,334
Less: Common stock in treasury, at cost— 101,951 shares	(1,595)	(1,595)
	198,301	183,065
Commitments and contingencies	$352,368	$421,769

Notes to Consolidated Financial Statements:

Note 14: Supplemental Financial Data Adjusted for Effects of Changing Prices (Unaudited)—Financial information reported on the conventional basis of historical cost does not reflect the impact of the continued high rate of inflation on the results of operations of business enterprises.

In recognition of this deficiency, the Financial Accounting Standards Board issued *Statement No. 33,* "Financial Reporting and Changing Prices," in September 1979. The statement prescribes two methods for measuring the effect of changing prices. The first method provides financial data adjusted for general inflation using the consumer price index for all urban consumers (CPI–U) as the broad-based measure of the general inflation rate. The restated amounts are referred to as constant-dollar income since The intent is to hold the purchasing power of the dollar constant for the period reported. The second method of measurement adjusts for changes in specific prices of resources actually used in the Company's operations. The restated amounts are referred to in current cost terms since the intent is to reflect the impact of the current cost of replacing these resources.

Since both of these methods involve the use of assumptions, approximations, and

Notes to Consolidated Financial Statements *(concluded)*

estimates, the Company makes no representations as to the usefulness of this data.

The Company uses the LIFO method of accounting for cost of sales in substantially all its operations which charges current costs to the results of operations for both financial reporting and income tax purposes. Accordingly, adjustments to cost of sales were necessary in determining the supplemental inflation accounting data to reflect the effect of LIFO inventory liquidations and translation of foreign LIFO inventories at current cost. Some companies in our industry use the FIFO method of accounting, which generally results in higher income for financial reporting purposes. However, these companies would have large inflation accounting adjustments to cost of sales that are not deductible for tax purposes.

Depreciation and amortization increased substantially due to the adjustment needed to reflect the impact of inflation on the Company's fixed assets, which have relatively long lives. Adjustments for current cost were based principally on external price indexes closely related to the resources being measured. Land, representing 2½ percent of total property, plant, and equipment was valued using the CPI–U average 1981 dollars for both constant-dollar and current cost. The data retain the same estimated useful lives and depreciation methods as used in computing historical depreciation.

The provision for income taxes has not been adjusted as the higher costs are not deductible for income tax purposes, highlighting the need for tax relief in these times of high inflation to enable companies to recover their investments before paying taxes on inflationary profits.

MOHASCO CORPORATION AND SUBSIDIARIES
Consolidated Statement of Income Information (Unaudited)
1981
($000, except per share amounts)

	As Reported in the Primary Statements	Adjusted for General Inflation	Adjusted for Specific Price Changes
Net sales and other revenues	$640,336	$640,336	$640,336
Cost of sales, excluding depreciation and amortization	461,789	467,315	474,355
Selling, administrative, and general and other expenses, excluding depreciation and amortization expense	136,953	136,953	136,953
Depreciation and amortization expense	17,665	26,475	26,249
Earnings before income taxes	23,929	9,593	2,779
Provision for income taxes	8,725	8,725	8,725
Net earnings (loss)	15,204	868	(5,946)
Gain from decline in purchasing power of net amounts owed	—	6,616	6,616
	$ 15,204	7,484	$ 670
Net earnings (loss) per common share	$ 2.30	$ .12	$ (.91)
Net earnings per common share after gain from decline in purchasing power of net amounts owed	$ 2.30	$ 1.12	$ .09

The gain from decline in purchasing power of net monetary liabilities is determined by calculating net monetary liabilities at the beginning and end of the year, adjusted for the change in these net liabilities held during the year, in terms of average 1981 dollars.

Net monetary liabilities are amounts owed that are fixed-dollar obligations less cash and claims to cash, which are fixed in dollar amounts. Since the Company held net monetary liabilities during a period of inflation, an unrealized gain in purchasing power resulted.

MOHASCO CORPORATION AND SUBSIDIARIES
Consolidated Balance Sheet Information (Unaudited)
December 31, 1981
($000, except per share amounts)

	As Reported in the Primary Financial Statements	Adjusted for General Inflation	Adjusted for Specific Price Changes
Monetary assets	$ 103,857	100,500	100,500
Monetary liabilities	(145,699)	(140,989)	(140,989)
Inventories	89,628	157,688	137,618
Property, plant, and equipment, net of accumulated depreciation	140,587	222,540	223,133
Other nonmonetary assets less nonmonetary liabilities	9,928	9,928	9,928
Common stock and other shareowners' equity	$ 198,301	349,667	330,190
Book value per common share	$ 30.16	53.20	50.23

Note 15: *Financial Information by Industry Segments*—During 1981 the Company reorganized into three strategic operating segments: Carpet, including the wholly owned distributors, with sales of a broad range of tufted, velvet, axminster and knitted carpet and rugs, and resilient floor coverings; Furniture, with sales of a variety of upholstered furniture, dining and family room furniture, office and institutional furniture, and metal furniture components; and Rental, with revenues from leasing furniture or residential and office use and the sale of rental return merchandise. In recognition of this reorganization, the financial information by industry segments for 1980 and 1979, as previously reported, has been restated to reflect the new strategic operating organization.

Financial information regarding the above industries in which the Company is engaged and its foreign operations as of and for the years ended December 31, 1981, 1980, and 1979 is as follows:

Industry Segment Information ($000)

	Carpet	Furniture	Rental	Corporate (2)	Volker Divestiture	Consolidated
Total revenues:						
1981	$305,930	295,858	39,402	—	—	641,190
1980	244,661	335,835	33,557	—	145,008	759,061
1979	251,667	324,731	29,238	—	161,127	766,763
Net sales and other revenues (3):						
1981	305,930	295,004 (1)	39,402	—	—	640,336
1980	231,793	334,855 (1)	33,557	—	145,008	745,213
1979	232,686	324,049 (1)	29,238	—	161,127	747,100
Operating income:						
1981	19,646	15,471	7,437	(9,087)	—	33,467 (4)
1980	5,264	11,792	5,190	(8,008)	2,303	16,541 (4)
1979	5,930	22,855	5,129	(9,038)	3,154	28,030 (4)
Total assets:						
1981	180,629	119,809	33,933	11,829	6,168	352,368
1980	187,967	143,866	31,498	7,468	50,970	421,769
1979	181,955	153,109	28,145	10,004	50,998	424,211

662

Industry Segment Information (concluded)

	Carpet	Furniture	Rental	Corporate (2)	Volker Divestiture	Consolidated
Capital additions (5):						
1981	9,006	3,183	11,877	7	18	24,091
1980	10,255	3,419	11,702	—	2,349	27,725
1979	14,235	6,879	12,758	—	2,606	36,478
Depreciation and amortization:						
1981	8,611	4,289	4,474	26	265	17,665
1980	8,434	5,121	3,956	—	561	18,072
1979	8,326	4,812	3,412	—	529	17,079

Geographic Segment Information ($000)

	United States	Foreign Operations	Corporate (2)	Consolidated
Net sales and other revenues:				
1981	$540,566	99,770	—	640,336
1980	630,886	114,327	—	745,213
1979	652,778	94,322	—	747,100
Operating income:				
1981	18,766	23,788	(9,087)	33,467 (4)
1980	13,713	10,836	(8,008)	16,541 (4)
1979	23,334	13,734	(9,038)	28,030 (4)
Total assets:				
1981	268,585	71,954	11,829	352,368
1980	332,444	81,857	7,468	421,769
1979	338,235	75,972	10,004	424,211

(1) 1981 excludes sales of Ranger, S.A. sold in early 1981. Included amounts for 1980 and 1979 were $45,921,000 and $38,590,000, respectively.

(2) Amounts related to charges for Corporate Headquarters functions are stated separately to avoid possible inequities in allocation by industry grouping or foreign operations. Corporate assets are principally cash.

(3) Intersegment sales are priced the same as sales to unaffiliated customers. The following intersegment sales were eliminated to arrive at the net sales and other revenues.

	Carpet	Furniture
1981	—	$854,000
1980	$12,868,000	980,000
1979	18,981,000	682,000

Intersegment Sales

(4) 1981 includes a provision of $5,300,000 primarily for anticipated costs in connection with relocating the domestic carpet headquarters and related operations. Charges for 1980 and 1979 were $5,570,000 (including $4,380,000 to write down the investment in Ranger, S.A.) and $2,000,000, respectively.

(5) Includes the following additions to rental furniture.

1981	$11,498,000
1980	10,590,000
1979	11,224,000

Required:

1.   Using historical cost data compute ROI for each of Mohasco's three segments. Use operating income in the numerator and total segment assets in the denominator.

2.   Suppose 1981 corporate assets of $11,829,000 and corporate operating income of ($9,087,000) are allocated to segments on the basis of their relative net operating incomes. Recompute the ratios that were computed in (1).

3.   Of what use are the ratios computed in (1)? In (2)?

4.   Using general price level adjusted and specific price level adjusted data, compute ROI for each of Mohasco's three segments. Assume that the ratio of historical cost operating income to price level adjusted operating income and the ratio of historical cost segment assets to price level adjusted segment assets are identical (and equal to the corporate ratios of historical cost net earnings to price level adjusted earnings and historical cost book value per common share to price level adjusted book values per common share) for all segments. How are these ratios useful?

5.   Which of the above ratios are most important in evaluating the performance of segment managers in evaluating the segments as economic investments? What other ratios or performance measures could you compute to aid in your evaluations?

25-3   Roadway*

Next time you take a long drive, chances are you will see a blue and orange Roadway Express rig. The Akron-based company owns 23,000 vehicles that are rarely idle. What's more Roadway operates in almost every state—making it the nation's largest and widest-ranging general freight carrier.

But size, as the people at Roadway Express, Inc., point out, isn't everything. Over 50 years of steady expansion, this publicity-shy company has outperformed competitors in a way almost unique in American business. Over the past decade, for example, Roadway's earnings have grown at a high-speed 22.5 percent annually—roughly twice the pace of aggressive transportation companies like Delta Airlines and even oil-rich Union Pacific.

Roadway's profitability is in overdrive, too. Its long-term return on capital averages 20 percent, and aftertax net margins of 6 percent are nearly three times the industry average.

Trucking isn't a complicated business. There is no black-box technology. Everybody drives similar Class 8 diesels that get about five miles to the gallon. With the exception of a few nonunion carriers—like Virginia-based

---

* Excerpted from *Forbes,* August 31, 1981, p. 91. "Easing into High Gear," by Jean A. Briggs. Reprinted by permission.

Overnite Transportation—nationwide Teamsters contracts give most competitors comparable labor costs. As tariffs are regulated, there's little opportunity for razzle-dazzle marketing. But such uniformity makes Roadway's record even more impressive. Its secret is decades of superior management, pure and simple.

A key part of Roadway's strategy is to make its variable costs match cargo service demand. "Our traffic fluctuates widely on a day-to-day basis," says Spitznagel [Roadway's chief executive officer]. "So we can't just set up a level of labor and say this is what we're going to use. Every day is different. Tuesday of this week is different from Tuesday of last week."

Fine—but how does Roadway make its expenses vary from Tuesday to Tuesday? Terminal managers—over 450 of them—handle their own staffing. Through a system of seniority and bidding for particular job slots, employees either work or stay home, depending on traffic volume at the terminal where they work. "Say we know we'll need 100 people every day, but three days per week we'll need 10 extras," says one manager. "We call them to come in just on those days."

Labor costs amount to roughly two thirds of Roadway's revenues so the ability to control them is crucial. Each terminal operates under its own local work rules. In the future, managers may have even more flexibility as deregulation is putting considerable pressure on the fabled Teamster intransigence.

Roadway's decentralization obviously gives local managers considerable responsibility. But Akron headquarters keeps watch. "We judge a man's results after the facts on a daily basis," says Spitznagel. "If costs get out of line we move in and find out what the problem is." Results: Each of Roadway's terminals is a profit center, and costs are controlled every day.

Spitznagel, who grew up in Alabama, studied marketing at Auburn University and has been with Roadway for his entire 31-year career, talks about "basic philosophies." The concept of matching labor costs to traffic flow is a typical example. Roadway's fundamental objective is to build its system from the bottom up. "We believe in small neighborhood terminals, close to the customer," he explains. "You can grow as large as you want as long as you have local identity as a hometown boy."

In other words, Roadway runs its terminals like small independent businesses. A local manager, who may be responsible for $5 million worth of equipment and 600 employees, has broad autonomy. "He's in charge of it all, it all reports to one," says Spitznagel. Still, if a manager's results look bad he finds out quickly—though Roadway's structure makes for a lean, 800-person home-office staff. Top terminal managers, however, can earn as much as $25,000 annually above their salary through Roadway's generous incentive compensation program.

Picking off the most profitable business is another part of Roadway's strategy. Instead of hauling bulk commodities the company concentrates on the motor-carrier equivalent of parcel post. Less-than-truckload (LTL) traffic accounts for 81 percent of its revenue—a higher proportion than at other big carriers.

These "small" cargoes can be anything up to 10,000 pounds, but Roadway's typical shipment is just over 1,000 pounds, and there is an average of 28 shipments to a trailer. At one time, few carriers wanted LTL business—much of which used to be handled by Railway Express. The problems are obvious: pickups and deliveries at a variety of destinations and the need for a complex billing and bookkeeping system. On the plus side, of course, per pound revenues are far greater. In other words, LTL carriers more than balance out the labor and time costs of constant loading and unloading by charging higher rates.

That's where efficiency comes in. Roadway keeps its trucks moving, and the profits from LTL business roll in. The company's breakbulk-relay system is the envy of the industry. All but 26 of its terminals are really just satellite depots where as many as 4,400 pickup and delivery tractors make regular "pedal runs" to nearby factories and warehouses. Ideally, trailers take pickups and deliveries at every customer's loading dock—so Roadway's trailers are infrequently heading home empty.

The 26 breakbulk terminals are the next rung. They consolidate shipments from satellite units within their service area using impressive automated shipping and hauling techniques. Roadway, for example, isn't worried just about getting the right shipment into the right trailer. Loading has to be done in the right order to reduce future handling to a minimum. Fuel economy is important, too. "The name of the game," says William Legg, a trucking analyst with Alex Brown, "is to have your highest load factor for the longest leg of the haul."

The result of Roadway's fabled efficiency is a service level second to none. Under its schedules a shipment dispatched from Stroudsburg, Pennsylvania, will arrive in Los Angeles 78½ hours later. "They can usually work within their own system rather than interlining with one carrier, then another," says Thomas Glodzik, traffic manager at Hasbro Industries, a Rhode Island toy manufacturer. Adds Richard Warren of Lever Brothers: "You're always better off to single-line. You can easily trace your shipment, and there's no split responsibility."

Roadway's size thus becomes a powerful marketing tool. The company already provides regular service to areas that include well over 90 percent of the nation's manufacturing capacity—more than any other carrier. Rather than presenting a competitive challenge, the freedom of deregulation makes expansion for Roadway easier. Sure, fledgling motor carriers can buy a few trucks and start serving bulk customers, but they can't profitably duplicate Roadway's nationwide capability. It isn't just a trucking company; it's a distribution network.

Controlling growth was part of Roush's credo. [Galen Roush and his brother Carroll founded Roadway in 1930.] But not earnings growth. "We grow as fast as possible there," says Spitznagel, allowing a tiny grin. What's more critical is expansion of operations and shipments handled. "We want that growth to be between 8 percent and 12 percent per year. In years we moved faster, we seemed to lose control. We're nothing more than the supervision of people. We are people-dependent. But we home-grow our people, so if we outstrip our people-development capacity we can get in trouble."

For the moment, Roadway is concentrating on the Pacific Northwest, building up its business terminal by terminal. But that is hardly uncharted territory. Consolidated Freightways, the industry's second-largest carrier, began in Portland, Oregon, in 1929. It gradually blanketed the western half of the United States, much as Roadway did the East. Now the two carriers' paths have crossed. "We've built for this day, and we're going to draw blood," says Lary Scott, who runs Consolidated's trucking operations.

For the moment, the toughest competition in the industry involves full truckload cargoes. Contract carriers and owner-operators have been bidding for this business, much of which they weren't allowed to haul until deregulation. That leaves all the big companies scrambling to increase their safer LTL revenues. The desperation strategy: Price-cutting.

Required:

1. What are the key factors of success for general freight carriers?

2. Does the current system of control and evaluation seem to be working?

3. Are individual terminals expense centers or profit centers?

4. What sort of dependencies exist among terminals? Is evaluating each terminal as a profit center counterproductive?

--- **25–4 Boeing Corporation*** ---

A good example of a reward system that recognizes the complexity of corporate objectives is that installed by the Boeing Corporation in the 1960s. About 50 percent of the compensation package is bonus-determined. One third of this bonus is tied to the profit target of the manager's program (say the 707 Jetliner or the 747 Jumbo). Another third stems from the profit of the commercial airplane division as a whole—an element designed to encourage sharing technical ideas across programs and pooling technical and managerial talent. The final third results from a technological audit which determines the program's contribution to the corporation's technical base.

The bonus element was thus designed to encourage achievement of four corporate objectives: (1) risk-taking—the high bonus element, of 50 percent (2) interprogram cooperation, (3) individual performance, (4) long-run technological development. Boeing's reward system, in other words, focuses on both the long term and the short—as it should; time-scales in incentive schemes are an important issue which is often overlooked.

Required:

1. Contrast the Boeing system with a system that rewards managers on the basis of pretax profit or return on assets.

---

* Excerpted with permission from Paul Miller, "The Rewards of Executive Incentives," *Management Today,* May 1982, p. 29.

2. If the main objective of a business is growth and expansion, what elements of a compensation scheme will encourage attainment of this objective?

3. What should the remuneration of a manager be based on if the main business objective is earnings? Cash flow?

25–5 Executive Compensation*

In the spring and early summer, the crescendo season for proxy statements and annual meetings, the chorus of hot complaints about the compensation paid top executives tends also to rise. From those linked to the system—corporate directors, consultants, executives themselves—the defenses shoot back. "These are big and complex organizations," the argument sometimes goes. "The people who run them deserve high pay. Look at the millions that Frank Sinatra gets, or Johnny Carson. Considering their pay, why should people get exercised about a corporate chief executive earning $1 million?"

In truth, there seems no way of judging whether the compensation of chief executives in general is too high or too low. But the Sinatra and Carson analogy has its weaknesses. As performers they are unremittingly on test in a free market. In the upper reaches of corporate America, the market frequently does not seem to work. In a totally rational world, top executives would get paid handsomely for first-class performance and would lose out when they flopped. But to an extraordinary extent, those who flop still get paid handsomely.

For this article and a portfolio of charts that follows, *Fortune* studied 140 large companies, comparing last year's return on stockholders' equity for each with the compensation paid its chief executive. Long-term forms of compensation—stock options and multiyear incentive plans—were excluded because the future payoffs on current plans are uncertain and payoffs already realized cannot logically be tied to a single year. The charts provide a perspective on pay and performance that a list cannot. They show some examples of consistency in which pay and performance match. They show many more examples of irrationality and contradiction.

If performance doesn't determine pay, what does? For one thing, size. Walton R. Winder, a Towers Perrin Foster & Crosby compensation consultant, says the firm's studies show that the correlation between size and pay, though by no means perfect, is relatively high and superior to any other single pay correlation tested. Performance, he says, correlates weakly with pay. Another consultant, Louis J. Brindisi, Jr., of Booz Allen & Hamilton, says it correlates not at all.

Most listings of compensation paid top executives don't tell you how it stacks up against performance. On these pages, *Fortune* presents "scatter

---

* Excerpted with permission from "The Madness of Executive Compensation" by Carol J. Loomis, FORTUNE, July 12, 1982, pp. 42–52. © 1982 Time Inc. All rights reserved.

plot" charts that compare pay with performance for 140 companies in 10 large industries. The grouping by industry allows the performance and pay policies of similar companies to be compared. Compensation among industries ranges widely, from a median of $1,030,781 last year for CEOs of the 10 largest conglomerates to $604,480 for the 10 top retailers.

The performance indicator we've used is each company's 1981 return on shareholders' equity, a ratio that shows how productively management is investing the shareholders' money. A one-year return is not a perfect indicator. But the returns of most companies reported do not swing violently; those that do tend to move with others in the same industry. Using an average of returns over several years would distort the standing of companies that had improved or lost ground.

On each chart the horizontal axis measures a company's 1981 return. The vertical axis shows the 1981 compensation of the chief executive.

In general, a plot point in the lower left-hand corner of a chart denotes poor performance punished by poor pay. A position at the upper right shows fine performance rewarded by fine pay. Taken together, the charts support the notion that pay and performance are poorly correlated.

Notable contrast can be seen between Johnson & Johnson and Upjohn. Both had about the same return on equity in 1981, and in recent years Upjohn has usually been the better performer of the two. Yet Burke of J&J gets more than double the compensation of Parfet at Upjohn. Part of the disparity is no doubt explained by size: J&J is the largest company

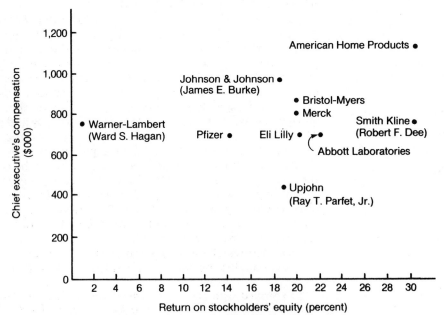

Pharmaceuticals Industry: 10 Largest Publicly Owned Companies

Source: Patricia Byrne, Jim Cavenagh for FORTUNE Magazine.

on the chart, Upjohn the smallest. Smith-Kline's enormous success with the ulcer drug Tagamet has swelled its profits. Dee's compensation, however, has not moved into the upper reaches, Warner-Lambert's return on equity is almost off the chart on the low side because the company was restructuring last year and took large losses on divestitures and phased-out product lines. By the rules in existence then, its low profits would have precluded bonuses. But this year the company got shareholders to agree that, in determining bonuses, unusual losses such as write-offs won't count in the profit calculation—and with that change, 1981 bonuses were retroactively paid. Eli Lilly has one of the oddest bonus deals around: its chief executive, Richard D. Wood, got .00535 percent of 1981 sales and .04305 percent of profits, with the two results averaged, as his bonus. By *Fortune*'s calculation, that worked out to $155,000 (which is included in the Lilly compensation figure on the chart).

Required:

Does return on equity measure executive performance? Why is it difficult to measure executive performance? How should executive compensation be determined? Do you agree with the above article?

Index

This book has been set CAP, in 10 and 9 point Primer, leaded 2 points. Chapter numbers are 36 point Spectra Extra Bold and chapter titles are 24 point Spectra Extra Bold. The overall size of the type page is 36 by 47 picas.